GARDNER'S

FRED S. KLEINER

ART through the AGES

A GLOBAL HISTORY

FOURTEENTH EDITION

BACKPACK EDITION

Modern Europe and America

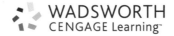

WADSWORTH
CENGAGE Learning™

Australia • Brazil • Japan • Korea • Mexico • Singapore • Spain • United Kingdom • United States

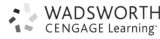

Gardner's Art through the Ages:
A Global History, Fourteenth Edition
Modern Europe and America, Book E
Fred S. Kleiner

Publisher: Clark Baxter

Senior Development Editor: Sharon Adams Poore

Assistant Editor: Ashley Bargende

Editorial Assistant: Elizabeth Newell

Associate Media Editor: Kimberly Apfelbaum

Senior Marketing Manager: Jeanne Heston

Marketing Coordinator: Klaira Markenzon

Senior Marketing Communications Manager: Heather Baxley

Senior Content Project Manager: Lianne Ames

Senior Art Director: Cate Rickard Barr

Senior Print Buyer: Mary Beth Hennebury

Rights Acquisition Specialist, Images: Mandy Groszko

Production Service & Layout: Joan Keyes, Dovetail Publishing Services

Text Designer: tani hasegawa

Cover Designer: tani hasegawa

Cover Image: © Giraudon/The Bridgeman Art Library

Compositor: Thompson Type, Inc.

For product information and technology assistance, contact us at
Cengage Learning Customer & Sales Support, 1-800-354-9706

For permission to use material from this text or product, submit all requests online at **www.cengage.com/permissions**. Further permissions questions can be emailed to **permissionrequest@cengage.com**.

Library of Congress Control Number: 2011931847
ISBN-13: 978-0-8400-3058-0
ISBN-10: 0-8400-3058-4

Wadsworth
20 Channel Center Street
Boston, MA 02210
USA

Cengage Learning is a leading provider of customized learning solutions with office locations around the globe, including Singapore, the United Kingdom, Australia, Mexico, Brazil and Japan. Locate your local office at **international.cengage.com/region**

Cengage Learning products are represented in Canada by Nelson Education, Ltd.

For your course and learning solutions, visit **www.cengage.com**. Purchase any of our products at your local college store or at our preferred online store **www.cengagebrain.com**.

Instructors: Please visit **login.cengage.com** and log in to access instructor-specific resources.

Printed in the United States of America
1 2 3 4 5 6 7 15 14 13 12 11

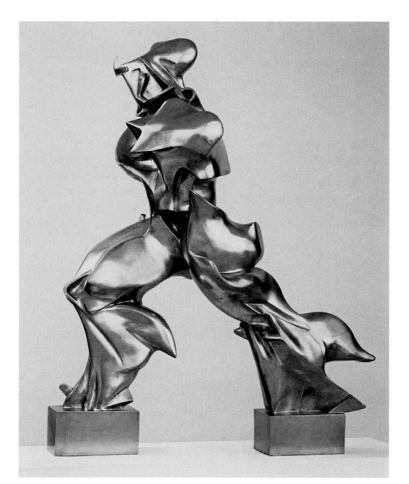

UMBERTO BOCCIONI, *Unique Forms of Continuity in Space,* 1913 (cast 1931). Bronze, 3′ 7⅞″ high. Museum of Modern Art, New York (acquired through the Lillie P. Bliss Bequest).

In 1909, the poet and playwright Filippo Tommaso Marinetti (1876–1944) founded the Futurist movement in Italy. Of particular interest to the Futurists were the speed and dynamism of modern technology. According to Marinetti, a racing "automobile adorned with great pipes like serpents with explosive breath . . . is more beautiful than the *Victory of Samothrace*" (cover of Book A). That ancient Greek statue lies behind the definitive work of Futurist sculpture, *Unique Forms of Continuity in Space* by UMBERTO BOCCIONI (1882–1916), which highlights the formal and spatial effects of motion rather than their source, the striding human figure. The figure is so expanded, interrupted, and broken in plane and contour it almost disappears behind the blur of its movement—just as people, buildings, and stationary objects become blurred when seen from an automobile traveling at great speed on a highway. Although Boccioni's figure resembles the *Victory of Samothrace*, the ancient sculptor suggested motion only through posture and agitated drapery, not through distortion and fragmentation of the human body. Boccioni has rarely if ever been surpassed for his ability to capture the sensation of motion in statuary.

That we know Boccioni's name and the details of his career is not surprising, because that has been the norm in Western art since the Renaissance, when the modern notion of individual artistic genius took root. But in many periods of the history of art, artists toiled in anonymity to fulfill the wishes of their patrons, whether Egyptian pharaohs, Roman emperors, or medieval monks. *Art through the Ages* surveys the art of all periods from prehistory to the present, and worldwide, and examines how artworks of all kinds have always reflected the historical contexts in which they were created.

BRIEF CONTENTS

CONTENTS

CHAPTER 31
CONTEMPORARY ART WORLDWIDE 940

FRAMING THE ERA | Art as Sociopolitical Message 941

PREFACE

THE GARDNER LEGACY IN THE 21ST CENTURY

I take great pleasure in introducing the extensively revised and expanded 14th edition of *Gardner's Art through the Ages: A Global History*, which, like the enhanced 13th edition, is a hybrid art history textbook—the first, and still the only, introductory survey of the history of art of its kind. This innovative new kind of "Gardner" retains all of the best features of traditional books on paper while harnessing 21st-century technology to increase by 25% the number of works examined—without increasing the size or weight of the book itself and at very low additional cost to students compared to a larger book.

When Helen Gardner published the first edition of *Art through the Ages* in 1926, she could not have imagined that more than 85 years later instructors all over the world would still be using her textbook in their classrooms. Indeed, if she were alive today, she would not recognize the book that, even in its traditional form, long ago became—and remains—the most widely read introduction to the history of art and architecture in the English language. During the past half-century, successive authors have constantly reinvented Helen Gardner's groundbreaking global survey, always keeping it fresh and current, and setting an ever-higher standard with each new edition. I am deeply gratified that both professors and students seem to agree that the 13th edition, released in 2008, lived up to that venerable tradition, for they made it the number-one choice for art history survey courses. I hope they will find the 14th edition of this best-selling book exceeds their high expectations.

In addition to the host of new features (enumerated below) in the book proper, the 14th edition follows the enhanced 13th edition in incorporating an innovative new online component. All new copies of the 14th edition are packaged with an access code to a web site with *bonus essays* and *bonus images* (with zoom capability) of more than 300 additional important paintings, sculptures, buildings, and other art forms of all eras, from prehistory to the present and worldwide. The selection includes virtually all of the works professors have told me they wished had been in the 13th edition, but were not included for lack of space. I am extremely grateful to Cengage Learning/Wadsworth for the considerable investment of time and resources that has made this remarkable hybrid textbook possible.

In contrast to the enhanced 13th edition, the online component is now fully integrated into the 14th edition. Every one of the more than 300 bonus images is cited in the text of the traditional book and a thumbnail image of each work, with abbreviated caption, is inset into the text column where the work is mentioned. The integration extends also to the maps, index, glossary, and chapter summaries, which seamlessly merge the printed and online information. The 14th edition is in every way a unified, comprehensive history of art and architecture, even though the text is divided into paper and digital components.

KEY FEATURES OF THE 14TH EDITION

In this new edition, I have added several important features while retaining the basic format and scope of the previous edition. Once again, the hybrid Gardner boasts roughly 1,700 photographs, plans, and drawings, nearly all in color and reproduced according to the highest standards of clarity and color fidelity, including hundreds of new images, among them a new series of superb photos taken by Jonathan Poore exclusively for *Art through the Ages* during three photographic campaigns in France and Italy in 2009, 2010, and 2011. The online component also includes custom videos made at each site by Sharon Adams Poore. This extraordinary new archive of visual material ranges from ancient Roman ruins in southern France to Romanesque and Gothic churches in France and Tuscany to Le Corbusier's modernist chapel at Ronchamp and the postmodern Pompidou Center and the Louvre Pyramid in Paris. The 14th edition also features the highly acclaimed architectural drawings of John Burge. Together, these exclusive photographs, videos, and drawings provide readers with a visual feast unavailable anywhere else.

The captions accompanying those illustrations contain, as before, a wealth of information, including the name of the artist or architect, if known; the formal title (printed in italics), if assigned, description of the work, or name of the building; the provenance or place of production of the object or location of the building; the date; the material(s) used; the size; and the present location if the work is in a museum or private collection. Scales accompany not only all architectural plans, as is the norm, but also appear next to each photograph of a painting, statue, or other artwork—another unique feature of the Gardner text. The works discussed in the 14th edition of *Art through the Ages* vary enormously in size, from colossal sculptures carved into mountain cliffs and paintings that cover entire walls or ceilings to tiny figurines, coins, and jewelry that one can hold in the hand. Although the captions contain the pertinent dimensions, it is difficult for students who have never seen the paintings or statues in person to translate those dimensions into an appreciation of the real size of the objects. The scales provide an effective and direct way to visualize how big or how small a given artwork is and its relative size compared with other objects in the same chapter and throughout the book.

Also retained in this edition are the Quick-Review Captions introduced in the 13th edition. Students have overwhelmingly reported that they found these brief synopses of the most significant aspects of each artwork or building illustrated invaluable when preparing for examinations. These extended captions accompany not only every image in the printed book but also all the digital images in the online supplement. Another popular tool introduced in the 13th edition to aid students in reviewing and mastering the material reappears in the 14th edition. Each chapter ends with a full-page feature called *The Big Picture*, which sets forth in bullet-point format the most important characteristics of each period or artistic movement discussed in the chapter. Small illustrations of characteristic works accompany the summary of major points. The 14th edition, however, introduces two new features in every chapter: a timeline summarizing the major developments during the era treated (again in bullet-point format for easy review) and a chapter-opening essay on a characteristic painting, sculpture, or building. Called *Framing the Era*, these in-depth essays are accompanied by a general view and four enlarged details of the work discussed.

The 14th edition of *Art through the Ages* is available in several different traditional paper formats—a single hardcover volume; two paperback volumes designed for use in the fall and spring semesters of a yearlong survey course; a six-volume "backpack" set; and an interactive e-book version. Another pedagogical tool not found in any other introductory art history textbook is the *Before 1300* section that appears at the beginning of the second volume of the paperbound version of the book and at the beginning of Book D of the backpack edition. Because many students taking the second half of a survey course will not have access to Volume I or to Books A, B, and C, I have provided a special set of concise primers on architectural terminology and construction methods in the ancient and medieval worlds, and on mythology and religion—information that is essential for understanding the history of art after 1300, both in the West and the East. The subjects of these special boxes are Greco-Roman Temple Design and the Classical Orders; Arches and Vaults; Basilican Churches; Central-Plan Churches; The Gods and Goddesses of Mount Olympus; The Life of Jesus in Art; Buddhism and Buddhist Iconography; and Hinduism and Hindu Iconography.

Boxed essays once again appear throughout the book as well. This popular feature first appeared in the 11th edition of *Art through the Ages*, which in 2001 won both the Texty and McGuffey Prizes of the Text and Academic Authors Association for a college textbook in the humanities and social sciences. In this edition the essays are more closely tied to the main text than ever before. Consistent with that greater integration, almost all boxes now incorporate photographs of important artworks discussed in the text proper that also illustrate the theme treated in the boxed essays. These essays fall under six broad categories:

Architectural Basics boxes provide students with a sound foundation for the understanding of architecture. These discussions are concise explanations, with drawings and diagrams, of the major aspects of design and construction. The information included is essential to an understanding of architectural technology and terminology. The boxes address questions of how and why various forms developed, the problems architects confronted, and the solutions they used to resolve them. Topics discussed include how the Egyptians built the pyramids; the orders of classical architecture; Roman concrete construction; and the design and terminology of mosques, stupas, and Gothic cathedrals.

Materials and Techniques essays explain the various media artists employed from prehistoric to modern times. Since materials and techniques often influence the character of artworks, these discussions contain essential information on why many monuments appear as they do. Hollow-casting bronze statues; fresco painting; Chinese silk; Andean weaving; Islamic tilework; embroidery and tapestry; engraving, etching, and lithography; and daguerreotype and calotype photography are among the many subjects treated.

Religion and Mythology boxes introduce students to the principal elements of the world's great religions, past and present, and to the representation of religious and mythological themes in painting and sculpture of all periods and places. These discussions of belief systems and iconography give readers a richer understanding of some of the greatest artworks ever created. The topics include the gods and goddesses of Egypt, Mesopotamia, Greece, and Rome; the life of Jesus in art; Buddha and Buddhism; Muhammad and Islam; and Aztec religion.

Art and Society essays treat the historical, social, political, cultural, and religious context of art and architecture. In some instances, specific monuments are the basis for a discussion of broader themes, as when the Hegeso stele serves as the springboard for an exploration of the role of women in ancient Greek society. Another essay discusses how people's evaluation today of artworks can differ from those of the society that produced them by examining the problems created by the contemporary market for undocumented archaeological finds. Other subjects include Egyptian mummification; Etruscan women; Byzantine icons and iconoclasm; artistic training in Renaissance Italy; 19th-century academic salons and independent art exhibitions; the Mesoamerican ball game; Japanese court culture; and art and leadership in Africa.

Written Sources present and discuss key historical documents illuminating important monuments of art and architecture throughout the world. The passages quoted permit voices from the past to speak directly to the reader, providing vivid and unique insights into the creation of artworks in all media. Examples include Bernard of Clairvaux's treatise on sculpture in medieval churches; Giovanni Pietro Bellori's biographies of Annibale Carracci and Caravaggio; Jean François Marmontel's account of 18th-century salon culture; as well as texts that bring the past to life, such as eyewitness accounts of the volcanic eruption that buried Roman Pompeii and of the fire that destroyed Canterbury Cathedral in medieval England.

Finally, in the *Artists on Art* boxes, artists and architects throughout history discuss both their theories and individual works. Examples include Sinan the Great discussing the mosque he designed for Selim II; Leonardo da Vinci and Michelangelo debating the relative merits of painting and sculpture; Artemisia Gentileschi talking about the special problems she confronted as a woman artist; Jacques-Louis David on Neoclassicism; Gustave Courbet on Realism; Henri Matisse on color; Pablo Picasso on Cubism; Diego Rivera on art for the people; and Judy Chicago on her seminal work *The Dinner Party*.

For every new edition of *Art through the Ages*, I also reevaluate the basic organization of the book. In the 14th edition, the unfolding narrative of the history of art in Europe and America is no longer interrupted with "excursions" to Asia, Africa, and Oceania. Those chapters are now grouped together at the end of Volumes I and II and in backpack Books D and F. And the treatment of the art of the later 20th century and the opening decade of the 21st century has been significantly reconfigured. There are now separate chapters on the art and architecture of the period from 1945 to 1980 and from 1980 to the present. Moreover, the second chapter (Chapter 31, "Contemporary Art Worldwide") is no longer confined to Western art but presents the art and architecture of the past three decades as a multifaceted global phenomenon. Furthermore, some chapters now appear in more than one of the paperbound versions of the book in order to provide enhanced flexibility to instructors who divide the global history of art into two or three semester-long courses. Chapter 14—on Italian art from 1200 to 1400—appears in both Volumes I and II and in backpack Books B and D. The Islamic and contemporary art chapters appear in both the Western and non-Western backpack subdivisions of the full global text.

Rounding out the features in the book itself is a greatly expanded Bibliography of books in English with several hundred new entries, including both general works and a chapter-by-chapter list of more focused studies; a Glossary containing definitions of all italicized terms introduced in both the printed and online texts; and, for the first time, a complete museum index listing all illustrated artworks by their present location .

The 14th edition of *Art through the Ages* also features a host of state-of-the-art online resources (enumerated on page xv).

WRITING AND TEACHING THE HISTORY OF ART

Nonetheless, some things have not changed in this new edition, including the fundamental belief that guided Helen Gardner so many years ago—that the primary goal of an introductory art history textbook should be to foster an appreciation and understanding of historically significant works of art of all kinds from all periods and from all parts of the globe. Because of the longevity and diversity of the history of art, it is tempting to assign responsibility for telling its story to a large team of specialists. The original publisher of *Art through the Ages* took this approach for the first edition prepared after Helen Gardner's death, and it has now become the norm for introductory art history surveys. But students overwhelmingly say the very complexity of the global history of art makes it all the more important for the story to be told with a consistent voice if they are to master so much diverse material. I think Helen Gardner would be pleased to know that *Art through the Ages* once again has a single storyteller—aided in no small part by invaluable advice from well over a hundred reviewers and other consultants whose assistance I gladly acknowledge at the end of this Preface.

I continue to believe that the most effective way to tell the story of art through the ages, especially to anyone studying art history for the first time, is to organize the vast array of artistic monuments according to the civilizations that produced them and to consider each work in roughly chronological order. This approach has not merely stood the test of time. It is the most appropriate way to narrate the *history* of art. The principle underlying my approach to every period of art history is that the enormous variation in the form and meaning of the paintings, sculptures, buildings, and other artworks men and women have produced over the past 30,000 years is largely the result of the constantly changing contexts in which

artists and architects worked. A historically based narrative is therefore best suited for a global history of art because it enables the author to situate each work discussed in its historical, social, economic, religious, and cultural context. That is, after all, what distinguishes art history from art appreciation.

In the 1926 edition of *Art through the Ages,* Helen Gardner discussed Henri Matisse and Pablo Picasso in a chapter entitled "Contemporary Art in Europe and America." Since then many other artists have emerged on the international scene, and the story of art through the ages has grown longer and even more complex. As already noted, that is reflected in the addition of a new chapter at the end of the book on contemporary art in which developments on all continents are treated together for the first time. Perhaps even more important than the new directions artists and architects have taken during the past several decades is that the discipline of art history has also changed markedly—and so too has Helen Gardner's book. The 14th edition fully reflects the latest art historical research emphases while maintaining the traditional strengths that have made previous editions of *Art through the Ages* so popular. While sustaining attention to style, chronology, iconography, and technique, I also ensure that issues of patronage, function, and context loom large in every chapter. I treat artworks not as isolated objects in sterile 21st-century museum settings but with a view toward their purpose and meaning in the society that produced them at the time they were produced. I examine not only the role of the artist or architect in the creation of a work of art or a building, but also the role of the individuals or groups who paid the artists and influenced the shape the monuments took. Further, in this expanded hybrid edition, I devote more space than ever before to the role of women and women artists in societies worldwide over time. In every chapter, I have tried to choose artworks and buildings that reflect the increasingly wide range of interests of scholars today, while not rejecting the traditional list of "great" works or the very notion of a "canon." Indeed, the expanded hybrid nature of the 14th edition has made it possible to illustrate and discuss scores of works not traditionally treated in art history survey texts without reducing the space devoted to canonical works.

CHAPTER-BY-CHAPTER CHANGES IN THE 14TH EDITION

All chapters feature many new photographs, revised maps, revised Big Picture chapter-ending summaries, and changes to the text reflecting new research and discoveries.

26: Rococo to Neoclassicism: The 18th Century in Europe and America. New Framing the Era essay "Art and Science in the Era of Enlightenment" and new timeline. Expanded discussion of Diderot as art critic. Adelaide Labille-Guiard added.

27: Romanticism, Realism, Photography: Europe & America, 1800 to 1870. New Framing the Era essay "Napoleon at Jaffa" and new timeline. Friedrich's *Wanderer above a Sea of Mist* and Altes Museum, Berlin, added.

28: Impressionism, Post-Impressionism, Symbolism: Europe and America, 1870 to 1900. New Framing the Era essay "Impressions of Modern Life" and new timeline. New discussion of Manet and Monet. Rodin's *Gates of Hell* and James Ensor added.

29: Modernism in Europe and America, 1900 to 1945. New Framing the Era essay "Global War, Anarchy, and Dada" and new timeline. New box on "Walter Gropius and the Bauhaus." Grosz's *Eclipse of the Sun,* de Chirico's *Song of Love,* Arthur Dove, Egon Schiele, Adolf Loos, and Margaret Bourke-White added.

30: Modernism and Postmodernism in Europe and America, 1945 to 1980. Former 1945–Present chapter significantly expanded and divided into two chapters. New Framing the Era essay "Art and Consumer Culture" and new timeline. Arshile Gorky, Lee Krasner, Franz Kline, Robert Motherwell, Joan Mitchell, Bridget Riley, Isamu Noguchi, George Segal, Niki de Saint-Phalle, Lucian Freud, Diane Arbus, Minor White, and Vanna Venturi house added.

31: Contemporary Art Worldwide. Former 1945–Present chapter significantly expanded and divided into two chapters. This chapter also now includes contemporary non-Western art. New Framing the Era essay "Art as Socio-Political Message" and new timeline. Robert Mapplethorpe, Shahzia Sikander, Carrie Mae Weems, Jean-Michel Basquiat, Kehinde Wiley, Shirin Neshat, Edward Burtynksy, Wu Guanzhong, Emily Kame Kngwarreye, Tara Donovan, Jenny Saville, Marisol, Rachel Whiteread, Andy Goldsworthy, Keith Haring, Andreas Gursky, Zaha Hadid, I.M. Pei, Daniel Libeskind, and green architecture added.

Go to the online instructor companion site or PowerLecture for a more detailed list of chapter-by-chapter changes and the figure number transition guide.

ACKNOWLEDGMENTS

A work as extensive as a global history of art could not be undertaken or completed without the counsel of experts in all areas of world art. As with previous editions, Cengage Learning/Wadsworth has enlisted more than a hundred art historians to review every chapter of *Art through the Ages* in order to ensure that the text lives up to the Gardner reputation for accuracy as well as readability. I take great pleasure in acknowledging here the important contributions to the 14th edition made by the following : Michael Jay Adamek, Ozarks Technical Community College; Charles M. Adelman, University of Northern Iowa; Christine Zitrides Atiyeh, Kutztown University; Gisele Atterberry, Joliet Junior College; Roann Barris, Radford University; Philip Betancourt, Temple University; Karen Blough, SUNY Plattsburgh; Elena N. Boeck, DePaul University; Betty Ann Brown, California State University Northridge; Alexandra A. Carpino, Northern Arizona University; Anne Walke Cassidy, Carthage College; Harold D. Cole, Baldwin Wallace College; Sarah Cormack, Webster University, Vienna; Jodi Cranston, Boston University; Nancy de Grummond, Florida State University; Kelley Helmstutler Di Dio, University of Vermont; Owen Doonan, California State University Northridge; Marilyn Dunn, Loyola University Chicago; Tom Estlack, Pittsburgh Cultural Trust; Lois Fichner-Rathus, The College of New Jersey; Arne R. Flaten, Coastal Carolina University; Ken Friedman, Swinburne University of Technology; Rosemary Gallick, Northern Virginia Community College; William V. Ganis, Wells College; Marc Gerstein, University of Toledo; Clive F. Getty, Miami University; Michael Grillo, University of Maine; Amanda Hamilton, Northwest Nazarene University; Martina Hesser, Heather Jensen, Brigham Young University; Grossmont College; Mark Johnson, Brigham Young University; Jacqueline E. Jung, Yale University; John F. Kenfield, Rutgers University; Asen Kirin, University of Georgia; Joanne Klein, Boise State University; Yu Bong Ko, Tappan Zee High School; Rob Leith, Buckingham Browne & Nichols School; Adele H.

Lewis, Arizona State University; Kate Alexandra Lingley, University of Hawaii–Manoa; Ellen Longsworth, Merrimack College; Matthew Looper, California State University–Chico; Nuria Lledó Tarradell, Universidad Complutense, Madrid; Anne McClanan, Portland State University; Mark Magleby, Brigham Young University; Gina Miceli-Hoffman, Moraine Valley Community College; William Mierse, University of Vermont; Amy Morris, Southeastern Louisiana University; Charles R. Morscheck, Drexel University; Johanna D. Movassat, San Jose State University; Carola Naumer, Truckee Meadows Community College; Irene Nero, Southeastern Louisiana University; Robin O'Bryan, Harrisburg Area Community College; Laurent Odde, Kutztown University of Pennsylvania; E. Suzanne Owens, Lorain County Community College; Catherine Pagani, The University of Alabama; Martha Peacock, Brigham Young University; Mabi Ponce de Leon, Bexley High School; Curtis Runnels, Boston University; Malia E. F. Serrano, Grossmont College; Molly Skjei, Normandale Community College; James Swensen, Brigham Young University; John Szostak, University of Hawaii–Manoa; Fred T. Smith, Kent State University; Thomas F. Strasser, Providence College; Katherine H. Tachau, University of Iowa; Debra Thompson, Glendale Community College; Alice Y. Tseng, Boston University; Carol Ventura, Tennessee Technological University; Marc Vincent, Baldwin Wallace College; Deborah Waite, University of Hawaii–Manoa; Lawrence Waldron, Saint John's University; Victoria Weaver, Millersville University; and Margaret Ann Zaho, University of Central Florida.

I am especially indebted to the following for creating the instructor and student materials for the 14th edition: William J. Allen, Arkansas State University; Ivy Cooper, Southern Illinois University Edwardsville; Patricia D. Cosper, The University of Alabama at Birmingham; Anne McClanan, Portland State University; and Amy M. Morris, Southeastern Louisiana University. I also thank the members of the Wadsworth Media Advisory Board for their input: Frances Altvater, University of Hartford; Roann Barris, Radford University; Bill Christy, Ohio University-Zanesville; Annette Cohen, Great Bay Community College; Jeff Davis, The Art Institute of Pittsburgh–Online Division; Owen Doonan, California State University-Northridge; Arne R. Flaten, Coastal Carolina University; Carol Heft, Muhlenberg College; William Mierse, University of Vermont; Eleanor F. Moseman, Colorado State University; and Malia E. F. Serrano, Grossmont College.

I am also happy to have this opportunity to express my gratitude to the extraordinary group of people at Cengage Learning/Wadsworth involved with the editing, production, and distribution of *Art through the Ages.* Some of them I have now worked with on various projects for nearly two decades and feel privileged to count among my friends. The success of the Gardner series in all of its various permutations depends in no small part on the expertise and unflagging commitment of these dedicated professionals, especially Clark Baxter, publisher; Sharon Adams Poore, senior development editor (as well as videographer extraordinaire); Lianne Ames, senior content project manager; Mandy Groszko, rights acquisitions specialist; Kimberly Apfelbaum, associate media editor; Robert White, product manager; Ashley Bargende, assistant editor; Elizabeth Newell, editorial assistant; Amy Bither and Jessica Jackson, editorial interns; Cate Rickard Barr, senior art director; Jeanne M. Heston, senior marketing manager, Heather Baxley, senior marketing communications manager, and the incomparable group of local sales representatives who have passed on to me the welcome advice offered by the hundreds of instructors they speak to daily during their visits to college campuses throughout North America.

I am also deeply grateful to the following out-of-house contributors to the 14th edition: the peerless and tireless Joan Keyes, Dovetail Publishing Services; Helen Triller-Yambert, development editor; Ida May Norton, copy editor; Do Mi Stauber and Michael Brackney, indexers; Susan Gall, proofreader; tani hasegawa, designer; Catherine Schnurr, Mary-Lise Nazaire, Lauren McFalls, and Corey Geissler, PreMediaGlobal, photo researchers; Alma Bell, Scott Paul, John Pierce, and Lori Shranko, Thompson Type; Jay and John Crowley, Jay's Publishing Services; Mary Ann Lidrbauch, art manuscript preparer; and, of course, Jonathan Poore and John Burge, for their superb photos and architectural drawings.

Finally, I owe thanks to my former co-author, Christin J. Mamiya of the University of Nebraska–Lincoln, for her friendship and advice, especially with regard to the expanded contemporary art section of the 14th edition, as well as to my colleagues at Boston University and to the thousands of students and the scores of teaching fellows in my art history courses since I began teaching in 1975. From them I have learned much that has helped determine the form and content of *Art through the Ages* and made it a much better book than it otherwise might have been.

Fred S. Kleiner

ABOUT THE AUTHOR

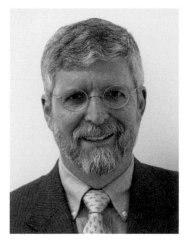

FRED S. KLEINER (Ph.D., Columbia University) is the author or co-author of the 10th, 11th, 12th, and 13th editions of *Art through the Ages: A Global History,* as well as the 1st, 2nd, and 3rd editions of *Art through the Ages: A Concise History,* and more than a hundred publications on Greek and Roman art and architecture, including *A History of Roman Art,* also published by Wadsworth, a part of Cengage Learning. He has taught the art history survey course for more than three decades, first at the University of Virginia and, since 1978, at Boston University, where he is currently Professor of Art History and Archaeology and Chair of the Department of History of Art and Architecture. From 1985 to 1998, he was Editor-in-Chief of the *American Journal of Archaeology.* Long acclaimed for his inspiring lectures and dedication to students, Professor Kleiner won Boston University's Metcalf Award for Excellence in Teaching as well as the College Prize for Undergraduate Advising in the Humanities in 2002, and he is a two-time winner of the Distinguished Teaching Prize in the College of Arts and Sciences Honors Program. In 2007, he was elected a Fellow of the Society of Antiquaries of London, and, in 2009, in recognition of lifetime achievement in publication and teaching, a Fellow of the Text and Academic Authors Association.

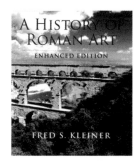

Also by Fred Kleiner: *A History of Roman Art, Enhanced Edition* (Wadsworth 2010; ISBN 9780495909873), winner of the 2007 Texty Prize for a new college textbook in the humanities and social sciences. In this authoritative and lavishly illustrated volume, Professor Kleiner traces the development of Roman art and architecture from Romulus's foundation of Rome in the eighth century BCE to the death of Constantine in the fourth century CE, with special chapters devoted to Pompeii and Herculaneum, Ostia, funerary and provincial art and architecture, and the earliest Christian art. The enhanced edition also includes a new introductory chapter on the art and architecture of the Etruscans and of the Greeks of South Italy and Sicily.

RESOURCES

FOR FACULTY

PowerLecture with Digital Image Library

This flashdrive is an all-in-one lecture and class presentation tool that makes it easy to assemble, edit, and present customized lectures for your course using Microsoft® PowerPoint®. The Digital Image Library provides high-resolution images (maps, diagrams, and most of the fine art images from the text, including the over 300 new images) for lecture presentations, either in PowerPoint format, or in individual file formats compatible with other image-viewing software. A zoom feature allows you to magnify selected portions of an image for more detailed display in class, or you can display images side by side for comparison. You can easily add your own images to those from the text. The Google Earth™ application allows you to zoom in on an entire city, as well as key monuments and buildings. There are links to specific figures for every chapter in the book. PowerLecture also includes an Image Transition Guide, an electronic Instructor's Manual and a Test Bank with multiple-choice, matching, short-answer, and essay questions in ExamView® computerized format. The text-specific Microsoft® PowerPoint® slides are created for use with JoinIn™, software for classroom personal response systems (clickers).

WebTutor™ with eBook on WebCT® and Blackboard®

WebTutor™ enables you to assign preformatted, text-specific content that is available as soon as you log on. You can also customize the WebTutor™ environment in any way you choose. Content includes the Interactive ebook, Test Bank, Practice Quizzes, Video Study Tools, and CourseMate™.

To order, contact your Cengage Learning representative.

FOR STUDENTS

CourseMate™ with eBook

Make the most of your study time by accessing everything you need to succeed in one place. Open the interactive eBook, take notes, review image and audio flashcards, watch videos, and take practice quizzes online with CourseMate™. You will find hundreds of zoomable, high-resolution bonus images (represented by thumbnail images in the text) along with discussion of the images, videos created specifically to enhanced your reading comprehension, audio chapter summaries, compare-and-contrast activities, Guide to Studying, and more.

Slide Guides

The Slide Guide is a lecture companion that allows you to take notes alongside thumbnails of the same art images that are shown in class. This handy booklet includes reproductions of the images from the book with full captions, page numbers, and space for note taking. It also includes Google Earth™ exercises for key cities, monuments, and buildings that will take you to these locations to better understand the works you are studying.

To order, go to www.cengagebrain.com

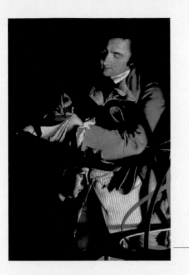

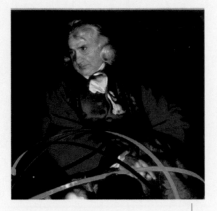

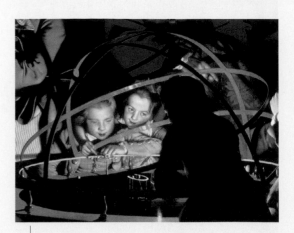

Joseph Wright of Derby specialized in dramatically lit paintings celebrating the scientific advances of the Enlightenment era. Here, a man listening to a learned lecture takes careful notes.

At the center of Wright's canvas, a scholar demonstrates an orrery, a mechanical model of the solar system in which each planet revolves around the sun at the correct relative velocity.

Awestruck children crowd close to the orbs representing the planets within the arcing bands symbolizing their orbits. Light from a lamp creates shadows, heightening the drama of the scene.

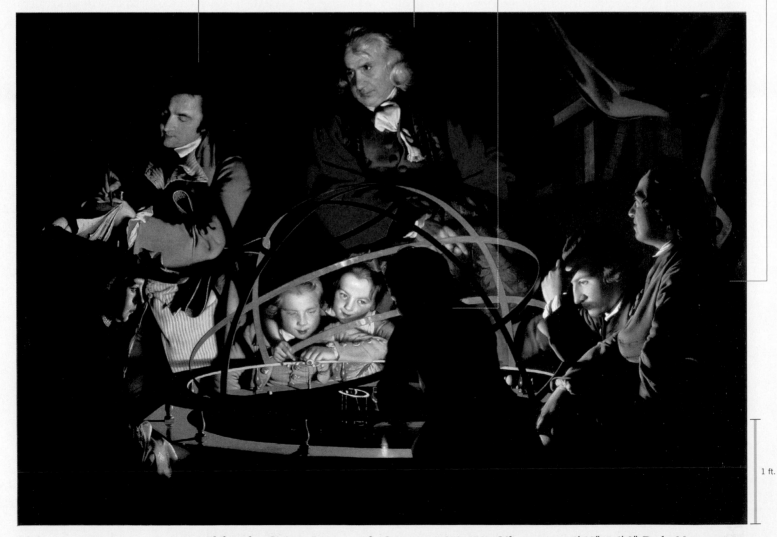

1 ft.

26-1 JOSEPH WRIGHT OF DERBY, *A Philosopher Giving a Lecture at the Orrery*, ca. 1763–1765. Oil on canvas, 4′ 10″ × 6′ 8″. Derby Museums and Art Gallery, Derby.

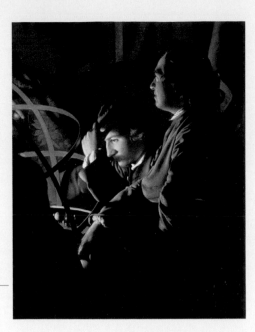

The wonders of scientific knowledge mesmerize everyone in Wright's painting, adults as well as children. At the right, two gentlemen pay rapt attention to the demonstration.

26

ROCOCO TO NEOCLASSICISM: THE 18TH CENTURY IN EUROPE AND AMERICA

FRAMING THE ERA

ART AND SCIENCE IN THE ERA OF ENLIGHTENMENT

The dawn of the *Enlightenment* in the 18th century brought a new way of thinking critically about the world and about humankind, independently of religion, myth, or tradition. Enlightenment thinkers rejected unfounded beliefs in favor of empirical evidence and promoted the questioning of all assertions. Thus, the Enlightenment encouraged and stimulated the habit and application of mind known as the "scientific method" and fostered technological invention. The scientific advances of the Enlightenment era affected the lives of everyone, and most people enthusiastically responded to wonders of the Industrial Revolution such as the steam engine, which gave birth to the modern manufacturing economy and the prospect of a seemingly limitless supply of goods and services.

The fascination science had for ordinary people as well as for the learned is the subject of *A Philosopher Giving a Lecture at the Orrery* (FIG. 26-1) by the English painter JOSEPH WRIGHT OF DERBY (1734–1797). Wright studied painting near Birmingham (MAP 27-2), the center of the Industrial Revolution, and specialized in dramatically lit scenes showcasing modern scientific instruments and experiments. In this painting, a scholar demonstrates a mechanical model of the solar system called an *orrery,* in which each planet (represented by a metal orb) revolves around the sun (a lamp) at the correct relative velocity. Light from the lamp pours forth from in front of the boy silhouetted in the foreground to create shadows that heighten the drama of the scene. Awestruck children crowd close to the tiny orbs representing the planets within the arcing bands symbolizing their orbits. An earnest listener makes notes, while the lone woman seated at the left and the two gentlemen at the right pay rapt attention. Scientific knowledge mesmerizes everyone in Wright's painting. The artist visually reinforced the fascination with the orrery by composing his image in a circular fashion, echoing the device's orbital design. The postures and gazes of all the participants and observers focus attention on the cosmic model. Wright scrupulously and accurately rendered every detail of the figures, the mechanisms of the orrery, and even the books and curtain in the shadowy background.

Wright's choice of subjects and realism in depicting them appealed to the great industrialists of his day, including Josiah Wedgwood (1730–1795), who pioneered many techniques of mass-produced pottery, and Sir Richard Arkwright (1732–1792), whose spinning frame revolutionized the textile industry. Both men often purchased paintings by Wright featuring scientific advances. To them, the Derby artist's elevation of the theories and inventions of the Industrial Revolution to the plane of history painting was exciting and appropriately in tune with the new era of Enlightenment.

A CENTURY OF REVOLUTIONS

In 1700, Louis XIV still ruled France as the Sun King (see Chapter 25), presiding over his realm and French culture from his palatial residence at Versailles (FIG. 25-26). The French king's palace in-

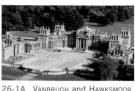

26-1A VANBRUGH and HAWKSMOOR, Blenheim Palace, 1705–1725.

spired the construction of many other grandiose homes on the Continent and across the English Channel during the early 18th century, including Blenheim Palace (FIG. 26-1A), which SIR JOHN VANBRUGH (1664–1726) and NICHOLAS HAWKSMOOR (1661–1736) designed for the duke of Marlborough. By 1800, however, revolutions had overthrown the monarchy in France and achieved independence for the British colonies in America (MAP 26-1). The 18th century also gave birth to a revolution of a different kind—the Industrial Revolution, which began in England and soon transformed the economies of continental Europe and North America and eventually the world.

Against this backdrop of revolutionary change, social as well as political, economic, and technological, came major transformations in the arts. Compare, for example, Antoine Watteau's *Pilgrimage to Cythera* (FIG. 26-7), painted 1717–1719, which unfolds in a lush landscape and celebrates the romantic dalliances of the moneyed elite, with Jacques-Louis David's 1784 *Oath of the Horatii* (FIG. 26-25), set in an austere Doric hall and glorifying the civic virtue and heroism of an ancient Roman family. The two works have little in common other than both are French oil paintings. In the 18th century, shifts in style and subject matter were both rapid and significant.

ROCOCO

The death of Louis XIV in 1715 brought many changes in French high society. The elite quickly abandoned the court of Versailles for the pleasures of town life. Although French citizens still owed allegiance to a monarch, the early 18th century brought a resurgence of aristocratic social, political, and economic power. Members of the nobility not only exercised their traditional privileges (for example, exemption from certain taxes and from forced labor on public works) but also sought to expand their power. In the cultural realm, aristocrats reestablished their predominance as art patrons.

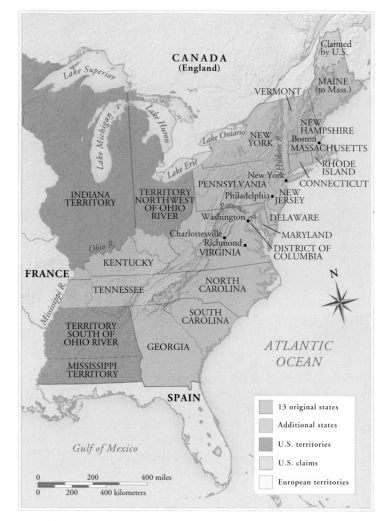

MAP 26-1 The United States in 1800.

The *hôtels* (townhouses) of Paris soon became the centers of a new, softer style called *Rococo*. Associated with the regency (1715–1723) following the death of Louis XIV and with the reign of Louis XV (r. 1723–1774), the Rococo style in art and architecture was the perfect expression of the lighthearted elegance the wealthy cultivated in their opulent homes (see "Femmes Savants and Salon Culture," page 729).

ROCOCO TO NEOCLASSICISM:
THE 18TH CENTURY IN EUROPE AND AMERICA

1700	1725	1750	1775	1800
▪ The Rococo style becomes the rage in the opulent townhouses of Paris ▪ Watteau creates a new painting genre—the *fête galante*	▪ Neumann adapts the intimate Rococo domestic style to ecclesiastical architecture ▪ Chardin rejects the frivolity of Rococo painting in favor of "natural" art ▪ Canaletto paints views of Venice as souvenirs of the Grand Tour of Italy	▪ The Enlightenment admiration for Greece and Rome prompts a Neoclassical revival in architecture ▪ During the Industrial Revolution, Wright celebrates scientific advances in dramatically lit paintings ▪ First use of iron in bridge construction at Coalbrookdale, England	▪ Reynolds achieves renown for Grand Manner portraits ▪ Vigée-Lebrun and Labille-Guiard gain admission to the French Royal Academy of Painting and Sculpture ▪ David becomes the painter-ideologist of the French Revolution ▪ Jefferson promotes Neoclassicism as the official architectural style of the new American republic	

Femmes Savants and Salon Culture

The feminine look of the Rococo style suggests the taste and social initiative of women, and to a large extent, women dominated the cultural sphere during the Rococo age. In the 18th century, aristocratic women—including Madame de Pompadour (1721–1764), mistress of Louis XV of France; Maria Theresa (1717–1780), archduchess of Austria and queen of Hungary and Bohemia; and Empresses Elizabeth (r. 1741–1762) and Catherine the Great (r. 1762–1796) of Russia—held some of the most influential positions in Europe. Female taste also was a defining factor in numerous smaller courts as well as in the private sphere.

In the early 1700s, Paris was the social capital of Europe, and the Rococo salon (FIG. 26-2) was the center of Parisian society. Wealthy, ambitious, and clever society hostesses competed to attract the most famous and accomplished people to their salons. The medium of social intercourse was conversation spiced with wit, repartee as quick and deft as a fencing match. Artifice reigned supreme, and participants considered enthusiasm or sincerity in bad taste.

The women who hosted these salons, whether in Paris or elsewhere in Europe (FIG. 26-3), referred to themselves as *femmes savants*—learned women. Chief among them was Julie de Lespinasse (1732–1776), one of the most articulate, urbane, and intelligent French women of the time. She held daily salons from five o'clock until nine in the evening. The memoirs of Jean François Marmontel (1723–1799), published in 1827, documented the liveliness of these gatherings and the remarkable nature of this hostess.

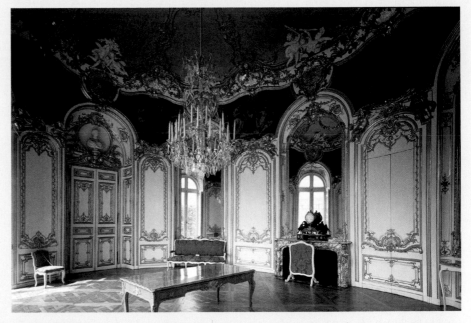

26-2 GERMAIN BOFFRAND, Salon de la Princesse, with paintings by CHARLES-JOSEPH NATOIRE and sculptures by JEAN-BAPTISTE LEMOYNE, Hôtel de Soubise, Paris, France, 1737–1740.

Rococo rooms such as this one, featuring sinuous curves, gilded moldings and mirrors, small sculptures and paintings, and floral ornamentation, were the center of Parisian social and intellectual life.

> The circle was formed of persons who were not bound together. She [Julie de Lespinasse] had taken them here and there in society, but so well assorted were they that once [in her salon] they fell into harmony like the strings of an instrument touched by an able hand. Following out that comparison, I may say that she played the instrument with an art that came of genius; she seemed to know what tone each string would yield before she touched it; I mean to say that our minds and our natures were so well known to her that in order to bring them into play she had but to say a word. Nowhere was conversation more lively, more brilliant, or better regulated than at her house. It was a rare phenomenon indeed, the

degree of tempered, equable heat which she knew so well how to maintain, sometimes by moderating it, sometimes by quickening it. The continual activity of her soul was communicated to our souls, but measurably; her imagination was the mainspring, her reason the regulator. Remark that the brains she stirred at will were neither feeble nor frivolous. . . . Her talent for casting out a thought and giving it for discussion to men of that class, her own talent in discussing it with precision, sometimes with eloquence, her talent for bringing forward new ideas and varying the topic— always with the facility and ease of a fairy . . . these talents, I say, were not those of an ordinary woman. It was not with the follies of fashion and vanity that daily, during four hours of conversation, without languor and without vacuum, she knew how to make herself interesting to a wide circle of strong minds.*

*Jean François Marmontel, *Memoirs of Marmontel* (1827), translated by Brigit Patmore (London: Routledge, 1930), 270.

Architecture

Rococo appeared in France in about 1700, primarily as a style of interior design. The French Rococo exterior was most often simple, or even plain, but Rococo exuberance took over the interior. The term derived from the French word *rocaille* (pebble), but it referred especially to the small stones and shells used to decorate grotto interiors. Shells or forms resembling shells were the principal motifs in Rococo ornamentation.

SALON DE LA PRINCESSE A typical French Rococo room is the Salon de la Princesse (FIG. **26-2**) in the Hôtel de Soubise in Paris, designed by GERMAIN BOFFRAND (1667–1754) in collaboration with the painter JOSEPH NATOIRE (1700–1777) and the sculptor JEAN-BAPTISTE LEMOYNE (1704–1778). Parisian salons such as this one were the center of Rococo social life. They usurped the role Louis XIV's Versailles palace (FIG. 25-26) played in the 17th century, when the Sun King set the tone for French culture. In the

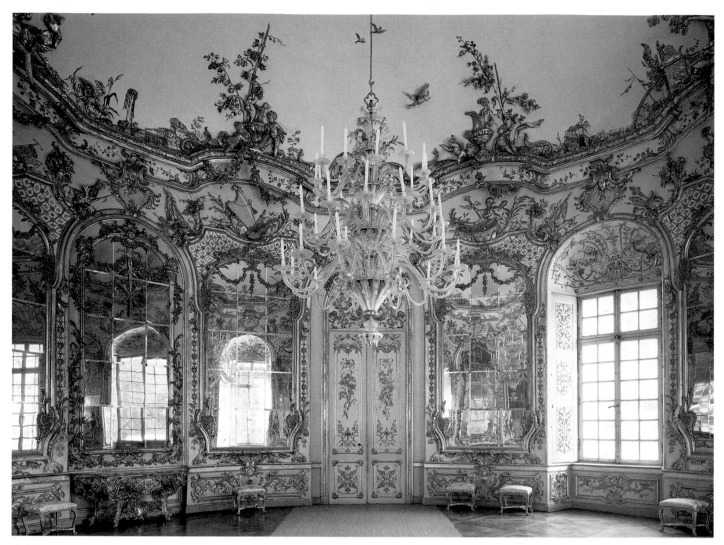

26-3 FRANÇOIS DE CUVILLIÉS, Hall of Mirrors, the Amalienburg, Nymphenburg Palace park, Munich, Germany, early 18th century.

Designed by a French architect, this circular hall in a German lodge displays the Rococo architectural style at its zenith, dazzling the eye with the organic interplay of mirrors, crystal, and stucco relief.

early 18th century, the centralized and grandiose palace-based culture of Baroque France gave way to a much more intimate and decentralized culture based in private homes. The new architectural style mirrored this social and cultural shift. A comparison between the Salon de la Princesse and the Galerie des Glaces (FIG. 25-27) at Versailles reveals how Boffrand softened the strong architectural lines and panels of the earlier style into flexible, sinuous curves luxuriantly multiplied in mirror reflections. The walls melt into the vault. Irregular painted shapes, surmounted by sculpture and separated by the ubiquitous rocaille shells, replace the hall's cornices. Painting, architecture, and sculpture combine to form a single ensemble. The profusion of curving tendrils and sprays of foliage blend with the shell forms to give an effect of freely growing nature, suggesting the designer permanently bedecked the Rococo room for a festival.

French Rococo interiors were lively total works of art. Exquisitely wrought furniture, enchanting small sculptures, ornamented mirror frames, delightful ceramics and silver, small paintings, and decorative *tapestries* complemented the architecture, relief sculptures, and mural paintings. Unfortunately, the Salon de la Princesse has lost most of the moveable furnishings that once contributed so much to its total ambience. Visitors can imagine, however, how this and similar Rococo rooms—with their alternating gilded moldings, vivacious relief sculptures, and daintily colored ornamentation of flowers and garlands—must have harmonized with the chamber music played in them, with the elaborate costumes of satin and brocade, and with the equally elegant etiquette and sparkling wit of the people who graced them.

AMALIENBURG The French Rococo style quickly spread beyond Paris. The Amalienburg, a small lodge the French architect FRANÇOIS DE CUVILLIÉS (1695–1768) built in the park of the Nymphenburg Palace in Munich, is a prime example of Germany's adoption of the Parisian style. The most spectacular room in the lodge is the circular Hall of Mirrors (FIG. **26-3**), a silver-and-blue ensemble of architecture, stucco relief, silvered bronze mirrors, and crystal. The hall dazzles the eye with myriad scintillating motifs, forms, and figurations and showcases the full ornamental repertoire of the Rococo style at its zenith. Silvery light, reflected and amplified by windows and mirrors, bathes the room and creates shapes and contours that weave rhythmically around the upper walls and the ceiling coves. Everything seems organic, growing, and in motion, an ultimate refinement of illusion the architect, artists, and artisans created with virtuoso flourishes.

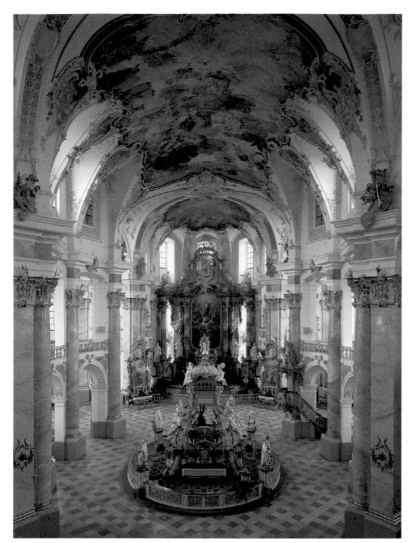

26-4 BALTHASAR NEUMANN, interior of the pilgrimage church of Vierzehnheiligen (looking east), near Staffelstein, Germany, 1743–1772.

Neumann adapted the intimate Rococo style to ecclesiastical architecture. Vierzehnheiligen's interior is light and delicate in contrast to the dynamic energy of Italian Baroque church designs.

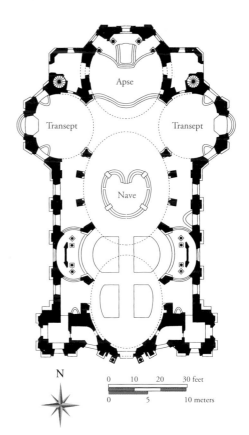

26-5 BALTHASAR NEUMANN, plan of the pilgrimage church of Vierzehnheiligen, near Staffelstein, Germany, 1743–1772.

Vierzehnheiligen's plan features undulating lines and a dynamic composition of tangent ovals and circles. It is even more complex than Borromini's influential church plans (FIGS. 24-10 and 24-13).

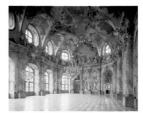

26-5A NEUMANN, Kaisersaal, Würzburg, 1719–1744.

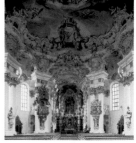

26-5B ZIMMERMANN, Wieskirche, Füssen, 1745–1754.

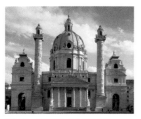

26-3A FISCHER VON ERLACH, Karlskirche, Vienna, 1716–1737.

VIERZEHNHEILIGEN Rococo style was not exclusively a domestic phenomenon, however. Although in the early 18th century, some architects, such as JOHANN BERNHARD FISCHER VON ERLACH (1656–1723), continued to design churches incorporating Baroque and classical elements—for example, Karlskirche (FIG. 26-3A) in Vienna— others eagerly adopted the Rococo style for ecclesiastical architecture. One of the most splendid examples is the pilgrimage church of Vierzehnheiligen (Fourteen Saints; FIGS. 26-4 and 26-5) near Staffelstein (MAP 25-1), which the German architect BALTHASAR NEUMANN (1687–1753) began as construction was about to be concluded on the grandiose palace (FIG. 26-5A) he had designed in 1719 for the prince-bishops of Würzburg. The interior (FIG. 26-4) of Neumann's church exhibits a vivacious play of architectural fantasy that retains the dynamic energy of Italian Baroque architecture (see Chapter 24) but not its drama. Numerous large windows in the richly decorated walls of Vierzehnheiligen flood the interior with an even, bright, and cheerful light. The feeling is one of lightness and delicacy.

Vierzehnheiligen's plan (FIG. 26-5) reveals the influence of Francesco Borromini (FIGS. 24-10 and 24-13), as does the contemporaneous Wieskirche (Church of the Meadow; FIG. 26-5B) by DOMINIKUS ZIMMERMANN (1685–1766). The Staffelstein plan, however, is even more complex than the plans for Borromini's churches in Rome. Neumann, perhaps deliberately, banished all straight lines. The composition, made up of tangent ovals and circles, achieves a quite different interior effect within the essential outlines of a traditional rectilinear basilican church with a nave, transept, and apse. Undulating space is in continuous motion, creating unlimited vistas bewildering in their variety and surprise effects. The structure's features pulse, flow, and commingle as if they were ceaselessly in the process of being molded. The design's fluidity of line, the floating and hovering surfaces, the interwoven spaces, and the dematerialized masses combine to suggest a "frozen" counterpart to the intricacy of voices in a Baroque fugue by Johann Sebastian Bach (1685–1750). The church is a brilliant ensemble of architecture, painting, sculpture, and music that dissolves the boundaries among the arts.

Painting and Sculpture

The unification of diverse artistic media that characterizes the Rococo style did not preclude the rise to prominence of painters of independent works. Chief among them were Antoine Watteau, François Boucher, and Jean-Honoré Fragonard in France.

ANTOINE WATTEAU The painter whom scholars most closely associate with French Rococo is ANTOINE WATTEAU (1684–1721). The sharp differences between the Rococo and Baroque ages in France quickly become evident by contrasting Watteau's *L'Indifférent* (*The Indifferent One*; FIG. 26-6) with Rigaud's portrait of Louis XIV (FIG. 25-24). Rigaud portrayed pompous majesty in supreme glory, as if the French monarch were reviewing throngs of bowing courtiers at Versailles. Watteau's painting is more delicate and lighter in both color and tone. The artist presented a languid, gliding dancer whose stilted minuet might constitute a parody of the monarch's solemnity if the paintings were hung together. (The contrast in scale would be equally stark: The portrait of Louis XIV is almost 10 feet tall. Watteau's dancer is 10 inches tall.) In Rigaud's portrait, stout architecture, bannerlike curtains, flowing ermine, and fleur-de-lis exalt the king. In Watteau's painting, the dancer moves in a rainbow shimmer of color, emerging onto the stage of the intimate comic opera to the silken sounds of strings. As in architecture, this contrast of paintings also highlights the shift in artistic patronage from one era to the next.

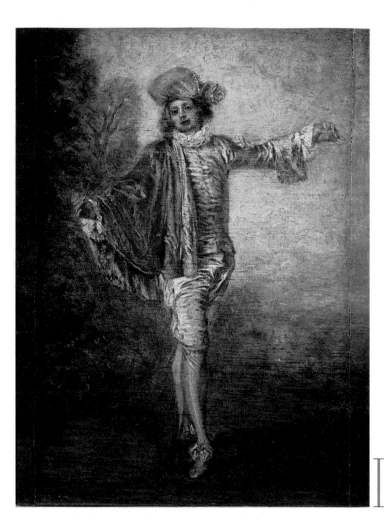

26-6 ANTOINE WATTEAU, *L'Indifférent*, ca. 1716. Oil on canvas, 10″ × 7″. Musée du Louvre, Paris. ■◀

This small Rococo painting of a dancer exhibits lightness and delicacy in both color and tone. It differs significantly from Rigaud's majestic portrait (FIG. 25-24) of the pompous Louis XIV.

1 in.

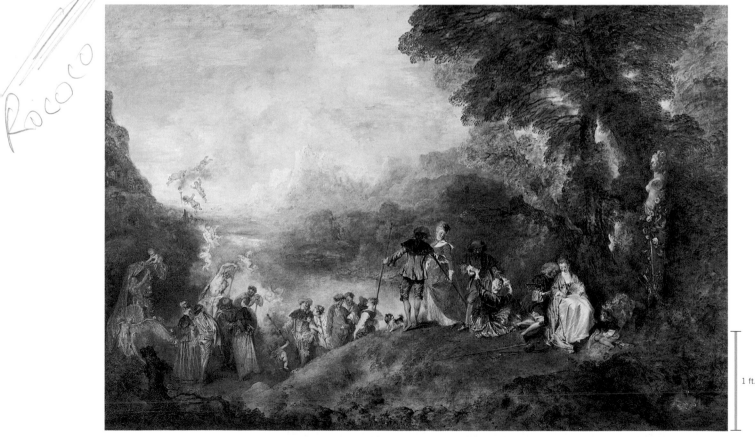

Rococo

26-7 ANTOINE WATTEAU, *Pilgrimage to Cythera*, 1717. Oil on canvas, 4′ 3″ × 6′ 4½″. Musée du Louvre, Paris. ■◀

Watteau's *fête galante* paintings depict the outdoor amusements of French upper-class society. The haze of color, subtly modeled shapes, gliding motion, and air of suave gentility match Rococo taste.

1 ft.

Whereas royal patronage, particularly on the part of Louis XIV, dominated the French Baroque period, Rococo was the culture of a wider aristocracy in which private patrons dictated taste.

PILGRIMAGE TO CYTHERA Watteau was largely responsible for creating a specific type of Rococo painting, called a *fête galante* (amorous festival) painting. These paintings depicted the outdoor entertainment or amusements of French high society. The premier example of a fête galante painting is Watteau's masterpiece (painted in two versions), *Pilgrimage to Cythera* (FIG. **26-7**). The painting was the artist's entry for admission to the French Royal Academy of Painting and Sculpture (see "Academic Salons," Chapter 28, page 802). In 1717 the fête galante was not an acceptable category for submission, but rather than reject Watteau's candidacy, the academy created a new category to accommodate his entry. At the turn of the 18th century, two competing doctrines sharply divided the membership of the French academy. Many members followed Nicolas Poussin in teaching that form was the most important element in painting, whereas "colors in painting are as allurements for persuading the eyes."[1] Colors were additions for effect and not really essential. The other group took Rubens as its model and proclaimed the natural supremacy of color and the coloristic style as the artist's proper guide. Depending on which doctrine they supported, academy members were either *Poussinistes* or *Rubénistes*. Watteau was Flemish and Rubens's coloristic style heavily influenced his work. With Watteau in their ranks, the Rubénistes carried the day, establishing Rococo painting as the preferred style of the early 18th century.

Watteau's *Pilgrimage to Cythera* (FIG. 26-7) presents luxuriously costumed lovers who have made a "pilgrimage" to Cythera, the island of eternal youth and love, sacred to Aphrodite. (Some art historians think the lovers are returning from Cythera rather than having just arrived. Watteau provided few clues to settle the question definitively.) The elegant figures move gracefully from the protective shade of a woodland park, filled with amorous cupids and voluptuous statuary. Watteau's figural poses blend elegance and sweetness. He composed his generally quite small paintings from albums of drawings in which he sought to capture slow movement from difficult and unusual angles, searching for the smoothest, most poised, and most refined attitudes. As he experimented with nuances of posture and movement, Watteau also strove for the most exquisite shades of color difference, defining in a single stroke the shimmer of silk at a bent knee or the iridescence that touches a glossy surface as it emerges from shadow. The haze of color, the subtly modeled shapes, the gliding motion, and the air of suave gentility appealed greatly to Watteau's wealthy patrons, whom, as he was dying from tuberculosis, he still depicted as carefree and at leisure in his most unusual painting, *Signboard of Gersaint* (FIG. **26-7A**).

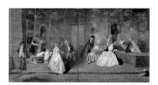

26-7A Watteau, *Signboard of Gersaint*, 1721.

FRANÇOIS BOUCHER After Watteau's death at age 36 brought his brilliant career to a premature end, FRANÇOIS BOUCHER (1703–1770) rose to the dominant position in French painting, in large part because he was Madame de Pompadour's favorite artist. Although Boucher was an excellent portraitist,

his success rested primarily on his graceful canvases depicting Arcadian shepherds, nymphs, and goddesses cavorting in shady glens engulfed in pink and sky-blue light. *Cupid a Captive* (FIG. **26-8**) presents a rosy pyramid of infant and female flesh set off against a cool, leafy background, with fluttering draperies both hiding and revealing the nudity of the figures. Boucher used the full range of Italian

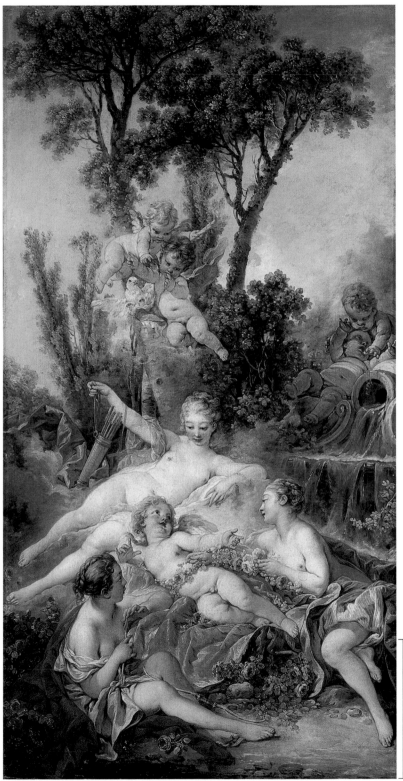

1 ft.

26-8 FRANÇOIS BOUCHER, *Cupid a Captive*, 1754. Oil on canvas, 5′ 6″ × 2′ 10″. Wallace Collection, London. ◼◀

Boucher was Madame de Pompadour's favorite artist. In this Rococo tableau, he painted a pyramid of rosy infant and female flesh and fluttering draperies set off against a cool, leafy background.

and French Baroque devices—the dynamic play of crisscrossing diagonals, curvilinear forms, and slanting recessions—to create his masterly composition. But he dissected powerful Baroque curves into a multiplicity of decorative flourishes, dissipating Baroque drama into sensual playfulness. Lively and lighthearted, Boucher's artful Rococo fantasies became mirrors for his affluent French patrons to behold the ornamental reflections of their cherished pastimes.

JEAN-HONORÉ FRAGONARD Boucher's greatest student, JEAN-HONORÉ FRAGONARD (1732–1806), was a first-rate colorist whose decorative skill almost surpassed his master's. An example of his manner can stand as characteristic not only of his work but also of the later Rococo in general. In *The Swing* (FIG. **26-9**), a young gentleman has convinced an unsuspecting old bishop to swing the young man's pretty sweetheart higher and higher, while her lover (and the work's patron), in the lower left corner, stretches out to admire her ardently from a strategic position on the ground. The young lady flirtatiously and boldly kicks off her shoe toward the little statue of Cupid. The infant love god holds his finger to his lips. The landscape emulates Watteau's—a luxuriant perfumed bower in

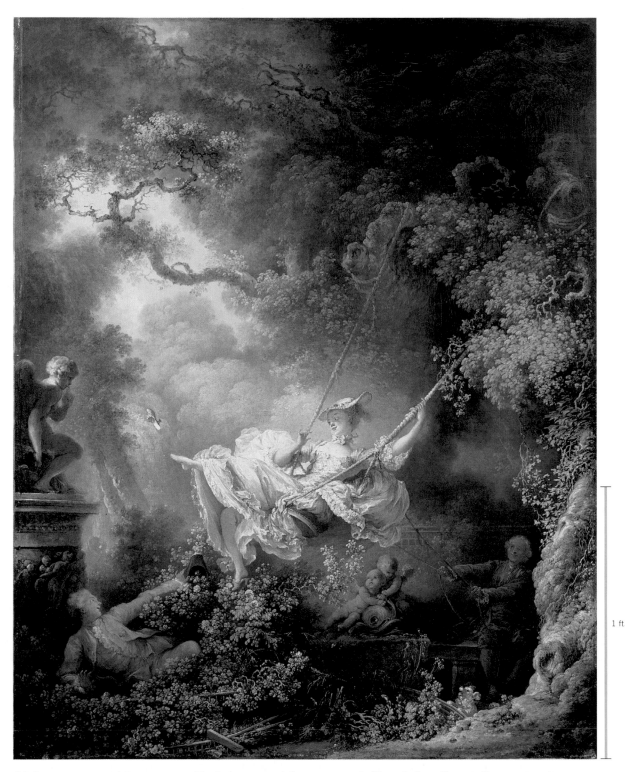

1 ft.

26-9 JEAN-HONORÉ FRAGONARD, *The Swing,* 1766. Oil on canvas, 2′ 8⅝″ × 2′ 2″. Wallace Collection, London. ◼◀

Fragonard's *Swing* epitomizes Rococo style. Pastel colors and soft light complement a scene in which a young lady flirtatiously kicks off her shoe at a statue of Cupid while her lover watches.

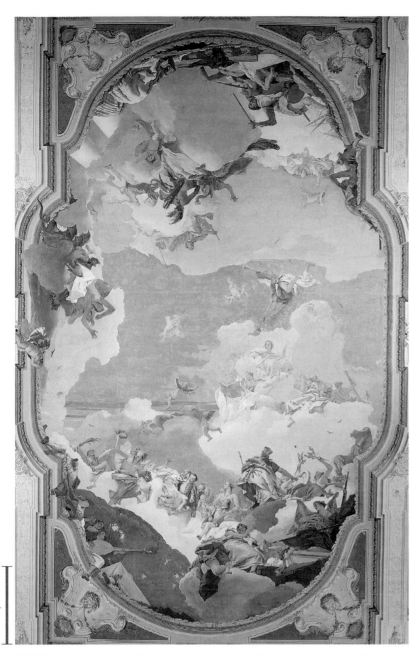

10 ft.

26-10 Giambattista Tiepolo, *Apotheosis of the Pisani Family,* ceiling painting in the Villa Pisani, Stra, Italy, 1761–1762. Fresco, 77′ 1″ × 44′ 3″.

A master of illusionistic ceiling painting in the Baroque tradition, Tiepolo adopted the bright and cheerful colors and weightless figures of Rococo easel paintings for huge frescoes.

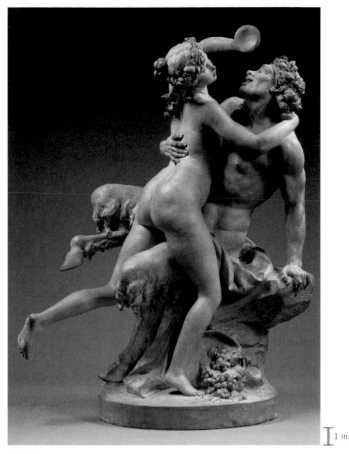

1 in.

26-11 Clodion, *Nymph and Satyr Carousing,* ca. 1780–1790. Terracotta, 1′ 11¼″ high. Metropolitan Museum of Art, New York (bequest of Benjamin Altman, 1913).

The erotic playfulness of Boucher and Fragonard is evident in Clodion's tabletop terracotta sculptures representing sensuous fantasies often involving satyrs and nymphs, the followers of Bacchus.

a park that very much resembles a stage scene for comic opera. The glowing pastel colors and soft light convey, almost by themselves, the theme's sensuality.

GIAMBATTISTA TIEPOLO *The Swing* is less than 3 feet in height and Watteau's *L'Indifférent* (FIG. 26-6), as already noted, barely 10 inches tall. But the intimate Rococo style could also be adapted for paintings of huge size, as the work of Giambattista Tiepolo (1696–1770) demonstrates. A Venetian, Tiepolo worked for patrons in Austria, Germany, and Spain, as well as in Italy. He was a master of illusionistic ceiling decoration in the Baroque tradition, but favored the bright, cheerful colors and relaxed compositions of Rococo easel paintings. In *Apotheosis of the Pisani Family* (FIG. 26-10), a ceiling fresco in the Villa Pisani at Stra in northern Italy (MAP 25-1), Tiepolo depicted seemingly weightless figures fluttering through vast sunlit skies and fleecy clouds, their forms casting dark accents

against the brilliant light of high noon. The painter elevated Pisani family members to the rank of gods in a heavenly scene recalling the ceiling paintings of Pozzo (FIG. 24-24). But while retaining 17th-century illusionism in his works, Tiepolo softened the rhetoric and created pictorial schemes of great elegance and grace, unsurpassed for their sheer effectiveness as decor.

CLODION Rococo was nontheless a style best suited for small-scale works projecting a mood of sensual intimacy. Claude Michel, called Clodion (1738–1814), specialized in small, lively sculptures representing sensuous Rococo fantasies. Clodion lived and worked in Rome for several years after winning a cherished Prix de Rome (Rome Prize) from the French royal academy to study art and paint or sculpt in the eternal city. Clodion's work incorporates echoes of Italian Mannerist sculpture. His small group, *Nymph and Satyr Carousing* (FIG. 26-11), depicts two followers of Bacchus, the Roman god of wine. The sensuous nymph who rushes to pour wine from a cup into the open mouth of a semihuman goat-legged satyr is reminiscent of the nude female figures of Benvenuto Cellini (FIGS. 22-52 and 22-52A), who worked at Fontainebleau for Francis I, and of Giovanni da Bologna (FIG. 22-53), a French Mannerist sculptor who moved to Italy. The erotic playfulness of Boucher and Fragonard is also evident in Clodion's 2-foot-tall terracotta group destined for display on a marble tabletop in an elegant Rococo salon.

THE ENLIGHTENMENT

The aristocratic culture celebrated in Rococo art did not go unchallenged during the 18th century. Indeed, the feudal system that served as the foundation of social and economic life in Europe dissolved, and the rigid social hierarchies that provided the basis for Rococo art and patronage relaxed. By the end of the 18th century, revolutions had erupted in France and America. A major factor in these political, social, and economic changes was the Enlightenment.

Philosophy and Science

Enlightenment thinkers championed an approach to the acquisition of knowledge based on empirical observation and scientific experimentation (see "Art and Science in the Era of Enlightenment," page 727). Enlightenment-era science had roots in the work of René Descartes (1596–1650), Blaise Pascal (1623–1662), Isaac Newton (1642–1727), and Gottfried Wilhelm von Leibnitz (1646–1716) in the 17th century. England and France were the principal centers of the Enlightenment, though its dictums influenced the thinking of intellectuals throughout Europe and in the American colonies. Benjamin Franklin (1706–1790), Thomas Jefferson (1743–1826), and other American notables embraced its principles.

NEWTON AND LOCKE Of particular importance for Enlightenment thought was the work of Isaac Newton and John Locke (1632–1704) in England. In his scientific studies, Newton insisted on empirical proof of his theories and encouraged others to avoid metaphysics and the supernatural—realms that extended beyond the natural physical world. This emphasis on both tangible data and concrete experience became a cornerstone of Enlightenment thought. In addition, Newton's experiments revealed rationality in the physical world, and Enlightenment thinkers transferred that concept to the sociopolitical world by promoting a rationally organized society. Locke, whose works acquired the status of Enlightenment gospel, developed these ideas further. According to Locke's "doctrine of empiricism," knowledge comes through sensory perception of the material world. From these perceptions alone people form ideas. Locke asserted human beings are born good, not cursed by original sin. The laws of nature grant them the natural rights of life, liberty, and property as well as the right to freedom of conscience. Government is by contract, and its purpose is to protect these rights. If and when government abuses these rights, the citizenry has the further natural right of revolution. Locke's ideas empowered people to take control of their own destinies.

PHILOSOPHES The work of Newton and Locke also inspired many French intellectuals, or *philosophes*. These thinkers conceived of individuals and societies at large as parts of physical nature. They shared the conviction the ills of humanity could be remedied by applying reason and common sense to human problems. They criticized the powers of church and state as irrational limits placed on political and intellectual freedom. They believed by accumulating and propagating knowledge, humanity could advance by degrees to a happier state than it had ever known. This conviction matured into the "doctrine of progress" and its corollary doctrine, the "perfectibility of humankind." Previous societies, for the most part, perceived the future as inevitable—the cycle of life and death. They believed religious beliefs determined fate. The notion of progress—the systematic and planned improvement of society—first developed during the 18th century and continues to influence 21st-century thought.

DIDEROT Animated by their belief in human progress and perfectibility, the philosophes took on the task of gathering knowledge and making it accessible to all who could read. Their program was, in effect, the democratization of knowledge. Denis Diderot (1713–1784) greatly influenced the Enlightenment's rationalistic and materialistic thinking. He became editor of the pioneering *Encyclopédie*, a compilation of articles written by more than a hundred contributors, including all the leading philosophes. The *Encyclopédie* was truly comprehensive (its formal title was *Systematic Dictionary of the Sciences, Arts, and Crafts*) and included all available knowledge—historical, scientific, and technical as well as religious and moral—and political theory. The first volume appeared in 1751 and the last of the 35 volumes of text and illustrations in 1780. Other Enlightenment authors produced different compilations of knowledge. Diderot's contemporary, Georges-Louis Leclerc (1707–1788), Comte de Buffon, undertook a kind of encyclopedia of the natural sciences. His *Natural History,* a monumental work of 44 volumes, was especially valuable for its zoological study. Buffon's contemporary, the Swedish botanist Carolus Linnaeus (1707–1778), established a system of plant classification.

The political, economic, and social consequences of this increase in knowledge and the doctrine of progress were explosive. It is no coincidence the French Revolution, the American Revolution, and the Industrial Revolution in England all occurred during this period. These upheavals precipitated yet other major changes, including the growth of cities and of an urban working class, and the expansion of colonialism as the demand for cheap labor and raw materials increased. This enthusiasm for growth gave birth to the doctrine of Manifest Destiny—the ideological justification for continued territorial expansion. Thus, the Age of Enlightenment ushered in a new way of thinking and affected historical developments worldwide.

VOLTAIRE François Marie Arouet, better known as Voltaire (1694–1778), was the most representative figure—almost the personification—of the Enlightenment spirit. Voltaire was instrumental in introducing Newton and Locke to the French intelligentsia. He hated, and attacked through his writings, the arbitrary despotic rule of kings, the selfish privileges of the nobility and the church, religious intolerance, and, above all, the injustice of the French *ancien regime* (the "old order"). In his numerous books and pamphlets, which the authorities regularly condemned and burned, he protested against government persecution of the freedoms of thought and religion. Voltaire believed humankind could never be happy until an enlightened society removed the traditional obstructions to the progress of the human mind. His personal and public involvement in the struggle against established political and religious authority gave authenticity to his ideas. Voltaire persuaded a whole generation that fundamental changes were necessary, paving the way for a revolution in France he never intended and probably would never have approved. Voltaire did not believe "all men are created equal," the credo of Jean-Jacques Rousseau, Thomas Jefferson, and the American Declaration of Independence.

INDUSTRIAL REVOLUTION The Enlightenment emphasis on scientific investigation and technological invention opened up new possibilities for human understanding of the world and for control of its material forces. Research into the phenomena of electricity and combustion, along with the discovery of oxygen and the power of steam, had enormous consequences. Steam power as an adjunct to, or replacement for, human labor initiated a new era in world history, beginning with the Industrial Revolution in England. These and other technological advances—admiringly

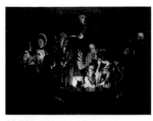

recorded in the paintings of Joseph Wright of Derby (FIGS. 26-1 and 26-11A)—epitomized the Enlightenment notion of progress and gave birth to the Industrial Revolution. Most scholars mark the dawn of that technological revolution in the 1740s with the invention of steam engines in England for industrial production. By 1850, England could boast the world's first manufacturing economy. Within a century, the harnessed power of steam, coal, oil, iron, steel, and electricity working in concert transformed Europe. These scientific and technological advances also affected the arts, particularly through the invention of photography (see Chapter 27) and the use of new materials for constructing buildings.

COALBROOKDALE BRIDGE The first use of iron in bridge design was in the cast-iron bridge (FIG. **26-12**) built over the Severn River, near Coalbrookdale in England (MAP 30-1), where ABRAHAM DARBY III (1750–1789), one of the bridge's two designers, ran his family's cast-iron business. The Darby family had spearheaded the evolution of the iron industry in England, and they vigorously supported the investigation of new uses for the material. The fabrication of cast-iron rails and bridge elements inspired Darby to work with architect THOMAS F. PRITCHARD (1723–1777) in designing the Coalbrookdale Bridge. The cast-iron armature supporting the roadbed springs from stone pier to stone pier until it leaps the final 100 feet across the Severn River gorge. The style of the graceful center arc echoes the grand arches of Roman aqueducts (FIG. 7-33). At the same time, the exposed structure of the bridge's cast-iron parts prefigured the skeletal use of iron and steel in the 19th century, when exposed structural armatures became expressive factors in the design of buildings such as the Crystal Palace (FIG. 27-47) in England and the Eiffel Tower (FIG. 28-38) in France.

ROUSSEAU The second key figure of the French Enlightenment, who was also instrumental in preparing the way ideologically for the French Revolution, was Jean-Jacques Rousseau (1712–1778). Voltaire believed the salvation of humanity lay in the advancement of science and the rational improvement of society. In contrast, Rousseau argued the arts, sciences, society, and civilization in general had corrupted "natural man"—people in their primitive state. He was convinced humanity's only salvation lay in a return to something like "the ignorance, innocence and happiness" of its original condition. According to Rousseau, human capacity for feeling, sensibility, and emotions came before reason: "To exist is to feel; our feeling is undoubtedly earlier than our intelligence, and we had feelings before we had ideas." Nature alone must be the guide: "All our natural inclinations are right." Fundamental to Rousseau's thinking was the notion "Man by nature is good . . . he is depraved and perverted by society." He rejected the idea of progress, insisting "Our minds have been corrupted in proportion as the arts and sciences have improved."[2] Rousseau's elevation of feelings above reason as the most primitive—and hence the most "natural"—of human expressions led him to exalt as the ideal the peasant's simple life, with its honest and unsullied emotions.

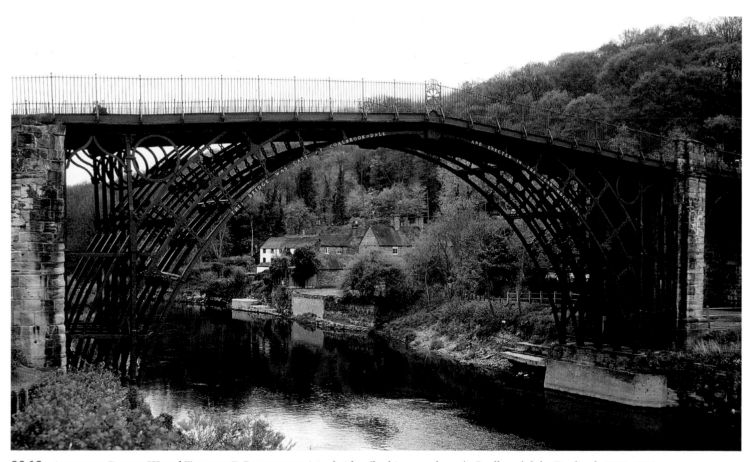

26-12 ABRAHAM DARBY III and THOMAS F. PRITCHARD, iron bridge (looking northwest), Coalbrookdale, England, 1776–1779.

The first use of iron in bridge design was in this bridge over the Severn River. The Industrial Revolution brought engineering advances and new materials that revolutionized architectural construction.

Diderot on Chardin and Boucher

Denis Diderot was a pioneer in the field of art criticism as well as in the encyclopedic compilation of human knowledge. Between 1759 and 1781, he contributed reviews of the biennial Salon of the French Royal Academy of Painting and Sculpture (see "Academic Salons," Chapter 28, page 802) to the Parisian journal *Correspondence littéraire*. In his review of the 1763 Salon, Diderot had the following praise for Chardin's still lifes and for naturalism in painting.

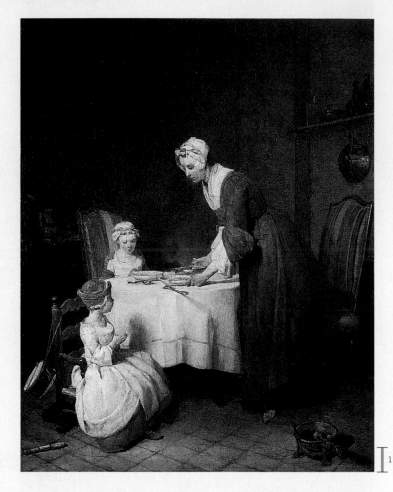

26-13 Jean-Baptiste-Siméon Chardin, *Saying Grace*, 1740. Oil on canvas, 1' 7" × 1' 3". Musée du Louvre, Paris.

Chardin embraced naturalism and celebrated the simple goodness of ordinary people, especially mothers and children, who lived in a world far from the frivolous Rococo salons of Paris.

1 in.

There are many small pictures by Chardin at the Salon, almost all of them depicting fruit with the accoutrements for a meal. This is nature itself. The objects stand out from the canvas and they are so real that my eyes are fooled by them. . . . In order to look at other people's paintings, I feel as though I need different eyes; but to look at Chardin's, I need only keep the ones nature gave me and use them properly. If I had painting in mind as a career for my child, I'd buy this one [and have him copy it]. . . . Yet nature itself may be no more difficult to copy. . . . O Chardin, it's not white, red or black pigment that you grind on your palette but rather the very substance of objects; it's real air and light that you take onto the tip of your brush and transfer onto the canvas. . . . It's magic, one can't understand how it's done: thick layers of colour, applied one on top of the other, each one filtering through from underneath to create the effect. . . . Close up, everything blurs, goes flat and disappears. From a distance, everything comes back to life and reappears.*

Diderot could write scathing reviews as well as lavish praise on the leading artists of his day. He admired Chardin (FIG. 26-13) because his work was the antithesis of the Rococo manner in painting, which Diderot deplored. Here, for example, is what Diderot had to say about François Boucher (FIG. 26-8), who also exhibited in the Salon of 1763, and his younger protégés emulating his Rococo style:

What a misuse of talent! How much time gone to waste! You could have had twice the effect for half the effort. . . . When one writes, does one have to write everything? And when one paints, does one have to paint everything? . . . This man is the ruination of all young apprentice painters. Barely able to handle a brush and hold a palette, they torture themselves stringing together infantile garlands, painting chubby crimson bottoms, and hurl themselves headlong into all kinds of follies which cannot be redeemed by originality, fire, tenderness nor by any magic in their models. For they lack all of these.†

*Translated by Kate Tunstall, in Charles Harrison, Paul Wood, and Jason Gaiger, eds., *Art in Theory 1648–1815: An Anthology of Changing Ideas* (Oxford: Blackwell, 2000), 604.
†Ibid., 603–604.

"NATURAL" ART

Rousseau's views, popular and widely read, were largely responsible for the turning away from the Rococo sensibility in the arts and the formation of a taste for the "natural," as opposed to the artificial and frivolous.

CHARDIN Reflecting Rousseau's values, Jean-Baptiste-Siméon Chardin (1699–1779) painted quiet scenes of domestic life, which offered the opportunity to praise the simple goodness of ordinary people, especially mothers and young children, who in spirit, occupation, and environment lived far from corrupt society. In *Saying Grace* (FIG. 26-13), Chardin ushers the viewer into a modest room where a mother and her two daughters are about to dine. The mood of quiet attention is at one with the hushed lighting and mellow color and with the closely studied still-life accessories whose worn surfaces tell their own humble domestic history. The viewer witnesses a moment of social instruction, when mother and older sister supervise the younger sister in the simple, pious ritual of giving thanks to God before a meal. The simplicity of the composition reinforces the subdued charm of this scene, with the three figures highlighted against the dark background. Chardin was the poet of the commonplace and the master of its nuances. A gentle sentiment

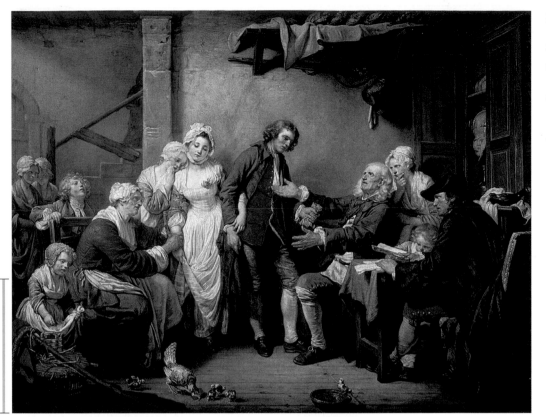

Greuze was a master of sentimental narrative, which appealed to a new audience that admired "natural" virtue. Here, in an unadorned room, a father blesses his daughter and her husband-to-be.

prevails in all his pictures, an emotion not contrived and artificial but born of the painter's honesty, insight, and sympathy. Chardin's paintings had wide appeal, even in unexpected places. Louis XV, the royal personification of the Rococo in his life and tastes, once owned *Saying Grace*. The painter was also a favorite of Diderot, the leading art critic of the day as well as the editor of the *Encyclopédie* (see "Diderot on Chardin and Boucher," page 738).

JEAN-BAPTISTE GREUZE The sentimental narrative in art became the specialty of French artist JEAN-BAPTISTE GREUZE (1725–1805), whose most popular work, *Village Bride* (FIG. 26-14), sums up the characteristics of the genre. The setting is an unadorned room in a rustic dwelling. In a notary's presence, the elderly father has passed his daughter's dowry to her youthful husband-to-be and blesses the pair, who gently take each other's arms. The old mother tearfully gives her daughter's arm a farewell caress, while the youngest sister melts in tears on the shoulder of the demure bride. An envious older sister broods behind her father's chair. Rosy-faced, healthy children play around the scene. The picture's story is simple—the happy climax of a rural romance. The picture's moral is just as clear—happiness is the reward of "natural" virtue.

Greuze produced this work at a time when the audience for art was expanding. The strict social hierarchy that provided the foundation for Rococo art and patronage gave way to a bourgeois economic and social system. The newly important bourgeois class embraced art, and paintings such as *Village Bride* particularly appealed to ordinary hard-working people. They carefully analyzed each gesture and each nuance of sentiment and reacted with tumultuous enthusiasm. At the 1761 Salon of the Royal Academy, Greuze's picture received enormous attention. Diderot, who reviewed the exhibition for *Correspondence littéraire*, reported it was difficult to get near the canvas because of the throngs of admirers.

ÉLISABETH-LOUISE VIGÉE-LEBRUN Another manifestation of the "naturalistic" impulse in 18th-century French art was the emergence of a new mode of portraiture exemplified by *Self-Portrait* (FIG. 26-15) by ÉLISABETH-LOUISE VIGÉE-LEBRUN (1755–1842). The painter looks directly at viewers and pauses in her work to return their gaze. Although her mood is lighthearted and her costume's details echo the serpentine curve Rococo artists and wealthy patrons loved, nothing about Vigée-Lebrun's pose or her mood speaks of Rococo frivolity. Hers is the self-confident stance of a woman whose art has won her an independent role in society. She

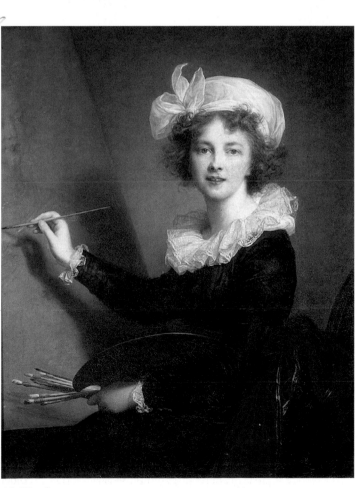

26-15 ÉLISABETH-LOUISE VIGÉE-LEBRUN, *Self-Portrait*, 1790. Oil on canvas, 8′ 4″ × 6′ 9″. Galleria degli Uffizi, Florence.

Vigée-Lebrun was one of the few women admitted to the Royal Academy of Painting and Sculpture. In this self-portrait, she depicted herself confidently painting the likeness of Queen Marie Antoinette.

natural and
ROCOCO Frivolity

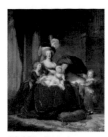

26-15A VIGÉE-LEBRUN, *Marie Antoinette*, 1787.

portrayed herself in a close-up, intimate view at work on one of the many portraits (for example, FIG. 26-15A) she painted of her most important patron, Queen Marie Antoinette (1755–1793). Like many of her contemporaries, Vigée-Lebrun lived a life of extraordinary personal and economic independence, working for the nobility throughout Europe. She was famous for the force and grace of her portraits, especially those of highborn ladies and royalty. She was successful during the age of the late monarchy in France and was one of the few women admitted to the Royal Academy of Painting and Sculpture. After the French Revolution, however, the academy rescinded her membership, because women were no longer welcome, but she enjoyed continued success owing to her talent, wit, and ability to forge connections with those in power in the postrevolutionary period.

ADÉLAÏDE LABILLE-GUIARD Six years older than Vigée-Lebrun, ADÉLAÏDE LABILLE-GUIARD (1749–1803) was the second-most important woman painter in Paris at the end of the 18th century, but she never achieved the renown enjoyed by her younger rival. She trained with François-Élie Vincent (1708–1790) and later with his son François-André Vincent (1746–1816), whom she married after her divorce from her first husband, Louis-Nicolas Guiard, a clerk. Like Vigée-Lebrun, Labille-Guiard boasted royal patronage but not of the same order. She became the official painter of the "mesdames"—the aunts of King Louis XVI—in 1787, four years after she was admitted to the royal painting academy on the same day as Vigée-Lebrun. The two painters captured the remaining two of four memberships reserved for women, a quota Labille-Guiard worked hard to lift after gaining admission. The two artists took opposite sides during the French Revolution, and Labille-Guiard painted portraits of some of the uprising's leaders, including one of the few known portraits of Maximilien Robespierre (1758–1794), the most prominent figure calling for the death of King Louis XVI.

A comparison between Labille-Guiard's *Self-Portrait with Two Pupils* (FIG. 26-16) and Vigée-Lebrun's *Self-Portrait* (FIG. 26-15) underscores the two women's different self-images. The younger painter presented herself at work on a portrait of her most important patron, Marie Antoinette. The subject of the canvas Labille-Guiard is painting is unknown. Her self-portrait focuses instead on her role as a teacher. She had as many as nine women in her studio at one time. Here, two apprentices—dressed more simply than their elegantly clad instructor—cluster behind her, one intently studying the painting in progress, the other, as Labille-Guiard, gazing at the viewer. The three figures form a classical pyramidal composition, echoed by the easel. In the V formed by the two triangles is a portrait bust of the artist's father. Appropriately for this early feminist, her muse is a man, a reversal of the traditional gender roles.

WILLIAM HOGARTH Across the Channel, a truly English style of painting emerged with WILLIAM HOGARTH (1697–1764), who satirized the lifestyle of the newly prosperous middle class with comic zest. Traditionally, the British imported painters from the Continent—Holbein, Rubens, and Van Dyck among them. Hogarth waged a lively campaign throughout his career against the English feeling of dependence on, and inferiority to, these artists. Although Hogarth would have been the last to admit it, his own painting owed much to the work of his contemporaries in France, the Rococo

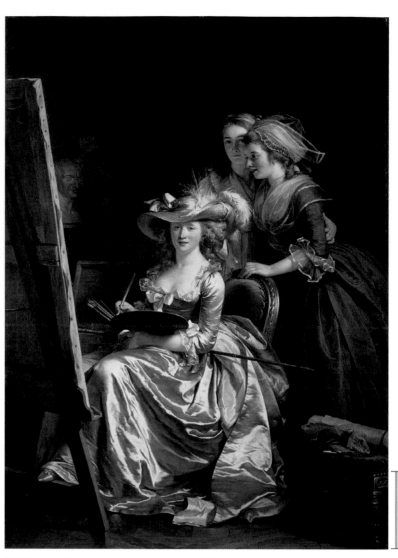

26-16 ADÉLAÏDE LABILLE-GUIARD, *Self-Portrait with Two Pupils*, 1785. Oil on canvas, 6′ 11″ × 4′ 11½″. Metropolitan Museum of Art, New York (gift of Julia A. Berwind, 1953).

In contrast to Vigée-Lebrun (FIG. 26-15), Labille-Guiard, her older contemporary, depicted herself as a teacher. Her father's bust portrait serves as her muse in a reversal of traditional gender roles.

artists. Yet his subject matter, frequently moral in tone, was distinctively English. This was the great age of English satirical writing, and Hogarth—who admired that literary genre and included Henry Fielding (1701–1754), the author of *Tom Jones,* among his closest friends—clearly saw himself as translating satire into the visual arts.

Hogarth's favorite device was to make a series of narrative paintings and prints, in a sequence similar to chapters in a book or scenes in a play, following a character or group of characters in their encounters with some social evil. *Breakfast Scene* (FIG. 26-17), from *Marriage à la Mode,* is one in a sequence of six paintings satirizing the marital immoralities of the moneyed classes in England. In it, the marriage of a young viscount is just beginning to founder. The husband and wife are tired after a long night spent in separate pursuits. While the wife stayed at home for an evening of cards and music-making, her young husband had been away from the house for a night of suspicious business. He thrusts his hands deep into the empty money-pockets of his breeches, while his wife's small dog sniffs inquiringly at a woman's lacy cap protruding from his coat pocket. A steward, his hands full of unpaid bills, raises his eyes in despair at the actions of his noble master and mistress. The house is palatial, but Hogarth filled it with witty clues to the dubious taste of

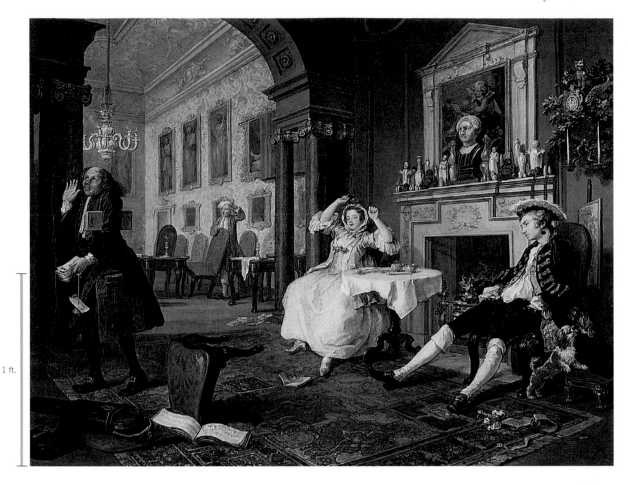

26-17 WILLIAM
HOGARTH, *Breakfast
Scene,* from *Marriage
à la Mode,* ca. 1745.
Oil on canvas,
2′ 4″ × 3′. National
Gallery, London.

Hogarth won fame for
his paintings and prints
satirizing English life with
comic zest. This is one of
a series of six paintings in
which he chronicled the
marital immoralities of
the moneyed class.

1 ft.

its occupants. For example, the row of pious religious paintings on the upper wall of the distant room concludes with a curtained canvas undoubtedly depicting an erotic subject. According to the custom of the day, ladies could not view this discretely hidden painting, but at the pull of a cord, the master and his male guests could enjoy a tableau of cavorting figures. In *Breakfast Scene,* as in all his work, Hogarth proceeded as a novelist might, elaborating on his subject with carefully chosen detail, the discovery of which heightens the comedy.

Hogarth designed the marriage series to be published as a set of engravings. The prints of this and his other moral narratives were so popular that unscrupulous entrepreneurs produced unauthorized versions almost as fast as the artist created his originals. The popularity of these prints speaks not only to the appeal of their subjects but also to the democratization of knowledge and culture the Enlightenment fostered and to the exploitation of new printing technologies that opened the way for a more affordable and widely disseminated visual culture.

THOMAS GAINSBOROUGH

A contrasting blend of "naturalistic" representation and Rococo setting is found in *Mrs. Richard Brinsley Sheridan* (FIG. **26-18**), a characteristic portrait by British painter THOMAS GAINSBOROUGH (1727–1788). Gainsborough presented Mrs. Sheridan as a lovely, informally dressed woman seated in a rustic landscape faintly reminiscent of Watteau (FIG. 26-7) in its soft-hued light and feathery brushwork. Gainsborough's goal was to match the natural, unspoiled

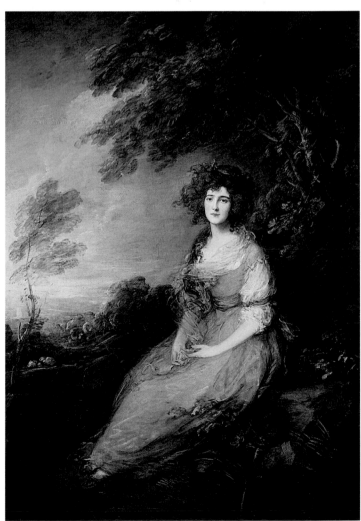

26-18 THOMAS
GAINSBOROUGH, *Mrs.
Richard Brinsley Sheridan,*
1787. Oil on canvas,
7′ 2⅝″ × 5′ ⅝″. National
Gallery of Art, Washington,
D.C. (Andrew W. Mellon
Collection).

In this life-size portrait,
Gainsborough sought to match
Mrs. Sheridan's natural beauty
with that of the landscape.
The rustic setting, soft-hued
light, and feathery brushwork
recall Rococo painting.

1 ft.

beauty of the landscape with that of his sitter. Mrs. Sheridan's dark brown hair blows freely in the slight wind, and her clear "English complexion" and air of ingenuous sweetness contrast sharply with the pert sophistication of the subjects of Continental Rococo portraits. Gainsborough planned to give the picture a more pastoral air by adding several sheep, but he did not live long enough to complete the canvas. Even without the sheep, the painting clearly expresses Gainsborough's deep interest in the landscape setting. Although he won greater fame in his time for his portraits, he had begun as a landscape painter and always preferred painting scenes of nature to depicting individual likenesses.

JOSHUA REYNOLDS Morality of a more heroic tone than found in the work of Greuze, yet in harmony with "naturalness," included the virtues of honor, valor, and love of country. The Enlightenment concept of "nobility," especially in the view of Rousseau, referred to character, not to aristocratic birth. As the century progressed and people felt the tremors of coming revolutions, the virtues of courage and resolution, patriotism, and self-sacrifice assumed greater importance. Having risen from humble origins, the modern military hero, not the decadent aristocrat, brought the excitement of war into the company of the "natural" emotions.

Sir Joshua Reynolds (1723–1792) specialized in what became known as *Grand Manner portraiture* and often painted likenesses of key participants in the great events of the latter part of the 18th century. Although clearly depicting specific individuals, Grand Manner portraits elevated the sitters by conveying refinement and elegance. Painters communicated a person's grace and class through certain standardized conventions, such as the large scale of the figure relative to the canvas, the controlled pose, the landscape setting, and the low horizon line.

Reynolds painted *Lord Heathfield* (FIG. **26-19**) in 1787. The sitter was a perfect subject for a Grand Manner portrait—a burly, ruddy English officer, the commandant of the fortress at Gibraltar. Heathfield had doggedly defended the British stronghold against the Spanish and French, and later received the honorary title Baron Heathfield of Gibraltar. Here, he holds the huge key to the fortress, the symbol of his victory. He stands in front of a curtain of dark smoke rising from the battleground, flanked by one cannon pointing ineffectively downward and another whose tilted barrel indicates it lies uselessly on its back. Reynolds portrayed the features of the general's heavy, honest face and his uniform with unidealized realism. But Lord Heathfield's posture and the setting dramatically suggest the heroic themes of battle, courage, and patriotism.

BENJAMIN WEST Some American artists also became well known in England. Benjamin West (1738–1820), born in Pennsylvania on what was then the colonial frontier (MAP 26-1), traveled to Europe early in life to study art and then went to England, where he met with almost immediate success. A cofounder of the Royal Academy of Arts, West succeeded Reynolds as its president. He became official painter to George III (r. 1760–1801) and retained that position even during the strained period of the American Revolution.

In *Death of General Wolfe* (FIG. **26-20**), West depicted the mortally wounded young English commander just after his defeat of the French in the decisive battle of Quebec in 1759, which gave Canada to Great Britain. Because his subject was a recent event, West clothed his characters in contemporary costumes (although the military uniforms are not completely accurate in all details). However, West blended this realism of detail with the grand tradition of history painting by arranging his figures in a complex and

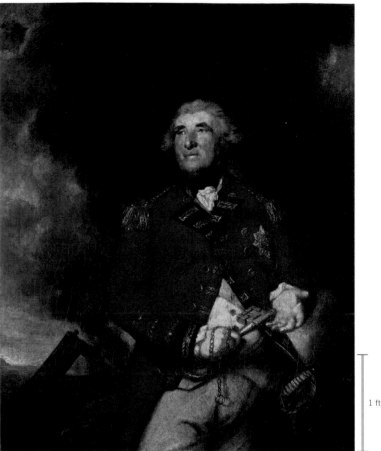

26-19 Sir Joshua Reynolds, *Lord Heathfield,* 1787. Oil on canvas, 4′ 8″ × 3′ 9″. National Gallery, London.

In this Grand Manner portrait, Reynolds depicted the English commander who defended Gibraltar. As is typical for this genre, Heathfield stands in a dramatic pose and his figure takes up most of the canvas.

theatrically ordered composition. His modern hero dies among grieving officers on the field of victorious battle in a way that suggests the death of a saint. (The composition, in fact, derives from paintings of the lamentation over the dead Christ.) West wanted to present this hero's death in the service of the state as a martyrdom charged with religious emotions. His innovative and highly effective combination of the conventions of traditional heroic painting with a look of modern realism influenced history painting well into the 19th century.

JOHN SINGLETON COPLEY American artist John Singleton Copley (1738–1815) matured as a painter in the Massachusetts Bay Colony. Like West, Copley later emigrated to England, where he absorbed the fashionable English portrait style. But unlike Grand Manner portraiture, Copley's *Paul Revere* (FIG. **26-21**), painted before the artist left Boston, conveys a sense of directness and faithfulness to visual fact that marked the taste for honesty and plainness noted by many late-18th- and 19th-century visitors to America. When Copley painted his portrait, Revere was not yet the familiar hero of the American Revolution. In the picture, he is working at his profession of silversmithing. The setting is plain, the lighting clear and revealing. Revere sits in his shirtsleeves, bent over a teapot in progress. He pauses and turns his head to look the observer straight in the eyes. The painter treated the reflections in the polished wood of the tabletop with as much care as he did Revere's

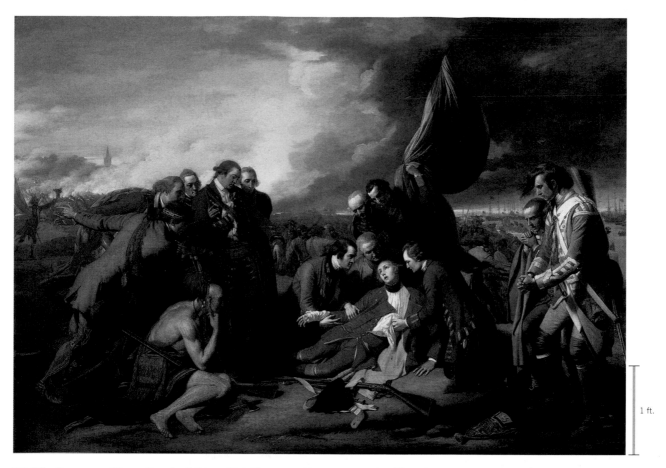

26-20 BENJAMIN WEST, *Death of General Wolfe*, 1771. Oil on canvas, 4' 11½" × 7'. National Gallery of Canada, Ottawa (gift of the Duke of Westminster, 1918).

West's great innovation was to blend contemporary subject matter and costumes with the grand tradition of history painting. Here, the painter likened General Wolfe's death to that of a martyred saint.

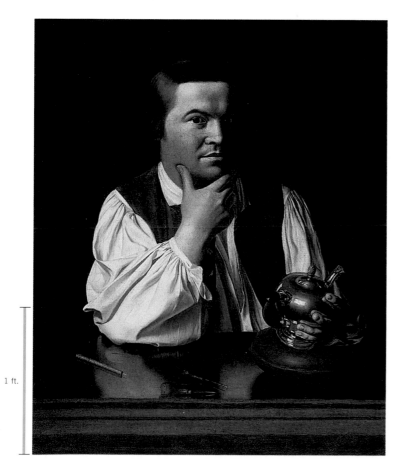

26-21 JOHN SINGLETON COPLEY, *Paul Revere*, ca. 1768–1770. Oil on canvas, 2' 11⅛" × 2' 4". Museum of Fine Arts, Boston (gift of Joseph W., William B., and Edward H. R. Revere).

In contrast to Grand Manner portraiture, Copley's *Paul Revere* emphasizes his subject's down-to-earth character, differentiating this American work from its European counterparts.

figure, his tools, and the teapot resting on its leather graver's pillow. Copley gave special prominence to Revere's eyes by reflecting intense reddish light onto the darkened side of his face and hands. The informality and the sense of the moment link this painting to contemporaneous English and Continental portraits. But the spare style and the emphasis on the sitter's down-to-earth character differentiate this American work from its European counterparts.

THE GRAND TOUR The 18th-century public also sought "naturalness" in artists' depictions of landscapes. Documentation of specific places became popular, in part due to growing travel opportunities and expanding colonialism. These depictions of geographic settings also served the needs of the many scientific expeditions mounted during the century and satisfied the desires of genteel tourists for mementos of their journeys. By this time, a Grand Tour of the major sites of Europe was an essential part of every well-bred person's education (see "The Grand Tour and Veduta Painting," page 744). Those who embarked on a tour of the Continent wished to return with souvenirs to help them remember their experiences and impress those at home with the wonders

The Grand Tour and Veduta Painting

Although travel throughout Europe was commonplace in the 18th century, Italy became an especially popular destination. This "pilgrimage" of aristocrats, the wealthy, politicians, and diplomats from France, England, Germany, Flanders, Sweden, the United States, Russia, Poland, and Hungary came to be known as the Grand Tour. Italy's allure fueled the revival of classicism, and the popularity of Neoclassical art drove the fascination with Italy. One British observer noted: "All our religion, all our arts, almost all that sets us above savages, has come from the shores of the Mediterranean."*

The Grand Tour was not simply leisure travel. The education available in Italy to the inquisitive mind made such a tour an indispensable experience for anyone who wished to make a mark in society. The Enlightenment had made knowledge of ancient Rome and Greece imperative, and a steady stream of Europeans and Americans traveled to Italy in the late 18th and early 19th centuries. These tourists aimed to increase their knowledge of literature, the visual arts, architecture, theater, music, history, customs, and folklore. Given this extensive agenda, it is not surprising a Grand Tour could take a number of years to complete. Most travelers moved from location to location, following an established itinerary.

The British were the most avid travelers, and they conceived the initial "tour code," including required itineraries to important destinations. Although they designated Rome early on as the primary destination in Italy, visitors traveled as far north as Venice and as far south as Naples. Eventually, Paestum, Sicily, Florence, Siena, Pisa, Genoa, Milan, Bologna, and Parma (MAP 25-1) all appeared in guidebooks and in paintings. Joseph Wright of Derby (FIGS. 26-1 and 26-11A) and Joseph Mallord William Turner (FIG. 27-22) were among the many British artists to undertake a Grand Tour.

Many visitors to Italy returned home from their Grand Tour with a painting by Antonio Canaletto, the leading painter of scenic views (*vedute*) of Venice. It must have been very cheering on a gray winter afternoon in England to look up and see a sunny, panoramic view such as that in Canaletto's *Riva degli Schiavoni, Venice* (FIG. 26-22), with its cloud-studded sky, picturesque water traffic, and well-known Venetian landmarks painted in scrupulous perspective and minute detail. (The Doge's Palace [FIG. 14-21] is at the left in *Riva degli Schiavoni*.) Canaletto usually made drawings "on

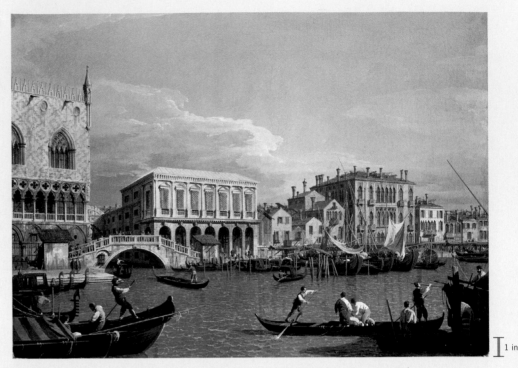

26-22 ANTONIO CANALETTO, *Riva degli Schiavoni, Venice*, ca. 1735–1740. Oil on canvas, 1′ 6½″ × 2′ ⅞″. Toledo Museum of Art, Toledo.

Canaletto was the leading painter of Venetian *vedute*, which were treasured souvenirs for 18th-century travelers visiting Italy on a Grand Tour. He used a camera obscura for his on-site drawings.

location" to take back to his studio and use as sources for paintings. To help make the on-site drawings true to life, he often used a camera obscura, as Vermeer (FIGS. 25-19 to 25-20A) did before him. These instruments were darkened chambers (some of them virtually portable closets) with optical lenses fitted into a hole in one wall through which light entered to project an inverted image of the subject onto the chamber's opposite wall. The artist could trace the main details from this image for later reworking and refinement. The camera obscura enabled artists to create convincing representations incorporating the variable focus of objects at different distances. Canaletto's paintings give the impression of capturing every detail, with no "editing." In fact, he presented each site according to Renaissance perspective conventions and exercised great selectivity about which details to include and which to omit to make a coherent and engagingly attractive veduta.

*Cesare de Seta, "Grand Tour: The Lure of Italy in the Eighteenth Century," in Andrew Wilton and Ilaria Bignamini, eds., *Grand Tour: The Lure of Italy in the Eighteenth Century* (London: Tate Gallery, 1996), 13.

---

they had seen. The English were especially eager collectors of travel pictures. Venetian artists in particular found it profitable to produce paintings of the most characteristic *vedute* (scenic views) of their city to sell to British visitors. Chief among those artists was

ANTONIO CANALETTO (1697–1768), whose works, for example *Riva degli Schiavoni, Venice* (*Bank of the Slaves, Venice*; FIG. **26-22**), English tourists avidly acquired as evidence of their visit to Italy's magical city of water.

The Excavations of Herculaneum and Pompeii

Among the developments stimulating the European fascination with classical antiquity was the initiation of systematic excavations at two ancient Roman cities on the Bay of Naples—Herculaneum and Pompeii—in 1738 and 1748, respectively. The violent eruption of Mount Vesuvius in August 79 CE had buried both cities under volcanic ash and lava (see "An Eyewitness Account of the Eruption of Mount Vesuvius," Chapter 7, page 188), protecting the sites for hundreds of years from looters and the ravages of nature. Consequently, the 18th-century excavations yielded an unprecedented number of well-preserved paintings, sculptures, vases, and other household objects, and provided rich evidence for reconstructing Roman art and life. As a result, European ideas about and interest in ancient Rome expanded tremendously, and collectors eagerly acquired as many of the newly discovered antiquities as they could. One of the most avid collectors was Sir William Hamilton (1731–1803), British consul in Naples from 1764 to 1800, who purchased numerous painted vases and other ancient objects and then sold them to the British Museum in 1772. The finds at Pompeii and Herculaneum, therefore, quickly became available to a wide public.

"Pompeian" style soon became all the rage in England, as is evident, for example, in Robert Adam's Etruscan Room (FIG. 26-23) at Osterley Park House, which was inspired by the frescoes of the Third and early Fourth Styles of Roman mural painting (FIGS. 7-21 and 7-22). Adam took decorative motifs (medallions, urns, vine scrolls, sphinxes, and tripods) from Roman art and arranged them sparsely within broad, neutral spaces and slender margins, as in his elegant, linear ancient models. This new Neoclassical style almost entirely displaced the curvilinear Rococo (FIGS. 26-2 and 26-3) in the homes of the wealthy after midcentury. Adam was also an archaeologist, and he had explored and written accounts of the ruins of Diocletian's palace (FIG. 7-74) at Split. Kedleston House in Derbyshire, Adelphi Terrace in London, and a great many other structures he designed show how the Split palace influenced his work.

The archaeological finds from Herculaneum and Pompeii also affected garden and landscape design, fashion, and tableware.

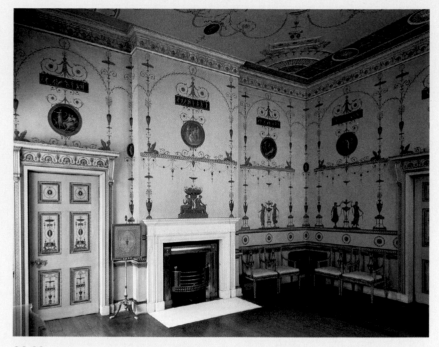

26-23 ROBERT ADAM, Etruscan Room, Osterley Park House, Middlesex, England, begun 1761. Reconstructed in the Victoria & Albert Museum, London.

Inspired by archaeological discoveries at Herculaneum and Pompeii in the mid-18th century, Adam incorporated decorative motifs from Roman mural painting into his Etruscan Room at Osterley Park.

Clothing based on classical garb became popular, and Emma, Lady Hamilton (1761–1815), Sir William's wife, often gave lavish parties dressed in delicate Greek-style drapery. Neoclassical taste also determined the pottery designs of John Flaxman (1755–1826) and Josiah Wedgwood. Wedgwood established his reputation in the 1760s with his creamware inspired by ancient art. He eventually produced vases based on what were then thought to be Etruscan designs (they were, in fact, imported Greek vases deposited in Etruscan tombs) and expanded his business by producing small busts of classical figures as well as cameos and medallions adorned with copies of antique reliefs and statues.

NEOCLASSICISM

One of the defining characteristics of the late 18th century was a renewed admiration for classical antiquity, which the Grand Tour was instrumental in fueling. This interest gave rise to the artistic movement known as *Neoclassicism,* which incorporated the subjects and styles of ancient art. Painting, sculpture, and architecture, however, were only the most prominent manifestations of Neoclassicism. Fascination with Greek and Roman culture was widespread and extended to the public culture of fashion and home decor. The Enlightenment's emphasis on rationality in part explains this classical focus, because the geometric harmony of classical art and architecture embodied Enlightenment ideals. In addition, classical cultures represented the pinnacle of civilized society. Greece and Rome served as models of enlightened political organization. With their traditions of liberty, civic virtue, morality, and sacrifice, these cultures were ideal models during a period of great political upheaval. Given these traditional associations, it is not coincidental that Neoclassicism was particularly appealing during the French and American revolutions.

Further whetting the public appetite for classicism were the excavations near Naples of Herculaneum and Pompeii, which the volcanic eruption of Mount Vesuvius had buried (see "The Excavations of Herculaneum and Pompeii," above). Soon, murals based on the paintings unearthed in the excavations began to appear in European townhouses, such as the Etruscan Room (FIG. **26-23**) by ROBERT ADAM (1728–1792) in Osterley Park House in Middlesex, begun in 1761.

26-24 ANGELICA KAUFFMANN, *Cornelia Presenting Her Children as Her Treasures*, or *Mother of the Gracchi*, ca. 1785. Oil on canvas, 3′ 4″ × 4′ 2″. Virginia Museum of Fine Arts, Richmond (Adolph D. and Wilkins C. Williams Fund).

Kauffmann's painting of a virtuous Roman mother who presented her children to a visitor as her jewels exemplifies the Enlightenment fascination with classical antiquity and with classical art.

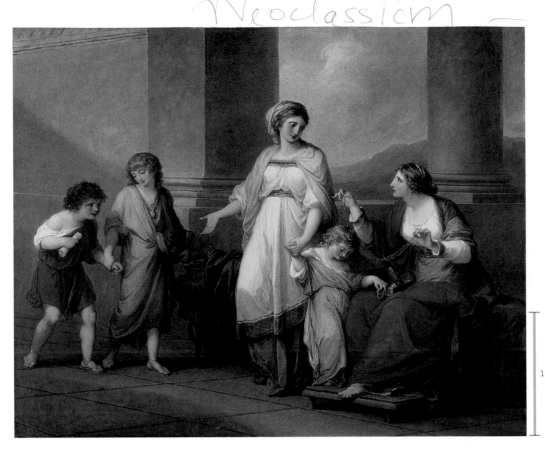

1 ft.

WINCKELMANN The enthusiasm for classical antiquity also permeated much of the scholarship of the time. In the late 18th century, the ancient world increasingly became the focus of academic research. A visit to Rome inspired Edward Gibbon (1737–1794) to begin his monumental *Decline and Fall of the Roman Empire*, which appeared between 1776 and 1788. Earlier, in 1755, Johann Joachim Winckelmann (1717–1768), widely recognized as the first modern art historian, published *Reflections on the Imitation of Greek Works in Painting and Sculpture*, in which the German scholar unequivocally designated Greek art as the most perfect to come from human hands. For Winckelmann, classical art was far superior to the "natural" art of his day.

> Good taste, which is becoming more prevalent throughout the world, had its origins under the skies of Greece. . . . The only way for us to become great . . . is to imitate the ancients. . . . In the masterpieces of Greek art, connoisseurs and imitators find not only nature at its most beautiful but also something beyond nature, namely certain ideal forms of its beauty. . . . A person enlightened enough to penetrate the innermost secrets of art will find beauties hitherto seldom revealed when he compares the total structure of Greek figures with most modern ones, especially those modelled more on nature than on Greek taste.[3]

In his later *History of Ancient Art* (1764), Winckelmann carefully described major works of classical art and positioned each one within a huge inventory organized by subject matter, style, and period. Before Winckelmann, art historians had focused on biography, as did Giorgio Vasari and Giovanni Pietro Bellori in the 16th and 17th centuries (see "Giovanni Pietro Bellori on Annibale Carracci and Caravaggio," Chapter 24, page 682). Winckelmann thus initiated one modern art historical method thoroughly in accord with Enlightenment ideas of ordering knowledge—a system of description and classification that provided a pioneering model for the understanding of stylistic evolution. Winckelmann's familiarity with classical art derived predominantly (as was the norm) from Roman works and Roman copies of Greek art in Italy. Yet Winckelmann was instrumental in bringing to scholarly attention the differences between Greek and Roman art. Thus, he paved the way for more thorough study of the distinct characteristics of the art and architecture of these two cultures.

Painting

Winckelmann's influence extended beyond the world of scholarship. He also was instrumental in promoting Neoclassicism as a major stylistic movement in late-18th-century painting. He was, for example, the scholar who advised his countryman ANTON RAPHAEL MENGS (1728–1779) on classical iconography when Mengs painted *Parnassus* (FIG. **26-23A**), the fresco many art historians regard as the first Neoclassical painting.

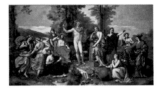

26-23A MENGS, *Parnassus*, 1761.

ANGELICA KAUFFMANN Another pioneer of Neoclassical painting was ANGELICA KAUFFMANN (1741–1807). Born in Switzerland and trained in Italy, Kauffmann spent many of her productive years in England. A student of Reynolds (FIG. 26-19), she was a founding member of the British Royal Academy of Arts and enjoyed an enviable reputation. Her *Cornelia Presenting Her Children as Her Treasures*, or *Mother of the Gracchi* (FIG. **26-24**), is an *exemplum virtutis* (example or model of virtue) drawn from Greek and Roman history and literature. The moralizing pictures of Greuze (FIG. 26-14) and Hogarth (FIG. 26-17) already had marked a change in taste, but Kauffmann replaced the modern setting and character of their works. She clothed her actors in ancient Roman garb and posed them in statuesque attitudes within Roman interiors. The theme of *Mother of the Gracchi* is the virtue of Cornelia, mother of the future political leaders Tiberius and Gaius Gracchus, who, in the second century BCE, attempted to reform the Roman Republic. Cornelia reveals her character in this scene, which takes place after a visitor had shown off her fine jewelry and then haughtily insisted Cornelia show hers. Instead of taking out her own precious adornments, Cornelia brought her sons forward, presenting them as her jewels. The architectural setting is severely Roman, with no

David on Greek Style and Public Art

Jacques-Louis David was the leading Neoclassical painter in France at the end of the 18th century. He championed a return to Greek style and the painting of inspiring heroic and patriotic subjects. In 1796 he made the following statement to his pupils:

> I want to work in a pure Greek style. I feed my eyes on antique statues, I even have the intention of imitating some of them. The Greeks had no scruples about copying a composition, a gesture, a type that had already been accepted and used. They put all their attention and all their art on perfecting an idea that had been already conceived. They thought, and they were right, that in the arts the way in which an idea is rendered, and the manner in which it is expressed, is much more important than the idea itself. To give a body and a perfect form to one's thought, this—and only this—is to be an artist.*

David also strongly believed paintings depicting noble events in ancient history, such as his *Oath of the Horatii* (FIG. 26-25), would serve to instill patriotism and civic virtue in the public at large in postrevolutionary France. In November 1793 he wrote:

> [The arts] should help to spread the progress of the human spirit, and to propagate and transmit to posterity the striking examples of the efforts of a tremendous people who, guided by reason and philosophy, are bringing back to earth the reign of liberty, equality, and law. The arts must therefore contribute forcefully to the education of the public. . . . The arts are the imitation of nature in her most beautiful and perfect form. . . .

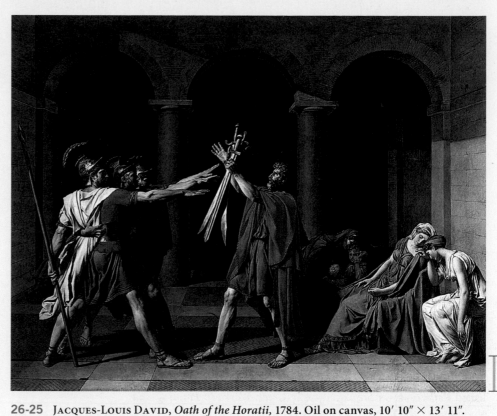

26-25 JACQUES-LOUIS DAVID, *Oath of the Horatii*, 1784. Oil on canvas, 10' 10" × 13' 11". Musée du Louvre, Paris. ◼◀

David was the Neoclassical painter-ideologist of the French Revolution. This huge canvas celebrating ancient Roman patriotism and sacrifice features statuesque figures and classical architecture.

> [T]hose marks of heroism and civic virtue offered the eyes of the people [will] electrify the soul, and plant the seeds of glory and devotion to the fatherland.†

*Translated by Robert Goldwater and Marco Treves, eds., *Artists on Art*, 3d ed. (New York: Pantheon Books, 1958), 206.
†Ibid., 205.

Rococo motif in evidence, and the composition and drawing have the simplicity and firmness of low-relief carving, qualities shared with Mengs's *Parnassus* (FIG. 26-23A).

JACQUES-LOUIS DAVID The Enlightenment idea of a participatory and knowledgeable citizenry lay behind the revolt against the French monarchy in 1789, but the immediate causes of the French Revolution were France's economic crisis and the clash between the Third Estate (bourgeoisie, peasantry, and urban and rural workers) and the First and Second Estates (the clergy and nobility, respectively). They fought over the issue of representation in the legislative body, the Estates-General, which had been convened to discuss taxation as a possible solution to the economic problem. However, the ensuing revolution revealed the instability of the monarchy and of French society's traditional structure and resulted in a succession of republics and empires as France struggled to find a way to adjust to these fundamental changes.

JACQUES-LOUIS DAVID (1748–1825) became the Neoclassical painter-ideologist of the French Revolution. A distant relative of François Boucher (FIG. 26-8), he followed the Rococo painter's style until a period of study in Rome won the younger man over to the classical art tradition. David favored academic teachings about using the art of the ancients and of the great Renaissance masters as models. He, as Winckelmann, rebelled against Rococo style as an "artificial taste" and exalted the "perfect form" of Greek art (see "David on Greek Style and Public Art," above).

OATH OF THE HORATII David concurred with the Enlightenment belief that the subject of an artwork should have a moral. Paintings representing noble deeds in the past could inspire virtue in the present. A milestone painting in the Neoclassical master's career, *Oath of the Horatii* (FIG. 26-25), depicts a story from pre-Republican Rome, the heroic phase of Roman history. The topic was not too obscure for David's audience. Pierre Corneille (1606–1684) had retold this story of conflict between love and patriotism, first recounted by the ancient Roman historian Livy, in a play performed in Paris several years earlier. According to the story, the leaders of the warring cities of Rome and Alba decided to resolve their conflicts in a series of encounters waged by three representatives from each side. The Romans chose as their champions the three Horatius brothers, who had to face the three sons of the Curatius family from Alba. A sister of the Horatii, Camilla, was the bride-to-be of one of the Curatius sons, and the wife of the youngest Horatius was the sister of the Curatii. David's painting shows the Horatii as they swear on their swords, held high by their father, to win or die for Rome, oblivious to the anguish and sorrow of the Horatii women.

Oath of the Horatii is a paragon of the Neoclassical style. Not only does the subject matter deal with a narrative of patriotism and sacrifice excerpted from Roman history, but the painter also employed formal devices to present the image with force and clarity. The action unfolds in a shallow space much like a stage setting, defined by a severely simple architectural framework. David deployed his statuesque and carefully modeled figures across the space, close to the foreground, in a manner reminiscent of ancient relief sculpture. The rigid, angular, and virile forms of the men on the left effectively contrast with the soft curvilinear shapes of the distraught women on the right. This juxtaposition visually pits virtues the Enlightenment leaders ascribed to men (such as courage, patriotism, and unwavering loyalty to a cause) against the emotions of love, sorrow, and despair the women in the painting express. The French viewing audience perceived such emotionalism as characteristic of the female nature. The message was clear and of a type readily identifiable to the prerevolutionary French public. The picture created a sensation at its first exhibition in Paris in 1785. Although David had painted it under royal patronage and did not intend the painting as a revolutionary statement, *Oath of the Horatii* aroused his audience to patriotic zeal. The Neoclassical style soon became the semiofficial voice of the French Revolution.

DEATH OF MARAT When the revolution broke out in 1789, David threw in his lot with the Jacobins, the radical and militant revolutionary faction. He accepted the role of de facto minister of propaganda, organizing political pageants and ceremonies requiring floats, costumes, and sculptural props. David believed art could play an important role in educating the public and that dramatic paintings emphasizing patriotism and civic virtue would prove effective as rallying calls. However, rather than continuing to create artworks focused on scenes from antiquity, David began to portray scenes from the French Revolution itself.

In 1793, David painted *Death of Marat* (FIG. **26-26**), which he wanted not only to serve as a record of an important event in the struggle to overthrow the monarchy but also to provide inspiration and encouragement to the revolutionary forces. The painting commemorates the assassination that year of Jean-Paul Marat (1743–1793), an influential writer who was David's friend. The artist depicted the martyred revolutionary in his bathtub after Charlotte Corday (1768–1793), a member of a rival political faction, stabbed him to death. (Marat suffered from a painful skin disease and required frequent medicinal baths.) David presented the scene with directness and clarity. The cold neutral space above Marat's figure slumped in the tub produces a chilling oppressiveness. The painter vividly placed all narrative details in the foreground—the knife, the wound, the blood, the letter with which Corday gained entrance— to sharpen the sense of pain and outrage. David masterfully composed the painting to present Marat as a tragic martyr who died

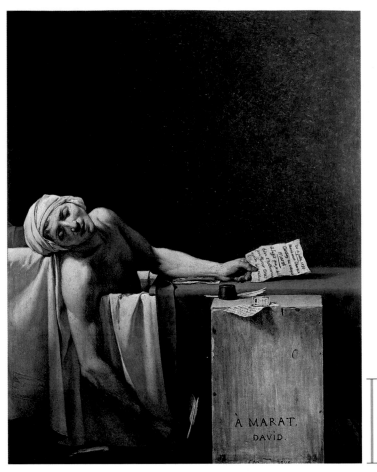

26-26 JACQUES-LOUIS DAVID, *Death of Marat*, 1793. Oil on canvas, 5′ 5″ × 4′ 2½″. Musées Royaux des Beaux-Arts de Belgique, Brussels. ◼◀

David depicted the revolutionary Marat as a tragic martyr, stabbed to death in his bath. Although the painting displays severe Neoclassical spareness, its convincing realism conveys pain and outrage.

in the service of the revolution. He based Marat's figure on Christ in Michelangelo's *Pietà* (FIG. 22-12) in Saint Peter's in Rome. The reference to Christ's martyrdom made the painting a kind of "altarpiece" for the new civic "religion," inspiring the French people with the saintly dedication of their slain leader.

Architecture and Sculpture

Architects in the Enlightenment era also formed a deep admiration for the Greco-Roman past. Fairly early in the 18th century, they began to turn away from the theatricality and ostentation of Baroque design, still evident in grandiose structures such as Blenheim Palace (FIG. 26-1A) in England and Karlskirche (FIG. 26-3A) in Austria, as well as from the delicate flourishes of Rococo salons (FIGS. 26-2 and 26-3), palaces (FIG. 26-5A), and churches (FIGS. 26-4 and 26-5B). The style they instead embraced offered a more streamlined antique look.

PANTHÉON The Parisian church of Sainte-Geneviève, now the Panthéon (FIG. **26-27**), by JACQUES-GERMAIN SOUFFLOT (1713–1780) stands as testament to the revived interest in classical architecture. The Roman ruins at Baalbek in Lebanon, especially the titanic colonnade of the temple of Jupiter, provided much of the inspiration for Soufflot's design. The columns, reproduced with studied archaeological precision, stand out from walls that are severely blank, except for a repeated garland motif near the top. The colonnaded dome, a Neoclassical version of the domes of Saint

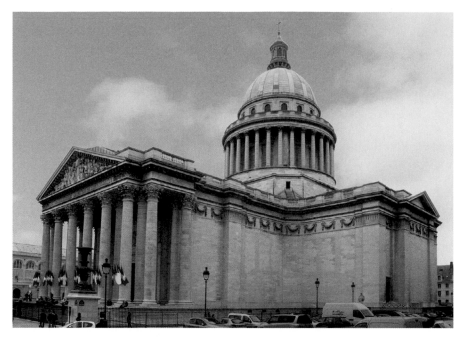

26-27 JACQUES-GERMAIN SOUFFLOT, Panthéon (Sainte-Geneviève; looking northeast), Paris, France, 1755–1792.

Soufflot's Panthéon is a testament to the Enlightenment admiration for Greece and Rome. It combines a portico based on an ancient Roman temple with a colonnaded dome and a Greek-cross plan.

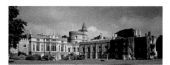

26-27A WALPOLE, Strawberry Hill, Twickenham, 1749–1777.

Peter's (FIG. 22-25) in Rome, the Église du Dôme (FIG. 25-30) in Paris, and Saint Paul's (FIG. 25-38) in London, rises above a Greek-cross plan. Both the dome and the vaults rest on an interior grid of splendid freestanding Corinthian columns, as if the portico's colonnade continued within. Although the whole effect, inside and out, is Roman, the structural principles employed were essentially Gothic. Soufflot was one of the first 18th-century builders to apply the logical engineering of Gothic cathedrals (see "The Gothic Cathedral," Chapter 13, page 373) to modern buildings. With few exceptions, however, such as Strawberry Hill (FIG. 26-27A), owned and largely designed by HORACE WALPOLE (1717–1797), the revival of interest in the Gothic architectural style did not take hold until the following century (see Chapter 27 and FIGS. 27-43 and 27-43A).

CHISWICK HOUSE The appeal of classical architecture extended well beyond French borders. The popularity of Greek and Roman cultures was due not only to their association with morality, rationality, and integrity but also to their connection to politi-

cal systems ranging from Athenian democracy to Roman imperial rule. Thus, parliamentary England joined revolutionary France in embracing Neoclassicism. In England, Neoclassicism's appeal also was due to its clarity and simplicity. These characteristics provided a stark contrast to the complexity and opulence of Baroque art, then associated with the flamboyant rule of absolute monarchy. In English architecture, the preference for a simple and rational style derived indirectly from the authority of the ancient Roman architect Vitruvius through Andrea Palladio (FIGS. 22-28 to 22-31) in the 16th century and Inigo Jones (FIG. 25-37) in the 17th.

RICHARD BOYLE (1695–1753), earl of Burlington, strongly restated Jones's Palladian doctrine in the new Neoclassical idiom in Chiswick House (FIG. **26-28**), which he built on London's outskirts with the help of WILLIAM KENT (ca. 1686–1748). Paving the way for this shift in style was, among other things, the publication of Colin Campbell's *Vitruvius Britannicus* (1715), three volumes of engravings of ancient buildings, prefaced by a denunciation of Italian Baroque and high praise for Palladio and Jones. Chiswick House is a free variation on the theme of Palladio's Villa Rotonda (FIG. 22-28). The exterior design provided a clear alternative to the colorful splendor of Versailles (FIG. 25-26). In its simple symmetry, unadorned planes, right angles, and precise proportions, Chiswick looks very classical and rational. But the Palladian-style villa's setting within informal gardens, where a charming irregularity of layout and freely growing uncropped foliage dominate the scene, mitigates the classical severity and rationality. Just as the owners of English villas cultivated irregularity in the landscaping surrounding their homes, they sometimes preferred interiors ornamented in a style more closely related to Rococo decoration. At Chiswick, the interior design creates a luxurious Baroque foil to the stern symmetry of the exterior and the plan.

Palladian classicism prevailed in English architecture until about 1760, when it began to evolve into Neoclassicism. Playing a pivotal role in the shift from a dependence on Renaissance examples to ancient models was the publication in 1762 of the first volume of *Antiquities of Athens*

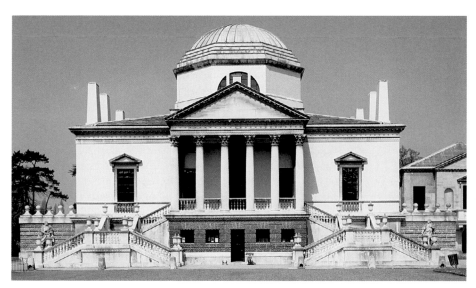

26-28 RICHARD BOYLE and WILLIAM KENT, Chiswick House (looking northwest), near London, England, begun 1725.

For this English villa, Boyle and Kent emulated the simple symmetry and unadorned planes of the Palladian architectural style. Chiswick House is a free variation on the Villa Rotonda (FIG. 22-28).

Neoclassicism **749**

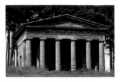

26-28A STUART, Doric Portico, Hagley Park, 1758.

by two British painters and architects, JAMES STUART (1713–1788) and Nicholas Revett (1720–1804). Indeed, the purest expression of Greek-inspired architecture in 18th-century England was Stuart's design for the Doric portico (FIG. 26-28A) at Hagley Park.

STOURHEAD PARK English architects also made a significant contribution to the history of architecture by developing the *picturesque garden* in the 18th century, a garden designed in accord with the Enlightenment taste for the "natural." This approach to landscape architecture was in strong opposition to the formality and symmetry of Continental gardens such as those of the palace at Versailles (FIG. 25-26), which epitomized the imposition of rational order on untamed nature. Despite their "unordered" appearance, English gardens were carefully planned and often made allusions to classical antiquity, satisfying the demands of their patrons to surround themselves with mementos of the Grand Tour (see "The Grand Tour," page 744) they undertook in their youth.

An early masterpiece of this genre is the park at Stourhead (FIG. 26-29), designed by HENRY FLITCROFT (1697–1769) in collaboration with the property's owner, HENRY HOARE (1705–1785), the son of a wealthy banker. Hoare's country estate in Wiltshire overlooked a lush valley in which Flitcroft created an irregularly shaped artificial lake by damming up the Stour River. Around it, he placed a winding path leading to and from a grotto adorned with statues of a river god and a nymph. The twisting road and the grotto conjured for Hoare the voyage of Aeneas and the entrance to the Underworld in Virgil's *Aeneid*, required reading (in the original Latin) for any properly educated British gentleman. Flitcroft also placed around Hoare's version of Lake Avernus a bridge with five arches modeled on Andrea Palladio's bridge at Vicenza and pavilions that are free variations on famous classical buildings, including the Temple of Venus (FIG. 7-72) at Baalbek and the Pantheon (FIG. 7-49) in Rome.

Flitcroft sited all the structures strategically to create vistas resembling those in the paintings of Claude Lorrain (FIG. 25-33), beloved by those who had completed a Grand Tour. In fact, the view reproduced here of Flitcroft's Pantheon beyond the Palladian bridge on the far side of the lake at Stourhead specifically emulates Claude's 1672 *Landscape with Aeneas at Delos* in the National Gallery in London, in turn inspired by the *Aeneid*. Still, consistent with the eclectic tastes of 18th-century patrons, Hoare's park also contains Chinese bridges, a Turkish tent, and a Gothic tower.

THOMAS JEFFERSON Because the appeal of Neoclassicism was due in part to the values with which it was associated—morality, idealism, patriotism, and civic virtue—it is not surprising that in the new American republic (MAP 26-1), THOMAS JEFFERSON (1743–1826) spearheaded a movement to adopt Neoclassicism as the national architectural style. Jefferson—economist, educational theorist, gifted amateur architect, as well as stateman—admired Palladio immensely and read carefully the Italian architect's *Four Books of Architecture.* Later, while minister to France, he studied 18th-century French classical architecture and city planning and visited the Maison Carrée (FIG. 7-32), an ancient Roman temple at Nîmes. After his European sojourn, Jefferson completely remodeled Monticello (FIG. 26-30), his home near Charlottesville, Virginia, which he originally had designed in a different style. The final version of Monticello is somewhat reminiscent of Palladio's Villa Rotonda (FIG. 22-28) and of Chiswick House (FIG. 26-28), but its materials are the local wood and brick used in Virginia.

UNIVERSITY OF VIRGINIA Jefferson's Neoclassicism was an extension of the Enlightenment belief in the perfectibility of human beings and in the power of art to help achieve that perfection. When he became president, he selected Benjamin Latrobe (1764–1820) to build the U.S. Capitol in Washington, D.C., specifying that Latrobe use a Roman style. Jefferson's choice in part reflected his admiration for the beauty of the Roman buildings he had seen in Europe and in part his association of those buildings

26-29 HENRY FLITCROFT and HENRY HOARE, the park at Stourhead, England, 1743–1765.

Flitcroft's design for Hoare's Wiltshire estate included a replica of the Pantheon overlooking an artificial lake and a grotto alluding to Aeneas's journey to the Underworld from Lake Avernus.

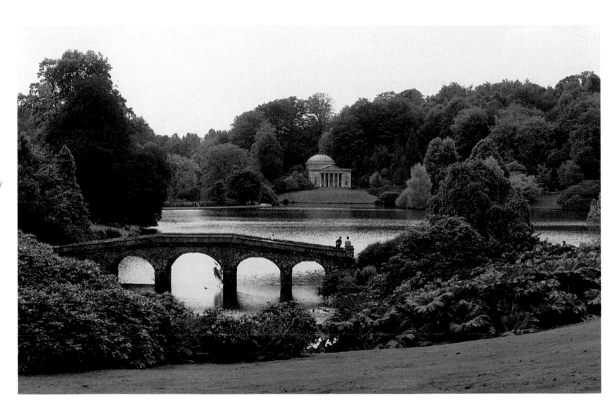

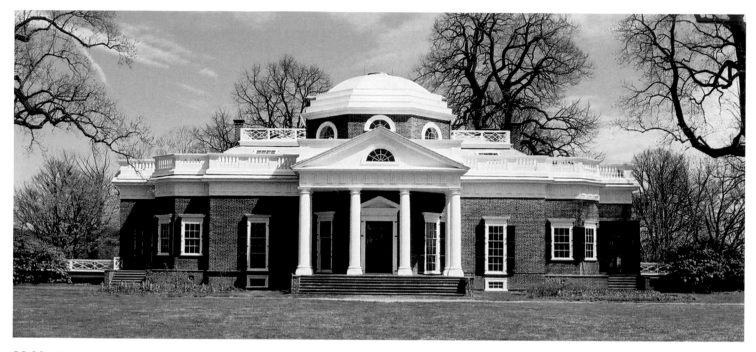

26-30 Thomas Jefferson, Monticello, Charlottesville, Virginia, 1770–1806. ◼◀

Jefferson led the movement to adopt Neoclassicism as the architectural style of the United States. Although built of local materials, his Palladian Virginia home recalls Chiswick House (FIG. 26-28).

with an idealized Roman republican government and, through that, with the democracy of ancient Greece.

In his own designs for public buildings, Jefferson also looked to Rome for models. He modeled the State Capitol in Richmond, Virginia, on the Maison Carrée (FIG. 7-32). For the University of Virginia, which he founded, Jefferson turned to the Pantheon (FIG. 7-49). The Rotunda (FIG. 26-31) is the centerpiece of Jefferson's "academical village" in Charlottesville. It sits on an elevated platform at one end of a grassy quadrangle ("the Lawn"), framed by Neoclassical pavilions and colonnades—just as temples in Roman forums (FIGS. 7-12 and 7-44) stood at one short end of a colonnaded square. Each of the ten pavilions (five on each side) resembles a small classical temple. No two are exactly alike. Jefferson ex-

perimented with variations of all the different classical orders in his pavilions. He had thoroughly absorbed the principles of classical architecture and clearly delighted in borrowing motifs from major buildings. Jefferson was no mere copyist, however. His designs were highly original—and, in turn, frequently emulated.

JEAN-ANTOINE HOUDON Neoclassicism also became the preferred style for public sculpture in the new American republic. When members of the Virginia legislature wanted to erect a life-size marble statue of Virginia-born George Washington (1732–1799), they awarded the commission to the leading French Neoclassical sculptor of the late 18th century, JEAN-ANTOINE HOUDON (1741–1828). Houdon had already carved a bust portrait of Benjamin Franklin

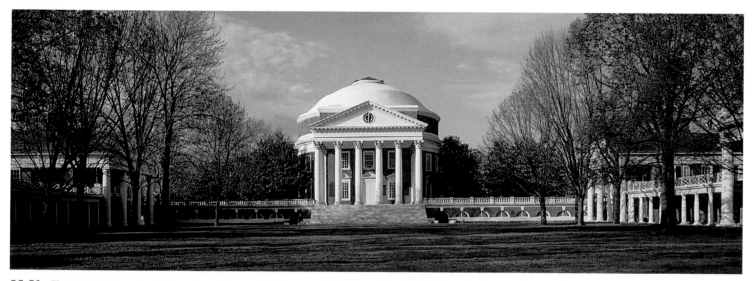

26-31 Thomas Jefferson, Rotunda and Lawn (looking north), University of Virginia, Charlottesville, Virginia, 1819–1826.

Modeled on the Pantheon (FIG. 7-49), Jefferson's Rotunda sits like a temple in a Roman forum on an elevated platform overlooking the colonnaded Lawn of the University of Virginia.

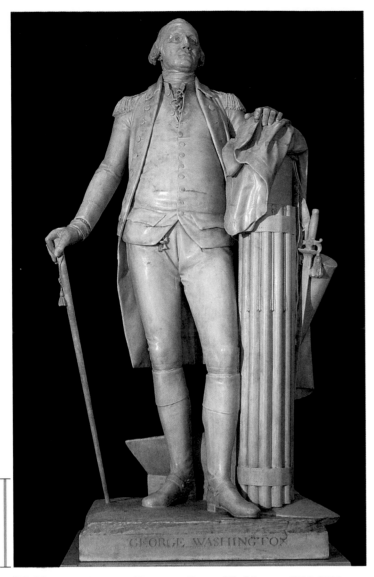

1 ft.

26-32 JEAN-ANTOINE HOUDON, *George Washington*, 1788–1792. Marble, 6′ 2″ high. State Capitol, Richmond.

Houdon portrayed Washington in contemporary garb, but he incorporated the Roman *fasces* and Cincinnatus's plow in the statue, because Washington similarly had returned to his farm after his war service.

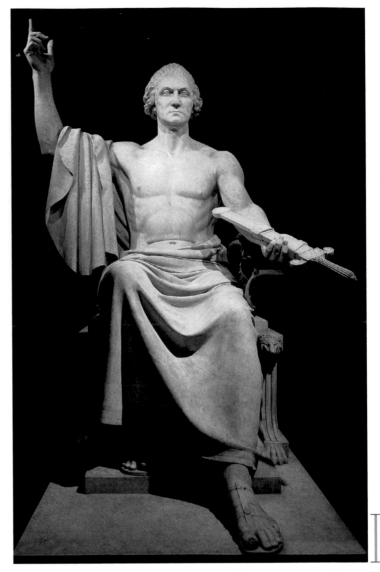

1 ft.

26-33 HORATIO GREENOUGH, *George Washington*, 1840. Marble, 11′ 4″ high. Smithsonian American Art Museum, Washington, D.C.

In this posthumous portrait, Greenough likened Washington to a god by depicting him seminude and enthroned in the manner of Phidias's Olympian statue of Zeus, king of the Greek gods.

(1706–1790) when he was America's ambassador to France. His portrait of Washington (FIG. **26-32**) is the sculptural equivalent of a painted Grand Manner portrait (FIG. 26-19). But although Washington wears 18th-century garb, the statue makes overt reference to the Roman Republic. The "column" on which Washington leans is a bundle of rods with an ax attached—the ancient Roman *fasces,* an emblem of authority (used much later as the emblem of Mussolini's Fascist—the term derives from "fasces"—government in 20th-century Italy). The 13 rods symbolize the 13 original states. The plow behind Washington alludes to Cincinnatus, a patrician of the early Roman Republic who was elected dictator during a time of war and resigned his position as soon as victory had been achieved in order to return to his farm. Washington wears the badge of the Society of the Cincinnati (visible beneath the bottom of his waistcoat), an association founded in 1783 for officers in the revolutionary army who had resumed their peacetime roles. Tellingly, Washington no longer holds his sword in Houdon's statue.

HORATIO GREENOUGH After his death, Washington gradually took on almost godlike stature as the "father of his country." In 1840 the U.S. Congress commissioned American sculptor HORATIO GREENOUGH (1805–1852) to create a statue (FIG. **26-33**) of the country's first president for the Capitol. Greenough used Houdon's portrait as his model for the head, but he portrayed Washington as seminude and enthroned, as Phidias depicted Zeus in the famous lost statue he made for the god's temple at Olympia in ancient Greece. The colossal statue—Washington is more than 11 feet tall, seated—epitomizes the Neoclassical style, but it did not win favor with either the Congress that commissioned it or the public. Although no one ever threw Greenough's statue into the Potomac River, as one congressman suggested, the legislators never placed it in its intended site beneath the Capitol dome. In fact, by 1840 the Neoclassical style itself was no longer in vogue. The leading artists of Europe and America had embraced a new style, Romanticism, examined in the next chapter.

ROCOCO TO NEOCLASSICISM:
THE 18TH CENTURY IN EUROPE AND AMERICA

ROCOCO

▌ In the early 18th century, the centralized and grandiose palace-based culture of Baroque France gave way to the much more intimate Rococo culture based in the townhouses of Paris. There, aristocrats and intellectuals gathered for witty conversation in salons featuring delicate colors, sinuous lines, gilded mirrors, elegant furniture, and small paintings and sculptures.

▌ The leading Rococo painter was Antoine Watteau, whose usually small canvases feature light colors and elegant figures in ornate costumes moving gracefully through lush landscapes. His *fête galante* paintings depict the outdoor amusements of French high society.

▌ Watteau's successors included François Boucher and Jean-Honoré Fragonard, who carried on the Rococo style late into the 18th century. In Italy, Giambattista Tiepolo adapted the Rococo manner to huge ceiling frescoes in the Baroque tradition.

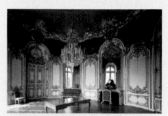

Boffrand, Salon de la Princesse, Paris 1737–1740

THE ENLIGHTENMENT

▌ By the end of the 18th century, revolutions had overthrown the monarchy in France and achieved independence for the British colonies in America. A major factor was the Enlightenment, a new way of thinking critically about the world independently of religion and tradition.

▌ The Enlightenment promoted scientific questioning of all assertions and embraced the doctrine of progress, epitomized by the Industrial Revolution, which began in England in the 1740s. The paintings of Joseph Wright of Derby celebrated the scientific inventions of the Enlightenment era.

▌ The Enlightenment also made knowledge of ancient Rome imperative for the cultured elite, and Europeans and Americans in large numbers undertook a Grand Tour of Italy. Among the most popular souvenirs of the Grand Tour were Antonio Canaletto's *vedute* of Venice rendered in precise Renaissance perspective with the aid of a camera obscura.

▌ Rejecting the idea of progress, Rousseau, one of the leading French *philosophes,* argued for a return to natural values and exalted the simple, honest life of peasants. His ideas had a profound impact on artists such as Jean-Baptiste-Siméon Chardin and Jean-Baptiste Greuze, who painted sentimental narratives about rural families.

▌ The taste for naturalism also led to the popularity of portrait paintings with landscape backgrounds, a specialty of Thomas Gainsborough, and to a reawakening of interest in realism. Benjamin West represented the protagonists in his history paintings wearing contemporary costumes.

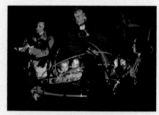

Wright, *A Lecture at the Orrery,* ca. 1763–1765

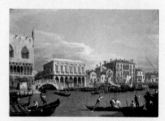

Canaletto, *Riva degli Schiavoni, Venice,* ca. 1735–1740

NEOCLASSICISM

▌ The Enlightenment revival of interest in Greece and Rome, which spurred systematic excavations at Herculaneum and Pompeii, also gave rise in the late 18th century to the artistic movement known as Neoclassicism, which incorporated the subjects and styles of ancient art.

▌ One pioneer of the new style was Angelica Kauffmann, who often chose subjects drawn from Roman history for her paintings. Jacques-Louis David, who exalted classical art as "the imitation of nature in her most beautiful and perfect form," also favored ancient Roman themes. Painted on the eve of the French Revolution, *Oath of the Horatii,* set in a severe classical hall, served as an example of patriotism and sacrifice.

▌ Architects also eagerly embraced the Neoclassical style. Ancient Roman and Italian Renaissance structures inspired Jacques-Germain Soufflot's Panthéon in Paris and Richard Boyle's Chiswick House near London. A Greek temple in Athens was the model for James Stuart's Doric portico in Worcestershire.

▌ In the United States, Thomas Jefferson adopted the Neoclassical style in his designs for Monticello and the University of Virginia. He championed Neoclassicism as the official architectural style of the new American republic because it represented for him idealism, patriotism, and civic virtue.

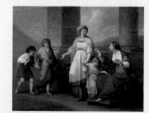

Kauffmann, *Mother of the Gracchi,* ca. 1785

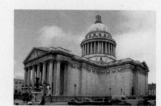

Soufflot, Panthéon, Paris, 1755–1792

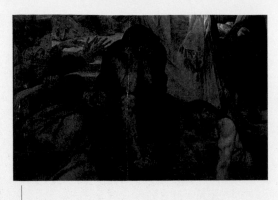

In the shadows of the left side of the huge canvas are dying and dead Arabs, including a seated man in despair. Gros based the figure on one of the damned in Michelangelo's *Last Judgment* (FIG. 22-19).

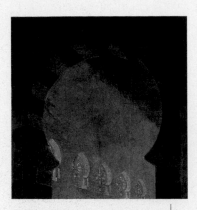

Foreshadowing Romanticism, Gros carefully recorded the exotic people, costumes, and architecture of Jaffa, including the distinctive Islamic striped horseshoe arches of the mosque-hospital.

Napoleon, fearless among the plague-stricken, reaches out to touch one man's sores. Gros portrayed the French general as Christlike, implying he possessed miraculous power to heal the sick.

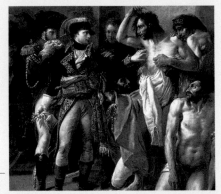

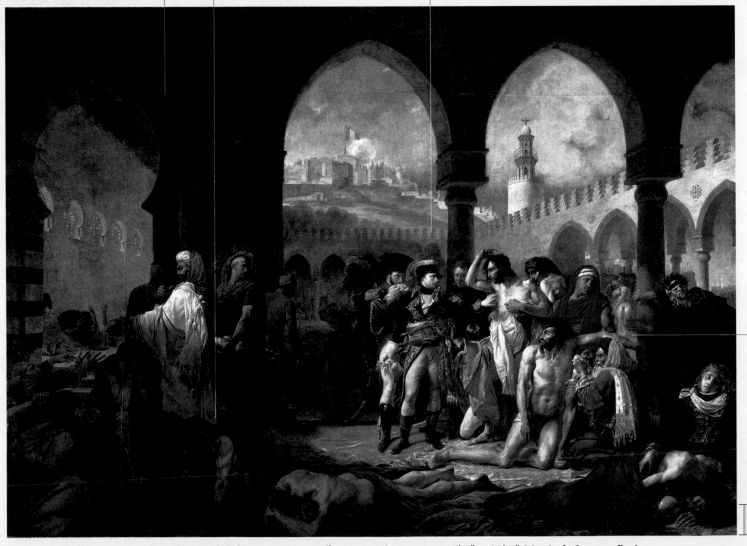

1 ft.

27-1 ANTOINE-JEAN GROS, *Napoleon at the Plague House at Jaffa,* 1804. Oil on canvas, 17′ 5″ × 23′ 7″. Musée du Louvre, Paris.

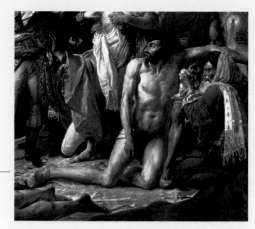

Among the dying whom Napoleon has come to comfort is a kneeling nude man with left arm extended. His posture recalls that of the dead Christ in Michelangelo's emotional *Pietà* (FIG. 22-20).

ROMANTICISM, REALISM, PHOTOGRAPHY: EUROPE AND AMERICA, 1800 TO 1870

NAPOLEON AT JAFFA

In the opening decade of the 19th century, many of the leading French artists produced major artworks glorifying the most powerful man in Europe at the time—Napoleon Bonaparte (1769–1821), since 1799 First Consul of the French Republic and from 1804 to 1815, Emperor of the French. One of those artists was ANTOINE-JEAN GROS (1771–1835), a pupil of Jacques-Louis David (FIGS. 26-25 and 26-26), Napoleon's favorite painter. Gros, like David, produced several paintings that contributed to Napoleon's growing mythic status. In *Napoleon at the Plague House at Jaffa* (FIG. 27-1), the artist, at Napoleon's request, recorded an incident during an outbreak of the bubonic plague in the course of the general's Syrian campaign of 1799. This fearsome disease struck Muslim and French forces alike, and to quell the growing panic and hysteria, on March 11, 1799, Napoleon himself visited the mosque at Jaffa that had been converted into a hospital for those who had contracted the dreaded disease. Gros depicted Napoleon's staff officers covering their noses against the stench of the place, whereas Napoleon, amid the dead and dying, is fearless and in control. He comforts those still alive, who are clearly awed by his presence and authority. Indeed, by depicting the French leader having removed his glove to touch the sores of a plague victim, Gros implied Napoleon possessed the miraculous power to heal. The composition recalls scenes of the doubting Thomas touching Christ's wound. Here, however, Napoleon is not Saint Thomas but a Christlike figure tending to the sick, as in Rembrandt's *Hundred-Guilder Print* (FIG. 25-16), which Gros certainly knew. The French painter also based the despairing seated figure at the lower left on the comparable figure (one of the damned) in Michelangelo's *Last Judgment* (FIG. 22-19). The kneeling nude man with extended arm at the right recalls the dead Christ in Michelangelo's late *Pietà* (FIG. 22-20).

The action in *Napoleon at the Plague House in Jaffa* unfolds against the exotic backdrop of the horseshoe arches and Moorish arcades of the mosque-hospital's courtyard (compare FIG. 10-9). On the left are Muslim doctors distributing bread and ministering to plague-stricken Arabs in the shadows. On the right, in radiant light, are Napoleon and his soldiers in their splendid tailored uniforms. David had used this polarized compositional scheme and an arcaded backdrop to great effect in his *Oath of the Horatii* (FIG. 26-25), and Gros emulated these features in this painting. However, the younger artist's fascination with the exoticism of the Muslim world, as is evident in his attention to the details of architecture and costume, represented a departure from Neoclassicism. This, along with Gros's emphasis on death, suffering, and an emotional rendering of the scene, presaged core elements of the artistic movement that would soon displace Neoclassicism—Romanticism.

ART UNDER NAPOLEON

The revolution of 1789 initiated a new era in France, but the overthrow of the monarchy also opened the door for Napoleon Bonaparte to exploit the resulting disarray and establish a different kind of monarchy with himself at its head. In 1799, after serving in various French army commands and leading major campaigns in Italy and Egypt, Napoleon became First Consul of the French Republic, a title with clear and intentional links to the ancient Roman Republic (see Chapter 7). During the next 15 years, the ambitious general gained control of almost all of continental Europe in name or through alliances

(MAP 27-1). In May 1804, for example, he became king of Italy. Later that year, the pope journeyed to Paris for Napoleon's coronation as Emperor of the French (FIG. 27-2). In 1812, however, Napoleon launched a disastrous invasion of Russia that ended in retreat, and in 1815 he suffered a devastating defeat at the hands of the British at Waterloo in present-day Belgium. Forced to abdicate the imperial throne, Napoleon went into exile on the island of Saint Helena in the South Atlantic, where he died six years later.

After Napoleon's death, the political geography of Europe changed dramatically (MAP 27-2, page 758), but in many ways the more significant changes during the first half of the 19th century

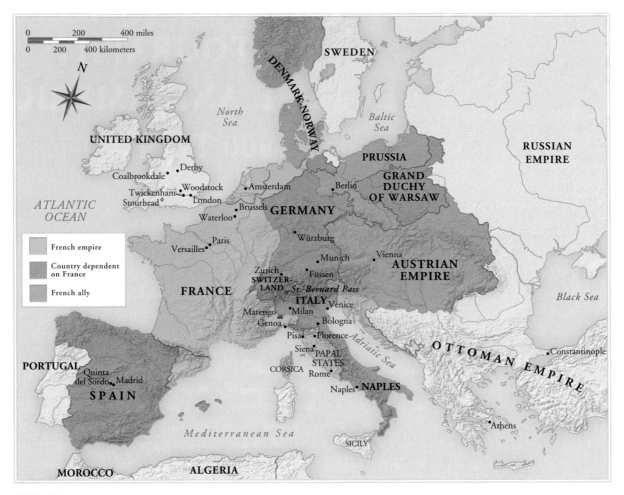

MAP 27-1 The Napoleonic Empire in 1815.

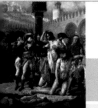

ROMANTICISM, REALISM, PHOTOGRAPHY: EUROPE AND AMERICA, 1800 TO 1870

1800	1815	1840	1870

- Napoleon appoints David as First Painter of the Empire and brings Canova from Rome to Paris
- Vignon designs La Madeleine, Napoleon's Neoclassical "temple of glory"
- Gros, Girodet, and Ingres form a bridge between Neoclassicism and Romanticism

- Romanticism is the leading art movement in Europe. Delacroix and other painters favor exotic and fantastic subjects featuring unleashed emotion, vibrant color, and bold brushstrokes
- Friedrich, Turner, Cole, and other Romantic artists specialize in painting transcendental landscapes
- Gothic style enjoys a revival in architecture
- Daguerre and Talbot invent photography

- Courbet exhibits his work in the Pavilion of Realism. He and other Realist painters in Europe and America insist people and events of their own time are the only valid subjects for art
- Manet's paintings get a hostile reception because of their shocking subject matter and nonillusionistic style
- Paxton pioneers prefabricated glass-and-iron construction in the Crystal Palace
- Technological advances enable artists to make on-the-spot photographs of the Civil War

were technological and economic. The Industrial Revolution caused a population boom in European cities, and railroads spread to many parts of the Continent, facilitating the transportation of both goods and people. Transformation also occurred in the art world. The century opened with Neoclassicism still supreme, but by 1870 Romanticism and Realism in turn had captured the imagination of artists and public alike. New construction techniques had a major impact on architectural design, and the invention of photography revolutionized picturemaking of all kinds.

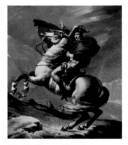

27-1A DAVID, *Napoleon Crossing Saint-Bernard*, 1800–1801.

DAVID AND NAPOLEON At the fall of the French revolutionary Maximilien Robespierre and his party in 1794, Jacques-Louis David, who had aligned himself personally and through his work with the revolutionary forces, barely escaped with his life. He stood trial and went to prison. After his release in 1795, he worked hard to resurrect his career. When Napoleon approached David in 1804 and offered him the position of First Painter of the Empire, David seized the opportunity. The artist, who had earlier painted a series of portraits of the emperor on horseback crossing the Alps (FIG. 27-1A), exemplified Neoclassicism, the artistic style Napoleon favored because he aspired to rule an empire that might one day rival ancient Rome's. The French emperor consequently embraced all links with the classical past as symbolic sources of authority.

CORONATION OF NAPOLEON The new emperor was well aware of the power of art for constructing a public image and of David's ability to produce inspiring patriotic images. The most grandiose work First Painter David produced for his new imperial patron was *Coronation of Napoleon* (FIG. **27-2**), an immense (20 by 32 feet) canvas documenting the pomp and pageantry of the crowning ceremony of December 1804. To a large extent, David adhered to historical fact in depicting Napoleon's coronation, duly recording, for example, the appearance of the interior of Paris's Notre Dame Cathedral as the emperor's architects Charles Percier (1764–1838) and Pierre-François-Léonard Fontaine (1762–1853) had decorated it for the occasion. David also faithfully portrayed those in attendance: Napoleon; his wife Josephine (1763–1814), who kneels to receive her crown; Pope Pius VII (r. 1800–1823), seated behind Napoleon; Joseph (1768–1814) and Louis (1778–1846) Bonaparte; Napoleon's ministers; the retinues of the emperor and empress; a representative group of the clergy; and David himself, seated among the rows of spectators in the balconies. Preliminary studies and drawings reveal, however, that, at Napoleon's request, David made changes to his initially accurate record of the event. For example, the emperor insisted the painter depict the pope with his hand raised in blessing. Further, Napoleon's mother, who had refused to attend the coronation, appears prominently in the center background.

Given the number of figures and details David had to incorporate in his painting, it is remarkable he was able to impose upon the lavish pageant the structured composition central to the Neoclassical style. As in his *Oath of the Horatii* (FIG. 26-25), David presented

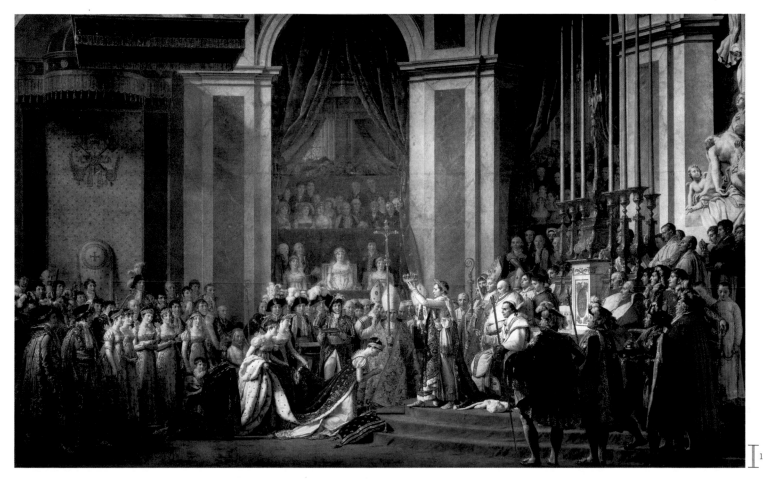

27-2 JACQUES-LOUIS DAVID, *Coronation of Napoleon,* 1805–1808. Oil on canvas, 20′ 4½″ × 32′ 1¾″. Musée du Louvre, Paris.

As First Painter of the Empire, David recorded Napoleon at his December 1804 coronation crowning his wife with the pope as witness, thus underscoring the authority of the state over the church.

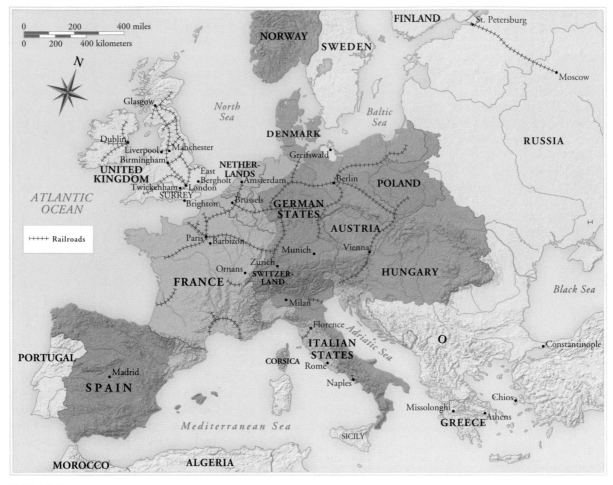

MAP 27-2 Europe around 1850.

the action as if on a theater stage—which in this instance was literally the case, even if the stage Percier and Fontaine constructed was inside a church. In addition, as he did in his arrangement of the men and women in *Oath of the Horatii,* David conceptually divided the painting to highlight polarities. The pope, prelates, and priests representing the Catholic Church appear on the right. The members of Napoleon's imperial court are on the left. The relationship between church and state was one of this period's most contentious issues. Napoleon's decision to crown himself, rather than to allow the pope to perform the coronation, as was traditional, reflected Napoleon's concern about the church-state power relationship. For the painting commemorating the occasion, the emperor insisted David depict the moment when, having already crowned himself,

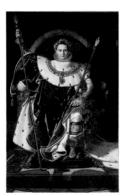

27-2A INGRES, *Napoleon on His Imperial Throne,* 1806.

Napoleon placed a crown on his wife's head, further underscoring his authority. Thus, although this painting appears at first to be a detailed, objective record of a historical event, it is, in fact, a carefully crafted tableau designed to present Napoleon in the way he wished to be seen. In that respect, as well as stylistically, David was emulating the artists in the employ of the ancient Roman emperors (see Chapter 7), as did his pupil, JEAN-AUGUSTE-DOMINIQUE INGRES (1780–1867) in a contemporaneous portrait (FIG. 27-2A) of Napoleon enthroned.

LA MADELEINE Napoleon also embraced Neoclassical architecture as an ideal vehicle for expressing his imperial authority. For example, the emperor resumed construction of the church of La Madeleine (FIG. 27-3) in Paris, which had been interrupted in 1790. However, he converted the building into a "temple of glory" for France's imperial armies. (The structure reverted again to a church after Napoleon's defeat and long before its completion in 1842.) Designed by PIERRE VIGNON (1763–1828), the grandiose Napoleonic temple includes a high podium and broad flight of stairs leading to a deep porch in the front. These architectural features, coupled with the Corinthian columns, recall Roman temples in France, such as the Maison Carrée (FIG. 7-32) at Nîmes, making La Madeleine a symbolic link between the Napoleonic and Roman empires. Curiously, the building's classical shell surrounds an interior covered by a sequence of three domes, a feature found in Byzantine and Romanesque churches. Vignon in essence clothed a traditional church in the costume of imperial Rome.

ANTONIO CANOVA Neoclassical sculpture also was in vogue under Napoleon. His favorite sculptor was ANTONIO CANOVA (1757–1822), who somewhat reluctantly left a successful career in Italy to settle in Paris and serve the emperor. Once in France, Canova became Napoleon's admirer and made numerous portraits, all in the Neoclassical style, of the emperor and his family. The most remarkable is the marble portrait (FIG. 27-4) of Napoleon's sister, Pauline Borghese (1780–1825), as Venus. Initially, Canova, who had gained renown for his sculptures of classical gods and heroes—for

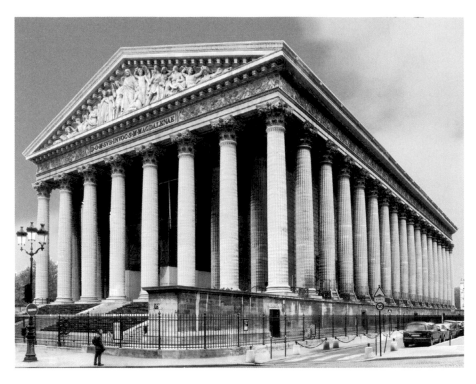

Napoleon constructed La Madeleine as a "temple of glory" for his armies. Based on ancient temples (FIG. 7-32) in France, Vignon's Neoclassical design linked the Napoleonic and Roman empires.

The French public never got to admire Canova's portrait, however. Napoleon had arranged the marriage of his sister to an heir of the noble Roman Borghese family. Once Pauline was in Rome, her behavior was less than dignified, and the public gossiped extensively about her affairs. Pauline's insistence on being represented as the goddess of love reflected her self-perception. Because of his wife's questionable reputation, Prince Camillo Borghese (1775–1832), the work's official patron, kept the sculpture sequestered in the Villa Borghese in Rome (where it still is). Borghese allowed relatively few people to see the portrait. Still, knowledge of the existence of the sculpture was widespread and increased the notoriety of both artist and subject.

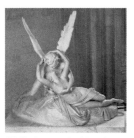

27-4A CANOVA, Cupid and Psyche, 1787–1793.

example, *Cupid and Psyche* (FIG. 27-4A)— had suggested depicting Borghese as Diana, goddess of the hunt. Pauline, however, demanded she be portrayed as Venus, the goddess of love. Thus she appears, reclining on a divan and gracefully holding the golden apple, the symbol of the goddess's triumph in the judgment of Paris. Canova clearly based his work on Greek statuary—the sensuous pose and seminude body recall Hellenistic works such as *Venus de Milo* (FIG. 5-83)—and the reclining figure has parallels on Roman sarcophagus lids (FIG. 7-61; compare FIG. 6-5).

DAVID'S STUDENTS Given David's stature as an artist in Napoleonic France, along with the popularity of Neoclassicism, it is not surprising the First Painter attracted numerous students and developed an active and flourishing teaching studio (see "David on Greek Style," Chapter 26, page 747). He gave practical instruction to and deeply influenced many important artists of the period. So strong was David's commitment to classicism that he encouraged all his students to learn Latin, the better to immerse themselves in and understand classical culture. David even initially demanded his pupils select their subjects from Plutarch, the ancient author of *Lives of the Noble Greeks and Romans* and a principal source of Neoclassical subject matter. Due to this thorough classical foundation, David's students all produced work that at its core retains Neoclassical elements. Yet David was far from authoritarian in his teaching, and he encouraged his students to find their own artistic identities. The work of his three most famous students—Gros (FIG. 27-1), Ingres (FIGS. 27-2A, 27-6, and 27-7), and Girodet-Trioson (FIGS. 27-5 and 27-5A)—represents a departure from the structured confines of Neoclassicism. David's pupils laid the foundation for the Romantic movement (see page 762) by exploring the realm of the exotic and the erotic, and often by turning to fictional narratives for the subjects of their paintings, as the Romantic artists would also do.

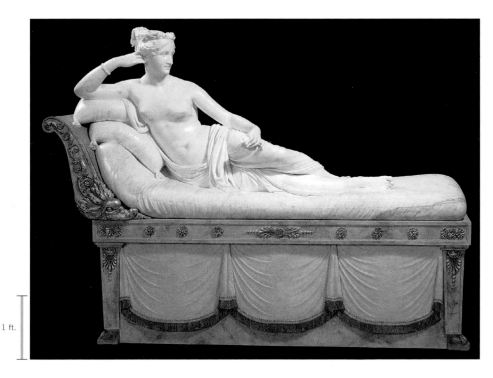

1 ft.

27-4 ANTONIO CANOVA, *Pauline Borghese as Venus*, 1808. Marble, 6′ 7″ long. Galleria Borghese, Rome.

Canova was Napoleon's favorite sculptor. Here, the artist depicted the emperor's sister—at her request—as the nude Roman goddess of love in a marble statue inspired by classical models.

27-5 Anne-Louis Girodet-Trioson, *Burial of Atala,* 1808. Oil on canvas, 6′ 11″ × 8′ 9″. Musée du Louvre, Paris.

Girodet's depiction of Native American lovers in the Louisiana wilderness appealed to the French public's fascination with what it perceived as the passion and primitivism of the New World.

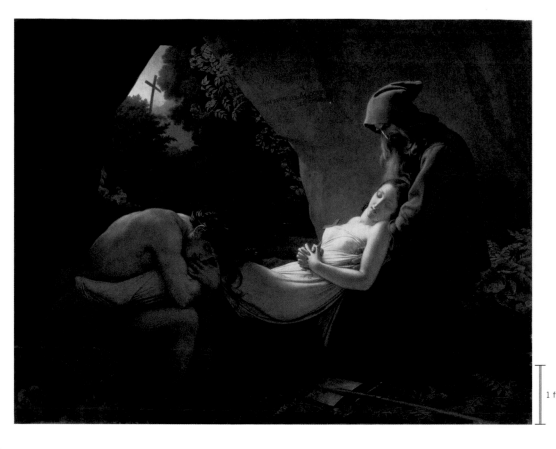

1 ft.

GIRODET-TRIOSON *Burial of Atala* (FIG. **27-5**) by Anne-Louis Girodet-Trioson (1767–1824) is an important bridge between Neoclassicism and Romanticism. Girodet based the painting on *The Genius of Christianity,* a novel by François René de Chateaubriand (1768–1848). The section of the novel dealing with Atala appeared as an excerpt a year before the publication of the entire book in 1802. Both the excerpt and the novel were enormously successful, and as a result, Atala became almost a cult figure. The exoticism and eroticism integral to the narrative accounted in large part for the public's interest in *The Genius of Christianity.* Set in Louisiana, Chateaubriand's work focuses on two young Native Americans, Atala and Chactas. The two, from different tribes, fall in love and run away together through the wilderness. Erotic passion permeates the story, and Atala, sworn to lifelong virginity, finally commits suicide rather than break her oath. Girodet's painting depicts this tragedy. Atala's grief-stricken lover, Chactas, buries the heroine in the shadow of a cross. Assisting in the burial is a cloaked priest, whose presence is appropriate given Chateaubriand's emphasis on the revival of Christianity (and the Christianization of the New World) in his novel. Like Gros's depiction of the exotic Muslim world of Jaffa (FIG. 27-1), Girodet's representation of American Indian lovers in the Louisiana wilderness appealed to the public's fascination (whetted by the Louisiana Purchase in 1803) with what it perceived as the passion and primitivism of Native American life in the New World. *Burial of Atala* speaks here to emotions, rather than inviting philosophical meditation or revealing some grand order of nature and form. Unlike David's appeal in *Oath of the Horatii* (FIG. 26-25) to feelings that inspire public action, the appeal here is to the viewer's private world of fantasy and emotion. But Girodet-Trioson also occasionally addressed contemporary themes in his work, as he did in his portrait (FIG. **27-5A**) of Jean-Baptiste Belley, a French legislator and former slave.

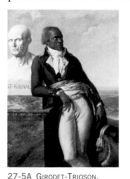

27-5A Girodet-Trioson, *Jean-Baptiste Belley,* 1797.

INGRES David's greatest pupil, J.-A.-D. Ingres (FIG. 27-2A), arrived at David's studio in the late 1790s after Girodet-Trioson had left to establish an independent career. Ingres's study there was to be short-lived, however, as he soon broke with David on matters of style. Ingres adopted what he believed to be a truer and purer Greek style than David's Neoclassical manner. The younger artist employed flat, linear forms approximating those found in Greek vase painting (see Chapter 5), and often placed the main figures in the foreground of his composition, emulating classical low-relief sculpture.

APOTHEOSIS OF HOMER Ingres exhibited his huge composition *Apotheosis of Homer* (FIG. **27-6**) at the Salon of 1827 (see "Academic Salons," Chapter 28, page 802). The painting presented in a single statement the doctrines of ideal form and of Neoclassical taste, and generations of academic painters remained loyal to that style. Winged Victory (or Fame) crowns the epic poet Homer, who sits like a god on a throne before an Ionic temple. At Homer's feet are two statuesque women, personifications of the *Iliad* and the *Odyssey,* the offspring of his imagination. Symmetrically grouped about him is a company of the "sovereign geniuses"—as Ingres called them—who expressed humanity's highest ideals in philosophy, poetry, music, and art. To Homer's left are the Greek poet Anacreon with his lyre, Phidias with his sculptor's hammer, the philosophers Plato and Socrates, and other ancient worthies of different eras. They gather together in the painter's world of suspended time as Raphael united them in *School of Athens* (FIG. 22-9), which was the inspiration for *Apotheosis of Homer.* To the far right in Ingres's assembly of literary and artistic giants are the Roman poets Horace and Vergil, and two Italians: Dante, and, conspicuously, Raphael. Among the forward group on the painting's left side are Poussin (pointing) and Shakespeare (half concealed). At the right are French writers Jean Baptiste Racine, Molière, Voltaire, and François de Salignac de la Mothe Fénelon. Ingres had planned a much larger and more inclusive group, but he never completed the project.

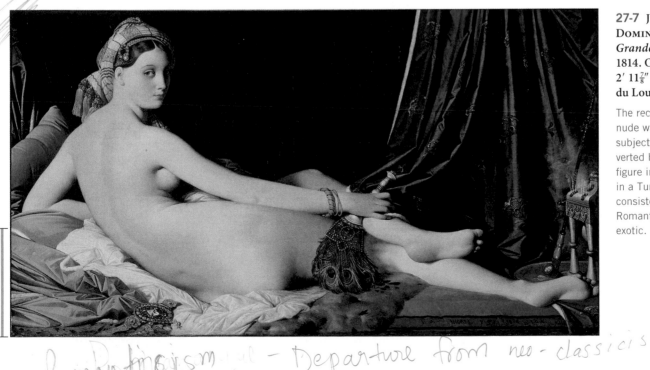

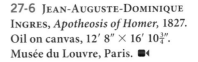

27-6 Jean-Auguste-Dominique Ingres, *Apotheosis of Homer,* 1827. Oil on canvas, 12′ 8″ × 16′ 10¾″. Musée du Louvre, Paris. ▣◀

Inspired by *School of Athens* (FIG. 22-9) by Raphael, Ingres's favorite painter, this monumental canvas is a Neoclassical celebration of Homer and other ancient worthies, Dante, and select French authors.

1 ft.

languid pose, small head and elongated limbs, and the generally cool color scheme reveal the painter's debt to Parmigianino (FIG. 22-44) and the Italian Mannerists. However, by converting the figure to an *odalisque* (woman in a Turkish harem), Ingres, unlike Canova, made a strong concession to the burgeoning Romantic taste for the exotic.

This rather strange mixture of artistic allegiances—the combination of precise classical form and Romantic themes—prompted confusion, and when Ingres first exhibited *Grande Odalisque* in 1814, the painting drew acid criticism. Critics initially saw Ingres as a rebel in terms of both the form and content of his works. They did not cease their attacks until the mid-1820s, when a greater enemy of David's Neoclassical style, Eugène Delacroix, appeared on the scene. Then critics suddenly perceived that Ingres's art, despite its innovations and deviations, still contained crucial elements adhering to the Neoclassical taste for the ideal. In fact, Ingres soon became the leader of the academic forces in their battle against the "barbarism" of Delacroix, Théodore Géricault, and the Romantic movement.

GRANDE ODALISQUE Despite his commitment to ideal form and careful compositional structure, Ingres also produced works that, like those of Gros and Girodet, his contemporaries saw as departures from Neoclassicism. The most famous is *Grande Odalisque* (FIG. **27-7**). The subject—the reclining nude female figure—followed the grand tradition of antiquity and the Renaissance (FIGS. 22 16 and 22-39) in sculpture as well as painting, as did Canova's *Pauline Borghese as Venus* (FIG. 27-4). *Grande Odalisque* again shows Ingres's admiration for Raphael in his borrowing of that master's type of female head (FIGS. 22-7 and 22-8). The figure's

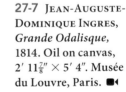

27-7 Jean-Auguste-Dominique Ingres, *Grande Odalisque,* 1814. Oil on canvas, 2′ 11⅞″ × 5′ 4″. Musée du Louvre, Paris. ▣◀

The reclining female nude was a Greco-Roman subject, but Ingres converted his Neoclassical figure into an odalisque in a Turkish harem, consistent with the new Romantic taste for the exotic.

1 ft.

Romanticism — Departure from neo-classicism

ROMANTICISM

Whereas Neoclassicism's rationality reinforced Enlightenment thought (see Chapter 26), particularly Voltaire's views, Rousseau's ideas contributed to the rise of *Romanticism*. Rousseau's exclamation "Man is born free, but is everywhere in chains!"—the opening line of his *Social Contract* (1762)—summarizes a fundamental Romantic premise. Romanticism emerged from a desire for freedom—not only political freedom but also freedom of thought, of feeling, of action, of worship, of speech, and of taste. Romantics asserted freedom was the right and property of all. They believed the path to freedom was through imagination rather than reason and functioned through feeling rather than through thinking.

The allure of the Romantic spirit grew dramatically during the late 18th century, when the term originated among German literary critics. Their aim was to distinguish peculiarly "modern" traits from the Neoclassical traits that already had displaced Baroque and Rococo design elements. Consequently, some scholars refer to Romanticism as a phenomenon that began around 1750 and ended about 1850, but most use the term more narrowly to denote a movement that flourished from about 1800 to 1840, between Neoclassicism and Realism.

Roots of Romanticism

The transition from Neoclassicism to Romanticism represented a shift in emphasis from reason to feeling, from calculation to intuition, and from objective nature to subjective emotion. Among Romanticism's manifestations were the interests in the medieval period and in the sublime. For people living in the 18th century, the Middle Ages were the "dark ages," a time of barbarism, superstition, dark mystery, and miracle. The Romantic imagination stretched its perception of the Middle Ages into all the worlds of fantasy open to it, including the ghoulish, the infernal, the terrible, the nightmarish, the grotesque, the sadistic, and all the imagery that comes from the chamber of horrors when reason sleeps. Related to the imaginative sensibility was the period's notion of the sublime. Among the individuals most involved in studying the sublime was the British politician and philosopher Edmund Burke (1729–1797). In *A Philosophical Enquiry into the Origins of Our Ideas of the Sublime and Beautiful* (1757), Burke articulated his definition of the sublime—feelings of awe mixed with terror. Burke observed that pain or fear evoked the most intense human emotions and that these emotions could also be thrilling. Thus, raging rivers and great storms at sea could be sublime to their viewers.

Accompanying this taste for the sublime was the taste for the fantastic, the occult, and the macabre—for the adventures of the soul voyaging into the dangerous reaches of the imagination.

HENRY FUSELI The concept of the nightmare is the subject of a 1781 painting (FIG. **27-8**) by HENRY FUSELI (1741–1825). Swiss by birth, Fuseli settled in England and eventually became a member of the Royal Academy and an instructor there. Largely self-taught, he contrived a distinctive manner to express the fantasies of his vivid imagination. Fuseli specialized in night moods of horror and in dark fantasies—in the demonic, in the macabre, and often in the sadistic. In *The Nightmare*, a beautiful young woman lies asleep, draped across the bed with her limp arm dangling over the side. An *incubus*, a demon believed in medieval times to prey, often sexually, on sleeping women, squats ominously on her body. In the background, a ghostly horse with flaming eyes bursts into the scene from beyond the curtain. Despite the temptation to see the painting's title as a pun because of this horse, the word *nightmare* in fact derives from "night" and "Mara." Mara was a spirit in Scandinavian mythology who tormented and suffocated sleepers. Fuseli was among the first to attempt to depict the dark terrain of the human subconscious that became fertile ground for later artists to harvest.

WILLIAM BLAKE In their images of the sublime and the terrible, Romantic artists often combined something of Baroque dynamism with naturalistic details in their quest for grippingly moving visions. These elements became the mainstay of Romantic art and contrasted with the more intellectual, rational Neoclassical themes and compositions. The two were not mutually exclusive, however. Gros, Girodet-Trioson, and Ingres effectively integrated elements of Neoclassicism with Romanticism. So, too, did the visionary English poet, painter, and engraver WILLIAM BLAKE (1757–1827). Blake greatly admired ancient Greek art because it exemplified for him the mathematical and thus the eternal, and his work often incorporated classical references. Yet Blake did not align himself with prominent Enlightenment figures. Like many other Romantic

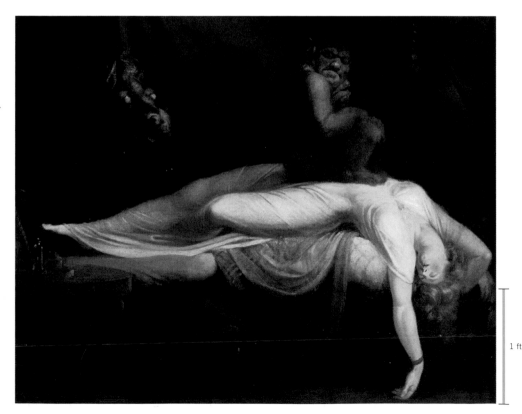

27-8 HENRY FUSELI, *The Nightmare*, 1781. Oil on canvas, 3' 3¾" × 4' 1½". Detroit Institute of the Arts (Founders Society purchase with funds from Mr. and Mrs. Bert L. Smokler and Mr. and Mrs. Lawrence A. Fleishman).

The transition from Neoclassicism to Romanticism marked a shift in emphasis from reason to feeling. Fuseli was among the first painters to depict the dark terrain of the human subconscious.

1 ft.

of his Michelangelesque physique keeps him firmly planted on his heavenly perch. In this image Blake merged ideal classical anatomy with the inner dark dreams of Romanticism.

Spain and France

From its roots in the work of Fuseli, Blake, and other late-18th-century artists, Romanticism gradually displaced Neoclassicism as the dominant painting style of the first half of the 19th century. Romantic artists, including Francisco Goya in Spain and Théodore Géricault and Eugène Delacroix in France, reveled in exploring the exotic, erotic, and fantastic.

FRANCISCO GOYA Although Francisco José de Goya y Lucientes (1746–1828) was David's contemporary, their work has little in common. Goya, however, did not arrive at his general dismissal of Neoclassicism without considerable thought about the Enlightenment and the Neoclassical penchant for rationality and order. In *The Sleep of Reason Produces Monsters* (FIG. 27-10), an

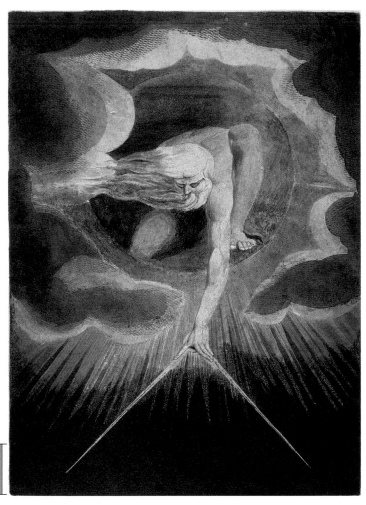

27-9 William Blake, *Ancient of Days*, frontispiece of *Europe: A Prophecy*, 1794. Metal relief etching, hand colored, $9\frac{1}{2}'' \times 6\frac{3}{4}''$. Pierpont Morgan Library, New York.

Although art historians classify Blake as a Romantic artist, he incorporated classical references in his works. Here, ideal classical anatomy merges with the inner dark dreams of Romanticism.

artists, he also found the art of the Middle Ages appealing. Blake derived the inspiration for many of his paintings and poems from his dreams. The importance he attached to these nocturnal experiences led him to believe the rationalist search for material explanations of the world stifled the spiritual side of human nature. He also believed the stringent rules of behavior that orthodox religions imposed killed the individual creative impulse.

Blake's vision of the Almighty in *Ancient of Days* (FIG. 27-9) combines his ideas and interests in a highly individual way. For Blake, this figure united the concept of the Creator with that of wisdom as a part of God. He chose *Ancient of Days* as the frontispiece for his book *Europe: A Prophecy,* and juxtaposed it with a quotation ("When he set a compass upon the face of the deep") from Proverbs 8:27. The speaker is Wisdom, who tells the reader how she was with the Lord through all the time of the creation (Prov. 8:22–23, 27–30). Energy fills Blake's composition. The Almighty leans forward from a fiery orb, peering toward earth and unleashing power through his outstretched left arm into twin rays of light. These emerge between his spread fingers like an architect's measuring instrument—a conception of creation with precedents in Gothic manuscript painting (FIG. 13-32). Here, however, a mighty wind surges through the Creator's thick hair and beard. Only the strength

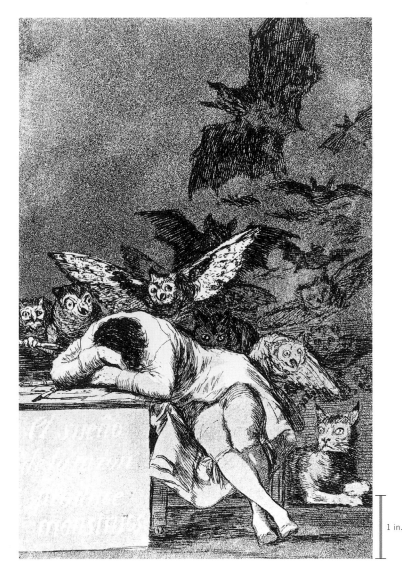

27-10 Francisco Goya, *The Sleep of Reason Produces Monsters,* from *Los Caprichos,* ca. 1798. Etching and aquatint, $8\frac{1}{2}'' \times 5\frac{7}{8}''$. Metropolitan Museum of Art, New York (gift of M. Knoedler & Co., 1918).

In this print, Goya depicted himself asleep while threatening creatures converge on him, revealing his commitment to the Romantic spirit—the unleashing of imagination, emotions, and nightmares.

etching from a series titled *Los Caprichos* (*The Caprices*), Goya depicted himself asleep, slumped onto a desk, while threatening creatures converge on him. Seemingly poised to attack the artist are owls (symbols of folly) and bats (symbols of ignorance). The viewer might read this as a portrayal of what emerges when reason is suppressed and, therefore, as advocating Enlightenment ideals. However, the print also can be interpreted as Goya's commitment to the creative process and the Romantic spirit—the unleashing of imagination, emotions, and even nightmares.

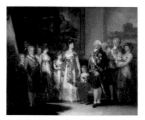

27-10A Goya, *Family of Charles IV*, 1800.

THIRD OF MAY, 1808 Much of Goya's multifaceted work deals not with Romantic fantasies but with contemporary events. In 1786, he became an official artist in the court of Charles IV (r. 1788–1808) and produced portraits of the king and his family (FIG. **27-10A**). Dissatisfaction with the king's rule increased dramatically during Goya's tenure at the court, and the Spanish people eventually threw their support behind the king's son, Ferdinand VII, in the hope he would initiate reform. To overthrow his father and mother, Queen Maria Luisa (1751–1819), Ferdinand enlisted the aid of Napoleon Bonaparte, who possessed uncontested authority and military expertise at that time. Napoleon had designs on the Spanish throne and thus readily agreed to send French troops to Spain. Not surprisingly, as soon as he ousted Charles IV, Napoleon revealed his plan to rule Spain himself by installing his brother Joseph Bonaparte (r. 1808–1813) on the Spanish throne.

The Spanish people, finally recognizing the French as invaders, sought a way to expel the foreign troops. On May 2, 1808, Spaniards attacked Napoleon's soldiers in a chaotic and violent clash. In retaliation and as a show of force, the French responded the next day by rounding up and executing Spanish citizens. This tragic event is the subject of Goya's most famous painting, *Third of*

May, 1808 (FIG. **27-11**), commissioned in 1814 by Ferdinand VII (r. 1813–1833), who had reclaimed the throne after the ouster of the French. In emotional fashion, Goya depicted the anonymous murderous wall of Napoleonic soldiers ruthlessly executing the unarmed and terrified Spanish peasants. The artist encouraged empathy for the Spaniards by portraying horrified expressions and anguish on their faces, endowing them with a humanity lacking in the French firing squad. Moreover, the peasant about to be shot throws his arms out in a cruciform gesture reminiscent of Christ's position on the cross. Goya enhanced the emotional drama of the massacre by using stark darks and lights and by extending the time frame depicted. Although Goya captured the specific moment when one man is about to be executed, he also recorded the bloody bodies of others lying dead on the ground. Still others have been herded together to be shot in a few moments.

SATURN Over time, Goya became increasingly disillusioned and pessimistic, and his declining health further contributed to this state of mind. Among Goya's later works are the "Black Paintings," frescoes he painted on the walls of his farmhouse in Quinta del Sordo, outside Madrid. Because Goya created these works solely on his terms and for his private viewing, they provide great insight into the artist's outlook, which is terrifying and disturbing. *Saturn Devouring One of His Children* (FIG. **27-12**) depicts the raw carnage and violence of Saturn (the Greek god Kronos; see "The Gods and Goddesses of Mount Olympus," Chapter 5, page 107, or page xxix in Volume II and Book D), wild-eyed and monstrous, as he consumes one of his offspring. Because of the similarity of Kronos and *khronos* (the Greek word for "time"), Saturn has come to be associated with time. This has led some to interpret Goya's painting as an expression of the artist's despair over the passage of time. Despite the simplicity of the image, it conveys a wildness, boldness, and brutality that evokes an elemental response from all viewers. Goya's work, rooted both in personal and national history, presents darkly emotional images well in keeping with Romanticism.

27-11 Francisco Goya, *Third of May, 1808*, 1814–1815. Oil on canvas, 8′ 9″ × 13′ 4″. Museo del Prado, Madrid. ◼◀

Goya encouraged empathy for the massacred Spanish peasants by portraying horrified expressions on their faces, endowing them with a humanity lacking in the French firing squad.

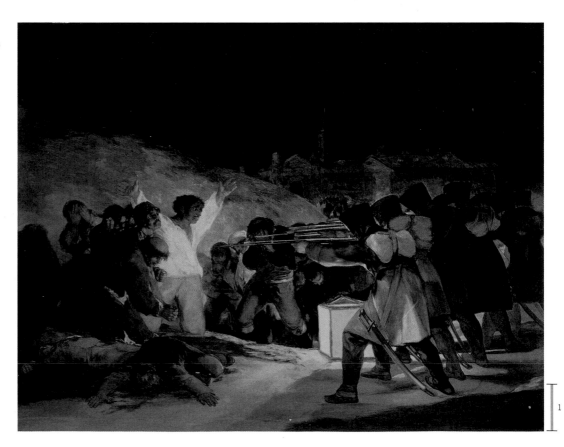

1 ft.

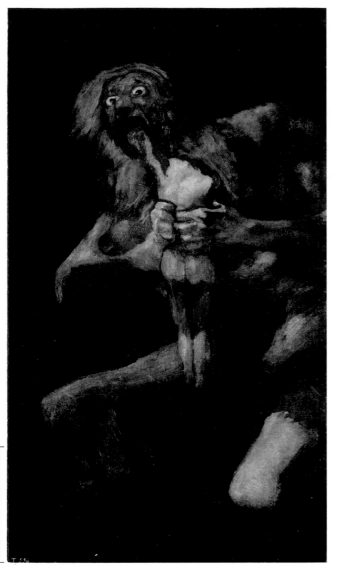

27-12 Francisco Goya, *Saturn Devouring One of His Children*, 1819–1823. Fresco, later detached and mounted on canvas, 4′ 9⅛″ × 2′ 8⅝″. Museo del Prado, Madrid.

This disturbing fresco in Goya's farmhouse uses a mythological tale to express the aging artist's despair over the passage of time. Saturn's Greek name *Kronos* is similar to the Greek word for "time."

1 ft.

THÉODORE GÉRICAULT In France, one of the artists most closely associated with the Romantic movement was THÉODORE GÉRICAULT (1791–1824), who studied with an admirer of David, PIERRE-NARCISSE GUÉRIN (1774–1833). Although Géricault retained an interest in the heroic and the epic and completed rigorous training in classical drawing, he chafed at the rigidity of the Neoclassical style, instead producing works that captivate viewers with their drama, visual complexity, and emotional force.

RAFT OF THE MEDUSA Géricault's most ambitious project was a gigantic canvas (approximately 16 by 23 feet) titled *Raft of the Medusa* (FIG. **27-13**), exhibited in the Salon of 1819, seven years after he burst onto the Parisian art scene with *Charging Chasseur* (FIG. **27-13A**). In both works, Géricault abandoned the idealism of Neoclassicism and embraced the theatricality of Romanticism. The subject of *Raft of the Medusa* is the 1816 shipwreck off the African coast of the French frigate *Medusa*, which ran aground on a reef due to the incompetence of the captain, a political appointee. In an attempt to survive, 150 passengers built a makeshift raft from pieces of the disintegrating ship. The raft drifted for 12 days, and the number still alive dwindled to 15. Finally, a ship spotted the raft and rescued the emaciated survivors. This horrendous event was political dynamite once it became public knowledge.

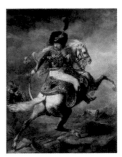

27-13A GÉRICAULT, *Charging Chasseur*, 1812.

In *Raft of the Medusa*, which took Géricault eight months to complete, the artist sought to capture the horror, chaos, and emotion of the tragedy yet invoke the grandeur and impact of Neoclassical history painting.

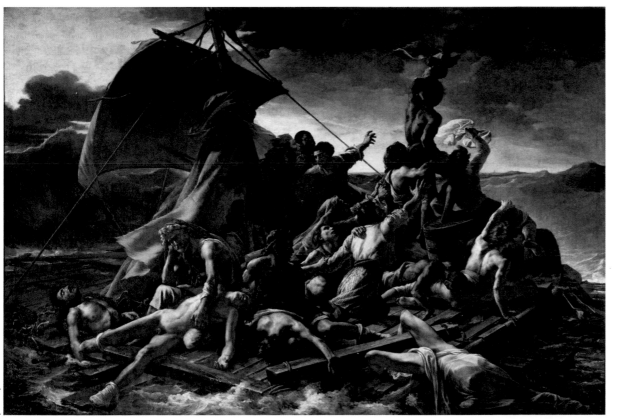

27-13 THÉODORE GÉRICAULT, *Raft of the Medusa*, 1818–1819. Oil on canvas, 16′ 1″ × 23′ 6″. Musée du Louvre, Paris. ◼◀

In this gigantic history painting, Géricault rejected Neoclassical compositional principles and, in the Romantic spirit, presented a jumble of writhing bodies in every attitude of suffering, despair, and death.

1 ft.

Romanticism   **765**

Géricault went to great lengths to ensure the accuracy of his representation. He visited hospitals and morgues to examine corpses, interviewed the survivors, and had a model of the raft constructed in his studio. In the painting, the few despairing survivors summon what little strength they have left to flag down the passing ship far on the horizon. The subdued palette and prominent shadows lend an ominous pall to the scene. Géricault departed from the straightforward organization of Neoclassical compositions and instead presented a jumble of writhing bodies. He arranged the survivors and several corpses in a powerful X-shaped composition, and piled one body on another in every attitude of suffering, despair, and death (recalling the plague-stricken figures in Gros's *Napoleon at the Plague House at Jaffa*, FIG. 27-1). One light-filled diagonal axis stretches from bodies at the lower left up to the black man raised on his comrades' shoulders and waving a piece of cloth toward the horizon. The cross axis descends from the dark, billowing sail at the upper left to the shadowed upper torso of the body trailing in the open sea. Géricault's decision to place the raft at a diagonal so that a corner juts outward further draws viewers into the tragic scene. Indeed, it seems as though some of the corpses are sliding off the raft into the viewing space.

Raft of the Medusa is also the artist's commentary on the practice of slavery. Géricault was a member of an abolitionist group that sought ways to end the slave trade in the colonies, the cause promoted in the French legislature by Jean-Baptiste Belley (FIG. 27-5A). Given Géricault's antipathy to slavery, it is appropriate he placed Jean Charles, a black soldier who was one of the few survivors, at the top of the pyramidal heap of bodies.

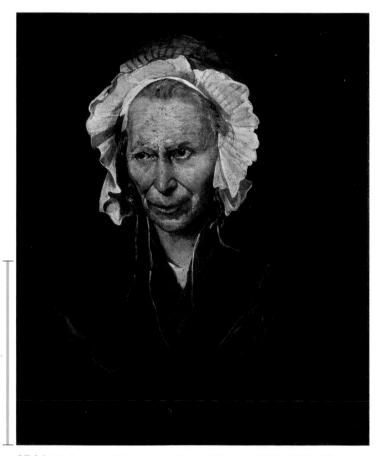

27-14 THÉODORE GÉRICAULT, *Insane Woman*, 1822–1823. Oil on canvas, 2′ 4″ × 1′ 9″. Musée des Beaux-Arts, Lyons.

The insane and the influence of aberrant states of mind on the appearance of the human face fascinated Géricault and other Romantic artists, who rebelled against Enlightenment rationality.

INSANE WOMAN Mental aberration and irrational states of mind could not fail to interest the rebels against Enlightenment rationality. Géricault, like Goya, examined the influence of mental states on the human face and believed, as many of his contemporaries did, that a face accurately revealed character, especially at the moment of death (FIG. 27-11) and in madness (FIG. 27-12). Géricault made many studies of the inmates of hospitals and institutions for the criminally insane, and he studied the severed heads of guillotine victims. Scientific and artistic curiosity often accompanied the morbidity of the Romantic interest in derangement and death.

Insane Woman (FIG. **27-14**) is one of several of Géricault's portraits of the insane possessing a peculiar hypnotic power. The woman looks away from the viewer, her mouth tense and her eyes red-rimmed with suffering. The portrait presents the psychic facts with astonishing authenticity and breaks sharply with traditional portraiture in which the sitter's visage is idealized, the expression placid, and the setting designed to communicate the elevated stature of the person portrayed.

EUGÈNE DELACROIX Art historians often present the history of painting during the first half of the 19th century as a contest between two major artists—Ingres, the Neoclassical draftsman, and EUGÈNE DELACROIX (1798–1863; FIG. 27-50), the Romantic colorist. Their dialogue recalls the quarrel between the Poussinistes and the Rubénistes at the end of the 17th century and the beginning of the 18th (see Chapter 26). The Poussinistes were conservative defenders of academism who insisted that drawing was superior to color, whereas the Rubénistes proclaimed the importance of color over line (line quality being more intellectual and thus more restrictive than color). Delacroix's works were products of his view that the artist's powers of imagination would in turn capture and inflame the viewer's imagination. Literature of imaginative power served Delacroix (and many of his contemporaries) as a useful source of subject matter (see "The Romantic Spirit in Art, Music, and Literature," page 767). Théophile Gautier (1811–1872), the prominent Romantic critic and novelist, recalled:

> In those days painting and poetry fraternized. The artists read the poets, and the poets visited the artists. We found Shakespeare, Dante, Goethe, Lord Byron and Walter Scott in the studio as well as in the study. There were as many splashes of color as there were blots of ink in the margins of those beautiful books which we endlessly perused. Imagination, already excited, was further fired by reading those foreign works, so rich in color, so free and powerful in fantasy.[1]

DEATH OF SARDANAPALUS Delacroix's 1827 *Death of Sardanapalus* (FIG. **27-15**) is perhaps the grandest Romantic pictorial drama ever painted. Although inspired by the 1821 narrative poem *Sardanapalus* by Lord Byron (1788–1824), the painting does not illustrate that text faithfully. Delacroix depicted the last hour of the Assyrian king Ashurbanipal (r. 668–627 BCE; FIG. 2-23), whom the Greeks called Sardanapalus. The king has just received news of his armies' defeat and the enemies' entry into his city. The setting Delacroix painted is much more tempestuous and crowded than Byron described, and orgiastic destruction has replaced the sacrificial suicide of the poem. Sardanapalus reclines on his funeral pyre, soon to be set alight, and gloomily watches the destruction of all of his most precious possessions—his women, slaves, horses, and treasure. The king's favorite concubine throws herself on the bed, determined to go up in flames with her master. The Assyrian ruler presides like a genius of evil over the tragic scene. Most conspicuous

1 ft.

The Romantic Spirit in Art, Music, and Literature

The appeal of Romanticism, with its emphasis on freedom and feeling, extended well beyond the realm of the visual arts. The imagination and vision that characterized Romantic paintings and sculptures were equally moving and riveting in musical or written form. In European music, literature, and poetry, the Romantic spirit was a dominant presence during the late 18th and early 19th centuries. Composers and authors alike rejected classicism's structured order in favor of the emotive and expressive. In music, the compositions of Franz Schubert (1797–1828), Franz Liszt (1811–1886), Frédéric Chopin (1810–1849), and Johannes Brahms (1833–1897) emphasized the melodic or lyrical. For these composers, music had the power to express the unspeakable and to communicate the subtlest and most powerful human emotions.

In literature, Romantic poets such as John Keats (1795–1821), William Wordsworth (1770–1850), and Samuel Taylor Coleridge (1772–1834) published volumes of poetry manifesting the Romantic interest in lyrical drama. *Ozymandias,* by Percy Bysshe Shelley (1792–1822), transported readers to faraway, exotic locales. The setting of Lord Byron's *Sardanapalus* is the ancient Assyrian Empire (see Chapter 2). Byron's poem conjures images of eroticism and fury unleashed—images Eugène Delacroix made concrete in his painting *Death of Sardanapalus* (FIG. 27-15). One of the best examples of the Romantic spirit is the engrossing novel *Frankenstein,* written in 1818 by Shelley's wife, Mary Wollstonecraft Shelley (1797–1851). This fantastic tale of a monstrous creature run amok remains popular to the present day. As was true of many Romantic artworks, the novel not only embraced emotionalism but also rejected the rationalism underlying Enlightenment thought. Dr. Frankenstein's monster was a product of science, and the novel is an indictment of the tenacious belief in science that Voltaire and other Enlightenment thinkers promoted. *Frankenstein* served as a cautionary tale of the havoc that could result from unrestrained scientific experimentation and from the arrogance of scientists.

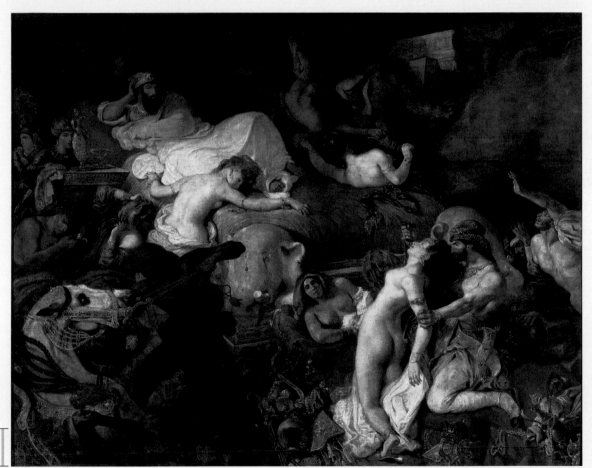

1 ft.

27-15 Eugène Delacroix, *Death of Sardanapalus,* 1827. Oil on canvas, 12′ 1½″ × 16′ 2⅞″. Musée du Louvre, Paris. ◼◀

Inspired by Byron's 1821 poem, Delacroix painted the Romantic spectacle of an Assyrian king on his funeral pyre. The richly colored and emotionally charged canvas is filled with exotic figures.

are the tortured and dying bodies of the harem women. In the foreground, a muscular slave plunges his knife into the neck of one woman. Delacroix filled this awful spectacle of suffering and death with the most daringly difficult and tortuous poses, and chose the richest intensities of hue. With its exotic and erotic overtones, *Death of Sardanapalus* tapped into the Romantic fantasies of 19th-century viewers.

Although *Death of Sardanapalus* is a seventh-century BCE drama, Delacroix, as Géricault, also turned to current events, particularly tragic or sensational ones, for his subject matter. For example, he produced several images based on the Greek War for Independence (1821–1829), including a huge canvas painted while the war was in progress recording the Turkish massacre of the Greeks of Chios (FIG. 27-15A). The French perception of the Greeks locked in a brutal struggle for freedom from the cruel and exotic Ottoman Turks generated great interest in Romantic circles.

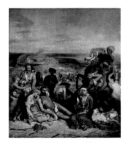

27-15A Delacroix, *Massacre at Chios,* 1822–1824.

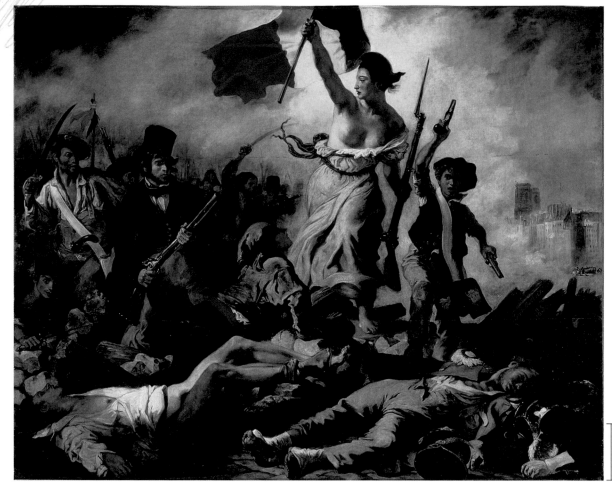

27-16 EUGÈNE DELACROIX, *Liberty Leading the People*, 1830. Oil on canvas, 8′ 6″ × 10′ 8″. Musée du Louvre, Paris. ◼◀

In a balanced mix of history and poetic allegory, Delacroix captured the passion and energy of the 1830 revolution in this painting of Liberty leading the Parisian uprising against Charles X.

1 ft.

LIBERTY LEADING THE PEOPLE Closer to home, Delacroix captured the passion and energy of the 1830 revolution in *Liberty Leading the People* (FIG. **27-16**). Based on the Parisian uprising against Charles X (r. 1824–1830) at the end of July 1830, it depicts the allegorical personification of Liberty defiantly thrusting forth the republic's tricolor banner as she urges the masses to fight on. The scarlet Phrygian cap (the symbol of a freed slave in antiquity) she wears reinforces the urgency of this struggle. Arrayed around Liberty are bold Parisian types—the street boy brandishing his pistols, the menacing worker with a cutlass, and the intellectual dandy in a top hat brandishing a musket. As in Géricault's *Raft of the Medusa* (FIG. 27-13), dead bodies are all around. In the background, the towers of Notre-Dame (FIG. 13-11) rise through the smoke and haze. The painter's inclusion of this recognizable Parisian landmark announces the specificity of locale and event, balancing contemporary historical fact with poetic allegory.

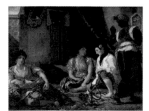

27-17A DELACROIX, *Women of Algiers*, 1834.

TIGER HUNT An enormously influential event in Delacroix's life that affected his art in both subject and form was his visit to North Africa in 1832 (see "Delacroix in Morocco," page 769). Things he saw there shocked his imagination with fresh impressions that lasted throughout his life and resulted in paintings such as *Tiger Hunt* (FIG. **27-17**), which he completed more than two decades after his trip. Among the canvases he painted immediately upon his return is *Women of Algiers* (FIG. **27-17A**), which captivated the public

when exhibited in the 1834 Salon. Delacroix's African experience further heightened his already considerable awareness of the expressive power of color and light. What Delacroix knew about color he passed on to later painters of the 19th century, particularly the Impressionists (see Chapter 28). He observed that pure colors are as rare in nature as lines and that color appears only in an infinitely varied scale of different tones, shadings, and reflections, which he tried to re-create in his paintings. He recorded his observations in his journal, which became for later painters and scholars a veritable handbook of pre-Impressionist color theory. Although Delacroix anticipated the later development of Impressionist color science, that art-science had to await the discoveries by Michel Eugène Chevreul (1786–1889) and Hermann von Helmholtz (1821–1894) of the laws of light decomposition and the properties of complementary colors. Only then could the problems of color perception and juxtaposition in painting be properly formulated (see "19th-Century Color Theory," Chapter 28, page 813). Nevertheless, Delacroix's observations were significant, and he advised other artists not to fuse their brushstrokes, as those strokes would appear to fuse naturally from a distance.

No other painter of the time explored the domain of Romantic subject and mood as thoroughly and definitively as Delacroix. His technique was impetuous, improvisational, and instinctive, rather than deliberate, studious, and cold. It epitomized Romantic colorist painting, catching the impression quickly and developing it in the execution process. His contemporaries commented on how furiously Delacroix worked once he had an idea, keeping the whole painting progressing at once. The fury of his attack matched the fury of his imagination and his subjects.

Delacroix in Morocco

Romantic painters often depicted exotic faraway places they had never seen, but Eugène Delacroix journeyed to Morocco in 1832 and discovered in the sun-drenched landscape—and in the hardy and colorful Moroccans dressed in robes reminiscent of the Roman toga—new insights into a culture built on proud virtues. He found in North Africa a culture more classical than anything European Neoclassicism could conceive. In a letter to his friend Fréderic Villot dated February 29, 1832, he wrote:

> This place is made for painters. . . . [B]eauty abounds here; not the over-praised beauty of fashionable paintings. The heroes of David and Co. with their rose-pink limbs would cut a sorry figure beside these children of the sun, who moreover wear the dress of classical antiquity with a nobler air, I dare assert.*

In a second letter, written June 4, 1832, he reported to Auguste Jal:

> You have seen Algiers and you can imagine what the natives of these regions are like. Here there is something even simpler and more primitive; there is less of the Turkish alloy; I have Romans and Greeks on my doorstep: it makes me laugh heartily at David's Greeks, apart, of course, from his sublime skill as a painter. I know now what they were really like; . . . If painting schools persist in [depicting classical subjects], I am convinced, and you will agree

with me, that they would gain far more from being shipped off as cabin boys on the first boat bound for the Barbary coast than from spending any more time wearing out the classical soil of Rome. Rome is no longer to be found in Rome.[†]

The gallantry, valor, and fierce love of liberty of the Moroccans made them, in Delacroix's eyes, unspoiled heroes uncontaminated by European decadence. The Moroccan voyage reinforced Delacroix's Romantic conviction that beauty exists in the fierceness of nature, natural processes, and natural beings, especially animals. After he experienced Morocco, more and more of Delacroix's subjects involved combats between beasts or between beasts and men. He painted snarling tangles of lions and tigers, battles between horses, and clashes of Muslims with great cats in swirling hunting scenes using compositions reminiscent of those of Rubens (FIG. I-14), as in his 1854 painting *Tiger Hunt* (FIG. 27-17), which clearly speaks to the Romantic interest in faraway lands and exotic cultures.

*Translated by Jean Stewart, in Charles Harrison, Paul Wood, and Jason Gaiger, eds., *Art in Theory 1815–1900: An Anthology of Changing Ideas* (Oxford: Blackwell, 1998), 87.
[†]Ibid., 88.

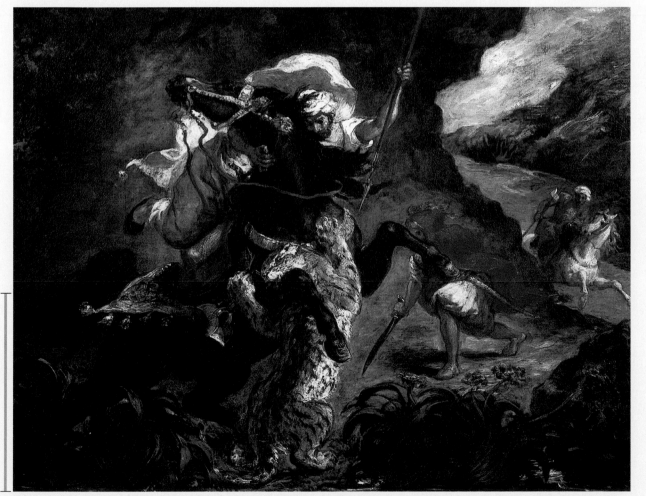

1 ft.

27-17 EUGÈNE DELACROIX, *Tiger Hunt*, 1854. Oil on canvas, 2′ 5″ × 3′. Musée d'Orsay, Paris.

Delacroix's 1832 trip to Morocco inspired *Tiger Hunt* and had a lasting impact on his art. His paintings of men battling ferocious beasts are consistent with the Romantic interest in exotic places.

FRANÇOIS RUDE The Romantic spirit pervaded all media during the early 19th century. As did the painters of the period, many sculptors produced work incorporating both Neoclassical and Romantic elements. The colossal limestone group *Departure of the Volunteers of 1792* (FIG. **27-18**), also called *La Marseillaise,* is one example. The relief, the work of FRANÇOIS RUDE (1784–1855), decorates one of the gigantic piers of the Arc de Triomphe in Paris. This French landmark was an 1806 Napoleonic commission designed by Jean François Thérèse Chalgrin (1739–1811) on the model of the triumphal arches of ancient Rome (FIGS. 7-40, 7-44B, and 7-75). Work on the arch stopped after Napoleon's defeat but resumed in 1833. Three years later, workmen inserted Rude's group (and three similar ones by other sculptors) into the completed arch. The sculpture depicts the volunteers of 1792 departing to defend France's borders against the foreign enemies of the revolution. The Roman goddess of war, Bellona (who here personifies liberty as well as the "Marseillaise," the revolutionary hymn that is now France's national anthem), soars above patriots of all ages, exhorting them forward with her thundering battle cry. The figures recall David's classically armored (FIG. 26-25) or nude heroes, as do the rhetorical gestures of the wide-flung arms and the striding poses. Yet the violence of motion, the jagged contours, and the densely packed, overlapping

masses relate more closely to the compositional method of dramatic Romanticism, as found in the canvases of Géricault (FIG. 27-13) and Delacroix (FIG. 27-16). Indeed, the allegorical figure in *La Marseillaise* is the spiritual sister of Delacroix's Liberty. Rude's stone figure shares the same Phrygian cap, the badge of liberty, with Delacroix's earlier painted figure, but Rude's soldiers wear classical costumes or are heroically nude, whereas those in Delacroix's painting appear in modern Parisian dress. Both works are allegorical, but one looks to the past and the other to the present.

Landscape Painting

Landscape painting came into its own in the 19th century as a fully independent and respected genre. Briefly eclipsed at the century's beginning by the taste for ideal form, which favored figural composition and history, landscape painting flourished as leading painters adopted the genre as their specialty. Increasing tourism, which came courtesy of improved and expanded railway systems both in Europe (MAP 27-2) and America, contributed to the popularity of landscape painting.

The notion of the picturesque became particularly resonant in the Romantic era. Already in the 18th century, artists had regarded the pleasurable, aesthetic mood that natural landscape inspired as making the landscape itself "picturesque"—that is, worthy of being painted. Rather than simply describe nature, Romantic poets and artists often used nature as allegory. In this manner, artists commented on spiritual, moral, historical, or philosophical issues. Landscape painting was a particularly effective vehicle for such commentary.

In the early 19th century, most northern European (especially German) landscape painting to some degree expressed the Romantic view (first extolled by Rousseau) of nature as a "being" that included the totality of existence in organic unity and harmony. In nature—"the living garment of God," as German poet and dramatist Johann Wolfgang von Goethe (1749–1832) called it—artists found an ideal subject to express the Romantic theme of the soul unified with the natural world. As all nature was mysteriously permeated by "being," landscape artists had the task of interpreting the signs, symbols, and emblems of universal spirit disguised within visible material things. Artists no longer merely beheld a landscape but participated in its spirit, becoming translators of nature's transcendent meanings.

CASPAR DAVID FRIEDRICH Among the first northern European artists to depict the Romantic transcendental landscape was CASPAR DAVID FRIEDRICH (1774–1840). For Friedrich, landscapes were temples, and his paintings were altarpieces. The reverential mood of his works demands from the viewer the silence appropriate to sacred places filled with a divine presence. *Abbey in the Oak Forest* (FIG. **27-19**) serves as a solemn requiem. Under a winter sky, through the leafless oaks of a snow-covered cemetery, a funeral procession bears a coffin into the ruins of a Gothic church Friedrich based on the remains of Eldana Abbey in Greifswald. The emblems of death are everywhere—the season's desolation, the leaning crosses and tombstones, the black of mourning the grieving wear, the skeletal trees, and the destruction time has wrought on the church. The painting is a kind of meditation on human mortality. As Friedrich himself remarked: "Why, it has often occurred to me to ask myself, do I so frequently choose death, transience, and the grave as subjects for my paintings? One must submit oneself many times to death in order some day to attain life everlasting."[2] The artist's sharp-focused rendering of details demonstrates his keen perception of everything in the physical environment relevant to his message. Friedrich's work

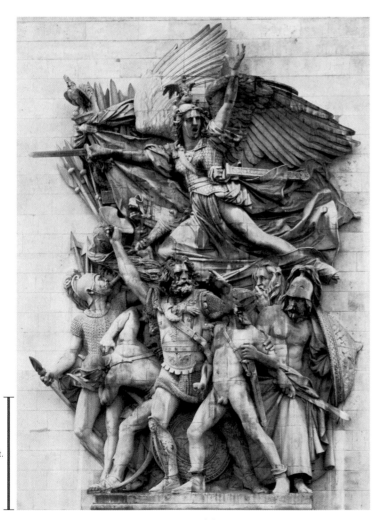

10 ft.

27-18 FRANÇOIS RUDE, *Departure of the Volunteers of 1792* (*La Marseillaise*), Arc de Triomphe, Paris, France, 1833–1836. Limestone, 41′ 8″ high. ◼◀

This historical-allegorical sculpture features the Roman war goddess Bellona, but the violent motion, jagged contours, and densely packed masses typify Romantic painting compositions.

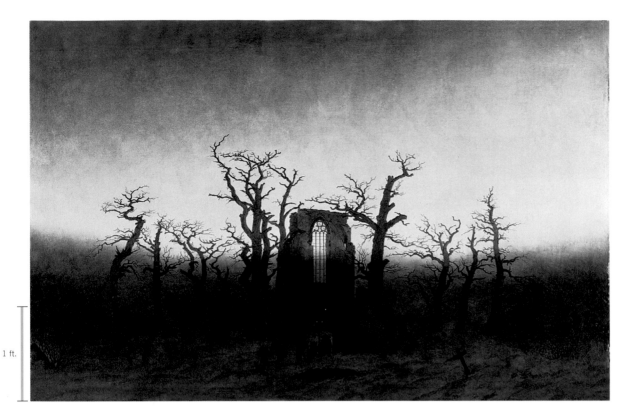

27-19 CASPAR DAVID
FRIEDRICH, *Abbey in
the Oak Forest*, 1810.
Oil on canvas, 4′ × 5′ 8½″.
Nationalgalerie, Staatliche
Museen zu Berlin, Berlin.
◼◀

Friedrich was a master of
the Romantic transcendental
landscape. The reverential
mood of this winter scene
with a ruined Gothic church
and cemetery demands the
silence appropriate to sacred
places.

1 ft.

balances inner and outer experience. "The artist," he wrote, "should not only paint what he sees before him, but also what he sees within him. If he does not see anything within him, he should give up painting what he sees before him."[3] Although Friedrich's works may not have the theatrical energy of the paintings of Géricault or Delacroix, a resonant and deep emotion pervades them.

WANDERER ABOVE A SEA OF MIST In *Abbey in the Oak Forest* and many of Friedrich's landscapes, the human figure plays an insignificant role. Indeed, in many instances the human actors are difficult even to discern. But in other paintings, one or more figures seen from behind gazing at the natural vista dominate the canvas. In *Wanderer above a Sea of Mist* (FIG. **27-20**), probably Friedrich's most famous painting, a solitary man dressed in German attire suggestive of a bygone era stands on a rocky promontory and leans on his cane. He surveys a vast panorama of clouds, mountains, and thick mist. Because Friedrich chose a point of view on the level of the man's head, the viewer has the sensation of hovering in space behind him—an impossible position that enhances the aura of mystery the scene conveys. Scholars dispute whether Friedrich intended the viewer to identify with the man seen from behind or if he wanted the viewer to contemplate the man gazing at the misty landscape. In either case, the painter communicated an almost religious awe at the beauty and vastness of the natural world. *Wanderer above a Sea of Mist* perfectly expresses the Romantic notion of the sublime in nature.

JOHN CONSTABLE In England, one of the most momentous developments in Western history—the Industrial Revolution—had a profound impact on the evolution of Romantic landscape painting. Although discussion of the Industrial Revolution invariably focuses on technological advances, factory development, and growth of urban centers (see Chapter 26), industrialization had no less pronounced an effect on the countryside and the land itself. The detrimental economic effect the Industrial Revolution had

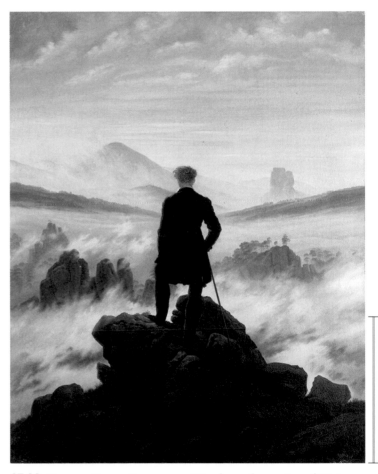

27-20 CASPAR DAVID FRIEDRICH, *Wanderer above a Sea of Mist*, 1817–1818. Oil on canvas, 3′ 1¾″ × 2′ 5⅜″. Hamburger Kunsthalle, Hamburg.

Friedrich's painting of a solitary man on a rocky promontory gazing at a vast panorama of clouds, mountains, and thick mist perfectly expresses the Romantic notion of the sublime in nature.

1 ft.

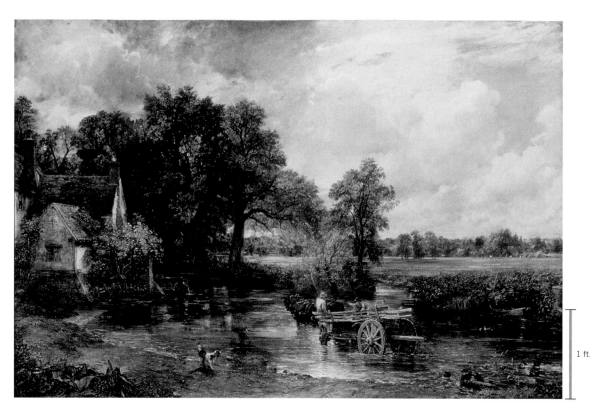

27-21 JOHN CONSTABLE, *The Haywain*, 1821. Oil on canvas, 4′ 3¼″ × 6′ 1″. National Gallery, London.

The Haywain is a nostalgic view of the disappearing English countryside during the Industrial Revolution. Constable had a special gift for capturing the texture that climate and weather give to landscape.

1 ft.

on prices for agrarian products produced significant unrest in the English countryside. In particular, increasing numbers of displaced farmers could no longer afford to farm their small land plots.

JOHN CONSTABLE (1776–1837) addressed this agrarian crisis in his landscape paintings. He made countless studies from nature for each of his canvases, which helped him produce in his paintings the convincing sense of reality that won so much praise from his contemporaries. In his quest for the authentic landscape, Constable studied it as a meteorologist (which he was by avocation). His special gift was for capturing the texture that climate and weather, which delicately veil what is seen, give to landscape. Constable's use of tiny dabs of local color, stippled with white, created a sparkling shimmer of light and hue across the canvas surface—the vibration itself suggestive of movement and process.

The Haywain (FIG. **27-21**) is representative of Constable's art and reveals much about his outlook. A small cottage sits on the left of this placid, picturesque scene of the countryside, and in the center foreground, a man leads a horse and wagon across the stream. Billowy clouds float lazily across the sky. The muted greens and golds and the delicacy of Constable's brushstrokes complement the scene's tranquility. The artist portrayed the oneness with nature the Romantic poets sought. The relaxed figures are not observers but participants in the landscape's "being."

In terms of content, *The Haywain* is significant for precisely what it does not show—the civil unrest of the agrarian working class and the resulting outbreaks of violence and arson. The people populating Constable's landscapes blend into the scenes and are at one with nature. Rarely does the viewer see workers engaged in tedious labor. Indeed, this painting has a nostalgic, wistful air to it, and reflects Constable's memories of a disappearing rural pastoralism. The artist's father was a rural landowner of considerable wealth, and many of the scenes Constable painted (*The Haywain* included) depict his family's property near East Bergholt in Suffolk, East Anglia. This nostalgia, presented in such naturalistic terms, renders Constable's works Romantic in tone. That the painter felt a kindred spirit with the Romantic artists is revealed by his comment, "Painting is but another word for feeling."[4]

J.M.W. TURNER Constable's contemporary in the English school of landscape painting, JOSEPH MALLORD WILLIAM TURNER (1775–1851), produced work that also responded to encroaching industrialization. However, whereas Constable's paintings are serene and precisely painted, Turner's feature turbulent swirls of frothy pigment. The passion and energy of Turner's works reveal the Romantic sensibility that was the foundation for his art and also clearly illustrate Edmund Burke's concept of the sublime—awe mixed with terror.

Among Turner's most notable works is *The Slave Ship* (FIG. **27-22**). Its subject is a 1783 incident reported in a widely read book titled *The History of the Abolition of the Slave Trade*, by Thomas Clarkson. Because the book had just been reprinted in 1839, Clarkson's account probably prompted Turner's choice of subject for this 1840 painting. The incident involved the captain of a slave ship who, on realizing his insurance company would reimburse him only for slaves lost at sea but not for those who died en route, ordered the sick and dying slaves thrown overboard. Appropriately, the painting's full title is *The Slave Ship (Slavers Throwing Overboard the Dead and Dying, Typhoon Coming On)*. Turner's frenzied emotional depiction of this act matches its barbaric nature. The artist transformed the sun into an incandescent comet amid flying scarlet clouds. The slave ship moves into the distance, leaving in its wake a turbulent sea choked with the bodies of slaves sinking to their deaths. The relative scale of the minuscule human forms compared with the vast sea and overarching sky reinforces the sense of the sublime, especially the immense power of nature over humans. Almost lost in the boiling colors are the event's particulars, but on close inspection, the viewer can discern the iron shackles and manacles around the wrists and ankles of the drowning slaves, cruelly denying them any chance of saving themselves.

A key ingredient of Turner's highly personal style is the emotive power of pure color. The haziness of the painter's forms and the indistinctness of his compositions intensify the colors and energetic brushstrokes. Turner's innovation in works such as *The Slave Ship* was to release color from any defining outlines so as to express both the forces of nature and the painter's emotional response to them. In his paintings, the reality of color is at one with the reality of feeling. Turner's methods had an incalculable effect on the later

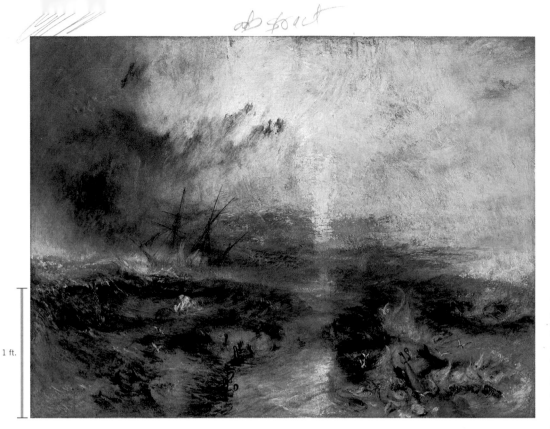

27-22 JOSEPH MALLORD WILLIAM TURNER, *The Slave Ship* (*Slavers Throwing Overboard the Dead and Dying, Typhoon Coming On*), 1840. Oil on canvas, 2′ 11¼″ × 4′. Museum of Fine Arts, Boston (Henry Lillie Pierce Fund).

The essence of Turner's innovative style is the emotive power of color. He released color from any defining outlines to express both the forces of nature and the painter's emotional response to them.

development of painting. His discovery of the aesthetic and emotive power of pure color and his pushing of the medium's fluidity to a point where the paint itself is almost the subject were important steps toward 20th-century abstract art, which dispensed with shape and form altogether (see Chapter 30).

THOMAS COLE In America, landscape painting was the specialty of a group of artists known as the Hudson River School, so named because its members drew their subjects primarily from the uncultivated regions of New York's Hudson River Valley, although many of these painters depicted scenes from across the country. As did the early-19th-century landscape painters in Germany and England, the artists of the Hudson River School not only presented Romantic panoramic landscape views but also participated in the

ongoing exploration of the individual's and the country's relationship to the land. American landscape painters frequently focused on identifying qualities that made America unique. One American painter of English birth, THOMAS COLE (1801–1848), often referred to as the leader of the Hudson River School, articulated this idea:

Whether he [an American] beholds the Hudson mingling waters with the Atlantic—explores the central wilds of this vast continent, or stands on the margin of the distant Oregon, he is still in the midst of American scenery—it is his own land; its beauty, its magnificence, its sublimity—all are his; and how undeserving of such a birthright, if he can turn towards it an unobserving eye, an unaffected heart![5]

Another issue that surfaced frequently in Hudson River School paintings was the moral question of America's direction as a civilization. Cole addressed this question in *The Oxbow* (*View from Mount Holyoke, Northampton, Massachusetts, after a Thunderstorm;* FIG. **27-23**). A splendid scene opens before the viewer, dominated by the lazy oxbow-shaped turning of the Connecticut River. Cole divided the composition in two, with the dark, stormy wilderness on the left and the more developed civilization on the right. The minuscule artist in the bottom center of the painting (wearing a top hat), dwarfed by the landscape's scale, turns to the viewer as if to ask for input in deciding the country's future course. Cole's depictions of expansive wilderness incorporated reflections and moods romantically appealing to the public.

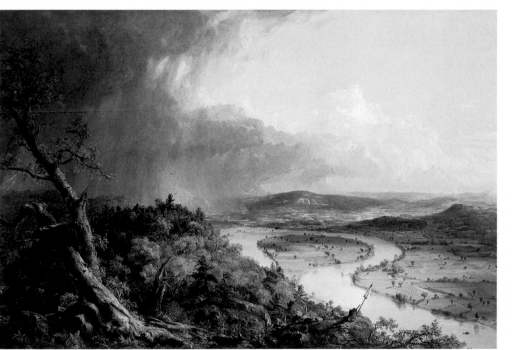

27-23 THOMAS COLE, *The Oxbow* (*View from Mount Holyoke, Northampton, Massachusetts, after a Thunderstorm*), 1836. Oil on canvas, 4′ 3½″ × 6′ 4″. Metropolitan Museum of Art, New York (gift of Mrs. Russell Sage, 1908). ◼◀

Cole divided his canvas into dark wilderness on the left and sunlit civilization on the right. The minuscule painter at the bottom center seems to be asking for advice about America's future course.

27-24 ALBERT BIERSTADT, *Among the Sierra Nevada Mountains, California*, 1868. Oil on canvas, 6′ × 10′. National Museum of American Art, Smithsonian Institution, Washington, D.C.

Bierstadt's panoramic landscape presents the breathtaking natural beauty of the American West, reinforcing the 19th-century doctrine of Manifest Destiny, which justified America's western expansion.

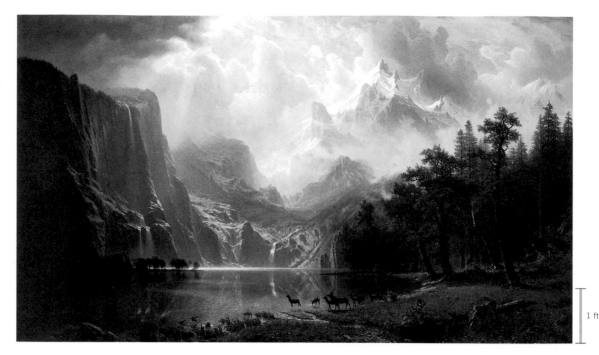

1 ft.

ALBERT BIERSTADT Other Hudson River artists used the landscape genre as an allegorical vehicle to address moral and spiritual concerns. ALBERT BIERSTADT (1830–1902) traveled west in 1858 and produced many paintings depicting the Rocky Mountains, Yosemite Valley, and other dramatic locales. These works, such as *Among the Sierra Nevada Mountains, California* (FIG. **27-24**), present breathtaking scenery and natural beauty. This panoramic view (the painting is 10 feet wide) is awe-inspiring. Deer and waterfowl appear at the edge of a placid lake, and steep and rugged mountains soar skyward on the left and in the distance. A stand of trees, uncultivated and wild, frames the lake on the right. To underscore the almost transcendental nature of this scene, Bierstadt depicted the sun's rays breaking through the clouds overhead, which suggests a heavenly consecration of the land. That Bierstadt's focus was the American West is not insignificant. By

calling national attention to the splendor and uniqueness of the regions beyond the Rocky Mountains, Bierstadt's paintings reinforced the idea of Manifest Destiny. This popular 19th-century doctrine held that westward expansion across the continent was the logical destiny of the United States. As John L. O'Sullivan (1813–1895) expounded in the earliest known use of the term in 1845, "Our manifest destiny [is] to overspread the continent allotted by Providence for the free development of our yearly multiplying millions."[6] Paintings of the scenic splendor of the West helped to mute growing concerns over the realities of conquest, the displacement of Native Americans, and the exploitation of the environment. It should come as no surprise that among those most eager to purchase Bierstadt's work were mail-service magnates and railroad builders—entrepreneurs and financiers involved in westward expansion.

27-25 FREDERIC EDWIN CHURCH, *Twilight in the Wilderness*, 1860s. Oil on canvas, 3′ 4″ × 5′ 4″. Cleveland Museum of Art, Cleveland (Mr. and Mrs. William H. Marlatt Fund).

Church's paintings eloquently express the Romantic notion of the sublime. Painted during the Civil War, this wilderness landscape presents an idealistic view of America free of conflict.

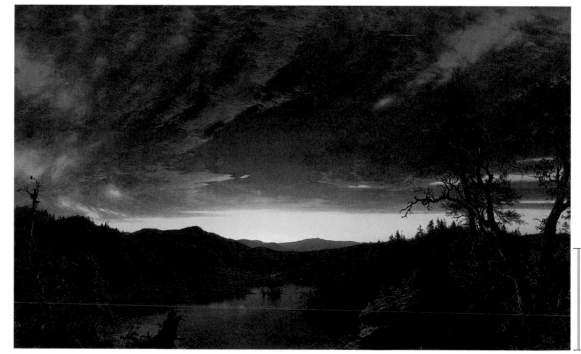

1 ft.

FREDERIC CHURCH Another painter usually associated with the Hudson River School was FREDERIC EDWIN CHURCH (1826–1900), but his interest in landscape scenes extended beyond America. He traveled widely—to South America, Mexico, Europe, the Middle East, Newfoundland, and Labrador. Church's paintings are firmly in the idiom of the Romantic sublime, yet they also reveal contradictions and conflicts in the constructed mythology of American providence and character. *Twilight in the Wilderness* (FIG. **27-25**) presents a panoramic view of the sun setting over the majestic landscape. Beyond Church's precise depiction of the magnificent spectacle of nature, the painting, like Constable's *Haywain* (FIG. 27-21), is remarkable for what it does not depict. As did Constable, Church and the other Hudson River School painters worked in a time of great upheaval. *Twilight in the Wilderness* dates to the 1860s, when the Civil War was tearing apart the no-longer-united states. Yet this painting does not display evidence of turbulence or discord. Indeed, it does not include even a single figure. By constructing such an idealistic and comforting view, Church contributed to the national mythology of righteousness and divine providence—a mythology that had become increasingly difficult to maintain in the face of conflict.

Landscape painting was immensely popular in the late 18th and early 19th centuries, in large part because it provided viewers with breathtaking and sublime spectacles of nature. Artists also could allegorize nature, and it was rare for a landscape painting not to touch on spiritual, moral, historical, or philosophical issues. Landscape painting became the perfect vehicle for artists (and the viewing public) to "naturalize" conditions, rendering debate about contentious issues moot and eliminating any hint of conflict.

REALISM

Advances in industrial technology during the early 19th century reinforced Enlightenment faith in the connection between science and progress. Both intellectuals and the general public increasingly embraced *empiricism* and *positivism*. To empiricists, the basis of knowledge is observation and direct experience. Positivists

ascribed to the philosophical model developed by Auguste Comte (1798–1857), who believed scientific laws governed the environment and human activity and could be revealed through careful recording and analysis of observable data. Comte's followers promoted science as the mind's highest achievement and advocated a purely empirical approach to nature and society.

France

Realism was a movement that developed in France around mid-century against this backdrop of an increasing emphasis on science. Consistent with the philosophical tenets of the empiricists and positivists, Realist artists argued that only the contemporary world—what people can see—was "real." Accordingly, Realists focused their attention on the people and events of their own time and disapproved of historical and fictional subjects on the grounds they were neither visible nor present and therefore were not real.

GUSTAVE COURBET The leading figure of the Realist movement in 19th-century art was GUSTAVE COURBET (1819–1877). In fact, even though he shunned labels, Courbet used the term *Realism* when exhibiting his own works (see "Courbet on Realism," page 776). The Realists' sincerity about scrutinizing their environment led them to paint subjects artists had traditionally deemed unworthy of depiction—the mundane and trivial, working-class laborers and peasants, and so forth. Moreover, by depicting these subjects on a scale and with an earnestness and seriousness previously reserved for historical, mythological, and religious painting, Realist artists sought to establish parity between contemporary subject matter and the traditional themes of "high art."

THE STONE BREAKERS An early work that exemplifies Courbet's championing of everyday life as the only valid subject for the modern artist is *The Stone Breakers* (FIG. **27-26**), in which the Realist painter presented a glimpse into the life of rural menial laborers. Courbet represented in a straightforward manner two men—one about 70, the other quite young—in the act of breaking stones, traditionally the lot of the lowest members of French society. By juxtaposing youth and age, Courbet suggested those born

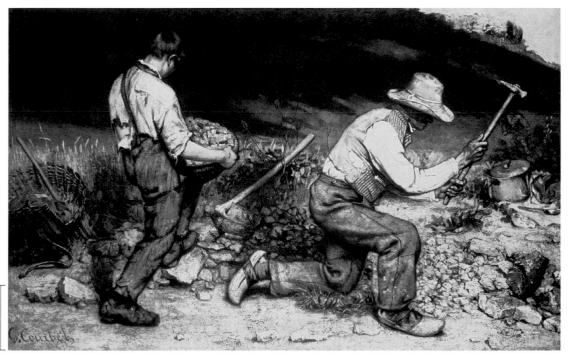

1 ft.

27-26 GUSTAVE COURBET, *The Stone Breakers*, 1849. Oil on canvas, 5' 3" × 8' 6". Formerly Gemäldegalerie, Dresden (destroyed in 1945).

Courbet was the leading figure in the Realist movement. Using a palette of dirty browns and grays, he conveyed the dreary and dismal nature of menial labor in mid-19th-century France.

Courbet on Realism

The academic jury selecting work for the 1855 Salon (part of the Exposition Universelle in Paris that year) rejected two of Courbet's paintings, declaring his subjects and figures were too coarse (so much so as to be plainly "socialistic") and too large. Typical of Courbet's work are *The Stone Breakers* (FIG. 27-26), which depicts menial laborers, and *Burial at Ornans* (FIG. 27-27), which represents the funeral of an ordinary man and is nearly 22 feet long. In response to the jury's decision, Courbet withdrew all of his works, including those that had been accepted, and set up his own exhibition outside the grounds, calling it the Pavilion of Realism. This was in itself a bold action. Courbet was the first artist ever known to have staged a private exhibition of his own work. His pavilion and the statement he issued to explain the paintings shown there amounted to the Realist movement's manifesto. Although Courbet maintained he founded no school and was of no school, he did, as the name of his pavilion suggests, accept the term *Realism* as descriptive of his art.

The statement Courbet distributed at his pavilion reads in part:

The title of "realist" has been imposed upon me . . . Titles have never given a just idea of things; were it otherwise, the work would be superfluous. . . . I have studied the art of the moderns, avoiding any preconceived system and without prejudice. I have no more wanted to imitate the former than to copy the latter; nor have I thought of achieving the idle aim of "art for art's sake." No! I have simply wanted to draw from a thorough knowledge of tradition the reasoned and free sense of my own individuality. . . . To be able to translate the customs, ideas, and appearances of my time as I see them—in a word, to create a living art—this has been my aim.*

Six years later, on Christmas Day, 1861, Courbet wrote an open letter, published a few days later in the *Courier du dimanche*, addressed to prospective students. In the letter, the painter reflected on the nature of his art.

[An artist must apply] his personal faculties to the ideas and the events of the times in which he lives. . . . [A]rt in painting should consist only of the representation of things that are visible and tangible to the artist. Every age should be represented only by its own artists, that is to say, by the artists who have lived in it. I also maintain that painting is an essentially concrete art form and can consist only of the representation of both real and existing things. . . . An abstract object, not visible, nonexistent, is not within the domain of painting.†

Courbet's most famous statement, however, is his blunt dismissal of academic painting, in which he concisely summed up the core principle of Realist painting:

I have never seen an angel. Show me an angel, and I'll paint one.‡

---

*Translated by Robert Goldwater and Marco Treves, eds., *Artists on Art from the XIV to the XX Century* (New York: Pantheon), 295.
†Translated by Petra ten-Doesschate Chu, *Letters of Gustave Courbet* (Chicago: University of Chicago Press, 1992), 203–204.
‡Quoted by Vincent van Gogh in a July 1885 letter to his brother Theo, in Ronald de Leeuw, *The Letters of Vincent van Gogh* (New York: Penguin, 1996), 302.

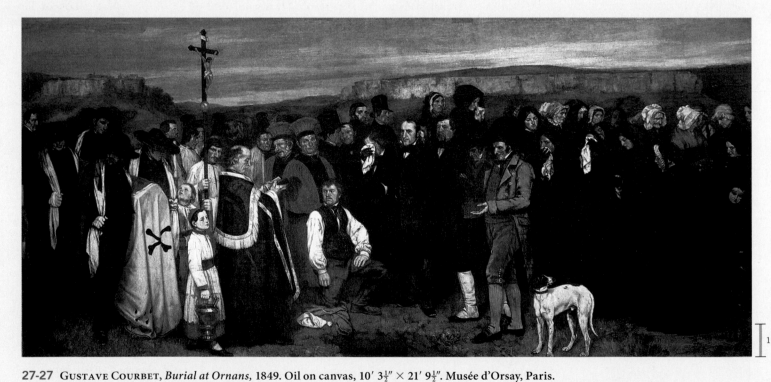

1 ft.

27-27 GUSTAVE COURBET, *Burial at Ornans*, 1849. Oil on canvas, 10′ 3½″ × 21′ 9½″. Musée d'Orsay, Paris.

Although as monumental in scale as a traditional history painting, *Burial at Ornans* horrified critics because of the ordinary nature of the subject and Courbet's starkly antiheroic composition.

to poverty remain poor their entire lives. The artist neither romanticized nor idealized the men's work but depicted their thankless toil with directness and accuracy. Courbet's palette of dirty browns and grays further conveys the dreary and dismal nature of the task, and the angular positioning of the older stone breaker's limbs suggests a mechanical monotony.

Courbet's interest in the working poor as subject matter had a special resonance for his mid-19th-century French audience. In 1848, laborers rebelled against the bourgeois leaders of the newly formed Second Republic and against the rest of the nation, demanding better working conditions and a redistribution of property. The army quelled the uprising in three days, but not without long-lasting trauma and significant loss of life. The 1848 revolution raised the issue of labor as a national concern. Courbet's depiction of stone breakers in 1849 was thus timely and populist.

BURIAL AT ORNANS Many art historians regard Courbet's *Burial at Ornans* (FIG. **27-27**) as his masterpiece. The huge (10 by 22 feet) canvas depicts a funeral set in a bleak provincial landscape outside the artist's home town. Attending the funeral are the types of ordinary people Honoré de Balzac (1799–1850) and Gustave Flaubert (1821–1880) presented in their novels. While an officious clergyman reads the Office of the Dead, those attending cluster around the excavated gravesite, their faces registering all degrees of response to the ceremony. Although the painting has the monumental scale of a traditional history painting, the subject's ordinariness and the starkly antiheroic composition horrified critics. Arranged in a wavering line extending across the enormous breadth of the canvas are three groups—the somberly clad women at the back right, a semicircle of similarly clad men by the open grave, and assorted churchmen at the left. This wall of figures blocks any view into deep space. The faces are portraits. Some of the models were Courbet's sisters (three of the women in the front row, toward the right) and friends. Behind and above the figures are bands of overcast sky and barren cliffs. The dark pit of the grave opens into the viewer's space in the center foreground. Despite the unposed look of the figures, Courbet controlled the composition in a masterful way by his sparing use of bright color. In place of the heroic, the sublime, and the dramatic, Courbet aggressively presented the viewer with the mundane realities of daily life and death. In 1857, Jules-François-Félix Husson Champfleury (1821–1889), one of the first critics to recognize and appreciate Courbet's work, wrote of *Burial at Ornans,* "[I]t represents a small-town funeral and yet reproduces the funerals of *all* small towns."[7] Unlike the theatricality of Romanticism, Realism captured the ordinary rhythms of daily life.

Of great importance for the later history of art, Realism also involved a reconsideration of the painter's primary goals and departed from the established emphasis on illusionism. Accordingly, Realists called attention to painting as a pictorial construction by the ways they applied pigment or manipulated composition. Courbet's intentionally simple and direct methods of expression in composition and technique seemed unbearably crude to many of his more traditional contemporaries, who called him a primitive. Although his bold, somber palette was essentially traditional, Courbet often used the *palette knife* for quickly placing and unifying large daubs of paint, producing a roughly wrought surface. His example inspired the young artists who worked for him (and later Impressionists such as Claude Monet and Auguste Renoir; see Chapter 28), but the public accused him of carelessness and critics wrote of his "brutalities."

JEAN-FRANÇOIS MILLET As did Courbet, JEAN-FRANÇOIS MILLET (1814–1878) found his subjects in the people and occupations of the everyday world. Millet was one of a group of French painters of country life who, to be close to their rural subjects, settled near the village of Barbizon in the forest of Fontainebleau. This Barbizon School specialized in detailed pictures of forest and countryside. Millet, their most prominent member, was of peasant stock and identified with the hard lot of the country poor. In *The Gleaners* (FIG. **27-28**), he depicted three impoverished women—members of the lowest level of peasant society—performing the backbreaking task of gleaning. Landowning nobles traditionally permitted peasants to glean, or collect, the wheat scraps left in the field after the harvest. Millet characteristically placed his monumental figures in the foreground, against a broad sky. Although the field stretches back to a rim of haystacks, cottages, trees, distant workers, and a flat horizon, the gleaners quietly doing their tedious and time-consuming work dominate the canvas.

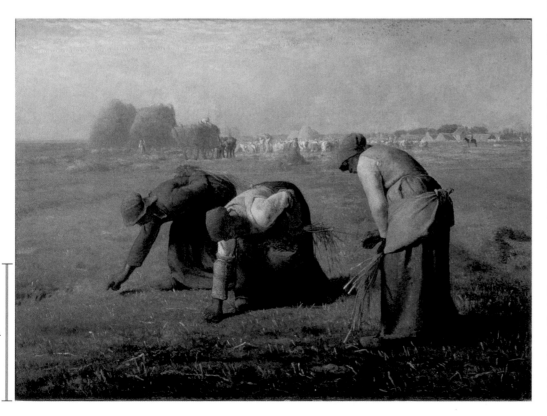

1 ft.

27-28 JEAN-FRANÇOIS MILLET, *The Gleaners,* 1857. Oil on canvas, 2′ 9″ × 3′ 8″. Musée d'Orsay, Paris.

Millet and the Barbizon School painters specialized in depictions of French country life. Here, Millet portrayed three impoverished women gathering the scraps left in the field after a harvest.

Lithography

In 1798, the German printmaker Alois Senefelder (1771–1834) created the first prints using stone instead of metal plates or wooden blocks. In contrast to earlier printing techniques (see "Woodcuts, Engravings, and Etchings," Chapter 20, page 556), in which the artist applied ink either to a raised or incised surface, in *lithography* (Greek, "stone writing") the printing and nonprinting areas of the plate are on the same plane.

The chemical phenomenon fundamental to lithography is the repellence of oil and water. The lithographer uses a greasy, oil-based crayon to draw directly on a stone plate and then wipes water onto the stone, which clings only to the areas the drawing does not cover.

Next, the artist rolls oil-based ink onto the stone, which adheres to the drawing but is repelled by the water. When the artist presses the stone against paper, only the inked areas—the drawing—transfer to the paper. Color lithography requires multiple plates, one for each color, and the printmaker must take special care to make sure each impression lines up perfectly with the previous one so that each color prints in its proper place.

One of the earliest masters of this new printmaking process was Honoré Daumier, whose politically biting lithographs (FIG. 27-29) published in a widely read French journal reached an audience of unprecedented size.

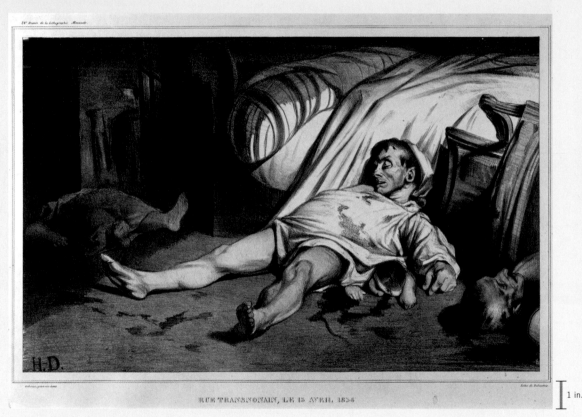

27-29 HONORÉ DAUMIER, *Rue Transnonain,* 1834. Lithograph, $1' \times 1' 5\frac{1}{2}''$. Philadelphia Museum of Art, Philadelphia (bequest of Fiske and Marie Kimball).

Daumier used the recent invention of lithography to reach a wide audience for his social criticism and political protest. This print records the horrific 1834 massacre in a workers' housing block.

Although Millet's paintings evoke a sentimentality absent from Courbet's, the French public still reacted to his work with disdain and suspicion. In the aftermath of the 1848 revolution, Millet's investiture of the poor with solemn grandeur did not meet with approval from the prosperous classes. In particular, middle-class landowners resisted granting gleaning rights, and thus Millet's relatively dignified depiction of gleaning antagonized them. The middle class also linked the poor with the dangerous, newly defined working class, which was finding outspoken champions in men such as Karl Marx (1818–1883), Friedrich Engels (1820–1895), and the novelists Émile Zola (1840–1902) and Charles Dickens (1812–1870). Socialism was a growing movement, and both its views on property and its call for social justice, even economic equality, threatened and frightened the bourgeoisie. Millet's sympathetic portrayal of the poor seemed to much of the public to be a political manifesto.

HONORÉ DAUMIER Because people widely recognized the power of art to serve political ends, the political and social agitation accompanying the violent revolutions in France and the rest of Europe in the later 18th and early 19th centuries prompted the French people to suspect artists of subversive intention. A person could be jailed for too bold a statement in the press, in literature, in art—even in music and drama. Realist artist HONORÉ DAUMIER (1808–1879) was a defender of the urban working classes, and in his art he boldly confronted authority with social criticism and political protest. In response, the authorities imprisoned the artist. A painter, sculptor, and, like Dürer, Rembrandt, and Goya, one of history's great printmakers, Daumier produced *lithographs* (see "Lithography," above) that enabled him to create an unprecedented number of prints, thereby reaching an exceptionally large and broad audience. In addition to producing individual prints for sale,

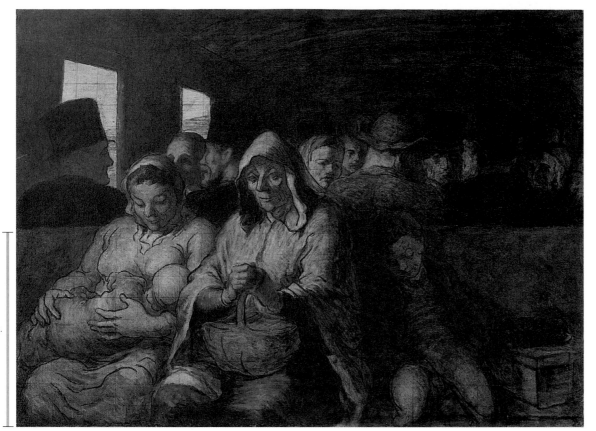

1 ft.

27-30 Honoré Daumier, *Third-Class Carriage*, ca. 1862. Oil on canvas, 2′ 1¾″ × 2′ 11½″. Metropolitan Museum of Art, New York (H. O. Havemeyer Collection, bequest of Mrs. H. O. Havemeyer, 1929).

Daumier frequently depicted the plight of the disinherited masses of 19th-century industrialization. Here, he portrayed the anonymous poor cramped together in a grimy third-class railway carriage.

Daumier also contributed satirical lithographs to the widely read, liberal French Republican journal *Caricature*, further increasing the number of people exposed to his work. In *Caricature*, Daumier mercilessly lampooned the foibles and misbehavior of politicians, lawyers, doctors, and the rich bourgeoisie in general.

RUE TRANSNONAIN Daumier's lithograph *Rue Transnonain* (FIG. **27-29**) depicts an atrocity having the same shocking impact as Goya's *Third of May, 1808* (FIG. 27-11). The title refers to a street in Paris where an unknown sniper killed a civil guard, part of a government force trying to repress a worker demonstration. Because the fatal shot had come from a workers' housing block, the remaining guards immediately stormed the building and massacred all of its inhabitants. With Goya's power, Daumier created a view of the slaughter from a sharp angle of vision. But unlike Goya, he depicted not the dramatic moment of execution but the terrible, quiet aftermath. The limp bodies of the workers—and of a child crushed beneath his father's corpse—lie amid violent disorder. The print's power lies in its factualness. Daumier's pictorial manner is rough and spontaneous, and that approach to representation, which is a central characteristic of Realist art, accounts in large measure for its remarkable force.

THIRD-CLASS CARRIAGE For his paintings, Daumier chose the same kind of subjects and representational manner as in his graphic work, especially after the 1848 revolution. His unfinished *Third-Class Carriage* (FIG. **27-30**) provides a glimpse into the cramped and grimy railway cars of the 1860s. The riders are poor and can afford only third-class tickets. First- and second-class carriages had closed compartments, but third-class passengers had to cram together on hard benches stretching from one end of their carriage to the other. The disinherited masses of 19th-century industrialization were Daumier's indignant concern. He depicted

them in the unposed attitudes and unplanned arrangements of the millions thronging the modern cities—anonymous, insignificant, dumbly patient with a lot they could not change. Daumier saw people as they ordinarily appeared, their faces vague, impersonal, and blank—unprepared for any observers. He tried to achieve the real by isolating a random collection of the unrehearsed details of human existence from the continuum of ordinary life. Daumier's vision anticipated the spontaneity and candor of scenes captured with the camera by the end of the century.

ROSA BONHEUR The most celebrated woman artist of the 19th century was Marie-Rosalie (Rosa) Bonheur (1822–1899). The winner of the gold medal at the Salon of 1848, Bonheur became in 1894 the first woman officer in the French Legion of Honor. As was typical for women since the Renaissance (see "The Artist's Profession," Chapter 20, page 545), Bonheur received her artistic training from her father, Oscar-Raymond Bonheur (1796–1849), who was a proponent of *Saint-Simonianism,* an early-19th-century utopian socialist movement that championed the education and enfranchisement of women. As a result of her father's influence, Bonheur launched her career believing that as a woman and an artist, she had a special role to play in creating a new and perfect society. A Realist passion for accuracy in painting drove Bonheur, but she resisted depicting the problematic social and political themes seen in the work of Courbet, Millet, Daumier, and other Realists. Rather, she turned to the animal world—not, however, to the exotic wild animals that so fascinated Delacroix (FIG. 27-17), but to animals common in the French countryside, especially horses, but also rabbits, cows, and sheep. She went to great lengths to observe the anatomy of living horses at the great Parisian horse fair and spent long hours studying the anatomy of carcasses in the Paris slaughterhouses.

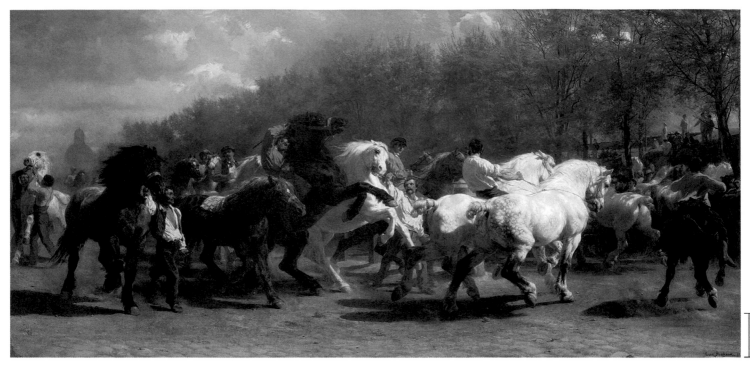

1 ft.

27-31 Rosa Bonheur, *The Horse Fair,* 1853–1855. Oil on canvas, 8′ $\frac{1}{4}$″ × 16′ 7$\frac{1}{2}$″. Metropolitan Museum of Art, New York (gift of Cornelius Vanderbilt, 1887).

Bonheur was the most celebrated woman artist of the 19th century. A Realist, she went to great lengths to record accurately the anatomy of living horses, even studying carcasses in slaughterhouses.

For *The Horse Fair* (FIG. **27-31**), Bonheur's best-known work, the artist chose a panoramic composition similar to that in Courbet's *Burial at Ornans* (FIG. 27-27). She filled her broad canvas with the sturdy farm Percherons and their grooms seen on parade at the annual Parisian horse sale. Some horses, not quite broken, rear up. Others plod or trot, guided on foot or ridden by their keepers. Bonheur recorded the Percherons' uneven line of march, their thunderous pounding, and their seemingly overwhelming power based on her close observation of living animals, even though she acknowledged some inspiration from the Parthenon frieze (FIG. 5-50, *top*). The dramatic lighting, loose brushwork, and rolling sky also reveal her admiration of Géricault's style (FIGS. 27-13 and 27-13A). The equine drama in *The Horse Fair* captivated viewers, who eagerly bought engraved reproductions of Bonheur's painting, making it one of the most popular artworks of the century.

ÉDOUARD MANET As pivotal a figure in 19th-century European art as Gustave Courbet was the painter ÉDOUARD MANET (1832–1883). Like Courbet, Manet was influential in articulating Realist principles, but the younger artist also played an important role in the development of Impressionism in the 1870s (see Chapter 28). Manet's *Le Déjeuner sur l'Herbe* (*Luncheon on the Grass;* FIG. **27-32**), widely recognized only later as a seminal work in the history of art, depicts two clothed men and one nude and one clothed woman at a picnic. Consistent with Realist principles, Manet based all four figures on real people. The seated nude is Victorine Meurend (Manet's favorite model at the time), and the gentlemen are his brother Eugène (with cane) and probably the sculptor Ferdinand Leenhof, although scholars have suggested other identifications. The two men wear fashionable Parisian attire of the 1860s. The nude woman is a distressingly unidealized figure who also seems disturbingly unabashed and at ease, gazing directly at the viewer without shame or flirtatiousness.

This audacious painting outraged the French public. Rather than a traditional pastoral scene, for example, Titian's *Pastoral Symphony* (FIG. 22-35), populated by anonymous idealized figures in an idyllic setting, *Le Déjeuner* featured ordinary men and promiscuous women in a Parisian park. One hostile critic, no doubt voicing public opinion, said: "A commonplace woman of the demi-monde, as naked as can be, shamelessly lolls between two dandies dressed to the teeth. These latter look like schoolboys on a holiday, perpetrating an outrage to play the man. . . . This is a young man's practical joke—a shameful, open sore."[8] Manet surely anticipated criticism of his painting, but shocking the public was not his primary aim. His goal was more complex and far more ambitious. With *Le Déjeuner,* he sought to reassess the nature of painting. The work contains sophisticated references and allusions to many artistic genres—history painting, portraiture, pastoral scenes, nudes, and even religious scenes. *Le Déjeuner* is Manet's impressive synthesis and critique of the entire history of painting.

The negative response to Manet's painting on the part of public and critics alike extended beyond subject matter. The painter's manner of presenting his figures also elicited severe criticism. He rendered the men and women in soft focus and broadly painted the landscape, including the pool in which the second woman bathes. The loose manner of painting contrasts with the clear forms of the harshly lit foreground trio and of the pile of discarded female clothes and picnic foods at the lower left. The lighting creates strong contrasts between dark and highlighted areas. In the main figures, many values are summed up in one or two lights or darks. The effect is both to flatten the forms and set them off sharply from the setting. Form, rather than a matter of line, is only a function of paint and light. Manet aimed to move away from illusionism toward an open acknowledgment of painting's properties, such as the flatness of the painting surface, which would become a core principle of many later 19th-century painters as well as their successors

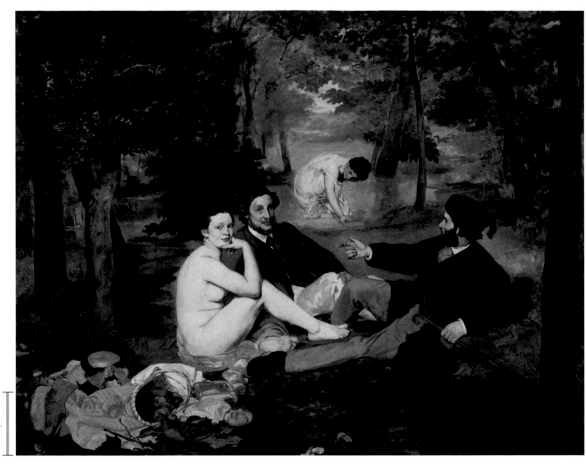

27-32 Édouard Manet, *Le Déjeuner sur l'Herbe* (*Luncheon on the Grass*), 1863. Oil on canvas, 7′ × 8′ 8″. Musée d'Orsay, Paris.

Manet shocked his contemporaries with both his subject matter and manner of painting. Moving away from illusionism, he used colors to flatten form and to draw attention to the painting surface.

to the present day. The mid-19th-century French public, however, saw only a crude sketch lacking the customary finish of paintings exhibited in the Paris Salon. The style of the painting, coupled with the unorthodox subject matter, made *Le Déjeuner sur l'Herbe* one of the most controversial artworks ever created.

OLYMPIA Even more scandalous to the French viewing public, however, was Manet's *Olympia* (FIG. **27-33**), painted the same year. Manet's subject was a young white prostitute (Olympia was a common "professional" name for prostitutes in 19th-century France). She reclines on a bed that extends across the full width of

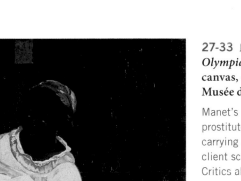

27-33 Édouard Manet, *Olympia*, 1863. Oil on canvas, 4′ 3″ × 6′ 2¼″. Musée d'Orsay, Paris. ◼◂

Manet's painting of a nude prostitute and her black maid carrying a bouquet from a client scandalized the public. Critics also faulted his rough brushstrokes and abruptly shifting tonalities.

the painting (and beyond) and is nude except for a thin black ribbon tied around her neck, a bracelet on her arm, an orchid in her hair, and fashionable slippers on her feet. Like the seated nude in *Le Déjeuner*, Olympia meets the viewer's eye with a look of cool indifference. The only other figure in the painting is a black maid, who presents Olympia a bouquet of flowers from a client.

Olympia horrified public and critics alike. Although images of prostitutes were not unheard of during this period, the shamelessness of Olympia and her look verging on defiance shocked viewers. The depiction of a black woman was also not new to painting, but the French public perceived Manet's inclusion of both a black maid and a nude prostitute as evoking moral depravity, inferiority, and animalistic sexuality. The contrast of the black servant with the fair-skinned courtesan also conjured racial divisions. One critic described Olympia as "a courtesan with dirty hands and wrinkled feet . . . her body has the livid tint of a cadaver displayed in the morgue; her outlines are drawn in charcoal and her greenish, bloodshot eyes appear to be provoking the public, protected all the while by a hideous Negress."[9] From this statement, it is clear viewers were responding not solely to the subject matter but to Manet's artistic style as well. The painter's

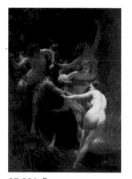

27-33A Bouguereau, *Nymphs and a Satyr*, 1873.

brushstrokes are much rougher and the shifts in tonality are far more abrupt than those found in traditional academic painting. This departure from accepted practice exacerbated the audacity of the subject matter. *Olympia*—indeed, all of Manet's work—represented a radical departure from the academic style then in favor, as exemplified by the work of ADOLPHE-WILLIAM BOUGUEREAU (1825–1905; FIG. 27-33A), an artist largely forgotten today, although he was a towering figure in the French art world during the second half of the 19th century.

Germany and the United States

Although French artists took the lead in promoting the depiction of the realities of modern life as the only valid goal for artists, the Realist movement was neither exclusively French nor confined to Europe.

WILHELM LEIBL In Germany, WILHELM LEIBL (1844–1900) shared French Realists' commitment to representing the contemporary world and real people in his paintings. *Three Women in a Village Church* (FIG. 27-34) is typical of Leibl's work, which focused on country life. The painting records a sacred moment—the moment of prayer—in the life of three women of different generations. Dressed in rustic costume, their Sunday-church best, they quietly pursue their devotions, their prayer books held in large hands roughened by work. Their manners and their dress reflect their unaffected nature, untouched by the refinements of urban life. Leibl highlighted their natural virtues: simplicity, honesty, steadfastness, patience. He spent three years working on this image of peasants in their village church, often under impossible conditions of lighting and temperature. Despite the meticulous application of paint and sharpness of focus, the picture is a moving expression of the artist's compassionate view of his subjects, a reading of character without sentimentality.

WINSLOW HOMER Realism received an especially warm welcome in the United States. One of the leading American Realist painters was WINSLOW HOMER (1836–1910) of Boston. Homer

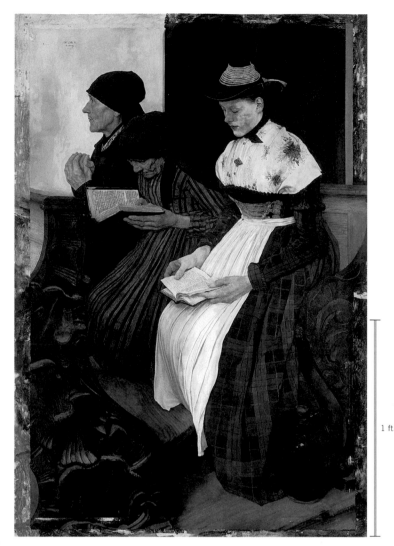

1 ft.

27-34 WILHELM LEIBL, *Three Women in a Village Church*, 1878–1882. Oil on canvas, 2′ 5″ × 2′ 1″. Hamburger, Kunsthalle, Hamburg.

French Realism spread quickly to Germany, where Leibl painted this moving depiction of simple peasant women of different generations holding their prayer books in hands roughened by work.

experienced at first hand the most momentous event of his era—the Civil War. In 1860, he joined the Union campaign as an artist-reporter for *Harper's Weekly*. At the end of the war, he painted *Veteran in a New Field* (FIG. 27-35). Although it is relatively simple and direct, Homer's painting is a significant commentary on the effects and aftermath of America's catastrophic national conflict. At the center of the canvas is a man with his back to the viewer, harvesting wheat. Homer identified him as a veteran by including his uniform and canteen carelessly thrown on the ground in the lower right corner. The man's current occupation, however, is as a farmer, and he has cast aside his former role as a soldier. The veteran's involvement in meaningful and productive work implies a smooth transition from war to peace. This postwar transition to work and the fate of disbanded soldiers were national concerns. Echoing the sentiments behind Houdon's portrayal of George Washington as the new Cincinnatus (FIG. 26-32), the *New York Weekly Tribune* commented: "Rome took her great man from the plow, and made him a dictator—we must now take our soldiers from the camp and make them farmers."[10] America's ability to effect a smooth transition was seen as evidence of its national strength. "The peaceful and harmonious

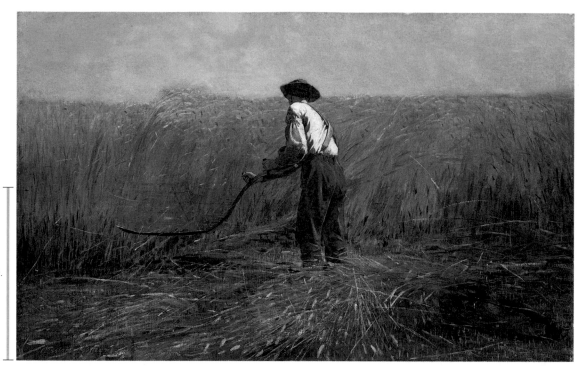

1 ft.

27-35 WINSLOW HOMER, *Veteran in a New Field*, 1865. Oil on canvas, 2' $\frac{1}{8}$" × 3' 2$\frac{1}{8}$". Metropolitan Museum of Art, New York (bequest of Miss Adelaide Milton de Groot, 1967).

This veteran's productive work implies a smooth transition to peace after the Civil War, but Homer placed a single-bladed scythe—the Grim Reaper's tool—in his hands, symbolizing the deaths of soldiers.

Veteran in a New Field also comments symbolically about death. By the 1860s, farmers used cradled scythes to harvest wheat. For this detail, however, Homer rejected realism in favor of symbolism. The former soldier's tool is a single-bladed scythe. The artist thus transformed the man who lived through the Civil War into a symbol of Death—the Grim Reaper himself. In addition to being a tribute to the successful transition to peace, *Veteran in a New Field* is an elegy to the thousands of soldiers who did not return from the war. It may also be a lamentation on the recent assassination of President Abraham Lincoln.

disbanding of the armies in the summer of 1865," poet Walt Whitman (1819–1892) wrote, was one of the "immortal proofs of democracy, unequall'd in all the history of the past."[11] Homer's painting thus reinforced the perception of the country's greatness.

THOMAS EAKINS Even more resolutely a Realist than Homer was Philadelphia-born THOMAS EAKINS (1844–1916), whose work reflects his keen appetite for recording the realities of the human experience. Eakins studied both painting and medical anatomy in Philadelphia before undertaking further study under French artist Jean-Léon Gérôme (1824–1904). Eakins aimed to paint things as he saw them rather than as the public might wish them portrayed. This attitude was very much in tune with 19th-century American taste, combining an admiration for accurate depiction with a hunger for truth.

The too-brutal Realism of Eakins's early masterpiece, *The Gross Clinic* (FIG. **27-36**), prompted the art jury to reject it for the Philadelphia exhibition celebrating the American independence centennial in 1876. The painting portrays the renowned surgeon Dr. Samuel Gross in the operating amphitheater of the Jefferson Medical College in Philadelphia, where the painting hung for 130 years until its sale in 2006 to raise funds for the college. Eakins's decision to depict

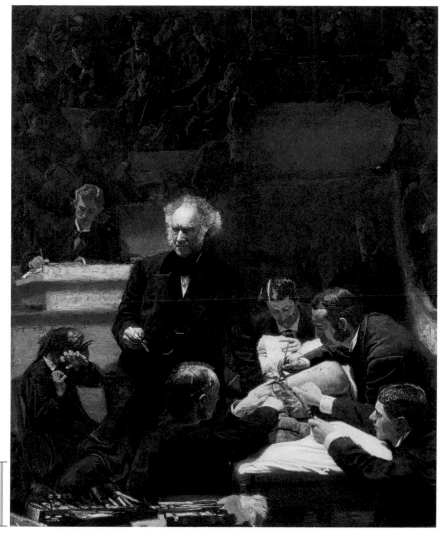

1 ft.

27-36 THOMAS EAKINS, *The Gross Clinic*, 1875. Oil on canvas, 8' × 6' 6". Philadelphia Museum of Art, Philadelphia. ◼◀

The too-brutal realism of Eakins's depiction of a medical college operating amphitheater caused this painting's rejection from the Philadelphia exhibition celebrating America's centennial.

an operation in progress reflects the public's increasing faith that scientific and medical advances could enhance—and preserve—lives. Dr. Gross, with bloody fingers and scalpel, lectures about his surgery on a young man's leg. The patient suffered from osteomyelitis, a bone infection. Watching the surgeon, acclaimed for his skill in this particular operation, are several colleagues—all of whom historians have identified—and the patient's mother, who covers her face. Also present is an anesthetist, who holds a cloth over the patient's face. Anesthetics had been introduced in 1846, and their development eliminated a major obstacle to extensive surgery. The painting is an unsparing description of an unfolding event, with a good deal more reality than many viewers could endure. "It is a picture," one critic said, "that even strong men find difficult to look at long, if they can look at it at all."[12]

Consistent with the dominance of empiricism in the latter half of the 19th century, Eakins believed careful observation—and, where relevant, scientific knowledge—were prerequisites for his art, and he created his paintings in a deliberate, methodical way based on firsthand study of his subject. For example, Eakins's focus on anatomical correctness led him to investigate the human form and humans in motion, both with regular photographic apparatuses and with a special camera devised by the French kinesiologist (a person who studies the physiology of body movement) Étienne-Jules Marey (1830–1904). Eakins later collaborated with Eadweard Muybridge (FIG. 27-54) in the photographic study of animal and human action of all types, anticipating the 20th-century invention of the motion picture.

JOHN SINGER SARGENT The expatriate American artist JOHN SINGER SARGENT (1856–1925), born in Florence, Italy, was a younger contemporary of Eakins. Sargent developed a looser, more dashing Realist portrait style, in contrast to Eakins's carefully rendered details. Sargent studied art in Paris before settling in London, where he won renown both as a cultivated and cosmopolitan gentleman and as an accomplished portrait painter. He learned his adept application of paint in thin layers and his effortless achievement of quick and lively illusion from his study of Velázquez, whose masterpiece, *Las Meninas* (FIG. 24-30), may have influenced Sargent's family portrait *The Daughters of Edward Darley Boit* (FIG. 27-37). The four girls (the children of one of Sargent's close friends) appear in a hall and small drawing room in their Paris home. The informal, eccentric arrangement of their slight figures suggests how much at ease they are within this familiar space and with objects such as the monumental Japanese vases, the red screen, and the fringed rug, whose scale subtly emphasizes the children's diminutive stature. Sargent must have known the Boit daughters well. Relaxed and trustful, they gave the artist an opportunity to record a gradation of young innocence. He sensitively captured the naive, wondering openness of the little girl in the foreground, the grave artlessness of the 10-year-old child, and the slightly self-conscious poise of the adolescents. Sargent's casual positioning of the figures and seemingly random choice of the setting communicate a sense of spontaneity. The children seem to be attending momentarily to an adult who has asked them to interrupt their activity. The painting embodies the Realist belief that the artist's business is to record modern people in modern contexts.

HENRY OSSAWA TANNER Typical of the Realist painter's desire to depict the lives of ordinary people engaged in everyday activities is the early work of African American artist HENRY OSSAWA TANNER (1859–1937). Tanner studied art with Eakins before moving to Paris. There he combined Eakins's belief in careful study from nature with a desire to portray with dignity the life of the working people he had been raised among as a minister's son in Pennsylvania. The mood in *The Thankful Poor* (FIG. 27-38) is one of quiet devotion not far removed from the Realism of Millet (FIG. 27-28) and

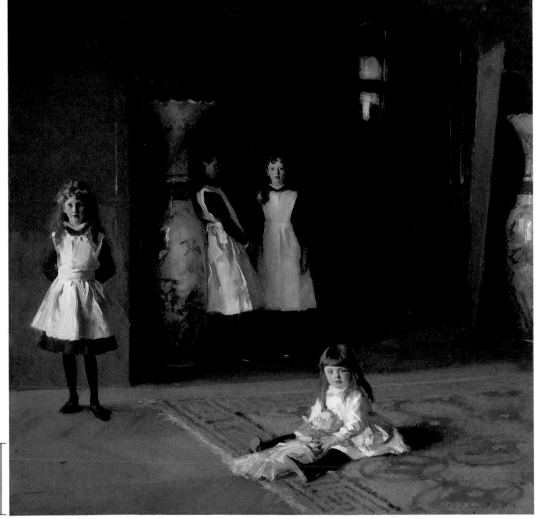

1 ft.

27-37 JOHN SINGER SARGENT, *The Daughters of Edward Darley Boit,* 1882. Oil on canvas, 7' 3⅜" × 7' 3⅝". Museum of Fine Arts, Boston (gift of Mary Louisa Boit, Florence D. Boit, Jane Hubbard Boit, and Julia Overing Boit, in memory of their father, Edward Darley Boit).

Sargent's casual positioning of the Boit sisters creates a sense of the momentary and spontaneous, consistent with Realist painters' interest in recording modern people in modern contexts.

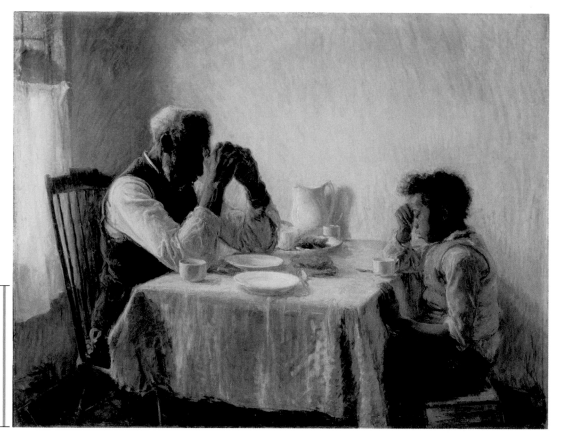

27-38 Henry Ossawa Tanner, *The Thankful Poor,* 1894. Oil on canvas, 2' 11½" × 3' 8¼". Collection of William H. and Camille Cosby.

Tanner combined the Realists' belief in careful study from nature with a desire to portray with dignity the life of African American families. Expressive lighting reinforces the painting's reverent spirit.

Leibl (FIG. 27-34). Tanner painted the grandfather, grandchild, and main objects in the room in great detail, whereas everything else dissolves into loose strokes of color and light. Expressive lighting reinforces the painting's reverent spirit, with deep shadows intensifying the man's devout concentration and golden light pouring in the window to illuminate the quiet expression of thanksgiving on the younger face. The deep sense of sanctity expressed here in terms of everyday experience became increasingly important for Tanner. Within a few years of completing *The Thankful Poor,* he began painting biblical subjects grounded in direct study from nature and in the love of Rembrandt that had inspired him from his days as a Philadelphia art student.

EDMONIA LEWIS About 15 years older than Tanner, the sculptor EDMONIA LEWIS (ca. 1845–after 1909), the daughter of a Chippewa mother and African American father, produced work stylistically indebted to Neoclassicism but depicting contemporary Realist themes. *Forever Free* (FIG. **27-39**) is a marble sculpture Lewis carved while living in Rome, surrounded by examples of both classical and Renaissance art. It represents two freed African American slaves. The man stands heroically in a contrapposto stance reminiscent of classical statues. His right hand rests on the shoulder of the kneeling woman, and his left hand holds aloft a broken manacle and chain as literal and symbolic references to his former servitude. Produced four years after President Lincoln's issuance of the Emancipation Proclamation, *Forever Free* (originally titled *The Morning*

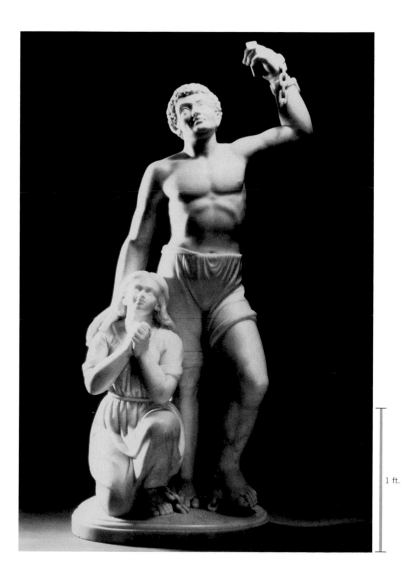

27-39 EDMONIA LEWIS, *Forever Free,* 1867. Marble, 3' 5¼" high. James A. Porter Gallery of Afro-American Art, Howard University, Washington, D.C.

Lewis was a sculptor whose work owes a stylistic debt to Neoclassicism but depicts contemporary Realist themes. She carved *Forever Free* four years after Lincoln's Emancipation Proclamation.

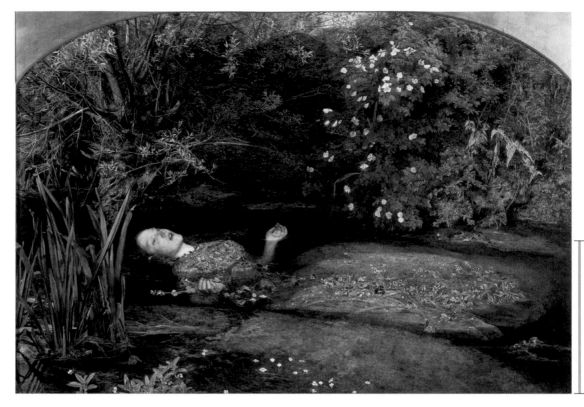

27-40 JOHN EVERETT MILLAIS, *Ophelia,* 1852. Oil on canvas, 2′ 6″ × 3′ 8″. Tate Gallery, London. ◼◀

Millet was a founder of the Pre-Raphaelite Brotherhood, whose members refused to be limited to the contemporary scenes that strict Realists portrayed. The drowning of Ophelia is a Shakespearean subject.

1 ft.

of Liberty) was widely perceived as an abolitionist statement. However, other factors caution against an overly simplistic reading. For example, scholars have debated the degree to which the sculptor attempted to inject a statement about gender relationships into this statue and whether the kneeling position of the woman is a reference to female subordination in the African American community.

Lewis's accomplishments as a sculptor speak to the increasing access to training available to women in the 19th century. Educated at Oberlin College (the first American college to grant degrees to women), Lewis financed her trip to Rome with the sale of medallions and marble busts. Her success in a field dominated by white male artists is a testament to both her skill and her determination.

Pre-Raphaelite Brotherhood

Realism did not appeal to all artists, of course. In England, a group of painters who called themselves the *Pre-Raphaelite Brotherhood* refused to be limited to the contemporary scenes strict Realists portrayed. These artists chose instead to represent fictional, historical, and fanciful subjects, albeit with a significant degree of convincing illusion.

JOHN EVERETT MILLAIS One of the founders of the Pre-Raphaelite Brotherhood was JOHN EVERETT MILLAIS (1829–1896). So painstakingly careful was Millais in his study of visual facts closely observed from nature that Charles Baudelaire (1821–1867) called him "the poet of meticulous detail." The Pre-Raphaelite Brotherhood, organized in 1848, wished to create fresh and sincere art, free from what its members considered the tired and artificial manner propagated in the academies by the successors of Raphael. Influenced by the critic, artist, and writer John Ruskin (1819–1900), the Pre-Raphaelites shared his distaste for the materialism and ugliness of the contemporary industrializing world. They also expressed appreciation for the spirituality and idealism (as well as the art and artisanship) of past times, especially the Middle Ages and the Early Renaissance.

Millais's *Ophelia* (FIG. **27-40**) garnered enthusiastic praise when the painter exhibited it in the Exposition Universelle in Paris in 1855—the exhibition at which Courbet set up his Pavilion of Realism. The subject, from Shakespeare's *Hamlet* (4.7.176–179), is the drowning of Ophelia, who, in her madness, is unaware of her plight:

> *Her clothes spread wide,*
> *And mermaidlike awhile they bore her up—*
> *Which time she chanted snatches of old tunes,*
> *As one incapable of her own distress.*

To make the pathos of the scene visible, Millais became a faithful and feeling witness of its every detail, reconstructing it with a lyricism worthy of the original poetry. Although the scene is fictitious and therefore one Realist painters would have rejected, Millais worked diligently to present it with unswerving fidelity to visual fact. He painted the background on site at a spot along the Hogsmill River in Surrey. For the figure of Ophelia, Millais had a friend lie in a heated bathtub full of water for hours at a time.

DANTE GABRIEL ROSSETTI Another founder of the Pre-Raphaelite Brotherhood was DANTE GABRIEL ROSSETTI (1828–1882), who established an enviable reputation as both a painter and poet. Like other members of the group, Rossetti focused on literary and biblical themes in his art. He also produced numerous portraits of women that projected an image of ethereal beauty and melded apparent opposites—for example, a Victorian prettiness with sensual allure. His *Beata Beatrix* (FIG. **27-41**) is ostensibly a portrait of a literary figure—Beatrice, from Dante's *Vita Nuova*—as she overlooks Florence in a trance after being mystically transported to Heaven. Yet the portrait also had personal resonance for Rossetti. It served as a memorial to his wife, Elizabeth Siddal (the model for Millais's *Ophelia*). Siddal had died shortly before Rossetti began this painting in 1862. In the image, the woman (Siddal-Beatrice) sits in a trancelike state, while a red dove (a messenger of both love

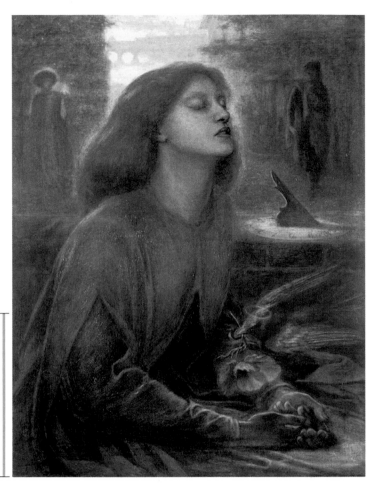

and death) deposits a poppy (symbolic of sleep and death) in her hands. Because Siddal died of an opium overdose, the presence of the poppy assumes greater significance.

1 ft.

27-41 DANTE GABRIEL ROSSETTI, *Beata Beatrix,* ca. 1863. Oil on canvas, 2′ 10″ × 2′ 2″. Tate Gallery, London.

This painting of a beautiful and sensuous woman is ostensibly a literary portrait of Dante's Beatrice, but the work also served as a memorial to Rossetti's wife, who died of an opium overdose.

ARCHITECTURE

At the opening of the 19th century, Napoleon had co-opted the classical style as the official architectural expression of his empire. Neoclassicism was in vogue elsewhere in Europe and in the new American republic too, but other historical styles also enjoyed revivals at the same time architects were exploring the expressive possibilities that new construction technologies had fostered. The buildings constructed during the 19th century are consequently among the most stylistically diverse in history.

ALTES MUSEUM, BERLIN After the fall of Napoleon, who had occupied the Prussian capital of Berlin from 1806 to 1808, a fervent nationalistic spirit emerged in Germany. One manifestation of Prussian nationalism was the decision to build Europe's first public art museum to house the extensive and growing royal collection. The commission went to KARL FRIEDRICH SCHINKEL (1781–1841), who worked in many revival styles during his career, including Romanesque, Gothic, and Italian Renaissance, but who chose the Neoclassical style for what he and Crown Prince Friedrich Wilhelm III (1755–1861) conceived as a "temple of culture."

The Altes (Old) Museum (FIG. **27-42**), constructed on an island in the Spree River across from the royal palace in Berlin, is not truly templelike, however. Rather, with its broad facade of 18 Ionic columns on a high podium, it more closely resembles a Greek stoa (FIG. 5-77) than a pediment-capped classical temple. Noteworthy for its perfect proportions, Schinkel's austere design expresses nobility, tradition, and elite culture, now made accessible to the public in a building whose style Europeans associated with the democratic values of ancient Greece and Rome.

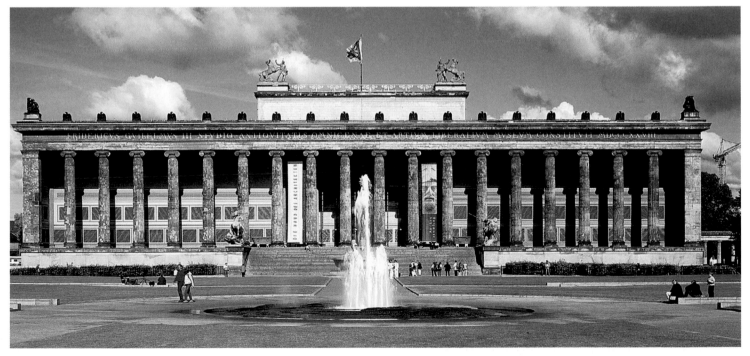

27-42 KARL FRIEDRICH SCHINKEL, Altes Museum, Berlin, Germany, 1822–1830.

Schinkel conceived the first public art museum in Europe as a Neoclassical "temple of culture." The Altes Museum's facade of 18 Ionic columns resembles an ancient Greek stoa (FIG. 5-77).

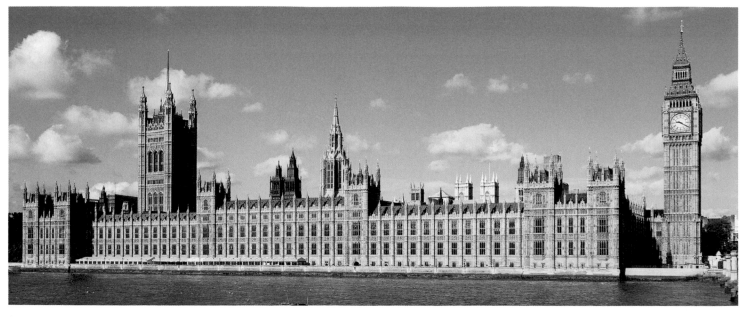

27-43 CHARLES BARRY and AUGUSTUS WELBY NORTHMORE PUGIN, Houses of Parliament, London, England, designed 1835. ◾◀

During the 19th century, architects revived many historical styles, often reflecting nationalistic pride. The Houses of Parliament have an exterior veneer and towers that recall English Late Gothic style.

The Neoclassical facade masks a very practical plan that has no model in classical temples or stoas. A broad central staircase leads into a foyer and then a cubical central block, which projects above the facade's colonnade. The central block houses a sculpture-filled domed rotunda loosely based on the Pantheon (FIGS. 7-50 and 7-51) in Rome. To either side is a courtyard whose windows provide light to the painting galleries all around. Large windows on the side and rear walls of the Altes Museum also illuminate the galleries. The museum was revolutionary in organizing the artworks it contained in chronological order, emphasizing the history of art, as opposed to simply displaying aesthetic treasures (compare FIG. 25-1A).

GOTHIC REVIVAL As 19th-century scholars gathered the documentary materials of European history in encyclopedic enterprises, each nation came to value its past as evidence of the validity of its ambitions and claims to greatness. Intellectuals appreciated the art of the remote past as a product of cultural and national genius. Italy, of course, had its Roman ruins, which had long inspired later architects. A reawakening of interest in Gothic architecture also surfaced at this time, even in France under Napoleon. In 1802, Chateaubriand published his influential *Genius of Christianity*—the source for Girodet-Trioson's *Burial of Atala* (FIG. 27-5)—which defended religion on the grounds of its beauty and mystery rather than on the grounds of truth. Gothic cathedrals, according to Chateaubriand, were translations of the sacred groves of the ancient Gauls into stone and should be cherished as manifestations of France's holy history. One result of this new nationalistic respect for the Gothic style was that Eugène Emmanuel Viollet-le-Duc (1814–1879) received a commission in 1845 to restore the interior of Paris's Notre Dame to its Gothic splendor after removing the Baroque and Napoleonic (FIG. 27-2) alterations.

HOUSES OF PARLIAMENT England also celebrated its medieval heritage with *Neo-Gothic* buildings. In London, when the old Houses of Parliament burned in 1834, the Parliamentary Commission decreed that designs for the new building be either Gothic or Elizabethan. CHARLES BARRY (1795–1860), with the assistance of AUGUSTUS WELBY NORTHMORE PUGIN (1812–1852), submitted

the winning design (FIG. 27-43) in 1835. By this time, architectural style had become a matter of selection from the historical past. Barry had traveled widely in Europe, Greece, Turkey, Egypt, and Palestine, studying the architecture of each place. He preferred the classical Renaissance styles, but he had designed some earlier Neo-Gothic buildings, and Pugin successfully influenced him in the direction of English Late Gothic. Pugin was one of a group of English artists and critics who saw moral purity and spiritual authenticity in the religious architecture of the Middle Ages and revered the careful medieval artisans who built the great cathedrals. The Industrial Revolution was flooding the market with cheaply made and ill-designed commodities. Machine work was replacing handicraft. Many, Pugin included, believed in the necessity of restoring the old artisanship, which they felt embodied honesty as well as quality. Pugin was also the author of the influential *True Principles of Pointed or Christian Architecture* (1841), which RICHARD UPJOHN (1802–1878) consulted for his Neo-Gothic Trinity Church (FIG. 27-43A) in New York City. The design of the Houses of Parliament, however, is not genuinely Gothic, despite its picturesque tower groupings (the Clock Tower, housing Big Ben, at one end, and the Victoria Tower at the other). The building has a formal axial plan and a kind of Palladian regularity beneath its Neo-Gothic detail. Pugin himself said of it, "All Grecian, Sir. Tudor [English Late Gothic] details on a classical body."[13]

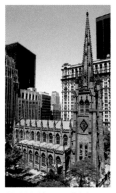

27-43A UPJOHN, Trinity Church, New York, 1841–1852.

ROYAL PAVILION Although the Neoclassical and Neo-Gothic styles dominated early-19th-century architecture, exotic new approaches of all manner soon began to appear, due in part to European imperialism and in part to the Romantic spirit permeating all the arts. Great Britain's forays throughout the world, particularly India, had exposed English culture to a broad range of non-Western artistic styles. The Royal Pavilion (FIG. 27-44), designed

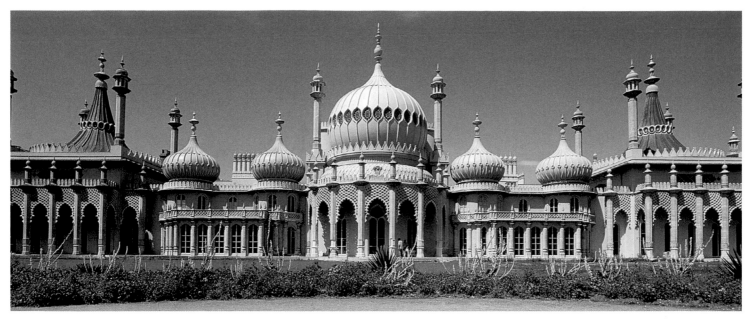

27-44 JOHN NASH, Royal Pavilion, Brighton, England, 1815–1818.

British territorial expansion brought a familiarity with many exotic styles. This palatial "Indian Gothic" seaside pavilion is a conglomeration of Islamic domes, minarets, and screens.

by JOHN NASH (1752–1835), exhibits a wide variety of these styles. Nash was an established architect, known for Neoclassical buildings in London, when the prince regent (later King George IV) asked him to design a royal pleasure palace in the seaside resort of Brighton. The architecture of Greece, Egypt, and China influenced the interior décor of the Royal Pavilion, but the fantastic exterior is a conglomeration of Islamic domes, minarets, and screens architectural historians describe as "Indian Gothic." Underlying the exotic facade is a cast-iron skeleton, an early (if hidden) use of this material in noncommercial construction. Nash also put this metal to fanciful use, creating life-size palm-tree columns in cast iron to support the Royal Pavilion's kitchen ceiling. The building, an appropriate enough backdrop for gala throngs pursuing pleasure by the seaside, has served as a prototype for countless playful architectural exaggerations still found in European and American resorts.

PARIS OPÉRA Another style that found favor in 19th-century architecture was the Baroque, because it was well suited to convey-ing a grandeur worthy of the riches the European elite acquired during this age of expansion. The Paris Opéra (FIG. **27-45**), designed by CHARLES GARNIER (1825–1898), mirrored the opulent lives of these privileged few. The opera house has a festive and spectacularly theatrical Neo-Baroque front and two wings resembling Baroque domed central-plan churches. Inside, intricate arrangements of corridors, vestibules, stairways, balconies, alcoves, entrances, and exits facilitate easy passage throughout the building and provide space for entertainment and socializing at intermissions.

The Baroque grandeur of the layout and of the building's ornamental appointments are characteristic of an architectural style called *Beaux-Arts,* which flourished in the late 19th and early 20th centuries in France. Based on ideas taught at the dominant École des Beaux-Arts (School of Fine Arts) in Paris, the Beaux-Arts style incorporated classical principles (such as symmetry in design, including interior spaces extending radially from a central core or axis) and featured extensive exterior ornamentation. As an example of a Beaux-Arts building, Garnier's Opéra proclaims, through its majesty and lavishness, its function as a gathering place for fashionable audiences in an era of conspicuous wealth. The style was so attractive to the moneyed classes who supported the arts that theaters and opera houses continued to reflect the Paris Opéra's design until World War I transformed society (see Chapter 29).

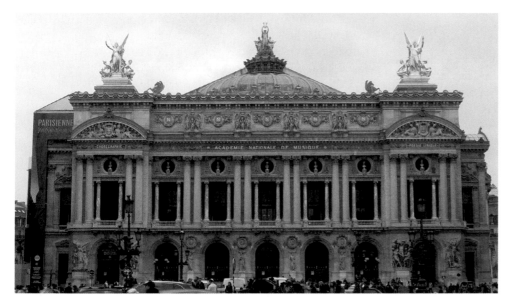

27-45 CHARLES GARNIER, Opéra (looking north), Paris, France, 1861–1874. ■◀

For Paris's opera house, Garnier chose a festive and spectacularly theatrical Neo-Baroque facade well suited to a gathering place for fashionable audiences in an age of conspicuous wealth.

The exterior of this Parisian library looks like a Renaissance palazzo, but the interior has an exposed cast-iron skeleton, which still incorporates classical Corinthian capitals and Renaissance scrolls.

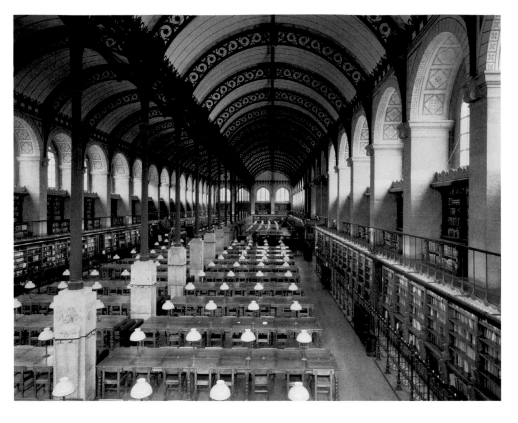

SAINTE-GENEVIÈVE LIBRARY

Work on Garnier's opera house began in 1861, but by the middle of the 19th century, many architects had already abandoned sentimental and Romantic designs from the past. Since the 18th century, bridges had been constructed of cast iron (FIG. 26-12) because of its tensile strength and resistance to fire, and steel became available after 1860 as a building material that enabled architects to create new designs involving vast enclosed spaces, as in the great train sheds of railroad stations (FIG. 28-4) and in exposition halls. Most other utilitarian architecture—factories, warehouses, dockyard structures, mills, and the like—long had been built simply and without historical ornamentation.

The Bibliothèque Sainte-Geneviève, built by HENRI LABROUSTE (1801–1875), is an interesting mix of Renaissance revival style and modern cast-iron construction. The library's two-story facade with arched windows recalls Renaissance palazzo designs, but Labrouste exposed the structure's metal skeleton on the interior. The lower story of the building housed the book stacks. The upper floor featured a spacious reading room (FIG. 27-46) consisting essentially of two barrel-vaulted halls, roofed in terracotta and separated by a row of slender cast-iron columns on concrete pedestals. The columns, recognizably Corinthian, support the iron roof arches pierced with intricate vine-scroll ornamentation derived from the Renaissance

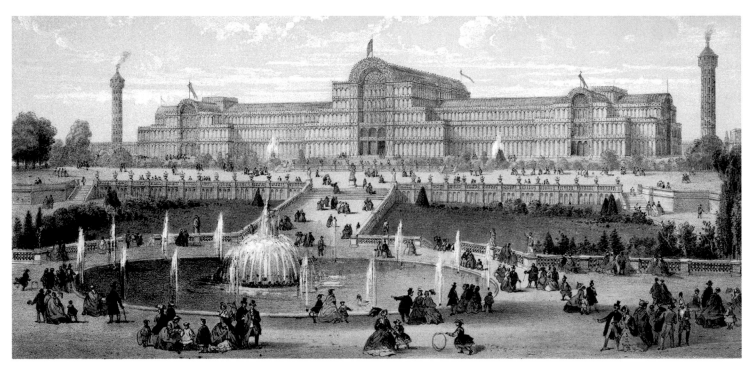

27-47 JOSEPH PAXTON, Crystal Palace, London, England, 1850–1851; enlarged and relocated at Sydenham, England, 1852–1854. Detail of a color lithograph by ACHILLE-LOUIS MARTINET, ca. 1862. Private collection.

The tensile strength of iron enabled Paxton to experiment with a new system of glass-and-metal roof construction. Constructed of prefabricated parts, the vast Crystal Palace required only six months to build.

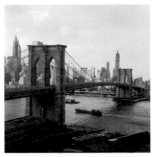

27-46A ROEBLING, Brooklyn Bridge, 1867–1883.

architectural repertoire. Labrouste's design highlights how the peculiar properties of the new structural material aesthetically transformed the shapes of traditional masonry architecture. But it is also clear how reluctant some 19th-century architects were to surrender traditional forms, even when fully aware of new possibilities for design and construction. Architects scoffed at "engineers' architecture" for many years and continued to clothe their steel-and-concrete structures in the Romantic "drapery" of a historical style. For example, the designer of the Brooklyn Bridge (FIG. 27-46A), JOHN AUGUSTUS ROEBLING (1806–1869), combined the latest steel technology with motifs from Gothic and Egyptian architecture.

CRYSTAL PALACE Completely "undraped" construction first became popular in the conservatories (greenhouses) of English country estates. JOSEPH PAXTON (1801–1865) built several of these structures for his patron, the duke of Devonshire. In the largest—300 feet long—he used an experimental system of glass-and-metal roof construction. Encouraged by the success of this system, Paxton submitted a winning glass-and-iron building design in the competition for the hall to house the Great Exhibition of 1851 in London, organized to present "works of industry of all nations." Paxton constructed the exhibition building, the Crystal Palace (FIG. 27-47), with prefabricated parts. This enabled workers to build the vast structure in the then-unheard-of time of six months and to dismantle it quickly at the exhibition's closing to avoid permanent obstruction of the park. The plan borrowed much from Roman and Christian basilicas, with a central flat-roofed "nave" and a barrel-vaulted crossing "transept." The design provided ample interior space to contain displays of huge machines as well as to accommodate decorative touches in the form of large working fountains and giant trees. The public admired the Crystal Palace so much that the workers who dismantled it put up an enlarged version of the glass-and-steel exhibition hall at a new location on the outskirts of London at Sydenham, where it remained until fire destroyed it in 1936. Fortunately, a few old black-and-white photographs and several color lithographs (FIG. 27-47) preserve a record of the Crystal Palace's appearance.

PHOTOGRAPHY

A technological device of immense consequence for the modern experience was invented shortly before the mid-19th century: the camera, with its attendant art of photography. From the time Frenchman LOUIS-JACQUES-MANDÉ DAGUERRE (1789–1851) and Briton William Henry Fox Talbot (1800–1877) announced the first practical photographic processes in 1839, people have celebrated photography's ability to make convincing pictures of people, places, and things. The relative ease of the process, even in its earliest and most primitive form, seemed a dream come true for scientists and artists, who for centuries had grappled with less satisfying methods of capturing accurate images of their subjects. Photography also perfectly suited an age that saw the emergence of Realism as an art movement and a pronounced shift of artistic patronage away from the elite few toward a broader base of support. The growing and increasingly powerful middle class embraced both the comprehensible images of the new artistic medium and their lower cost.

For the traditional artist, photography suggested new answers to the great debate about what is real and how to represent the real in art. Because photography easily and accurately enabled the reproduction of three-dimensional objects on a two-dimensional surface, the new medium also challenged the place of traditional modes of pictorial representation originating in the Renaissance. Artists as diverse as Delacroix, Ingres, Courbet, and the Impressionist Edgar Degas (see Chapter 28) welcomed photography as a helpful auxiliary to painting. Other artists, however, feared the camera was a mechanism that would displace the painstaking work of skilled painters. From the moment of its invention, photography threatened to expropriate the realistic image, until then the exclusive property of painting. But just as some painters looked to the new medium of photography for answers on how best to render an image in paint, so some photographers looked to painting for suggestions about ways to imbue the photographic image with qualities beyond simple reproduction. Indeed, the first subjects photographers chose to record were traditional painting themes, for example, still lifes and portraits—in part to establish photography as a legitimate artistic medium on a par with painting. A debate immediately began over whether the photograph was an art form or if the camera was merely a scientific instrument. An 1862 court case provided the answer: Photography was an art, and photographs were entitled to copyright protection.

Artists themselves were instrumental in the development of the new photographic technology. The camera obscura was familiar to 18th-century artists. In 1807, the invention of the *camera lucida* (lighted room) replaced the enclosed chamber of the camera obscura. Now the photographer aimed a small prism lens, hung on a stand, downward at an object. The lens projected the image of the object onto a sheet of paper. Artists using either of these devices found the process long and arduous, no matter how accurate the resulting work. All yearned for a more direct way to capture a subject's image. Two very different scientific inventions that accomplished this—the *daguerreotype* and the *calotype* (see "Daguerreotypes, Calotypes, and Wet-Plate Photography," page 792)—appeared almost simultaneously in France and England in 1839.

DAGUERREOTYPES The French government presented the new daguerreotype process at the Academy of Science in Paris on January 7, 1839, with the understanding that its details would be made available to all interested parties without charge (although the inventor received a large annuity in appreciation). Soon, people worldwide began making pictures with the daguerreotype "camera" (a name shortened from camera obscura) in a process almost immediately christened "photography," from the Greek *photos* (light) and *graphos* (writing). From the start, the possibilities of the process as a new art medium intrigued painters. Paul Delaroche (1797–1856), a leading academic painter of the day, wrote in an official report to the French government that anticipated the 1862 legal ruling:

> Daguerre's process completely satisfies all the demands of art, carrying certain essential principles of art to such perfection that it must become a subject of observation and study even to the most accomplished painters. The pictures obtained by this method are as remarkable for the perfection of the details as for the richness and harmony of the general effect. Nature is reproduced in them not only with truth, but also with art.[14]

Daguerreotypes, Calotypes, and Wet-Plate Photography

The earliest photographic processes were the *daguerreotype* (FIGS. 27-48 and 27-49), named after L.J.M. Daguerre, and the *calotype* (FIG. 27-54). Daguerre was an architect and theatrical set painter and designer. This background led Daguerre and a partner to open a popular entertainment called the Diorama. Audiences witnessed performances of "living paintings" created by changing the lighting effects on a "sandwich" composed of a painted backdrop and several layers of painted translucent front curtains. Daguerre used a camera obscura for the Diorama, but he wanted to find a more efficient and effective procedure. Through a mutual acquaintance, he met Joseph Nicéphore Niépce (1765–1833), who in 1826 had successfully made a permanent picture of the cityscape outside his upper-story window by exposing, in a camera obscura, a metal plate covered with a light-sensitive coating. Niépce's process, however, had the significant drawback that it required an eight-hour exposure time. After Niépce died in 1833, Daguerre continued his work, making two important discoveries. Latent development—that is, bringing out the image through treatment in chemical solutions—considerably shortened the length of time needed for exposure. Daguerre also discovered a better way to "fix" the image by chemically stopping the action of light on the photographic plate, which otherwise would continue to darken until the image turned solid black.

The daguerreotype reigned supreme in photography until the 1850s, but the second major photographic invention, the ancestor of the modern negative-print system, eventually replaced it. On January 31, 1839, less than three weeks after Daguerre unveiled his method in Paris, William Henry Fox Talbot presented a paper on his "photogenic drawings" to the Royal Institution in London. As early as 1835, Talbot made "negative" images by placing objects on sensitized paper and exposing the arrangement to light. This created a design of light-colored silhouettes recording the places where opaque or translucent objects had blocked light from darkening the paper's emulsion. In his experiments, Talbot next exposed sensitized papers inside simple cameras and, with a second sheet, created "positive" images. He further improved the process with more light-sensitive chemicals and a chemical development of the negative image. This technique enabled multiple prints. However, in Talbot's process, which he named the calotype (from the Greek word *kalos,* "beautiful"), the photographic images incorporated the texture of the paper. This produced a slightly blurred, grainy effect very different from the crisp detail and wide tonal range available with the daguerreotype. Also discouraging widespread adoption of the calotype were the stiff licensing and equipment fees charged for many years after Talbot patented his new process in 1841.

One of the earliest masters of an improved kind of calotype photography was the multitalented Frenchman known as Nadar (FIGS. 27-50 and 27-51). He used glass negatives and albumen (prepared with egg white) printing paper (FIGS. 27-52 and 27-53), which could record finer detail and a wider range of light and shadow than Talbot's calotype process. The new *wet-plate* technology (so named because the photographic plate was exposed, developed, and fixed while wet) almost at once became the universal way of making negatives until 1880. However, wet-plate photography had drawbacks. The plates had to be prepared and processed on the spot. Working outdoors meant taking along a portable darkroom—a wagon, tent, or box with light-tight sleeves for the photographer's arms.

Refinements of these early processes served photographers well for a century and a half but have been largely supplanted today by digital photography (see Chapter 31).

27-48 LOUIS-JACQUES-MANDÉ DAGUERRE, *Still Life in Studio,* 1837. Daguerreotype, 6¼″ × 8¼″. Société Française de Photographie, Paris. ◼◀

One of the first plates Daguerre produced after perfecting his new photographic process was this still life, in which he was able to capture amazing detail and finely graduated tones of light and shadow.

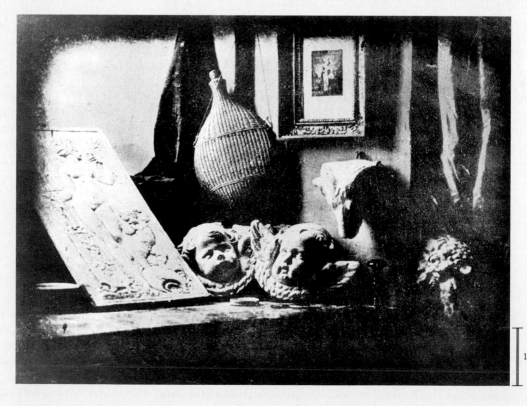

1 in.

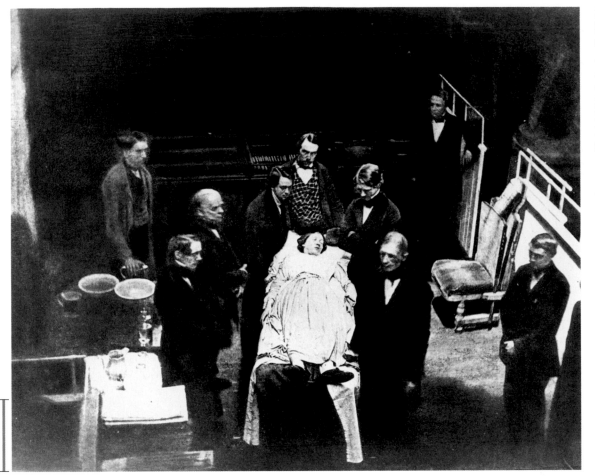

27-49 Josiah Johnson Hawes and Albert Sands Southworth, *Early Operation under Ether, Massachusetts General Hospital,* ca. 1847. Daguerreotype, $6\frac{1}{2}'' \times 8\frac{1}{2}''$. Massachusetts General Hospital Archives and Special Collections, Boston. ◼◄

In this early daguerreotype, which predates Eakins's *The Gross Clinic* (FIG. 27-36) by almost 30 years, Hawes and Southworth demonstrated the documentary power of the new medium of photography.

1 in.

Unlike photographs people make today, whether printed from traditional film negatives or from computerized digital images, each daguerreotype is a unique work. *Still Life in Studio* (FIG. **27-48**) is one of the first successful plates Daguerre produced after perfecting his method. The process captured every detail—the subtle forms, the varied textures, the finely graduated tones of light and shadow—in Daguerre's carefully constructed tableau. The three-dimensional forms of the sculptures, the basket, and the bits of cloth spring into high relief. The inspiration for the composition came from 17th-century Dutch vanitas still lifes, such as those of Pieter Claesz (FIG. 25-1). As did Claesz, Daguerre arranged his objects to reveal their textures and shapes clearly. Unlike a painter, Daguerre could not alter anything within his arrangement to create a stronger image. However, he could suggest a symbolic meaning through his choice of objects. Like the skull and timepiece in Claesz's painting, Daguerre's sculptural and architectural fragments and the framed print of an embrace suggest even art is vanitas and will not endure forever.

HAWES AND SOUTHWORTH In the United States, photographers began to make daguerreotypes within two months of Daguerre's presentation in Paris. Two particularly avid and resourceful advocates of the new medium were JOSIAH JOHNSON HAWES (1808–1901), a painter, and ALBERT SANDS SOUTHWORTH (1811–1894), a pharmacist and teacher. Together, they ran a daguerreotype studio in Boston specializing in portraiture, then popular due to the shortened exposure time required for the process (although it was still long enough to require head braces to help subjects remain motionless while photographers recorded their images).

The partners also took their equipment outside the studio to record places and events of particular interest to them. One resultant image is *Early Operation under Ether, Massachusetts General Hospital* (FIG. **27-49**). This daguerreotype, taken from the vantage point of the gallery of a hospital operating room, put the viewer in the position of medical students looking down on a lecture-demonstration typical throughout the 19th century. An image of historical record, this early daguerreotype predates Eakins's *Gross Clinic* (FIG. 27-36) by almost three decades. The focus of attention in *Early Operation* is the white-draped patient surrounded by a circle of darkly clad doctors. The details of the figures and the room's furnishings are in sharp focus, but the slight blurring of several of the figures betrays motion during the exposure. The elevated viewpoint flattens the spatial perspective and emphasizes the relationships of the figures in ways the Impressionists, especially Degas, found intriguing.

NADAR Portraiture was one of the first photography genres to use a technology that improved the calotype. Making portraits was an important economic opportunity for most photographers, as Southworth and Hawes proved, but the greatest of the early portrait photographers was undoubtedly Gaspar-Félix Tournachon. Known simply as NADAR (1820–1910), Tournachon was a French novelist, enthusiastic balloonist, and caricaturist, who became an early champion of photography. Photographic studies for his caricatures led Nadar to open a portrait studio. So talented was he at capturing the essence of his subjects that the most important people in France, including Delacroix, Daumier, Courbet, and Manet, flocked to his studio to have their portraits made. Nadar said he sought in his work "that instant of understanding that puts you in touch with the model—helps you sum him up,

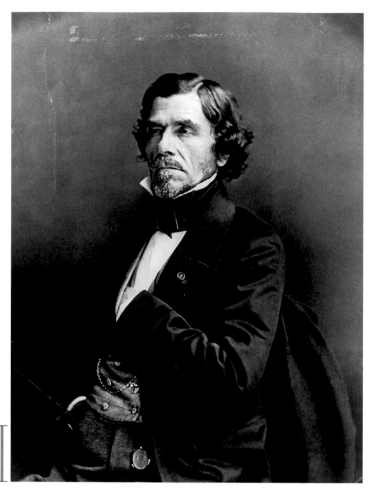

27-50 NADAR, *Eugène Delacroix,* ca. 1855. Modern print, $8\frac{1}{2}'' \times 6\frac{2}{3}''$, from the original negative. Bibliothèque Nationale, Paris.

Nadar was one of the earliest portrait photographers. His prints of the leading artists of the day, such as this one of Delacroix, reveal the sitters' personalities as well as record their features.

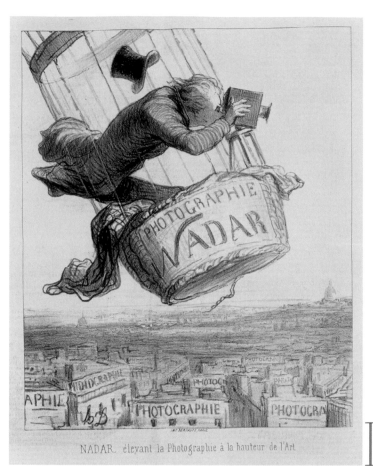

NADAR. élevant la Photographie à la hauteur de l'Art

27-51 HONORÉ DAUMIER, *Nadar Raising Photography to the Height of Art,* 1862. Lithograph, $10\frac{3}{4}'' \times 8\frac{3}{4}''$. Museum of Fine Arts, Boston.

Daumier's lithograph of Nadar (FIG. 27-50) in a balloon "elevating the art of photography" commemorates a court decision acknowledging photographs as artworks protected by copyright.

guides you to his habits, his ideas, and character and enables you to produce . . . a really convincing and sympathetic likeness, an intimate portrait."[15]

Nadar's *Eugène Delacroix* (FIG. **27-50**) shows the painter at the height of his career. In this photograph, the artist appears with remarkable presence. Even in half-length, his gesture and expression create a mood that seems to reveal much about him. Perhaps Delacroix responded to Nadar's famous gift for putting his clients at ease by assuming the pose that best expressed his personality. The new photographic materials made possible the rich range of tones in Nadar's images.

Nadar achieved so much fame for his wet-plate photographic portraits (see "Daguerreotypes, Calotypes, and Wet-Plate Photography," page 792) that he became the subject of a Daumier lithograph (FIG. **27-51**) that provides incisive and amusing commentary about the struggle of photography to be recognized as a fine art. Daumier made his print in response to the 1862 court decision acknowledging photographs were indeed artworks. In the lithograph, Nadar energetically takes pictures with his camera as his balloon rises over Parisian rooftops—Daumier's literal representation of the elevation of photography's status the French judge reaffirmed. The image also refers to the fact that Nadar was a staunch advocate of balloon transportation and aerial reconnaissance. He produced the first aerial photographs of Paris in 1858 from his balloon *Le Géant* (The Giant).

JULIA MARGARET CAMERON Among the most famous portrait photographers in 19th-century England was JULIA MARGARET CAMERON (1815–1879), who did not take up photography seriously until the age of 48. Although she produced images of many well-known men of the period, including Charles Darwin, Alfred Tennyson, and Thomas Carlyle, she photographed more women than men, as was true of many women photographers. *Ophelia, Study No. 2* (FIG. **27-52**) typifies her portrait style. Cameron often depicted her female subjects as characters in literary or biblical narratives. The slightly blurred focus also became a distinctive feature of her work—the byproduct of photographing with a lens with a short focal length, which allowed only a small area of sharp focus. The blurriness adds an ethereal, dreamlike tone to the photographs, appropriate for Cameron's fictional "characters." Her photograph of Ophelia has a mysterious, fragile quality reminiscent of Pre-Raphaelite paintings (FIG. 27-41) of literary heroines.

TIMOTHY O'SULLIVAN Photographers were quick to realize the documentary power of their new medium. Thus began the story of photography's influence on modern life and of the immense changes it brought to communication and information management. Historical events could be recorded in permanent form on the spot for the first time. The photographs taken of the Crimean War (1856) by Roger Fenton (1819–1869) and of the American Civil War by Mathew B. Brady (1823–1896), ALEXANDER GARDNER (1821–1882),

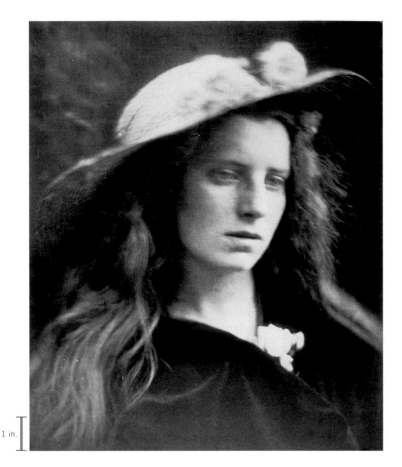

27-52 JULIA MARGARET CAMERON, *Ophelia, Study No. 2,* 1867. Albumen print, 1' 1" × 10⅔". George Eastman House, Rochester (gift of Eastman Kodak Company; formerly Gabriel Cromer Collection).

Cameron was a prominent 19th-century photographer who often depicted her female subjects as characters in literary or biblical narratives. The slightly blurred focus is a distinctive feature of her work.

1 in.

and TIMOTHY O'SULLIVAN (1840–1882) remain unsurpassed as incisive accounts of military life, unsparing in their truth to detail and poignant as expressions of human experience.

Of the Civil War photographs, the most moving are the inhumanly objective records of combat deaths. Perhaps the most reproduced of these Civil War photographs is Gardner's print of O'Sullivan's *A Harvest of Death, Gettysburg, Pennsylvania* (FIG. **27-53**). Although viewers could regard this image as simple reportage, it also functions to impress on people the high price of war. Corpses litter the battlefield as far as the eye can see. O'Sullivan presented a scene stretching far to the horizon. As the photograph modulates from the precise clarity of the bodies of Union soldiers in the foreground, boots stolen and pockets picked, to the indistinct corpses in the distance, the suggestion of innumerable other dead soldiers is unavoidable. This "harvest" is far more sobering and depressing than that in Winslow Homer's Civil War painting, *Veteran in a New Field* (FIG. 27-35). Though it was years before photolithography could reproduce photographs such as this in newspapers, photographers exhibited them publicly. They made an impression newsprint engravings never could.

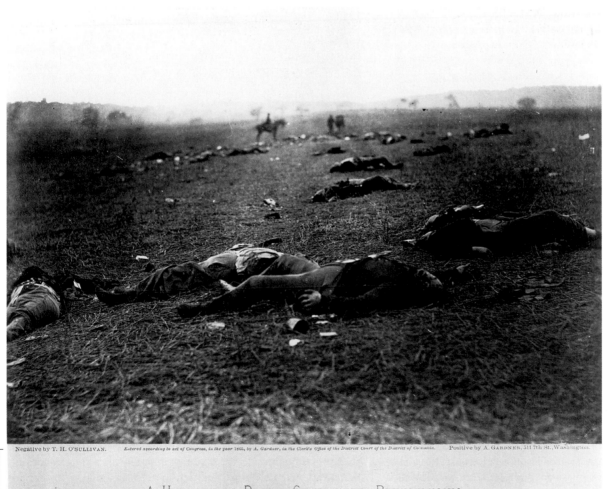

Negative by T. H. O'SULLIVAN.   *Entered according to act of Congress, in the year 1865, by A. Gardner, in the Clerk's Office of the District Court of the District of Columbia.*   Positive by A. GARDNER, 511 7th St., Washington.

A HARVEST OF DEATH, GETTYSBURG, PENNSYLVANIA.

1 in.

27-53 TIMOTHY O'SULLIVAN, *A Harvest of Death, Gettysburg, Pennsylvania,* 1863. Negative by Timothy O'Sullivan. Albumen print by ALEXANDER GARDNER, 6¾" × 8¾". New York Public Library (Astor, Lenox and Tilden Foundations, Rare Books and Manuscript Division), New York.

Wet-plate technology enabled photographers to record historical events on the spot— and to comment on the high price of war, as in this photograph of dead Union soldiers at Gettysburg in 1863.

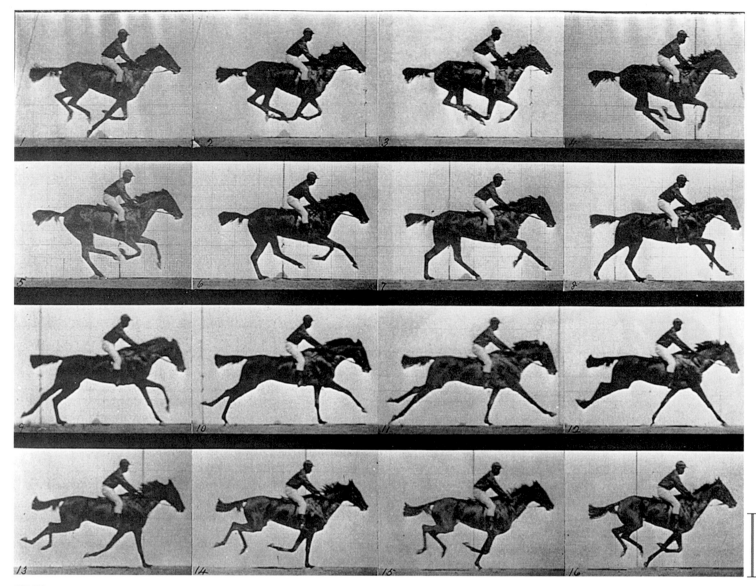

1 in.

27-54 Eadweard Muybridge, *Horse Galloping*, 1878. Calotype print, 9″ × 12″. George Eastman House, Rochester. ◼◀

Muybridge specialized in photographic studies of the successive stages in human and animal motion—details too quick for the human eye to capture. Modern cinema owes a great deal to his work.

EADWEARD MUYBRIDGE The Realist photographer and scientist EADWEARD MUYBRIDGE (1830–1904) came to the United States from England in the 1850s and settled in San Francisco, where he established a prominent international reputation for his photographs of the western United States. In 1872, the governor of California, Leland Stanford (1824–1893), sought Muybridge's assistance in settling a bet about whether, at any point in a stride, all four feet of a horse galloping at top speed are off the ground. Through his sequential photography, as seen in *Horse Galloping* (FIG. 27-54), Muybridge proved they were. This experience was the beginning of Muybridge's photographic studies of the successive stages in human and animal motion—details too quick for the human eye to capture. These investigations culminated in 1885 at the University of Pennsylvania with a series of multiple-camera motion studies that recorded separate photographs of progressive moments in a single action. Muybridge's discoveries received extensive publicity through the book *Animal Locomotion* (1887), and his motion photographs earned him a place in the history of science, as well

as art. These sequential motion studies, along with those of Eakins and Marey, influenced many other artists, including their contemporary, the painter and sculptor Edgar Degas (FIG. 28-10), and 20th-century artists such as Marcel Duchamp (FIG. 29-35).

Muybridge presented his work to scientists and general audiences with a device called the *zoopraxiscope,* which he invented to project his sequences of images (mounted on special glass plates) onto a screen. The result was so lifelike one viewer said it "threw upon the screen apparently the living, moving animals. Nothing was wanting but the clatter of hoofs upon the turf."[16] The illusion of motion in Muybridge's photographic exhibits was the result of a physical fact of human eyesight called "persistence of vision." Stated simply, it means the brain retains whatever the eye sees for a fraction of a second after the eye stops seeing it. Thus, viewers saw a rapid succession of different images merging one into the next, producing the illusion of continuous change. This illusion lies at the heart of the motion-picture industry that debuted in the 20th century. Thus, with Muybridge's innovations in photography, yet another new art form was born—the cinema.

ROMANTICISM, REALISM, PHOTOGRAPHY: EUROPE AND AMERICA, 1800 TO 1870

ART UNDER NAPOLEON

▌ As Emperor of the French from 1804 to 1815, Napoleon embraced the Neoclassical style in order to associate his regime with the empire of ancient Rome. Roman temples were the models for La Madeleine in Paris, which Pierre Vignon built as a temple of glory for France's imperial armies.

▌ Napoleon chose Jacques-Louis David as First Painter of the Empire. His favorite sculptor was Antonio Canova, who carved marble Neoclassical portraits of the imperial family, including a reclining image of Napoleon's sister, Pauline Borghese, in the guise of Venus.

▌ The beginning of a break from Neoclassicism can already be seen in the work of some of David's students, including Gros, Girodet-Trioson, and Ingres, all of whom painted some exotic subjects reflecting Romantic taste.

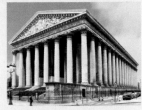

Vignon, La Madeleine, Paris, 1807–1842

ROMANTICISM

▌ The roots of Romanticism are in the 18th century, but usually the term more narrowly denotes the artistic movement that flourished from 1800 to 1840, between Neoclassicism and Realism. Romantic artists gave precedence to feeling and imagination over Enlightenment reason. Romantic painters explored the exotic, erotic, and fantastic in their art.

▌ In Spain, Francisco Goya's *Los Caprichos* series celebrated the unleashing of imagination, emotions, and even nightmares. In France, Eugène Delacroix led the way in depicting Romantic narratives set in faraway places and distant times. Ancient Assyria, for example, is the subject of his colorful *Death of Sardanapalus*.

▌ Romantic painters often chose landscapes as an ideal subject to express the theme of the soul unified with the natural world. Masters of the transcendental landscape include Friedrich in Germany, Constable and Turner in England, and Cole, Bierstadt, and Church in the United States.

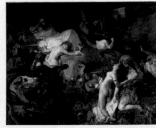

Delacroix, *Death of Sardanapalus*, 1827

REALISM

▌ Realism developed as an artistic movement in mid-19th-century France. Its leading proponent was Gustave Courbet, whose paintings of menial laborers and ordinary people exemplify his belief that painters should depict only their own time and place. Honoré Daumier boldly confronted authority with his satirical lithographs commenting on the plight of the urban working classes. Édouard Manet shocked the public with his paintings featuring promiscuous women, and his rough brushstrokes, which emphasized the flatness of the painting surface, paved the way for modern abstract art.

▌ Among the leading American Realists were Winslow Homer, Thomas Eakins, and John Singer Sargent. Eakins's painting of surgery in progress was too brutally realistic for the Philadelphia art jury that rejected it.

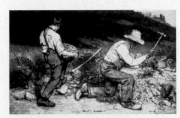

Courbet, *The Stone Breakers,* 1849

ARCHITECTURE

▌ Territorial expansion, the Romantic interest in exotic locales and earlier eras, and nationalistic pride led to the revival in the 19th century of older architectural styles, especially the Gothic, exemplified by London's Houses of Parliament.

▌ By the middle of the century, many architects had already abandoned sentimental and Romantic designs from the past in favor of exploring the possibilities of cast-iron construction, as in Henri Labrouste's Saint-Geneviève Library in Paris and Joseph Paxton's Crystal Palace in London.

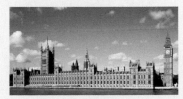

Barry and Pugin, Houses of Parliament, London, 1835

PHOTOGRAPHY

▌ In 1839, Daguerre in Paris and Talbot in London invented the first practical photographic processes. In 1862, a French court formally recognized photography as an art form subject to copyright protection. Many of the earliest photographers, including Nadar and Cameron, specialized in portrait photography, but others, including Hawes, Southworth, and O'Sullivan in the United States quickly realized the documentary power of the new medium. Muybridge's sequential photos of human and animal motion were the forerunners of the modern cinema.

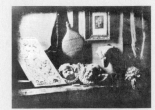

Daguerre, *Still Life in Studio,* 1837

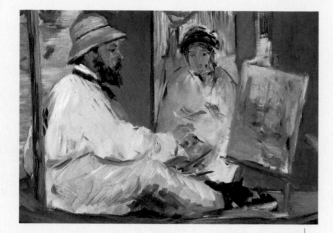

In summer 1874, Manet recorded Monet painting—*en plein air* directly on canvas without any preliminary sketchpreliminar—in his floating studio on the Seine at Argenteuil, 22 minutes from Paris by train.

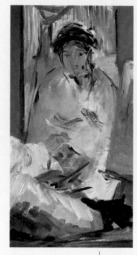

With Monet is his wife, Camille Doncieux. Monet, underappreciated as an artist, had recently sold some paintings, enabling the couple to purchase the small boat he equipped with a cabin and easel.

In this painting, Manet adopted not only Monet's Impressionist subject matter but also the younger artist's short brushstrokes and fascination with the reflection of sunlight on water.

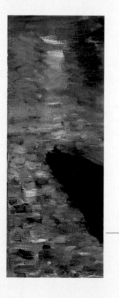

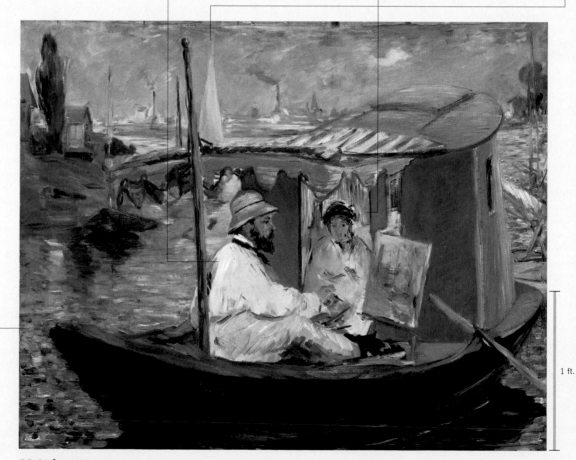

1 ft.

28-1 ÉDOUARD MANET, *Claude Monet in His Studio Boat*, 1874. Oil on canvas, 2′ 8″ × 3′ 3¼″. **Neue Pinakothek, Munich.** ◼◀

28

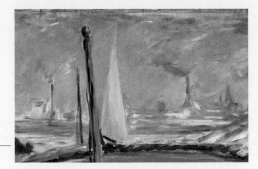

In the distance are the factories and smokestacks of Argenteuil. Manet thus recorded the two poles of modern life—the leisure activities of the bourgeosie and the industrialization along the Seine.

IMPRESSIONISM, POST-IMPRESSIONISM, SYMBOLISM: EUROPE AND AMERICA, 1870 TO 1900

FRAMING THE ERA

IMPRESSIONS OF MODERN LIFE

Impressionism was an art movement born in late-19th-century industrialized, urbanized Paris as a reaction to the sometimes brutal and chaotic transformation of French life, which made the world seem unstable and insubstantial. As the poet and critic Charles Baudelaire (1821–1867) observed in his 1860 essay *The Painter of Modern Life:* "[M]odernity is the transitory, the fugitive, the contingent."[1] Accordingly, Impressionist painters built upon the innovations of the Realists in turning away from traditional mythological and religious themes in favor of daily life, but they sought to convey the elusiveness and impermanence of the subjects they portrayed.

In 1872, the painter CLAUDE MONET (1840–1926), a leading Impressionist, moved to Argenteuil, a prosperous industrial town on the Seine (MAP **28-1**) that was also a favorite leisure destination of the city dwellers of Paris—only 22 minutes by train from the Saint-Lazare train station (FIG. 28-4). Situated at a point where the river widened into a deep basin, Argenteuil was an ideal spot for boating of all kinds, from casual rowing to formal regattas. In 1873, after accumulating enough money from recent sales of his paintings, the underappreciated and financially strapped Monet was able to purchase a small boat, which he equipped with a tiny wooden cabin and a striped awning and used as his floating studio.

During the summer of 1874, Édouard Manet (FIGS. 27-32 and 27-33) joined Monet at Argenteuil and painted side-by-side with the younger artist. One day, Manet recorded Monet in his studio boat (FIG. **28-1**) at work on *Sailboats on the Seine, Argenteuil,* a painting now in the Fine Arts Museum of San Francisco. Monet, wearing a straw hat, sits at the front of the boat with his easel before him. Camille Doncieux, Monet's wife (compare FIG. 28-2A), is at once the painter's admirer and his muse. In the distance are the factories and smokestacks that represent the opposite pole of life at Argenteuil. In capturing both the leisure activities of the bourgeoisie and the industrialization along the Seine in the 1870s on the same canvas, Manet, like Monet, was fulfilling Baudelaire's definition of "the painter of modern life."

Claude Monet in His Studio Boat is noteworthy as a document of Monet's preference for painting outdoors (*en plein air*)—a radical practice at the time—in order to record his "impression" of the Seine by placing colors directly on a white canvas without any preliminary sketch—also a sharp break from traditional studio techniques. The painting further attests to Monet's influence on his older friend Manet, who here adopted the younger painter's subject matter, short brushstrokes, and fascination with the reflection of light on water.

MARXISM, DARWINISM, MODERNISM

The momentous developments of the early 19th century in Europe—industrialization, urbanization, and increased economic and political interaction worldwide—matured during the latter half of the century. The Industrial Revolution born in England spread so rapidly to the Continent and the United States that historians often refer to the third quarter of the 19th century as the second Industrial Revolution. Whereas the first Industrial Revolution centered on textiles, steam, and iron, the second focused on steel, electricity, chemicals, and oil. The discoveries in these fields provided the foundation for developments in plastics, machinery, building construction, and automobile manufacturing and paved the way for the invention of the radio, electric light, telephone, and electric streetcar.

A significant consequence of industrialization was urbanization. The number and size of Western cities grew dramatically during the latter part of the 19th century, largely due to migration from the countryside. Farmers in large numbers relocated to urban centers because expanded agricultural enterprises squeezed smaller property owners from their land. The widely available work opportunities in the cities, especially in the factories, were also a major factor in this population shift. Improving health and living conditions in the cities further contributed to their explosive growth.

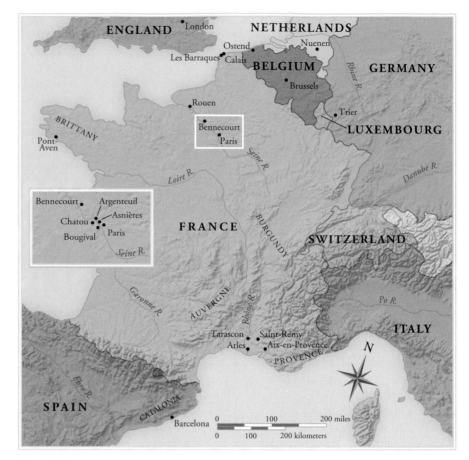

MAP 28-1 France around 1870.

MARXISM AND DARWINISM The rise of the urban working class was fundamental to the ideas of Karl Marx (1818–1883), one of the era's dominant figures. Born in Trier, Germany, Marx received a doctorate in philosophy from the University of Berlin. After moving to Paris, he met fellow German Friedrich Engels (1820–1895), who became his lifelong collaborator. Together they wrote *The Communist Manifesto* (1848), which called for the working class to overthrow the capitalist system. As did other 19th-century empiricists, Marx believed scientific, rational law governed nature and, indeed, all human history. For Marx, economic forces based on class struggle induced historical change. Throughout history, insisted Marx, those who controlled the means of production conflicted with those whose labor they exploited for their own enrichment—a dynamic he called "dialectical materialism." Marx advocated the creation of a socialist state in which the working class seized power and destroyed capitalism. This new political, social, and economic system—Marxism—held great appeal for the oppressed as well as for many intellectuals.

Equally influential was the English naturalist Charles Darwin (1809–1882), whose theory of natural selection did much to increase interest in science. Darwin and his compatriot Alfred Russel Wallace (1823–1913), working independently, proposed a model for the process of evolution based on mechanistic laws, rather than attributing evolution to random chance or God's plan. They postulated a competitive system in which only the fittest survived. Darwin's controversial ideas, as presented in *On the Origin of Species by Means of Natural Selection* (1859), contradicted the biblical narrative of creation. By challenging traditional religious beliefs, Darwinism contributed to growing secularism.

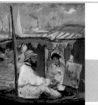

IMPRESSIONISM, POST-IMPRESSIONISM, SYMBOLISM: EUROPE AND AMERICA, 1870 TO 1900

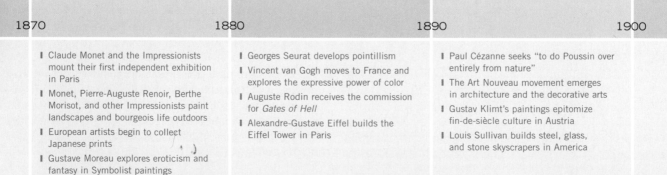

1870	1880	1890	1900
▮ Claude Monet and the Impressionists mount their first independent exhibition in Paris	▮ Georges Seurat develops pointillism	▮ Paul Cézanne seeks "to do Poussin over entirely from nature"	
▮ Monet, Pierre-Auguste Renoir, Berthe Morisot, and other Impressionists paint landscapes and bourgeois life outdoors	▮ Vincent van Gogh moves to France and explores the expressive power of color	▮ The Art Nouveau movement emerges in architecture and the decorative arts	
▮ European artists begin to collect Japanese prints	▮ Auguste Rodin receives the commission for *Gates of Hell*	▮ Gustav Klimt's paintings epitomize fin-de-siècle culture in Austria	
▮ Gustave Moreau explores eroticism and fantasy in Symbolist paintings	▮ Alexandre-Gustave Eiffel builds the Eiffel Tower in Paris	▮ Louis Sullivan builds steel, glass, and stone skyscrapers in America	

Other theorists and social thinkers, most notably British philosopher Herbert Spencer (1820–1903), applied Darwin's principles to the rapidly changing socioeconomic realm. As in the biological world, they asserted, industrialization's intense competition led to the survival of the most economically fit companies, enterprises, and countries. The social Darwinists provided Western nations with justification for the colonization of peoples and cultures they deemed less advanced. By 1900, the major economic and political powers had divided up much of the world. The French had colonized most of North Africa and Indochina, while the British occupied India, Australia, and large areas of Africa, including Nigeria, Egypt, Sudan, Rhodesia, and the Union of South Africa. The Dutch were a major presence in the Pacific, and the Germans, Portuguese, Spanish, and Italians all established themselves in various areas of Africa.

MODERNISM The combination of extensive technological changes and increased exposure to other cultures, coupled with the rapidity of these changes, led to an acute sense in Western cultures of the world's impermanence. Darwin's ideas of evolution and Marx's emphasis on a continuing sequence of conflicts reinforced this awareness of a constantly shifting reality. These societal changes in turn fostered a new and multifaceted artistic approach that art historians call *modernism*. Modernist artists seek to capture the images and sensibilities of their age, but modernism transcends the simple depiction of the contemporary world—the goal of Realism (see Chapter 27). Modernist artists also critically examine the premises of art itself, as Manet did in his seminal 1863 painting *Le Déjeuner sur l'Herbe* (FIG. 27-32). Modernism thus implies certain concerns about art and aesthetics internal to art production, regardless of whether the artist is portraying modern life. Clement Greenberg (1909–1994), an influential American art critic who wrote about the revolutionary art movements of the decades following World War II (see Chapter 30), explained:

> The essence of Modernism lies . . . in the use of the characteristic methods of a discipline to criticize the discipline itself—not in order to subvert it, but to entrench it more firmly in its area of competence. . . . Realistic, illusionist art had dissembled the medium, using art to conceal art. Modernism used art to call attention to art. The limitations that constitute the medium of painting—the flat surface, the shape of the support, the properties of pigment—were treated by the Old Masters as negative factors that could be acknowledged only implicitly or indirectly. Modernist painting has come to regard these same limitations as positive factors that are to be acknowledged openly.[2]

Although the work of Gustave Courbet and the Realists already expressed this modernist viewpoint, modernism emerged even more forcefully in the late-19th-century movements that art historians call Impressionism, Post-Impressionism, and Symbolism.

IMPRESSIONISM

A hostile critic applied the term *Impressionism* in response to Claude Monet's *Impression: Sunrise* (FIG. 28-2), exhibited in the first Impressionist show in 1874 (see "Academic Salons and Independent Art Exhibitions," page 802). Although the critic intended the label to be derogatory, by the third Impressionist show in 1878, the artists had embraced it and were calling themselves Impressionists.

CLAUDE MONET Artists and critics had used the term *Impressionism* before, but only in relation to sketches. Impression-ist paintings do incorporate the qualities of sketches—abbreviation, speed, and spontaneity. This is apparent in *Impression: Sunrise* (FIG. **28-2**), in which Monet made no attempt to disguise the brushstrokes or blend the pigment to create smooth tonal gradations and an optically accurate scene. This concern with acknowledging the paint and the canvas surface continued the modernist exploration the Realists began. Beyond this connection to the sketch, Impressionism operated at the intersection of what the artists saw and what they felt. In other words, the "impressions" these artists recorded in their paintings were neither purely objective descriptions of the exterior world nor solely subjective responses, but the interaction between the two. They were sensations—the Impressionists' subjective and personal responses to nature.

In sharp contrast to traditional studio artists, Monet painted outdoors, often on the banks of the Seine (FIG. 28-2A) northwest of Paris or in a boat on the river (FIG. 28-1). Painting *en plein air* sharpened Monet's focus on the roles light and color play in capturing an instantaneous representation of atmosphere and climate. Monet carried the

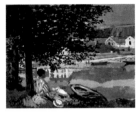

28-2A MONET, *Bank of the Seine, Bennecourt*, 1868.

systematic investigation of light and color further than any other Impressionist, but all of them recognized the importance of carefully observing and understanding how light and color operate. Such thorough study enabled the Impressionists to present images that truly conveyed a sense of the momentary and transitory. Lila Cabot Perry (1848–1933), a student of Monet's late in his career, gave this description of Monet's approach:

> I remember his once saying to me: "When you go out to paint, try to forget what objects you have before you—a tree, a house, a field, or whatever. Merely think, here is a little square of blue, here an oblong of pink, here a streak of yellow, and paint it just as it looks to you, the exact color and shape, until it gives your own naïve impression of the scene before you."[3]

Scientific studies of light and the invention of chemically synthesized pigments increased artists' sensitivity to the multiplicity of colors in nature and gave them new colors for their work. After scrutinizing the effects of light and color on forms, the Impressionists concluded that *local color*—an object's color in white light—becomes modified by the quality of the light shining on it, by reflections from other objects, and by the effects juxtaposed colors produce. Shadows do not appear gray or black, as many earlier painters thought, but seem to be composed of colors modified by reflections or other conditions. If artists use complementary colors (see "19th-Century Color Theory," page 813) side by side over large enough areas, the colors intensify each other, unlike the effect of small quantities of adjoining mixed pigments, which blend into neutral tones. Furthermore, the "mixing" of colors by juxtaposing them on a canvas produces a more intense hue than the same colors mixed on the palette. It is not strictly true the Impressionists used only primary hues, placing them side by side to create secondary colors (blue and yellow, for example, to create green). But they did achieve remarkably brilliant effects with their characteristically short, choppy brushstrokes, which so accurately caught the vibrating quality of light. The fact their canvas surfaces look unintelligible at close range and their forms and objects appear only when the eye fuses the strokes at a certain distance accounts for much of the early adverse criticism leveled at their work. Some critics even accused the Impressionists of firing their paint at the canvas with pistols.

Academic Salons and Independent Art Exhibitions

For both artists and art historians, modernist art stands in marked contrast—indeed in forceful opposition—to academic art, that is, to the art promoted by the established art schools such as the Royal Academy of Painting and Sculpture in France (founded in 1648) and the Royal Academy of Arts in Britain (founded in 1768). These academies provided instruction for art students and sponsored exhibitions, exerting tight control over the art scene. The annual exhibitions, called "Salons" in France, were highly competitive, as was membership in these academies. Subsidized by the government, the French Royal Academy supported a limited range of artistic expression, focusing on traditional subjects and highly polished technique. Because of the challenges modernist art presented to established artistic conventions, the juries for the Salons and other exhibitions often rejected the works more adventurous artists wished to display, thereby preventing the public from viewing any art other than the officially sanctioned forms of expression. When, however, the 1855 jury rejected some of Gustave Courbet's paintings, the artist reacted by setting up his own Pavilion of Realism (see "Courbet on Realism," Chapter 27, page 776). Years later, he wrote:

> [I]t is high time that someone have the courage to be an honest man and that he say that the Academy is a harmful, all-consuming institution, incapable of fulfilling the goal of its so-called mission.*

Growing dissatisfaction with the decisions of the French Academy's jurors prompted Napoleon III (r. 1852–1870) in 1863 to establish the Salon des Refusés (Salon of the Rejected) to show all of the works not accepted for exhibition in the regular Salon. Édouard Manet's *Le Déjeuner sur l'Herbe* (FIG. 27-32) was among them. The public greeted it and the entire exhibition with derision. One reviewer of the rejected works summed up the prevailing attitude:

> This exhibition, at once sad and grotesque, . . . offers abundant proof . . . that the jury always displays an unbelievable leniency. Save for one or two questionable exceptions there is not a painting which deserves the honor of the official galleries . . . There is even something cruel about this exhibition; people laugh as they do at a farce.†

In 1867, after further rejections, Manet, following Courbet, mounted a private exhibition of 50 of his paintings outside the Paris World's Fair. Six years later, Claude Monet (FIG. 28-2) and the other Impressionists formed their own society and began mounting shows of their works in Paris. This action provided the Impressionists much freedom, for they did not have to contend with the Royal Academy's authoritative and confining viewpoint. The Impressionist exhibitions took place at one- or two-year intervals from 1874 until 1886.

Another group of artists unhappy with the official Salon's conservative nature adopted the same renegade idea. In 1884, these artists formed the Société des Artistes Indépendants (Society of Independent Artists) and held annual Salons des Indépendants. Georges Seurat's *A Sunday on La Grande Jatte* (FIG. 28-16) was one of the paintings in the Independents' 1886 salon.

As the art market expanded, venues for the exhibition of art increased. Art circles and societies sponsored private shows in which both amateurs and professionals participated. Dealers became more aggressive in promoting the artists they represented by mounting exhibitions in a variety of spaces, some fairly intimate and small, others large and grandiose. All of these proliferating opportunities for exhibition gave French artists alternatives to the traditional constraints of the Salon and provided fertile breeding ground for the development of radically new art forms and styles.

*Letter to Jules-Antoine Castagnary, October 17, 1868. Translated by Petra ten-Doesschate Chu, *Letters of Gustave Courbet* (Chicago: University of Chicago Press, 1992), 346.
†Maxime du Camp, in *Revue des deux mondes,* 1863, quoted in George Heard Hamilton, *Manet and His Critics* (New Haven: Yale University Press, New Haven, Conn., 1986), 42–43.

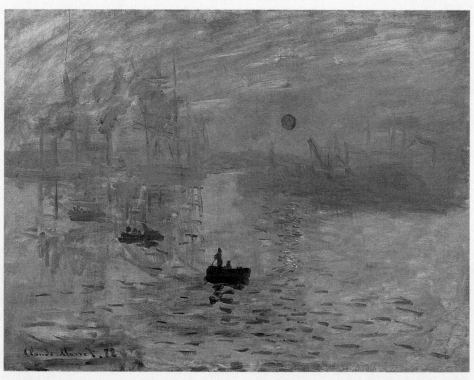

28-2 CLAUDE MONET, *Impression: Sunrise,* 1872. Oil on canvas, 1′ 7½″ × 2′ 1½″. Musée Marmottan, Paris.

A hostile critic applied the derogatory term *Impressionism* to this painting because of its sketchy quality and undisguised brushstrokes. Monet and his circle embraced the label for their movement.

1 in.

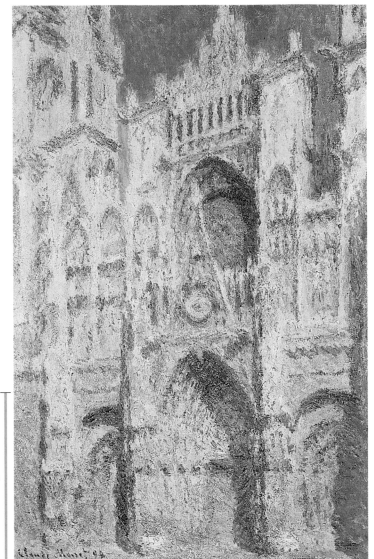

28-3 CLAUDE MONET, *Rouen Cathedral: The Portal (in Sun)*, 1894. Oil on canvas, 3' 3¼" × 2' 1⅞". Metropolitan Museum of Art, New York (Theodore M. Davis Collection, bequest of Theodore M. Davis, 1915).

Monet painted a series of views of Rouen Cathedral at different times of day and under various climatic conditions. The real subject of this painting is not the building but the sunlight shining on it.

ROUEN CATHEDRAL Monet's intensive study of the phenomena of light and color is especially evident in several series of paintings he made of the same subject. In one series, he painted more than three dozen views of Rouen Cathedral, northwest of Paris. For each canvas in the series, Monet observed the cathedral from nearly the same viewpoint but at different times of the day or under various climatic conditions. In the painting illustrated here (FIG. **28-3**), Monet depicted the church bathed in bright light. With scientific precision, he carefully recorded the passing of time as seen in the movement of light over identical forms. In fact, the real subject of Monet's painting—as the title *Rouen Cathedral: The Portal (in Sun)* implies—is not the cathedral, which he showed only in part, but the sunlight on the building's main portal. Later critics accused Monet and his companions of destroying form and order for fleeting atmospheric effects, but Monet focused on light and color precisely to reach a greater understanding of the appearance of form.

SAINT-LAZARE Most of the Impressionists painted scenes in and around Paris, the heart of modern life in France. Monet's *Saint-Lazare Train Station* (FIG. **28-4**) depicts a dominant aspect of the contemporary urban scene. The expanding railway network had made travel more convenient, bringing throngs of people into Paris and enabling city dwellers to reach rural areas quickly. In this painting, Monet captured the energy and vitality of Paris's modern transportation hub. The train, emerging from the steam and smoke it emits, rumbles into the station. In the background haze are the tall buildings that were becoming a major component of the Parisian landscape. Monet's agitated paint application contributes to the sense of energy and conveys the atmosphere of urban life.

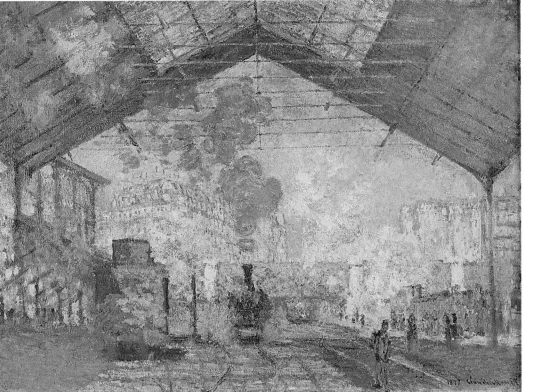

28-4 CLAUDE MONET, *Saint-Lazare Train Station*, 1877. Oil on canvas, 2' 5¾" × 3' 5". Musée d'Orsay, Paris.

Impressionist paintings are unintelligible at close range, but the eye fuses the brushstrokes at a distance. The agitated application of paint contributes to the sense of energy in this urban scene.

Georges Rivière (1855–1943), a critic and friend of some of the Impressionists, saw this painting in the third Impressionist exhibition and recorded the essence of what Monet had tried to achieve:

> Like a fiery steed, stimulated rather than exhausted by the long trek that it has only just finished, [the locomotive] tosses its mane of smoke, which lashes the glass roof of the main hall. . . . We see the vast and manic movements at the station where the ground shakes with every turn of the wheel. The platforms are sticky with soot, and the air is full of that bitter scent exuded by burning coal. As we look at this magnificent picture, we are overcome by the same feelings as if we were really there, and these feelings are perhaps even more powerful, because in the picture the artist has conveyed his own feelings as well.[4]

GUSTAVE CAILLEBOTTE Other Impressionists also represented facets of city life, although not always using Monet's impressionistic brushstrokes. The setting of *Paris: A Rainy Day* (FIG. **28-5**) by GUSTAVE CAILLEBOTTE (1849–1893) is a junction of spacious boulevards resulting from the redesigning of Paris begun in 1852. The city's population had reached close to 1.5 million by midcentury. To accommodate this congregation of humanity—and to facilitate the movement of troops in the event of another revolution—Napoleon III ordered Paris rebuilt. The emperor named Baron Georges Haussmann (1809–1891), a city superintendent, to oversee the entire project. In addition to new water and sewer systems, street lighting, and new residential and commercial buildings, a major component of the new Paris was the creation of the wide, open boulevards seen in Caillebotte's painting. These great avenues, whose construction caused the demolition of thousands of old buildings and streets, transformed medieval Paris into the present-day city, with its superb vistas and wide uninterrupted arteries for the flow of vehicular and pedestrian traffic. Caillebotte chose to focus on these markers of the city's rapid urbanization.

Although Caillebotte did not dissolve his image into the broken color and brushwork characteristic of Impressionism, he did use an informal and asymmetrical composition. The figures seem randomly placed, with the frame cropping them arbitrarily, suggesting the transitory nature of the street scene. Well-dressed Parisians of the leisure class share the viewer's space. Despite the sharp focus of *Paris: A Rainy Day,* the picture captures the artist's "impression" of urban life.

CAMILLE PISSARRO Other Impressionists also found Paris's spacious boulevards and avenues—the product of "Haussmannization"—attractive subjects for paintings. *La Place du Théâtre Français* (FIG. **28-6**) is one of many panoramic scenes of the city CAMILLE PISSARRO (1830–1903) painted. The artist recorded the blurred dark accents against a light ground that constituted his visual sensations of a crowded Parisian square viewed from several stories above street level. The moment Pissarro captured on his canvas is not so much of fugitive light effects as it is of the street life, achieved through a deliberate casualness in the arrangement of figures. To accomplish this sense of spontaneity, Pissarro sometimes used photography to record the places he wished to paint, as did many of his fellow Impressionists. Indeed, the visual parallels between Impressionist paintings and photographs are striking. In *La Place du Théâtre Français,* these parallels include the arbitrary cutting off of figures at the edges of the painting and the curious flattening spatial effect produced by the high viewpoint.

BERTHE MORISOT Many Impressionist paintings depict scenes from resort areas on the seashore or along the Seine River, such as Argenteuil (FIG. 28-1), Bennencourt (FIG. 28-2A), Bougival, and Chatou (MAP 28-1). The railway line running to and from Saint-Lazare station connected Argenteuil to Paris, so transportation was not an obstacle. Parisians often would take the train out to these resort areas for a day of sailing, picnicking, and strolling

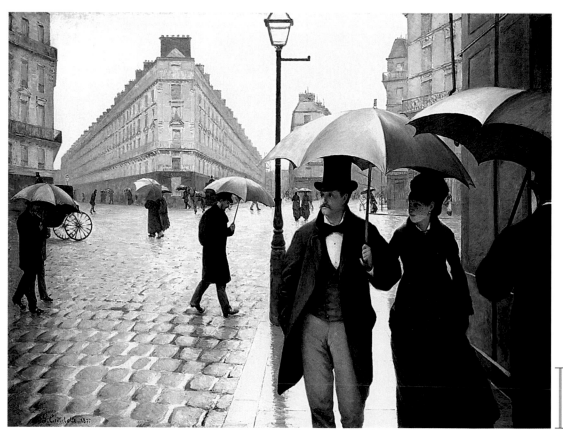

28-5 GUSTAVE CAILLEBOTTE, *Paris: A Rainy Day,* 1877. Oil on canvas, 6′ 9″ × 9′ 9″. Art Institute of Chicago, Chicago (Worcester Fund).

Although Caillebotte did not use Impressionistic broken brushstrokes, the seemingly randomly placed figures and the arbitrary cropping of the vista suggest the transitory nature of modern life.

1 ft.

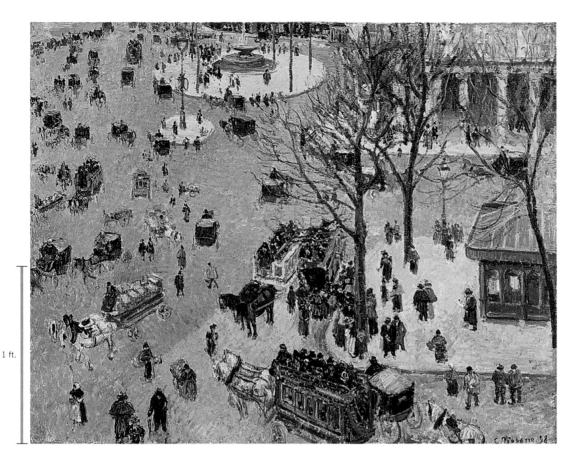

28-6 CAMILLE PISSARRO, *La Place du Théâtre Français*, 1898. Oil on canvas, 2′ 4½″ × 3′ ½″. Los Angeles County Museum of Art, Los Angeles (Mr. and Mrs. George Gard De Sylva Collection).

This Impressionist view of a busy Paris square seen from several stories above street level has much in common with photographs, especially the flattening spatial effect of the high viewpoint.

along the Seine. BERTHE MORISOT (1841–1895), Édouard Manet's sister-in-law, regularly exhibited with the Impressionists. Most of her paintings focus on domestic subjects, the one realm of Parisian life where society allowed an upper-class woman such as Morisot free access, but she also produced many outdoor scenes, including *Villa at the Seaside* (FIG. **28-7**), painted in 1874, and *Summer's Day* (FIG. **28-7A**), in 1879. The subject and style of both works correlate well with Impressionist concerns.

The setting of *Villa at the Seaside* is the shaded veranda of a summer hotel at a fashionable seashore resort. A woman elegantly but not ostentatiously dressed sits gazing out across the railing to a sunlit beach. Her child, its discarded toy boat a splash of red, gazes at the passing sails on the placid sea. The mood is of relaxed leisure. Morisot used the

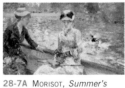

28-7A MORISOT, *Summer's Day*, 1879. ◼◀

open brushwork and the *plein air* lighting characteristic of Impressionism. Sketchy brushstrokes record her quick perceptions. Nowhere did Morisot linger on contours or enclosed details. She presented the scene in a slightly filmy, soft focus conveying a feeling of airiness. The composition also recalls the work of other Impressionists. The figures fall informally into place, as someone who shared their intimate space would perceive them. Morisot was both immensely ambitious and talented, as her ability to catch the pictorial moment demonstrates. She escaped the hostile criticism directed at most of the other Impressionists. People praised her work for its sensibility, grace, and delicacy.

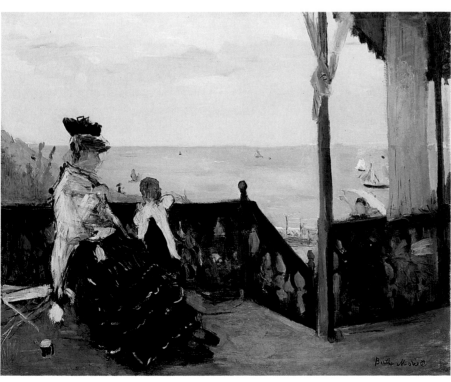

28-7 BERTHE MORISOT, *Villa at the Seaside*, 1874. Oil on canvas, 1′ 7¾″ × 2′ ⅛″. Norton Simon Art Foundation, Los Angeles. ◼◀

In this informal view of a woman and child enjoying their leisure time at a fashionable seashore resort, Morisot used swift, sketchy strokes of light colors to convey a feeling of airiness.

Renoir on the Art of Painting

Many 19th-century artists were concerned with the theoretical basis of picturemaking. One of the most cogent statements on this subject is Pierre-Auguste Renoir's concise summary of how he, as an Impressionist, painted pictures and what he hoped to achieve as an artist.

I arrange my subject as I want it, then I go ahead and paint it, like a child. I want a red to be sonorous, to sound like a bell; if it doesn't turn out that way, I add more reds and other colors until I get it. I am no cleverer than that. I have no rules and no methods; . . . I have no secrets. I look at a nude; there are myriads of tiny tints. I must find the ones that will make the flesh on my canvas live and quiver. . . . [I]f they could explain a picture, it wouldn't be art. Shall I tell you what I think are the two qualities of art? It must be indescribable and it must be inimitable. . . . The work of art must seize upon you, wrap you up in itself, carry you away. It is the means by which the artist conveys his passions. . . . I want people to feel that neither the setting nor the figures are dull and lifeless.*

There is certainly nothing dull or lifeless about *Le Moulin de la Galette* (FIG. 28-8), in which Renoir depicted throngs of people gathered in a popular Parisian dance hall. Some crowd the tables and chatter, while others dance energetically. So lively is the atmosphere the viewer can virtually hear the sounds of music, laughter, and tinkling glasses. The painter dappled the whole scene with sunlight and shade, artfully blurred into the figures to produce precisely the effect of floating and fleeting light the Impressionists so cultivated. Renoir's casual unposed placement of the figures and the suggested continuity of space, spreading in all directions and only accidentally limited by the frame, position the viewer as a participant rather than as an outsider. Whereas classical art sought to express universal and timeless qualities, Impressionism attempted to depict just the opposite—the incidental, momentary, and passing aspects of reality.

*Quoted in Eric Protter, ed., *Painters on Painting* (New York: Grosset & Dunlap, 1971), 145.

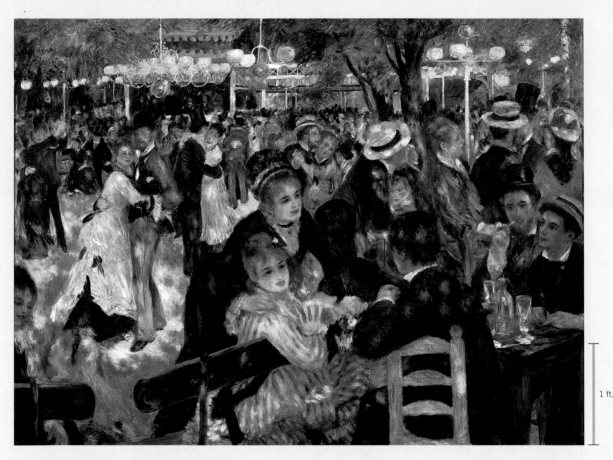

28-8 PIERRE-AUGUSTE RENOIR, *Le Moulin de la Galette*, 1876. Oil on canvas, 4′ 3″ × 5′ 8″. Musée d'Orsay, Paris. ◼◀

Renoir's painting of this popular Parisian dance hall is dappled by sunlight and shade, artfully blurred into the figures to produce the effect of floating and fleeting light the Impressionists cultivated.

1 ft.

PIERRE-AUGUSTE RENOIR Ample time for leisure activities was another facet of the new, industrialized Paris, and scenes of dining and dancing, café-concerts, opera, ballet, and other forms of urban recreation became mainstays of Impressionism. Although seemingly unrelated, industrialization facilitated these pursuits. With the advent of set working hours, people's schedules became more regimented, enabling them to plan their favorite pastimes. One Impressionist who turned repeatedly to Parisian nightlife for the subjects of his canvases was PIERRE-AUGUSTE RENOIR (1841–1919), who in 1874 painted *en plein air* alongside Monet and Manet at Argenteuil (FIG. 28-1) and was also one of the most eloquent writers on the aims of Impressionism (see "Renoir on the Art of Painting," above). His *Le Moulin de la Galette* (FIG. 28-8) of 1876 is a superb example of this Impressionist genre.

Art 102 H

Professor
Lauren Evans

Name: Ruchi Tyagi

Curatorial PowerPoint Presentation

40/40 points

Create a virtual exhibition in a museum in Southern California. Choose a contemporary theme; this could be a social or political current event, (an example would be the drought in California). Utilizing the work we have studied in class and contemporary artists you have researched to curate your exhibition. The artwork you chose should span work we have studied throughout the course.

You will want to do some research on the museum/gallery you choose to know the size and feel of the space you will be working with. Do not just pick an entire museum but a particular gallery/space within that museum. You want to make sure you select the correct amount of work for your exhibition and how the work will be displayed. Too much or too little work can become an issue and make for a confusing exhibition.

Notes: Inspiring and brilliant. Such an important topic, Climate Change and fantastic way to begin the exhibition with the quote from Ashworth, and wonderful beginning with The Art of Climate Modeling by the Los Alamos National Laboratory. I was so impressed with your inclusion of Monet and the research about his use of color and climate change. Also the inclusion of Dali's work added a fantastic interpretation. Your addition of your contemporary artist such as Elizabeth Kyle and Duga C I thought was brilliant, ending with hope is a good thing and when you think about it allows the viewer to take it in. For those who do not believe in climate change (as we discussed in class) allowing a hopeful take opens the door for greater communication and perhaps ones defenses will go down and they may take in the message. Truly brilliant and I do hope you continue to communicate/teach/present with art in this manner.

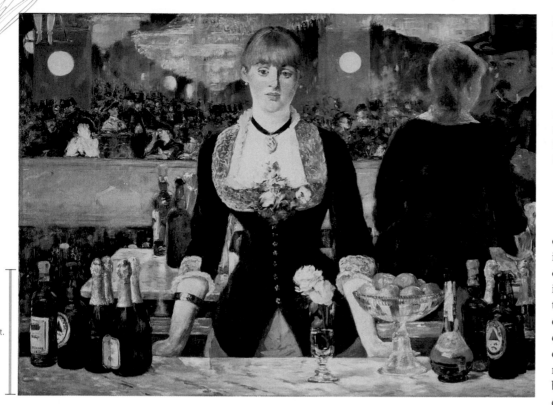

28-9 ÉDOUARD MANET, *A Bar at the Folies-Bergère*, 1882. Oil on canvas, 3′ 1″ × 4′ 3″. Courtauld Institute of Art Gallery, London. ◼◀

In this painting set in a Parisian café, Manet called attention to the canvas surface by creating spatial inconsistencies, such as the relationship between the barmaid and her apparent reflection in a mirror.

1 ft.

ÉDOUARD MANET

The immensely versatile Manet, whose career bridged Realism (FIGS. 27-32 and 27-33) and Impressionism (FIG. 28-1), also depicted Parisian nightlife. One of his later works in the Impressionist mode is *A Bar at the Folies-Bergère* (FIG. **28-9**), painted in 1882. The Folies-Bergère was a popular café with music-hall performances, one of the fashionable gathering places for Parisian revelers that many Impressionists frequented. In Manet's painting, a barmaid, centrally placed, looks out from the canvas but seems disinterested or lost in thought, divorced from her patrons as well as from the viewer. Manet blurred and roughly applied the brushstrokes, particularly those in the background, and the effects

of modeling and perspective are minimal. This painting method further calls attention to the surface by forcing the viewer to scrutinize the work to make sense of the scene. But it is difficult to do so, because visual discrepancies immediately emerge. For example, what initially seems easily recognizable as a mirror behind the barmaid creates confusion throughout the rest of the painting. Is the woman on the right the barmaid's reflection? If both figures are the same person, it is impossible to reconcile the spatial relationship between the barmaid, the mirror, the bar's frontal horizontality, and the barmaid's seemingly displaced reflection. These visual contradictions reveal Manet's insistence on calling attention to the pictorial structure of his painting, in keeping with his modernist interest in examining the basic premises of the medium.

EDGAR DEGAS

Impressionists also depicted more-formal leisure activities. The fascination EDGAR DEGAS (1834–1917) had with patterns of motion brought him to the Paris Opéra (FIG. 27-45) and its ballet school. There, his keen observational power took in the formalized movements of classical ballet, one of his favorite subjects. In *The Rehearsal* (FIG. **28-10**), Degas used several devices to bring the observer into the pictorial space. The frame cuts off the spiral stair, the windows in the background, and the group of figures in the right foreground. The figures are not at the center of a

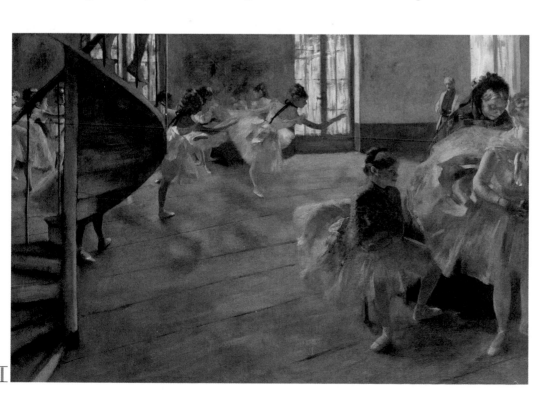

1 in.

28-10 EDGAR DEGAS, *The Rehearsal*, 1874. Oil on canvas, 1′ 11″ × 2′ 9″. Glasgow Art Galleries and Museum, Glasgow (Burrell Collection). ◼◀

The arbitrarily cut-off figures of dancers, the patterns of light splotches, and the blurry images reveal Degas's interest in reproducing fleeting moments, as well as his fascination with photography.

Japonisme

Despite Europe's and America's extensive colonization during the 19th century, Japan avoided Western intrusion until 1853–1854, when Commodore Matthew Perry (1794–1858) and American naval forces exacted trading and diplomatic privileges from Japan. From the increased contact, Westerners became familiar with Japanese culture. So intrigued were the French with Japanese art and culture that they coined a specific term—*Japonisme*—to describe the Japanese aesthetic, which, because of both its beauty and exoticism, greatly appealed to the fashionable segment of Parisian society. In 1867 at the Exposition Universelle in Paris, the Japanese pavilion garnered more attention than any other. Soon, Japanese kimonos, fans, lacquer cabinets, tea caddies, folding screens, tea services, and jewelry flooded Paris. Japanese-themed novels and travel books were immensely popular as well. As demand for Japanese merchandise grew in the West, the Japanese began to develop import-export businesses, and the foreign currency flowing into Japan helped to finance much of its industrialization.

Artists in particular were great admirers of Japanese art. Among those the Japanese aesthetic influenced were the Impressionists and Post-Impressionists, especially Édouard Manet, Edgar Degas, Mary Cassatt, James Abbott McNeill Whistler, Henri de Toulouse-Lautrec, Paul Gauguin, and Vincent van Gogh. Indeed, van Gogh collected and copied Japanese prints (FIG. 28-16B; compare FIG. 34-1). For the most part, the Japanese presentation

of space in woodblock prints (see "Japanese Woodblock Prints," Chapter 34, page 1016), which were more readily available in the West than any other Asian art form, intrigued these artists. Because of the simplicity of the woodblock printing process, the Japanese prints feature broad areas of flat color with a limited amount of modulation or gradation. This flatness interested modernist painters, who sought ways to call attention to the picture surface. The right side of Degas's *The Tub* (FIG. 28-11), for example, has this two-dimensional quality. Degas, in fact, owned a print by Japanese artist Torii Kiyonaga depicting eight women at a bath in various poses and states of undress. That print inspired Degas's painting. A comparison between Degas's bather and a detail (FIG. 28-12) of a bather from another of Kiyonaga's prints is striking, although Degas did not closely copy any of the Japanese artist's figures. Instead, he absorbed the essence of Japanese compositional style and the distinctive angles employed in representing human figures, and he translated them into the Impressionist mode.

The decorative quality of Japanese images also appealed to the artists associated with the Arts and Crafts movement in England. Artists such as William Morris (FIG. 28-34) and Charles Rennie Mackinstosh (FIG. 28-35) found Japanese prints attractive because those artworks intersected nicely with two fundamental Arts and Crafts principles: art should be available to the masses, and functional objects should be artistically designed.

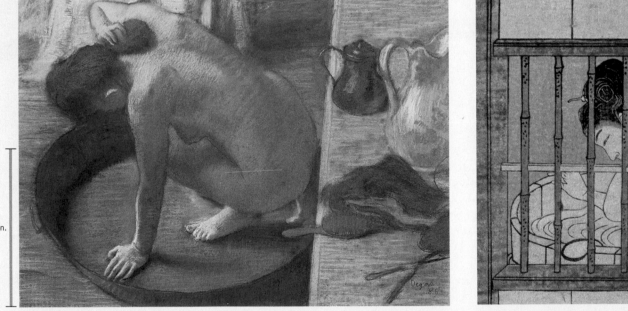

1 in.

28-11 EDGAR DEGAS, *The Tub*, 1886. Pastel, 1' 11½" × 2' 8⅜". Musée d'Orsay, Paris. ◼◀

1 in.

28-12 TORII KIYONAGA, detail of *Two Women at the Bath*, ca. 1780. Color woodblock, full print 10½" × 7½", detail 3¾" × 3½". Musée Guimet, Paris.

The Tub reveals the influence of Japanese prints, especially the sharp angles that artists such as Kiyonaga used in representing figures. Degas translated his Japanese model into the Impressionist mode.

classically balanced composition. Instead, Degas arranged them in a seemingly random manner. The prominent diagonals of the wall bases and floorboards lead the viewer's eye into and along the directional lines of the dancers. Finally, as is customary in Degas's ballet pictures, a large, off-center, empty space creates the illusion of a continuous floor connecting the observer with the pictured figures.

The often arbitrarily cut-off figures, the patterns of light splotches, and the blurriness of the images in this and other Degas works indicate the artist's interest in reproducing single moments. They also reveal his fascination with photography. Degas not only studied the photographs of others but regularly used a camera to make preliminary studies for his works, particularly photographing figures in interiors. Japanese woodblock prints (see "Japonisme," page 808) were another inspirational source for paintings such as *The Rehearsal*. The cunning spatial projections in Degas's paintings probably derived in part from Japanese prints, such as those by Suzuki Harunobu (FIG. 34-12). Japanese artists used diverging lines not only to organize the flat shapes of figures but also to direct the viewer's attention into the picture space. The Impressionists, acquainted with these woodblocks as early as the 1860s, greatly admired the spatial organization, familiar and intimate themes, and flat unmodeled color areas of the Japanese prints, and avidly incorporated these features into their own paintings.

THE TUB Although color and light were major components of the Impressionists' quest to capture fleeting sensations, these artists considered other formal elements as well. Degas, for example, became a master of line, so much so his works often differ significantly from those of Monet and Renoir. Degas specialized in studies of figures in rapid and informal action, recording the quick impression of arrested motion, as is evident in *The Rehearsal* (FIG. 28-10). He often employed lines to convey this sense of movement. In *The Tub* (FIG. **28-11**), inspired by a Japanese print similar to the one illustrated here (FIG. **28-12**) by Torii Kiyonaga (1752–1815), a young woman crouches in a washing tub. Degas outlined the major objects in the painting— the woman, tub, and pitchers—and covered all surfaces with linear hatch marks. He was able to achieve this leaner quality by using *pastels,* his favorite medium. With these dry sticks of powdered pigment, Degas drew directly on the paper, as one would with a piece of chalk, thus accounting for the linear basis of his work. Although the applied pastel is subject to smudging, the colors tend to retain their autonomy, so they appear fresh and bright.

The Tub also reveals how Degas's work, like that of the other Impressionists, continued the modernist exploration of the premises of painting by acknowledging the artwork's surface. Although the viewer clearly perceives the woman as a depiction of a three-dimensional form in space, the tabletop or shelf on the right of the image appears severely tilted, so much so it seems to parallel the picture plane. The two pitchers on the table complicate this visual conflict between the table's flatness and the illusion of the bathing woman's three-dimensional volume. The limited foreshortening of the pitchers and their shared edge, in conjunction with the rest of the image, create a visual perplexity for the viewer.

MARY CASSATT In the Salon of 1874, Degas admired a painting by a young American artist, Mary Cassatt (1844–1926), the daughter of a Philadelphia banker. Degas befriended and influ-

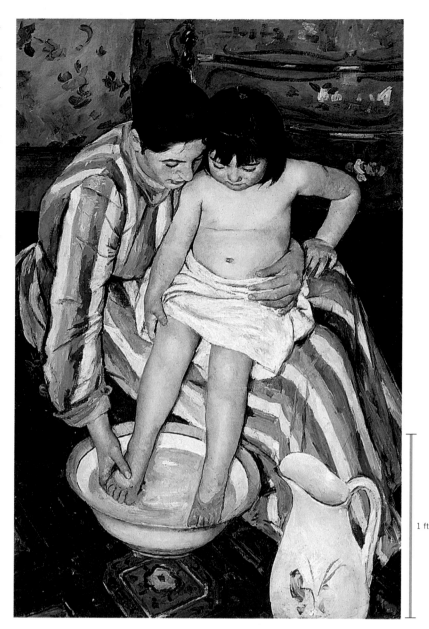

28-13 Mary Cassatt, *The Bath,* ca. 1892. Oil on canvas, 3′ 3″ × 2′ 2″. Art Institute of Chicago, Chicago (Robert A. Walker Fund). ◼◀

Cassatt's compositions owe much to Degas and Japanese prints, but her subjects differ from those of most Impressionist painters, in part because, as a woman, she could not frequent cafés.

enced Cassatt, who exhibited regularly with the Impressionists. She had trained as a painter before moving to Europe to study masterworks in France and Italy. As a woman, she could not easily frequent the cafés with her male artist friends, and she had the responsibility of caring for her aging parents, who had moved to Paris to join her. Because of these restrictions, Cassatt's subjects, like Morisot's (FIG. 28-7), were principally women and children, whom she presented with a combination of objectivity and genuine sentiment. Works such as *The Bath* (FIG. **28-13**) show the tender relationship between a mother and child. As in Degas's *The Tub,* the visual solidity of the mother and child contrasts with the flattened patterning of the wallpaper and rug. Cassatt's style in this work owed much to the compositional devices of Degas and of Japanese prints, but the painting's design has an originality and strength all its own.

Whistler on "Artistic Arrangements"

Underscoring the insistence by late-19th-century artists, both in Europe and America, that paintings are independent two-dimensional artworks and not windows opening onto the three-dimensional world, American-born James Abbott Mc-Neill Whistler, who produced his most famous works in London, called his paintings "arrangements" or "nocturnes." *Nocturne in Black and Gold* (FIG. 28-14) is a daring painting with gold flecks and splatters representing an exploded firework punctuating the darkness of the night sky. More interested in conveying the atmospheric effects than in providing details of the scene, Whistler emphasized creating a harmonious arrangement of shapes and colors on the rectangle of his canvas, an approach many 20th-century artists adopted. Whistler's works angered many 19th-century viewers, however. The British critic John Ruskin (1819–1900) responded to this painting by writing a scathing review accusing Whistler of "flinging a pot of paint in the public's face" with his style. In reply, Whistler sued Ruskin for libel. During the trial, Ruskin's attorney asked Whistler about the subject of *Nocturne*:

"What is your definition of a Nocturne?"

"It is an arrangement of line, form, and colour first; . . . Among my works are some night pieces; and I have chosen the word Nocturne because it generalizes and amplifies the whole set of them. . . . The nocturne in black and gold is a night piece and represents the fireworks at Cremorne [Gardens in London]."

"Not a view of Cremorne?"

"If it were a view of Cremorne, it would certainly bring about nothing but disappointment on the part of the beholders. It is an artistic arrangement."*

The court transcript notes the spectators in the courtroom laughed at that response, but Whistler won the case. However, his victory

28-14 JAMES ABBOTT MCNEILL WHISTLER, *Nocturne in Black and Gold (The Falling Rocket)*, ca. 1875. Oil on panel, 1′ 11⅝″ × 1′ 6½″. Detroit Institute of Arts, Detroit (gift of Dexter M. Ferry Jr.).

In this painting, Whistler displayed an Impressionist's interest in conveying the atmospheric effects of fireworks at night, but he also emphasized the abstract arrangement of shapes and colors.

1 in.

had sadly ironic consequences for him. The judge in the case, showing where his—and the public's—sympathies lay, awarded the artist only one farthing (less than a penny) in damages and required him to pay all of the court costs, which ruined him financially.

*Quoted in Charles Harrison, Paul Wood, and Jason Gaiger, *Art in Theory, 1815–1900* (Oxford: Blackwell, 1998), 835–836.

JAMES WHISTLER Another American expatriate artist in Europe was JAMES ABBOTT MCNEILL WHISTLER (1834–1903), who spent time in Paris before settling finally in London. He met many of the French Impressionists, and his art, for example, *Nocturne in Black and Gold,* or *The Falling Rocket* (FIG. 28-14), is a unique combination of some of their concerns and his own (see "Whistler on 'Artistic Arrangements,'" above). Whistler shared the Impressionists' interests in the subject of contemporary life and the sensations color produces on the eye. To these influences

he added his own desire to create harmonies paralleling those achieved in music.

Nature contains the elements, in color and form, of all pictures, as the keyboard contains the notes of all music. But the artist is born to pick, and choose, and group with science, these elements, that the result may be beautiful—as the musician gathers his notes, and forms his chords, until he brings forth from chaos glorious harmony.[5]

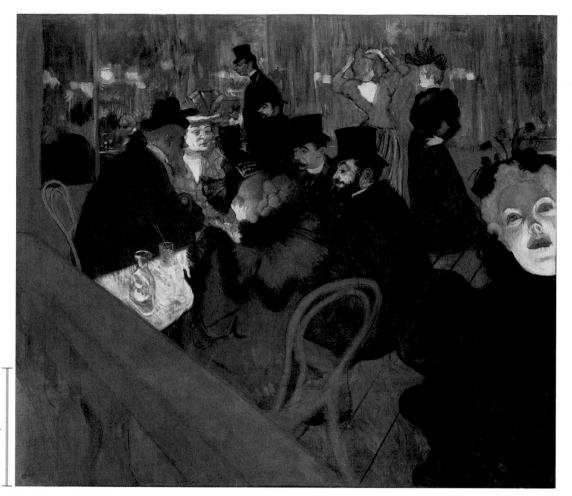

28-15 HENRI DE TOULOUSE-LAUTREC, *At the Moulin Rouge,* 1892–1895. Oil on canvas, 4′ × 4′ 7″. Art Institute of Chicago, Chicago (Helen Birch Bartlett Memorial Collection).

Degas, Japanese prints, and photography influenced this painting's oblique composition, but the glaring lighting, masklike faces, and dissonant colors are distinctly Toulouse-Lautrec's.

1 ft.

POST-IMPRESSIONISM

By 1886 most critics and a large segment of the public accepted the Impressionists as serious artists. Just when their images of contemporary life no longer seemed crude and unfinished, however, some of these painters and a group of younger followers came to feel the Impressionists were neglecting too many of the traditional elements of picturemaking in their attempts to capture momentary sensations of light and color on canvas. In a conversation with the influential art dealer Ambroise Vollard (1866–1939) in about 1883, Renoir commented: "I had wrung impressionism dry, and I finally came to the conclusion that I knew neither how to paint nor how to draw. In a word, impressionism was a blind alley, as far as I was concerned."[6] By the 1880s, some artists were more systematically examining the properties and the expressive qualities of line, pattern, form, and color. Among them were Dutch-born Vincent van Gogh and the French painter Paul Gauguin, who focused their artistic efforts on exploring the expressive capabilities of formal elements, and Georges Seurat and Paul Cézanne, also from France, who were more analytical in orientation. Because their art had its roots in Impressionist precepts and methods, but was not stylistically homogeneous, these artists and others, including Henri de Toulouse-Lautrec, became known as the *Post-Impressionists.*

HENRI DE TOULOUSE-LAUTREC Closest to the Impressionists in many ways was the French artist HENRI DE TOULOUSE-LAUTREC (1864–1901), who deeply admired Degas and shared the Impressionists' interest in capturing the sensibility of modern life. His work, however, has an added satirical edge to it and often borders on caricature. Genetic defects stunted his growth and partially crippled him, leading to his self-exile from the high society his ancient aristocratic name entitled him to enter. He became a denizen of the night world of Paris, consorting with a tawdry population of entertainers, prostitutes, and other social outcasts. He reveled in the energy of the city's music halls, such as the Moulin Rouge (FIG. **28-15**) and the Jardin de Paris (FIG. **28-15A**), cafés, and bordellos. *At the Moulin Rouge* reveals the influ-

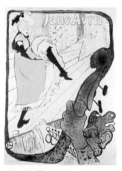

28-15A TOULOUSE-LAUTREC, *Jane Avril,* 1893.

ences of Degas, of Japanese prints, and of photography in the oblique and asymmetrical composition, the spatial diagonals, and the strong line patterns with added dissonant colors. But although Toulouse-Lautrec based everything he painted on firsthand observation and the scenes he captured were already familiar to viewers in the work of the Impressionists, he so emphasized or exaggerated each element that the tone is new. Compare, for instance, the mood of *At the Moulin Rouge* with the relaxed and casual atmosphere of Renoir's *Le Moulin de la Galette* (FIG. 28-8). Toulouse-Lautrec's scene is nightlife, with its glaring artificial light, brassy music, and assortment of corrupt, cruel, and masklike faces. (He included himself in the background—the diminutive man wearing a derby hat accompanying the very tall man, his cousin.) Such distortions by simplification of the figures and faces anticipated Expressionism (see Chapter 29), when artists' use of formal elements—for example, brighter colors and bolder lines than ever before—increased the effect of the images on observers.

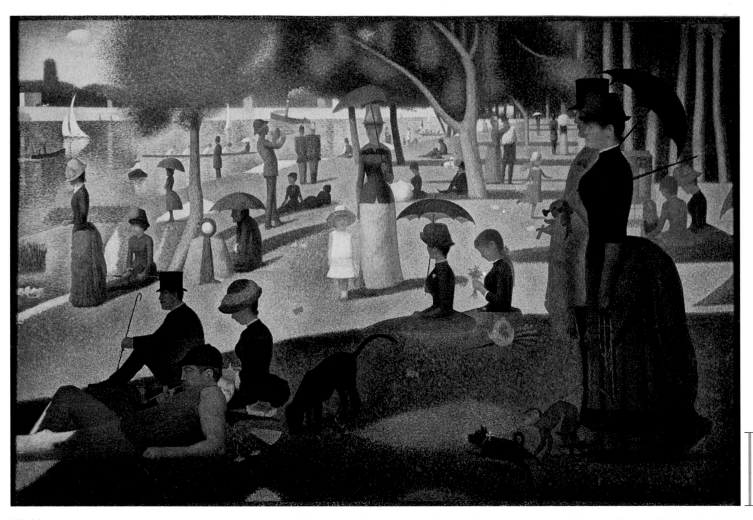

1 ft.

28-16 Georges Seurat, *A Sunday on La Grande Jatte,* 1884–1886. Oil on canvas, 6′ 9″ × 10′. Art Institute of Chicago, Chicago (Helen Birch Bartlett Memorial Collection, 1926). ◼◀

Seurat's color system—pointillism—involved dividing colors into their component parts and applying those colors to the canvas in tiny dots. The forms become comprehensible only from a distance.

GEORGES SEURAT The themes Georges Seurat (1859–1891) addressed in his paintings were also Impressionist subjects, but he depicted them in a resolutely intellectual way. He devised a disciplined and painstaking system of painting focused on color analysis. Seurat was less concerned with the recording of immediate color sensations than he was with their careful and systematic organization into a new kind of pictorial order. He disciplined the free and fluent play of color characterizing Impressionism into a calculated arrangement based on scientific color theory. Seurat's system, known as *pointillism* or *divisionism,* involved carefully observing color and separating it into its component parts (see "Pointillism and 19th-Century Color Theory," page 813). The artist then applies these pure component colors to the canvas in tiny dots (points) or daubs. Thus, the shapes, figures, and spaces in the image become comprehensible only from a distance, when the viewer's eyes blend the many pigment dots.

Seurat introduced pointillism to the French public at the eighth and last Impressionist exhibition in 1886, where he displayed *A Sunday on La Grande Jatte* (FIG. **28-16**). The subject of the painting is consistent with Impressionist recreational themes, and Seurat also shared the Impressionists' interest in analyzing light and color. But Seurat's rendition of Parisians at leisure is rigid and remote, unlike the spontaneous representations of Impressionism. Seurat's pointillism instead produced a carefully composed and painted image. By using meticulously calculated values, the painter carved out a deep rectangular space. He played on repeated motifs both to

create flat patterns and to suggest spatial depth. Reiterating the profile of the female form, the parasol, and the cylindrical forms of the figures, Seurat placed each in space to set up a rhythmic movement in depth as well as from side to side. Sunshine fills the picture, but the painter did not break the light into transient patches of color. Light, air, people, and landscape are formal elements in an abstract design in which line, color, value, and shape cohere in a precise and tightly controlled organization. Seurat's orchestration of the many forms across the monumental (almost 7 by 10 feet) canvas created a rhythmic cadence harmonizing the entire composition.

Seurat once stated: "They see poetry in what I have done. No, I apply my method, and that is all there is to it."[7] Despite this claim, Seurat's art is much more than a scientifically based system. *La Grande Jatte* reveals the painter's recognition of the tenuous and shifting social and class relationships at the time. La Grande Jatte (The Big Bowl) is an island in the Seine River near Asnières, one of late-19th-century Paris's rapidly growing industrial suburbs. Seurat's painting captures public life on a Sunday—a congregation of people from various classes, from the sleeveless worker lounging in the left foreground, to the middle-class man and woman seated next to him. Most of the people wear their Sunday best, making class distinctions less obvious.

VINCENT VAN GOGH In marked contrast to Seurat, Vincent van Gogh (1853–1890) explored the capabilities of colors

Pointillism and 19th-Century Color Theory

In the 19th century, advances in the sciences contributed to changing theories about color and how people perceive it. Many physicists and chemists immersed themselves in studying optical reception and the behavior of the human eye in response to light of differing wavelengths. They also investigated the psychological dimension of color. These new ideas about color and its perception provided a framework within which artists such as Georges Seurat (FIG. 28-16) worked. Although historians do not know which publications on color Seurat himself read, he no doubt relied on aspects of these evolving theories to develop pointillism.

Discussions of color often focus on *hue* (for example, red, yellow, and blue), but it is important to consider the other facets of color—*saturation* (the hue's brightness or dullness) and *value* (the hue's lightness or darkness). Most artists during the 19th century understood the concepts of *primary colors* (red, yellow, and blue), *secondary colors* (orange, purple, and green), and *complementary colors* (red and green, yellow and purple, blue and orange; see Introduction, page 7).

Chemist Michel-Eugène Chevreul (1786–1889) extended artists' understanding of color dynamics by formulating the law of *simultaneous contrasts* of colors. Chevreul asserted juxtaposed colors affect the eye's reception of each, making the two colors as dissimilar as possible, both in hue and value. For example, placing light green next to dark green has the effect of making the light green look even lighter and the dark green darker. Chevreul further provided an explanation of *successive contrasts*—the phenomenon of colored afterimages. When a person looks intently at a color (green, for example) and then shifts to a white area, the fatigued eye momentarily perceives the complementary color (red).

Charles Blanc (1813–1882), who coined the term *optical mixture* to describe the visual effect of juxtaposed complementary colors, asserted the smaller the areas of adjoining complementary colors, the greater the tendency for the eye to "mix" the colors, so that the viewer perceives a grayish or neutral tint. Seurat used this principle frequently in his paintings.

Also influential for Seurat was the work of physicist Ogden Rood (1831–1902), who published his ideas in *Modern Chromatics, with Applications to Art and Industry* in 1879. Expanding on the ideas of Chevreul and Blanc, Rood constructed an accurate and understandable diagram of contrasting colors. Further (and particularly significant to Seurat), Rood explored representing color gradation. He suggested artists could achieve gradation by placing small

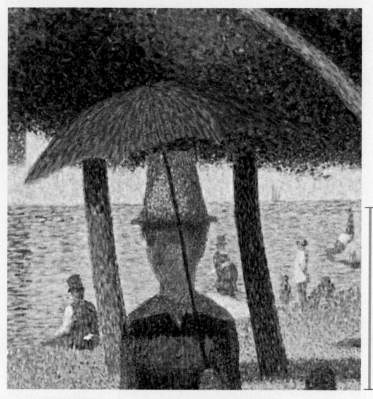

Detail of *A Sunday on La Grande Jatte* (FIG. 28-16).

1 ft.

dots or lines of color side by side, which he observed blended in the eye of the beholder when viewed from a distance.

The color experiments of Seurat and other late-19th-century artists were also part of a larger discourse about human vision and how people see and understand the world. The theories of physicist Ernst Mach (1838–1916) focused on the psychological experience of sensation. He believed humans perceive their environments in isolated units of sensation the brain then recomposes into a comprehensible world. Another scientist, Charles Henry (1859–1926), also pursued research into the psychological dimension of color—how colors affect people, and under what conditions. He went even further to explore the physiological effects of perception. Seurat's work, though characterized by a systematic and scientifically minded approach, also incorporated his concerns about the emotional tone of the images.

and distorted forms to express his emotions as he confronted nature. The son of a Dutch Protestant pastor, van Gogh believed he had a religious calling and did missionary work in the coal-mining area of Belgium. Repeated professional and personal failures brought him close to despair. Only after he turned to painting did he find a way to communicate his experiences. He completed his first major work, *The Potato Eaters* (FIG. 28-16A), when he was 32 years old. Five years later, considering himself a failure as an artist and an outcast not only from artistic circles but also from society at large, van Gogh fatally shot himself. He sold only one painting during his lifetime. Since his death, however, van Gogh's reputation and the

appreciation of his art have grown dramatically. Subsequent painters, especially the Fauves and German Expressionists (see Chapter 29), built on van Gogh's use of color and the expressiveness of his art. This kind of influence is an important factor in determining artistic significance, and it is no exaggeration to state that today van Gogh is one of the most revered artists in history.

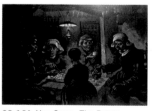

28-16A VAN GOGH, *The Potato Eaters*, 1885.

The Letters of Vincent van Gogh

Throughout his life, Vincent van Gogh wrote letters to his brother Theo van Gogh (1857–1891), a Parisian art dealer, on matters both mundane and philosophical. The letters are precious documents of the vicissitudes of the painter's life and reveal his emotional anguish. In many of the letters, van Gogh also forcefully stated his views about art, including his admiration for Japanese prints (FIG. 28-16B). In one letter, he told Theo: "In both my life and in my painting, I can very well do without God but I cannot, ill as I am, do without something which is greater than I, . . . the power to create."* For van Gogh, the power to create involved the expressive use of color. "Instead of trying to reproduce exactly what I have before my eyes, I use color more arbitrarily so as to express myself forcibly."† Color in painting, he argued, is "not locally true from the point of view of the delusive realist, but color suggesting some emotion of an ardent temperament."‡

Some of van Gogh's letters contain vivid descriptions of his paintings, which are invaluable to art historians in gauging his intentions and judging his success. For example, about *Night Café* (FIG. 28-17), he wrote:

> I have tried to express the terrible passions of humanity by means of red and green. The room is blood red and dark yellow with a green billiard table in the middle; there are four citron-yellow lamps with a glow of orange and green. Everywhere there is a clash and contrast of the most disparate reds and greens in the figures

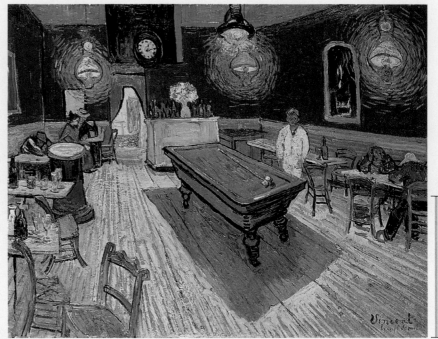

28-17 VINCENT VAN GOGH, *Night Café*, 1888. Oil on canvas, 2' 4½" × 3'. Yale University Art Gallery, New Haven (bequest of Stephen Carlton Clark).

In *Night Café*, van Gogh explored ways colors and distorted forms can express emotions. The thickness, shape, and direction of the brushstrokes create a tactile counterpart to the intense colors.

1 ft.

of little sleeping hooligans, in the empty, dreary room, in violet and blue. The blood-red and the yellow-green of the billiard table, for instance, contrast with the soft, tender Louis XV green of the counter, on which there is a pink nosegay. The white coat of the landlord, awake in a corner of that furnace, turns citron-yellow, or pale luminous green.§

*Vincent van Gogh to Theo van Gogh, September 3, 1888, in W. H. Auden, ed., *Van Gogh: A Self-Portrait. Letters Revealing His Life as a Painter* (New York: Dutton, 1963), 319.
†August 11, 1888. Ibid., 313.
‡September 8, 1888. Ibid., 321.
§September 8, 1888. Ibid., 320.

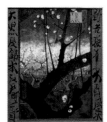

28-16B VAN GOGH, *Flowering Plum Tree*, 1887.

NIGHT CAFÉ Van Gogh moved to Paris in 1886, where he began to collect—and copy (FIG. 28-16B)—Japanese prints. In 1888, he relocated to Arles in southern France, where he painted *Night Café* (FIG. 28-17), one of his most important and innovative canvases. Although the subject is apparently benign, van Gogh invested it with a charged energy. As he stated in a letter to his brother Theo (see "The Letters of Vincent van Gogh," above), he wanted the painting to convey an oppressive atmosphere—" a place where one can ruin oneself, go mad, or commit a crime."§ The proprietor rises like a specter from the edge of the billiard table, which the painter depicted in such a steeply tilted perspective that it threatens to slide out of the painting into the viewer's space. Van Gogh communicated the "madness" of the place by selecting vivid hues whose juxtaposition augmented their intensity. His insistence

on the expressive values of color led him to develop a corresponding expressiveness in his paint application. The thickness, shape, and direction of his brushstrokes created a tactile counterpart to his intense color schemes. He moved the brush vehemently back and forth or at right angles, giving a textilelike effect, or squeezed dots or streaks onto his canvas from his paint tube. This bold, almost slapdash attack enhanced the intensity of his colors.

STARRY NIGHT Similarly illustrative of van Gogh's "expressionist" method is *Starry Night* (FIG. 28-18), which the artist painted in 1889, the year before his death. At this time, van Gogh was living at the asylum of Saint-Paul-de-Mausole in Saint-Rémy, near Arles, where he had committed himself. In *Starry Night*, the artist did not represent the sky's appearance. Rather, he communicated his feelings about the electrifying vastness of the universe, filled with whirling and exploding stars, with the earth and humanity huddling beneath it. The church nestled in the center of the village is, perhaps, van

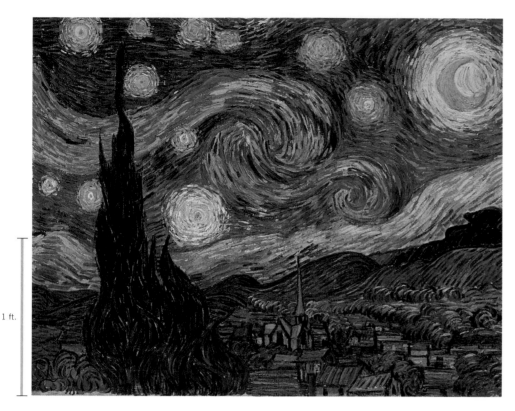

28-18 Vincent van Gogh, *Starry Night*, 1889. Oil on canvas, 2′ 5″ × 3′ ¼″. Museum of Modern Art, New York (acquired through the Lillie P. Bliss Bequest). ◼◀

In this late work, van Gogh painted the vast night sky filled with whirling and exploding stars, the earth huddled beneath it. The painting is an almost abstract pattern of expressive line, shape, and color.

lent brushstrokes, the color suggests a quiet but pervasive depression. A letter van Gogh wrote to his brother on July 16, 1888, reveals his contemplative state of mind:

> Perhaps death is not the hardest thing in a painter's life. . . . [L]ooking at the stars always makes me dream, as simply as I dream over the black dots representing towns and villages on a map. Why, I ask myself, shouldn't the shining dots of the sky be as accessible as the black dots on the map of France? Just as we take the train to get to Tarascon or Rouen, we take death to reach a star.[9]

PAUL GAUGUIN After painting as an amateur, PAUL GAUGUIN (1848–1903) took lessons with Camille Pissarro and then resigned from his prosperous brokerage business in 1883 to devote his time entirely to painting. As van Gogh did, Gauguin rejected objective representation in favor of subjective expression. He also broke with the Impressionists' studies of minutely contrasted hues because he believed color above all must be expressive. For Gauguin, the artist's power to determine the colors in a painting was a central element of creativity. However, whereas van Gogh's heavy, thick brushstrokes were an important component of his expressive style, Gauguin's color areas appear flatter, often visually dissolving into abstract patches or patterns.

In 1886, attracted by Brittany's unspoiled culture, its ancient Celtic folkways, and the still-medieval Catholic piety of its people, Gauguin moved to Pont-Aven. Although in the 1870s and 1880s, Brittany had been transformed into a profitable market economy, Gauguin still viewed the Bretons as "natural" men and women, perfectly at ease in their unspoiled peasant environment. At Pont-Aven, he painted *Vision after the Sermon* (FIG. **28-19**), also known as *Jacob Wrestling with the Angel*, a work in which he decisively rejected both Realism and Impressionism. The painting shows Breton women, wearing their starched white Sunday caps and black dresses, visualizing the

Gogh's attempt to express or reconcile his conflicted views about religion. Although the style of *Starry Night* suggests a very personal vision, this work does correspond in many ways to the view available to the painter from the window of his room in Saint-Paul-de-Mausole. The existence of cypress trees and the placement of the constellations have been confirmed as matching the view visible to van Gogh during his stay in the asylum. Still, the artist translated everything he saw into his unique vision. Given van Gogh's determination to "use color . . . to express [him]self forcibly," the dark, deep blue suffusing the entire painting cannot be overlooked. Together with the turbu-

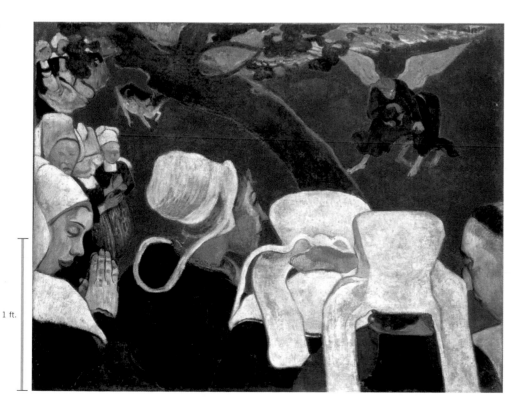

28-19 Paul Gauguin, *Vision after the Sermon* (*Jacob Wrestling with the Angel*), 1888. Oil on canvas, 2′ 4¾″ × 3′ ½″. National Gallery of Scotland, Edinburgh. ◼◀

Gauguin admired Japanese prints, stained glass, and cloisonné enamels. Their influences are evident in this painting of Breton women, in which firm outlines enclose large areas of unmodulated color.

Gauguin on *Where Do We Come From?*

Paul Gauguin's *Where Do We Come From? What Are We? Where Are We Going?* (FIG. 28-20), painted in Tahiti in 1897, was, in the artist's judgment, his most important work. It can be read as a summary of his artistic methods and of his views on life. The scene is a tropical landscape, populated with native women and children. Despite the setting, most of the canvas surface, other than the figures, consists of broad areas of flat color, which convey a lushness and intensity.

Two of Gauguin's letters to friends contain lengthy discussions of this work and shed important light on the artist's intentions and on the painting's meaning.

> Where are we going? Near to death an old woman.... What are we? Day to day existence.... Where do we come from? Source. Child. Life begins.... Behind a tree two sinister figures, cloaked in garments of sombre colour, introduce, near the tree of knowledge, their note of anguish caused by that very knowledge in contrast to some simple beings in a virgin nature, which might be paradise as conceived by humanity, who give themselves up to the happiness of living.*

> I wanted to kill myself. I went to hide in the mountains, where my corpse would have been eaten up by ants. I didn't have a revolver but I did have arsenic... Was the dose too large, or was it the fact of vomiting, which overcame the effects of the poison by getting rid of it? I know not..... Before I died I wanted to paint a large canvas that I had worked out in my head, and all month long I worked day and night at fever pitch. I can assure you it's nothing like a canvas by Puvis de Chavannes [FIG. 28-23], with studies from nature, then a preparatory cartoon, etc. No, it's all done without a model, feeling my way with the tip of the brush on a piece of sackcloth that is full of knots and rough patches; so it looks terribly unpolished. [Contrary to this assertion, Gauguin did make a detailed preliminary drawing, now in the Louvre, for *Where Do We Come From?* He is here altering the facts in order to establish a persona for himself as an inspired genius who created great works without recourse to traditional studio methods.] People will say it is slipshod, unfinished ... [but] I do believe that not only is this painting worth more than all the previous ones but also that I will never do a better one or another like it. I put all my energy into it before dying, such painful passion amid terrible circumstances ... and life burst from it.†

Where Do We Come From? is, therefore, a sobering, pessimistic image of the life cycle's inevitability.

*Letter to Charles Morice, March 1898. Translated by Belinda Thompson, *Gauguin by Himself* (Boston: Little, Brown, 1993), 270–271.
†Letter to Daniel de Monfreid, February 1898. Translated by Thompson, ibid., 257–258.

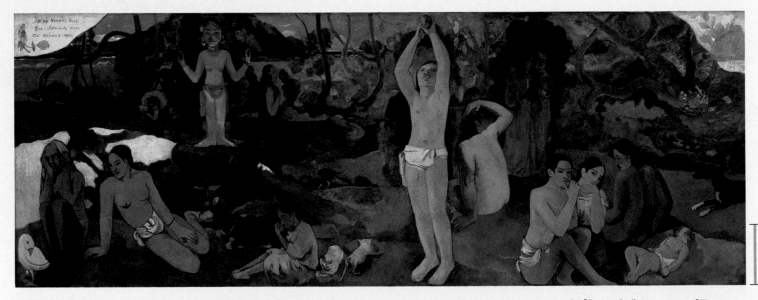

28-20 PAUL GAUGUIN, *Where Do We Come From? What Are We? Where Are We Going?* 1897. Oil on canvas, 4′ 6¾″ × 12′ 3″. Museum of Fine Arts, Boston (Tompkins Collection).

In search of a place far removed from European materialism, Gauguin moved to Tahiti, where he used native women and tropical colors to present a pessimistic view of the inevitability of the life cycle.

sermon they have just heard in church on Jacob's encounter with the Holy Spirit (Gen. 32:24–30). The women pray devoutly before the apparition, as they would have before the roadside crucifix shrines that were characteristic features of the Breton countryside. Gauguin departed from optical realism and composed the picture elements to focus the viewer's attention on the idea and intensify its message.

The images are not what the Impressionist eye would have seen and replicated but what memory would have recalled and imagination would have modified. Thus the artist twisted the perspective and allotted the space to emphasize the innocent faith of the unquestioning women, and he shrank Jacob and the angel, wrestling in a ring enclosed by a Breton stone fence, to the size of fighting cocks.

Wrestling matches were regular features at the entertainment held after high mass, so Gauguin's women are spectators at a contest that was, for them, a familiar part of their culture.

Gauguin did not unify the picture with a horizon perspective, light and shade, or naturalistic use of color. Instead, he abstracted the scene into a pattern. Pure unmodulated color fills flat planes and shapes bounded by firm line: white caps, black dresses, and the red field of combat. The shapes are angular, even harsh. The caps, the sharp fingers and profiles, and the hard contours suggest the austerity of peasant life and ritual. Gauguin admired Japanese prints, stained glass, and *cloisonné* metalwork (FIGS. 11-2 and 11-3). These art forms contributed to his daring experiment to transform traditional painting and Impressionism into abstract, expressive patterns of line, shape, and pure color. His revolutionary method found its first authoritative expression in *Vision after the Sermon*.

WHERE DO WE COME FROM? After a brief period of association with van Gogh in Arles in 1888, Gauguin, in his restless search for provocative subjects and for an economical place to live, settled in Tahiti (MAP 36-1). The South Pacific island attracted Gauguin because he believed it offered him a life far removed from materialistic Europe and an opportunity to reconnect with nature. Upon his arrival, he discovered that Tahiti, under French control since 1842, had been extensively colonized. Disappointed, Gauguin tried to maintain his vision of an untamed paradise by moving to the Tahitian countryside, where he expressed his fascination with primitive life in a series of canvases in which he often based the design, although indirectly, on native motifs. The tropical flora of the island inspired the colors he chose for these paintings—unusual harmonies of lilac, pink, and lemon.

Despite the allure of the South Pacific, Gauguin continued to struggle with life. His health suffered, and his art had a hostile reception. In 1897, worn down by these obstacles, Gauguin decided to take his own life, but not before painting a large canvas titled *Where Do We Come From? What Are We? Where Are We Going?* (FIG. 28-20), which he wrote about in letters to his friends (see "Gauguin on *Where Do We Come From?*" page 816). His attempt to commit suicide in Tahiti was unsuccessful, but Gauguin died a few years later, in 1903, in the Marquesas Islands, his artistic genius still unrecognized.

PAUL CÉZANNE Although a lifelong admirer of Delacroix, PAUL CÉZANNE (1839–1906) allied himself early in his career with the Impressionists, especially Pissarro (FIG. 28-6). He at first accepted their color theories and their faith in subjects chosen from everyday life, but his own studies of the Old Masters in the Louvre persuaded him Impressionism lacked form and structure. Cézanne declared he wanted to "make of Impressionism something solid and durable like the art of the museums."[10]

The basis of Cézanne's art was his unique way of studying nature in works such as *Mont Sainte-Victoire* (FIG. 28-21), one of many views he painted of this mountain near his home in Aix-en-Provence. His aim was not truth in appearance, especially not photographic truth, nor was it the "truth" of Impressionism. Rather, he sought a lasting structure behind the formless and fleeting visual information the eyes absorb. Instead of employing the Impressionists' random approach when he was face-to-face with nature, Cézanne developed a more analytical style. His goal was to order the lines, planes, and colors comprising nature. He constantly and painstakingly checked his painting against the part of the scene—he called it the "motif"—he was studying at the moment. In a March 1904 letter, Cézanne stated his goal as a painter: "[to do] Poussin over entirely from nature . . . in the open air, with color and light, instead of one of those works imagined in a studio, where

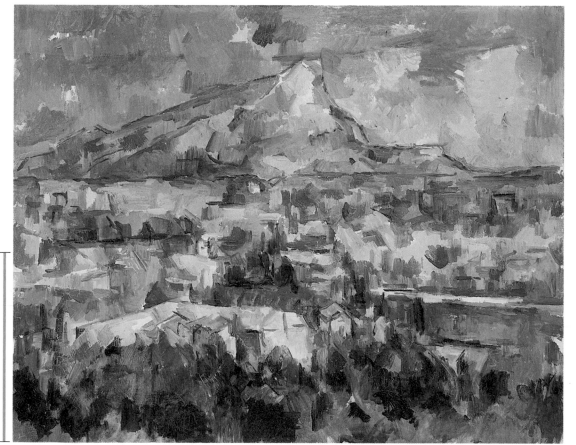

28-21 PAUL CÉZANNE, *Mont Sainte-Victoire*, 1902–1904. Oil on canvas, 2′ 3½″ × 2′ 11¼″. Philadelphia Museum of Art, Philadelphia (George W. Elkins Collection). ◼◀

In his landscapes, Cézanne replaced the transitory visual effects of changing atmospheric conditions—the Impressionists' focus—with careful analysis of the lines, planes, and colors of nature.

1 ft.

everything has the brown coloring of feeble daylight without reflections from the sky and sun."[11] He sought to achieve Poussin's effects of distance, depth, structure, and solidity not by using traditional perspective and chiaroscuro but by recording the color patterns he deduced from an optical analysis of nature.

With special care, Cézanne explored the properties of line, plane, and color and their interrelationships. He studied the effect of every kind of linear direction, the capacity of planes to create the sensation of depth, the intrinsic qualities of color, and the power of colors to modify the direction and depth of lines and planes. To create the illusion of three-dimensional form and space, Cézanne focused on carefully selecting colors. He understood the visual properties—hue, saturation, and value—of different colors vary (see "Color Theory," page 813). Cool colors tend to recede, whereas warm ones advance. By applying to the canvas small patches of juxtaposed colors, some advancing and some receding, Cézanne created volume and depth in his works. On occasion, the artist depicted objects chiefly in one hue and achieved convincing solidity by modulating the intensity (or saturation). At other times, he juxtaposed contrasting colors—for example, green, yellow, and red—of similar saturation (usually in the middle range rather than the highest intensity) to compose specific objects, such as fruit or bowls.

In *Mont Sainte-Victoire,* Cézanne replaced the transitory visual effects of changing atmospheric conditions, effects that preoccupied Monet, with a more concentrated, lengthier analysis of the colors in large lighted spaces. The main space stretches out behind and beyond the canvas plane and includes numerous small elements, such as roads, fields, houses, and the viaduct at the far right, each seen from a slightly different viewpoint. Above this shifting, receding perspective rises the largest mass of all, the mountain, with an effect—achieved by equally stressing background and foreground contours—of being simultaneously near and far away. This portrayal approximates the experience a person has when viewing the landscape forms piecemeal. The relative proportions of objects vary rather than being fixed by strict perspective, such as that normally found in a photograph. Cézanne immobilized the shifting colors of Impressionism into an array of clearly defined planes composing the objects and spaces in his scene. Describing his method in a letter to a fellow painter, he wrote:

> [T]reat nature by the cylinder, the sphere, the cone, everything in proper perspective so that each side of an object or a plane is directed towards a central point. Lines parallel to the horizon give breadth . . . Lines perpendicular to this horizon give depth. But nature for us men is more depth than surface, whence the need of introducing into our light vibrations, represented by reds and yellows, a sufficient amount of blue to give the impression of air.[12]

BASKET OF APPLES Still life was another good vehicle for Cézanne's experiments, as he could arrange a limited number of selected objects to provide a well-ordered point of departure. So analytical was Cézanne in preparing, observing, and painting still lifes (in contrast to the Impressionist emphasis on spontaneity) that he had to abandon using real fruit and flowers because they tended to rot. In *Basket of Apples* (FIG. **28-22**), the objects have lost something of their individual character as bottles and fruit and have almost become cylinders and spheres. Cézanne captured the solidity of each object by juxtaposing color patches. His interest in the study of volume and solidity is evident from the disjunctures in the painting—the table edges are discontinuous, and various objects seem to be depicted from different vantage points. In his zeal to understand three-dimensionality and to convey the placement of forms relative to the space around them, Cézanne explored his still-life arrangements from different viewpoints. This resulted in paintings that, though conceptually coherent, do not appear optically realistic. Cézanne created what might be called, paradoxically, an architecture of color.

In keeping with the modernist concern with the integrity of the painting surface, Cézanne's methods never allow the viewer to disregard the actual two-dimensionality of the picture plane.

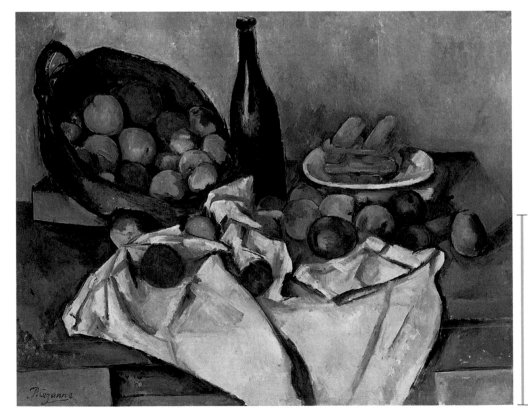

28-22 PAUL CÉZANNE, *Basket of Apples,* ca. 1895. Oil on canvas, 2' $\frac{3}{8}$" × 2' 7". Art Institute of Chicago, Chicago (Helen Birch Bartlett Memorial Collection, 1926). ◼◀

Cézanne's still lifes reveal his analytical approach to painting. He captured the solidity of bottles and fruit by juxtaposing color patches, but the resulting abstract shapes are not optically realistic.

1 ft.

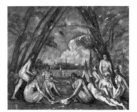

In this manner, Cézanne achieved a remarkable feat—presenting the viewer with two-dimensional and three-dimensional images simultaneously. His late works, such as his unfinished *The Large Bathers* (FIG. **28-22A**), profoundly influenced the development of Cubism in the early 20th century (see Chapter 29).

SYMBOLISM

The Impressionists and Post-Impressionists believed their emotions and sensations were important elements for interpreting nature, but the depiction of nature remained a primary focus of their efforts. By the end of the 19th century, the representation of nature became completely subjective. Artists no longer sought to imitate nature but created free interpretations of it, concerned solely with expressing their individual spirit. They rejected the optical world as observed in favor of a fantasy world, of forms they conjured in their free imagination, with or without reference to things conventionally seen. Color, line, and shape, divorced from conformity to the optical image, became symbols of personal emotions in response to the world. Deliberately choosing to stand outside of convention and tradition, artists spoke in signs and symbols, as if they were prophets.

Many of the artists following this path adopted an approach to subject and form that associated them with a general European movement called *Symbolism*. Symbolists, whether painters or writers, disdained Realism as trivial. The task of Symbolist artists, both visual and verbal, was not to see things but to see through them to a significance and reality far deeper than what superficial appearance revealed. In this function, as the poet Arthur Rimbaud (1854–1891) insisted, artists became beings of extraordinary insight. (One group of Symbolist painters called itself the *Nabis,* the Hebrew word for "prophet.") Rimbaud, whose poems had great influence on the artistic community, went so far as to say, in his *Letter from a Seer* (1871), that to achieve the seer's insight, artists must become deranged. In effect, they must systematically unhinge and confuse the everyday faculties of sense and reason, which served only to blur artistic vision. The artists' mystical vision must convert the objects of the commonsense world into symbols of a reality beyond that world and, ultimately, a reality from within the individual. Elements of Symbolism appeared in the works of van Gogh and Gauguin, but their art differed from mainstream Symbolism in their insistence on showing unseen powers as linked to a physical reality, instead of attempting to depict an alternate, wholly interior life.

The extreme subjectivism of the Symbolists led them to cultivate all the resources of fantasy and imagination, no matter how deeply buried or obscure. Moreover, they urged artists to stand against the vulgar materialism and conventional mores of industrial and middle-class society. Above all, the Symbolists wished to purge literature and art of anything utilitarian, to cultivate an exquisite aesthetic sensitivity. The subjects of the Symbolists, conditioned by this reverent attitude toward art and exaggerated aesthetic sensation, became increasingly esoteric and exotic, mysterious, visionary, dreamlike, and fantastic. Perhaps not coincidentally, contemporary with the Symbolists, Sigmund Freud (1856–1939), the founder of psychoanalysis, began the age of psychiatry with his *Interpretation of Dreams* (1900), an introduction to the concept and the world of unconscious experience.

PIERRE PUVIS DE CHAVANNES Although he never formally identified himself with the Symbolists, the French painter PIERRE PUVIS DE CHAVANNES (1824–1898) became the "prophet" of those artists. Puvis rejected Realism and Impressionism and went his own way in the 19th century, serenely unaffected by these movements. He produced an ornamental and reflective art—a dramatic rejection of Realism's noisy everyday world. In *Sacred Grove* (FIG. **28-23**), which may have influenced Seurat's *Grande Jatte*

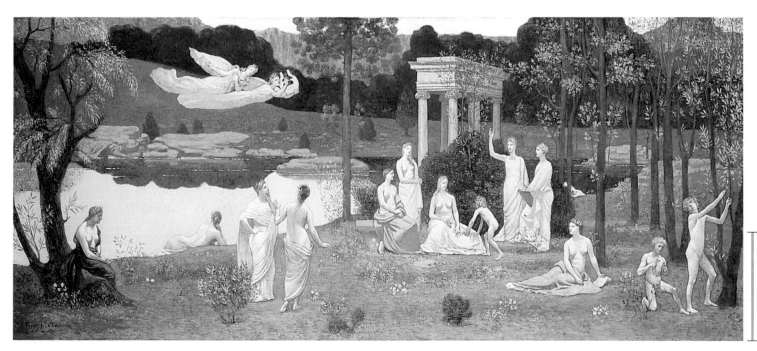

1 ft.

28-23 PIERRE PUVIS DE CHAVANNES, *Sacred Grove*, 1884. Oil on canvas, 2′ 11½″ × 6′ 10″. Art Institute of Chicago, Chicago (Potter Palmer Collection).

The Symbolists revered Puvis de Chavannes for his rejection of Realism. His statuesque figures in timeless poses inhabit a tranquil landscape, their gestures suggesting a symbolic ritual significance.

(FIG. 28-16), he deployed statuesque figures in a tranquil landscape with a classical shrine. Suspended in timeless poses, the figures' contours are simple and sharp, and their modeling is as shallow as *bas-relief*. The calm and still atmosphere suggests some consecrated place where all movements and gestures have a permanent ritual significance. The stillness and simplicity of the forms, the linear patterns their rhythmic contours create, and the suggestion of their symbolic weight constitute a type of anti-Realism. Puvis garnered support from a wide range of artists. The conservative French Academy and the government applauded his classicism. The Symbolists revered Puvis for his vindication of imagination and his independence from the capitalist world of materialism and the machine.

GUSTAVE MOREAU In keeping with Symbolist tenets, GUSTAVE MOREAU (1826–1898) gravitated toward subjects inspired by dreaming, which was as remote as possible from the everyday world. Moreau presented these subjects sumptuously, and his natural love of sensuous design led him to incorporate gorgeous color, intricate line, and richly detailed shape in all his paintings.

The Apparition (FIG. **28-24**), one of two versions of the same subject Moreau submitted to the Salon of 1876, treats a theme that fascinated him and many of his contemporaries—the *femme fatale* (fatal woman), the destructive temptress of men. The seductive heroine here is the biblical Salome (Mark 6:211–28), who danced enticingly before her stepfather, King Herod, and demanded in return the head of Saint John the Baptist (compare FIG. 21-8). In Moreau's representation of the story, Herod sits in the background, enthroned not in a Middle Eastern palace but in a classical columnar hall resembling a Roman triumphal arch. Salome is in the foreground, scantily clad in a gold- and gem-encrusted costume. She points to an apparition hovering in the air at the level of Herod's head. In a radiant circle of light is the halo-framed head of John the Baptist that Salome

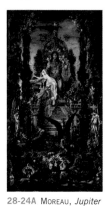

28-24A MOREAU, *Jupiter and Semele*, ca. 1875.

desired, dripping with blood but with eyes wide open. The combination of hallucinatory imagery, eroticism, precise drawing, rich color, and opulent setting is the hallmark of Moreau's highly original style (compare FIG. **28-24A**). His paintings foreshadow the work of the Surrealists in the next century (see Chapter 29).

ODILON REDON Like Moreau, fellow French Symbolist ODILON REDON (1840–1916) was a visionary. He had been aware of an intense inner world since childhood and later wrote of "imaginary things" haunting him. Redon adapted the Impressionist palette and stippling brushstroke for a very different purpose. In *The Cyclops* (FIG. **28-25**), Redon projected a figment of the imagination as if it were visible, coloring it whimsically with a rich profusion of fresh saturated hues that harmonized with the mood he felt fit the subject. The fetal head of the shy, simpering Polyphemus, with its single huge loving eye, rises balloonlike above the sleeping Galatea. The image born of the dreaming world and the color

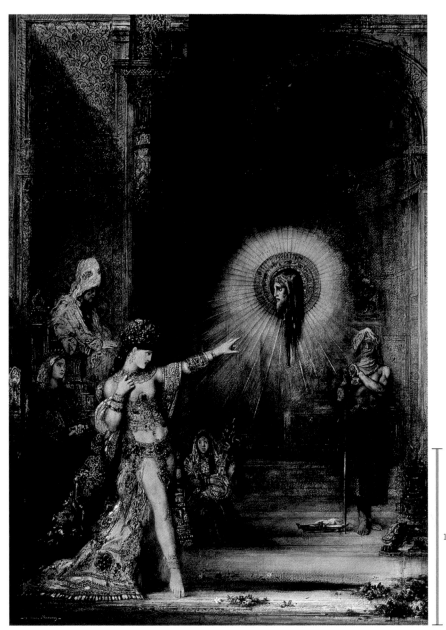

28-24 GUSTAVE MOREAU, *The Apparition*, 1874–1876. Watercolor on paper, 3′ 5¾″ × 2′ 4⅜″. Musée du Louvre, Paris.

Moreau's painting of Salome, a biblical femme fatale, combines hallucinatory imagery, eroticism, precise drawing, rich color, and an opulent setting—hallmarks of Moreau's Symbolist style.

1 ft.

analyzed and disassociated from the waking world come together here at the artist's will. The contrast with Raphael's representation of the same subject (FIG. 22-11) could hardly be more striking. As Redon himself observed: "All my originality consists . . . in making unreal creatures live humanly by putting, as much as possible, the logic of the visible at the service of the invisible."[13]

HENRI ROUSSEAU The imagination of HENRI ROUSSEAU (1844–1910) engaged a different but equally powerful world of personal fantasy. Gauguin had journeyed to the South Seas in search of primitive innocence. Rousseau was a "primitive" without leaving Paris—a self-taught amateur who turned to painting full-time only after his retirement from service in the French government. Nicknamed "Le Douanier" (The Customs Inspector), he first exhibited in the Salon of 1885 when he was 41. Derided by the critics, Rousseau turned to the Salon des Indépendants in 1886 and thereafter

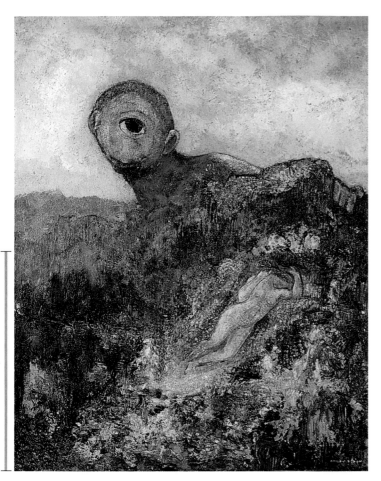

28-25 ODILON REDON, *The Cyclops,* 1898. Oil on canvas, 2′ 1″ × 1′ 8″. Kröller-Müller Foundation, Otterlo.

In *The Cyclops,* the Symbolist painter Odilon Redon projected a figment of the imagination as if it were visible, coloring it whimsically with a rich profusion of hues adapted from the Impressionist palette.

exhibited his works there almost every year until his death. Even in that more liberal venue, Rousseau still received almost universally unfavorable reviews because of his lack of formal training, imperfect perspective, doll-like figures, and settings resembling constructed theater sets more than natural landscapes. Rousseau compensated for his apparent visual, conceptual, and technical na-iveté with a natural talent for design and an imagination teeming with exotic images of mysterious tropical landscapes, which are the setting for two of his most famous works, *Sleeping Gypsy* (FIG. **28-26**) of 1897 and *The Dream* (FIG. **28-26A**), painted 13 years later. In the earlier painting, the recumbent figure occupies a desert

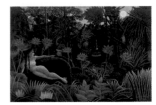

28-26A ROUSSEAU, *The Dream,* 1910.

world, silent and secret, and dreams beneath a pale, perfectly round moon. In the foreground, a lion resembling a stuffed, but somehow menacing, animal doll sniffs at the gypsy. A critical encounter impends—an encounter of the type that recalls the uneasiness of a person's vulnerable subconscious self during sleep—a subject of central importance to Rousseau's contemporary, Sigmund Freud. Rousseau's art of drama and fantasy has its own sophistication and, after the artist's death, influenced the development of Surrealism (see Chapter 29).

JAMES ENSOR Not all Symbolist artists were French. The leading Belgian painter of the late 19th century was JAMES ENSOR (1860–1949), the son of an expatriate Englishman and a Flemish mother, who spent most of his life in the seaside resort village of Ostend, far from the artistic centers of Europe. In 1883 he cofounded Les Vingts (The Twenty), a group of Belgian artists who staged unjuried exhibitions in Brussels modeled on the independent salons of Paris. A fervent nationalist, he left the group when it began to exhibit the work of foreign artists. In fact, Ensor's most monumental

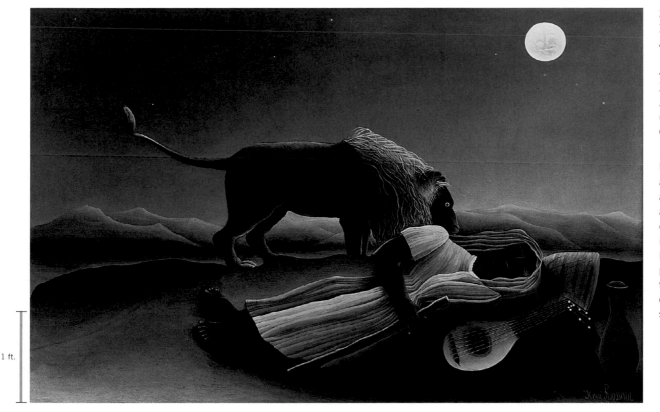

28-26 HENRI ROUSSEAU, *Sleeping Gypsy,* 1897. Oil on canvas, 4′ 3″ × 6′ 7″. **Museum of Modern Art, New York (gift of Mrs. Simon Guggenheim).**

In *Sleeping Gypsy,* Rousseau depicted a doll-like but menacing lion sniffing at a recumbent dreaming figure in a mysterious landscape. The painting suggests the vulnerable subconscious during sleep.

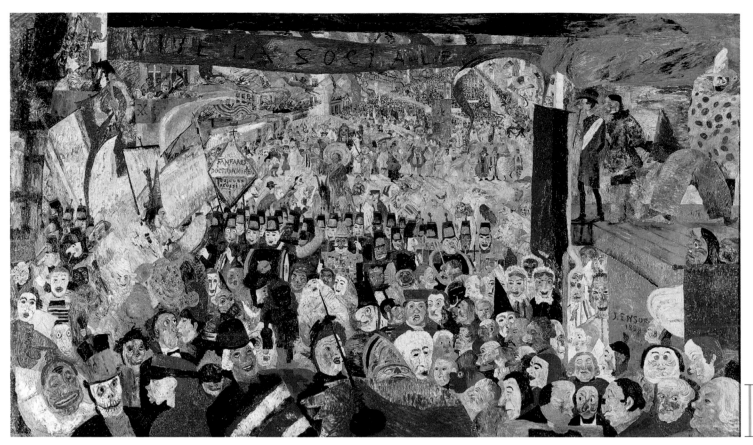

28-27 JAMES ENSOR, *Christ's Entry into Brussels in 1889,* 1888. Oil on canvas, 8′ 3½″ × 14′ 1½″. J. Paul Getty Museum, Los Angeles.

Ensor's gigantic canvas is an indictment of corrupt modern values. Christ enters Brussels on a donkey in 1889, ignored by the dense crowd of soldiers and citizens wearing grotesque, grimacing masks.

work, *Christ's Entry into Brussels in 1889* (FIG. **28-27**), is very likely a critical response to Georges Seurat's *La Grande Jatte* (FIG. 28-16), exhibited by Les Vingt in 1887.

Whereas Seurat's canvas celebrates the leisure activities of contented bourgeois Parisians, Ensor's even larger (14 feet long) painting is a socialist commentary on the decadence and alienation of urban life at the end of the 19th century. The giant canvas is the artist's pessimistic vision of how Christ would be greeted if he entered the Belgian capital in 1889. Christ is a small and insignificant figure on a donkey in the background of the painting, ignored by the dense crowd of soldiers and citizens wearing grotesque masks inspired by the papier-mâché carnival masks Ensor's family sold in their curio shop in Ostend. Some of the people carry banners and signs. One reads "Long Live Jesus, King of Brussels," another "Long Live Socialism." Complementing the ugly, grimacing masked faces of the anonymous crowd, which eloquently express Ensor's condemnation of the corrupt values of modern society, are the discordant combination of reds, blues, and greens and the coarse texture of the thickly applied oil pigment. As an indictment of the immorality of modern life, Ensor's canvas has few equals.

EDVARD MUNCH Also linked in spirit to the Symbolists were the English artist AUBREY BEARDSLEY (1872–1898; FIG. **28-27A**) and the Norwegian EDVARD MUNCH (1863–1944). Munch felt deeply the pain of human life. He believed humans were powerless before the great natural forces of death and love. The emotions associated with them—jealousy, loneliness, fear, desire, despair— became the theme of most of his art. Because Munch's goal was

to describe the conditions of "modern psychic life," as he put it, Realist and Impressionist techniques were inappropriate, focusing as they did on the tangible world. In the spirit of Symbolism, Munch used color, line, and figural distortion for expressive ends. Influenced by Gauguin, Munch produced both paintings and prints whose high emotional charge was a major source of inspiration for the German Expressionists in the early 20th century (see Chapter 29).

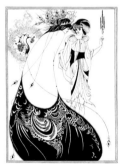

28-27A BEARDSLEY, *The Peacock Skirt,* 1894.

Munch's *The Scream* (FIG. **28-28**) exemplifies his style. The image—a man standing on a bridge or jetty in a landscape—comes from the real world, but Munch's treatment of the image departs significantly from visual reality. *The Scream* evokes a visceral, emotional response from the viewer because of the painter's dramatic presentation. The man in the foreground, simplified to almost skeletal form, emits a primal scream. The landscape's sweeping curvilinear lines reiterate the shapes of the man's mouth and head, almost like an echo, as the cry seems to reverberate through the setting. The fiery red and yellow stripes that give the sky an eerie glow also contribute to this work's resonance. Munch wrote a revealing epigraph to accompany the painting: "I stopped and leaned against the balustrade, almost dead with fatigue. Above the blue-black fjord hung the clouds, red as blood and tongues of fire. My friends had left me, and alone, trembling with anguish, I became aware of the vast, infinite cry of nature."[14] Appropriately, the original title of this work was *Despair.*

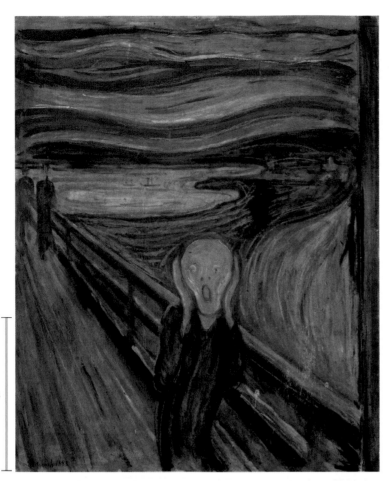

28-28 EDVARD MUNCH, *The Scream*, 1893. Tempera and pastels on cardboard, 2′ 11¾″ × 2′ 5″. National Gallery, Oslo.

Although grounded in the real world, *The Scream* departs significantly from visual reality. Munch used color, line, and figural distortion to evoke a strong emotional response from the viewer.

FIN-DE-SIÈCLE Historians have adopted the term *fin-de-siècle,* which literally means "end of the century," to describe the spirit of dissolution and anxiety that characterized European, and especially Austrian, culture of the late 1800s. This designation is not merely chronological but also refers to a certain sensibility. The increasingly large and prosperous middle classes aspired to the advantages the aristocracy traditionally enjoyed. They too strove to live "the good life," which evolved into a culture of decadence and indulgence. Characteristic of the fin-de-siècle period was an intense preoccupation with sexual drives, powers, and perversions. People at the end of the century also immersed themselves in an exploration of the unconscious. This culture was unrestrained and freewheeling, but the determination to enjoy life masked an anxiety prompted by significant political upheaval and an uncertain future. The country most closely associated with fin-de-siècle culture was Austria.

GUSTAV KLIMT The Viennese artist GUSTAV KLIMT (1863–1918) captured this period's flamboyance in his work but tempered it with unsettling undertones. In *The Kiss* (FIG. **28-29**), his best-known work, Klimt depicted a couple locked in an embrace. The setting is ambiguous, an indeterminate place apart from time and space. Moreover, all the viewer sees of the embracing couple is a small segment of each body—and virtually nothing of the man's face. The rest of the canvas dissolves into shimmering, extravagant flat patterning. This patterning has clear ties to Art Nouveau and to the Arts and Crafts movement (discussed later) and also evokes the conflict between two- and three-dimensionality intrinsic to the work of Degas and other modernists. In *The Kiss*, however, those patterns also signify gender contrasts—rectangles for the man's garment, circles for the woman's. Yet the patterning also unites the two lovers into a single formal entity, underscoring their erotic union.

GERTRUDE KÄSEBIER Photography, which during the 19th century most people regarded as the ultimate form of Realism, could also be manipulated by artists to produce effects more akin to painting than to factual records of contemporary life. After the first great breakthroughs (see Chapter 27), which bluntly showed what was before the eye, some photographers began to pursue

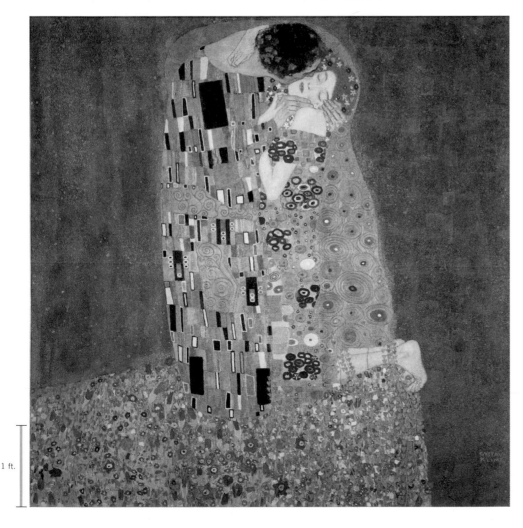

28-29 GUSTAV KLIMT, *The Kiss,* 1907–1908. Oil on canvas, 5′ 10¾″ × 5′ 10¾″. Österreichische Galerie Belvedere, Vienna. ◼◀

In this opulent Viennese fin-de-siècle painting, Klimt revealed only a small segment of each lover's body. The rest of his painting dissolves into shimmering, extravagant flat patterning.

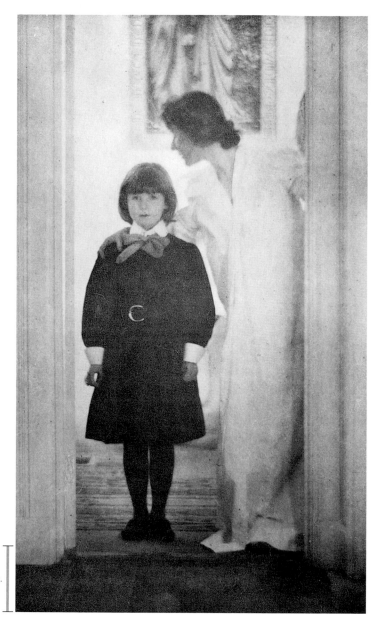

1 ft.

28-30 GERTRUDE KÄSEBIER, *Blessed Art Thou among Women,* 1899. Platinum print on Japanese tissue, 9⅜″ × 5½″. Museum of Modern Art, New York (gift of Mrs. Hermine M. Turner).

Symbolist Käsebier injected a sense of the spiritual and the divine into scenes from everyday life. The deliberately soft focus of this photograph invests the scene with an aura of otherworldly peace.

new ways of using the medium as a vehicle of artistic expression. A leading practitioner of what might be called the pictorial style in photography was the American GERTRUDE KÄSEBIER (1852–1934), who took up the camera in 1897 after raising a family and working as a portrait painter. She soon became famous for photographs with Symbolist themes, such as *Blessed Art Thou among Women* (FIG. **28-30**). The title repeats the phrase the angel Gabriel used to announce to the Virgin Mary that she will be the mother of Jesus. In the context of Käsebier's photography, the words suggest a parallel between the biblical Mother of God and the modern mother in the image, who both protects and sends forth her daughter. The white setting and the mother's pale gown shimmer in soft focus behind the serious girl, who wears darker tones and whom the photographer captured with sharper focus. Käsebier deliberately combined an out-of-focus background with a sharp or almost-sharp foreground in order to achieve an expressive effect by blurring the

entire image slightly. In *Blessed Art Thou among Women,* the soft focus invests the whole scene with an aura of otherworldly peace. The photograph showcases Käsebier's ability to inject a sense of the spiritual and the divine into scenes from everyday life.

SCULPTURE

The three-dimensional art of sculpture could not capture the optical sensations many painters favored in the later 19th century. Its very nature—its tangibility and solidity—suggests permanence. Consequently, the sculptors of this period pursued artistic goals markedly different from those of contemporaneous painters and photographers.

JEAN-BAPTISTE CARPEAUX In France, JEAN-BAPTISTE CARPEAUX (1827–1875) combined an interest in Realism with a love of ancient, Renaissance, and Baroque sculpture. He based his group *Ugolino and His Children* (FIG. **28-31**) on a passage in Dante's *Inferno* (33.58–75) in which Count Ugolino and his four sons starve to death while shut up in a tower. In Hell, Ugolino relates to Dante how, in a moment of extreme despair, he bit both his hands in grief. His children, thinking he did it because of his hunger, offered him

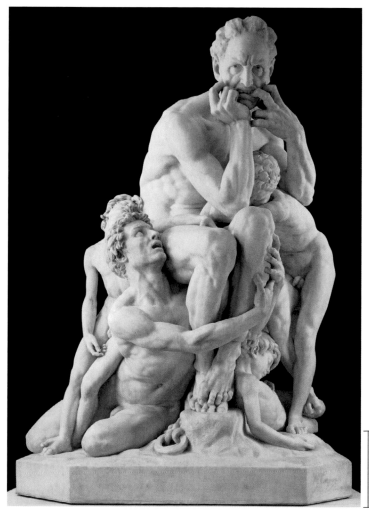

1 ft.

28-31 JEAN-BAPTISTE CARPEAUX, *Ugolino and His Children,* 1865–1867. Marble, 6′ 5″ high. Metropolitan Museum of Art, New York (Josephine Bay Paul and C. Michael Paul Foundation, Inc., and the Charles Ulrich and Josephine Bay Foundation, Inc., gifts, 1967).

As in Dante's *Inferno,* Carpeaux represented Ugolino biting his hands in despair as he and his sons await death by starvation. The twisted forms suggest the self-devouring torment of frustration.

Rodin on Movement in Art and Photography

Photography had a profound effect on 19th-century art, and many artists used photographs as an aid in capturing "reality" on canvas or in stone. Eadweard Muybridge's photographs of a galloping horse (FIG. 27-54), for example, definitively established that at certain times all four hooves of the animal are in the air. But not all artists believed photography was "true to life." The sculptor Auguste Rodin (FIGS. 28-32, 28-32A, and 28-33) was one of the doubters.

I have always sought to give some indication of movement [in my statues]. I have very rarely represented complete repose. I have always endeavoured to express the inner feelings by the mobility of the muscles. . . . The illusion of life is obtained in our art by good modelling and by movement. . . . [M]ovement is the transition from one attitude to another. . . . Have you ever attentively examined instantaneous photographs of walking figures? . . . [Photographs] present the odd appearance of a man suddenly stricken with paralysis and petrified in his pose. . . . If, in fact, in instantaneous photographs, the figures, though taken while moving, seem suddenly fixed in mid-air, it is because, all parts of the body being reproduced exactly at the same twentieth or fortieth of a second, there is no progressive development of movement as there is in art. . . . [I]t is the artist who is truthful and it is photography which lies, for in reality time does not stop.*

* Translated by Robin Fedden, in Elizabeth Gilmore Holt, ed., *From the Classicists to the Impressionists: Art and Architecture in the 19th Century* (New Haven, Conn.: Yale University Press, 1966; reprint 1986), 406–409.

28-32 AUGUSTE RODIN, *Walking Man,* **1905. Bronze, 6′ 11¾″ high. Musée d'Orsay, Paris.**

In this study for a statue of Saint John the Baptist, Rodin depicted a headless and armless figure in midstride. *Walking Man* demonstrates Rodin's mastery of anatomy and ability to capture transitory motion.

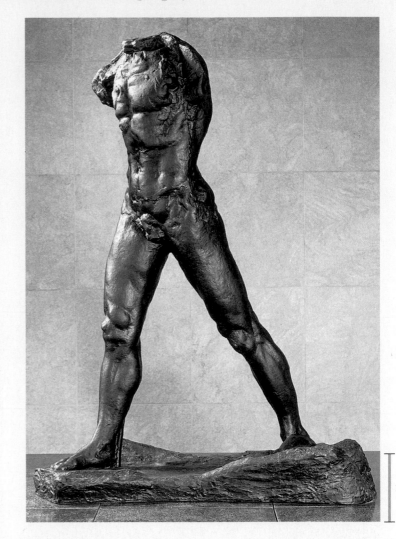

1 ft.

---

their own flesh as food. In Carpeaux's statuary group, the powerful forms—twisted, intertwined, and densely concentrated—suggest the self-devouring torment of frustration and despair wracking the unfortunate Ugolino. A careful student of Michelangelo's male figures, Carpeaux also said he had the Laocoön group (FIG. 5-89) in mind. Certainly, the storm and stress of *Ugolino and His Children* recall similar characteristics of that ancient work. Regardless of these influences, the sense of vivid reality in the anatomy of Carpeaux's figures shows the artist's interest in study from life. The French public did not share that interest, however, and preferred the idealized bodies of classical sculptures—one of the reasons Carpeaux was forced to remove *The Dance* (FIG. **28-31A**) from the facade of the Paris opera house (FIG. 27-45).

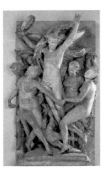

28-31A CARPEAUX, *The Dance,* 1867–1869.

AUGUSTE RODIN The leading French sculptor of the later 19th century was AUGUSTE RODIN (1840–1917), who conceived and executed his sculptures with a Realist sensibility. The human body in

motion (see "Rodin on Movement in Art and Photography," above) fascinated Rodin, as it did Eakins and Muybridge (FIG. 27-54) before him. Rodin was also well aware of the Impressionists' innovations. Although color was not a significant factor in Rodin's work, the influence of Impressionism is evident in the artist's abiding concern for the effect of light on sculpted surfaces. When focusing on the human form, he joined his profound knowledge of anatomy and movement with special attention to the body's exterior, saying, "The sculptor must learn to reproduce the surface, which means all that vibrates on the surface, soul, love, passion, life. . . . Sculpture is thus the art of hollows and mounds, not of smoothness, or even polished planes."[15] Primarily a modeler of pliable material rather than a carver of hard wood or stone, Rodin worked his surfaces with fingers sensitive to the subtlest variations of surface, catching the fugitive play of constantly shifting light on the body. In his studio, he often would have a model move around in front of him while he created preliminary versions of his sculptures with coils of clay.

In *Walking Man* (FIG. **28-32**), a preliminary study for the sculptor's *Saint John the Baptist Preaching*, Rodin succeeded in representing a fleeting moment in cast bronze. He portrayed a headless and armless figure in midstride at the moment when weight is

Sculpture **825**

transferred across the pelvis from the back leg to the front. In addition to capturing the sense of the transitory, Rodin demonstrated his mastery of realistic detail in his meticulous rendition of muscle, bone, and tendon.

GATES OF HELL Rodin also made many nude and draped studies for each of the figures in two of his most ambitious works—the life-size group *Burghers of Calais* (FIG. **28-32A**) and the *Gates of Hell* (FIG. **28-33**), which occupied the sculptor for two decades. After he failed to gain admission to the École des Beaux-Arts, Rodin enrolled in the École Impériale Spéciale de Dessin et Mathématiques, the French school of decorative arts, known as the "Petit École" (Little School) because it was a lesser version of the more prestigious Beaux-Arts academy. Nonetheless, Rodin gained attention for the outstanding realism of some of his early sculptures, and on August 16, 1880, he received a major governmental commission to design a pair of doors for a planned Museum of Decorative Arts in Paris. Rodin worked on the project for 20 years, but the museum was never built (the Musée d'Orsay now occupies the intended site). It was not until after the sculptor's death that others cast his still-unfinished doors in bronze.

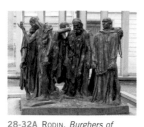

28-32A RODIN, *Burghers of Calais*, 1884–1889.

The commission permitted Rodin to choose his own subject. He selected *The Gates of Hell,* based on Dante's *Inferno* and Baudelaire's *Flowers of Evil.* Originally inspired by Lorenzo Ghiberti's *Gates of Paradise* (FIG. 21-9), which he had seen in Florence, Rodin quickly abandoned the idea of a series of framed narrative panels and decided instead to cover each of the doors with a continuous writhing mass of tormented men and women, sinners condemned to Dante's second circle of Hell for their lust. Because of the varying height of the relief and the variegated surfaces, the figures seem to be in flux, moving in and out of an undefined space in a reflection of their psychic turmoil. The dreamlike (or rather, the nightmarish) vision connects Rodin with the Symbolists, and the pessimistic mood exemplifies the fin-de-siècle spirit. The swirling composition and emotionalism recall Eugène Delacroix's *Death of Sardanapalus* (FIG. 27-15) and Michelangelo's *Last Judgment* (FIG. 22-19). But Rodin's work defies easy stylistic classification.

The nearly 200 figures of *The Gates of Hell* spill over onto the jambs and the lintel. Rodin also included freestanding figures, which, cast separately in multiple versions, are among his most famous works. Above the doors, *The Three Shades* is a trio of twisted nude male figures, essentially the same figure with elongated arms in three different positions. The group evokes Jean Baptiste Carpeaux's *Ugolino and His Children* (FIG. 28-31). *The Thinker,* Rodin's famous seated nude man with a powerful body who rests his chin

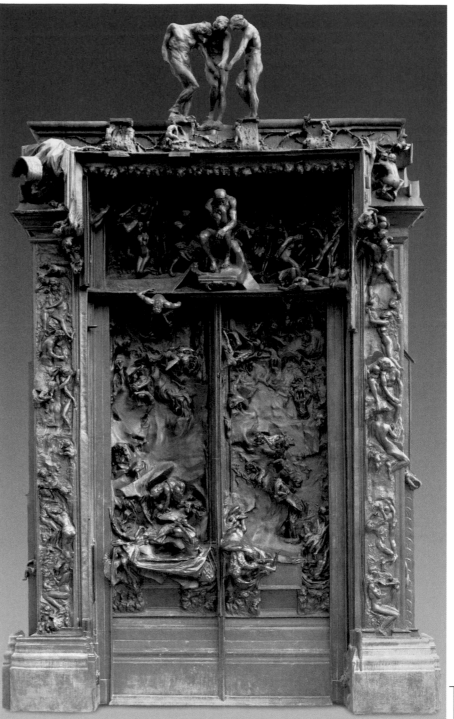

28-33 AUGUSTE RODIN, *The Gates of Hell,* 1880–1900 (cast in 1917). Bronze, 20′ 10″ × 13′ 1″. Musée Rodin, Paris.

Rodin's most ambitious work, inspired by Dante's *Inferno* and Ghiberti's *Gates of Paradise* (FIG. 21-9), presents nearly 200 tormented sinners in relief below *The Three Shades* and *The Thinker.*

on his clenched right hand, ponders the fate of the tormented souls on the doors below. *The Gates of Hell,* more than 20 feet tall, was Rodin's most ambitious project. It greatly influenced the painters and sculptors of the Expressionist movements of the early 20th century (see Chapter 29).

Rodin's ability to capture the quality of the transitory through his highly textured surfaces while revealing larger themes and deeper, lasting sensibilities is one of the reasons he had a strong influence on 20th-century artists. Because many of his works, such as

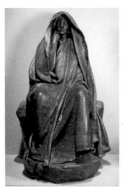

28-33A SAINT-GAUDENS, *Adams Memorial*, 1886–1891.

Walking Man, were deliberate fragments, he was also instrumental in creating a taste for the incomplete, an aesthetic many later sculptors embraced enthusiastically.

AUGUSTUS SAINT-GAUDENS

Other leading sculptors of the late 19th century pursued more traditional goals, however. In America, for example, AUGUSTUS SAINT-GAUDENS (1848–1907) produced monumental statues expressing the majestic calm of ancient Greek and Roman sculpture, as in his *Adams Memorial* (FIG. 28-33A) in Washington, D.C.

ARCHITECTURE AND DECORATIVE ARTS

The decisive effects of industrialization were impossible to ignore, and although many artists embraced this manifestation of "modern life" or at least explored its effects, other artists, especially those associated with the Arts and Crafts movement in England, decried the impact of rampant industrialism. This movement, which developed during the last decades of the 19th century, was shaped by the ideas of John Ruskin, the critic who skewered Whistler's "arrangements" (see "Whistler," page 810), and the artist William Morris. Both men shared a distrust of machines and industrial capitalism, which they believed alienated workers from their own nature. Accordingly, they advocated an art "made by the people for the people

as a joy for the maker and the user."[16] This condemnation of capitalism and support for manual laborers were consistent with the tenets of socialism, and many artists in the Arts and Crafts movement, especially in England, considered themselves socialists and participated in the labor movement.

This democratic, or at least populist, attitude carried over to the art they produced as well. Members of the Arts and Crafts movement dedicated themselves to making functional objects with high aesthetic value for a wide public. They advocated a style based on natural, rather than artificial, forms, which often consisted of repeated designs of floral or geometric patterns. For Ruskin, Morris, and others in the Arts and Crafts movement, high-quality artisanship and honest labor were crucial ingredients of superior works of decorative art.

WILLIAM MORRIS To promote these ideals, WILLIAM MORRIS (1834–1896) formed a decorating firm dedicated to Arts and Crafts principles: Morris, Marshall, Faulkner, and Company, Fine Arts Workmen in Painting, Carving, Furniture, and Metals. His company did a flourishing business producing wallpaper, textiles, furniture, books, rugs, stained glass, tiles, and pottery. In 1867, Morris received the commission to decorate the Green Dining Room (FIG. 28-34) at London's South Kensington Museum (now the Victoria & Albert Museum), the center of public art education and home of decorative art collections. The range of room features—windows, lights, and *wainscoting* (paneling on the lower part of interior walls)—Morris created for this unified, beautiful, and functional environment was all-encompassing. Nothing escaped his eye. Morris's design for this room also reveals the penchant of Arts and Crafts designers for intricate patterning.

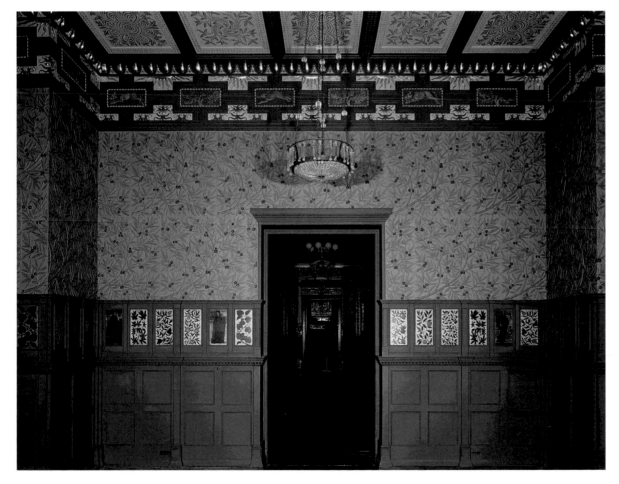

28-34 WILLIAM MORRIS, Green Dining Room, South Kensington Museum (now Victoria & Albert Museum), London, England, 1867.

William Morris was a founder of the Arts and Crafts movement. His Green Dining Room exemplifies the group's dedication to creating intricately patterned yet unified and functional environments.

The Mackintoshes' Ladies' Luncheon Room in Glasgow features functional and exquisitely designed Arts and Crafts decor, including stained-glass windows and pristinely geometric furnishings.

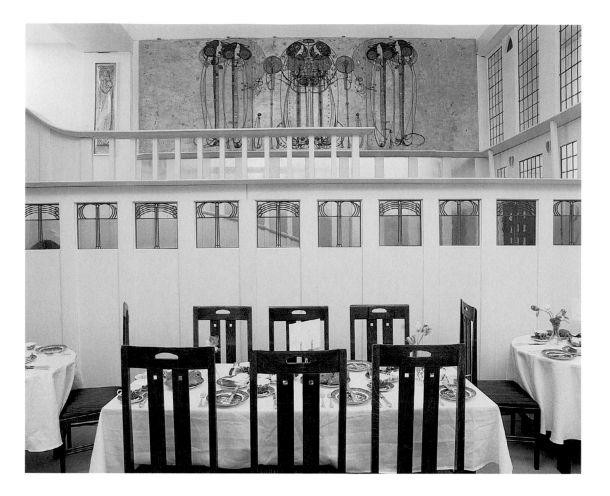

CHARLES RENNIE MACKINTOSH Numerous Arts and Crafts societies in America, England, and Germany carried on this ideal of artisanship. In Scotland, CHARLES RENNIE MACKINTOSH (1868–1929) designed a number of tea rooms, including the Ladies' Luncheon Room (FIG. 28-35) located in the Ingram Street Tea Room in Glasgow. The room decor is consistent with Morris's vision of a functional, exquisitely designed art. The chairs, stained-glass windows, and large panels of colored gesso with twine, glass beads, thread, mother-of-pearl, and tin leaf—made by MARGARET MACDONALD MACKINTOSH (1864–1933), an artist-designer and Mackintosh's wife, who collaborated with him on many projects—are all pristinely geometric and rhythmical in design.

ART NOUVEAU An important international architectural and design movement that developed out of the ideas the Arts and Crafts movement promoted was *Art Nouveau* (New Art), which took its name from a shop in Paris called L'Art Nouveau. Known by that name in France, Belgium, Holland, England, and the United States, the style had other names in other places: *Jugendstil* in Austria and Germany (after the magazine *Jugend,* "youth"), *Modernismo* in Spain, and *Floreale* in Italy. Proponents of this movement tried to synthesize all the arts in a determined attempt to create art based on natural forms that could be mass-produced for a large audience. The Art Nouveau style adapted the twining plant form to the needs of architecture, painting, sculpture, and all of the decorative arts.

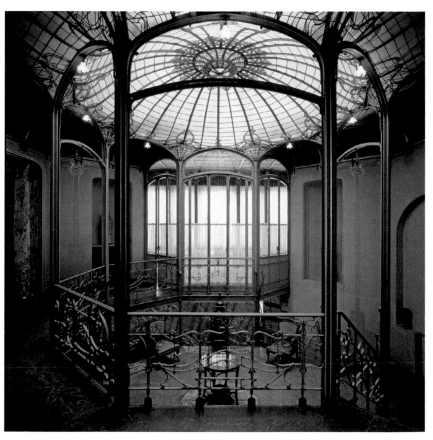

28-36 VICTOR HORTA, staircase in the Van Eetvelde House, Brussels, 1895.

The Art Nouveau movement was an attempt to create art and architecture based on natural forms. Here, every detail conforms to the theme of the twining plant and functions as part of a living whole.

VICTOR HORTA The mature Art Nouveau style of the 1890s is on display in the houses the Belgian architect VICTOR HORTA (1861–1947) designed. A characteristic example is the staircase (FIG. **28-36**) in the Van Eetvelde House, which Horta built in Brussels in 1895, three years after designing the Tassel House (FIG. **28-36A**), his first major commission. Every detail of the Van Eetvelde interior functions as part of a living whole. Furniture, drapery folds, veining in the lavish stone paneling, and the patterning of the door moldings join with real plants to provide graceful counterpoints for the twining-plant theme. Metallic tendrils curl around the railings and posts, delicate metal tracery fills the glass dome, and floral and leaf motifs spread across the fabric panels of the screen. Flower and plant motifs also figure prominently in the immensely popular stained-glass lamps (FIG. **28-36B**) of LOUIS COMFORT TIFFANY (1848–1933).

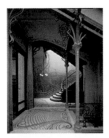

28-36A HORTA, Tassel House, Brussels, 1892–1893.

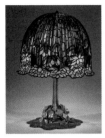

28-36B TIFFANY, water lily lamp, 1904–1915.

The Art Nouveau style reflects several influences. In addition to the rich, foliated two-dimensional ornamentation of Arts and Crafts design and that movement's respect for materials, the sinuous whiplash curve of Japanese print designs (FIG. 34-13) inspired Art Nouveau artists. Art Nouveau also borrowed from the expressively patterned styles of van Gogh (FIGS. 28-17 and 28-18), Gauguin (FIGS. 28-19 and 28-20), and their Post-Impressionist and Symbolist contemporaries.

ANTONIO GAUDI Art Nouveau achieved its most personal expression in the work of the Spanish architect ANTONIO GAUDI (1852–1926). Before becoming an architect, Gaudi had trained as an ironworker. As many young artists of his time, he longed to create a style both modern and appropriate to his country. Taking inspiration from Moorish architecture and from the simple architecture of his native Catalonia, Gaudi developed a personal aesthetic. He conceived a building as a whole and molded it almost as a sculptor might shape a figure from clay. Although work on his designs proceeded slowly under the guidance of his intuition and imagination, Gaudi was a master who invented many new structural techniques that facilitated construction of his visions. His Barcelona apartment house, Casa Milá (FIG. **28-37**), is a wondrously free-form mass wrapped around a street corner. Lacy iron railings enliven the swelling curves of the cut-stone facade. Dormer windows peep from the undulating tiled roof, from which fantastically writhing chimneys poke energetically into the air above. The rough surfaces of the stone walls suggest naturally worn rock. The entrance portals look like eroded sea caves, but their design also may reflect the excitement that swept Spain following the 1879 discovery of Paleolithic cave paintings at Altamira (FIG. 1-9). Gaudi felt each of his buildings was symbolically a living thing, and the passionate naturalism of his Casa Milá is the spiritual kin of early-20th-century Expressionist painting and sculpture (see Chapter 29).

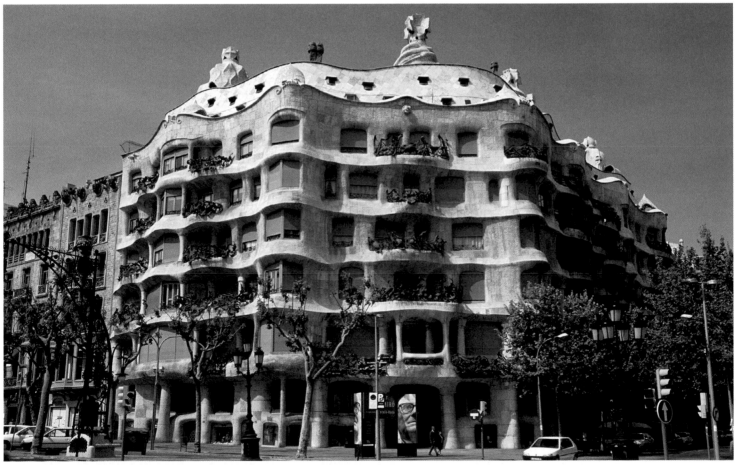

28-37 ANTONIO GAUDI, Casa Milá (looking north), Barcelona, Spain, 1907.

Spanish Art Nouveau architect Gaudi conceived this apartment house as if it were a gigantic sculpture to be molded from clay. Twisting chimneys cap the undulating roof and walls.

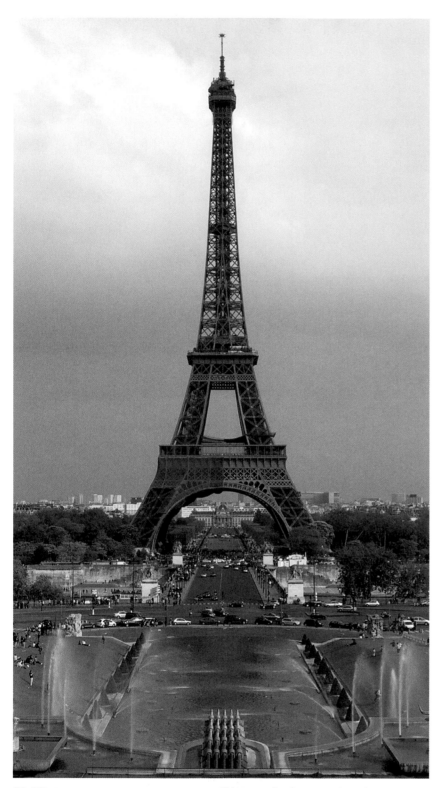

28-38 ALEXANDRE-GUSTAVE EIFFEL, Eiffel Tower (looking southeast), Paris, France, 1889. ◼◀

New materials and technologies and the modernist aesthetic fueled radically new architectural designs in the late 19th century. Eiffel jolted the world with the exposed iron skeleton of his tower.

ALEXANDRE-GUSTAVE EIFFEL In the later 19th century, new technologies and the changing needs of urbanized, industrialized society affected architecture throughout the Western world. Since the 18th century, bridges had been built of cast iron (FIG. 26-12), which enabled engineering advancements in the construction of larger, stronger, and more fire-resistant structures. Steel, available after 1860, made it possible for architects to enclose ever larger spaces, such as those found in railroad stations (FIG. 28-4) and exposition halls. The Realist impulse also encouraged architectural designs that honestly expressed a building's purpose, rather than elaborately disguising its function. The elegant metal-skeleton structures of the French engineer-architect ALEXANDRE-GUSTAVE EIFFEL (1832–1923) were responses to this idea, and they constituted an important contribution to the development of the 20th-century skyscraper. A native of Burgundy, Eiffel trained in Paris before beginning a distinguished career designing exhibition halls, bridges, and the interior armature for France's anniversary gift to the United States—the *Statue of Liberty* by Frédéric Auguste Bartholdi (1834–1904).

Eiffel designed his best-known work, the Eiffel Tower (FIG. **28-38**), for an exhibition in Paris in 1889. Originally seen as a symbol of modern Paris and still considered a symbol of 19th-century civilization, the elegant iron tower thrusts its needle shaft 984 feet above the city, making it at the time of its construction (and for some time thereafter) the world's tallest structure. The tower rests on four giant supports connected by gracefully arching open-frame skirts that provide a pleasing mask for the heavy horizontal girders needed to strengthen the legs. Visitors can take two successive elevators to the top, or they can use the internal staircase. Either way, the view of Paris and the Seine from the tower is incomparable, as is the design of the tower itself. The transparency of Eiffel's structure blurs the distinction between interior and exterior to an extent never before achieved or even attempted. This interpenetration of inner and outer space became a hallmark of 20th-century art and architecture. Eiffel's tower and the earlier iron skeletal frames designed by Labrouste (FIG. 27-46) and Paxton (FIG. 27-47) jolted the architectural profession into a realization that modern materials and processes could germinate a completely new style and a radically innovative approach to architectural design.

AMERICAN SKYSCRAPERS The desire for greater speed and economy in building, as well as for a reduction in fire hazards, prompted the use of cast and wrought iron for many building programs, especially commercial ones. Designers in both England and the United States enthusiastically developed cast-iron architecture until a series of disastrous fires in the early 1870s in New York, Boston, and Chicago demonstrated that cast iron by itself was far from impervious to fire. This discovery led to encasing the metal in masonry, combining the first material's strength with the second's fire resistance.

In cities, convenience required closely grouped buildings, and increased property values forced architects literally to raise the roof. Even an attic could command high rentals if the builders installed one of the new elevators, used for the first time in the Equitable Building in New York (1868–1871). Metal, which could support these towering structures, gave birth to the American skyscraper.

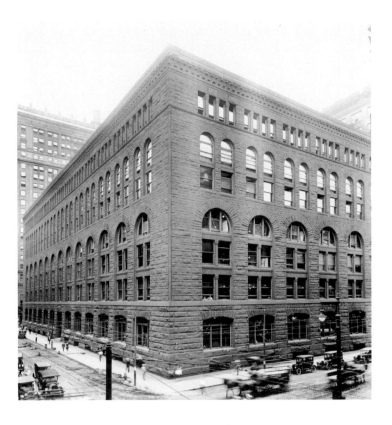

28-39 HENRY HOBSON RICHARDSON, Marshall Field wholesale store, Chicago, 1885–1887 (demolished 1930).

Richardson was a pioneer in designing commercial structures using a cast-iron skeleton encased in fire-resistant masonry. This construction technique enabled the insertion of large windows in the walls.

HENRY HOBSON RICHARDSON One of the pioneers in designing these modern commercial structures was HENRY HOBSON RICHARDSON (1838–1886), but he also had a profound respect for earlier architectural styles. Because Richardson had a special fondness for the Romanesque architecture of the Auvergne area in France, he frequently used heavy round arches and massive masonry walls. Architectural historians sometimes consider his work to constitute a Romanesque revival related to the Neo-Gothic style (FIGS. 27-43 and 27-43A). This designation does not do credit to the originality and quality of most of the buildings Richardson designed during his brief 18-year practice. Trinity Church in Boston and his smaller public libraries, residences, railroad stations, and courthouses in New England and elsewhere best demonstrate his vivid imagination and the solidity (the sense of enclosure and permanence) so characteristic of his style. However, his most important and influential building was the Marshall Field wholesale store (FIG. 28-39) in Chicago, begun in 1885 and demolished in 1930. This vast building occupied an entire city block. Designed for the most practical of purposes, it nonetheless recalled historical styles without imitating them. The tripartite elevation of a Renaissance palace (FIG. 21-37) or of the Roman aqueduct (FIG. 7-33) near Nîmes, France, may have been close to Richardson's mind. But he used no classical ornamentation, made much of the massive courses of masonry, and, in the strong horizontality of the window-sills and the interrupted courses defining the levels, stressed the long sweep of the building's lines, as well as the edifice's ponderous weight. Although the structural frame still lay behind and in conjunction with the masonry screen, the great glazed arcades opened up the walls of the monumental store. They pointed the way to the modern total penetration of walls and the transformation of them into mere screens or curtains that serve both to echo the underlying structural grid and to protect it from the weather.

LOUIS HENRY SULLIVAN As skyscrapers proliferated, architects refined the visual vocabulary of these buildings. LOUIS HENRY SULLIVAN (1856–1924), whom many architectural historians call the first truly modern architect, arrived at a synthesis of industrial structure and ornamentation that perfectly expressed the spirit of late-19th-century commerce. To achieve this, he used the latest technological developments to create light-filled, well-ventilated office buildings and adorned both exteriors and interiors with ornate embellishments. Such decoration served to connect commerce and culture, and imbued these white-collar workspaces with a sense of refinement and taste. These characteristics are evident in the Guaranty (Prudential) Building (FIG. 28-40) in Buffalo, built

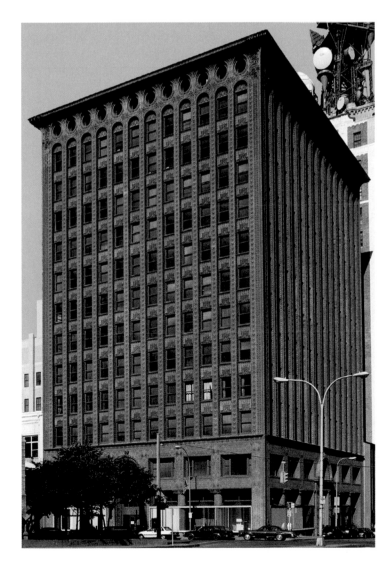

28-40 LOUIS HENRY SULLIVAN, Guaranty (Prudential) Building (looking southwest), Buffalo, New York, 1894–1896.

Sullivan drew on the latest technologies to create this light-filled, well-ventilated Buffalo office building. He added ornate surface embellishments to impart a sense of refinement and taste.

Architecture and Decorative Arts **831**

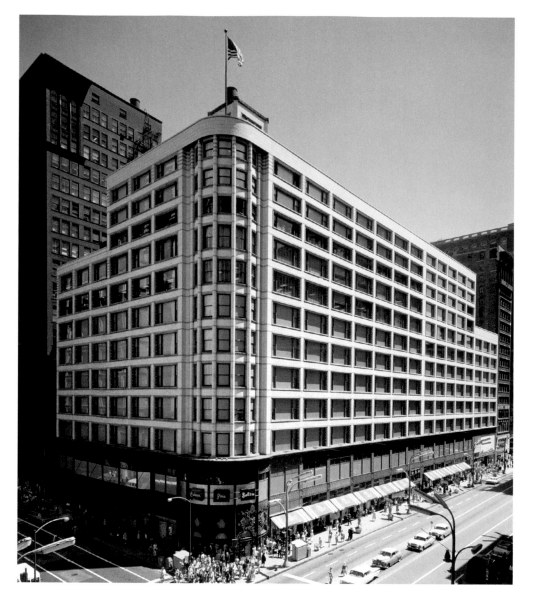

28-41 Louis Henry Sullivan, Carson, Pirie, Scott Building (looking southeast), Chicago, 1899–1904.

Sullivan's slogan was "form follows function." He tailored the design of this steel, glass, and stone Chicago department store to meet the needs of its employees and customers.

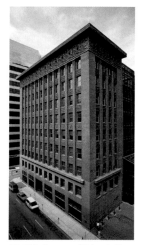

28-40A Sullivan, Wainwright Building, St. Louis, 1890–1891.

between 1894 and 1896, and in his earlier Wainwright Building (FIG. **28-40A**) in St. Louis. The Buffalo skyscraper is steel, sheathed with terracotta. The imposing scale of the building and the regularity of the window placements served as an expression of the large-scale, refined, and orderly office work taking place within. Sullivan tempered the severity of the structure with lively ornamentation, both on the piers and cornice on the exterior of the building and on the stairway balustrades, elevator cages, and ceiling in the interior. The Guaranty Building illustrates Sullivan's famous dictum "form follows function," which became the slogan of many early-20th-century architects. Still, Sullivan did not advocate a rigid and doctrinaire correspondence between exterior and interior design. Rather, he espoused a free and flexible relationship—one his pupil

Frank Lloyd Wright (see Chapter 29) later described as similar to that between the hand's bones and tissue.

Sullivan also designed the Carson, Pirie, Scott Building (FIG. **28-41**) in Chicago. Built between 1899 and 1904, this department store required broad, open, well-illuminated display spaces. Sullivan again used a minimal structural steel skeleton to achieve this goal. The architect gave over the lowest two levels of the building to an ornament in cast iron (of his invention) made of wildly fantastic motifs. He regarded the display windows as pictures, which merited elaborate frames. As in the Guaranty Building, Sullivan revealed his profound understanding of the maturing consumer economy and tailored the Carson, Pirie, Scott Building to meet the functional and symbolic needs of its users.

Thus, in architecture as well as in the pictorial arts, the late 19th century was a period during which artists challenged traditional modes of expression, often emphatically rejecting the past. Architects and painters as different as Sullivan, Monet, van Gogh, and Cézanne, each in his own way, contributed significantly to the entrenchment of modernism as the new cultural orthodoxy of the early 20th century (see Chapter 29).

IMPRESSIONISM, POST-IMPRESSIONISM, SYMBOLISM: EUROPE AND AMERICA, 1870 TO 1900

IMPRESSIONISM

I A hostile critic applied the term *Impressionism* to the paintings of Claude Monet because of their sketchy quality. The Impressionists—Monet, Pierre-Auguste Renoir, Edgar Degas, and others—strove to capture fleeting moments and transient effects of light and climate on canvas. They also focused on recording the contemporary urban scene in Paris, frequently painting bars, dance halls, the ballet, wide boulevards, and railroad stations.

I Complementing the Impressionists' sketchy, seemingly spontaneous brushstrokes are the compositions of their paintings. Reflecting the influence of Japanese prints and photography, Impressionist works often have arbitrarily cut-off figures and settings seen at sharply oblique angles.

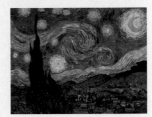

Renoir, *Le Moulin de la Galette*, 1876

POST-IMPRESSIONISM AND SYMBOLISM

I Post-Impressionism is not a unified style. The term refers to the group of late-19th-century artists, including Georges Seurat, Vincent van Gogh, Paul Gauguin, and Paul Cézanne, who followed the Impressionists and took painting in new directions. Seurat refined the Impressionist approach to color and light into pointillism—the disciplined application of pure color in tiny daubs. Van Gogh explored the capabilities of colors and distorted forms to express emotions. Gauguin, an admirer of Japanese prints, moved away from Impressionism in favor of large areas of flat color bounded by firm lines. Cézanne replaced the transitory visual effects of the Impressionists with a rigorous analysis of the lines, planes, and colors that make up landscapes and still lifes.

I Gustave Moreau, Odilon Redon, and Henri Rousseau were the leading French Symbolists. They disdained Realism as trivial and sought to depict a reality beyond that of the everyday world, rejecting materialism and celebrating fantasy and imagination. Their subjects were often mysterious, exotic, and sensuous.

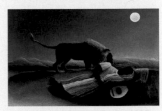

van Gogh, *Starry Night*, 1889

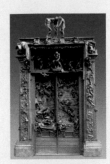

Rousseau, *Sleeping Gypsy*, 1897

SCULPTURE

I Sculpture cannot capture transitory optical effects or explore the properties of color and line, and late-19th-century sculptors pursued goals different from those of contemporaneous painters.

I The leading figure of the era was Auguste Rodin, who explored Realist themes and the representation of movement. His vision of tormented, writhing figures in Hell connects his work with the Symbolists. Rodin also made statues that were deliberate fragments, creating a taste for the incomplete that appealed to many later sculptors.

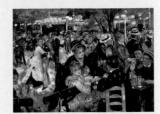

Rodin, *Gates of Hell*, 1880–1900

ARCHITECTURE AND DECORATIVE ARTS

I Not all artists embraced the industrialization transforming daily life during the 19th century. The Arts and Crafts movement in England and the international Art Nouveau style formed in opposition to modern mass production. Both schools advocated natural forms and high-quality craftsmanship.

I New technologies and the changing needs of urbanized, industrialized society transformed architecture in the late 19th century. The exposed iron skeleton of the Eiffel Tower jolted architects into realizing how modern materials and processes could revolutionize architectural design. Henry Hobson Richardson and Louis Sullivan were pioneers in designing the first metal, stone, and glass skyscrapers.

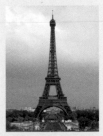

Eiffel, Eiffel Tower, Paris, 1889

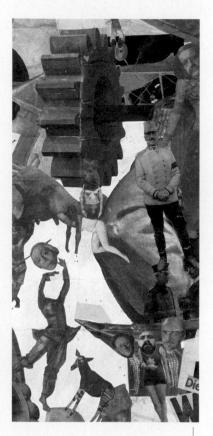

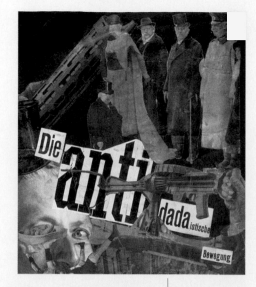

The cut-out photos in Höch's photomontage appear to be randomly selected, but they are carefully arranged. The leading figures of the Weimar Republic (the "anti-Dadaists") are at the top right.

The many photos pasted together in *Cut with a Kitchen Knife* include mass-produced machine parts. In the lower left of this detail, the artist Käthe Kollwitz's head floats above a dancer's body.

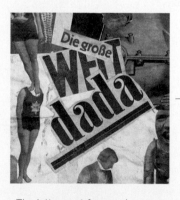

The letters cut from various publications are of different typefaces and font sizes, contributing to the sense of dislocation throughout. Near the center are the words "The great Dada world."

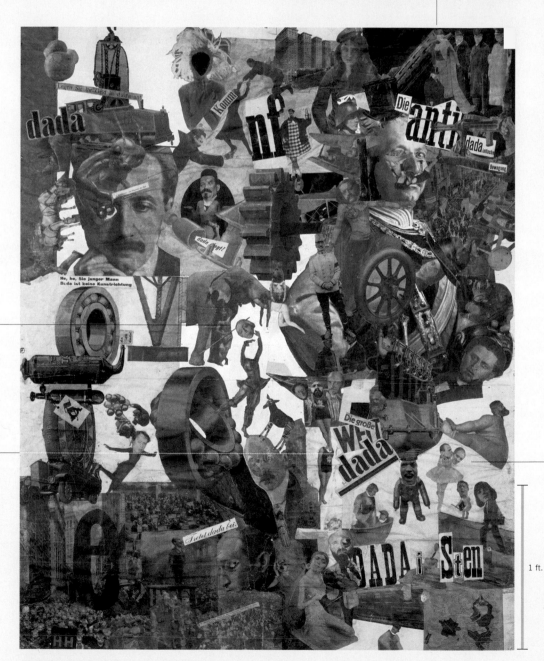

1 ft.

29-1 HANNAH HÖCH, *Cut with the Kitchen Knife Dada through the Last Weimar Beer Belly Cultural Epoch of Germany,* 1919–1920. Photomontage, 3′ 9″ × 2′ 11½″. Neue Nationalgalerie, Staatliche Museen zu Berlin, Berlin. ◼◖

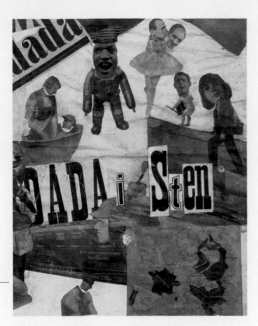

MODERNISM IN EUROPE AND AMERICA, 1900 TO 1945

At the lower right, in the section labeled "Dadaists," Höch juxtaposed a photo of her own face with a map of Europe showing those countries that had granted women the right to vote.

FRAMING THE ERA

GLOBAL WAR, ANARCHY, AND DADA

World War I—the "Great War"—broke out in 1914, unleashing slaughter and devastation on a scale unprecedented in history. More than nine million soldiers died in four years. Britain alone lost 60,000 men on the opening day of the battle of the Somme. The negotiated formal end of hostilities in 1919 redrew the political map of Europe (MAP **29-1**). Peace, however, could not erase the scars of a global conflict that had altered the worldview of millions. One major consequence of the Great War was the emergence of an artistic movement known as *Dada*. The Dadaists believed reason and logic had been responsible for the insane spectacle of collective homicide that was World War I, and they concluded the only route to salvation was through political anarchy, the irrational, and the intuitive.

In Berlin, Dada took on an activist political edge. The Berlin Dadaists pioneered a variation of the technique called *collage* in French (FIG. 29-17)—creating artistic compositions from cut pieces of paper. The Berliners christened their version *photomontage,* because their assemblages consisted almost entirely of pieces of magazine photographs, usually combined into deliberately antilogical compositions. Collage lent itself well to the Dada desire to exploit chance in the creation of art—and anti-art.

One of the Berlin Dadaists who perfected the photomontage technique was HANNAH HÖCH (1889–1978). Höch's photomontages advanced the absurd illogic of Dada by presenting viewers with chaotic, contradictory, and satiric compositions. They also provided scathing and insightful commentary on two of the most dramatic developments during the Weimar Republic (1918–1933) in Germany—the redefinition of women's social roles and the explosive growth of mass print media. Höch incorporated both themes in *Cut with the Kitchen Knife Dada through the Last Weimar Beer Belly Cultural Epoch of Germany* (FIG. **29-1**), in which she arranged in seemingly haphazard fashion—often with a touch of typically wicked Dada humor—an eclectic mixture of cutout photos. Closer inspection, however, reveals the artist's careful selection and placement of the photographs. For example, the key figures in the Weimar Republic are together at the upper right (identified as the "anti-Dada movement"). Some of Höch's fellow Dadaists appear among images of Karl Marx and Vladimir Lenin, aligning Dada with other revolutionary forces in what she prominently labeled with cutout lettering "Die grosse Welt dada" (the great Dada world). Höch also positioned herself in the topsy-turvy Dada world she created. A photograph of her head appears in the lower right corner, juxtaposed with a map of Europe showing which countries had granted women the right to vote—a commentary on the power both women and Dada had to destabilize society.

GLOBAL UPHEAVAL
AND ARTISTIC REVOLUTION

The first half of the 20th century was a period of significant upheaval worldwide. Between 1900 and 1945, the major industrial powers fought two global wars, witnessed the rise of Communism, Fascism, and Nazism, and suffered the Great Depression. These decades were also a time of radical change in the arts when painters and sculptors challenged some of the most basic assumptions about the purpose of art and what form an artwork should take. Throughout history, artistic revolution has often accompanied political, social, and economic upheaval, but never before had the new directions artists explored been as pronounced or as long-lasting as those born during the first half of the last century.

AVANT-GARDE As did other members of society, artists felt deeply the effects of the political and economic disruptions of the early 20th century. As the old social orders collapsed and new ones, from communism to corporate capitalism, took their places, artists searched for new definitions of and uses for art in a changed world. Already in the 19th century, each successive modernist movement had challenged artistic conventions with ever-greater intensity. This relentless questioning of the status quo gave rise to the notion of an artistic *avant-garde*. The term, which means "front guard," derives from 19th-century French military usage. The avant-garde were the troops sent ahead of the army's main body to reconnoiter and make occasional raids on the enemy. Politicians who deemed themselves visionary and forward-thinking subsequently adopted the term. It then migrated to the art world in the 1880s, when artists and critics used it to refer to the Realists, Impressionists, and Post-Impressionists—artists who were ahead of their time and who transgressed the limits of established art forms.

These trailblazing rebels rejected the classical, academic, and traditional, and zealously explored the premises and formal qualities of painting, sculpture, and other media. Although the general public found avant-garde art incomprehensible, the principles underlying 19th-century modernism appealed to increasing numbers of artists as the 20th century dawned.

EUROPE, 1900 TO 1920

Avant-garde artists in all their diversity became a major force during the opening decades of the 20th century, beginning with the artistic movement known as *Fauvism*.

Fauvism

In 1905, at the third Salon d'Automne (Autumn Salon) in Paris, a group of young painters exhibited canvases so simplified in design and so shockingly bright in color that a startled critic, Louis Vauxcelles (1870–1943), described the artists as *fauves* (wild beasts). The Fauves were totally independent of the French Academy and the "official" Salon (see "Academic Salons and Independent Art Exhibitions," Chapter 28, page 802). Driving the Fauve movement was a desire to develop an art having the directness of Impressionism but employing intense color juxtapositions for expressive ends.

Building on the legacy of artists such as Vincent van Gogh and Paul Gauguin (see Chapter 28), the Fauves went even further in liberating color from its descriptive function and exploring the effects different colors have on emotions. The Fauves produced portraits, landscapes, still lifes, and nudes of spontaneity and verve, with rich surface textures, lively linear patterns, and, above all, bold colors. They employed startling contrasts of vermilion and emerald green and of cerulean blue and vivid orange held together by sweeping brushstrokes and bold patterns in an effort to release internal feelings.

The Fauve painters never officially organized, and the looseness of both personal connections and stylistic affinities caused the Fauve movement to begin to disintegrate almost as soon as it emerged. Within five years, most of the artists had departed from a strict adherence to Fauve principles and developed their own more

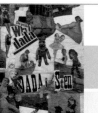

MODERNISM IN EUROPE AND AMERICA, 1900 TO 1945

1900	1910	1920	1930	1945

- European artists build on the innovations of the Impressionists and Post-Impressionists and explore new avenues of artistic expression
- Henri Matisse and the Fauves free color from its descriptive function
- German Expressionist groups—Die Brücke and Der Blaue Reiter—produce paintings featuring bold colors and distorted forms
- In America, Frank Lloyd Wright promotes "natural architecture" in his expansive "prairie houses"

- Pablo Picasso and Georges Braque radically challenge the traditional Western way of making pictures with their Cubist dissection of forms
- The Italian Futurists celebrate dynamic motion and modern technology in paintings and statues
- Vassily Kandinsky pursues complete abstraction in painting
- The Dadaists explore the role of chance in often irreverent artworks
- The Armory Show introduces American artists and the public to avant-garde developments in Europe

- In the wake of World War I, German Neue Sachlichkeit painters depict the horrors of global conflict
- The Surrealists seek ways to visualize the world of the unconscious and investigate automatism as a means of creating art
- De Stijl artists create "pure plastic art" using geometric forms and primary colors
- Constantine Brancusi and Barbara Hepworth promote abstraction in sculpture
- The Bauhaus advocates the integration of all the arts in its vision of "total architecture"
- Photography emerges as an important art form in the work of Alfred Stieglitz and Edward Weston

- Aaron Douglas and Jacob Lawrence explore African American history in the Harlem Renaissance
- Alexander Calder creates abstract sculptures with moving parts
- Grant Wood and the Regionalists celebrate life in rural America in paintings rejecting European abstraction
- José Orozco and Diego Rivera paint vast mural cycles recording Mexican history
- Dorothea Lange and Margaret Bourke-White achieve renown for their documentary photography

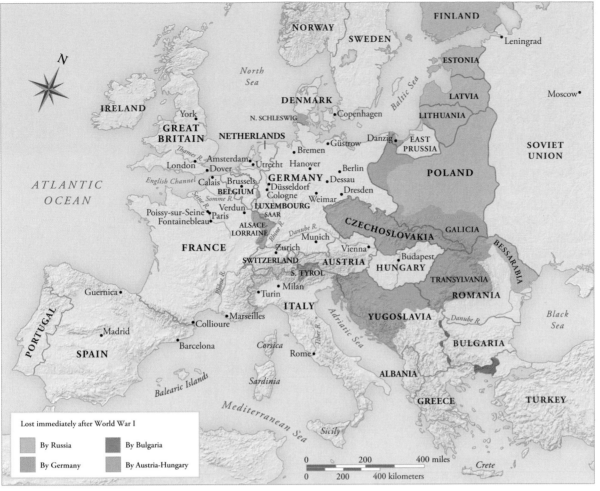

MAP 29-1 Europe at the end of World War I

Lost immediately after World War I

By Russia	By Bulgaria
By Germany	By Austria-Hungary

0 200 400 miles
0 200 400 kilometers

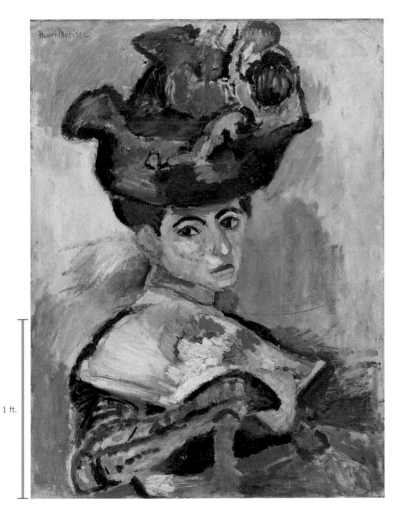

29-2 HENRI MATISSE, *Woman with the Hat,* 1905. Oil on canvas, 2′ 7¾″ × 1′ 11½″. San Francisco Museum of Modern Art, San Francisco (bequest of Elise S. Haas).

Matisse's portrayal of his wife, Amélie, features patches and splotches of seemingly arbitrary colors. He and the other Fauve painters used color not to imitate nature but to produce a reaction in the viewer.

personal styles. During its brief existence, however, Fauvism made a remarkable contribution to the direction of art by demonstrating color's structural, expressive, and aesthetic capabilities.

HENRI MATISSE The dominant figure of the Fauve group was HENRI MATISSE (1869–1954), who believed color could play a primary role in conveying meaning and focused his efforts on developing this notion. In an early painting, *Woman with the Hat* (FIG. **29-2**), Matisse depicted his wife, Amélie, in a rather

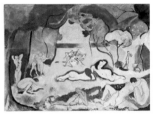

29-2A MATISSE, *Le Bonheur de Vivre,* 1905–1906.

conventional manner compositionally, but the seemingly arbitrary colors immediately startle the viewer, as does the sketchiness of the forms. The entire image—the woman's face, clothes, hat, and background—consists of patches and splotches of color juxtaposed in ways that sometimes produce jarring contrasts. Matisse explained his approach: "What characterized fauvism was that we rejected imitative colors, and that with pure colors we obtained stronger reactions."[1] For Matisse and the Fauves, therefore, color became the formal element most responsible for pictorial coherence and the primary conveyor of meaning (see "Matisse on Color," page 838, and FIG. **29-2A**).

Matisse on Color

In an essay entitled "Notes of a Painter," published in the Parisian journal *La Grande Revue* on Christmas Day, 1908, Henri Matisse responded to his critics and set forth his principles and goals as a painter. The following excerpts help explain what Matisse was trying to achieve in paintings such as *Harmony in Red* (FIG. 29-3).

> What I am after, above all, is expression. . . . Expression, for me, does not reside in passions glowing in a human face or manifested by violent movement. The entire arrangement of my picture is expressive: the place occupied by the figures, the empty spaces around them, the proportions, everything has its share. Composition is the art of arranging in a decorative manner the diverse elements at the painter's command to express his feelings. . . .
>
> Both harmonies and dissonances of colour can produce agreeable effects. . . . Suppose I have to paint an interior: I have before me a cupboard; it gives me a sensation of vivid red, and I put down a red which satisfies me. A relation is established between this red and the white of the canvas. Let me put a green near the red, and make the floor yellow; and again there will be relationships between the green or yellow and the white of the canvas which will satisfy me. . . . A new combination of colours will succeed the first and render the totality of my representation. I am forced to transpose until finally my picture may seem completely changed when, after successive modifications, the red has succeeded the green as the dominant colour. I cannot copy nature in a servile way; I am forced to interpret nature and submit it to the spirit of the picture. From the relationship I have found in all the tones there must result a living harmony of colours, a harmony analogous to that of a musical composition. . . .
>
> The chief function of colour should be to serve expression as well as possible. . . . My choice of colours does not rest on any scientific theory; it is based on observation, on sensitivity, on felt experiences. . . . I simply try to put down colours which render my sensation. There is an impelling proportion of tones that may lead me to change the shape of a figure or to transform my composition. Until I have achieved this proportion in all parts of the composition I strive towards it and keep on working. Then a moment comes when all the parts have found their definite relationships, and from then on it would be impossible for me to add a stroke to my picture without having to repaint it entirely.*

*Translated by Jack D. Flam, *Matisse on Art* (London: Phaidon, 1973), 32–40.

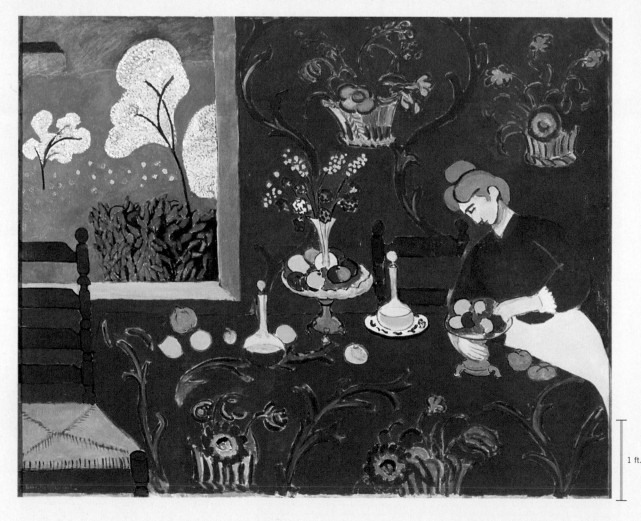

29-3 HENRI MATISSE, *Red Room* (*Harmony in Red*), 1908–1909. Oil on canvas, 5′ 11″ × 8′ 1″. State Hermitage Museum, Saint Petersburg. ◼◀

Matisse believed painters should choose compositions and colors that express their feelings. Here, the table and wall seem to merge because they are the same color and have identical patterning.

1 ft.

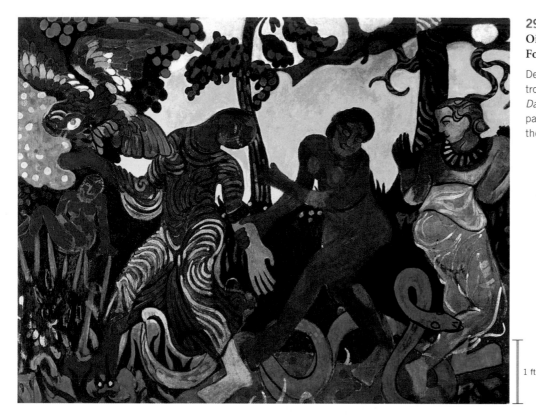

1 ft.

HARMONY IN RED These color discoveries reached maturity in Matisse's *Red Room* (*Harmony in Red*; FIG. 29-3). The subject is the interior of a comfortable, prosperous household with a maid placing fruit and wine on the table, but Matisse's canvas is radically different from traditional paintings of domestic interiors (for example, FIGS. 25-19 and 25-20A). The Fauve painter depicted objects in simplified and schematized fashion and flattened out the forms. For example, Matisse eliminated the front edge of the table, rendering the table, with its identical patterning, as flat as the wall behind it. The window at the upper left could also be a painting on the wall, further flattening the space. Everywhere, the colors contrast richly and intensely. Matisse's process of overpainting reveals the importance of color for striking the right chord in the viewer. Initially, this work was predominantly green. Then Matisse repainted it blue, but blue also did not seem appropriate. Not until he repainted the canvas red did Matisse feel he had found the right color for the "harmony" he wished to compose.

ANDRÉ DERAIN Another leading Fauve painter was ANDRÉ DERAIN (1880–1954). As did Matisse, with whom he worked closely, Derain sought to employ color for aesthetic and compositional coherence and to elicit emotional responses. *The Dance* (FIG. 29-4), in which several figures, some nude, others clothed, frolic in a lush

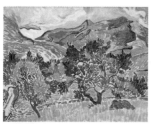

29-4A DERAIN, *Mountains at Collioure*, 1905.

landscape (compare FIG. 29-4A), is one of Derain's best paintings. The tropical setting and the bold colors reflect in part Derain's study of Gauguin's canvases (FIGS. 28-19 and 28-20), as does the flattened perspective. Derain used color to delineate space, and he indicated light and shadow not by differences in value but by contrasts of hue. For the Fauves, as for Gauguin and van Gogh, color does not describe the local tones of objects but expresses the picture's content.

German Expressionism

The immediacy and boldness of the Fauve images appealed to many artists, including the German *Expressionists*. However, although color plays a prominent role in German painting of the early 20th century, the "expressiveness" of the German images is due as much to the Expressionists' wrenching distortions of form, ragged outlines, and agitated brushstrokes.

ERNST LUDWIG KIRCHNER The first group of German Expressionists—*Die Brücke* (The Bridge)—gathered in Dresden in 1905 under the leadership of ERNST LUDWIG KIRCHNER (1880–1938). The group members thought of themselves as paving the way for a more perfect age by bridging the old age and the new, hence their name. Kirchner's early studies in architecture, painting, and the graphic arts had instilled in him a deep admiration for German medieval art. As did the British artists associated with the Arts and Crafts movement, such as William Morris (FIG. 28-34), Die Brücke artists modeled themselves on medieval craft guilds whose members lived together and practiced all the arts equally. Kirchner described their lofty goals in a ringing 1913 statement published in the form of a woodcut titled *Chronik der Brücke:*

> With faith in progress and in a new generation of creators and spectators we call together all youth. As youth, we carry the future and want to create for ourselves freedom of life and of movement against the long-established older forces. Everyone who reproduces that which drives him to creation with directness and authenticity belongs to us.[2]

Die Brücke artists protested the hypocrisy and materialistic decadence of those in power. Kirchner, in particular, focused much of his attention on the detrimental effects of industrialization, such as the alienation of individuals in cities, which he felt fostered a mechanized and impersonal society. The tensions leading to World War I further exacerbated the discomfort and anxiety of the German Expressionists.

29-5 ERNST LUDWIG KIRCHNER, *Street, Dresden,* 1908 (dated 1907). Oil on canvas, 4' 11¼" × 6' 6⅞". Museum of Modern Art, New York. ■◀

Kirchner's perspective distortions, disquieting figures, and color choices reflect the influence of the Fauves and of Edvard Munch (FIG. 28-28), who made similar expressive use of formal elements.

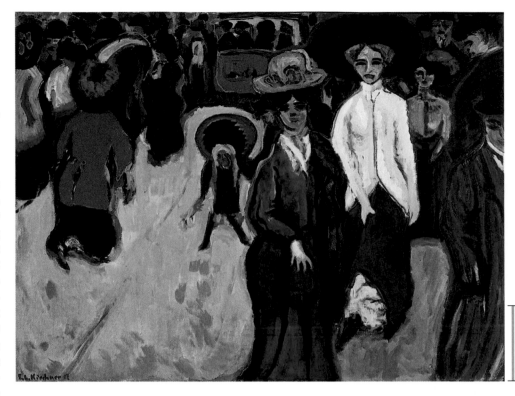

Kirchner's *Street, Dresden* (FIG. **29-5**) provides a glimpse into the frenzied urban activity of a bustling German city before World War I. Rather than offering the distant, panoramic urban view of the Impressionists (FIG. 28-5), Kirchner's street scene is jarring and dissonant in both composition and color. The women in the foreground loom large, approaching somewhat menacingly. The steep perspective of the street, which threatens to push the women directly into the viewer's space, increases their confrontational nature. Harshly rendered, the women's features make them appear ghoulish, and the garish, clashing colors—juxtapositions of bright orange, emerald green, chartreuse, and pink—add to the expressive impact of the image. Kirchner's perspective distortions, disquieting figures, and color choices reflect the influence of the work of Edvard Munch, who made similar expressive use of formal elements in *The Scream* (FIG. 28-28).

EMIL NOLDE Much older than most Die Brücke artists was Emil Hansen, who changed his name in 1902 to EMIL NOLDE (1867–1956) after his birthplace in northern Germany. The younger artists invited him to join their group in 1906, but Nolde, an introvert who preferred to work alone, left Die Brücke the next year. By 1913, the group had dissolved, but a commonality of interests and painterly style continued to link Nolde and the other Die Brücke artists throughout their careers. The content of Nolde's work centered, for the most part, on religious imagery. In contrast to the quiet spirituality and restraint of traditional religious images, however, Nolde's paintings, for example, *Saint Mary of Egypt among Sinners* (FIG. **29-6**), are visceral and forceful. Mary, before her conversion, entertains lechers whose lust magnifies their brutal ugliness. The distortions of form and color (especially the jarring juxtaposition of blue and orange) and the rawness of the brushstrokes amplify the harshness of the leering faces.

Borrowing ideas from van Gogh, Munch, the Fauves, and African and Oceanic art (see "Primi-

tivism and Colonialism," page 846, and FIG. **29-6A**), Nolde and the other Die Brücke artists created images that derive much of their power from a dissonance and seeming lack of finesse. The harsh colors, aggressively brushed paint, and distorted forms expressed the painters' feelings about the injustices of society and their belief in a healthful union of human beings and nature.

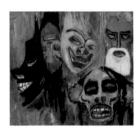

29-6A NOLDE, *Masks,* 1911.

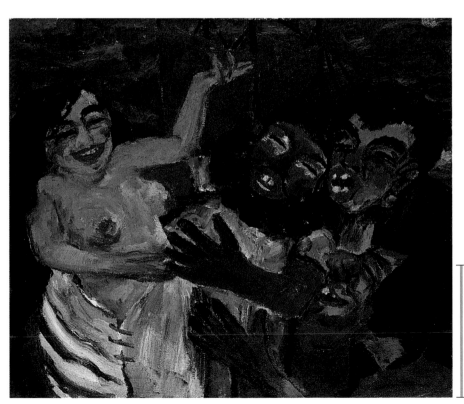

29-6 EMIL NOLDE, *Saint Mary of Egypt among Sinners,* 1912. Left panel of a triptych, oil on canvas, 2' 10" × 3' 3". Hamburger Kunsthalle, Hamburg.

In contrast to the quiet spirituality of traditional religious images, Nolde's paintings produce visceral emotions and feature distorted forms, jarring color juxtapositions, and raw brushstrokes.

Science and Art in the Early 20th Century

In the early 20th century, radical new ways of thinking emerged in both science and art, forcing people to revise how they understood the world. In particular, the values and ideals that were the legacy of the Enlightenment (see Chapter 26) began to yield to new perspectives. Intellectuals countered 18th- and 19th-century assumptions about progress and reason with ideas challenging traditional notions about the physical universe, the structure of society, and human nature. Modernist artists fully participated in this reassessment and formulated innovative theoretical bases for their work. Accordingly, much early-20th-century Western art is a rejection of traditional limitations and definitions both of art and of the universe.

Fundamental to the Enlightenment was faith in science. Because of its basis in empirical, or observable, fact, science provided a mechanistic conception of the universe, which reassured a populace that was finding traditional religions less certain. As promoted in the classic physics of Isaac Newton (1642–1727), the universe was a huge machine consisting of time, space, and matter. In the early 20th century, many scientists challenged this model of the universe in what amounted to a second scientific and technological revolution. Particularly noteworthy was the work of physicists Max Planck (1858–1947), Albert Einstein (1879–1955), Ernest Rutherford (1871–1937), and Niels Bohr (1885–1962). With their discoveries, each of these scientists shattered the existing faith in the objective reality of matter and, in so doing, paved the way for a new model of the universe. Planck's quantum theory (1900) raised questions about the emission of atomic energy. In his 1905 paper "The Electrodynamics of Moving Bodies," Einstein carried Planck's work further by introducing his theory of relativity. He argued that space and time are not absolute, as postulated in Newtonian physics. Rather, Einstein explained, time and space are relative to the observer and linked in

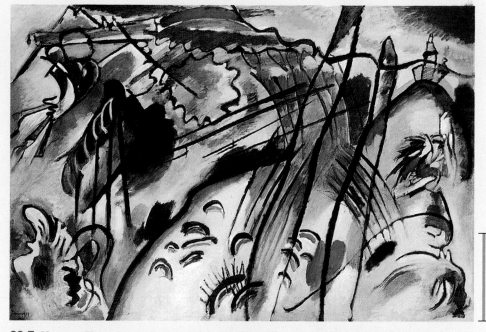

29-7 VASSILY KANDINSKY, *Improvisation 28* (second version), 1912. Oil on canvas, 3′ 7⅞″ × 5′ 3⅞″. Solomon R. Guggenheim Museum, New York (gift of Solomon R. Guggenheim, 1937).

The theories of Einstein and Rutherford convinced Kandinsky that material objects had no real substance. He was one of the first painters to explore complete abstraction in his canvases.

what he called a four-dimensional space-time continuum. He also concluded that matter, rather than a solid, tangible reality, was another form of energy. Einstein's famous equation, $E = mc^2$, where E stands for energy, m for mass, and c for the speed of light, provided a formula for understanding atomic energy. Rutherford's and Bohr's exploration of atomic structure between 1906 and 1913 contributed to this new perception of matter and energy. Together, all these scientific discoveries constituted a changed view of physical nature and contributed to the growing interest in abstraction, as opposed to the mimetic representation of the world, among early-20th-century artists such as Vassily Kandinsky (FIG. 29-7).

VASSILY KANDINSKY A second major German Expressionist group, *Der Blaue Reiter* (The Blue Rider), formed in Munich in 1911. The two founding members, Vassily Kandinsky and Franz Marc, whimsically selected this name because of their mutual interest in the color blue and horses. As did Die Brücke, this group produced paintings that captured their feelings in visual form while also eliciting intense visceral responses from viewers.

Born in Russia, VASSILY KANDINSKY (1866–1944) moved to Munich in 1896 and soon developed a spontaneous and aggressively avant-garde expressive style. Indeed, Kandinsky was one of the first artists to explore complete abstraction, as in *Improvisation 28* (FIG. **29-7**), painted in 1912. Kandinsky fueled his elimination of representational elements with his interest in theosophy (a religious and philosophical belief system incorporating a wide

range of tenets from, among other sources, Buddhism and mysticism) and the occult, as well as with advances in the sciences. A true intellectual, widely read in philosophy, religion, history, and the other arts, especially music, Kandinsky was also one of the few early modernists to read with some comprehension the new scientific theories of the era (see "Science and Art in the Early 20th Century," above). Scientists' exploration of atomic structure, for example, convinced Kandinsky that material objects had no real substance, thereby shattering his faith in a world of tangible things. He articulated his ideas in an influential treatise, *Concerning the Spiritual in Art,* published in 1912. Artists, Kandinsky believed, must express their innermost feelings by orchestrating color, form, line, and space. *Improvisation 28* is one of numerous works Kandinsky produced that convey feelings with color juxtapositions, intersecting

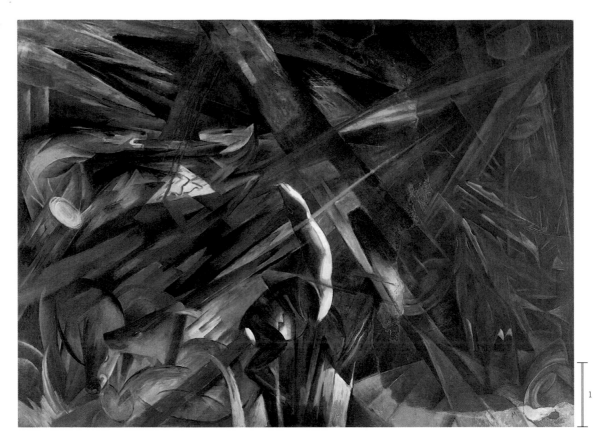

29-8 FRANZ MARC, *Fate of the Animals,* 1913. Oil on canvas, 6′ 4¾″ × 8′ 9½″. Kunstmuseum Basel, Basel.

Marc developed a system of correspondences between specific colors and feelings or ideas. In this apocalyptic scene of animals trapped in a forest, the colors of severity and brutality dominate.

1 ft.

linear elements, and implied spatial relationships. Ultimately, Kandinsky saw these abstractions as evolving blueprints for a more enlightened and liberated society emphasizing spirituality.

FRANZ MARC As did many of the other German Expressionists, FRANZ MARC (1880–1916), the cofounder of Der Blaue Reiter, grew increasingly pessimistic about the state of humanity, especially as World War I loomed on the horizon. His perception of human beings as deeply flawed led him to turn to the animal world for his subjects. Animals, he believed, were more pure than humanity and thus more appropriate vehicles to express an inner truth. In his quest to imbue his paintings with greater emotional intensity, Marc focused on color and developed a system of correspondences between specific colors and feelings or ideas. In a letter to a fellow Blaue Reiter, Marc explained: "Blue is the *male* principle, severe and spiritual. Yellow is the *female* principle, gentle, happy and sensual. Red is *matter,* brutal and heavy."[3]

Fate of the Animals (FIG. **29-8**) represents the culmination of Marc's efforts to create, in a sense, an iconography of color. Painted in 1913, when the tension of impending cataclysm had pervaded society, the animals appear trapped in a forest amid falling trees, some apocalyptic event destroying both the forest and the animals inhabiting it. The painter distorted the entire scene and shattered it into fragments. Significantly, the lighter and brighter colors—the passive, gentle, and cheerful ones—are absent, and the colors of severity and brutality dominate the work. On the back of the canvas Marc wrote: "All being is flaming suffering." The artist discovered just how well his painting portended war's anguish and tragedy when he ended up at the front the following year. His experiences in battle prompted him to tell his wife in a letter: "[*Fate of the Animals*] is like a premonition of this war—horrible and shattering. I can hardly conceive that I painted it."[4] Marc's contempt for people's inhumanity and his attempt to express that through his art ended, with tragic irony, in his death in action in 1916.

KÄTHE KOLLWITZ The emotional range of German Expressionism extends from passionate protest and satirical bitterness to the poignantly expressed pity for the poor in the prints of KÄTHE KOLLWITZ (1867–1945), for example, *Woman with Dead Child* (FIG. **29-9**). Kollwitz and her younger contemporary PAULA MODERSOHN-BECKER (1876–1907; FIG. **29-9A**) studied at the Union of Berlin Women Artists and had no formal association with any Expres-

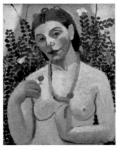

29-9A MODERSOHN-BECKER, *Self-Portrait,* 1906.

sionist group. Working in a variety of printmaking techniques, including woodcut, lithography, and etching, Kollwitz explored a range of issues from the overtly political to the deeply personal.

One image Kollwitz explored in depth, producing a number of print variations, was a mother with her dead child. Although she initially derived the theme from the Christian *Pietà,* Kollwitz transformed it into a universal statement of maternal loss and grief. In the etching and lithograph illustrated here (FIG. 29-9), she replaced the reverence and grace pervading most depictions of Mary holding the dead Christ (FIG. 22-12) with an animalistic passion. The grieving mother ferociously grips the body of her dead child. The primal nature of the undeniably powerful image is in keeping with the aims of the Expressionists. Not since the Gothic age in Germany (FIG. 13-50) had any artist produced a mother-and-son group with a comparable emotional impact. Because Kollwitz used her son Peter as the model for the dead child, the image was no doubt all the more personal to her. The print stands as a poignant premonition. Peter died fighting in World War I at age 21.

EGON SCHIELE Also related in spirit to but not associated with any German Expressionist group was the Austrian artist EGON SCHIELE (1890–1918), who during his tragically brief but

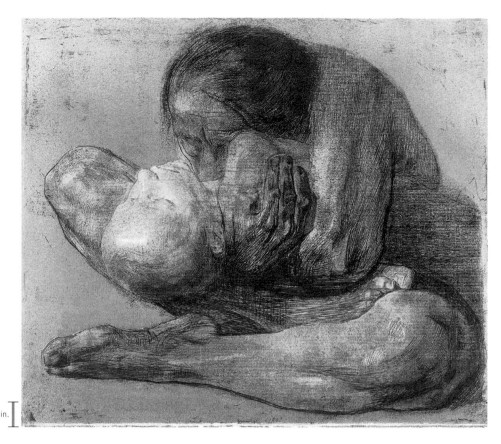

29-9 Käthe Kollwitz, *Woman with Dead Child*, 1903. Etching and soft-ground etching, overprinted lithographically with a gold tone plate, 1′ 4⅝″ × 1′ 7⅛″. British Museum, London.

The theme of a mother mourning over her dead child comes from images of the *Pietà* in Christian art, but Kollwitz transformed it into a powerful universal statement of maternal loss and grief.

prolific career produced more than 3,000 paintings and drawings. The bulk of them are nude figure studies of men and women in *gouache* and watercolor on paper, including approximately a hundred self-portraits (FIG. **29-10**) exemplifying early-20th-century Expressionist painters' intense interest in emotional states. As a teenager, Schiele watched the slow, painful deterioration of his father, who contracted syphilis and died when Egon was 15. The experience had a profound impact on the artist, who ever after associated sex with physical and emotional pain and death.

Schiele began formal art training the year after his father died. He enrolled in Vienna's Academy of Fine Art in 1906, where he became a protégé of Gustav Klimt (FIG. 28-29), who invited Schiele to exhibit some of his works with his own and those of, among others, Vincent van Gogh and Edvard Munch. The emotional content of their work made a deep impression upon Schiele, who nonetheless far surpassed van Gogh, Munch, and all of his contemporaries, including the sculptor WILHELM LEHMBRUCK (1881–1919; FIG. **29-10A**), in the portrayal of emaciated bodies and tormented psyches. Indeed, Schiele once spent 24 days in prison for producing what a judge ruled was pornographic art.

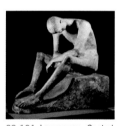

29-10A LEHMBRUCK, *Seated Youth*, 1917.

Schiele's 1910 nude portrait of himself grimacing (FIG. 29-10) is a characteristic example of his mature work. He stands frontally, staring at himself in the large mirror he kept in his studio. There is no background. The edges of the paper sever his lower legs and right elbow. In some portraits Schiele portrayed himself with amputated limbs, and his body is always that of a malnourished man whose muscles show through transparent flesh. The pose is awkward, twisted, and pained. The elongated fingers of the hands seem useless, incapable of holding anything. It is hard to imagine a nude body breaking more sharply with the classical tradition of heroic male nudity. Schiele's self-portrait is that of a martyr who has suffered both physically and psychologically. (He portrayed himself in several paintings as Saint Sebastian pierced by arrows.) Schiele's unhappy life ended when he contracted the Spanish flu in 1918. He was only 28 years old.

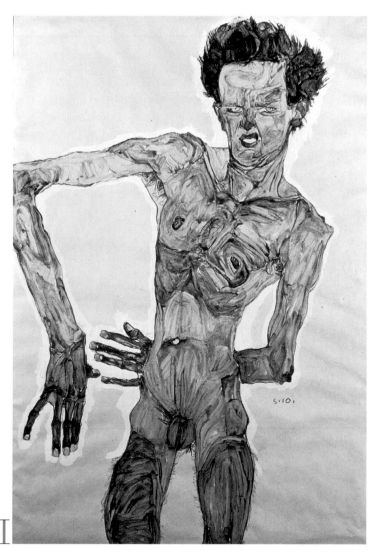

29-10 EGON SCHIELE, *Nude Self-Portrait, Grimacing*, 1910. Gouache, watercolor, and pencil on paper, 1′ 10″ × 1′ 2⅜″. Albertina, Vienna.

Breaking sharply with the academic tradition of heroic male nudity, Schiele, a Viennese Expressionist, often portrayed himself with an emaciated body, twisted limbs, and a grimacing expression.

Gertrude and Leo Stein and the Avant-Garde

One of the many unexpected developments in the history of art is that two Americans—Gertrude (1874–1946) and Leo (1872–1947) Stein—played pivotal roles in the history of the European avant-garde. The Steins provided a hospitable environment in their Paris home for artists, writers, musicians, collectors, and critics to socialize and discuss progressive art and ideas. Born in Pennsylvania, the Stein siblings moved to 27 rue de Fleurus in Paris in 1903. Gertrude's experimental writing stimulated her interest in the latest developments in the arts. Conversely, the avant-garde ideas discussed in her home influenced Gertrude's unique poetry, plays, and other works. She is perhaps best known for *The Autobiography of Alice B. Toklas* (1933), a unique memoir written in the persona of her longtime lesbian companion.

The Steins' interest in the exciting and invigorating debates taking place in avant-garde circles led them to welcome visitors to their Saturday salons, which included lectures, thoughtful discussions, and spirited arguments. Often, these gatherings lasted until dawn and included not only their French friends but also visiting Americans, Britons, Swedes, Germans, Hungarians, Spaniards, Poles, and Russians. Among the hundreds who visited the Steins were artists Henri Matisse, Pablo Picasso, Georges Braque, Mary Cassatt, Marcel Duchamp, Alfred Stieglitz, and Arthur B. Davies; writers Ernest Hemingway, F. Scott Fitzgerald, John dos Passos, Jean Cocteau, and Guillaume Apollinaire; art dealers Daniel Kahnweiler and Ambroise Vollard; critics Roger Fry and Clive Bell; and collectors Sergei Shchukin and Ivan Morozov.

The Steins were avid art collectors, and the works they hung in their home attracted many visitors. One of the first paintings Leo purchased was Matisse's notorious *Woman with the Hat* (FIG. 29-2), and he subsequently bought many more by Matisse—including *Le Bonheur de Vivre* (FIG. 29-2A)—along with works by Gauguin, Cézanne, Renoir, Picasso, and Braque. Picasso, who developed a close friendship with Gertrude, painted her portrait (FIG. 29-11) in 1907. Gertrude loved the painting so much she kept it by her all her life and bequeathed it to the Metropolitan Museum of Art only upon her death in 1946.

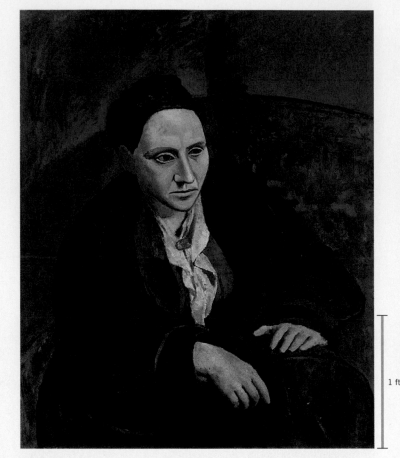

1 ft.

29-11 PABLO PICASSO, *Gertrude Stein*, 1906–1907. Oil on canvas, 3′ 3⅜″ × 2′ 8″. Metropolitan Museum of Art, New York (bequest of Gertrude Stein, 1947). ◼◀

Picasso had left this portrait of his friend and patron unfinished until he decided to incorporate the planar simplicity of ancient Iberian stone sculptures into his depiction of her face.

Primitivism and Cubism

The Expressionist departure from any strict adherence to illusionism in art was a path other artists followed. Among those who most radically challenged prevailing artistic conventions and moved most aggressively into the realm of abstraction was Pablo Picasso.

PABLO PICASSO Born in Spain four years after Gustave Courbet's death, PABLO PICASSO (1881–1973) mastered all aspects of late-19th-century Realist technique by the time he entered the Barcelona Academy of Fine Art in the late 1890s. His prodigious talent led him to experiment with a wide range of visual expression, first in Spain and then in Paris, where he settled in 1904. An artist whose importance to the history of art is uncontested, Picasso made staggering contributions to new ways of representing the surrounding world. Perhaps the most prolific artist in history, he explored virtually every artistic medium during his lengthy career, but remained a traditional artist in making careful preparatory studies for each major work. Nonetheless, Picasso epitomized modernism in his enduring quest for innovation, which resulted in sudden shifts from one style to another. By the time he settled permanently in Paris, Picasso's work had evolved from Spanish painting's sober Realism through an Impressionistic phase to the so-called Blue Period (1901–1904), when, in a melancholy state of mind, he used primarily blue colors to depict worn, pathetic, and alienated figures. In 1904, Picasso's palette changed to lighter and brighter colors during his Rose (or Pink) Period (1904–1906), but some of the canvases he painted during those years, such as *Family of Saltimbanques* (FIG. 29-11A), retain the pessimistic overtones of the Blue Period.

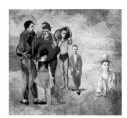

29-11A PICASSO, *Family of Saltimbanques*, 1905.

GERTRUDE STEIN By 1906, Picasso was searching restlessly for new ways to depict form. He found clues in the ancient Iberian sculpture of his homeland and other "primitive" cultures.

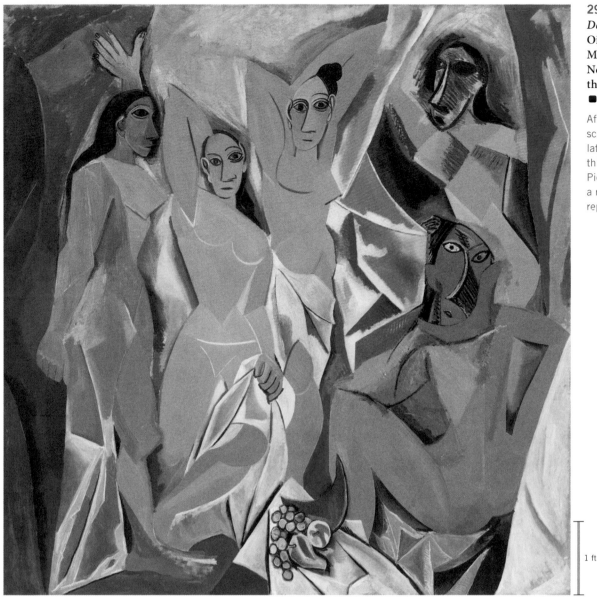

29-12 PABLO PICASSO, *Les Demoiselles d'Avignon*, 1907. Oil on canvas, 8′ × 7′ 8″. Museum of Modern Art, New York (acquired through the Lillie P. Bliss Bequest). ▣◀

African and ancient Iberian sculpture and Cézanne's late paintings influenced this pivotal work, with which Picasso opened the door to a radically new method of representing forms in space.

1 ft.

Inspired by these sources, Picasso returned to a portrait of *Gertrude Stein* (FIG. **29-11**), his friend and patron (see "Gertrude and Leo Stein and the Avant-Garde," page 844). Picasso had left the portrait unfinished after Stein posed for more than 80 sittings earlier in the year. On resuming work, Picasso painted Stein's head as a simplified planar form, incorporating aspects derived from Iberian stone heads. Although the disparity between the style of the face and the rest of the figure is striking, together they provide an insightful portrait of a forceful, vivacious woman. More important, Picasso had discovered a new approach to the representation of the human form.

DEMOISELLES D'AVIGNON The influence of "primitive" art also surfaces in *Les Demoiselles d'Avignon* (*The Young Ladies of Avignon*; FIG. **29-12**), which opened the door to a radically new method of representing form in space. Picasso began the work as a symbolic picture to be titled *Philosophical Bordello,* portraying two male clients (who, based on surviving drawings, had features resembling Picasso's) intermingling with women in the reception room of a brothel on Avignon Street in Barcelona. One was a sailor. The other carried a skull, an obvious reference to death. By the time the artist finished, he had eliminated the male figures and simpli-

fied the room's details to a suggestion of drapery and a schematic foreground still life. Picasso had become wholly absorbed in the problem of finding a new way to represent the five female figures in their interior space. Instead of depicting the figures as continuous volumes, he fractured their shapes and interwove them with the equally jagged planes representing drapery and empty space. Indeed, the space, so entwined with the bodies, is virtually illegible. Here Picasso pushed Cézanne's treatment of form and space (FIGS. 28-21 to 28-22A) to a new level. The tension between Picasso's representation of three-dimensional space and his conviction a painting is a two-dimensional design on the surface of a stretched canvas is a tension between representation and abstraction.

The artist extended the radical nature of *Les Demoiselles d'Avignon* even further by depicting the figures inconsistently. Ancient Iberian sculptures inspired the calm, ideal features of the three young women at the left, as they had the head of Gertrude Stein (FIG. 29-11). The energetic, violently striated features of the two heads to the right emerged late in Picasso's production of the work and grew directly from his increasing fascination with the power of African sculpture (see "'Primitivism' and Colonialism," page 846), which the artist studied in Paris's Trocadéro ethnography museum

Primitivism and Colonialism

The art of Africa, Oceania, and the native peoples of the Americas was a major source of inspiration for many early-20th-century modernist artists. Art historians refer to the incorporation of stylistic elements from these "non-Western" cultures as *primitivism*. Both terms imply the superiority of Western civilization and Western art, but many modernist artists admired these artworks precisely because they embodied different stylistic preferences and standards. Some artists, for example Henri Matisse and Pablo Picasso (FIG. 29-13), became enthusiastic collectors of "primitive art," but all of them could view non-Western objects in the many European and American anthropological and ethnographic museums that had begun to proliferate during the second half of the 19th century.

In 1882, the Musée d'Ethnographie du Trocadéro (now the Musée du quai Branly) in Paris opened its doors to the public. The Musée Permanent des Colonies (now the Musée National des Arts d'Afrique et d'Océanie) in Paris also provided the public with a wide array of objects—weapons, tools, basketwork, headdresses—from colonial territories, as did the Musée Africain in Marseilles. In Berlin, the Museum für Völkerkunde housed almost 10,000 African objects by 1886, when it opened for public viewing. Even the Expositions Universelles—regularly scheduled exhibitions in France designed to celebrate industrial progress—included products from Oceania and Africa after 1851. By the beginning of the 20th century, significant non-Western collections were on view in museums in Liverpool, Glasgow, Edinburgh, London, Hamburg, Stuttgart, Vienna, Berlin, Munich, Leiden, Copenhagen, and Chicago.

The formation of these collections was a by-product of the frenzied imperialist expansion central to the geopolitical dynamics of the 19th century and much of the 20th century. Most of the Western powers maintained colonies as raw-material sources, as manufacturing markets, and as territorial acquisitions. For example, the United States, France, and Holland all kept a colonial presence in the Pacific. Britain, France, Germany, Belgium, Holland, Spain, and Portugal divided up the African continent. People often perceived these colonial cultures as "primitive" and referred to many of the non-Western artifacts displayed in museums as "artificial curiosities" or "fetish objects." Indeed, the exhibition of these objects collected during expeditions to the colonies served to reinforce the "need" for a colonial presence in these countries. Colonialism often had a missionary dimension. These objects, which often depicted strange gods or creatures, reinforced the perception these peoples were "barbarians" who needed to be "civilized" or "saved," and this perception justified colonialism and its missionary aspects worldwide.

Whether avant-garde artists were aware of the imperialistic implications of their appropriation of non-Western culture is unclear. Certainly, however, many artists reveled in the energy and freshness of non-Western images and forms. These different cultural products provided Western artists with new ways of looking at their own art. Matisse always maintained he saw African sculptures as simply "good sculptures . . . like any other."* Picasso, in contrast, believed "the masks weren't just like any other pieces of

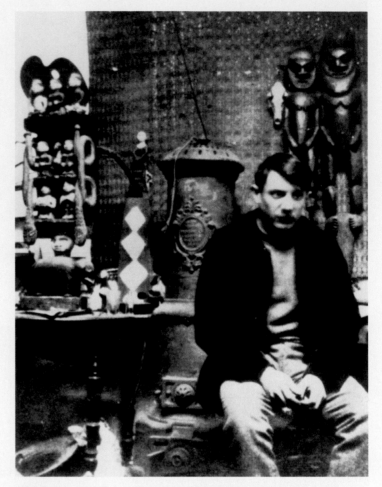

29-13 FRANK GELETT BURGESS, photograph of Pablo Picasso in his studio in the rue Ravignan, Paris, France, 1908. Musée Picasso, Paris. ◼◀

Picasso was familiar with ancient Iberian art from his homeland and studied African and other "primitive" art in Paris's Trocadéro museum. He kept his own collection of primitive art in his studio.

sculpture. Not at all. They were magic things. . . . mediators" between humans and the forces of evil, and he sought to capture their power as well as their forms in his paintings. "[In the Trocadéro] I understood why I was a painter. . . . All alone in that awful museum, with masks, dolls . . . *Les Demoiselles d'Avignon* [FIG. 29-12] must have come to me that day."† "Primitive art" seemed to embody a directness, closeness to nature, and honesty that appealed to modernist artists determined to reject conventional models. Non-Western art served as an important revitalizing and energizing force in Western art.

*Jean-Louis Paudrat, "From Africa," in William Rubin, ed., *"Primitivism" in 20th Century Art: Affinity of the Tribal and the Modern* (New York: Museum of Modern Art, 1984), 1:141.
†Ibid.

and collected and kept in his Paris studio (FIG. 29-13). Perhaps responding to the energy of these two new heads, Picasso also revised their bodies. He broke them into more ambiguous planes suggesting a combination of views, as if the observer sees the figures from more than one place in space at once. The woman seated at the lower right shows these multiple angles most clearly, seeming to present the viewer simultaneously with a three-quarter back view from the left, another from the right, and a front view of the head that suggests seeing the figure frontally as well. Gone is the traditional concept of an orderly, constructed, and unified pictorial space mirroring the world. In its place are the rudimentary beginnings of a new representation of the world as a dynamic interplay of time and space. Clearly, *Les Demoiselles d'Avignon* represents a dramatic departure from the careful presentation of a visual reality. Explained Picasso: "I paint forms as I think them, not as I see them."[5]

GEORGES BRAQUE AND CUBISM

For many years, Picasso showed *Les Demoiselles* only to other painters. One of the first to see it was GEORGES BRAQUE (1882–1963), a Fauve painter who found it so challenging he began to rethink his own painting style. Using the painting's revolutionary elements as a point of departure, together Braque and Picasso formulated *Cubism* around 1908 in the belief the art of painting had to move far beyond the description of visual reality. Cubism represented a radical turning point in the history of art, nothing less than a dismissal of the pictorial illusionism that had dominated Western art since the Renaissance. The Cubists rejected naturalistic depictions, preferring compositions of shapes and forms abstracted from the conventionally perceived world. They pursued the analysis of form central to Cézanne's artistic explorations by dissecting everything around them into their many constituent features, which they then recomposed, by a new logic of design, into a coherent, independent aesthetic picture. The Cubists' rejection of accepted artistic practice illustrates both the period's aggressive avant-garde critique of pictorial convention and the public's dwindling faith in a safe, concrete Newtonian world in the face of the physics of Einstein and others (see "Science and Art," page 841).

The new style received its name after Matisse described some of Braque's work to the critic Louis Vauxcelles as having been painted "with little cubes." In his review, Vauxcelles described the new paintings as "cubic oddities."[6] The French writer and theorist Guillaume Apollinaire (1880–1918) summarized well the central concepts of Cubism in 1913:

> Authentic cubism [is] the art of depicting new wholes with formal elements borrowed not from the reality of vision, but from that of conception. This tendency leads to a poetic kind of painting which stands outside the world of observation; for, even in a simple cubism, the geometrical surfaces of an object must be opened out in order to give a complete representation of it. . . . Everyone must agree that a chair, from whichever side it is viewed, never ceases to have four legs, a seat and a back, and that, if it is robbed of one of these elements, it is robbed of an important part.[7]

Most art historians refer to the first phase of Cubism, developed jointly by Picasso and Braque, as *Analytic Cubism,* because in essence it is a painterly analysis of the structure of form. Because Cubists could not achieve the kind of total view Apollinaire described by the traditional method of drawing or painting models from one position, they began to dissect the forms of their subjects and to present their analysis of form across the canvas surface.

THE PORTUGUESE Georges Braque's painting *The Portuguese* (FIG. 29-14) exemplifies Analytic Cubism. The subject is a Portuguese musician the artist recalled seeing years earlier in a bar in Marseilles. Braque dissected the man and his instrument and placed the resulting forms in dynamic interaction with the space around them. Unlike the Fauves and German Expressionists, who used vibrant colors, the Cubists chose subdued hues—here solely brown tones—in order to focus attention on form. In *The Portuguese,* Braque carried his analysis so far viewers must work diligently to discover clues to the subject. The construction of large intersecting planes suggests the forms of a man and a guitar. Smaller shapes interpenetrate and hover in the large planes. The way Braque treated light and shadow reveals his departure from conventional artistic practice. Light and dark passages suggest both chiaroscuro modeling and transparent planes that enable viewers to see through one level to another. Solid forms emerge only to be canceled almost immediately by a different reading of the subject.

The stenciled letters and numbers Braque included add to the painting's complexity. Letters and numbers are flat shapes, but as elements of a Cubist painting such as *The Portuguese,* they enable the

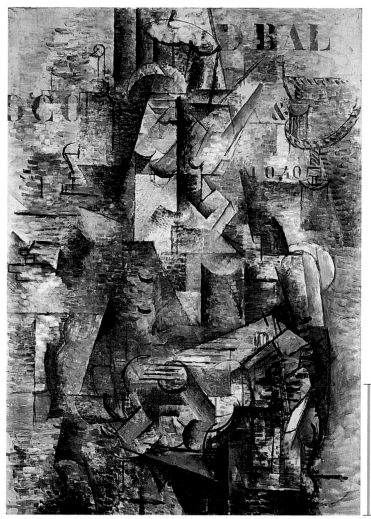

29-14 GEORGES BRAQUE, *The Portuguese,* 1911. Oil on canvas, 3′ 10⅛″ × 2′ 8″. Kunstmuseum Basel, Basel (gift of Raoul La Roche, 1952). ◼◂

The Cubists rejected the pictorial illusionism that had dominated Western art for centuries. Here, Braque concentrated on dissecting form and placing it in dynamic interaction with space.

painter to play with viewers' perception of two- and three-dimensional space. The letters and numbers lie flat on the painted canvas surface, yet the shading and shapes of other forms seem to flow behind and underneath them, pushing the letters and numbers forward into the viewing space. Occasionally, they seem attached to the surface of some object within the painting. Ultimately, the constantly shifting imagery makes it impossible to arrive at any definitive or final reading of the image. Examining this kind of painting is a disconcerting excursion into ambiguity and doubt, especially since the letters and numbers seem to anchor the painting in the world of representation, thereby exacerbating the tension between representation and abstraction. Analytical Cubist paintings radically disrupt expectations about the representation of space and time.

ROBERT DELAUNAY Art historians generally regard the suppression of color as crucial to Cubism's success, but ROBERT DELAUNAY (1885–1941), Picasso's and Braque's contemporary, worked toward a kind of color Cubism. Apollinaire gave the name *Orphism* to Delaunay's version of Cubism, after Orpheus, the Greek god of music. Apollinaire believed art, like music, was distinct from the representation of the visible world. But Delaunay's own name for his art was *Simultanéisme*. "Simultaneity" for Delaunay meant the application of 19th-century theories about the perception and psychology of color (see "19th-Century Color Theory," Chapter 28, page 813) to create spatial effects and kaleidoscopic movement solely through color contrasts. He insisted color in painting was both form and subject, and as early as 1912 he began to paint purely abstract compositions with titles such as *Simultaneous Disks, Simultaneous Windows,* and *Simultaneous Contrasts.* Delaunay developed his ideas about color use in dialogue with his Russian-born wife, Sonia (1885–1974), also an important modernist artist. She created paintings, quilts, and other textile arts, and book covers that exploited the expressive capabilities of color. As a result of their artistic explorations, both Delaunays became convinced the rhythms of modern life could best be expressed through color harmonies and dissonances.

A salient feature of modern life for Delaunay was technological innovation, and the engineering marvels of the late 19th and early 20th centuries figure prominently in his paintings. In 1914 he immortalized the engineer, inventor, and aviator Louis Blériot (1872–1936) in one of his boldest Orphic canvases. *Homage to Blériot* (FIG. **29-15**) is an almost purely abstract composition that celebrates Blériot's great achievement of being the first person to fly across the English Channel, which he accomplished in a monoplane of his own design. The 22-mile flight from Les Barraques, near Calais, France, to Dover, England, on July 25, 1909, lasted 37 minutes and made Blériot an instant international celebrity. It also brought him a prize of 1,000 British pounds, which a London newspaper had offered as a challenge to all aviators. At the time Delaunay commemorated the event, Blériot was manufacturing warplanes for use by French pilots and their allies during World War I. Blériot's monoplane appears at the upper right of Delaunay's painting, above another triumph of French engineering, the Eiffel

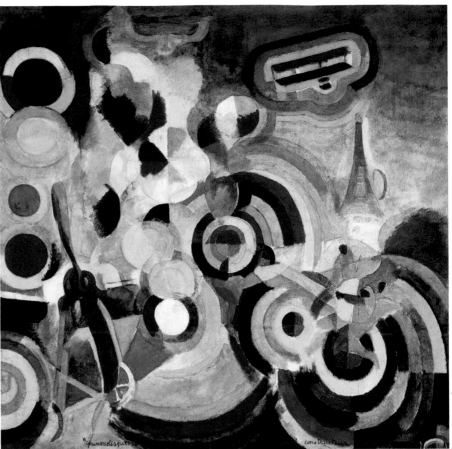

29-15 ROBERT DELAUNAY, *Homage to Blériot*, 1914. Oil on canvas, 8′ 2½″ × 8′ 3″. Kunstmuseum Basel, Basel (Emanuel Hoffman Foundation).

In this Orphic Cubist composition, Delaunay paid tribute to Louis Blériot, the first person to fly across the English Channel. Blériot's monoplane is at the upper right, above the Eiffel Tower.

Tower (FIG. 28-38), one of Delaunay's favorite subjects (FIG. **29-15A**). Filling the rest of the canvas are a propeller (at the lower left) and mostly circular abstract shapes suggestive of whirling propellers and blazing suns.

SYNTHETIC CUBISM In 1912, Cubism entered a new phase that art historians have dubbed *Synthetic Cubism.* In this later Cubist style, instead of dissecting forms, artists constructed paintings and

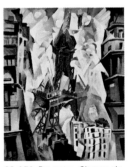

29-15A DELAUNAY, *Champs de Mars,* 1911.

drawings from objects and shapes cut from paper or other materials. The work marking the point of departure for this new style was Picasso's *Still Life with Chair-Caning* (FIG. **29-16**), a mixed-media painting in which Picasso imprinted a photolithographed pattern of a cane chair seat on the canvas and then pasted a piece of oilcloth on it. Framed with rope, this work challenges viewers' understanding of reality. The photographically replicated chair caning seems so "real" one expects the holes to break any brushstrokes laid upon it. But the chair caning, although optically suggestive of the real, is only an illusion or representation of an object. In contrast, the painted abstract areas do not refer to tangible objects in the real world. Yet the fact they do not imitate anything makes them more "real" than the chair caning. No pretense exists. Picasso extended the visual play by making the letter *U* escape from the space of the accompanying *J* and *O*

Picasso on Cubism

In 1923, almost a decade after Picasso and Braque launched an artistic revolution with their Analytic (FIG. 29-14) and Synthetic (FIG. 29-16) Cubist paintings, Picasso granted an interview to the painter and critic Marius de Zayas (1880–1961). Born in Mexico, de Zayas had settled in New York City in 1907, and in 1911 had been instrumental in mounting the first exhibition in the United States of Picasso's works. In their conversation, the approved English translation of which appeared in the journal *The Arts* under the title "Picasso Speaks," the artist set forth his views about Cubism and the nature of art in general.

> We all know that Art is not truth. Art is a lie that makes us realize truth, at least the truth that is given us to understand. The artist must know the manner whereby to convince others of the truthfulness of his lies. . . . They speak of naturalism in opposition to modern painting. I would like to know if anyone has ever seen a natural work of art. Nature and art, being two different things, cannot be the same thing. Through art we express our conception of what nature is not. . . .
>
> Cubism is no different from any other school of painting. The same principles and the same elements are common to all. . . . Many think that Cubism is an art of transition, an experiment which is to bring ulterior results. Those who think that way have not understood it. Cubism is not either a seed or a foetus, but an art dealing primarily with forms, and when a form is realized it is there to live its own life. . . . Mathematics, trigonometry, chemistry, psychoanalysis, music, and whatnot, have been related to Cubism to give it an easier interpretation. All this has been pure literature, not to say nonsense, . . . Cubism has kept itself within the limits and limitations of painting, never pretending to go beyond it. Drawing, design, and color are understood and practiced in Cubism in the spirit and manner that they are understood and practiced in all other schools. Our subjects might be different, as we have introduced into painting objects and forms that were formerly ignored. . . . [I]n our subjects, we keep the joy of discovery, the pleasure of the unexpected; our subject itself must be a source of interest.*

*Marius de Zayas, "Picasso Speaks," *The Arts* (May 1923), 315–326. Reprinted in Herschel B. Chipp, *Theories of Modern Art: A Source Book by Artists and Critics* (Berkeley and Los Angeles: University of California Press, 1968), 263–266.

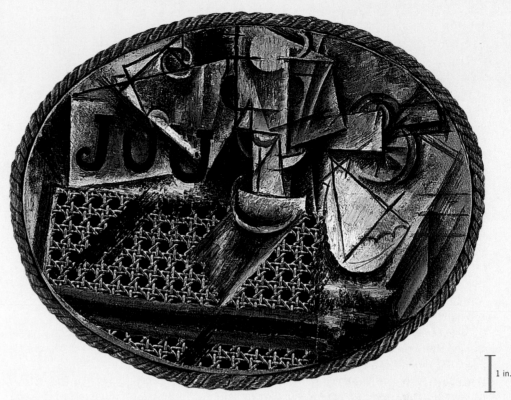

29-16 PABLO PICASSO, *Still Life with Chair-Caning,* 1912. Oil, oilcloth, and rope on canvas, $10\frac{5}{8}'' \times 1'\ 1\frac{3}{4}''$. Musée Picasso, Paris. ◼◀

This painting includes a piece of oilcloth imprinted with the photolithographed pattern of a cane chair seat. Framed with a piece of rope, the still life challenges the viewer's understanding of reality.

1 in.

and partially covering it with a cylindrical shape that pushes across its left side. The letters *JOU,* which appear in many Cubist paintings, formed part of the masthead of the daily French newspapers (*journaux*) often found among the objects represented. Picasso and Braque especially delighted in the punning references to *jouer* and *jouir*—the French verbs meaning "to play" and "to enjoy."

Although most discussions of Cubism focus on the formal innovations of Picasso, Braque, and Delaunay, it is important to note that the public also viewed the revolutionary nature of Cubism in sociopolitical terms. Many people considered Cubism's challenge to artistic convention and tradition a subversive attack on 20th-century society. In fact, many modernist artists and writers of the period allied themselves with various anarchist groups whose social critiques and utopian visions appealed to progressive thinkers. It was, therefore, not difficult to see radical art, such as Cubism, as having political ramifications. Many critics in the French press consistently equated Cubism's disdain for tradition with anarchism and revolution. Picasso himself, however, never viewed Cubism as a protest movement or even different in kind from traditional painting (see "Picasso on Cubism," above).

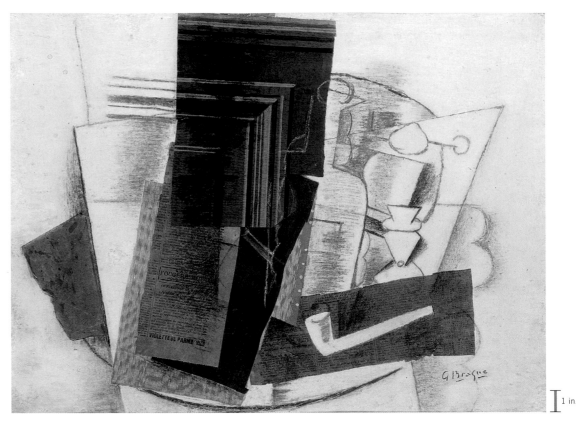

29-17 Georges Braque, *Bottle, Newspaper, Pipe, and Glass*, 1913. Charcoal and various papers pasted on paper, 1′ 6⅞″ × 2′ 1¼″. Private collection, New York. ◼◀

This Cubist collage of glued paper is a visual game to be deciphered. The pipe in the foreground, for example, seems to lie on the newspaper, but it is a cutout revealing the canvas surface.

⌶ 1 in.

COLLAGE After *Still Life with Chair-Caning*, both Picasso and Braque continued to explore the medium of *collage* introduced into the realm of "high art" (as opposed to unselfconscious "folk art") in that work. From the French word *coller*, meaning "to stick," a collage is a composition of bits of objects, such as newspaper or cloth, glued to a surface. Braque's *Bottle, Newspaper, Pipe, and Glass* (FIG. **29-17**) is a type of collage called *papier collé* ("stuck paper") in which the artist glues assorted paper shapes to a drawing or painting. In Braque's papier collé, charcoal lines and shadows provide clues to the Cubist multiple views of various surfaces and objects. Roughly rectangular strips of printed and colored paper dominate the composition. The paper imprinted with wood grain and moldings provides an illusion whose concreteness contrasts with the lightly rendered objects on the right. Five pieces of paper overlap one another in the center of the composition to create a layering of flat planes that both echo the space the lines suggest and establish the flatness of the work's surface. All shapes in the image seem to oscillate, pushing forward and dropping back in space. Shading seems to carve space into flat planes in some places and to turn planes into transparent surfaces in others. The pipe in the foreground illustrates this complex visual interplay especially well. Although it appears to lie on the newspaper, it is in fact a form cut through the printed paper to reveal the canvas surface, which Braque lightly modeled with charcoal. The artist thus kept his audience aware that *Bottle, Newspaper, Pipe, and Glass* is an artwork, a visual game to be deciphered, and not an attempt to reproduce nature.

Picasso explained the goals of Cubist collage in this way:

> Not only did we try to displace reality; reality was no longer in the object.... [In] the *papier collé*... [w]e didn't any longer want to fool the eye; we wanted to fool the mind.... If a piece of newspaper can be a bottle, that gives us something to think about in connection with both newspapers and bottles, too.[8]

Like all collage, the papier collé technique was modern in its medium—mass-produced materials never before found in high art—and modern in the way the artist embedded the art's "message" in the imagery and in the nature of these everyday materials.

GUERNICA Picasso continued to experiment with different artistic styles and media right up until his death in 1973. Celebrated primarily for his brilliant formal innovations, he was nonetheless acutely aware of politics throughout his life. As Picasso watched his homeland descend into civil war in the late 1930s, his involvement in political issues grew even stronger. He declared: "[P]ainting is not made to decorate apartments. It is an instrument for offensive and defensive war against the enemy."[9] Picasso got the opportunity to use art as a weapon in January 1937 when the Spanish Republican government-in-exile in Paris asked Picasso to produce a major work for the Spanish Pavilion at the Paris International Exposition that summer. He did not formally accept the invitation, however, until he received word that Guernica, the capital of the Basque region (an area in southern France and northern Spain populated by Basque speakers), had been almost totally destroyed in an air raid on April 26, 1937. Nazi pilots acting on behalf of the rebel general Francisco Franco (1892–1975) bombed the city at the busiest hour of a market day, killing or wounding many of Guernica's 7,000 citizens as well as leveling buildings. The event jolted Picasso into action. By the end of June, he had completed *Guernica* (FIG. **29-18**), a mural-sized canvas of immense power.

Despite the painting's title, Picasso made no specific reference to the event in *Guernica*. The imagery includes no bombs and no German planes. It is a universal visceral outcry of human grief. In the center, along the lower edge of the painting, lies a slain warrior clutching a broken and useless sword. A gored horse tramples him and rears back in fright as it dies. On the left, a shrieking, anguished woman cradles her dead child. On the far right, a woman on fire runs screaming from a burning building, while another woman flees mindlessly. In the upper right corner, a woman, represented by only a head, emerges from the burning building, thrusting forth a light to illuminate the horror. Overlooking the destruction is a bull, which, according to the artist, represents "brutality and darkness."[10]

In *Guernica*, Picasso brilliantly used aspects of his earlier Cubist discoveries to expressive effect, particularly the fragmentation of objects and the dislocation of anatomical features. This Cubist

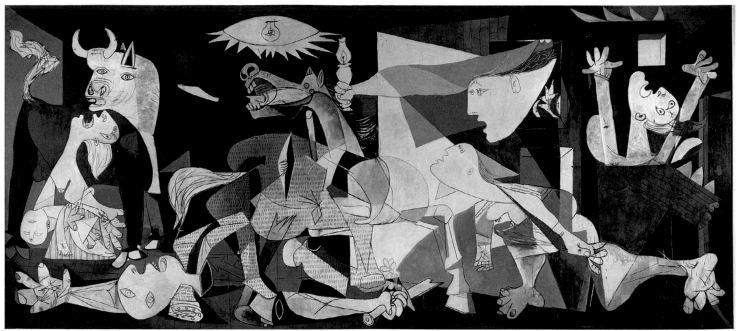

29-18 PABLO PICASSO, *Guernica,* 1937. Oil on canvas, 11′ 5½″ × 25′ 5¾″. Museo Nacional Centro de Arte Reina Sofía, Madrid. ◼◀

Picasso used Cubist techniques, especially the fragmentation of objects and dislocation of anatomical features, to expressive effect in this condemnation of the Nazi bombing of the Basque capital.

fragmentation gave visual form to the horror of the aerial bombardment of the Basque people. What happened to these figures in the artist's act of painting—the dissections and contortions of the human form—paralleled what happened to them in real life. To emphasize the scene's severity and starkness, Picasso reduced his palette to black, white, and shades of gray, suppressing color once again, as he had in his Analytic Cubist works.

GUITAR Cubism not only opened new avenues for representing form on two-dimensional surfaces. It also inspired new approaches to sculpture. Picasso created *Guitar* (FIG. **29-19**) in 1912. As in his Cubist paintings, this sculpture operates at the intersection of two- and three-dimensionality. Picasso took the form of a guitar—an image that surfaces in many of his paintings as well, including *Three Musicians* (FIG. **29-19A**)—and explored its volume via flat planar cardboard surfaces. (FIG. 29-19 reproduces the *maquette,* or model. The finished sculpture was to be made of sheet metal.) By presenting what is essentially a cutaway view of a guitar, Picasso allowed viewers to examine both surface and interior space, both mass and void. This, of course, was completely in keeping with the Cubist program. Some scholars have suggested Picasso

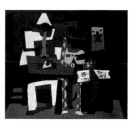

29-19A PICASSO, *Three Musicians,* 1921.

derived the cylindrical form that serves as the sound hole on the guitar from the eyes on masks from the Ivory Coast of Africa. African masks were a continuing and persistent source of inspiration for the artist (see "Primitivism," page 846). Here, however, Picasso seems to have transformed the anatomical features of African masks into a part of a musical instrument—dramatic evidence of his unique, innovative artistic vision. Ironically—and intentionally—the sound hole, the central void in a real guitar, is, in Picasso's *Guitar,* the only solid form.

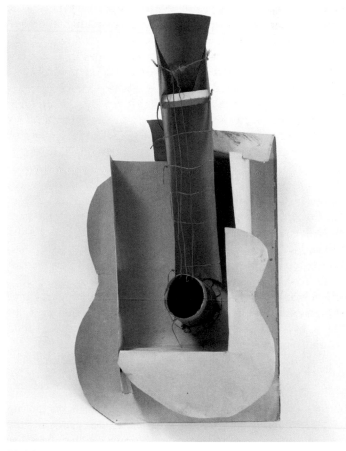

29-19 PABLO PICASSO, maquette for *Guitar,* 1912. Cardboard, string, and wire (restored), 2′ 1¼″ × 1′ 1″ × 7½″. Museum of Modern Art, New York.

In this model for a sculpture of sheet metal, Picasso presented what is essentially a cutaway view of a guitar, allowing the viewer to examine both surface and interior space, both mass and void.

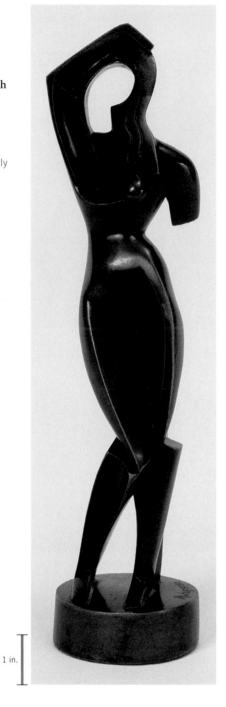

29-20 Aleksandr Archipenko, *Woman Combing Her Hair*, 1915. Bronze, 1' 1¾" × 3¼" × 3⅛". Museum of Modern Art, New York (acquired through the Lillie P. Bliss Bequest).

In this statuette, Archipenko introduced, in place of the head, a void with a shape of its own that figures importantly in the whole design. The void is not simply the negative counterpart of the volume.

1 in.

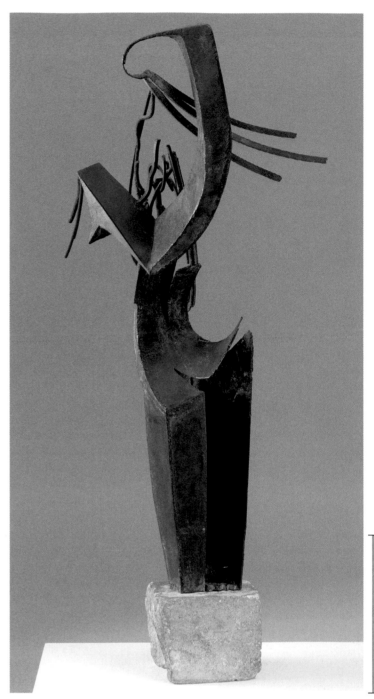

1 ft.

29-21 Julio González, *Woman Combing Her Hair*, 1936. Iron, 4' 4" × 1' 11½" × 2' ⅝". Museum of Modern Art, New York (Mrs. Simon Guggenheim Fund).

Using prefabricated metal pieces, González reduced his figure to an interplay of curves, lines, and planes—virtually a complete abstraction without any vestiges of traditional representational art.

ALEKSANDR ARCHIPENKO The Russian sculptor Aleksandr Archipenko (1887–1964) similarly explored the Cubist notion of spatial ambiguity and the relationship between solid forms and space. In *Woman Combing Her Hair* (FIG. 29-20), Archipenko introduced, in place of the head, a void with a shape of its own that figures importantly in the whole design. Enclosed spaces have always existed in figurative sculpture—for example, the space between the arm and the body when the hand rests on the hip (FIG. 21-13). But in Archipenko's statuette the space penetrates the figure's continuous mass and is a defined form equal in importance to the mass of the bronze. It is not simply the negative counterpart to the volume as it is in traditional statues. Archipenko's *Woman* shows the same fluid intersecting planes seen in Cubist painting, and the relation of the planes to each other is equally complex. Thus, both in painting and sculpture, the Cubists broke through traditional limits and transformed these media.

JULIO GONZÁLEZ Among the other notable sculptors of the early 20th century were Julio González (1876–1942; FIG. 29-21) and Jacques Lipchitz (1891–1973). Lipchitz's works, such as *Bather* (FIG. 29-21A), are three-dimensional equivalents of the Analytical Cubist canvases of Picasso and Braque (FIG. 29-14). González was a friend of Picasso who shared his interest in the artistic possibilities of new materials and new methods borrowed from both industrial technology and

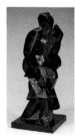

29-21A Lipchitz, *Bather*, 1917.

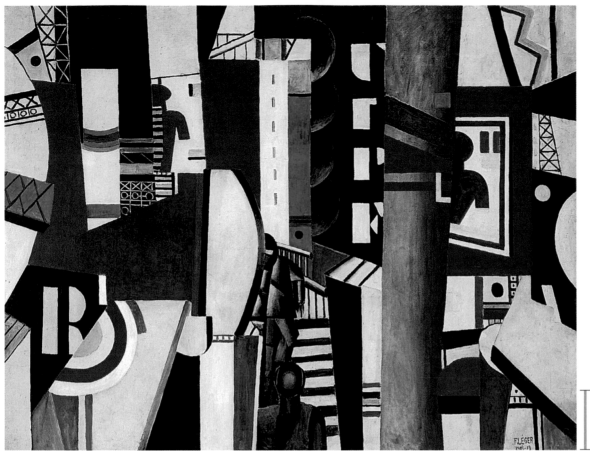

29-22 Fernand Léger, *The City*, 1919. Oil on canvas, 7′ 7″ × 9′ 9½″. Philadelphia Museum of Art, Philadelphia (A. E. Gallatin Collection).

Léger championed the "machine aesthetic." In *The City*, he captured the mechanical commotion of urban life, incorporating the effects of billboard ads, flashing lights, and noisy traffic.

1 ft.

traditional metalworking. Born into a family of metalworkers in Barcelona, González helped Picasso construct a number of welded sculptures. This contact with Picasso in turn enabled González to refine his own sculptural vocabulary. Using prefabricated bars, sheets, or rods of welded or wrought iron and bronze, González created dynamic sculptures with both linear elements and volumetric forms. A comparison between his *Woman Combing Her Hair* (FIG. 29-21) and Archipenko's version of the same subject (FIG. 29-20) is instructive. Archipenko's figure still incorporates the basic shapes of a woman's body. González reduced his figure to an interplay of curves, lines, and planes—virtually a complete abstraction without any vestiges of traditional representational art. Although González's sculpture received only limited exposure during his lifetime, his work greatly influenced later abstract artists working in welded metal (FIG. 30-16).

FERNAND LÉGER AND PURISM Best known today as one of the most important modernist architects, Le Corbusier (FIG. 29-68) was also a painter. In 1918 he founded a movement called *Purism*, which opposed Synthetic Cubism on the grounds it was becoming merely an esoteric, decorative art out of touch with the machine age. Purists maintained machinery's clean functional lines and the pure forms of its parts should direct artists' experiments in design, whether in painting, architecture, or industrially produced objects. This "machine aesthetic" inspired FERNAND LÉGER (1881–1955), a French artist who had painted with the Cubists. He devised an effective compromise of tastes, bringing together meticulous Cubist analysis of form with Purism's broad simplification and machinelike finish of the design components. He retained from his Cubist practice a preference for cylindrical and tube-shaped motifs, suggestive of machined parts such as pistons and cylinders.

Léger's works have the sharp precision of the machine, whose beauty and quality he was one of the first artists to appreciate. For example, in his film *Ballet Mécanique* (1924), Léger contrasted inanimate objects such as functioning machines with humans in dancelike variations. Preeminently the painter of modern urban life, Léger incorporated into works such as *The City* (FIG. **29-22**) the massive effects of modern posters and billboard advertisements, the harsh flashing of electric lights, and the noise of traffic. The monumental scale of *The City*, an early work incorporating the aesthetic of Synthetic Cubism, suggests Léger, had he been given the opportunity, would have been one of the

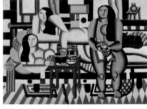

29-22A Léger, *Three Women*, 1921.

great mural painters of his age. In a definitive way, he depicted the mechanical commotion of urban life, including the robotic movements of mechanized people (FIG. **29-22A**).

Futurism

Artists associated with another early-20th-century movement, *Futurism*, pursued many of the ideas the Cubists explored. Equally important to the Futurists, however, was their well-defined sociopolitical agenda. Inaugurated and given its name by the charismatic Italian poet and playwright Filippo Tommaso Marinetti (1876–1944) in 1909, Futurism began as a literary movement but soon encompassed the visual arts, cinema, theater, music, and architecture. Indignant over the political and cultural decline of Italy, the Futurists published numerous manifestos in which they aggressively

Futurist Manifestos

On April 11, 1910, a group of young Italian artists published *Futurist Painting: Technical Manifesto* in Milan in an attempt to apply the writer Filippo Tommaso Marinetti's views on literature to the visual arts. Signed jointly by Umberto Boccioni, Carlo Carrà, Luigi Russolo, Giacomo Balla, and Gino Severini, the manifesto also appeared in an English translation supervised by Marinetti himself. It states in part:

> On account of the persistency of an image on the retina, moving objects constantly multiply themselves [and] their form changes . . . Thus a running horse has not four legs, but twenty. . . .

> What was true for the painters of yesterday is but a falsehood today. . . . To paint a human figure you must not paint it; you must render the whole of its surrounding atmosphere. . . . [T]he vivifying current of science [must] soon deliver painting from academic tradition. . . . The shadows which we shall paint shall be more luminous than the highlights of our predecessors, and our pictures, next to those of the museums, will shine like blinding daylight compared with deepest night. . . .

> We declare . . . that all forms of imitation must be despised, all forms of originality glorified . . . that all subjects previously used must be swept aside in order to express our whirling life of steel, of pride, of fever and of speed . . . that movement and light destroy the materiality of bodies.*

Two years later, Boccioni published a *Technical Manifesto of Futurist Sculpture,* in which he argued traditional sculpture was "a monstrous anachronism" and modern sculpture should be

> a translation, in plaster, bronze, glass, wood or any other material, of those atmospheric planes which bind and intersect things. . . . Let's . . . proclaim the absolute and complete abolition of finite lines and the contained statue. Let's split open our figures and place the environment inside them. We declare that the environment must form part of the plastic whole.†

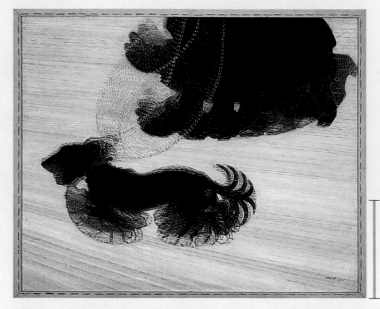

29-23 GIACOMO BALLA, *Dynamism of a Dog on a Leash,* 1912. Oil on canvas, 2′ 11⅜″ × 3′ 7¼″. Albright-Knox Art Gallery, Buffalo (bequest of A. Conger Goodyear, gift of George F. Goodyear, 1964). ◼◀

The Futurists' interest in motion and in the Cubist dissection of form is evident in Balla's painting of a passing dog and its owner. Simultaneity of views was central to the Futurist program.

The sculptures of Boccioni (FIG. 29-24) and the paintings of Balla (FIG. 29-23) and Severini (FIG. 29-25) are the perfect expressions of these Futurist principles and goals.

*Futurist Painting: Technical Manifesto (Poesia, April 11, 1910). Translated by Filippo Tommaso Marinetti, in Umbro Apollonio, ed., *Futurist Manifestos* (Boston: Museum of Fine Arts, 1970), 27–31.*
*†Translated by Robert Brain, in Apollonio, *Futurist Manifestos,* 51–65.*

advocated revolution, both in society and in art. As did Die Brücke, the Futurists aimed at ushering in a new, more enlightened era.

In their quest to launch Italian society toward a glorious future, the Futurists championed war as a means of washing away the stagnant past. Indeed, they saw war as a cleansing agent. Marinetti declared: "We will glorify war—the only true hygiene of the world."[11] The Futurists agitated for the destruction of museums, libraries, and similar repositories of accumulated culture, which they described as mausoleums. They also called for radical innovation in the arts. Of particular interest to the Futurists were the speed and dynamism of modern technology, an interest shared by Delaunay (FIGS. 29-15 and 29-15A) and Léger (FIGS. 29-22 and 29-22A). Marinetti insisted a racing "automobile adorned with great pipes like serpents with explosive breath . . . is more beautiful than the *Victory of Samothrace*"[12]—a reference to the Greek statue (FIG. 5-82) in the Musée du Louvre that for early-20th-century artists represented classicism and the glories of past civilizations.

Appropriately, Futurist art often focused on motion in time and space, incorporating the Cubist discoveries derived from the analysis of form.

GIACOMO BALLA The Futurists' interest in motion and in the Cubist dissection of form is evident in *Dynamism of a Dog on a Leash* (FIG. 29-23), in which GIACOMO BALLA (1871–1958) represented a passing dog and its owner, whose skirts are just within visual range. Balla achieved the effect of motion by repeating shapes, for example, the dog's legs and tail and the swinging line of the leash. Simultaneity of views, as in Cubism, was central to the Futurist program (see "Futurist Manifestos," above).

UMBERTO BOCCIONI One of the cosigners of the Futurist manifesto was UMBERTO BOCCIONI (1882–1916), who produced what is perhaps the definitive work of Futurist sculpture, *Unique Forms of Continuity in Space* (FIG. **29-24**). This piece highlights the formal and spatial effects of motion rather than their source,

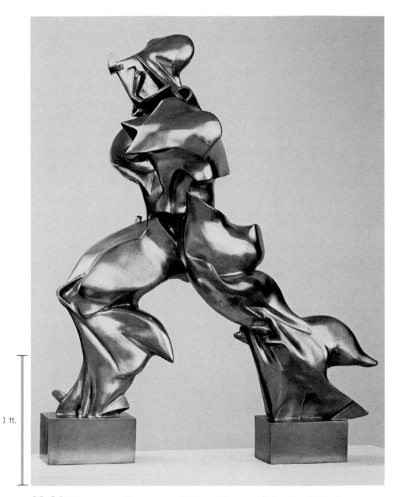

29-24 UMBERTO BOCCIONI, *Unique Forms of Continuity in Space,* 1913 (cast 1931). Bronze, 3′ 7⅞″ × 2′ 10⅞″ × 1′ 3¾″. Museum of Modern Art, New York (acquired through the Lillie P. Bliss Bequest). ◼◀

Boccioni's Futurist manifesto for sculpture advocated abolishing the enclosed statue. This running figure's body is so expanded it almost disappears behind the blur of its movement.

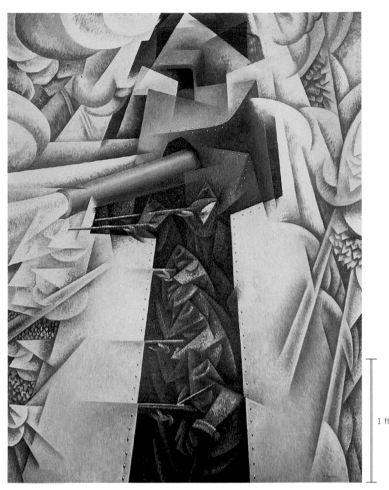

29-25 GINO SEVERINI, *Armored Train,* 1915. Oil on canvas, 3′ 10″ × 2′ 10⅛″. Collection of Richard S. Zeisler, New York. ◼◀

Severini's glistening armored train with protruding cannon reflects the Futurist faith in the cleansing action of war. The painting captures the dynamism and motion central to the Futurist manifesto.

the striding human figure. The figure is so expanded, interrupted, and broken in plane and contour it almost disappears behind the blur of its movement—just as people, buildings, and stationary objects become blurred when seen from an automobile traveling at great speed on a highway. Boccioni's search for sculptural means for expressing dynamic movement reached a monumental expression in *Unique Forms.* In its power and sense of vital activity, this sculpture surpasses similar efforts in Futurist painting to create images symbolic of the dynamic quality of modern life. Although Boccioni's figure bears a curious resemblance to the *Nike of Samothrace* (FIG. 5-82), the ancient sculptor suggested motion only through posture and agitated drapery, not through distortion and fragmentation of the human body.

This Futurist representation of motion in sculpture has its limitations, however. The eventual development of the motion picture, based on the rapid sequential projection of fixed images, produced more convincing illusions of movement. And several decades later in sculpture, Alexander Calder (FIG. 29-78) pioneered the development of kinetic sculpture—sculptures with parts that really move. But in the early 20th century, Boccioni was unsurpassed for his ability to capture the sensation of motion in statuary.

GINO SEVERINI The painting *Armored Train* (FIG. **29-25**) by GINO SEVERINI (1883–1966) also encapsulates the Futurist program—politically as well as artistically. Severini depicted a high-tech armored train with its rivets glistening and a huge booming cannon protruding from the top. Submerged in the bowels of the train, soldiers in a row point guns at an unseen target. In Cubist fashion, Severini depicted all of the elements of the painting, from the soldiers to the smoke emanating from the cannon, broken into facets and planes, suggesting action and movement. *Armored Train* reflects the Futurists' passion for speed and the "whirling life of steel," and their faith in the cleansing action of war. Not only are the colors predominantly light and bright, but death and destruction—the tragic consequences of war—are absent from Severini's painting. This sanitized depiction of armed conflict contrasts sharply with Francisco Goya's *The Third of May, 1808* (FIG. 27-11), which also depicts a uniform row of anonymous soldiers in the act of shooting. Goya, however, graphically presented the dead and those about to be shot, and the dark tones he used cast a dramatic and sobering pall.

Once World War I broke out, the Futurist group began to disintegrate, largely because so many of them felt compelled (given the Futurist support for the war) to join the Italian Army. Some of them, including Umberto Boccioni, died in the war.

Dada

Although the Futurists celebrated World War I and the changes they hoped it would effect, the mass destruction and chaos that conflict unleashed horrified other artists. Humanity had never before witnessed such wholesale slaughter on so grand a scale over such an extended period. Millions died or sustained grievous wounds in great battles. For example, in 1916, the battle of Verdun (lasting five months) produced a half million casualties. The new technology of armaments, bred from the age of steel, made the Great War a "war of the guns." In the face of massed artillery hurling millions of tons of high explosives and gas shells and in the sheets of fire from thousands of machine guns in armored vehicles of the kind celebrated in Futurist canvases (FIG. 29-25), attack was suicidal. Battle movement congealed into the stalemate of trench warfare, stretching from the English Channel almost to Switzerland. The mud, filth, and blood of the trenches, the pounding and shattering of incessant shell fire, and the terrible deaths and mutilations were a devastating psychological, as well as physical, experience for a generation brought up with the doctrine of progress and a belief in the fundamental values of civilization. The introduction of poison gas in 1915 added to the horror of humankind's inhumanity.

With the war as a backdrop, many artists contributed to the artistic and literary movement that became known as *Dada* (see page 835). This movement emerged, in large part, in reaction to what many of these artists saw as nothing more than an insane spectacle of collective homicide. Although Dada began independently in New York and Zurich, it also emerged in Paris, Berlin, and Cologne, among other cities. Dada was more a mindset or attitude than a single identifiable style. As André Breton (1896–1966), founder of the slightly later Surrealist movement, explained: "Cubism was a school of painting, futurism a political movement: DADA is a state of mind."[13] The Dadaists believed Enlightenment reasoning had produced global devastation, and consequently they turned away from logic in favor of the irrational. Thus, an element of absurdity is a cornerstone of Dada—reflected in the movement's very name. Many explanations exist for the choice of "Dada," but according to an oft-repeated anecdote, the Dadaists chose the word at random by sticking a knife into a French-German dictionary (hence the title Hannah Höch chose for her Dada photomontage (FIG. 29-1). *Dada* is French for "a child's hobby horse." The word satisfied the Dadaists' desire for something nonsensical.

The Dadaists' pessimism and disgust surfaced in their disdain for convention and tradition. These artists made a concerted and sustained attempt to undermine cherished notions and assumptions about art. Because of this destructive dimension, art historians often describe Dada as a nihilistic enterprise. Dada's nihilism and its derisive iconoclasm can be read at random from the Dadaists' numerous manifestos and declarations of intent:

> Dada knows everything. Dada spits on everything. Dada says "knowthing," Dada has no fixed ideas. Dada does not catch flies. Dada is bitterness laughing at everything that has been accomplished, sanctified. . . . Dada is never right. . . . No more painters, no more writers, no more religions, no more royalists, no more anarchists, no more socialists, no more police, no more airplanes, no more urinary passages. . . . Like everything in life, Dada is useless, everything happens in a completely idiotic way. . . . We are incapable of treating seriously any subject whatsoever, let alone this subject: ourselves.[14]

Although cynicism and pessimism inspired the Dadaists, what they developed was phenomenally influential and powerful. By attacking convention and logic, the Dada artists unlocked new avenues for creative invention, thereby fostering a more serious examination of the basic premises of art than had prior movements. But the Dadaists could also be lighthearted in their subversiveness. Although horror and disgust about the war initially prompted Dada, an undercurrent of humor and whimsy—sometimes sardonic or irreverent—runs through much of the art. For example, Marcel Duchamp painted a moustache and goatee on a reproduction of Leonardo's *Mona Lisa* (FIG. 29-27A). The French painter Francis Picabia (1879–1953), Duchamp's collaborator in setting up Dada in New York, nailed a toy monkey to a board and labeled it *Portrait of Cézanne*.

In its emphasis on the spontaneous and intuitive, Dada paralleled the views of Sigmund Freud (1856–1939) and Carl Jung (1875–1961). Freud was a Viennese doctor who developed the fundamental principles for what became known as psychoanalysis. In his book *The Interpretation of Dreams* (1900), Freud argued unconscious and inner drives (of which people are largely unaware) control human behavior. Jung, a Swiss psychiatrist who developed Freud's theories further, believed the unconscious is composed of two facets, a personal unconscious and a collective unconscious. The collective unconscious comprises memories and associations all humans share, such as archetypes and mental constructions. According to Jung, the collective unconscious accounts for the development of myths, religions, and philosophies.

Particularly interested in the exploration of the unconscious that Freud advocated, the Dada artists believed art was a powerfully practical means of self-revelation and catharsis, and the images arising out of the subconscious mind had a truth of their own, independent of conventional vision. A Dada filmmaker, Hans Richter (1888–1976), summarized the attitude of the Dadaists:

> Possessed, as we were, of the ability to entrust ourselves to "chance," to our conscious as well as our unconscious minds, we became a sort of public secret society. . . . We laughed at everything. . . . But laughter was only the expression of our new discoveries, not their essence and not their purpose. Pandemonium, destruction, anarchy, anti-everything of the World War? How could Dada have been anything but destructive, aggressive, insolent, on principle and with gusto?[15]

JEAN ARP One prominent Dada artist whose works illustrate Richter's element of chance was Zurich-based JEAN (HANS) ARP (1887–1966). Arp pioneered the use of chance in composing his images. Tiring of the look of some Cubist-related collages he was making, he took some sheets of paper, tore them into roughly shaped squares, haphazardly dropped them onto a sheet of paper on the floor, and glued them into the resulting arrangement. The rectilinearity of the shapes guaranteed a somewhat regular design (which Arp no doubt enhanced by adjusting the random arrangement into a quasi-grid), but chance had introduced an imbalance that seemed to Arp to restore to his work a special mysterious vitality he wanted to preserve. *Collage Arranged According to the Laws of Chance* (FIG. **29-26**) is one of the works he created by this method. The operations of chance were for Dadaists a crucial part of this kind of improvisation. As Richter stated: "For us chance was the 'unconscious mind' that Freud had discovered in 1900. . . . Adoption of chance had another purpose, a secret one. This was to restore to the work of art its primeval magic power and to find a way back to the immediacy it had lost through contact with . . . classicism."[16] Arp's

1 in.

29-26 JEAN (HANS) ARP, *Collage Arranged According to the Laws of Chance*, 1916–1917. Torn and pasted paper, 1′ 7⅛″ × 1′ 1⅝″. Museum of Modern Art, New York. ◼◀

In this collage, Arp dropped torn paper squares onto a sheet of paper and then glued them where they fell. His reliance on chance in composing images reinforced the anarchy inherent in Dada.

renunciation of artistic control and reliance on chance when creating his compositions reinforced the anarchy and subversiveness inherent in Dada.

MARCEL DUCHAMP Perhaps the most influential Dadaist was MARCEL DUCHAMP (1887–1968), a Frenchman who became the central artist of New York Dada but was also active in Paris. In 1913, he exhibited his first "readymade" sculptures, which were mass-produced common objects—"found objects" the artist selected and sometimes "rectified" by modifying their substance or combining them with another object. The creation of readymades, he insisted, was free from any consideration of either good or bad taste, qualities shaped by a society he and other Dada artists found aesthetically bankrupt. Perhaps his most outrageous readymade was *Fountain* (FIG. **29-27**), a porcelain urinal presented on its back, signed "R. Mutt," and dated (1917). The "artist's signature" was, in fact, a witty pseudonym derived from the Mott plumbing company's name and that of the shorter man of the then-popular Mutt and Jeff comic-strip duo. As with Duchamp's other readymades and "assisted readymades" such as *L.H.O.O.Q.* (FIG. **29-27A**), he did not select the urinal for exhibition because of its aesthetic qualities. The "art" of this "artwork" lay in the artist's choice of object, which had the effect of conferring the status of art on it and forcing viewers to see the object in a new light. As Duchamp wrote in a "defense" published in 1917, after an exhibition committee rejected *Fountain* for display: "Whether Mr. Mutt with his own hands made the fountain or not has no importance. He CHOSE it. He took an ordinary article of life, placed it so that its useful significance disappeared under the new title and point of view—created a new thought for that object."[17] It is hard to imagine a more aggressive challenge to artistic conventions than Dada works such as *Fountain*.

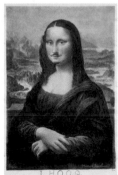

29-27A DUCHAMP, *L.H.O.O.Q.*, 1919.

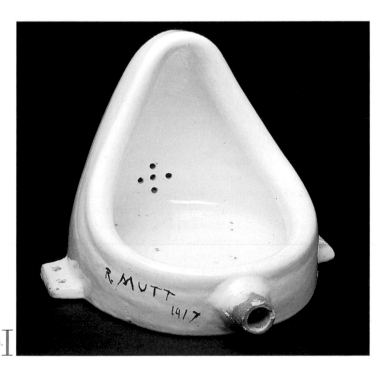

1 in.

29-27 MARCEL DUCHAMP, *Fountain* (second version), 1950 (original version produced 1917). Glazed sanitary china with black paint, 1′ high. Philadelphia Museum of Art, Philadelphia.

Duchamp's "readymade" sculptures were mass-produced objects the Dada artist modified. In *Fountain,* he conferred the status of art on a urinal and forced people to see the object in a new light.

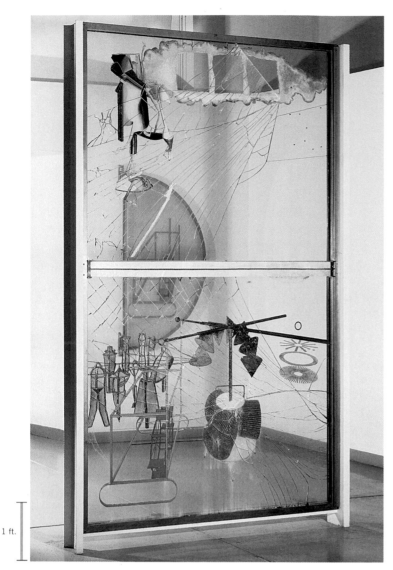

29-28 MARCEL DUCHAMP, *The Bride Stripped Bare by Her Bachelors, Even (The Large Glass)*, 1915–1923. Oil, lead, wire, foil, dust, and varnish on glass, 9′ 1½″ × 5′ 9⅛″. Philadelphia Museum of Art, Philadelphia (Katherine S. Dreier Bequest).

The Large Glass is a simultaneously playful and serious examination of humans as machines. The bride is a motor fueled by "love gasoline," and the male figures in the lower half also move mechanically.

THE LARGE GLASS Among the most visually and conceptually challenging of Duchamp's works is *The Bride Stripped Bare by Her Bachelors, Even* (FIG. 29-28), often called *The Large Glass*. Begun in 1915 and abandoned by Duchamp as unfinished in 1923, *The Large Glass* is a simultaneously playful and serious examination of humans as machines. Consisting of oil paint, wire, and lead foil sandwiched in between two large glass panels, the artwork presents an array of images, some apparently mechanical, others diagrammatic, and yet others seemingly abstract in nature. Duchamp provided some clues to the intriguing imagery in a series of notes accompanying the work. The top half of *The Large Glass* represents "the bride," whom Duchamp has depicted as "basically a motor" fueled by "love gasoline." In contrast, the bachelors appear as uniformed male figures in the lower half of the composition. They too move mechanically. The chocolate grinder in the center of the lower glass pane represents masturbation ("the bachelor grinds his own chocolate"). In *The Large Glass*, Duchamp provided his own whimsical but insightful ruminations into the ever-confounding realm of desire and sexuality. In true

Dadaist fashion, chance completed the work. During the transportation of *The Large Glass* from an exhibition in 1927, the glass panes shattered. Rather than replace the broken glass, Duchamp painstakingly pieced together the glass fragments. After encasing the reconstructed work, broken panes and all, between two heavier panes of glass, Duchamp declared the work completed "by chance."

Duchamp (and the generations of artists after him profoundly influenced by his art and especially his attitude) considered life and art matters of chance and choice freed from the conventions of society and tradition. In Duchamp's approach to art and life, each act was individual and unique. Every person's choice of found objects would be different, for example, and each person's throw of the dice would be at a different instant and probably would yield a different number. This philosophy of utter freedom for artists was fundamental to the history of art in the 20th century—in America as well as Europe. Duchamp spent much of World War I in New York, where he painted *Nude Descending a Staircase* (FIG. 29-35) and inspired a group of American artists and collectors with his radical rethinking of the role of artists and of the nature of art.

KURT SCHWITTERS Early on, Dada spread to Germany. In Berlin, Hannah Höch produced photomontages (FIG. 29-1) featuring sharp political commentary. In Hanover, KURT SCHWITTERS (1887–1948) followed a gentler muse. Inspired by Cubist collage but working nonobjectively, Schwitters found visual poetry in the cast-off junk of modern society and scavenged in trash bins for materials, which he pasted and nailed together into designs such as *Merz 19* (FIG. **29-29**). The term *Merz*, which Schwitters used as a generic title for a whole series of collages, derived nonsensically from the German word *Kommerzbank* (commerce bank) and appeared as a word fragment in one of his compositions. Although nonobjective, his collages still resonate with the meaning of the fragmented found objects they contain. The recycled elements of Schwitters's collages, like Duchamp's readymades, acquire new meanings through their new uses and locations. Elevating objects that are essentially trash to the status of high art certainly fits within the parameters of the Dada program and parallels the absurdist dimension of much of Dada art. Contradiction, paradox, irony, and even blasphemy were Dada's bequest to later artists.

Suprematism and Constructivism

Dada was a movement born of pessimism and cynicism. Not all early-20th-century artists, however, reacted to the profound turmoil of the times by retreating from society. Some artists promoted utopian ideals, believing staunchly in art's ability to contribute to improving society and all humankind. These efforts often surfaced in the face of significant political upheaval, as was the case with Suprematism and Constructivism in Russia.

KAZIMIR MALEVICH Despite Russia's distance from Paris, the center of the international art world in the early 20th century, Russians had a long history of cultural contact and interaction with western Europe. Wealthy Russians, such as Ivan Morozov (1871–1921) and Sergei Shchukin (1854–1936), amassed extensive collections of Impressionist, Post-Impressionist, and avant-garde paintings. Shchukin, who participated in the salons at the Steins' home in Paris (see "Gertrude and Leo Stein," page 844), became particularly enamored with the work of both Picasso and Matisse. By the mid-1910s, he had acquired 37 paintings by Matisse and 51 by Picasso. Because of their access to collections such as these, Russian artists were familiar with the latest artistic developments, especially Fauvism, Cubism, and Futurism.

One Russian artist who pursued the revolutionary direction Cubism introduced was KAZIMIR MALEVICH (1878–1935). Malevich

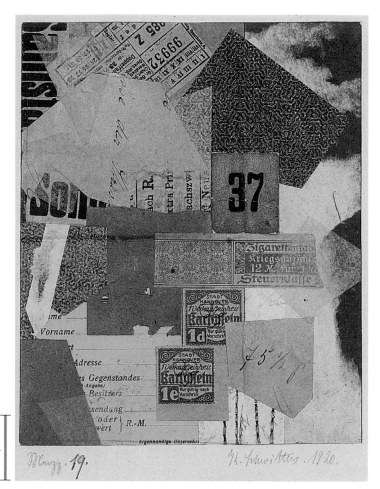

29-29 KURT SCHWITTERS, *Merz 19*, 1920. Paper collage, $7\frac{1}{4}'' \times 5\frac{7}{8}''$. Yale University Art Gallery, New Haven (gift of Collection Société Anonyme).

Inspired by Cubist collage but working nonobjectively, Schwitters found visual poetry in the cast-off junk of modern society, which he pasted and nailed together into striking Dada compositions.

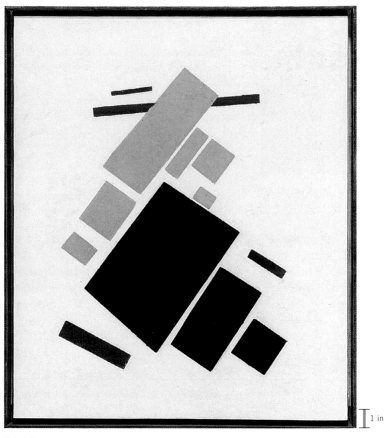

29-30 KAZIMIR MALEVICH, *Suprematist Composition: Airplane Flying,* 1915 (dated 1914). Oil on canvas, $1'\ 10\frac{7}{8}'' \times 1'\ 7''$. Museum of Modern Art, New York. ◼◀

Malevich developed an abstract style he called Suprematism to convey that the supreme reality in the world is pure feeling. Here, the brightly colored rectilinear shapes float against white space.

developed an abstract style to convey his belief that the supreme reality in the world is "pure feeling," which attaches to no object. Thus, this belief called for new, nonobjective forms in art—shapes not related to objects in the visible world. Malevich had studied painting, sculpture, and architecture and had worked his way through most of the avant-garde styles of his youth before deciding none could express pure feeling. He christened his new artistic approach *Suprematism,* explaining: "Under Suprematism I understand the supremacy of pure feeling in creative art. To the Suprematist, the visual phenomena of the objective world are, in themselves, meaningless; the significant thing is feeling, as such, quite apart from the environment in which it is called forth."[18]

The basic form of Malevich's new Suprematist nonobjective art was the square. Combined with its relatives, the straight line and the rectangle, the square soon filled his paintings, such as *Suprematist Composition: Airplane Flying* (FIG. **29-30**). In this work, the brightly colored shapes float against and within a white space, and the artist placed them in dynamic relationship to one another. Malevich believed all peoples would easily understand his new art because of the universality of its symbols. It used the pure language of shape and color, to which everyone could respond intuitively.

Having formulated his artistic approach, Malevich welcomed the Russian Revolution, which broke out in 1917 as a result of

widespread dissatisfaction with the regime of Tsar Nicholas II (r. 1894–1917). Russian workers staged a general strike in protest, and the tsar abdicated in March. In late 1917, the Bolsheviks, a faction of Russian Social Democrats that promoted violent revolution, wrested control of the country from the ruling provisional government. Once in power, their leader, Vladimir Lenin (1870–1924), nationalized the land and turned it over to the local rural soviets (councils of workers' and soldiers' deputies). After extensive civil war, the Communists, as they now called themselves, succeeded in retaining control of Russia and taking over an assortment of satellite countries in eastern Europe. This new state adopted the official name Union of Soviet Socialist Republics (USSR, or Soviet Union) in 1923.

Malevich viewed the revolution as an opportunity to wipe out past traditions and begin a new culture. He believed his art could play a major role in that effort because of its universal accessibility. But, after a short period when the new regime heralded avant-garde art, the political leaders of the Soviet Union decided their new communist society needed a more "practical" art. Soviet authorities promoted a "realistic," illusionistic art that they thought a wide public could understand and that they hoped would teach citizens about their new government. This horrified Malevich. To him, true art could never have a practical connection with life:

> Every social idea, however great and important it may be, stems
> from the sensation of hunger; every art work, regardless of how
> small and insignificant it may seem, originates in pictorial or

plastic feeling. It is high time for us to realize that the problems of art lie far apart from those of the stomach or the intellect.[19]

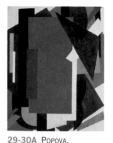

Disappointed and unappreciated by the public, Malevich eventually gravitated toward other disciplines, such as mathematical theory and geometry, logical fields given his interest in pure abstraction, but his work and his theories made a profound impression on other artists, especially in Russia. These included Lyubov Popova (1889–1924), who joined Malevich's Suprematist movement in 1916. Popova's most notable works are the series of canvases she named *Architectonic Paintings* (FIG. 29-30A).

NAUM GABO The Russian-born sculptor Naum Gabo (1890–1977) also wanted to create an innovative art to express a new reality, and like Malevich, he believed art should spring from sources separate from the everyday world. For Gabo, the new reality was the space-time world described by early-20th-century scientists (see "Science and Art," page 841). As he wrote in *The Realistic Manifesto*, published with his brother Anton Pevsner (1886–1962) in 1920:

> Space and time are the only forms on which life is built and hence art must be constructed. . . . The realization of our perceptions of the world in the forms of space and time is the only aim of our pictorial and plastic art. . . . We renounce the thousand-year-old delusion in art that held the static rhythms as the only elements of the plastic and pictorial arts. We affirm in these arts a new element, the kinetic rhythms, as the basic forms of our perception of real time.[20]

Gabo was one of the Russian sculptors known as Constructivists. The name *Constructivism* may have come originally from the title *Construction*, which the Russian artist Vladimir Tatlin (FIG. 29-32) used for some relief sculptures he made in 1913 and 1914. Gabo explained he called himself a Constructivist partly because he built up his sculptures piece by piece in space, instead of carving or modeling them in the traditional way. Although Gabo experimented briefly with real motion in his work, most of his sculptures relied on the relationship of mass and space to suggest the nature of space-time. To indicate the volumes of mass and space more clearly in his sculpture, Gabo used some of the new synthetic plastic materials, including celluloid, nylon, and Lucite, to create constructions whose space seems to flow through as well as around the transparent materials. In works such as *Column* (FIG. 29-31), Gabo opened up the column's circular mass so viewers could experience the volume of space it occupies. Two transparent planes extend through its diameter, crossing at right angles at the center of the implied cylindrical column shape. The opaque colored planes at the base and the inclined open ring set up counter-rhythms to the crossed upright planes. They establish the sense of dynamic kinetic movement Gabo always sought to express as an essential part of reality.

Architecture

A third art movement that emerged in the Soviet Union in the years immediately following the Russian Revolution was *Productivism*, which was an offshoot of the Constructivist movement. The Productivists sought to design a better environment for human beings.

VLADIMIR TATLIN One of the most gifted leaders of the Productivism movement was Vladimir Tatlin (1885–1953). The Russian Revolution was the signal to Tatlin, as it had been to Malevich, that the hated old order was about to end. In utopian fashion, he and the other Productivists aspired to play a significant role in creating

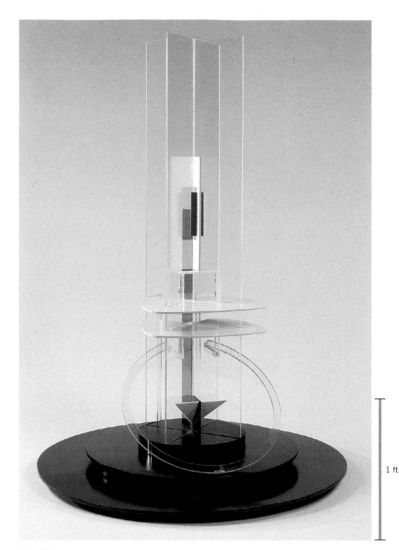

1 ft.

29-31 NAUM GABO, *Column*, ca. 1923 (reconstructed 1937). Perspex, wood, metal, glass, 3′ 5″ × 2′ 5″ × 2′ 5″. Solomon R. Guggenheim Museum, New York.

Gabo's Constructivist sculptures rely on the relationship of mass and space to suggest the nature of space-time. Space seems to flow through as well as around the transparent materials he used.

a new world, one that would fully use the power of industrialization to benefit all people. Initially, like Malevich and Gabo, Tatlin believed nonobjective art was ideal for the new society, free as such art was from any past symbolism. But after the 1917 revolution, Tatlin enthusiastically abandoned abstract art for "functional art" and designed products such as an efficient stove and workers' clothing.

Tatlin's most famous work is *Monument to the Third International* (FIG. 29-32), which, in its reductive geometry, connects Productivism to the artistic programs of the Suprematists and Constructivists. Tatlin received the commission from the Department of Artistic Work of the People's Commissariat for Enlightenment in early 1919 to honor the Russian Revolution. He envisioned a huge glass-and-iron building that—at 1,300 feet—would have been one-third taller than the Eiffel Tower (FIG. 28-38). Widely influential, "Tatlin's Tower," as it became known, served as a model for those seeking to encourage socially committed and functional art. On its proposed site in the center of Moscow, it would have functioned as a propaganda and news center for the Soviet people. Within a dynamically tilted spiral cage, three geometrically shaped chambers were to rotate around a central axis, each chamber housing

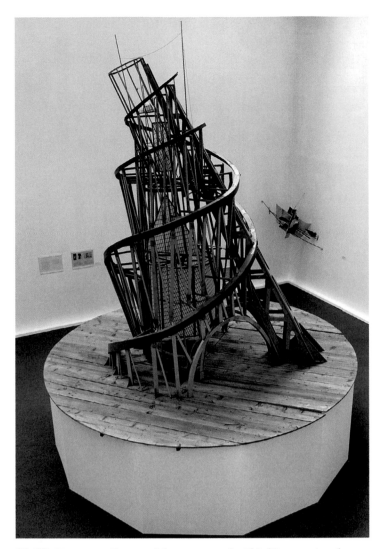

29-32 VLADIMIR TATLIN, *Monument to the Third International*, 1919–1920. Reconstruction of the lost model, 1992-1993. Kunsthalle, Düsseldorf.

"Tatlin's Tower" was an ambitious avant-garde design for a Soviet governmental building with three geometrically shaped chambers rotating at different speeds within a dynamically tilted spiral cage.

facilities for a different type of governmental activity and rotating at a different speed. The one at the bottom, a huge cylindrical glass structure for lectures and meetings, was to revolve once a year. Higher up was a cone-shaped chamber that would rotate monthly and serve administrative functions. At the top, a cubic information center would have revolved daily, issuing news bulletins and proclamations via the most modern means of communication. These included an open-air news screen (illuminated at night) and a special instrument designed to project words on the clouds on any overcast day. The proposed decreasing size of the chambers as visitors ascended the monument paralleled the decision-making hierarchy in the political system, with the most authoritative, smallest groups near the building's apex. The design thus served as a visual reinforcement of a social and political reality. Unfortunately, due to Russia's desperate economic situation in the 1920s, Tatlin's Tower was never built. But Tatlin worked out his ambitious design in now-lost metal and wood models exhibited on various official occasions. The only records of these models are a few drawings and photographs, but they have permitted faithful reconstructions of the design, such as the one reproduced in FIG. 29-32.

ADOLF LOOS In Germany, ADOLF LOOS (1870–1933) was the most influential architectural theorist during the opening decades of the 20th century. Loos trained as an architect at the Dresden College of Technology and then traveled to the United States to attend the 1893 Columbia Exposition in Chicago. Although he apparently found no work as an architect in Chicago, he remained there three years. During that time he became familiar with the buildings (FIGS. 28-40, 28-40A, and 28-41) and theories of Louis Sullivan, whose 1892 essay *Ornament in Architecture* affected Loos profoundly. In that treatise, Sullivan suggested architects consider banishing all ornamentation from their buildings for a period of years "in order that our thought might concentrate acutely upon the production of buildings well formed and comely in the nude."

Loos carried Sullivan's ideas even further in a series of essays in which he railed against the excesses of the Art Nouveau style (FIGS. 28-40 and 28-40A), which was the rage in Europe at the turn of the century. He published his major statement on the subject in 1908 under the title *Ornament and Crime*. Loos equated architectural ornamentation with the "amoral" tattoos of Papua New Guinea (see "Tattoo in Polynesia," Chapter 36, page 1055, and FIGS. I-19 and 36-16) and asserted that modern men who tattooed themselves were either criminals or degenerates. Ornamentation in architecture was also a crime, both on aesthetic grounds and because it wasted labor and materials.

Loos put his ideas to work in his 1910 design for the Viennese home of the painter Lilly Steiner (1884–1962). Cubical in form with a garden facade in the shape of a shallow U, the Steiner House (FIG. 29-33) has a reinforced-concrete skeleton and a severe white stucco shell devoid of ornamentation of any kind, even moldings separating the floors. The windows are simple unframed sheets of plate glass, symmetrically arranged. Walter Gropius would later build upon Loos's ideas about pure, functional architectural design at the Bauhaus (see "Walter Gropius and the Bauhaus," page 885, and FIG. 29-66), where he promoted "avoiding all romantic embellishment and whimsy."

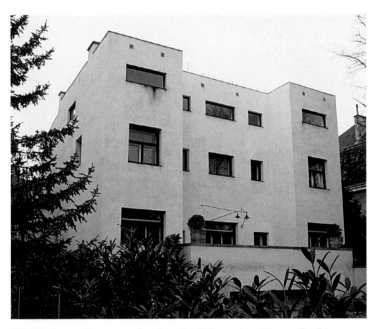

29-33 ADOLF LOOS, garden facade of the Steiner House (looking northwest), Vienna, Austria, 1910.

For Loos, decoration was a "criminal" waste of labor and materials. His Steiner House is a cubical mass with a white stucco shell devoid of ornamentation and without even moldings separating floors.

UNITED STATES, 1900 TO 1930

Avant-garde experiments in the arts were not limited to Europe. Increasingly common transatlantic travel during the later 19th and early 20th centuries resulted in a lively exchange of artistic ideas among European and American artists. For example, John Singer Sargent (FIG. 27-37), Mary Cassatt (FIG. 28-13), and James Abbott McNeill Whistler (FIG. 28-14) spent much of their productive careers in Europe, whereas many European artists ended their careers in the United States, especially in anticipation of and, later, in the wake of World War I. American artists wishing to pursue modernist ideas at home received encouragement from a number of wealthy and visionary patrons, mostly women (see "Art 'Matronage' in the United States," page 865).

Painting and Sculpture

In the opening decade of the 20th century, when most American artists knew little about the revolutionary work of their European counterparts, the goal of many of the leading painters was to present a realistic, unvarnished look at American life. In this regard, their work paralleled that of the French Realists in the mid-19th century (see Chapter 27).

JOHN SLOAN AND THE EIGHT The most important group of American Realist artists was The Eight—eight painters who gravitated into the circle of the influential and evangelical artist and teacher Robert Henri (1865–1929). Henri urged his followers to make "pictures from life,"[21] and accordingly, these artists pursued with zeal the production of images depicting the rapidly changing urban landscape of New York City. Because these vignettes often captured the bleak and seedy aspects of city life, The Eight eventually became known as the Ash Can School. Some critics referred to them as "the apostles of ugliness."

A prominent member of The Eight was JOHN SLOAN (1871–1951). A self-described "incorrigible window watcher,"[22] Sloan constantly wandered the streets of New York, observing human drama. He focused much of his attention on the working class, which he perceived as embodying the realities of life. So sympathetic was Sloan to the plight of workers that he joined the Socialist Party in 1909 and eventually ran for public office on the Socialist ticket. In paintings such as *Sixth Avenue and 30th Street* (FIG. **29-34**), Sloan revealed his ability to capture both the visual and social realities of American urban life. When he painted this image in 1907, Sloan lived on West 23rd Street, on the outskirts of the Tenderloin District, an area cluttered with brothels, dance halls, saloons, gambling dens, and cheap hotels. *Sixth Avenue* depicts a bustling intersection. Bracketing the throngs of people filling the intersection are elevated train tracks on the left and a row of storefronts and apartment buildings on the right. These two defining elements of city life converge in the far center background of the painting. Sloan's portrayals of New York also feature a cross-section of the population of the city at the opening of the 20th century. In the foreground of *Sixth Avenue,* Sloan prominently placed three women. One, in a shabby white dress, is a drunkard, stumbling along with her pail of beer. Two streetwalkers stare at her. In turn, two well-dressed men gaze at the prostitutes. Sloan's depiction of the women allied him with reformers of the time, who saw streetwalkers not as immoral but as victims of an unfair social and economic system. At a time when traditional art centered on genteel and proper society, Sloan's forthright depiction of prostitutes was categorically "Realist."

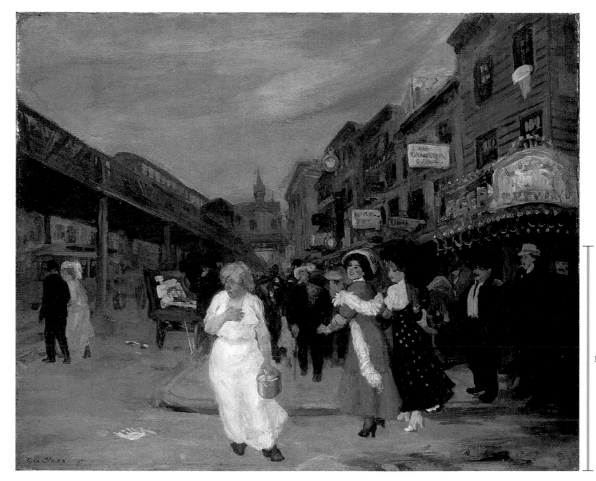

29-34 JOHN SLOAN, *Sixth Avenue and Thirtieth Street, New York City,* 1907. Oil on canvas, 2′ $\frac{1}{4}$″ × 2′ 8″. Philadelphia Museum of Art, Philadelphia (gift of Meyer P. Potamkin and Vivian O. Potamkin, 2000).

A prominent member of the American Realist group called The Eight, Sloan captured in his paintings the bleak and seedy aspects of the rapidly changing urban landscape of New York City.

1 ft.

The Armory Show

From February 17 to March 15, 1913, the American public flocked in large numbers to view the International Exhibition of Modern Art at the 69th Regiment Armory in New York City. The "Armory Show," as it came universally to be called, was an ambitious endeavor organized primarily by two artists, Walt Kuhn (1877–1949) and Arthur B. Davies (1862–1928). The show included more than 1,600 artworks by American and European artists. Among the European artists represented were Matisse, Derain, Picasso, Braque, Duchamp (FIG. 29-35), Kandinsky, Kirchner, Lehmbruck, and Brancusi. In addition to exposing Americans to the latest European artistic developments, the Armory Show also provided American artists with a prime showcase for their work. The foreword to the exhibition catalog spelled out the goals of the organizers:

> The American artists exhibiting here consider the exhibition of equal importance for themselves as for the public. The less they find their work showing signs of the developments indicated in the Europeans, the more reason they will have to consider whether or not painters or sculptors here have fallen behind . . . the forces that have manifested themselves on the other side of the Atlantic.*

On its opening, this provocative exhibition served as a lightning rod for commentary, immediately attracting heated controversy. The *New York Times* described the show as "pathological" and called the modernist artists "cousins to the anarchists," while the magazine *Art and Progress* compared them to "bomb throwers, lunatics, depravers."[†] Other critics demanded the exhibition be closed as a menace to public morality. The *New York Herald,* for example, asserted: "The United States is invaded by aliens, thousands of whom constitute so many perils to the health of the body politic. Modernism is of precisely the same heterogeneous alien origin and is imperiling the republic of art in the same way."[‡]

Nonetheless, the exhibition was an important milestone in the history of art in the United States. The Armory Show traveled to Chicago and Boston after it closed in New York and was a significant catalyst for the reevaluation of the nature and purpose of American art.

*Quoted in Herschel B. Chipp, *Theories of Modern Art: A Source Book by Artists and Critics* (Berkeley and Los Angeles: University of California Press, 1968), 503.
[†]Quoted in Sam Hunter, John Jacobus, and Daniel Wheeler, *Modern Art,* rev. 3d. ed. (Upper Saddle River, N.J.: Prentice Hall, 2005), 250.
[‡]Quoted in Francis K. Pohl, *Framing America: A Social History of American Art,* 2d ed. (New York: Thames & Hudson, 2002), 341.

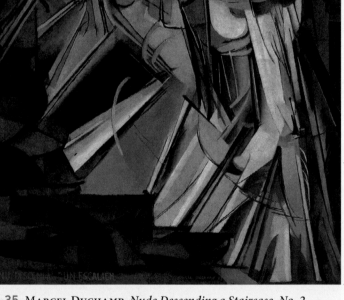

1 ft.

29-35 MARCEL DUCHAMP, *Nude Descending a Staircase, No. 2,* 1912. Oil on canvas, 4′ 10″ × 2′ 11″. Philadelphia Museum of Art, Philadelphia (Louise and Walter Arensberg Collection).

The Armory Show introduced European modernism to America. Duchamp's figure moving in a time continuum owes a debt to Cubism and Futurism. The press gave it a hostile reception.

ARMORY SHOW The relative isolation of American artists from developments across the Atlantic came to an abrupt end in early 1913 when the Armory Show opened in New York City (see "The Armory Show," above). Although later recognized as the seminal event in the development of American modernist art, the exhibition received a hostile response from the press. The work the journalists and critics most maligned was Marcel Duchamp's *Nude Descending a Staircase, No. 2* (FIG. 29-35). The painting represents a single figure in motion down a staircase in a time continuum and suggests the effect of a sequence of overlaid film stills. Unlike the Dada works by Duchamp (FIGS. 29-27, 29-27A, and 29-28), *Nude Descending a Staircase* shares many characteristics with the work of the Cubists and the Futurists. The monochromatic palette is reminiscent of Analytic Cubism, as is Duchamp's faceted presentation of the human form. The artist's interest in depicting the figure in motion reveals an affinity for the Futurists' ideas. One critic described this work as "an explosion in a shingle factory,"[23] and newspaper cartoonists delighted in lampooning the painting.

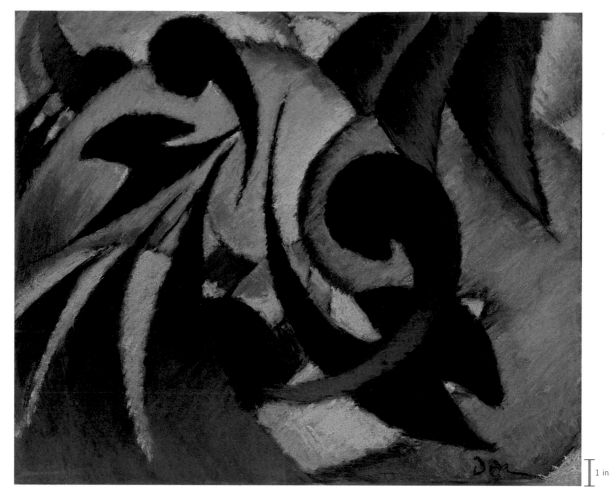

1 in.

29-36 ARTHUR DOVE, *Nature Symbolized No. 2*, ca. 1911. Pastel on paper, 1′ 6″ × 1′ 9⅝″. Art Institute of Chicago, Chicago (Alfred Stieglitz Collection).

Dove was one of the first painters to produce completely nonobjective canvases. Using only abstract shapes and color, he sought to capture the essence of nature and of pulsating organic growth.

ARTHUR DOVE Among the American modernists who exhibited their work in the Armory Show was ARTHUR DOVE (1880–1946). After graduating from Cornell University, Dove worked briefly as a commercial artist in New York and then in 1907 left for Paris, where he encountered the paintings of Henri Matisse (FIGS. 29-2, 29-2A, and 29-3) and André Derain (FIGS. 29-4 and 29-4A). Dove returned to New York in 1910. He occupies a special place in the evolution of modernist art in the United States because he began painting completely nonobjective paintings at about the same time as Vassily Kandinsky but apparently without any knowledge of Kandinsky's *Improvisation* series (FIG. 29-7).

Dove spent most of his life on farms in rural New York and Connecticut and loved the textures and colors of the American landscape. He sought to capture in his paintings the essence of nature, especially its pulsating energy, but without representing nature directly. A characteristic and aptly named example of his abstract renditions of fields, vegetation, and sky is *Nature Symbolized No. 2* (FIG. **29-36**), which he probably painted in 1911. Incorporating some of the principles and forms of Cubism but without representing any identifiable objects or landscape elements, Dove used swirling and jagged lines and a palette of mostly green, black, and sandy yellow to capture the essence of vegetation sprouting gloriously from fertile soil beneath patches of blue sky. He once described his goal as the creation of "rhythmic paintings" expressing nature's "spirit" through shape and color.

MAN RAY Another American artist who incorporated the latest European trends in his work was Emmanuel Radnitzky, who assumed the name MAN RAY (1890–1976). Ray was a close associate of Duchamp's in the 1920s. During that decade, Ray produced art having a decidedly Dada spirit, and he often incorporated found objects in his paintings, sculptures, movies, and photographs.

Trained as an architectural draftsman and engineer, Ray earned his living as a graphic designer and portrait photographer, and developed an innovative photographic technique relying on chance. In contrast to traditional photographs, Ray produced his images without using a camera. He placed objects directly on photographic paper and then exposed the paper to light. Ray dubbed these photographs, which in effect created themselves, *Rayographs*.

As did many other artists of this period, Ray had a keen interest in mass-produced objects and technology, as well as a dedication to exploring the psychological realm of human perception of the exterior world. Like Schwitters, he used the dislocation of ordinary things from their everyday settings to surprise his viewers into new awareness. His displacement of found objects was particularly effective in works such as *Cadeau* (*Gift*; FIG. **29-37**). For this sculpture, with characteristic Dada humor, he equipped a laundry iron with a row of wicked-looking tacks, subverting its proper function. Ray's "gift" would rip to shreds any garment the recipient tried to press with it.

Art "Matronage" in the United States

Until the 20th century, a leading reason for the dearth of women artists was that professional institutions restricted women's access to artistic training. For example, the proscription against women participating in life-drawing classes, a staple of academic artistic training, in effect denied women the opportunity to become professional artists. Another explanation for the absence of women from the traditional art historical canon is that art historians have not considered as "high art" many of the art objects women have traditionally produced (for example, quilts or basketry).

By the early 20th century, however, many of the impediments to a woman's becoming a recognized artist had been removed. Today, women are a major presence in the art world. One of the developments in the early 20th century that laid the groundwork for this change was the prominent role American women played as art patrons. These "art matrons" provided financial, moral, and political support to cultivate the advancement of the arts in America. Chief among them were Gertrude Vanderbilt Whitney, Lillie P. Bliss, Mary Quinn Sullivan, Abby Aldrich Rockefeller, Isabella Stewart Gardner, Peggy Guggenheim, and Jane Stanford.*

Gertrude Vanderbilt Whitney (1875–1942) was a practicing sculptor and enthusiastic collector. To assist young American artists such as Robert Henri and John Sloan (FIG. 29-34) in exhibiting their work, she opened the Whitney Studio in 1914. By 1929, dissatisfied with the recognition accorded young, progressive American artists, she offered her entire collection of 500 works to the Metropolitan Museum of Art in New York City. Her offer rejected, she founded her own museum in New York, the Whitney Museum of American Art. She chose as the first director a visionary and energetic woman, Juliana Force (1876–1948), who inaugurated a pioneering series of monographs on living American artists and organized lecture series by influential art historians and critics. Through the efforts of these two women, the Whitney Museum became a major force in American art.

A trip to Paris in 1920 whetted the interest of Peggy Guggenheim (1898–1979) in avant-garde art. As did Whitney, Guggenheim collected art and eventually opened a gallery in England to exhibit the work of innovative artists. She continued her support for modernist art after her return to the United States. Guggenheim's New York gallery, called Art of This Century, was instrumental in advancing the careers of many artists, including her husband, Max Ernst (FIG. 29-53). She eventually moved her art collection to a lavish Venetian palace, where the public can still view the important artworks she acquired.

Other women who contributed significantly to the arts were Lillie P. Bliss (1864–1931), Mary Quinn Sullivan (1877–1939), and Abby Aldrich Rockefeller (1874–1948). Philanthropists, art collectors, and educators, these influential and far-sighted women saw the need for a museum to collect and exhibit modernist art. Together they established the Museum of Modern Art in New York City in 1929, which became (and continues to be) the most influential museum of modern art in the world (see "The Museum of Modern Art," page 895), and collects American as well as European modernist art, for example, Man Ray's *Cadeau* (FIG. 29-37).

Isabella Stewart Gardner (1840–1924) and Jane Stanford (1828–1905) also undertook the ambitious project of founding museums. The Isabella Stewart Gardner Museum in Boston, established in 1903,

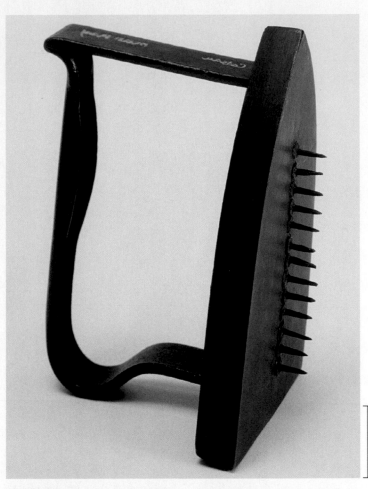

1 in.

29-37 **MAN RAY**, *Cadeau* (*Gift*), ca. 1958 (replica of 1921 original). Painted flatiron with row of 13 tacks with heads glued to the bottom, $6\frac{1}{8}'' \times 3\frac{5}{8}'' \times 4\frac{1}{2}''$. Museum of Modern Art, New York (James Thrall Soby Fund).

With characteristic Dada humor, the American artist Man Ray equipped a laundry iron with a row of wicked-looking spikes, subverting its proper function of smoothing and pressing.

houses a well-chosen and comprehensive collection of art of many periods. The Stanford Museum, the first American museum west of the Mississippi, got its start in 1905 on the grounds of Stanford University, which Leland Stanford Sr. and Jane Stanford founded after the tragic death of their son. The Stanford Museum houses a wide range of objects, including archaeological and ethnographic artifacts. These two driven women committed much of their time, energy, and financial resources to ensure the success of their museums, and were intimately involved in their institutions' day-to-day operations.

The museums these women established flourish today, attesting to the extraordinary vision of these "art matrons" and the remarkable contributions they made to the advancement of art in the United States.

*Art historian Wanda Corn coined the term *art matronage* in the catalog *Cultural Leadership in America: Art Matronage and Patronage* (Boston: Isabella Stewart Gardner Museum, 1997).

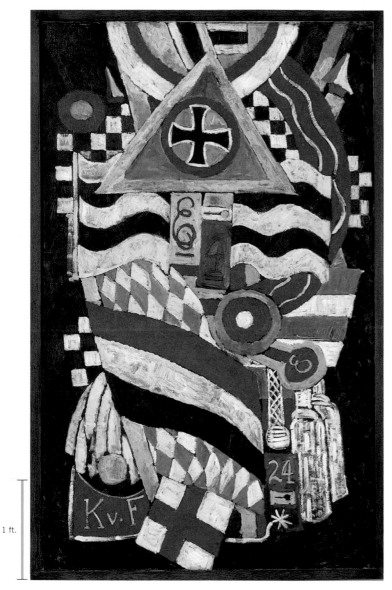

29-38 MARSDEN HARTLEY, *Portrait of a German Officer,* 1914. Oil on canvas, 5' 8¼" × 3' 5⅜". Metropolitan Museum of Art, New York (Alfred Stieglitz Collection).

In this elegy to a lover killed in battle, Hartley arranged military-related images against a somber black background. The flattened, planar presentation reveals the influence of Synthetic Cubism.

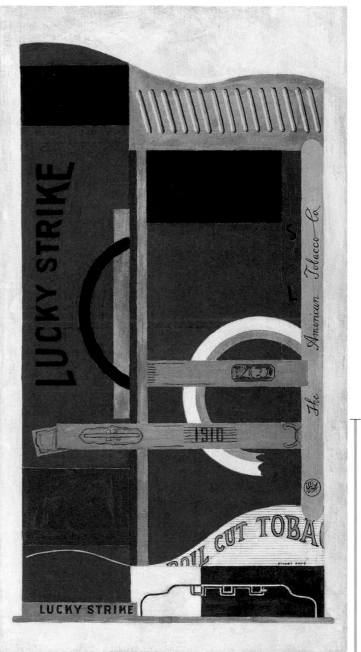

29-39 STUART DAVIS, *Lucky Strike,* 1921. Oil on canvas, 2' 9¼" × 1' 6". Museum of Modern Art, New York (gift of the American Tobacco Company, Inc.). © Estate of Stuart Davis/Licensed by VAGA, New York.

Tobacco products fascinated Davis, a heavy smoker. In *Lucky Strike,* he depicted a cigarette package in fragmented form, recalling Cubism, and imbued his painting with an American jazz rhythm.

MARSDEN HARTLEY One American artist who developed a personal style influenced by Cubism and German Expressionism was MARSDEN HARTLEY (1877–1943). In 1912, Hartley traveled to Europe, visiting Paris, where he became acquainted with the work of the Cubists, and Munich, where he gravitated to the Blaue Reiter circle. Kandinsky's work particularly impressed Hartley, and he developed a style he called "Cosmic Cubism." In 1913, he moved to Berlin. With the heightened militarism in Germany and the eventual outbreak of World War I, Hartley immersed himself in military imagery.

Portrait of a German Officer (FIG. **29-38**) is one of Hartley's best paintings of this period. It depicts an array of military-related images: German imperial flags, regimental insignia, badges, and emblems such as the Iron Cross. Although this image resonates in the general context of wartime militarism, important elements in the painting had personal significance for Hartley. In particular,

the painting includes references to his lover, Lieutenant Karl von Freyberg, who lost his life in battle a few months before Hartley painted this "portrait." Von Freyberg's initials appear in the lower left corner. His age when he died (24) appears in the lower right corner, and his regiment number (4) appears in the center of the painting. Also incorporated is the letter E for von Freyberg's regiment, the Bavarian Eisenbahn. The influence of Synthetic Cubism is evident in the flattened, planar presentation of the elements, which almost appear as abstract patterns. The somber black background against which the artist placed the colorful stripes, patches, and shapes casts an elegiac pall over the painting.

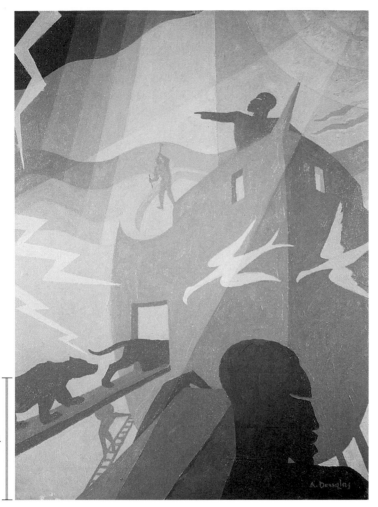

29-40 AARON DOUGLAS, *Noah's Ark,* ca. 1927. Oil on Masonite, 4′ × 3′. Fisk University Galleries, University of Tennessee, Nashville.

In *Noah's Ark* and other paintings of the cultural history of African Americans, Douglas incorporated motifs from African sculpture and the transparent angular planes characteristic of Synthetic Cubism.

1 ft.

STUART DAVIS Philadelphia-born STUART DAVIS (1894–1964) created what he believed was a modern American art style by combining the flat shapes of Synthetic Cubism with his sense of jazz tempos and his perception of the energy of fast-paced American culture. *Lucky Strike* (FIG. 29-39) is one of several tobacco still lifes Davis began in 1921. Davis was a heavy smoker, and tobacco products and their packaging fascinated him. He insisted the introduction of packaging in the late 19th century was evidence of high civilization and therefore, he concluded, of the progressiveness of American culture. Davis depicted the Lucky Strike package in fragmented form, reminiscent of Synthetic Cubist collages. However, although the work does incorporate flat printed elements, these are illusionistically painted, rather than glued onto the canvas. The discontinuities and the interlocking planes imbue *Lucky Strike* with a dynamism and rhythm not unlike American jazz or the pace of life in a lively American metropolis. *Lucky Strike* is resolutely both American and modern.

AARON DOUGLAS Also deriving his personal style from Synthetic Cubism was African American artist AARON DOUGLAS (1898–1979), who used the style to represent symbolically the historical and cultural memories of his people. Born in Kansas,

Douglas studied in Nebraska and Paris before settling in New York City, where he became part of the flowering of art and literature in the 1920s known as the Harlem Renaissance. Spearheaded by writers and editors Alain Locke (1886–1953) and Charles Spurgeon Johnson (1883–1956), the Harlem Renaissance was a manifestation of the desire of African Americans to promote their cultural accomplishments. They also aimed to cultivate pride among fellow African Americans and to foster racial tolerance across the United States. Expansive and diverse, the fruits of the Harlem Renaissance included the writings of authors such as Langston Hughes, Countee Cullen, and Zora Neale Hurston; the jazz and blues of Duke Ellington, Bessie Smith, Eubie Blake, Fats Waller, and Louis Armstrong; the photographs of James Van Der Zee and Prentice H. Polk; and the paintings and sculptures of Meta Warrick Fuller and Augusta Savage.

Douglas arrived in New York City in 1924 and became one of the most sought-after graphic artists in the African American community. Encouraged to create art that would express the cultural history of his race, Douglas incorporated motifs from African sculpture into compositions painted in a version of Synthetic Cubism stressing transparent angular planes. *Noah's Ark* (FIG. 29-40) was one of seven paintings based on a book of poems by James Weldon Johnson (1871–1938) called *God's Trombones: Seven Negro Sermons in Verse.* Douglas used flat planes to evoke a sense of mystical space and miraculous happenings. In *Noah's Ark,* lightning strikes and rays of light crisscross the pairs of animals entering the ark, while men load supplies in preparation for departure. The artist suggested deep space by differentiating the size of the large human head and shoulders of the worker at the bottom and the small person at work on the far deck of the ship. Yet the composition's unmodulated color shapes create a pattern on the Masonite surface that cancels any illusion of three-dimensional depth. Here, Douglas used Cubism's formal language to express a powerful religious vision. Seven years later, employed by the U.S. government to create murals for the Harlem branch of the New York Public Library, he addressed a contemporary rather than a biblical subject: the history of Africans in America (FIG. 29-40A).

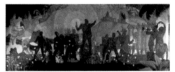

29-40A DOUGLAS, *Slavery through Reconstruction,* 1934.

PRECISIONISM Another distinctly American art movement in the post–Armory Show period was *Precisionism.* Although not an organized group, the Precisionists shared a fascination with the machine's "precision" and its importance in modern life. Although new technologies captured the imaginations of many European artists, especially the Futurists, Americans generally seemed more enamored by the prospects of a mechanized society than did Europeans. Even the Frenchman Francis Picabia, Duchamp's collaborator, noted: "Since machinery is the soul of the modern world, and since the genius of machinery attains its highest expression in America, why is it not reasonable to believe that in America the art of the future will flower most brilliantly?"[24] Precisionism, however, expanded beyond the exploration of machine imagery. Many artists associated with this group gravitated toward Synthetic Cubism's flat, sharply delineated planes as an appropriate visual idiom for their imagery, adding to the clarity and precision of their work. Eventually, Precisionism came to be characterized by a merging of a familiar native style in American architecture and artifacts with a modernist vocabulary derived largely from Synthetic Cubism.

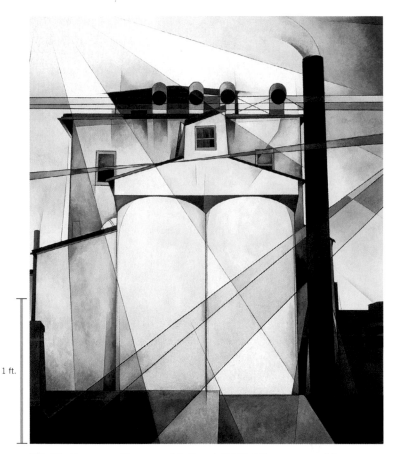

29-41 CHARLES DEMUTH, *My Egypt,* 1927. Oil on composition board, 2′ 11¾″ × 2′ 6″. Whitney Museum of American Art, New York (purchased with funds from Gertrude Vanderbilt Whitney).

Demuth was one of the leading Precisionists—American artists who extolled the machine age. This painting depicts grain elevators reduced to geometric forms amid Cubist transparent diagonal planes.

CHARLES DEMUTH Two of the leading Precisionists hailed from Pennsylvania—Charles Sheeler (1883–1965) and CHARLES DEMUTH (1883–1935). Sheeler traveled to Italy and France in 1909, and Demuth spent the years 1912–1914 in Paris, but both artists rejected pure abstraction and favored American subjects, especially industrial landscapes. Demuth's *My Egypt* (FIG. **29-41**) incorporates the spatial discontinuities characteristic of Cubism into a typically Precisionist depiction of an industrial site near Lancaster, the painter's birthplace. Demuth reduced the John W. Eshelman and Sons grain elevators to simple geometric forms. The grain elevators remain recognizable and solid, but the "beams" of transparent planes and the diagonal force lines threaten to destabilize the image and recall Cubist fragmentation of space. The degree to which Demuth intended to extol the American industrial scene is unclear. The title, *My Egypt,* is sufficiently ambiguous in tone to accommodate differing readings. On the one hand, Demuth could have been suggesting a favorable comparison between the Egyptian pyramids and American grain elevators as cultural icons. On the other hand, the title could be read cynically, as a negative comment on the limitations of American culture.

GEORGIA O'KEEFFE The work of Wisconsin-born GEORGIA O'KEEFFE (1887–1986) changed stylistically throughout her career. During the 1920s, O'Keeffe was a Precisionist. She had moved from the tiny town of Canyon, Texas, to New York City in 1918, and although she had visited the city before, what she found there excited her. "You have to live in today," she told a friend. "Today the

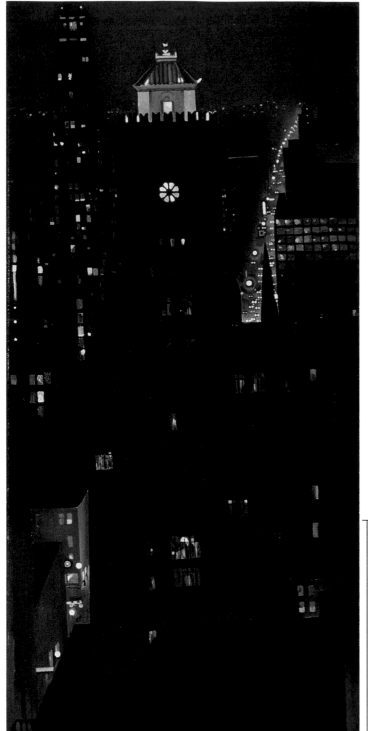

29-42 GEORGIA O'KEEFFE, *New York, Night,* 1929. Oil on canvas, 3′ 4⅛″ × 1′ 7⅛″. Sheldon Memorial Art Gallery, Lincoln (Nebraska Art Association, Thomas C. Woods Memorial Collection).

O'Keeffe's Precisionist representation of New York's soaring skyscrapers reduces the buildings to large, simple, dark planes punctuated by small windows that add rhythm and energy to the image.

city is something bigger, more complex than ever before in history. And nothing can be gained from running away. I couldn't even if I could."[25] While in New York, O'Keeffe met Alfred Stieglitz (FIGS. 29-43 and 29-43A), who played a major role in promoting the avant-garde in the United States. Stieglitz had established an art gallery at 291 Fifth Avenue in New York. In "291," as the gallery came to be called, he exhibited the latest in both European and

American art. Thus, 291, like the Armory Show, played an important role in the history of early-20th-century art in America. Stieglitz had seen and exhibited some of O'Keeffe's earlier work, and he drew her into his avant-garde circle of painters and photographers. He became one of O'Keeffe's staunchest supporters and, eventually, her husband. The interest of Stieglitz and his circle in capturing the sensibility of the machine age intersected with O'Keeffe's fascination with the fast pace of city life, and she produced paintings during this period, such as *New York, Night* (FIG. **29-42**), featuring the soaring skyscrapers dominating the city. As did other Precisionists, O'Keeffe reduced her images to simple planes, here punctuated by small rectangular windows that add rhythm and energy to the image, countering the monolithic darkness of the looming buildings.

Despite O'Keeffe's affiliation with the Precisionist movement and New York, she is best known for her paintings of cow skulls and of flowers. For example, in *Jack in the Pulpit No. 4* (FIG. I-5), she reveals her interest in stripping subjects to their purest forms and colors to heighten their expressive power. In this work, O'Keeffe reduced the incredible details of a flower to a symphony of basic colors, shapes, textures, and vital rhythms. Exhibiting the natural flow of curved planes and contour, O'Keeffe simplified the form almost to the point of complete abstraction. The fluid planes unfold like undulant petals from a subtly placed axis—the white jetlike streak—in a vision of the slow, controlled motion of growing life. O'Keeffe's painting, in its graceful, quiet poetry, reveals the organic reality of the object by strengthening its characteristic features.

Photography

Among the most significant artistic developments during the decades between the two world wars was the emergence of photography as a respected branch of the fine arts. The person most responsible for elevating the stature of photography was Alfred Stieglitz.

ALFRED STIEGLITZ Taking his camera everywhere he went, ALFRED STIEGLITZ (1864–1946) photographed whatever he saw around him, from the bustling streets of New York City to cloudscapes in upstate New York and the faces of friends and relatives. He believed in making only "straight, unmanipulated" photographs. Thus, he exposed and printed them using basic photographic processes, without resorting to techniques such as double-exposure or double-printing that would add information absent in the subject when he released the shutter. Stieglitz said he wanted the photographs he made with this direct technique "to hold a moment, to record something so completely that those who see it would relive an equivalent of what has been expressed."[26]

Stieglitz began a lifelong campaign to win a place for photography among the fine arts while he was a student of photochemistry in Germany. Returning to New York, he founded the Photo-Secession group, which mounted traveling exhibitions in the United States and sent loan collections abroad, and he published an influential journal titled *Camera Work*. In his own works, Stieglitz specialized in photographs of his environment and saw these subjects in terms of arrangements of forms and of the "colors" of his black-and-white materials. His aesthetic approach crystallized during the making of *The Steerage* (FIG. **29-43**), taken during a voyage to Europe with his first wife and daughter in 1907. Traveling first class, Stieglitz rapidly grew bored with the company of the prosperous passengers in his section of the ship. He walked as far forward on the first-class level as he could, when the rail around the opening onto the lower deck brought him up short. This level was for the steerage passengers the U.S. government sent back to Europe after refusing them entrance into the country. Later, Stieglitz described what happened next:

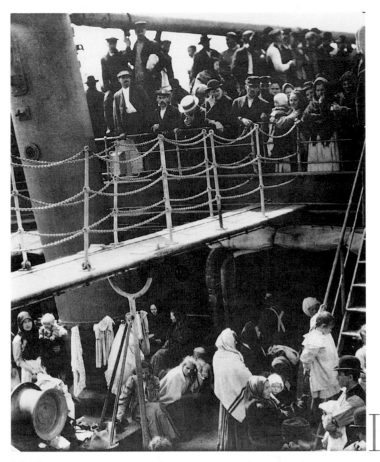

29-43 ALFRED STIEGLITZ, *The Steerage,* 1907 (print 1915). Photogravure (on tissue), 1′ $\frac{3}{8}$″ × 10$\frac{1}{8}$″. Amon Carter Museum, Fort Worth. ◼◀

Stieglitz waged a lifelong campaign to win a place for photography among the fine arts. This 1907 image is a haunting mixture of found patterns of forms and human activity. It stirs deep emotions.

The scene fascinated me: A round hat; the funnel leaning left, the stairway leaning right; the white drawbridge, its railing made of chain; white suspenders crossed on the back of a man below; circular iron machinery; a mast that cut into the sky, completing a triangle. I stood spellbound. I saw shapes related to one another—a picture of shapes, and underlying it, a new vision that held me: simple people; the feeling of ship, ocean, sky; a sense of release that I was away from the mob called rich. Rembrandt came into my mind and I wondered would he have felt as I did. . . . I had only one plate holder with one unexposed plate. Could I catch what I saw and felt? I released the shutter. If I had captured what I wanted, the photograph would go far beyond any of my previous prints. It would be a picture based on related shapes and deepest human feeling—a step in my own evolution, a spontaneous discovery.[27]

This description reveals Stieglitz's abiding interest in the formal elements of the photograph—an insistently modernist focus that emerges in even more extreme form in his *Equivalent* series (FIG. **29-43A**) of the 1920s. The finished print fulfilled Stieglitz's vision so well that it shaped his future photographic work, and its haunting mixture of found patterns and human activity has continued to stir viewers' emotions to this day.

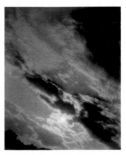

29-43A STIEGLITZ, *Equivalent,* 1923. ◼◀

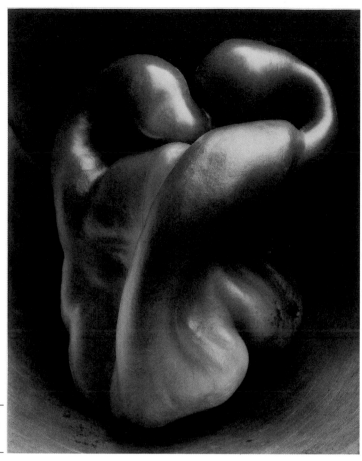

29-44 EDWARD WESTON, *Pepper No. 30,* 1930. Gelatin silver print, $9\frac{1}{2}'' \times 7\frac{1}{2}''$. Center for Creative Photography, University of Arizona, Tucson.

Weston "previsualized" his still lifes, choosing the exact angle, lighting, and framing he desired. His vegetables often resemble human bodies, in this case a seated nude seen from behind.

EDWARD WESTON Like Alfred Stieglitz, in whose 291 Gallery he exhibited his work, EDWARD WESTON (1886–1958) played a major role in establishing photography as an important artistic medium. But unlike Stieglitz, who worked outdoors and sought to capture transitory moments in his photographs, Weston meticulously composed and carefully lit his subjects in a controlled studio setting, whether he was doing still lifes of peppers, shells, and other natural forms of irregular shape, or figure studies. The 1930

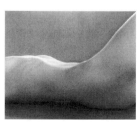

29-44A WESTON, *Nude,* 1925.

photograph of a pepper illustrated here (FIG. 29-44) is the 30th in a large series and an outstanding example of this genre. In contrast to Weston's photographs of sections of nude human bodies (FIG. 29-44A), his still-life photographs show the entire object, albeit tightly framed. (Compare Georgia O'Keeffe's *Jack-in-the-Pulpit No. 4* [FIG. I-5] painted the same year.) The artificial lighting accentuates the undulating surfaces and crevices of the vegetable. Weston left nothing to chance, choosing the exact angle and play of light over the object, "previsualizing" the final photographic print before snapping the camera's shutter.

In a kind of reversal of his approach to photographing nudes, which he often transformed into landscapes, Weston frequently chose peppers whose shapes reminded him of human bodies. *Pepper No. 30* looks like a seated nude figure seen from behind with raised arms emerging from broad shoulders. Viewers can read the vertical crease down the center of the vegetable as the spinal column leading to the buttocks. Although highly successful as a purely abstract composition of shapes and of light and dark, Weston's still life also conveys mystery and sensuality through its dramatic lighting and rich texture.

Architecture

As did other artists, many early-20th-century architects in the United States looked to Europe for inspiration, but distinctive American styles also emerged that in turn had a major influence on architectural design worldwide.

FRANK LLOYD WRIGHT One of the most striking personalities in the development of modern architecture on either side of the Atlantic was FRANK LLOYD WRIGHT (1867–1959). Born in Wisconsin, Wright moved to Chicago, where he eventually joined the firm headed by Louis Sullivan (FIGS. 28-40, 28-40A, and 28-41). Wright set out to create an American "architecture of democracy."[28] Always a believer in "natural" and "organic" buildings, Wright saw architecture as serving free individuals who have the right to move within a "free" space, envisioned as a nonsymmetrical design interacting spatially with its natural surroundings. He sought to develop an organic unity of planning, structure, materials, and site. Wright identified the principle of continuity as fundamental to understanding his view of organic unity:

> Classic architecture was all fixation.... Now why not let walls, ceilings, floors become seen as component parts of each other?... You may see the appearance in the surface of your hand contrasted with the articulation of the bony structure itself. This ideal, profound in its architectural implications . . . I called . . . continuity.[29]

Wright manifested his vigorous originality early, and by 1900 he had arrived at a style entirely his own. In his work during the first decade of the 20th century, his cross-axial plan and his fabric of continuous roof planes and screens defined a new American domestic architecture.

ROBIE HOUSE Wright fully expressed these elements and concepts in the Robie House (FIG. 29-45), built between 1907 and 1909. Like other buildings in the Chicago area Wright designed at about the same time, he called this home a "prairie house." Wright conceived the long, sweeping, ground-hugging lines, unconfined by abrupt wall limits, as reaching out toward and capturing the expansiveness of the Midwest's great flatlands. Abandoning all symmetry, he eliminated a facade, extended the roofs far beyond the walls, and all but concealed the entrance. Wright filled the house's "wandering" plan (FIG. 29-46) with intricately joined spaces (some large and open, others closed), grouped freely around a great central fireplace. (He believed strongly in the hearth's age-old domestic significance.) Wright designed enclosed patios, overhanging roofs, and strip windows to provide unexpected light sources and glimpses of the outdoors as the inhabitants moved through the interior space. These elements, together with the open ground plan, created a sense of space in motion, inside and out. Wright matched his new and fundamental interior spatial arrangement in his exterior treatment. For example, the flow of interior space determined the sharp angular placement of exterior walls.

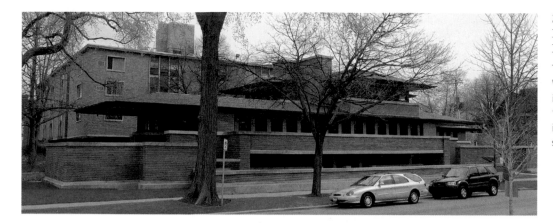

29-45 FRANK LLOYD WRIGHT, Robie House (looking northeast), Chicago, Illinois, 1907–1909.

The Robie House is an example of Wright's "architecture of democracy," in which free individuals move within a "free" space—a nonsymmetrical design interacting spatially with its natural surroundings.

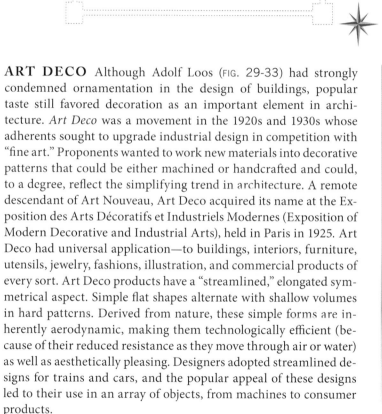

29-46 FRANK LLOYD WRIGHT, plan of the second (main) level of the Robie House, Chicago, Illinois, 1907–1909.

Typical of Wright's "prairie houses," the Robie House has a bold "wandering" asymmetrical plan with intricately joined open and closed spaces grouped freely around a great central fireplace.

ART DECO Although Adolf Loos (FIG. 29-33) had strongly condemned ornamentation in the design of buildings, popular taste still favored decoration as an important element in architecture. *Art Deco* was a movement in the 1920s and 1930s whose adherents sought to upgrade industrial design in competition with "fine art." Proponents wanted to work new materials into decorative patterns that could be either machined or handcrafted and could, to a degree, reflect the simplifying trend in architecture. A remote descendant of Art Nouveau, Art Deco acquired its name at the Exposition des Arts Décoratifs et Industriels Modernes (Exposition of Modern Decorative and Industrial Arts), held in Paris in 1925. Art Deco had universal application—to buildings, interiors, furniture, utensils, jewelry, fashions, illustration, and commercial products of every sort. Art Deco products have a "streamlined," elongated symmetrical aspect. Simple flat shapes alternate with shallow volumes in hard patterns. Derived from nature, these simple forms are inherently aerodynamic, making them technologically efficient (because of their reduced resistance as they move through air or water) as well as aesthetically pleasing. Designers adopted streamlined designs for trains and cars, and the popular appeal of these designs led to their use in an array of objects, from machines to consumer products.

Art Deco's exemplary masterpiece is the stainless-steel spire of the Chrysler Building (FIG. **29-47**) in New York City, designed by WILLIAM VAN ALEN (1882–1954). The building and spire are

29-47 WILLIAM VAN ALEN, Art Deco spire of the Chrysler Building (looking south), New York, New York, 1928–1930. ◼◀

The Chrysler Building's stainless steel spire epitomizes Art Deco architecture. The skyscraper's glittering crown of diminishing fan shapes has a streamlined form popular during the 1920s.

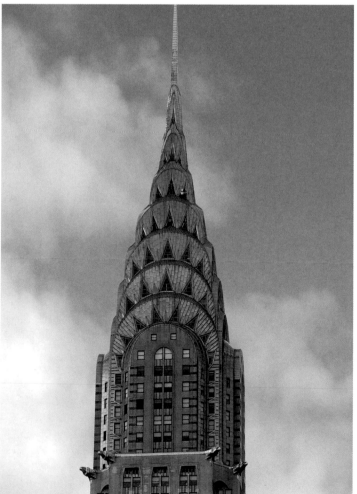

monuments to the fabulous 1920s, when American millionaires and corporations competed with one another to raise the tallest skyscrapers in the biggest cities. Built up of diminishing fan shapes, the spire glitters triumphantly in the sky, a resplendent crown honoring the business achievements of the great auto manufacturer. As a temple of commerce, the Chrysler Building celebrated the principles and success of American business before the onset of the Great Depression.

EUROPE, 1920 TO 1945

Because World War I was fought entirely on European soil, European artists experienced its devastating effects to a much greater degree than did American artists. The war had a profound effect on Europe's geopolitical terrain, on individual and national psyches, and on the art of the 1920s and 1930s.

Neue Sachlichkeit

In Germany, World War I gave rise to an artistic movement called *Neue Sachlichkeit* (New Objectivity). All of the artists associated with Neue Sachlichkeit served, at some point, in the German army. Their military experiences deeply influenced their worldviews and informed their art. "New Objectivity" captures the group's aim—

to present a clear-eyed, direct, and honest image of the war and its effects.

GEORGE GROSZ One of the Neue Sachlichkeit artists was GEORGE GROSZ (1893–1958), who was, for a time, associated with the Dada group in Berlin. Grosz observed the onset of World War I with horrified fascination that soon turned to anger and frustration. He reported:

> Of course, there was a kind of mass enthusiasm at the start. But this intoxication soon evaporated, leaving a huge vacuum.... And then after a few years when everything bogged down, when we were defeated, when everything went to pieces, all that remained, at least for me and most of my friends, were disgust and horror.[30]

The largest canvas Grosz ever painted— *The Eclipse of the Sun* (FIG. **29-48**)—does not depict the Great War itself, but, as are many of his other paintings and drawings (FIG. **29-48A**), it is a stinging indictment of the militarism and capitalism he believed were the root causes of the global conflict. The painting takes its name from the large red German coin at the upper left blocking the sun and signifying capitalism has

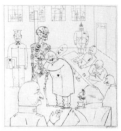

29-48A GROSZ, *Fit for Active Service*, 1916–1917.

brought darkness to the world. Also at the top are burning buildings. At the lower right are a skull and bones. Filling the rest of the canvas are the agents of this destruction seated at a table seen at a sharp angle from above. The main figure is the president of Germany, Paul von Hindenburg (r. 1925–1934), who wears his army uniform and war medals. His bloody sword is on the table before him, and on his head is the laurel wreath of victory. He presides over a meeting with four headless ministers—men who act on his orders without question. Grosz, however, also portrayed the president as a puppet leader. A wealthy industrialist wearing a top hat whispers instructions in von Hindenburg's ear. The painting is also a commentary on the gullibility of the public, personified here as a donkey who eats newspapers, that is, as a mindless creature who swallows the propagandistic lies promoted by the government- and business-friendly press.

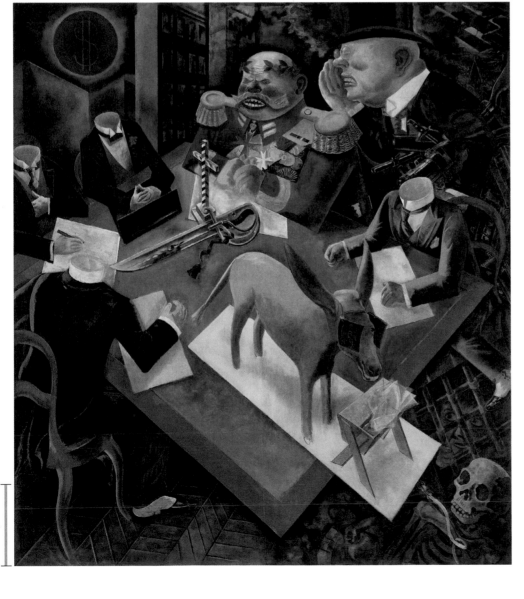

29-48 GEORGE GROSZ, *The Eclipse of the Sun*, 1926. Oil on canvas, 6′ 9⅝″ × 5′ 11⅞″. Heckscher Museum of Art, Huntington.

In Grosz's indictment of militarism and capitalism, an industrialist whispers instructions in the ear of the uniformed president of Germany, who meets with four of his headless ministers.

1 ft.

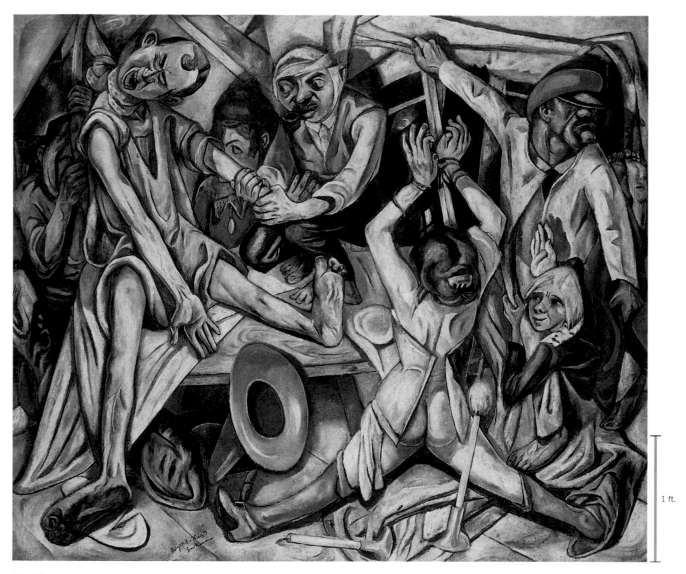

29-49 MAX BECKMANN, *Night,* 1918–1919. Oil on canvas, 4′ 4⅜″ × 5′ ¼″. Kunstsammlung Nordrhein-Westfalen, Düsseldorf.

Beckmann's treatment of forms and space in *Night* matched his view of the brutality of early-20th-century society. Objects seem dislocated and contorted, and the space appears buckled and illogical.

MAX BECKMANN Another major German artist who enlisted in the German army and initially rationalized the Great War was MAX BECKMANN (1884–1950). He believed the chaos would lead to a better society, but over time the massive loss of life and widespread destruction increasingly disillusioned him. Soon his work began to emphasize the horrors of war and of a society he saw descending into madness. His disturbing view of society is evident in *Night* (FIG. **29-49**), which depicts a cramped room three intruders have forcefully invaded. A bound woman, apparently raped, is splayed across the foreground of the painting. Her husband appears on the left. One of the intruders hangs him, while another one twists his left arm out of its socket. An unidentified woman cowers in the background. On the far right, the third intruder prepares to flee with the child.

Although this image does not depict a war scene, the wrenching brutality and violence pervading the home are searing and horrifying comments on society's condition. Beckmann also injected a personal reference by using himself, his wife, and his son as the models for the three family members. The stilted angularity of the figures and the roughness of the paint surface contribute to the image's savageness. In addition, the artist's treatment of forms and space reflects the world's violence. Objects seem dislocated and contorted, and the space appears buckled and illogical. For example, the woman's hands are bound to the window opening from the room's back wall, but her body appears to hang vertically, rather than lying across the plane of the intervening table.

OTTO DIX The third artist most closely associated with Neue Sachlichkeit was OTTO DIX (1891–1959). Having served as both a machine gunner and an aerial observer, Dix was well acquainted with war's effects. As did Grosz and Beckmann, Dix initially tried to find redeeming value in the apocalyptic event: "The war was a horrible thing, but there was something tremendous about it, too. . . . You have to have seen human beings in this unleashed state to know what human nature is. . . . I need to experience all the depths of life for myself, that's why I go out, and that's why I volunteered."[31] This idea of experiencing the "depths of life" stemmed from Dix's interest in the philosophy of Friedrich Nietzsche (1844–1900). In particular, Dix avidly read Nietzsche's *The Joyous Science,* deriving from it a belief in life's cyclical nature—procreation and death, building up and tearing down, and growth and decay.

As the war progressed, however, Dix's faith in the potential improvement of society dissipated, and he began to produce

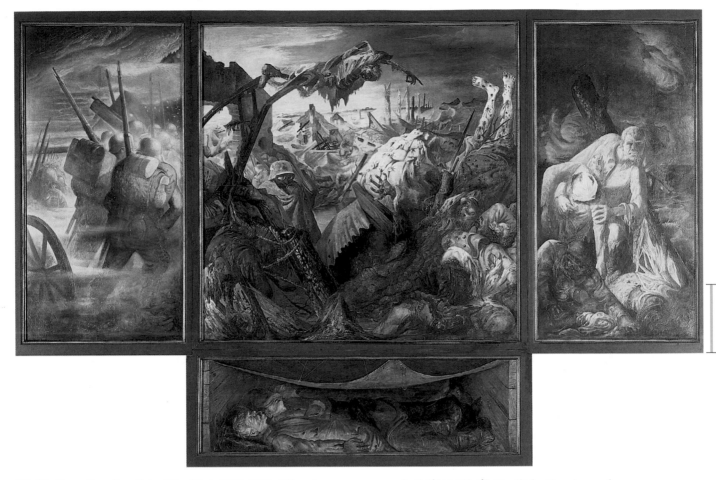

29-50 OTTO DIX, *Der Krieg* (*The War*), 1929–1932. Oil and tempera on wood, 6′ 8⅓″ × 13′ 4¾″. Staatliche Kunstsammlungen, Gemäldegalerie Neue Meister, Dresden.

In this triptych recalling earlier altarpieces, Dix captured the panoramic devastation war inflicts on the terrain and on humans. He depicted himself as a soldier dragging a comrade to safety.

unflinchingly direct and provocative artworks. His triptych titled *Der Krieg* (*The War*; FIG. 29-50) vividly captures the panoramic devastation war inflicts, both on the terrain and on humans. In the left panel, armed and uniformed soldiers march off into the distance. Dix graphically displayed the horrific results in the center and right panels, where mangled bodies, many riddled with bullet holes, are scattered throughout the eerily lit apocalyptic landscape. As if to emphasize the intensely personal nature of this scene, the artist painted himself into the right panel as the ghostly but determined soldier who drags a comrade to safety. In the bottom panel, in a coffinlike bunker, lie soldiers asleep—or perhaps dead. Dix significantly chose to present this sequence of images in the format of an altarpiece, and the work recalls triptychs such as Matthias Grünewald's *Isenheim Altarpiece* (FIG. 23-2). However, Dix's "altarpiece" presents a bleaker outlook than Grünewald's. The hope of salvation extended to viewers of the *Isenheim Altarpiece* through Christ's eventual resurrection is absent from *Der Krieg*. As did his fellow Neue Sachlichkeit artists, Dix felt compelled to lay bare the realities of his time, which the war's violence dominated. Even years later, Dix still maintained:

> You have to see things the way they are. You have to be able to say yes to the human manifestations that exist and will always exist. That doesn't mean saying yes to war, but to a fate that approaches you under certain conditions and in which you have to prove yourself. Abnormal situations bring out all the depravity, the bestiality of human beings. . . . I portrayed states, states that the war brought about, and the results of war, as states.[32]

ERNST BARLACH A work more spiritual in its expression is the *War Monument* (FIG. 29-51), which the German sculptor ERNST BARLACH (1870–1938) created for the cathedral in his hometown of Güstrow in 1927. Working often in wood, Barlach sculpted single figures usually dressed in flowing robes and portrayed in strong, simple poses embodying deep human emotions and experiences such as grief, vigilance, or self-comfort. Barlach's works combine sharp, smoothly planed forms with intense expression. The cast-bronze hovering figure of his *War Monument* is one of the poignant memorials of World War I. Unlike traditional war memorials depicting heroic military figures, often engaged in battle, the hauntingly symbolic figure Barlach created speaks to the experience of all caught in the conflict of war. The floating human form, suspended above a tomb inscribed with the dates 1914–1918 (and later also 1939–1945), suggests a dying soul at the moment when it is about to awaken to everlasting life—the theme of death and transfiguration. The rigid economy of surfaces concentrates attention on the simple but expressive head. So powerful was this sculpture the Nazis had it removed from the cathedral in 1937 and melted it down for ammunition. Luckily, a friend hid another version Barlach made. A Protestant parish in Cologne purchased it, and bronze workers made a new cast of the figure for the Güstrow cathedral.

Surrealism

The exuberantly aggressive momentum of the Dada movement that emerged during World War I lasted for only a short time. By 1924, with the publication in France of the *First Surrealist Manifesto,*

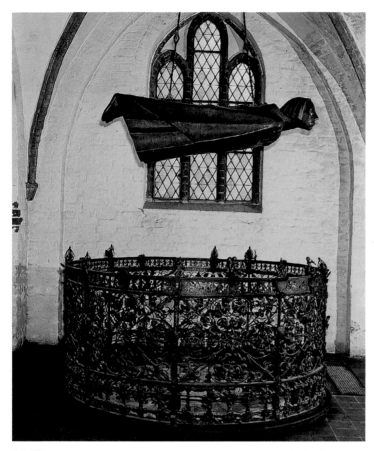

29-51 ERNST BARLACH, *War Monument,* Güstrow Cathedral, Güstrow, Germany, 1927. Bronze.

In this World War I memorial, which the Nazis melted down for ammunition, a human form floating above a tomb suggests a dying soul at the moment it is about to awaken to everlasting life.

most of the artists associated with Dada joined the *Surrealism* movement and its determined exploration of ways to express in art the world of dreams and the unconscious. Not surprisingly, the Surrealists incorporated many of the Dadaists' improvisational techniques. They believed these methods important for engaging the elements of fantasy and activating the unconscious forces deep within every human being. The Surrealists sought to explore the inner world of the psyche, the realm of fantasy and the unconscious. Inspired in part by the ideas of the psychoanalysts Sigmund Freud and Carl Jung, the Surrealists had a special interest in the nature of dreams. They viewed dreams as occurring at the level connecting all human consciousness and as constituting the arena in which people could move beyond their environment's constricting forces to reengage with the deeper selves society had long suppressed. In the words of André Breton, one of the leading Surrealist thinkers:

> Surrealism is based on the belief in the superior reality of certain forms of association heretofore neglected, in the omnipotence of dreams, in the undirected play of thought. . . . I believe in the future resolution of the states of dream and reality, in appearance so contradictory, in a sort of absolute reality, or surreality.[33]

Thus, the Surrealists' dominant motivation was to bring the aspects of outer and inner "reality" together into a single position, in much the same way life's seemingly unrelated fragments combine in the vivid world of dreams. The projection in visible form of this new conception required new techniques of pictorial construction. The Surrealists adapted some Dada devices and invented new

methods such as automatic writing (spontaneous writing using free association), not so much to reveal a world without meaning as to provoke reactions closely related to subconscious experience.

Surrealism developed along two lines. In *Naturalistic Surrealism,* artists presented recognizable scenes that seem to have metamorphosed into a dream or nightmare image. The artists Salvador Dalí (FIG. 29-55) and René Magritte (FIGS. 29-56 and 29-56A) were the most famous practitioners of this variant of Surrealism. In contrast, some artists gravitated toward an interest in *Biomorphic Surrealism.* In Biomorphic (life forms) Surrealism, *automatism*—the creation of art without conscious control—predominated. Biomorphic Surrealists such as Joan Miró (FIG. 29-58) produced largely abstract compositions, although the imagery sometimes suggests organisms or natural forms.

GIORGIO DE CHIRICO The widely recognized precursor of Surrealism was the Italian painter GIORGIO DE CHIRICO (1888–1978). De Chirico's emphatically ambiguous paintings of cityscapes are the most famous examples of a movement called *Pittura Metafisica,* or Metaphysical Painting. Returning to Italy after studying in Munich, de Chirico found hidden reality revealed through strange juxtapositions, such as those seen on late autumn afternoons, when the long shadows of the setting sun transformed vast open squares and silent public monuments into what the painter called "metaphysical towns." De Chirico translated this vision into paint in works such as *The Song of Love* (FIG. 29-52), a dreamlike scene set in the deserted piazza of an Italian town. A huge marble head—a fragment of the

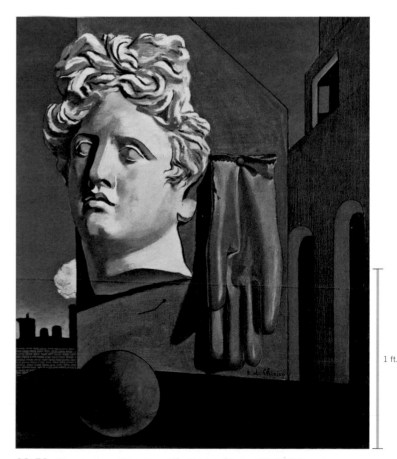

1 ft.

29-52 GIORGIO DE CHIRICO, *The Song of Love,* 1914. Oil on canvas, 2′ 4¾″ × 1′ 11⅜″. Museum of Modern Art, New York (Nelson A. Rockefeller bequest).

De Chirico's Metaphysical Painting movement was a precursor of Surrealism. Here, a classical head of Apollo floats mysteriously next to a gigantic red glove in a deserted, shadow-filled Italian city square.

famous *Apollo Belvedere* in the Vatican—is suspended in midair above a large green ball. To the right is a gigantic red glove nailed to a wall. The buildings and the three over-life-size objects cast shadows that direct the viewer's eye to the left and to a locomotive puffing smoke—a favorite Futurist motif, here shown in slow motion and incongruously placed near the central square. The choice of the term *metaphysical* to describe de Chirico's paintings suggests these images transcend their physical appearances. *The Song of Love*, for all of its clarity and simplicity, takes on a rather sinister air. The sense of strangeness de Chirico could conjure with familiar objects and scenes recalls Nietzsche's "foreboding that underneath this reality in which we live and have our being, another and altogether different reality lies concealed."[34]

Reproductions of De Chirico's paintings appeared in periodicals almost as soon as he completed them, and his works quickly influenced artists outside Italy, including both the Dadaists and, later, the Surrealists. The incongruities in his work intrigued the Dadaists, whereas the eerie mood and visionary quality of paintings such as *The Song of Love* excited and inspired Surrealist artists who sought to portray the world of dreams.

MAX ERNST Originally a Dada activist in Germany, MAX ERNST (1891–1976) became one of the early adherents of the Surrealist circle André Breton anchored. As a child living in a small community near Cologne, Ernst had found his existence fantastic and filled with marvels. In autobiographical notes, written mostly in the third person, he said of his birth: "Max Ernst had his first contact with the world of sense on the 2nd April 1891 at 9:45 a.m., when he emerged from the egg which his mother had laid in an eagle's nest and which the bird had incubated for seven years."[35] Ernst's service in the German army during World War I swept away his early success as an Expressionist. In his own words:

> Max Ernst died on 1st August 1914. He returned to life on 11th November 1918, a young man who wanted to become a magician and find the central myth of his age. From time to time he consulted the eagle which had guarded the egg of his prenatal existence. The bird's advice can be detected in his work.[36]

Before joining the Surrealists, Ernst explored every means to achieve the sense of the psychic in his art. As other Dadaists did, Ernst set out to incorporate found objects and chance into his works, often combining fragments of images he had cut from old books, magazines, and prints to form one hallucinatory collage. He also began making paintings that shared the mysterious dreamlike effect of his collages.

In 1920, Ernst met Breton, who instantly recognized the German artist's affinity with the Surrealist group. In 1922, Ernst moved to Paris, where he painted *Two Children Are Threatened by a Nightingale* (FIG. **29-53**). In it, Ernst displayed a private dream challenging the post-Renaissance idea that a painting should resemble a window looking into a "real" scene rendered illusionistically three-dimensional through mathematical perspective. He painted the landscape, the distant city, and the tiny flying bird in conventional fashion, following all the established rules of linear and atmospheric perspective. The three sketchily rendered figures, however, clearly belong to a dream world, and the literally three-dimensional miniature gate, the odd button knob, and the strange closed building "violate" the bulky frame's space. Additional dislocation occurs in the traditional museum identification label, which Ernst displaced into a cutaway part of the frame. Handwritten, it announces the work's title (taken from a poem Ernst wrote before he painted this), adding another note of irrational mystery.

As is true of many Surrealist works, the title, *Two Children Are Threatened by a Nightingale*, is ambiguous and relates uneasily to what the spectator sees. The viewer must struggle to decipher connections between the image and the words. When Surrealists (and Dadaists and Metaphysical artists before them) used puzzling titles, they intended the seeming contradiction between title and picture to knock the audience off balance with all expectations challenged. Much of the impact of Surrealist works begins with the viewer's sudden awareness of the incongruity and absurdity of what the artist pictured. These were precisely the qualities that subjected the Dadaists and

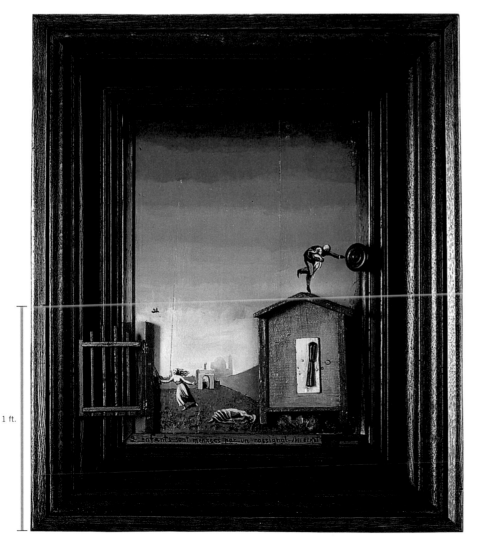

1 ft.

29-53 MAX ERNST, *Two Children Are Threatened by a Nightingale*, 1924. Oil on wood with wood construction, 2' 3½" × 1' 10½" × 4½". Museum of Modern Art, New York.

In this early Surrealist painting with an intentionally ambiguous title, Ernst used traditional perspective to represent the setting, but the three sketchily rendered figures belong to a dream world.

Degenerate Art

Although avant-garde artists often had to endure public ridicule both in Europe and America (see "The Armory Show," page 863), they suffered outright political persecution in Germany in the 1930s and 1940s. The most dramatic example of this persecution was the infamous "Entartete Kunst" (Degenerate Art) exhibition Adolf Hitler (1889–1945) and the Nazis mounted in 1937.

Hitler aspired to become an artist himself and produced numerous drawings and paintings reflecting his firm belief that 19th-century realistic genre painting represented the zenith of Aryan art development. Accordingly, Hitler denigrated anything that did not conform to that standard—in particular, avant-garde art. Turning his criticism into action, Hitler ordered the confiscation of more than 16,000 artworks he considered "degenerate." To publicize his condemnation of this art, he ordered his minister for public enlightenment and propaganda, Joseph Goebbels (1897–1945), to organize a massive exhibition of this "degenerate art." Hitler designated as degenerate those artworks that "insult German feeling, or destroy or confuse natural form, or simply reveal an absence of adequate manual and artistic skill."* The term *degenerate* also had other specific connotations at the time. The Nazis used it to identify supposedly inferior racial, sexual, and moral types. Hitler's order to Goebbels to target 20th-century avant-garde art for inclusion in the Entartete Kunst exhibition aimed to impress on the public the general inferiority of the artists producing this work. To make that point all the more dramatic, Hitler ordered the organization of another exhibition, the Grosse Deutsche Kunstausstellung (Great German Art Exhibition), which ran concurrently and presented an extensive array of Nazi-approved conservative art.

Entartete Kunst opened in Munich on July 19, 1937, and included more than 650 paintings, sculptures, prints, and books. The exhibition was immensely popular. Roughly 20,000 viewers visited the show daily. By the end of its four-month run, it had attracted more than two million viewers, and nearly a million more viewed it as it traveled through Germany and Austria. Among the 112 artists whose works the Nazis presented for ridicule were Ernst Barlach, Max Beckmann, Otto Dix, Max Ernst, George Grosz, Vassily Kandinsky, Ernst Kirchner, Paul Klee, Wilhelm Lehmbruck, Franz Marc, Emil Nolde, and Kurt Schwitters. In a memorable photograph (FIG. 29-54) taken during Hitler's preview visit to the exhibition on July 16, 1937, the Nazi leader pauses in front of the Dada wall. Behind him are works by Schwitters, Klee, and Kandinsky, which the organizers deliberately hung askew on the wall. (They subsequently straightened them for the duration of the exhibition.)

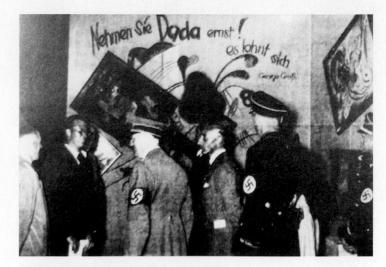

29-54 Adolf Hitler, accompanied by Nazi commission members, including photographer Heinrich Hoffmann, Wolfgang Willrich, Walter Hansen, and painter Adolf Ziegler, viewing the "Entartete Kunst" show on July 16, 1937.

For Hitler's visit, the curators deliberately hung askew the works of Kandinsky, Klee, and Schwitters. In Nazi Germany, no modernist artist was safe from persecution, and many fled the country.

In Germany in the 1930s and 1940s, in the face of Nazi persecution, artists committed to pursuing avant-garde ideas required courage and a resoluteness that extended beyond issues of aesthetics and beyond the confines of the art world. No modernist artist was safe from Hitler's attack. (Only six of the artists in the exhibition were Jewish.) For example, despite his status as a charter member of the Nazi party, Emil Nolde received particularly harsh treatment. The Nazis confiscated more than 1,000 of Nolde's works from German museums and included 27 of them in the exhibition, more than for almost any other artist. Max Beckmann and his wife fled to Amsterdam on the opening day of the Entartete Kunst exhibit, never to return to their homeland. Ernst Kirchner responded to the stress of Nazi pressure by destroying all his woodblocks and burning many of his works. A year later, in 1938, he committed suicide.

*Stephanie Barron, *"Degenerate Art": The Fate of the Avant-Garde in Nazi Germany* (Los Angeles: Los Angeles County Museum of Art, 1991), 19.

Surrealists to public condemnation and, in Germany under Adolf Hitler (1889–1945), to governmental persecution (see "Degenerate Art," above, and FIG. **29-54**).

SALVADOR DALÍ The Surrealists' exploration of the human psyche and dreams reached new heights in the works of Spanish-born SALVADOR DALÍ (1904–1989). In his paintings, sculptures, jewelry, and designs for furniture and movies, Dalí probed a deeply erotic dimension, studying the writings of Richard von Krafft-Ebing (1840–1902) and Sigmund Freud, and inventing what he called the "paranoiac-critical method" to assist his creative process. As he described it, in his painting he aimed "to materialize the images of concrete irrationality with the most imperialistic fury of precision . . . in order that the world of imagination and of concrete irrationality may be as objectively evident . . . as that of the exterior world of phenomenal reality."[37]

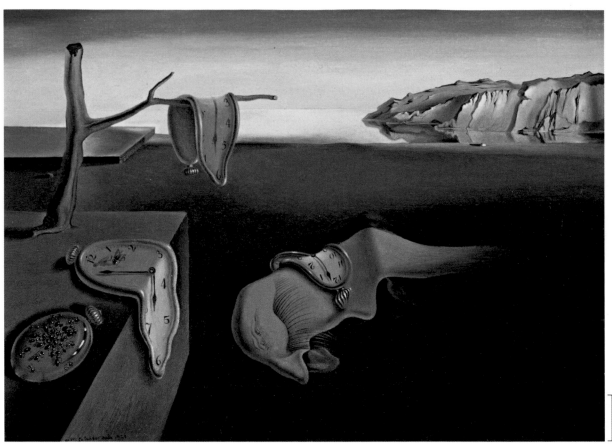

29-55 Salvador Dalí, *The Persistence of Memory*, 1931. Oil on canvas, 9¼″ × 1′ 1″. Museum of Modern Art, New York. ■◀

Dalí painted "images of concrete irrationality." In this realistically rendered landscape featuring three "decaying" watches, he created a haunting allegory of empty space where time has ended.

1 in.

In *The Persistence of Memory* (FIG. **29-55**), Dalí created a haunting allegory of empty space where time has ended. An eerie, never-setting sun illuminates the barren landscape. An amorphous creature draped with a limp pocket watch sleeps in the foreground. Another watch hangs from the branch of a dead tree springing unexpectedly from a blocky architectural form. A third watch hangs half over the edge of the rectangular form, beside a small timepiece

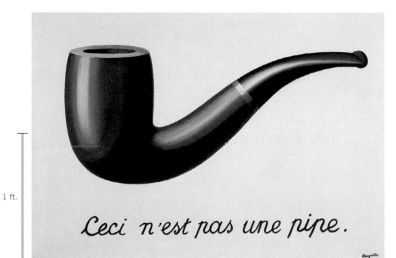

1 ft.

29-56 René Magritte, *The Treachery (or Perfidy) of Images*, 1928–1929. Oil on canvas, 1′ 11⅝″ × 3′ 1″. Los Angeles County Museum of Art, Los Angeles (purchased with funds provided by the Mr. and Mrs. William Preston Harrison Collection). ■◀

The discrepancy between Magritte's meticulously painted briar pipe and his caption, "This is not a pipe," challenges the viewer's reliance on the conscious and rational in the reading of visual art.

resting dial-down on the block's surface. Ants swarm mysteriously over the small watch, while a fly walks along the face of its large neighbor, almost as if this assembly of watches were decaying organic life—soft and sticky. Dalí rendered every detail of this dreamscape with precise control, striving to make the world of his paintings convincingly real—in his words, to make the irrational concrete.

RENÉ MAGRITTE The Belgian painter René Magritte (1898–1967) encountered the work of Giorgio de Chirico (FIG. 29-52) in 1922. The Italian artist's disquieting combinations of motifs rendered in a realistic manner deeply impressed the younger Belgian artist, who produced his first Surrealist painting, *The Lost Jockey*, in 1926. The next year Magritte moved to Paris, where he joined the intellectual circle of André Breton and remained in France until 1930. In 1929, Magritte published an important essay in the Surrealist journal *La revolution surréaliste* in which he discussed the disjunction between objects, pictures of objects, and names of objects and pictures. The essay explains the intellectual basis for *The Treachery (or Perfidy) of Images* (FIG. **29-56**), in which Magritte presented a meticulously rendered *trompe l'oeil* depiction of a briar pipe. The caption beneath the image, however, contradicts what seems obvious: "Ceci n'est pas une pipe" ("This is not a pipe"). The discrepancy between image and caption clearly challenges the assumptions underlying the reading of visual art. As is true of the other Surrealists' work, Magritte's paintings for example, *The False Mirror* (FIG. **29-56A**), wreak havoc on the viewer's reliance on the conscious and the rational.

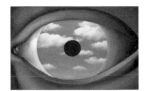

29-56A Magritte, *The False Mirror*, 1928.

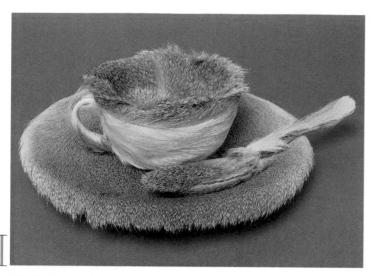

29-57 MERET OPPENHEIM, *Object* (*Le Déjeuner en fourrure*), 1936. Fur-covered cup, 4⅜″ diameter; saucer, 9⅜″ diameter; spoon, 8″ long. Museum of Modern Art, New York.

The Surrealists loved the concrete tangibility of sculpture, which made their art even more disquieting. Oppenheim's functional fur-covered object captures the Surrealist flair for magical transformation.

MERET OPPENHEIM Sculpture especially appealed to the Surrealists because its concrete tangibility made their art all the more disquieting. *Object* (FIG. **29-57**), also called *Le Déjeuner en fourrure* (*Luncheon in Fur*), by Swiss artist MERET OPPENHEIM (1913–1985) captures the incongruity, humor, visual appeal, and, often, eroticism characterizing Surrealism. The artist presented a fur-lined teacup inspired by a conversation she had with Picasso.

After admiring a bracelet Oppenheim had made from a piece of brass covered with fur, Picasso noted anything might be covered with fur. When her tea grew cold, Oppenheim responded to Picasso's comment by ordering "un peu plus de fourrure" (a little more fur), and the sculpture had its genesis. *Object* takes on an anthropomorphic quality, animated by the quirky combination of the fur with a functional object. Further, the sculpture captures the Surrealist flair for alchemical, seemingly magical or mystical, transformation. It incorporates a sensuality and eroticism (seen here in the seductively soft, tactile fur lining the concave form) that are also components of much of Surrealist art.

JOAN MIRÓ Like the Dadaists, the Surrealists used many methods to free the creative process from reliance on the kind of conscious control they believed society had shaped too much. Dalí used his paranoiac-critical approach to encourage the free play of association as he worked. Other Surrealists used automatism and various types of planned "accidents" to provoke reactions closely related to subconscious experience. Dalí's older countryman JOAN MIRÓ (1893–1983) was a master of this approach. Although Miró resisted formal association with any movement or group, including the Surrealists, André Breton identified him as "the most Surrealist of us all."[38] From the beginning, Miró's work contained an element of fantasy and hallucination. After Surrealist poets in Paris introduced him to the use of chance in the creation of art, the young Spaniard devised a new painting method that enabled him to create works such as *Painting* (FIG. **29-58**). Miró began this painting by making a scattered collage composition with assembled fragments cut from a catalog for machinery. The shapes in the collage became motifs the artist freely reshaped on the canvas to create black silhouettes—solid or in outline, with dramatic accents of white and vermilion. They suggest, in the painting, a host of amoebic organisms or constellations in outer space floating in an immaterial background space filled with soft reds, blues, and greens.

Miró described his creative process as a switching back and forth between unconscious and conscious image-making: "Rather than setting out to paint something, I begin painting and as I paint the picture begins to assert itself, or suggest itself under my brush. The form becomes a sign for a woman or a bird as I work. . . . The first stage is free, unconscious. . . . The second stage is carefully calculated."[39] Even the artist could not always explain the meanings of pictures such as *Painting*. They are, in the truest sense, spontaneous and intuitive expressions of the little-understood, submerged unconscious part of life.

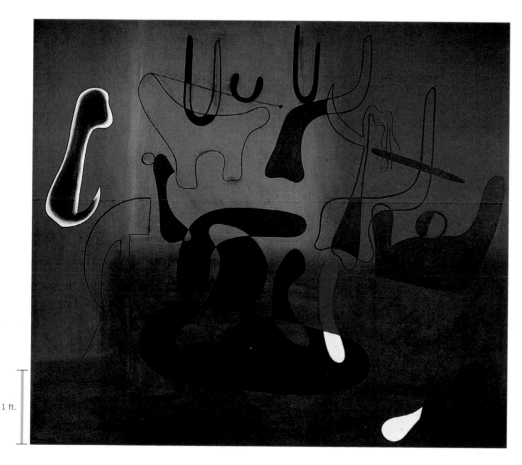

29-58 JOAN MIRÓ, *Painting*, 1933. Oil on canvas, 5′ 8″ × 6′ 5″. Museum of Modern Art, New York (Loula D. Lasker bequest by exchange). ◼◄

Miró promoted automatism, the creation of art without conscious control. He began this painting with a scattered collage and then added forms suggesting floating amoebic organisms.

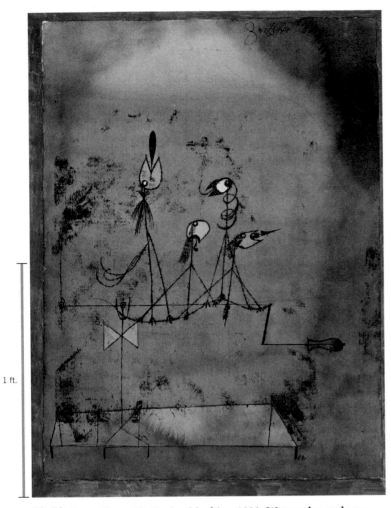

29-59 PAUL KLEE, *Twittering Machine*, 1922. Watercolor and pen and ink, on oil transfer drawing on paper, mounted on cardboard, 2′ 1″ × 1′ 7″. Museum of Modern Art, New York. ◼◀

1 ft.

Although based on forms in the tangible world easily read as birds, Klee's *Twittering Machine* is a fanciful vision of a mysterious world presented in a simplified, almost childlike manner.

PAUL KLEE Perhaps the most inventive artist using fantasy images to represent the nonvisible world was the Swiss-German painter PAUL KLEE (1879–1940). Like Miró, he shunned formal association with groups such as the Dadaists and Surrealists but pursued their interest in the subconscious. Klee sought clues to humanity's deeper nature in primitive shapes and symbols. Like Jung, Klee seems to have accepted the existence of a collective unconscious that reveals itself in archaic signs and patterns and is everywhere evident in the art of "primitive" cultures (see "Primitivism," page 846). The son of a professional musician and himself an accomplished violinist, Klee thought of painting as similar to music in its ability to express feelings through color, form, and line. In 1920, Klee set down his "creative credo," which reads in part:

> Art does not reproduce the visible; rather it makes visible. . . . The formal elements of graphic art are dot, line, plane, and space—the last three charged with energy of various kinds. . . . Formerly we used to represent things visible on earth, things we either liked to look at or would have liked to see. Today we reveal the reality that is behind visible things.[40]

To penetrate the reality behind visible things, Klee studied nature avidly, taking special interest in analyzing processes of growth and change. He coded these studies in diagrammatic form

in notebooks. The root of his work was thus nature, but nature filtered through his mind. Upon starting an image, he would allow the pencil or brush to lead him until an image emerged, to which he would then respond to complete the idea.

Twittering Machine (FIG. **29-59**) reveals Klee's fanciful vision. The painting, although based on forms in the tangible world easily read as birds, is far from illusionistic. Klee presented the scene in a simplified, almost childlike manner, imbuing the work with a poetic lyricism. The inclusion of a crank-driven mechanism added a touch of whimsy. The small size of Klee's works enhances their impact. A viewer must draw near to decipher the delicately rendered forms and enter his mysterious dream world. Perhaps no other artist of the 20th century matched Klee's subtlety as he deftly created a world of ambiguity and understatement that draws each viewer into finding a unique interpretation of the work.

Also associated with the Surrealists was WIFREDO LAM (1902–1982), a Cuban painter who studied in Madrid and Paris and whose work (FIG. **29-59A**) was greatly influenced by Picasso. It was Picasso who introduced Lam to Braque, Breton, and other avant-garde artists and critics.

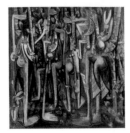

29-59A LAM, *The Jungle*, 1943.

De Stijl

The utopian spirit and ideals of the Suprematists and Constructivists (FIGS. 29-30 and 29-31) in Russia were shared in western Europe by a group of young Dutch artists. They formed a new movement in 1917 and began publishing a magazine, calling both movement and magazine *De Stijl* (*The Style*). The group's cofounders were the painters Piet Mondrian (FIG. 29-60) and Theo van Doesburg (1883–1931). In addition to promoting utopian ideals, De Stijl artists believed in the birth of a new age in the wake of World War I. They felt it was a time of balance between individual and universal values, when the machine would assure ease of living. In their first manifesto of De Stijl, the artists declared: "There is an old and a new consciousness of time. The old is connected with the individual. The new is connected with the universal."[41] The goal, according to van Doesburg and architect Cor van Eesteren (1897–1988), was a total integration of art and life:

> We must realize that life and art are no longer separate domains. That is why the "idea" of "art" as an illusion separate from real life must disappear. The word "Art" no longer means anything to us. In its place we demand the construction of our environment in accordance with creative laws based upon a fixed principle. These laws, following those of economics, mathematics, technique, sanitation, etc., are leading to a new, plastic unity.[42]

PIET MONDRIAN Toward this goal of integration, PIET MONDRIAN (1872–1944) created a new style based on a single ideal principle. The choice of the term *De Stijl* reflected Mondrian's confidence that this style—*the* style—revealed the underlying eternal structure of existence. Accordingly, De Stijl artists reduced their artistic vocabulary to simple geometric elements. Time spent in Paris, just before World War I, introduced Mondrian to Cubism and other modes of abstraction. However, as his attraction to theological writings grew, Mondrian sought to purge his art of every overt reference to individual objects in the external world. He initially favored the teachings of theosophy, a tradition basing knowledge of nature and the human condition on knowledge of the divine nature or spiritual powers. (His fellow theosophist Vassily Kandinsky pursued a similar path.) Mondrian, however, quickly abandoned the strictures of

1 in.

29-60 PIET MONDRIAN, *Composition with Red, Blue, and Yellow,* 1930. Oil on canvas, 1′ 6⅛″ × 1′ 6⅛″. Kunsthaus, Zürich. © Mondrian/ Holtzman Trust c/o HCR International, VA, USA. ◼◀

Mondrian's "pure plastic" paintings consist of primary colors locked into a grid of intersecting vertical and horizontal lines. By altering the grid patterns, he created a dynamic tension.

theosophy and turned toward a conception of nonobjective design— "pure plastic art"—that he believed expressed universal reality. He articulated his credo with great eloquence in 1914:

> What first captivated us does not captivate us afterward (like toys). If one has loved the surface of things for a long time, later on one will look for something more. . . . The interior of things shows through the surface; thus as we look at the surface the inner image is formed in our soul. It is this inner image that should be represented. For the natural surface of things is beautiful, but the imitation of it is without life. . . . Art is higher than reality and has no direct relation to reality. . . . To approach the spiritual in art, one will make as little use as possible of reality, because reality is opposed to the spiritual. . . . [W]e find ourselves in the presence of an abstract art. Art should be above reality, otherwise it would have no value for man.[43]

Mondrian soon moved beyond Cubism because he felt "Cubism did not accept the logical consequences of its own discoveries; it was not developing towards its own goal, the expression of pure plastics."[44] Caught by the outbreak of hostilities while on a visit to Holland, Mondrian remained there during World War I, developing his theories for what he called *Neoplasticism*—the new "pure plastic art." He believed all great art had polar but coexistent goals, the attempt to create "universal beauty" and the desire for "aesthetic expression of oneself."[45] The first goal is objective in nature, whereas the second is subjective, existing within the individual's mind and heart. To create a universal expression, an artist must communicate "a real equation of the universal and the individual."[46]

To express this vision, Mondrian eventually limited his formal vocabulary to the three primary colors (red, yellow, and blue), the three primary values (black, white, and gray), and the two primary directions (horizontal and vertical). Basing his ideas on a combination of teachings, he concluded primary colors and values are the

purest colors and therefore are the perfect tools to help an artist construct a harmonious composition. Using this system, he created numerous paintings locking color planes into a grid of intersecting vertical and horizontal lines, as in *Composition with Red, Blue, and Yellow* (FIG. **29-60**). In each of these paintings, Mondrian altered the grid patterns and the size and placement of the color planes to create an internal cohesion and harmony. This did not mean inertia. Rather, Mondrian worked to maintain a dynamic tension in his paintings from the size and position of lines, shapes, and colors.

Sculpture

It was impossible for early-20th-century artists to ignore the increasingly intrusive expansion of mechanization and growth of technology. However, not all artists embraced these developments, as had the Futurists. In contrast, many artists attempted to overcome the predominance of mechanization in society by immersing themselves in a search for the organic and natural.

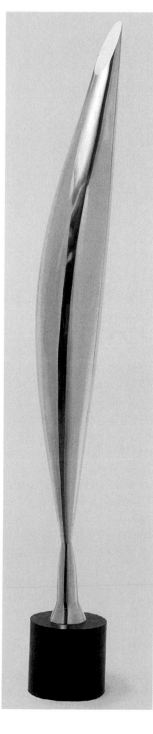

1 ft.

CONSTANTIN BRANCUSI One artist who was eager to produce works emphasizing the natural or organic was Romanian sculptor CONSTANTIN BRANCUSI (1876–1957). Brancusi sought to move beyond surface appearances to capture the essence or spirit of the object depicted (see "Brancusi, Hepworth, and Moore on Abstract Sculpture," page 882) in rhythmic, elegant sculptures. The softly curving surfaces and ovoid form of his sculptures refer, directly or indirectly, to the cycle of life. *Bird in Space* (FIG. **29-61**) is not a literal depiction of a bird, nor does his *Newborn* (FIG. **29-61A**) mimic a real baby's head. The abstract form of both works is the final result of a long process. For *Bird in Space,* Brancusi started with the image of a bird at rest with its wings folded at its sides and ended with a gently

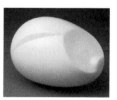

29-61A BRANCUSI, *The Newborn,* 1915.

29-61 CONSTANTIN BRANCUSI, *Bird in Space,* 1924. Bronze, 4′ 2 5/16″ high. Philadelphia Museum of Art, Philadelphia (Louise and Walter Arensberg Collection, 1950). ◼◀

Although not a literal depiction of a bird, Brancusi's softly curving light-reflecting abstract sculpture in polished bronze suggests a bird about to soar in free flight through the heavens.

Brancusi, Hepworth, and Moore on Abstract Sculpture

Many early-20th-century sculptors rejected the notion that reproducing the physical world of nature was the purpose of sculpture. Instead, they championed abstraction as the sculptor's proper goal. Among those who not only produced enduring masterpieces of abstract sculpture but also wrote eloquently about the theoretical basis of their work were Constantin Brancusi (FIG. 29-61), Barbara Hepworth (FIG. 29-62), and Henry Moore (FIG. 29-63). Some excerpts from their writings on sculpture illustrate their commitment to abstraction as their guiding principle.

▌ *Constantin Brancusi* Simplicity is not an objective in art, but one achieves simplicity despite oneself by entering into the real sense of things.* . . . What is real is not the external form but the essence of things. Starting from this truth it is impossible for anyone to express anything essentially real by imitating its exterior surface.[†]

▌ *Barbara Hepworth* The forms which have had special meaning for me since childhood have been the standing form (which is the translation of my feeling towards the human being standing in landscape); the two forms (which is the tender relationship of one living thing beside another); and the closed form, such as the oval, spherical, or pierced form (sometimes incorporating colour) which translates for me the association and meaning of gesture in the landscape. . . . In all these shapes the translation of what one feels about man and nature must be conveyed by the sculptor in terms of mass, inner tension, and rhythm, scale in relation to our human size, and the quality of surface which speaks through our hands and eyes.[‡]

▌ *Henry Moore* Since the Gothic, European sculpture had become overgrown with moss, weeds—all sorts of surface excrescences which completely concealed shape. It has been Brancusi's special mission to get rid of this overgrowth, and to make us once more shape-conscious. To do this he has had to concentrate on very simple direct shapes . . . Abstract qualities of design are essential to the value of a work . . . Because a work does not aim at reproducing natural appearances, it is not, therefore, an escape from life—but may be a penetration into reality. . . . My sculpture is becoming less representational, less an outward visual copy . . . but only because I believe that in this way I can present the

29-62 BARBARA HEPWORTH, *Oval Sculpture* (*No. 2*), 1943, cast 1958, plaster, $11\frac{1}{4}''\times 1'\,4\frac{1}{4}''\times 10''$. Tate.

Hepworth's major contribution to the history of sculpture was the introduction of the hole, or negative space, as an abstract element that is as integral and important to the sculpture as its mass.

human psychological content of my work with greatest directness and intensity.[§]

*Quoted in Herschel B. Chipp, *Theories of Modern Art: A Source Book by Artists and Critics* (Berkeley and Los Angeles: University of California Press, 1968), 364–365.
[†]Quoted in George Heard Hamilton, *Painting and Sculpture in Europe, 1880–1940*, 6th ed. (New Haven, Conn.: Yale University Press, 1993), 426.
[‡]Barbara Hepworth, *A Pictorial Autobiography* (London: Tate Gallery, 1978), 9, 53.
[§]Quoted in Robert L. Herbert, *Modern Artists on Art,* 2d ed. (Mineola, N.Y.: Dover, 2000), 173–179.

curving columnar form sharply tapered at each end. Despite the abstraction, the sculpture retains the suggestion of a bird about to soar in free flight through the heavens. The highly reflective surface of the polished bronze does not allow the viewer's eye to linger on the sculpture itself (as do, for example, Rodin's agitated and textured surfaces; FIGS. 28-32, 28-32A, and 28-33). Instead, the eye follows the gleaming reflection along the delicate curves right off the tip of the work, thereby inducing a feeling of flight. Brancusi stated, "All my life I have sought the essence of flight. Don't look for mysteries. I give you pure joy. Look at the sculptures until you see them. Those nearest to God have seen them."[47]

BARBARA HEPWORTH In England, BARBARA HEPWORTH (1903–1975) developed her own kind of essential sculptural form,

combining pristine shape with a sense of organic vitality. She sought a sculptural idiom that would express her sense both of nature and the landscape and of the person who is in and observes nature (see "Brancusi, Hepworth, and Moore," above). By 1929, Hepworth arrived at a breakthrough that evolved into an enduring and commanding element in her work from that point on. It represents her major contribution to the history of sculpture: the use of the hole, or void. Earlier sculptors, such as Archipenko (FIG. 29-20) had experimented with sculptural voids, but Hepworth introduced holes in her sculptures as abstract elements. The holes do not represent anything specific. They are simply negative space, but are as integral and important to the sculptures as their mass. *Oval Sculpture* (*No. 2*) is a plaster cast (FIG. 29-62) of an earlier wood sculpture Hepworth carved in 1943. Pierced in four places, the work is as

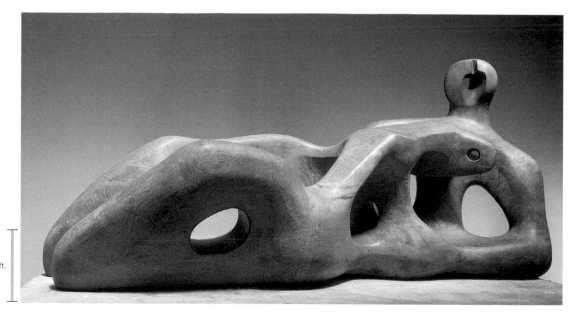

much defined by the smooth, curving holes as by the volume of white plaster. Like the forms in all of Hepworth's mature works, those in *Oval Sculpture* are basic and universal, expressing a sense of eternity's timelessness.

HENRY MOORE Fellow Briton HENRY MOORE (1898–1986) shared Hepworth's interest in the hole, or void, as an important element in sculptural design, but his sculptures, such as *Reclining Figure* (FIG. 29-63), although abstracted, always remain recognizable. This statue is one of a long series of reclining female nudes inspired originally by a photograph Moore acquired of a *chacmool* (FIG. 18-17) from pre-Columbian Mexico. Moore believed the simple and massive shapes of his statues expressed a universal truth beyond the physical world (see "Brancusi, Hepworth, and Moore," page 882).

Reclining Figure is also characteristic of Moore's work in exploiting the natural beauty of different materials—here, elm. Moore maintained every "material has its own individual qualities" and these qualities could play a role in the creative process: "It is only when the sculptor works direct, when there is an active relationship with his material, that the material can take its part in the shaping of an idea."[48] Accordingly, the contours of *Reclining Figure* follow the grain of the wood. The abstracted shapes suggest Surrealist biomorphic forms (FIG. 29-58), but Moore's recumbent woman is also a powerful earth mother whose undulant forms and hollows suggest nurturing human energy. Similarly, the body shapes evoke the contours of the Yorkshire hills of Moore's childhood and the wind-polished surfaces of weathered wood and stone. Moore heightened the allusions to landscape and to Surrealist organic forms in his work by interplaying mass and void, based on the intriguing qualities of cavities in nature. For Moore, the hole was not an abstract shape. It represented "the mysterious fascination of caves in hillsides and cliffs."[49] *Reclining Figure* combines the organic vocabulary central to Moore's philosophy—bone shapes, eroded rocks, and geologic formations—to communicate the human form's fluidity, dynamism, and evocative nature.

VERA MUKHINA Not all European sculptors of this period pursued abstraction, however. *The Worker and the Collective Farm Worker* (FIG. 29-64) by Russian artist VERA MUKHINA (1889–1963) presents a vivid contrast with the work of Brancusi, Hepworth, and Moore. Produced in 1937 for the International Exposition

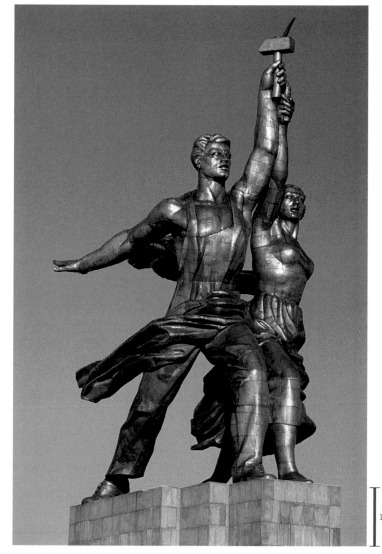

29-64 VERA MUKHINA, *The Worker and the Collective Farm Worker*, Soviet Pavilion, Paris Exposition, 1937. Stainless steel, 78′ high. © Estate of Vera Mukhina/RAO, Moscow/VAGA, New York.

In contrast to contemporaneous abstract sculpture, Mukhina's realistic representation of a male factory worker and a female farm worker glorified the communal labor of the Soviet people.

in Paris—the same venue in which Picasso displayed *Guernica* (FIG. 29-18)—Mukhina's monumental stainless-steel sculpture glorifies the communal labor of the Soviet people. Whereas Picasso employed Cubist abstraction to convey the horror of wartime bombing, Mukhina relied on realism to represent exemplars of the Soviet citizenry. Her sculpture, which stood on the top of the Soviet Pavilion at the exposition, depicts a male factory worker, holding aloft the tool of his trade, the hammer. Alongside him is a female farm worker, raising her sickle to the sky. The juxtaposed hammer and sickle at the apex of the sculpture replicate their appearance on the Soviet flag. Mukhina augmented the heroic tenor of the work by emphasizing the solidity of the figures, who stride forward with their clothes blowing dramatically behind them. Mukhina had studied in Paris and was familiar with abstraction, especially Cubism, but felt a commitment to realism produced the most powerful sculpture. The Soviet government officially approved this realist style and Mukhina earned high praise for her sculpture. Indeed, Russian citizens celebrated the work as a national symbol for decades.

Architecture

As in the opening decades of the century, developments in European architecture after World War I closely paralleled the stylistic and theoretical concerns of painters and sculptors.

GERRIT THOMAS RIETVELD The ideas Piet Mondrian, Theo van Doesburg, and De Stijl artists advanced found their architectural equivalent in the designs of GERRIT THOMAS RIETVELD (1888–1964). His Schröder House (FIG. 29-65) in Utrecht, built in 1924, perfectly expresses van Doesburg's definition of De Stijl architecture:

> The new architecture is anti-cubic, i.e., it does not strive to contain the different functional space cells in a single closed cube, but it throws the functional space (as well as canopy planes, balcony volumes, etc.) out from the centre of the cube, so that height, width, and depth plus time become a completely new plastic expression in open spaces. . . . The plastic architect . . . has to construct in the new field, time-space.[50]

The main living rooms of the Schröder House are on the second floor, with more private rooms on the ground floor. However, Rietveld's house has an open plan and a relationship to nature more like the houses of American architect Frank Lloyd Wright (FIGS. 29-45 and 29-46). Rietveld designed the entire second floor with sliding partitions that can be closed to define separate rooms or pushed back to create one open space broken into units only by the furniture arrangement. This shifting quality appears also on the outside, where railings, free-floating walls, and long rectangular windows give the effect of cubic units breaking up before the viewer's eyes. Rectangular planes seem to slide across each other on the Schröder House facade like movable panels, making this structure a kind of three-dimensional projection of the rigid but carefully proportioned flat color rectangles in Mondrian's paintings (FIG. 29-60).

WALTER GROPIUS De Stijl architects not only developed an appealing simplified geometric style but also promoted the notion art should be thoroughly incorporated into living environments. As Mondrian had insisted, "[A]rt and life are *one*; art and life are both expressions of truth."[51] In Germany, WALTER GROPIUS (1883–1969) developed a particular vision of "total architecture." He made this concept the foundation of not only his own work but also the work of generations of pupils under his influence at a school called the *Bauhaus* (see "Walter Gropius and the Bauhaus," page 885).

The building Gropius designed for the Bauhaus in 1925 after the school relocated to Dessau was the Bauhaus's architectural manifesto. The Dessau Bauhaus consisted of workshop and class areas, a dining room, a theater, a gymnasium, a wing with studio apartments, and an enclosed two-story bridge housing administrative offices. Of the major wings, the most dramatic was the Shop Block (FIG. 29-66). Three stories tall, the Shop Block housed a printing shop and dye works facility, in addition to other work areas. The builders constructed the skeleton of reinforced concrete but set these supports well back, sheathing the entire structure in glass, creating a streamlined and light effect. This design's simplicity followed Gropius's dictum that architecture should avoid "all romantic embellishment and whimsy." Further, he realized the "economy in the use of space" articulated in his list of Bauhaus principles in his interior layout of the Shop Block, which consisted of large areas of free-flowing undivided space. Gropius believed this kind of spatial organization encouraged interaction and the sharing of ideas.

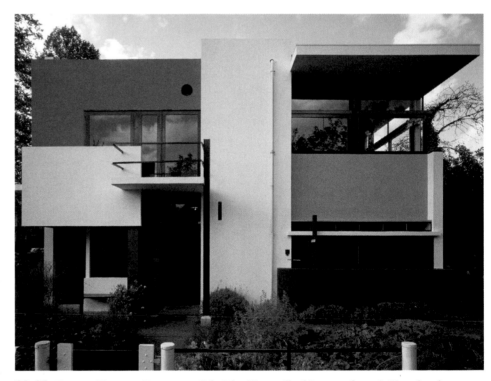

29-65 GERRIT THOMAS RIETVELD, Schröder House (looking northwest), Utrecht, the Netherlands, 1924.

The De Stijl Schröder House has an open plan and an exterior that is a kind of three-dimensional projection of the carefully proportioned flat color rectangles in Mondrian's paintings (FIG. 29-60).

Walter Gropius and the Bauhaus

In 1919, Walter Gropius became the director of the Weimar School of Arts and Crafts in Germany, founded in 1906. Under Gropius, the school assumed a new name—Das Staatliche Bauhaus (State School of Building). Gropius's goal was to train artists, architects, and designers to accept and anticipate 20th-century needs. He developed an extensive curriculum based on certain principles set forth in a formal Bauhaus *Manifesto* published in April 1919.

BAUHAUS MANIFESTO

The first principle Gropius staunchly advocated in the 1919 manifesto was the importance of strong basic design (including principles of composition, two- and three-dimensionality, and color theory) and craftsmanship as fundamental to good art and architecture. He asserted there was no essential difference between the artist and the craftsperson.

> The Bauhaus strives to coordinate all creative effort, to achieve, in a new architecture, the unification of all training in art and design. The ultimate, if distant, goal of the Bauhaus is the collective work of art—the Building—in which no barriers exist between the structural and the decorative arts.*

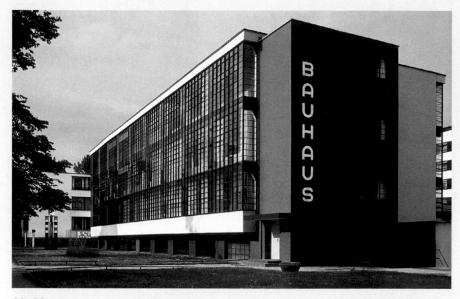

29-66 WALTER GROPIUS, Shop Block (looking northeast), the Bauhaus, Dessau, Germany, 1925–1926.

Gropius constructed this Bauhaus building by sheathing a reinforced concrete skeleton in glass. The design followed his dictum that architecture should avoid "all romantic embellishment and whimsy."

29-66A BREUER, Wassily chair, 1925.

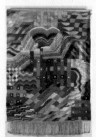

29-66B STÖLZL, Gobelin tapestry, 1927–1928.

To encourage the elimination of those boundaries that traditionally separated art from architecture and art from craft, the Bauhaus offered courses in a wide range of artistic disciplines. These included carpentry, furniture design (by MARCEL BREUER [1902–1981]; FIG. **29-66A**), weaving (by GUNTA STÖLZL [1897–1983]; FIG. **29-66B**), pottery, bookbinding, metalwork, stained glass, mural painting, stage design, and advertising and typography, in addition to painting, sculpture, and architecture. Both a technical instructor and a "teacher of form"—an artist—taught in each department. Among the teachers Gropius hired were Vassily Kandinsky (FIG. 29-7) and Paul Klee (FIG. 29-59).

In addition, because Gropius wanted the Bauhaus to produce graduates who could design progressive environments that satisfied 20th-century needs, he emphasized thorough knowledge of machine-age technologies and materials. He felt that to produce truly successful designs, the artist-architect-craftsperson had to understand industry and mass production. Ultimately, Gropius hoped for a marriage between art and industry—a synthesis of design and production. As did the De Stijl movement, the Bauhaus philosophy had its roots in utopian principles. Gropius's declaration reveals the idealism of the entire Bauhaus enterprise:

> Let us collectively desire, conceive, and create the new building of the future, which will be everything in one structure: architecture and sculpture and painting, which, from the million hands of craftsmen, will one day rise towards heaven as the crystalline symbol of a new and coming faith.†

In its reference to a unity of workers, this statement also reveals the undercurrent of socialism present in Germany at the time.

BAUHAUS IN DESSAU

After encountering increasing hostility from a new government elected in 1924, the Bauhaus moved north from Weimar to Dessau (FIG. 29-66) in early 1925. By this time, the Bauhaus program had matured. In a new statement, Gropius listed the school's goals more clearly:

I A decidedly positive attitude to the living environment of vehicles and machines

I The organic shaping of things in accordance with their own current laws, avoiding all romantic embellishment and whimsy

I Restriction of basic forms and colors to what is typical and universally intelligible

I Simplicity in complexity, economy in the use of space, materials, time, and money‡

*Quoted in Charles Harrison and Paul Wood, eds., *Art in Theory, 1900–2000: An Anthology of Changing Ideas,* 2d ed. (Oxford: Blackwell, 2003), 311.
†Translated by Charles W. Haxthausen, in Barry Bergdoll, ed., *Bauhaus 1919–1933* (New York: Museum of Modern Art, 2009), 64.
‡Quoted in John Willett, *Art and Politics in the Weimar Period: The New Sobriety, 1917–1933* (New York: Da Capo Press, 1978), 119.

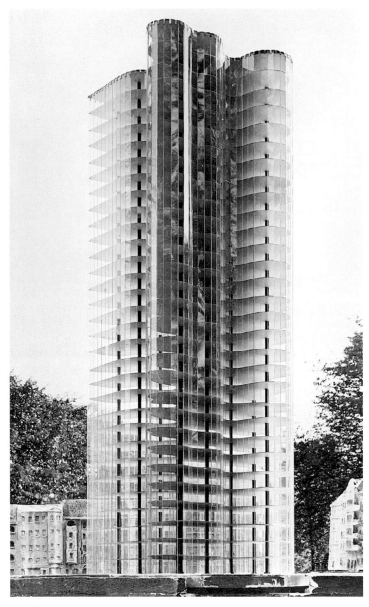

29-67 Ludwig Mies van der Rohe, **model for a glass skyscraper, Berlin, Germany, 1922 (no longer extant).**

In this technically and aesthetically adventurous design, the architect whose motto was "less is more" proposed a transparent building that revealed its cantilevered floor planes and thin supports.

LUDWIG MIES VAN DER ROHE In 1928, Gropius left the Bauhaus, and LUDWIG MIES VAN DER ROHE (1886–1969) eventually took over the directorship, moving the school to Berlin. Taking as his motto "less is more" and calling his architecture "skin and bones," the new Bauhaus director had already fully formed his aesthetic when he conceived the model (FIG. 29-67) for a glass skyscraper building in 1921. In the glass model, which was on display at the first Bauhaus exhibition in 1923, three irregularly shaped towers flow outward from a central court designed to hold a lobby, a porter's room, and a community center. Two cylindrical entrance shafts rise at the ends of the court, each containing elevators, stairways, and toilets. Wholly transparent, the perimeter walls reveal the regular horizontal patterning of the cantilevered floor planes and their thin vertical supporting elements. The bold use of glass sheathing and inset supports was, at the time, technically and aesthetically adventurous. The weblike delicacy of the lines of the

model, as well as the illusion of movement created by reflection and by light changes seen through the glass, appealed to many other architects. A few years later, Gropius pursued it in his design for the Bauhaus building (FIG. 29-66) in Dessau. The legacy of Mies van der Rohe's design can be seen in the glass-and-steel skyscrapers found in major cities throughout the world today.

END OF THE BAUHAUS One of Hitler's first acts after coming to power was to close the Bauhaus in 1933. During its 14-year existence, the beleaguered school graduated fewer than 500 students, yet it achieved legendary status. Its phenomenal influence extended beyond painting, sculpture, and architecture to interior design, graphic design, and advertising. Moreover, art schools everywhere began to structure their curricula in line with the program the Bauhaus pioneered. The numerous Bauhaus instructors who fled Nazi Germany disseminated the school's philosophy and aesthetic. Many Bauhaus members came to the United States. Gropius and Breuer (FIG. 29-66A) ended up at Harvard University. Mies van der Rohe moved to Chicago and taught there.

LE CORBUSIER The simple geometric aesthetic developed by Gropius and Mies van der Rohe became known as the *International style* because of its widespread popularity. The first and purest exponent of this style was the Swiss architect Charles-Edouard Jeanneret, who adopted his maternal grandfather's name—LE CORBUSIER (1887–1965). Trained in Paris and Berlin, he was also a painter, but Le Corbusier had the greatest influence as an architect and theorist on modern architecture. As such, he applied himself to designing a functional living space, which he described as a "machine for living."[52]

Le Corbusier maintained the basic physical and psychological needs of every human being were sun, space, and vegetation combined with controlled temperature, good ventilation, and insulation against harmful and undesired noise. He also advocated basing dwelling designs on human scale, because the house is humankind's assertion within nature. All these qualities characterize Le Corbusier's Villa Savoye (FIG. **29-68**), located at Poissy-sur-Seine near Paris. The country house sits at the center of a large plot of land cleared of trees and shrubs, but windows on all sides and the villa's roof-terrace provide the residents with broad views of the surrounding landscape. Several colors appear on the exterior—originally, a dark-green base, cream walls, and a rose-and-blue windscreen on top. They were a deliberate analogy for the colors in the machine-inspired Purist style of painting (FIG. 29-22) Le Corbusier practiced.

A cube of lightly enclosed and deeply penetrated space, the Villa Savoye has only a partially confined ground floor (containing, originally, a three-car garage, bedrooms, a bathroom, and utility rooms, and today a ticket counter and small gift shop for visitors). Much of the house's interior is open space, with thin columns supporting the main living floor and the roof garden area. The major living rooms in the Villa Savoye are on the second floor, wrapping around an open central court. Strip windows running along the membranelike exterior walls provide illumination to the rooms as well as views out to nature. From the second floor court, a ramp leads up to the roof-terrace and an interior garden protected by a curving windbreak along the north side.

The Villa Savoye has no traditional facade. The ostensible approach to the house does not define an entrance. Visitors must walk around and through the house to comprehend its layout, which incorporates several changes of direction and spiral staircases. Spaces and masses interpenetrate so fluidly that inside and outside space intermingle. The machine-planed smoothness of the unadorned

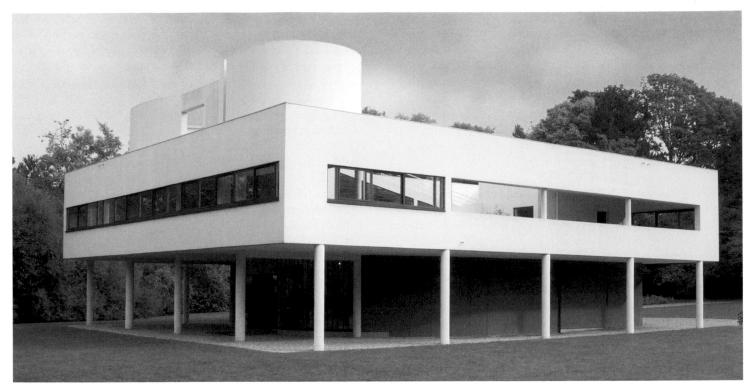

29-68 LE CORBUSIER, Villa Savoye (looking southeast), Poissy-sur-Seine, France, 1929. ■◀

Steel and ferroconcrete made it possible for Le Corbusier to invert the traditional practice of placing light architectural elements above heavy ones and to eliminate weight-bearing walls on the ground story.

surfaces, the slender ribbons of continuous windows, and the buoyant lightness of the whole fabric—all combine to reverse the effect of traditional country houses (FIG. 22-28). By placing heavy elements above and light ones below, and by refusing to enclose the ground story of the Villa Savoye with masonry walls, Le Corbusier inverted traditional design practice. This openness, made possible by the use of steel and ferroconcrete as construction materials, makes the "load" of the Villa Savoye's upper stories appear to hover lightly on the slender columnar supports.

MARSEILLES AND CHANDIGARH Le Corbusier designed the Villa Savoye as a private home, but as did De Stijl architects, he dreamed of extending his ideas of the house as a "machine for living" to designs for efficient and humane cities. He saw great cities as spiritual workshops and he proposed to correct the deficiencies in existing cities caused by poor traffic circulation, inadequate living units, and the lack of space for recreation and exercise. He proposed replacing traditional cities with three types of new communities. Vertical cities would house workers and the business and service industries. Linear-industrial cities would run as belts along the routes between the vertical cities and would serve as centers for the people and processes involved in manufacturing. Finally, separate centers would be constructed for people involved in intensive agricultural activity. Le Corbusier's cities would provide for human cultural needs in addition to serving every person's physical, mental, and emotional comfort needs.

Later in his career, Le Corbusier designed a few vertical cities, most notably the Unité d'Habitation in Marseilles (1945–1952). He also created the master plan for the entire city of Chandigarh, the capital city of the Punjab, India (1950–1957). He ended his career with a personal expressive style in his design of the Chapel of Notre Dame du Haut (FIG. 30-40) at Ronchamp, France.

UNITED STATES AND MEXICO, 1930 TO 1945

In the 1930s, much of the Western world was plunged into the Great Depression, which had a particularly acute effect in the United States. The decade following the catastrophic stock market crash of October 1929 dramatically changed the nation, and artists were among the millions of economic victims. The limited art market virtually disappeared, and museums curtailed both their purchases and exhibition schedules. Many artists sought financial support from the federal government, which established numerous programs to provide relief, assist recovery, and promote reform. Among the programs supporting artists were the Treasury Relief Art Project, founded in 1934 to commission art for federal buildings, and the Works Progress Administration (WPA), founded in 1935 to relieve widespread unemployment. Under the WPA, varied activities of the Federal Art Project paid artists, writers, and theater people a regular wage in exchange for work in their professions.

Despite the economic hardships facing artists during the Great Depression, the United States became a haven for European painters, sculptors, and architects seeking to escape from Hitler and the Nazis. Among those who abandoned their homelands for America during the years leading up to World War II in search of freedom from political and religious persecution and a more hospitable environment for their art were Léger, Lipchitz, Beckmann, Grosz, Ernst, and Dalí. This influx of European artists was as significant a factor in exposing American artists to modernist European art as was the Armory Show of 1913 (see "The Armory Show," page 863).

A complementary factor was the desire on the part of American museums to demonstrate their familiarity and connection with the most progressive European art by mounting exhibitions centered on the latest European artistic developments. In 1938, for example, the City Art Museum of Saint Louis presented an exhibition of Beckmann's work, and the Art Institute of Chicago organized *George Grosz: A Survey of His Art from 1918–1938*. This interest in exhibiting the work of persecuted artists driven from their homelands also had political overtones. In the highly charged atmosphere of the late 1930s leading to the onset of World War II, Americans often perceived support for these artists and their work as support for freedom and democracy. In 1942, Alfred H. Barr Jr. (1902–1981), the director of the Museum of Modern Art, stated:

> Among the freedoms which the Nazis have destroyed, none has been more cynically perverted, more brutally stamped upon, than the Freedom of Art. For not only must the artist of Nazi Germany bow to political tyranny, he must also conform to the personal taste of that great art connoisseur, Adolf Hitler. . . . But German artists of spirit and integrity have refused to conform. They have gone into exile or slipped into anxious obscurity. . . . Their paintings and sculptures, too, have been hidden or exiled. . . . But in free countries they can still be seen, can still bear witness to the survival of a free German culture.[53]

Despite this moral support for exiled artists, once the United States formally entered the war, Germany officially became the enemy. It became much more difficult for the American art world to promote German artists, however persecuted. Many émigré artists, including Léger, Grosz, Ernst, and Dalí, returned to Europe after the war ended. Their collective presence in the United States until then, however, was critical for the development of American art.

Painting

Although the political, social, and economic developments of the 1930s and 1940s brought many modernist European artists to the United States, the leading American painters of this period were primarily figural artists who had only a limited interest in abstract composition.

BEN SHAHN Born in Lithuania, BEN SHAHN (1898–1969) came to the United States in 1906 and trained as a lithographer before broadening the media in which he worked to include easel painting, photography, and murals. He focused on the lives of ordinary people and the injustices often done to them by the structure of an impersonal, bureaucratic society. In the early 1930s, he completed a cycle of 23 paintings and prints inspired by the trial and execution of the two Italian anarchists Nicola Sacco and Bartolomeo Vanzetti. Accused of killing two men in a holdup in 1920 in South Braintree, Massachusetts, the Italians were convicted in a trial many people thought resulted in a grave miscarriage of justice. Shahn felt he had found in this story a subject the equal of any in Western art history: "Suddenly I realized . . . I was living through another crucifixion."[54] Basing many of the works in this cycle on newspaper photographs of the events, Shahn devised a style that adapted his knowledge of Synthetic Cubism and his training in commercial art to an emotionally expressive use of flat, intense color in figural compositions filled with sharp, dry, angular forms. He called the major work in the series *The Passion of Sacco and Vanzetti* (FIG. I-6), drawing a parallel to Christ's Passion. This tall, narrow painting condenses the narrative in terms of both time and space. The two executed men lie in coffins at the bottom of the composition. Presiding over them are the three members of the commission chaired by Harvard University president A. Laurence Lowell, who declared the original trial fair and cleared the way for the executions to take place. A framed portrait of Judge Webster Thayer, who handed down the initial sentence, hangs on the wall of a simplified government building. The gray pallor of the dead men, the stylized mask-faces of the mock-pious mourning commissioners, and the sanctimonious, distant judge all contribute to the mood of anguished commentary making this image one of Shahn's most powerful works.

EDWARD HOPPER Trained as a commercial artist, EDWARD HOPPER (1882–1967) studied painting and printmaking in New York and then in Paris. When he returned to the United States, he concentrated on scenes of contemporary American city and

29-69 EDWARD HOPPER, *Nighthawks*, 1942. Oil on canvas, $2' 6'' \times 4' 8\frac{11}{16}''$. Art Institute of Chicago, Chicago (Friends of American Art Collection).

The seeming indifference of Hopper's characters to one another, and the echoing spaces surrounding them, evoke the overwhelming loneliness and isolation of Depression-era life in the United States.

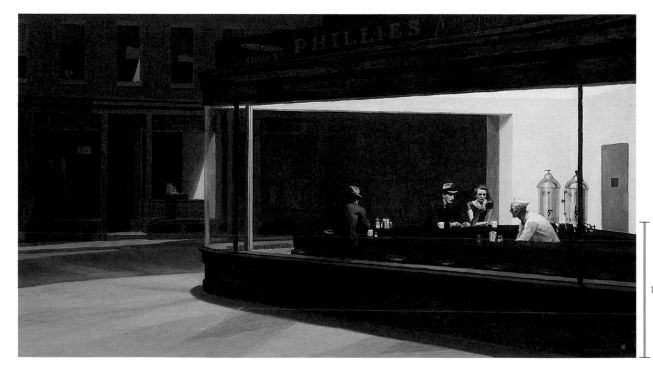

1 ft.

country life. His paintings depict buildings, streets, and landscapes that are curiously muted, still, and filled with empty spaces, evoking the national mind-set during the Depression era. Hopper did not paint historically specific scenes. He took as his subject the more generalized theme of the overwhelming loneliness and echoing isolation of modern life in the United States. In his paintings, motion is stopped and time suspended.

From the darkened streets outside a restaurant in Hopper's *Nighthawks* (FIG. **29-69**), the viewer glimpses the lighted interior through huge plate-glass windows, which lend the inner space the paradoxical sense of being both a safe refuge and a vulnerable place for the three customers and the man behind the counter. The seeming indifference of Hopper's characters to one another as well as the echoing spaces surrounding them evoke the pervasive loneliness of modern humans. In *Nighthawks* and other works, Hopper created a Realist vision recalling that of 19th-century artists such as Thomas Eakins (FIG. 27-36) and Henry Ossawa Tanner (FIG. 27-38), but in keeping with more recent trends in painting, he simplified the shapes, moving toward abstraction.

JACOB LAWRENCE African American artist JACOB LAWRENCE (1917–2000) moved to Harlem, New York, in 1927 while still a boy. There, he came under the spell of the African art and the African American history he found in lectures and exhibitions and in the special programs sponsored by the 135th Street branch of the New York Public Library, which had outstanding collections of African American art and archival data. Inspired by the politically oriented art of Goya (FIG. 27-11), Daumier (FIG. 27-29), and Orozco (FIG. 29-73), and influenced by the many artists and writers of the Harlem Renaissance whom he met, including Aaron Douglas (FIGS. 29-40 and 29-40A), Lawrence found his subjects in the everyday life of Harlem and in African American history.

In 1941, Lawrence began a 60-painting series titled *The Migration of the Negro* in which he defined his vision of the continuing African American struggle against discrimination. Unlike his earlier historical paintings depicting important figures in American history, such as the abolitionists Frederick Douglass and Harriet Tubman, this series called attention to a contemporaneous event—the ongoing exodus of black labor from the southern United States. Disillusioned with their lives in the South, hundreds of thousands of African Americans migrated north in the years following World War I, seeking improved economic opportunities and a more hospitable political and social environment. But the conditions African Americans encountered both during their migration and in the North were often as difficult and discriminatory as those they had left behind in the South, as Lawrence knew from his own experience:

> I was part of the migration, as was my family, my mother, my sister, and my brother. . . . I grew up hearing tales about people "coming up," another family arriving. . . . I didn't realize what was happening until about the middle of the 1930s, and that's when the *Migration* series began to take form in my mind.[55]

Lawrence's *Migration* paintings provide numerous vignettes capturing the experiences of the African Americans who had moved to the North. Often, a sense of the bleakness and degradation of their new life dominates the images. *No. 49* (FIG. **29-70**) of this series bears the caption "They also found discrimination in the North although it was much different from that which they had known in the South." Lawrence depicted a blatantly segregated dining room with a barrier running down the room's center separating

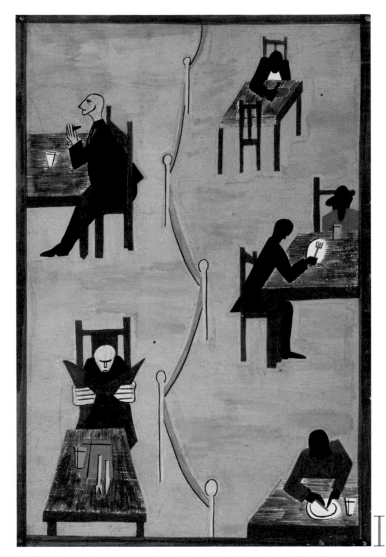

29-70 JACOB LAWRENCE, *No. 49* from *The Migration of the Negro*, 1940–1941. Tempera on Masonite, 1′ 6″ × 1′. Phillips Collection, Washington, D.C.

The 49th in a series of 60 paintings documenting African American life in the North, Lawrence's depiction of a segregated dining room underscored that the migrants had not left discrimination behind.

the whites on the left from the African Americans on the right. To ensure a continuity and visual integrity among all 60 paintings, Lawrence interpreted his themes systematically in rhythmic arrangements of bold, flat, and strongly colored shapes. His style drew equally from his interest in the push-pull effects of Cubist space and his memories of the patterns made by the colored scatter rugs brightening the floors of his childhood homes. He unified the narrative with a consistent palette of bluish green, orange, yellow, and grayish brown throughout the entire series.

GRANT WOOD Although many American artists, such as the Precisionists (FIGS. 29-41 and 29-42), preferred to depict the city or rapidly developing technological advances, others avoided subjects tied to modern life. At a 1931 arts conference, GRANT WOOD (1891–1942) announced a new movement developing in the Midwest, known as *Regionalism,* which he described as focused on American subjects and as standing in reaction to the modernist abstraction of Europe and New York. Four years later, Wood published an essay titled "Revolt against the City" that underscored their new focus.

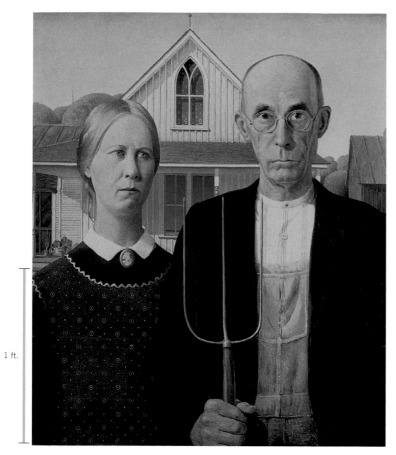

1 ft.

29-71 GRANT WOOD, *American Gothic*, 1930. Oil on beaverboard, 2′ 5⅞″ × 2′ ⅞″. Art Institute of Chicago, Chicago (Friends of American Art Collection). ◼◀

In reaction to modernist abstract painting, the Midwestern Regionalism movement focused on American subjects. Wood's painting of an Iowa farmer and his daughter became an American icon.

Wood and the Regionalists, sometimes referred to as the American Scene Painters, turned their attention instead to rural life as America's cultural backbone. Wood's paintings, for example, portray the people of rural Iowa, where he was born and raised.

The work that catapulted Wood to national prominence was *American Gothic* (FIG. **29-71**), which became an American icon. The artist depicted a farmer and his spinster daughter standing in front of a neat house with a small *lancet* window, a motif originating in Gothic architecture and associated with churches and religious piety. The man and woman wear traditional attire. He appears in worn overalls and she in an apron trimmed with rickrack. The dour expression on both faces gives the painting a severe quality, which Wood enhanced with his meticulous brushwork. The public and professional critics agreed *American Gothic* was "quaint, humorous, and AMERICAN" and embodied "strength, dignity, fortitude, resoluteness, integrity," qualities that represented the true spirit of America.[56]

Wood's Regionalist vision involved more than his subjects. It extended to a rejection of avant-garde styles in favor of a clearly readable, Realist style. Surely this approach appealed to many people alienated by the increasing presence of abstraction in art. However, despite the accolades this painting received, it also attracted criticism. Not everyone saw the painting as a sympathetic portrayal of Midwestern life. Indeed, some Iowans considered the depiction of life in their state insulting. In addition, despite the seemingly reportorial nature of *American Gothic,* some viewed it as a political statement—one of staunch nationalism. In light of the problematic

nationalism in Germany at the time, many observers found Wood's nationalistic attitude disturbing. Nonetheless, during the Great Depression, Regionalist paintings had a popular appeal because they often projected a reassuring image of America's heartland. The public saw Regionalism as a means of coping with the national crisis through a search for cultural roots. Thus, people deemed acceptable any nostalgia implicit in Regionalist paintings or mythologies these works perpetuated because they served a larger purpose.

THOMAS HART BENTON Another major Regionalist artist was THOMAS HART BENTON (1889–1975). Whereas Wood focused his attention on Iowa, Benton turned to scenes from his native Missouri. He produced one of his major works, a series of murals titled *A Social History of the State of Missouri,* in 1936 for the Missouri State Capitol. The murals depict a collection of images from the state's historic and legendary past, such as primitive agriculture, horse trading, a vigilante lynching, and an old-fashioned political meeting. Other scenes portray the mining industry, grain elevators, Native Americans, and family life. One segment, *Pioneer Days and Early Settlers* (FIG. **29-72**), shows a white man using whisky as a bartering tool with a Native American (*left*), along with scenes documenting the building of Missouri (*right*). Part documentary and part invention, Benton's images include both positive and negative aspects of Missouri's history, as these examples illustrate. Although the public perceived the Regionalists as dedicated to glorifying Midwestern life, that was not their aim. Indeed, Grant Wood observed, "Your true regionalist is not a mere eulogist; he may even be a severe critic."[57] Benton, like Wood, championed a visually accessible style, but he developed a highly personal aesthetic that included complex compositions, a fluidity of imagery, and simplified figures depicted with a rubbery distortion.

JOSÉ CLEMENTE OROZCO During the period between the two world wars, several Mexican painters achieved international renown for their work both in Mexico and the United States. The eldest of the three was JOSÉ CLEMENTE OROZCO (1883–1949), one of a group of Mexican artists determined to base their art on the indigenous history and culture existing in Mexico before Europeans arrived. The movement these artists formed was part of the idealistic rethinking of society that occurred in conjunction with the Mexican Revolution (1910–1920) and the lingering political turmoil of the 1920s. Among the projects these politically motivated artists undertook were vast mural cycles placed in public buildings to dramatize and validate the history of Mexico's native peoples. Orozco worked on one of the first major cycles, painted in 1922 on the walls of the National Training School in Mexico City. He carried the ideas of this mural revolution to the United States, completing many commissions for wall paintings between 1927 and 1934. From 1932 to 1934, he painted a major mural cycle in the Baker Library at Dartmouth College in New Hampshire. The college let Orozco choose the subject, and he designed 14 large panels and 10 smaller ones that together formed a panoramic and symbolic history of ancient and modern Mexico. The murals recount Mexican history from the early mythic days of the feathered-serpent god Quetzalcoatl (see Chapters 18 and 35) to a contemporary and bitterly satiric vision of modern education.

The imagery in panel 16, *Epic of American Civilization: Hispano-America* (FIG. **29-73**), revolves around the monumental figure of a heroic Mexican peasant armed to participate in the Mexican Revolution. Looming on either side of him are mounds crammed with symbolic figures of his oppressors—bankers, government soldiers, officials, gangsters, and the rich. Money-grubbers empty huge bags of gold coins at the incorruptible peon's feet, cannons threaten him,

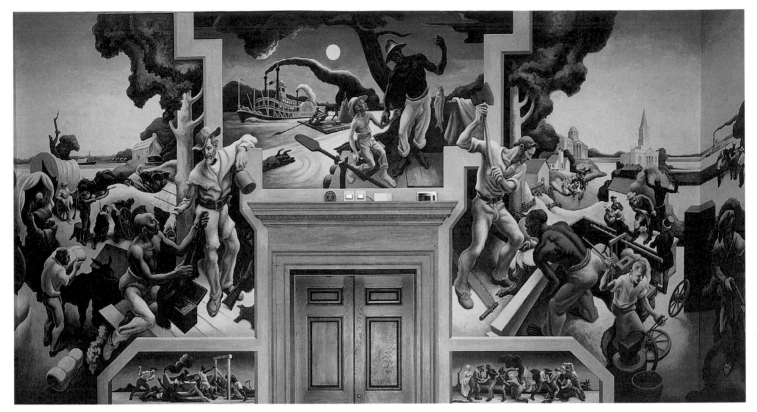

29-72 THOMAS HART BENTON, *Pioneer Days and Early Settlers,* fresco in the State Capitol, Jefferson City, Missouri, 1936. © T. H. Benton and R. P. Benton Testamentary Trusts/UMB Bank Trustee/Licensed by VAGA, New York.

Benton's mural for Missouri's State Capitol is one of the major Regionalist artworks. Part documentary and part invention, the images include both positive and negative aspects of state history.

and a general bedecked with medals raises a dagger to stab him in the back. Orozco's training as an architect gave him a sense of the framed wall surface, which he easily commanded, projecting his clearly defined figures onto the solid mural plane in monumental scale. In addition, Orozco's early experience as a maker of politi-cal prints and as a newspaper artist had taught him the rhetorical strength of graphic brevity, which he used here to assure his alle-gory could be read easily. His special merging of the graphic and mural media effects gives his work an originality and force rarely seen in mural painting after the Renaissance and Baroque periods.

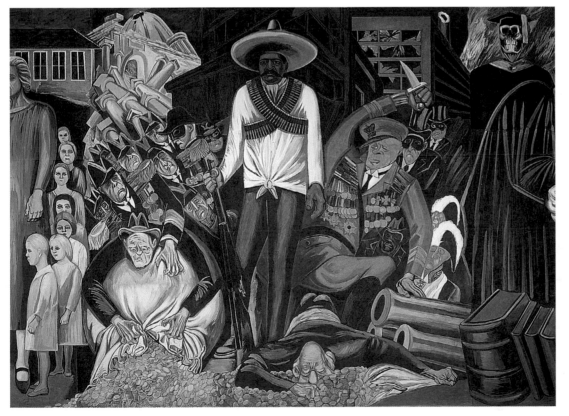

29-73 JOSÉ CLEMENTE OROZCO, *Epic of American Civilization: Hispano-America* (panel 16), fresco in Baker Memorial Library, Dartmouth College, Hanover, New Hampshire, ca. 1932–1934.

One of 24 panels depicting the history of Mexico from ancient times, this scene focuses on a heroic peasant soldier of the Mexican Revolution surrounded by symbolic figures of his oppressors.

United States and Mexico, 1930 to 1945   **891**

Rivera on Art for the People

Diego Rivera was an avid proponent of a social and political role for art in the lives of common people and wrote passionately about the proper goals for an artist—goals he fully met in his own murals depicting Mexican history (FIG. 29-74). Rivera's views stand in sharp contrast to the growing interest in abstraction on the part of many early-20th-century painters and sculptors.

Art has always been employed by the different social classes who hold the balance of power as one instrument of domination—hence, as a political instrument. One can analyze epoch after epoch—from the stone age to our own day—and see that there is no form of art which does not also play an essential political role. . . . What is it then that we really need? . . . An art with revolution as its subject: because the principal interest in the worker's life has to be touched first. It is necessary that he find aesthetic satisfaction and the highest pleasure appareled in the essential interest of his life. . . . The subject is to the painter what the rails are to a locomotive. He cannot do without it. In fact, when he refuses to seek or accept a subject, his own plastic methods and his own aesthetic theories become his subject instead. . . . [H]e himself becomes the subject of his work. He becomes nothing but an illustrator of his own state of mind . . . That is the deception practiced under the name of "Pure Art."*

*Quoted in Robert Goldwater and Marco Treves, eds., *Artists on Art from the XIV to the XX Century* (New York: Pantheon, 1945), 475–477.

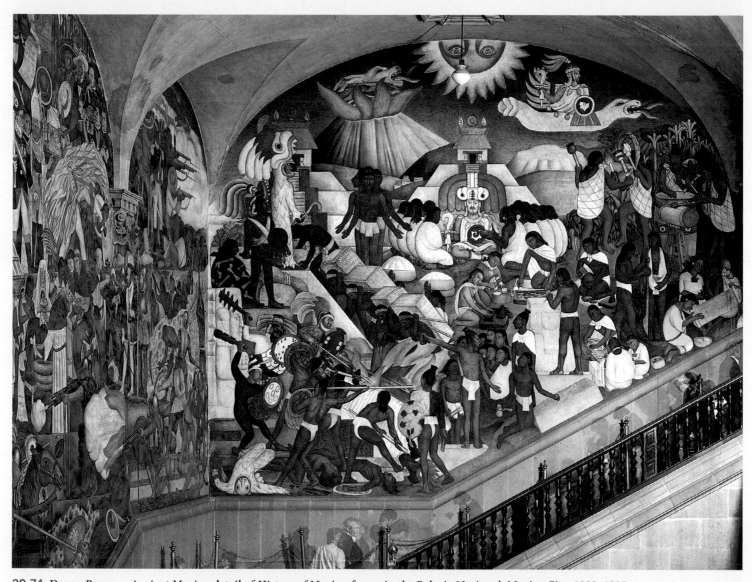

29-74 DIEGO RIVERA, *Ancient Mexico,* detail of *History of Mexico,* fresco in the Palacio Nacional, Mexico City, 1929–1935.

A staunch Marxist, Rivera painted vast mural cycles in public buildings to dramatize the history of his native land. This fresco depicts the conflicts between indigenous Mexicans and Spanish colonizers.

DIEGO RIVERA A second Mexican who received great acclaim for his murals, both in Mexico and in the United States was DIEGO RIVERA (1886–1957). A staunch Marxist, Rivera strove to develop an art that served his people's needs (see "Rivera on Art for the People," page 892). Toward that end, he sought to create a national Mexican style focusing on Mexico's history and also incorporating a popular, generally accessible aesthetic in keeping with the socialist spirit of the Mexican Revolution. Rivera produced numerous large murals in public buildings, among them a series lining the staircase of the National Palace in Mexico City. In these images, painted between 1929 and 1935, he depicted scenes from Mexico's history, of which *Ancient Mexico* (FIG. **29-74**) is one. This section of the mural represents the conflicts between the indigenous people and the Spanish colonizers. Rivera included portraits of important figures in Mexican history, especially those involved in the struggle for Mexican independence. Although the composition is complex, the simple monumental shapes and areas of bold color make the story easily legible.

FRIDA KAHLO Born to a Mexican mother and German father, the painter FRIDA KAHLO (1907–1954), who married Diego Rivera, used the details of her life as powerful symbols for the psychological pain of human existence. Art historians often consider Kahlo a Surrealist due to the psychic, autobiographical issues she dealt with in her art. Indeed, André Breton himself deemed her

a Natural Surrealist. (The work of her older contemporary, RUFINO TAMAYO [1899–1991; FIG. **29-74A**] has also been compared to Natural Surrealism.) Kahlo herself, however, rejected any association with the Surrealists. She began painting seriously as a young student, during convalescence from an accident that tragically left her in constant pain. Her life became a heroic and tumultuous battle for survival against illness and stormy personal relationships.

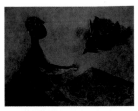

29-74A TAMAYO, *Friend of the Birds,* 1944.

Typical of her long series of unflinching self-portraits is *The Two Fridas* (FIG. **29-75**), one of the few large-scale canvases Kahlo ever produced. The twin figures sit side by side on a low bench in a barren landscape under a stormy sky. The figures suggest different sides of the artist's personality, inextricably linked by the clasped hands and by the thin artery stretching between them, joining their exposed hearts. The artery ends on one side in surgical forceps and on the other in a miniature portrait of her husband as a child. Her deeply personal paintings touch sensual and psychological memories in her audience.

To read Kahlo's paintings solely as autobiographical overlooks the powerful political dimension of her art. Kahlo was deeply nationalistic and committed to her Mexican heritage. Politically active, she joined the Communist Party in 1920 and participated in public political protests. *The Two Fridas* incorporates Kahlo's commentary on the struggle facing Mexicans in the early 20th century in defining their national cultural identity. The Frida on the right (representing indigenous culture) appears in a Tehuana dress, the traditional costume of Zapotec women from the Isthmus of Tehuantepec, whereas the Frida on the left (representing imperialist forces) wears a European-style white lace dress. The heart, depicted here in such dramatic fashion, was an important symbol in the art of the Aztecs, whom Mexican nationalists idealized as the last independent rulers of their land. Thus *The Two Fridas* represents both Kahlo's personal struggles and the struggles of her homeland.

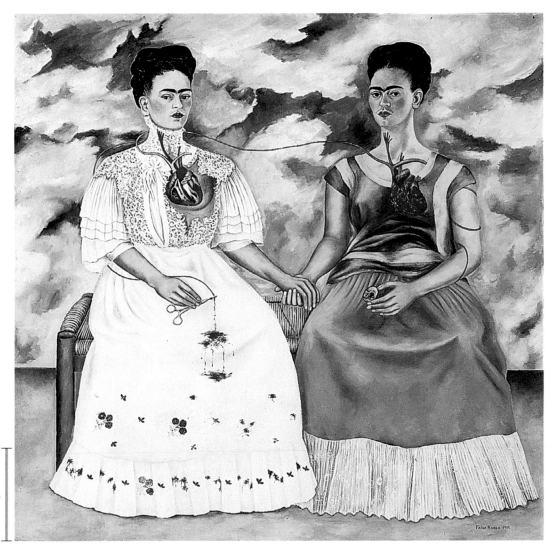

1 ft.

29-75 FRIDA KAHLO, *The Two Fridas,* 1939. Oil on canvas, 5′ 7″ × 5′ 7″. Museo de Arte Moderno, Mexico City.

Kahlo's deeply personal paintings touch sensual and psychological memories in her audience. Here, twin self-portraits linked by clasped hands and a common artery suggest two sides of her personality.

Photography

Frida Kahlo is the most famous female artist of her generation, but other women achieved prominence in the arts, especially the photographers Dorothea Lange and Margaret Bourke-White.

DOROTHEA LANGE One of the most important programs the U.S. government initiated during the 1930s was the Resettlement Administration (RA), better known by its later name, the Farm Security Administration. The RA oversaw emergency aid programs for farm families struggling to survive the Great Depression. The RA hired DOROTHEA LANGE (1895–1965) in 1936, and dispatched her to document the deplorable living conditions of the rural poor. At the end of an assignment photographing migratory pea pickers in California, Lange stopped at a camp in Nipomo and found the migrant workers there starving because the crops had frozen in the fields. Among the pictures Lange made on this occasion was *Migrant Mother, Nipomo Valley* (FIG. **29-76**), in which she captured the mixture of strength and worry in the raised hand and careworn face of a young mother, who holds a baby on her lap. Two older children cling to their mother trustfully while turning their faces away from the camera. Lange described how she got the picture:

> [I] saw and approached the hungry and desperate mother, as if drawn by a magnet. I do not remember how I explained my presence or my camera to her, but I remember she asked me no questions. I made five exposures, working closer and closer from the same direction. . . . There she sat in that lean-to tent with her children huddled around her, and she seemed to know that my pictures might help her, and so she helped me.[58]

Within days after Lange's photograph appeared in a San Francisco newspaper, people rushed food to Nipomo to feed the hungry workers.

MARGARET BOURKE-WHITE Almost 10 years younger than Dorothea Lange, MARGARET BOURKE-WHITE (1904–1971) also made her reputation as a photojournalist in Depression-era America. She was the first staff photographer Henry Luce (1898–1967) hired to furnish illustrations for the magazines in his publishing empire. Beginning in 1929, Bourke-White worked for *Fortune*, then for *Life* when Luce launched the famous newsweekly in 1936. During her long career, she photographed Midwestern farmers in their drought-stricken fields, impoverished Southern sharecroppers, black gold miners in South Africa, the Nazi concentration camp at Buchenwald, and the Korean War.

Bourke-White's most famous photographs, however, were not of people or events but of the triumphs of 20th-century engineering, many of which appeared in Luce's magazines and served to instill pride in an American public severely lacking in confidence during the Depression. She photographed the Chrysler Building (FIG. 29-47) while it was under construction in New York, attracting media attention for her daring balancing act on steel girders high above the pavement. She also achieved renown as the first woman to fly a combat mission when she was an official U.S. Air Force photographer during World War II.

For the first issue of *Life* (November 23, 1936), Bourke-White not only provided the cover photograph (FIG. **29-77**) of *Fort Peck Dam*,

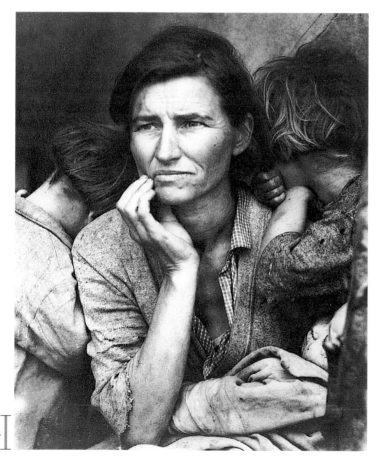

29-76 DOROTHEA LANGE, *Migrant Mother, Nipomo Valley*, 1935. Gelatin silver print, 1′ 1″ × 9″. Oakland Museum of California, Oakland (gift of Paul S. Taylor). ◼▸

While documenting the lives of migratory farm workers during the Depression, Lange made this unforgettable photograph of a mother in which she captured the woman's strength and worry.

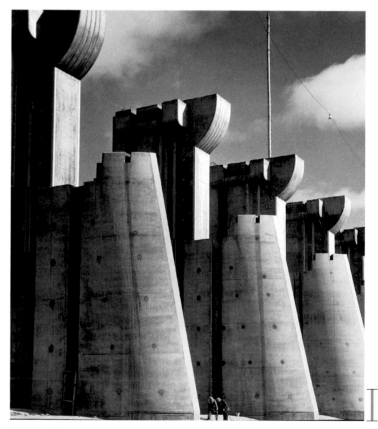

29-77 MARGARET BOURKE-WHITE, *Fort Peck Dam, Montana*, 1936. Gelatin silver print, 1′ 1″ × 10½″. Metropolitan Museum of Art, New York (gift of Ford Motor Company and John C. Waddell, 1987).

Bourke-White's dramatic photograph of Fort Peck Dam graced the cover of the first issue of *Life* magazine and celebrated the achievements of modern industry at the height of the Great Depression.

The Museum of Modern Art and the Avant-Garde

Established in 1929, the Museum of Modern Art (MoMA) in New York City owes its existence to a trio of women—Lillie P. Bliss, Mary Quinn Sullivan, and Abby Aldrich Rockefeller (see "Art 'Matronage' in the United States," page 865)—who saw the need for a museum to collect and exhibit modernist art. Together they founded MoMA, which quickly became the most influential museum of modern art in the world. Their success was extraordinary considering the skepticism and hostility greeting modernist art at the time of the museum's inception. Indeed, in the 1920s and 1930s, few American museums exhibited any late-19th- and 20th-century art.

In its quest to expose the public to the energy and challenge of modernist, particularly avant-garde, art, MoMA developed unique and progressive exhibitions. Among those the museum mounted during the early years of its existence were *Cubism and Abstract Art* and *Fantastic Art, Dada, Surrealism* (1936). Two other noteworthy shows were *American Sources of Modern Art* (*Aztec, Maya, Inca*) in 1933 and *African Negro Art* in 1935, both among the first exhibitions to deal with "primitive" artifacts in artistic rather than anthropological terms (see "Primitivism and Colonialism," page 846).

The organization of MoMA's administrative structure and the scope of the museum's early activities were also remarkable. MoMA's first director, Alfred H. Barr Jr., insisted on establishing departments not only for painting and sculpture but also for photography, prints and drawing, architecture, and the decorative arts. He developed a library of books on modern art and a film library, both of which have become world-class collections, as well as an extensive publishing program.

It is the museum's art collection, however, that has drawn the most attention. By cultivating an influential group of patrons, MoMA has developed an extensive and enviable collection of late-19th- and 20th-century art. The museum boasts such important works as van Gogh's *Starry Night* (FIG. 28-18), Picasso's *Les Demoi-*

29-78 ALEXANDER CALDER, *Lobster Trap and Fish Tail,* 1939. Painted sheet aluminum and steel wire, 8′ 6″ × 9′ 6″. Museum of Modern Art, New York.

Using his thorough knowledge of engineering to combine nonobjective organic forms and motion, Calder created a new kind of sculpture—the mobile—that expressed nature's innate dynamism.

selles d'Avignon (FIG. 29-12), and Dalí's *The Persistence of Memory* (FIG. 29-55), as well as many others illustrated in this book, including 22 in this chapter alone. MoMA has also served as an art patron itself. For example, in 1939, just a decade after the institution's founding, it commissioned Alexander Calder to produce the mobile *Lobster Trap and Fish Tail* (FIG. 29-78).

Montana, but also wrote and illustrated with 16 additional photographs the lead story on the town of New Deal, home to the workers who constructed the dam during the depths of the Depression. Fort Peck Dam was at the time the largest earth-filled dam in the world. Bourke-White photographed its towers (designed to conjure a crenellated medieval fortress) at a sharp angle from below to communicate the dam's soaring height, underscoring the immense scale by including two dwarfed figures of men in the foreground. The tight framing, which shuts out all of the landscape and much of the sky, transforms the dam into an almost-abstract composition, a kind of still life, like Edward Weston's peppers (FIG. 29-44). Bourke-White's photographs celebrate modern industry as heir to the architectural achievements of the ancient world's great civilizations, and bear comparison with the paintings of Charles Demuth (FIG. 29-41).

Sculpture

In striking contrast to the leading American painters and photographers of the 1930s, the most renowned sculptor of this period rose to international prominence because of his contributions to the development of abstract art.

ALEXANDER CALDER The son and grandson of sculptors, ALEXANDER CALDER (1898–1976) initially studied mechanical engineering. Fascinated all his life by motion, he explored movement in relationship to three-dimensional form in much of his work. As a young artist in Paris in the late 1920s, Calder invented a circus full of wire-based miniature performers he activated into analogues of the motion of their real-life counterparts. After a visit to Piet Mondrian's studio in the early 1930s, Calder set out to put the Dutch painter's brightly colored rectangular shapes (FIG. 29-60) into motion. (Marcel Duchamp, intrigued by Calder's early motorized and hand-cranked examples of moving abstract pieces, named them *mobiles.*) Calder's engineering skills soon helped him to fashion a series of balanced structures hanging from rods, wires, and colorful, organically shaped plates. This new kind of sculpture, which combined nonobjective organic forms and motion, succeeded in expressing the innate dynamism of the natural world.

An early Calder mobile is *Lobster Trap and Fish Tail* (FIG. 29-78), which the artist created in 1939 under a commission from the Museum of Modern Art in New York City for the stairwell of the museum's new building on West 53rd Street (see "The

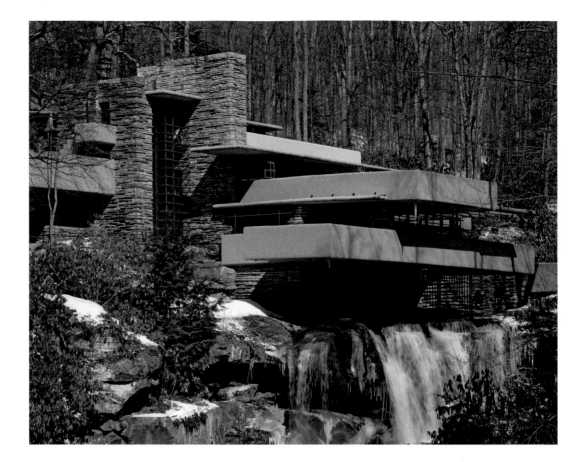

29-79 Frank Lloyd Wright, Kaufmann House (Fallingwater; looking northeast), Bear Run, Pennsylvania, 1936–1939.

Perched on a rocky hillside over a waterfall, Wright's Fallingwater has long sweeping lines, unconfined by abrupt wall limits, reaching out and capturing the expansiveness of the natural environment.

Museum of Modern Art and the Avant-Garde," page 895). Calder carefully planned each nonmechanized mobile so any air current would set the parts moving to create a constantly shifting dance in space. Mondrian's studio may have provided the initial inspiration for the mobiles, but their organic shapes resemble those in Joan Miró's Surrealist paintings (FIG. 29-58). Indeed, viewers can read Calder's forms as either geometric or organic. Geometrically, the lines suggest circuitry and rigging, and the shapes derive from circles and ovoid forms. Organically, the lines suggest nerve axons, and the shapes resemble cells, leaves, fins, wings, and other bioforms.

Architecture

The most influential American architect of the 1930s, as during the opening decades of the century, was the ever-inventive Frank Lloyd Wright.

FALLINGWATER Wright's universally acclaimed masterpiece of this period is the Kaufmann House (FIG. **29-79**), which he designed as a weekend retreat at Bear Run, Pennsylvania, for Pittsburgh department store magnate Edgar Kaufmann Sr. Perched on a rocky hillside over a small waterfall, the house, nicknamed Fallingwater, has become an icon of modernist architectural design. In keeping with his commitment to an "architecture of democracy," Wright sought to find a way to incorporate the structure fully into its site in order to ensure a fluid, dynamic exchange between the interior of the house and the natural environment outside. Rather than build the house overlooking or next to the waterfall, Wright decided to build it over the waterfall, because he believed the inhabitants would become desensitized to the waterfall's presence and power if they merely overlooked it. In Fallingwater, Wright took the blocky masses characterizing his earlier Robie House (FIGS. 29-45 and 29-46) and extended them in all four directions. To take ad-

vantage of the location, he designed a series of terraces that extend on three levels from a central core structure. The contrast in textures among concrete, painted metal, and natural stones in the house's terraces and walls enlivens its shapes, as does Wright's use of full-length strip windows to create a stunning interweaving of interior and exterior space.

The implied message of Wright's new architecture was space, not mass—a space designed to fit the patron's life and enclosed and divided as required. Wright took special pains to meet his clients' requirements, often designing all the accessories of a house (including, in at least one case, gowns for his client's wife). In the late 1930s, he acted on a cherished dream to provide good architectural design for less prosperous people by adapting the ideas of his prairie houses (see page 870) to plans for smaller, less expensive dwellings with neither attics nor basements. These residences, known as *Usonian* houses (for "United States of North America"), became templates for suburban housing developments in the post–World War II housing boom.

The publication of Wright's plans brought him a measure of fame in Europe, especially in Holland and Germany. The issuance in Berlin in 1910 of a portfolio of his work and an exhibition of his designs the following year stimulated younger architects to adopt some of his ideas about open plans that afforded clients freedom. Some 40 years before his career ended, his work was already of revolutionary significance. Mies van der Rohe wrote in 1940: "[The] dynamic impulse from [Wright's] work invigorated a whole generation. His influence was strongly felt even when it was not actually visible."[59]

Frank Lloyd Wright's influence in Europe was exceptional, however, for any American artist before World War II. But in the decades following that global conflict, American painters, sculptors, and architects often took the lead in establishing new styles artists elsewhere quickly emulated. This new preeminence of the United States in the arts is the subject of Chapter 30.

MODERNISM IN EUROPE AND AMERICA, 1900 TO 1945

EUROPE 1900 to 1920

▌ In the early 1900s, avant-garde artists searched for new definitions of art in a changed world. Matisse and the Fauves used bold colors as the primary means of conveying feeling. German Expressionist paintings featured clashing colors, disquieting figures, and perspective distortions.

▌ Pablo Picasso and Georges Braque radically challenged prevailing artistic conventions with Cubism, in which artists dissect forms and place them in interaction with the space around them.

▌ The Futurists focused on motion in time and space in their effort to create paintings and sculptures that captured the dynamic quality of modern life. The Dadaists celebrated the spontaneous and intuitive, exploring the role of chance in art and often incorporating found objects in their works.

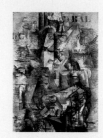

Braque, *The Portuguese*, 1911

UNITED STATES 1900 to 1930

▌ The Armory Show of 1913 introduced avant-garde European art to American artists. Man Ray, for example, embraced Dada's fondness for chance and the displacement of ordinary items, and Stuart Davis adopted the Cubist interest in fragmented form.

▌ The Harlem Renaissance brought African American artists to the forefront, including Aaron Douglas, whose paintings drew on Cubist principles. Charles Demuth, Georgia O'Keeffe, and the Precisionists used European modernist techniques to celebrate contemporary American subjects.

▌ Photography emerged as an important American art form in the work of Alfred Stieglitz and Edward Weston, who emphasized the careful arrangement of forms and patterns of light and dark.

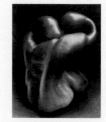

Weston, *Pepper No. 30*, 1930

EUROPE 1920 to 1945

▌ World War I gave rise to the Neue Sachlichkeit movement in Germany. "New Objectivity" artists depicted the horrors of war and explored the themes of death and transfiguration.

▌ The Surrealists investigated ways to express in art the world of dreams and the unconscious. Natural Surrealists aimed for "concrete irrationality" in their naturalistic paintings of dreamlike scenes. Biomorphic Surrealists experimented with automatism and employed abstract imagery.

▌ Many European modernists pursued utopian ideals. The Suprematists developed an abstract style to express pure feeling. The Constructivists used nonobjective forms to suggest the nature of space-time. De Stijl artists reduced their formal vocabulary to simple geometric forms in their search for "pure plastic art."

▌ Brancusi, Hepworth, Moore, and other sculptors increasingly turned to abstraction, often emphasizing voids as well as masses in their work.

▌ The Bauhaus in Germany promoted the vision of "total architecture," which called for the integration of all the arts in constructing modern living environments. Bauhaus buildings were simple glass and steel designs devoid of "romantic embellishment and whimsy." In France, Le Corbusier used modern construction materials to build "machines for living"—simple houses with open plans and unadorned surfaces.

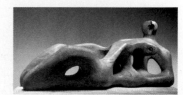

Moore, *Reclining Figure*, 1939

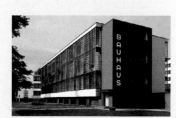

Gropius, Bauhaus, Dessau, 1925–1926

UNITED STATES AND MEXICO 1930 to 1945

▌ Although Alexander Calder created abstract works between the wars, other American artists favored figural art. Lange and Shahn chronicled social injustice. Hopper explored the loneliness of life in the Depression era. Lawrence recorded the struggle of African Americans. Wood depicted life in rural Iowa.

▌ Mexican artists Orozco and Rivera painted epic mural cycles of the history of Mexico. Kahlo's powerful paintings explored the human psyche and were frequently autobiographical.

▌ The leading American architect of the first half of the 20th century was Frank Lloyd Wright, who promoted the "architecture of democracy," in which free individuals move in a "free" space.

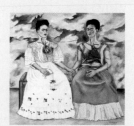

Kahlo, *The Two Fridas*, 1939

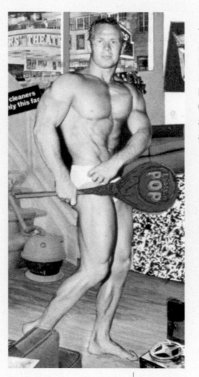

Toying with mass-media imagery typifies British Pop Art. The central motif in Hamilton's modern home is the body builder Charles Atlas, who holds a Tootsie Pop in place of a weightlifter's barbell.

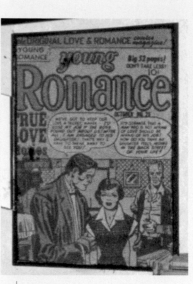

Hanging on the wall like a framed traditional painting is a cutout of a page from a 1950s romance comic book. Modern mass media fascinated Pop artists as an aspect of popular culture.

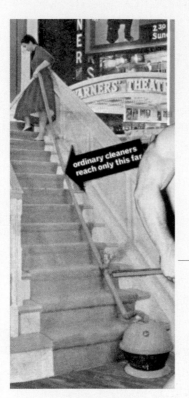

The fantasy interior in Hamilton's collage reflects the values of modern consumer culture. The figures and objects cut from glossy magazines include an advertisement for Hoover vacuum cleaners.

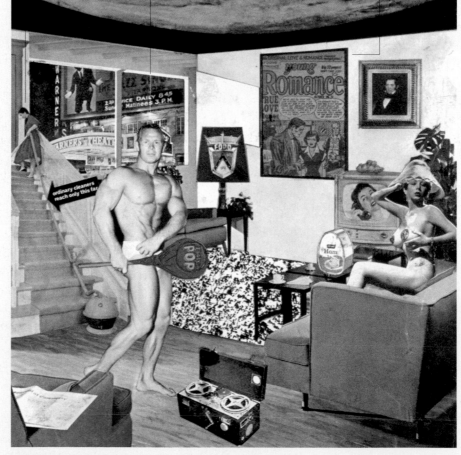

1 in.

30-1 RICHARD HAMILTON, *Just What Is It That Makes Today's Homes So Different, So Appealing?* 1956. Collage, 10¼″ × 9¾″. Kunsthalle Tübingen, Tübingen.

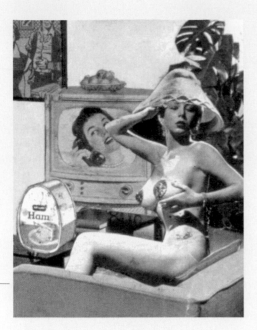

Also included in Hamilton's "appealing" modern home are a television, a can of Armour ham, and a photograph taken from a "girlie magazine" to stimulate speculation about society's values.

MODERNISM AND POSTMODERNISM IN EUROPE AND AMERICA, 1945 TO 1980

ART AND CONSUMER CULTURE

The interest in abstraction that emerged so forcefully in avant-garde artistic circles during the first half of the 20th century gained even greater momentum in the decades after the end of World War II. However, a reaction to pure formalism in painting and sculpture also set in. The artists of the *Pop Art* movement reintroduced all of the devices the postwar abstractionists had purged from their artworks. Pop artists revived the tools traditionally used to convey meaning in art, such as signs, symbols, metaphors, allusions, illusions, and figural imagery. They not only embraced representation but also firmly grounded their art in the consumer culture and mass media of the postwar period, thereby making it much more accessible and understandable to the average person. Indeed, the name "Pop Art"—credited to the British art critic Lawrence Alloway (1926–1990)—is short for "popular art" and referred to the popular mass culture and familiar imagery of the contemporary urban environment.

Art historians trace the roots of Pop Art to the young British artists, architects, and writers who formed the Independent Group at the Institute of Contemporary Art in London in the early 1950s. They sought to initiate fresh thinking in art, in part by sharing their fascination with the aesthetics and content of such facets of popular culture as advertising, comic books, and movies. In 1956, an Independent Group member, RICHARD HAMILTON (b. 1922), made a small collage, *Just What Is It That Makes Today's Homes So Different, So Appealing?* (FIG. **30-1**), which exemplifies British Pop Art. Trained as an engineering draftsman, exhibition designer, and painter, Hamilton studied the way advertising shapes public attitudes. Long intrigued by Marcel Duchamp's ideas (see Chapter 29), Hamilton consistently combined elements of popular art and fine art, seeing both as belonging to the whole world of visual communication. He created *Just What Is It?* for the poster and catalog of one section of an exhibition titled *This Is Tomorrow*, which included images from Hollywood cinema, science fiction, and the mass media.

The fantasy interior in Hamilton's collage reflects the values of mid-20th-century consumer culture through figures and objects cut from glossy magazines. *Just What Is It?* includes references to mass media (the television, the theater marquee outside the window, the newspaper), to advertising (Hoover vacuum cleaners, Ford cars, Armour hams, Tootsie Pops), and to popular culture (the "girlie magazine," the body builder Charles Atlas, romance comic books). Artworks of this sort stimulated viewers' wide-ranging speculation about society's values. This kind of intellectual toying with mass-media meaning and imagery typified Pop Art both in Europe and America.

THE AFTERMATH OF WORLD WAR II

World War II, with the global devastation it unleashed on all dimensions of life—political, economic, and psychological—set the stage for the second half of the 20th century. The dropping of atomic bombs by the United States on the Japanese cities of Hiroshima and Nagasaki in 1945 signaled a turning point not only in the war itself but in the geopolitical balance and the nature of international conflict as well. For the postwar generation, nuclear attack became a very real threat. Indeed, the two nuclear superpowers, the United States and the Soviet Union, divided the world into spheres of influence, and each regularly intervened politically, economically, and militarily wherever and whenever it considered its interests to be at stake.

The cessation of global warfare did not bring global peace. On the contrary, regional conflicts erupted throughout the world during the decades after World War II. In 1947, the British left India, which precipitated a murderous Hindu-Muslim war that divided South Asia into two new hostile nations—India and Pakistan. After a bloody civil war, Communists came to power in China in 1949. North Korea invaded South Korea in 1950 and fought a grim war with the United States and its allies. The Soviets brutally suppressed uprisings in their subject nations—East Germany, Poland, Hungary, and Czechoslovakia. The United States intervened in disputes in Central and South America. Almost as soon as many colonized nations of Africa—Kenya, Uganda, Nigeria, Angola, Mozambique, the Sudan, Rwanda, and the Congo—won their independence, civil wars devastated them. In Indonesia, civil war left more than 100,000 dead. Algeria expelled France in 1962 after the French waged a prolonged war with Algeria's Muslim natives. After 15 years of bitter war in Southeast Asia, the United States suffered defeat in Vietnam.

The period from 1945 to 1980 also brought upheaval in the cultural sphere. In the United States, for example, various groups forcefully questioned the status quo. The struggles for civil rights for African Americans, for free speech on university campuses, and for disengagement from the Vietnam War led to a rebellion of the young, who took to the streets in often raucous demonstrations, some with violent repercussions. The prolonged ferment produced a new system of values, a "youth culture," expressed in the radical rejection not only of national policies but often also of the society generating them. Young Americans derided their elders' lifestyles and adopted unconventional dress, manners, habits, and morals deliberately subversive of mainstream social standards. The youth era witnessed the sexual revolution, the widespread use and abuse of drugs, and the development of rock music, then an exclusively youthful art form. Young people "dropped out" of regulated society, embraced alternative belief systems, and rejected Western university curricula as irrelevant.

This counterculture had considerable societal impact. The civil rights movement of the 1960s and later the women's liberation movement of the 1970s reflected the spirit of rebellion, coupled with the rejection of racism and sexism. In keeping with the growing resistance to established authority, women systematically began to challenge the male-dominated culture, which they perceived as having limited their political power and economic opportunities for centuries. Feminists charged that the institutions of Western society, particularly the traditional family unit headed by a patriarch, perpetuated male power and the subordination of women. They further contended that monuments of Western culture—its arts and sciences, as well as its political, social, and economic institutions—masked the realities of male power.

Increasingly, individuals and groups actively sought to combat the inappropriate exercise of power or to change the balance of power. For example, following patterns developed first in the civil rights movement and later in feminism, various ethnic groups and gays and lesbians mounted challenges to discriminatory policies and attitudes. These groups fought for recognition, respect, and legal protection and battled discrimination with political action. In addition, the growing scrutiny in numerous academic fields—cultural studies, literary theory, and colonial and postcolonial studies—of the dynamics and exercise of power also contributed to the dialogue on these issues. As a result of this concern for the dynamics of power, identity (both individual and group) emerged as a potent arena for discussion and action—and as a persistent and compelling subject for painters, sculptors, and photographers.

PAINTING, SCULPTURE, AND PHOTOGRAPHY

The end of World War II in 1945 left devastated cities, ruptured economies, and governments in chaos throughout Europe. These factors, coupled with the massive loss of life and the indelible horrors of the bombing of Hiroshima and Nagasaki and of the

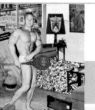

MODERNISM AND POSTMODERNISM IN EUROPE AND AMERICA, 1945 TO 1980

1945	1960	1970	1980

- European Expressionists capture in their paintings and sculptures the revulsion and cynicism that emerged in the wake of World War II
- New York School painters develop Abstract Expressionism, emphasizing form and raw energy over subject matter
- Sleek, geometrically rigid modernist skyscrapers become familiar sights in cities throughout the world

- Post-Painterly Abstractionists reject the passion and texture of action painting and celebrate the flatness of pigment on canvas
- Op artists produce the illusion of motion and depth using only geometric forms
- Minimalists reduce sculpture to basic shapes and emphasize their works' "objecthood"
- Pop artists find inspiration in popular culture and commonplace commercial products
- Superrealists create paintings and sculptures characterized by scrupulous reproduction of the appearance of people and objects
- Performance artists replace traditional stationary artworks with temporal action-artworks

- Artists play a leading role in the feminist movement by promoting women's themes and employing materials traditionally associated with women, such as china and fabric
- Postmodern architects erect complex and eclectic buildings that often incorporate references to historical styles
- Environmental artists redefine what constitutes "art" by manipulating natural materials in monumental earthworks
- Artists increasingly embrace new media—video recorders, computers—as tools for creating artworks

Holocaust, in which six million Jews died at the hands of the Nazis, resulted in a pervasive sense of despair, disillusionment, and skepticism. Although many people (for example, the Futurists in Italy; see Chapter 29) had tried to find redemptive value in World War I, it was nearly impossible to do the same with World War II, coming as it did so soon after the "war to end all wars." Additionally, World War I was largely a European conflict that left roughly 10 million people dead, whereas World War II was a truly global catastrophe, claiming 35 million lives.

Postwar Expressionism in Europe

The cynicism pervading Europe in the 1940s found voice in existentialism, a philosophy asserting the absurdity of human existence and the impossibility of achieving certitude. Many who embraced existentialism also promoted atheism and questioned the possibility of situating God within a systematic philosophy. Scholars trace the roots of existentialism to the Danish theologian Søren Kierkegaard (1813–1855), but in the postwar period, the writings of French author Jean-Paul Sartre (1905–1980) most clearly captured the existentialist spirit. According to Sartre, if God does not exist, then individuals must constantly struggle in isolation with the anguish of making decisions in a world without absolutes or traditional values. This spirit of pessimism and despair emerged frequently in European art of the immediate postwar period. A brutality or roughness appropriately expressing both the artist's state of mind and the larger cultural sensibility characterized the work of many European sculptors and painters.

ALBERTO GIACOMETTI The sculpture of Swiss artist ALBERTO GIACOMETTI (1901–1966) perhaps best expresses the spirit of existentialism. Although Giacometti never claimed he pursued existentialist ideas in his art, his works capture the spirit of that philosophy. Indeed, Sartre, Giacometti's friend, saw the artist's figurative sculptures as the epitome of existentialist humanity—alienated, solitary, and lost in the world's immensity. Giacometti's sculptures of the 1940s, such as *Man Pointing, No. 5* (FIG. **30-2**), are thin, nearly featureless figures with rough, agitated surfaces. Rather than conveying the solidity and mass of conventional bronze sculpture, these severely attenuated figures seem swallowed up by the space surrounding them, imparting a sense of isolation and fragility. Giacometti's evocative, moving sculptures spoke to the pervasive despair that emerged in the aftermath of world war.

FRANCIS BACON Although born in Dublin, Ireland, FRANCIS BACON (1910–1992) was the son of a well-to-do Englishman. He spent most of his life in London, where he experienced firsthand the destruction of lives and property the Nazi bombing wrought on the city during World War II. *Painting* (FIG. **30-3**) is Bacon's indictment of humanity and a reflection of war's butchery. The artist presented a compelling and revolting image of a powerful, stocky man with a gaping mouth and a vivid red stain on his upper lip, as if he were a carnivore devouring the raw meat sitting on the railing

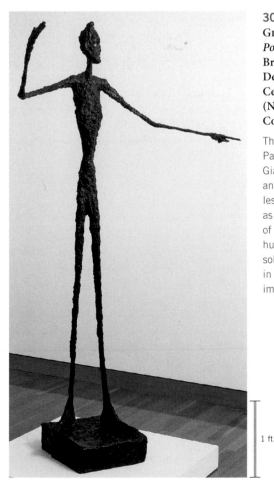

30-2 ALBERTO GIACOMETTI, *Man Pointing No. 5,* 1947. Bronze, 5′ 10″ high. Des Moines Art Center, Des Moines (Nathan Emory Coffin Collection).

The writer Jean-Paul Sartre saw Giacometti's thin and virtually featureless sculpted figures as the epitome of existentialist humanity—alienated, solitary, and lost in the world's immensity.

1 ft.

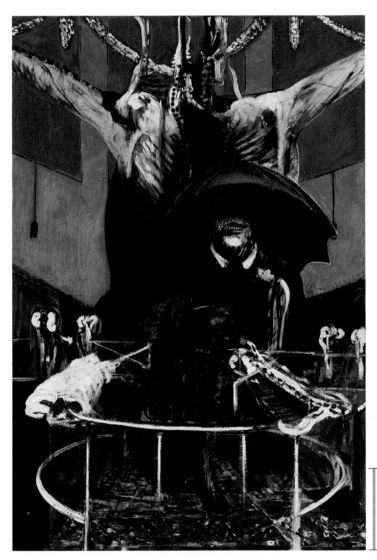

1 ft.

30-3 FRANCIS BACON, *Painting,* 1946. Oil and pastel on linen, 6′ 5⅞″ × 4′ 4″. Museum of Modern Art, New York.

Painted in the aftermath of World War II, this intentionally revolting image of a powerful figure presiding over a slaughter is Bacon's indictment of humanity and a reflection of war's butchery.

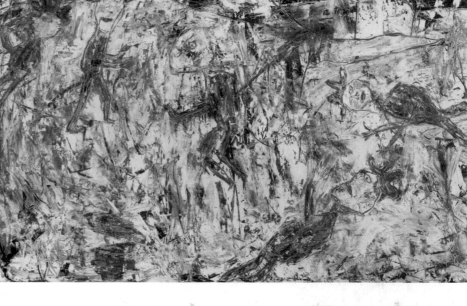

1 ft.

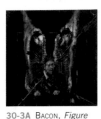

surrounding him (compare FIG. **30-3A**). Bacon may have based his depiction of this central figure on news photos of similarly dressed European and American officials. The umbrella in par-

30-3A BACON, *Figure with Meat*, 1954.

ticular recalls images of Neville Chamberlain (1869–1940), the wartime British prime minister who frequently appeared in photographs with an umbrella. Bacon added to the visceral impact of the painting by depicting the flayed carcass hanging behind the central figure like a crucified human form. Although the specific sources for the imagery in *Painting* are uncertain, the work is unmistakably "an attempt to remake the violence of reality itself," as Bacon often described his art, based on what he referred to as "the brutality of fact."[1]

JEAN DUBUFFET Although less specific, the works of French artist JEAN DUBUFFET (1901–1985) also express a tortured vision of the world through manipulated materials. In works such as *Vie Inquiète* (*Uneasy Life*; FIG. **30-4**), Dubuffet first built up an *impasto* (a layer of thickly applied pigment) of plaster, glue, sand, asphalt, and other common materials, over which he painted or incised crude images of the kind produced by children, the insane, and scrawlers of graffiti. Scribblings interspersed with the images heighten the impression of smeared and gashed surfaces of crumbling walls and worn pavements marked by random individuals. Dubuffet believed the art of children, the mentally unbalanced, prisoners, and outcasts was more direct and genuine because those who created it did so unrestrained by conventional standards of art. He promoted "art brut"—untaught and coarse art.

Abstract Expressionism

In the 1960s, the center of the Western art world shifted from Paris to New York because of the devastation World War II had inflicted across Europe and the resulting influx of émigré artists escaping to the United States. It was in New York that the first major American avant-garde art movement—Abstract Expressionism—emerged. The most important forerunner of the Abstract Expressionists, however, was an Armenian immigrant who arrived in New York in 1924.

ARSHILE GORKY Born a Christian in Islamic Turkish Armenia, Vosdanik Manoog Adoian was four years old when his father escaped being drafted into the Turkish army by fleeing the country. His mother died of starvation in her 15-year-old son's arms in a refugee camp for victims of the Turkish campaign of genocide against the Christian minority. The penniless Vosdanik managed in 1920 to make his way to America, where a relative

took him into his home near Boston. Four years later, then a young man, Vosdanik changed his name to ARSHILE GORKY (1904–1948)—"Bitter Achilles" in Russian—and moved to New York City, where he continued the art education he had begun in Boston. In 1948, he hanged himself after an automobile accident robbed him of the use of his right arm. The injury might have been only temporary, but the depressed Gorky thought he would never be able to paint again. In a career lasting only two decades, Gorky contributed significantly to the artistic revolution born in New York. His work is the bridge between the Biomorphic Surrealism of Joan Miró (FIG. 29-58) and the totally abstract canvases of Jackson Pollock (FIG. 30-6).

Garden in Sochi (FIG. **30-5**), painted in 1943, is the third in a series of canvases with identical titles named after a Black Sea resort but inspired by Gorky's childhood memories of the Garden of Wish Fulfillment in his birthplace. The women of the Armenian village of Khorkom believed their wishes would be granted if they rubbed their bare breasts against a rock in that garden beneath a tree to which they tied strips of their clothing. The brightly colored and thinly outlined forms in *Garden in Sochi*, which initially appear to be purely abstract biomorphic shapes, are loose sketches representing, at the left, a bare-breasted woman, and, at the center, a tree trunk with fluttering fabric. At the bottom are two oversized shoes—the Armenian slippers Gorky's father gave his son shortly before abandoning the family.

CLEMENT GREENBERG The few traces of representational art in Gorky's work disappeared in *Abstract Expressionism*. As the name suggests, the artists associated with the New York School of Abstract Expressionism produced paintings that are, for the most part, abstract but express the artist's state of mind, with the goal also of striking emotional chords in the viewer. The most important champion of this strict *formalism*—an emphasis on an artwork's visual elements rather than its subject—was the American art critic Clement Greenberg (1909–1994), who wielded considerable influence from the 1940s through the 1970s. Greenberg helped redefine the parameters of modernism by advocating the rejection of illusionism and the exploration of the properties of each artistic medium. So dominant was Greenberg that scholars often refer to the general modernist tenets during this period as Greenbergian formalism.

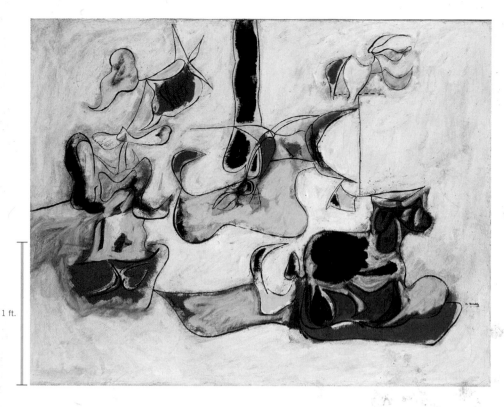

1 ft.

30-5 Arshile Gorky, *Garden in Sochi*, ca. 1943. Oil on canvas, 2′ 7″ × 3′ 3″. Museum of Modern Art, New York (acquired through the Lillie P. Bliss Bequest).

Gorky's paintings of the 1940s, which still incorporate recognizable forms, are the bridge between the Biomorphic Surrealist canvases of Miró and the Abstract Expressionist paintings of Pollock.

Among other things, this means renouncing illusion and explicit subject matter. The arts are to achieve concreteness, "purity," by dealing solely with their respective selves—that is, by becoming "abstract" or nonfigurative.[3]

The Abstract Expressionists turned inward to create, and the resulting works convey a rough spontaneity and palpable energy. The New York School painters wanted the viewer to grasp the content of their art intuitively, in a mental state free from structured thinking. One of the leading painters of this group, Mark Rothko (FIG. 30-10), eloquently wrote:

Although Greenberg modified his complex ideas about art over the years, he consistently expounded certain basic concepts. In particular, Greenberg promoted the idea of artistic purity: "Purity in art consists in the acceptance, willing acceptance, of the limitations of the medium of the specific art."[2] In other words, Greenberg believed artists should strive for a more explicit focus on the properties exclusive to each medium—for example, two-dimensionality or flatness in painting, and three-dimensionality in sculpture.

> It follows that a modernist work of art must try, in principle, to avoid communication with any order of experience not inherent in the most literally and essentially construed nature of its medium.

> We assert man's absolute emotions. We don't need props or legends. We create images whose realities are self evident. Free ourselves from memory, association, nostalgia, legend, myth. Instead of making cathedrals out of Christ, man or life, we make it out of ourselves, out of our own feelings. The image we produce is understood by anyone who looks at it without nostalgic glasses of history.[4]

The Abstract Expressionist movement developed along two lines—*gestural abstraction* and *chromatic abstraction*. The gestural abstractionists relied on the expressiveness of energetically applied pigment. In contrast, the chromatic abstractionists focused on color's emotional resonance.

JACKSON POLLOCK The artist whose work best exemplifies gestural abstraction is Jackson Pollock (1912–1956), who developed his signature style in the mid-1940s. By 1950, Pollock had refined his technique and was producing large-scale abstract paintings such as *Number 1, 1950* (*Lavender Mist*; FIG. **30-6**), which consist of rhythmic drips, splatters, and dribbles of paint. The mural-sized fields of energetic skeins of pigment envelop viewers, drawing them into a lacy spider web. Using sticks or brushes, Pollock flung,

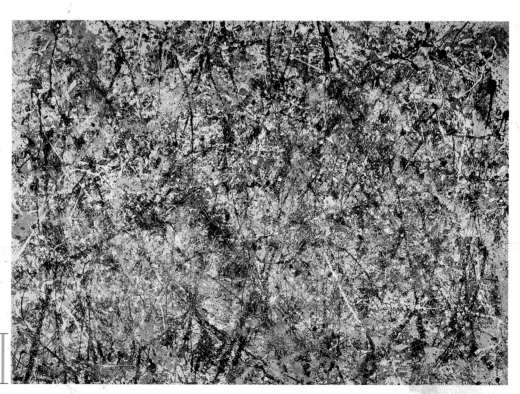

1 ft.

30-6 Jackson Pollock, *Number 1, 1950* (*Lavender Mist*), 1950. Oil, enamel, and aluminum paint on canvas, 7′ 3″ × 9′ 10″. National Gallery of Art, Washington, D.C. (Ailsa Mellon Bruce Fund).

Pollock's paintings emphasize the creative process. His mural-size canvases consist of rhythmic drips, splatters, and dribbles of paint that envelop viewers, drawing them into a lacy spider web.

Jackson Pollock on Easel and Mural Painting

Jackson Pollock's canvases (FIG. 30-6) constitute a revolution in the art of painting not only because of their purely abstract form but also in the artist's rejection of the centuries-old tradition of applying pigment to stretched canvases supported vertically before the painter on an easel. In two statements Pollock made in 1947, one as part of his application for a Guggenheim Fellowship and one in a published essay, the artist explained the motivations for his new kind of "action painting" and described the tools he used and the way he produced his monumental canvases (FIG. 30-7).

> I intend to paint large movable pictures which will function between the easel and mural. . . . I believe the easel picture to be a dying form, and the tendency of modern feeling is towards the wall picture or mural.*

> My painting does not come from the easel. I hardly ever stretch my canvas before painting. I prefer to tack the unstretched canvas to the hard wall or the floor. I need the resistance of a hard surface. On the floor I am more at ease. I feel nearer, more a part of the painting, since this way I can walk around it, work from the four sides and literally be *in* the painting. This is akin to the method of the Indian sand painters of the West [see Chapter 35, page 1032]. I continue to get further away from the usual painter's tools such as easel, palette, brushes, etc. I prefer sticks, trowels, knives and dripping fluid paint or a heavy impasto with sand, broken glass and other foreign matter added. When I am *in* my painting, I'm not aware of what I'm doing. . . . [T]he painting has a life of its own. I try to let it come through. . . . The source of my painting is the unconscious.†

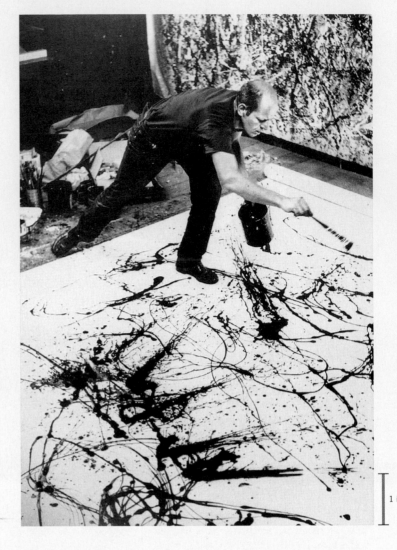

30-7 HANS NAMUTH, Jackson Pollock painting in his studio in Springs, Long Island, New York, 1950. Gelatin silver print, 10″ × 8″. Center for Creative Photography, University of Arizona, Tucson.

"Gestural abstraction" nicely describes Pollock's working technique. Using sticks or brushes, he flung, poured, and dripped paint onto a section of canvas he simply unrolled across his studio floor.

1 in.

*Quoted in Francis V. O'Connor, *Jackson Pollock* (New York: Museum of Modern Art, 1967), 39.
†Ibid., 39-40.

poured, and dripped paint (not only traditional oil paints but aluminum paints and household enamels as well) onto a section of canvas he simply unrolled across his studio floor (FIG. **30-7**). This working method earned Pollock the derisive nickname "Jack the Dripper." Responding to the image as it developed, he created art that was spontaneous yet choreographed. Pollock's painting technique highlights the most significant aspect of gestural abstraction—its emphasis on the creative process. Indeed, Pollock literally immersed himself in the painting during its creation.

Art historians have linked Pollock's ideas about improvisation in the creative process to his interest in what psychiatrist Carl Jung called the collective unconscious. The improvisational nature of Pollock's work and his reliance on the subconscious also have parallels in the "psychic automatism" of Surrealism and the work of Vassily Kandinsky (FIG. 29-7), whom critics described as an Abstract Expressionist as early as 1919. In addition to Pollock's

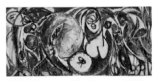

30-7A KRASNER, *The Seasons*, 1957.

unique working methods and the expansive scale of his canvases, the lack of a well-defined compositional focus in his paintings significantly departed from conventional easel painting (see "Jackson Pollock on Easel and Mural Painting," above). A towering figure in 20th-century art, Pollock tragically died in a car accident at age 44, cutting short the development of his innovative artistic vision. Surviving him was his wife, LEE KRASNER (1908–1984), whom art historians recognize as a major Abstract Expressionist painter (FIG. **30-7A**), although overshadowed by Pollock during her lifetime.

WILLEM DE KOONING Despite the public's skepticism about Pollock's art, other artists enthusiastically pursued similar avenues of expression. Dutch-born WILLEM DE KOONING (1904–1997)

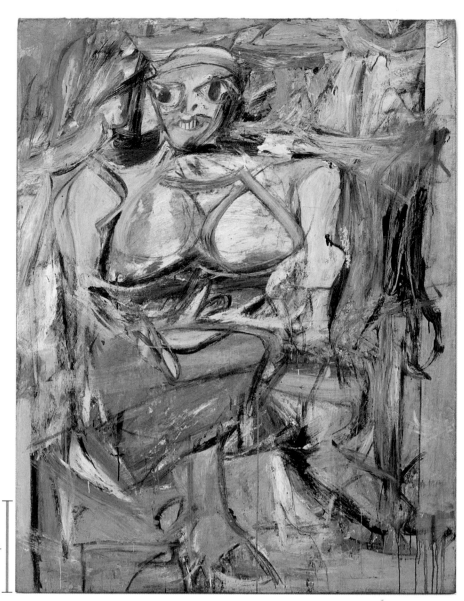

1 ft.

30-8 WILLEM DE KOONING, *Woman I,* 1950–1952. Oil on canvas, 6′ 3⅞″ × 4′ 10″. Museum of Modern Art, New York. ◼◀

Although rooted in figuration, including pictures of female models on advertising billboards, de Kooning's *Woman I* displays the energetic application of pigment typical of gestural abstraction.

In addition to this *Woman* series, de Kooning created nonrepresentational works dominated by huge swaths and splashes of pigment. The images suggest rawness and intensity. His dealer, Sidney Janis (1896–1989), confirmed this impression, recalling de Kooning occasionally brought him paintings with ragged holes in them, the result of overly vigorous painting. Like Pollock, de Kooning was very much "in" his paintings. Vigorous physical interaction between the painter and the canvas led the critic Harold Rosenberg (1906–1978) to describe the work of the New York School as *action painting.* In his influential 1952 article "The American Action Painters," Rosenberg described the attempts of Pollock, de Kooning, and others to get "inside the canvas."

> At a certain moment the canvas began to appear to one American painter after another as an arena in which to act—rather than as a space in which to reproduce, re-design, analyze or "express" an object, actual or imagined. What was to go on the canvas was not a picture but an event. The painter no longer approached his easel with an image in his mind; he went up to it with material in his hand to do something to that other piece of material in front of him. The image would be the result of this encounter.[5]

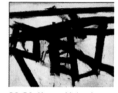

30-8A KLINE, *Mahoning,* 1956.

Among the other prominent New York School Abstract Expressionists were Pennsylvania-born FRANZ KLINE (1910–1962), whose predominantly black-and-white paintings (FIG. **30-8A**) resemble Chinese and Japanese calligraphy; ROBERT MOTHERWELL (1915–1991), best known for his series of paintings inspired by the Spanish civil war (FIG. **30-8B**);

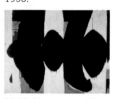

30-8B MOTHERWELL, *Elegy to the Spanish Republic,* 1953–1954.

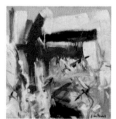

30-8C MITCHELL, *Untitled,* ca. 1953–1954.

and JOAN MITCHELL (1925–1992), the leading woman action painter (FIG. **30-8C**) of the 1950s. In the 1970s and later, a new generation of artists, including SUSAN ROTHENBERG (b. 1945; FIG. **30-8D**) reinvigorated Abstract Expressionism in a movement art historians have dubbed *Neo-Expressionism* (see Chapter 31).

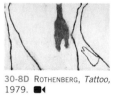

30-8D ROTHENBERG, *Tattoo,* 1979. ◼◀

also developed a gestural abstractionist style. Even images such as *Woman I* (FIG. **30-8**), although rooted in figuration, display the sweeping gestural brushstrokes and energetic application of pigment typical of gestural abstraction. Out of the jumbled array of slashing lines and agitated patches of color appears a ferocious-looking woman with staring eyes and ponderous breasts. Her toothy smile, inspired by an ad for Camel cigarettes, seems to devolve into a grimace. Female models on advertising billboards partly inspired *Woman I,* one of a series of images of women, but de Kooning's female forms also suggest fertility figures and a satiric inversion of the traditional image of Venus, goddess of love.

Process was important to de Kooning, as it was to Pollock. Continually working on *Woman I* for almost two years, de Kooning painted an image and then scraped it away the next day and began anew. His wife Elaine, also an accomplished painter, estimated he painted approximately 200 scraped-away images of women on this canvas before settling on the final one.

BARNETT NEWMAN In contrast to the aggressively energetic images of the gestural abstractionists, the work of the chromatic abstractionists exudes a quieter aesthetic, exemplified by the work of Barnett Newman and Mark Rothko. The emotional resonance of their works derives from their eloquent use of color. In his early paintings, New York native BARNETT NEWMAN (1905–1970) presented organic abstractions inspired by his study of biology and his fascination with Native American art. He soon simplified his

30-9 BARNETT NEWMAN, *Vir Heroicus Sublimis,* 1950–1951. Oil on canvas, 7′ 11⅜″ × 17′ 9¼″. Museum of Modern Art, New York (gift of Mr. and Mrs. Ben Heller). ■◄

Newman's canvases consist of a single slightly modulated color field split by "zips" (narrow bands) running from one edge of the painting to the other, energizing the color field and giving it scale.

compositions so that each canvas—for example, the monumental (almost 8 by 18 feet) Latin-titled *Vir Heroicus Sublimis* (*Sublime Heroic Man;* FIG. **30-9**)—consists of a single slightly modulated color field split by narrow bands the artist called "zips," which run from one edge of the painting to the other. As Newman explained it, "The streak was always going through an atmosphere; I kept trying to create a world around it."[6] He did not intend the viewer to perceive the zips as specific entities, separate from the ground, but as accents energizing the field and giving it scale. By simplifying his compositions, Newman increased color's capacity to communicate and to express his feelings about the tragic condition of modern life and the human struggle to survive. He claimed "the artist's problem . . . [is] the idea-complex that makes contact with mystery—of life, of men, of nature, of the hard black chaos that is death, or the grayer, softer chaos that is tragedy."[7] Confronted by one of Newman's grandiose colored canvases, viewers truly feel as if they are in the presence of the epic.

MARK ROTHKO The work of MARK ROTHKO (1903–1970) also deals with universal themes. Born in Russia, Rothko moved with his family to the United States when he was 10. His early paintings were figural, but he soon came to believe that references to anything specific in the physical world conflicted with the sublime idea of the universal, supernatural "spirit of myth," which he saw as the core of meaning in art. In a statement cowritten with Newman and artist Adolph Gottlieb (1903–1974), Rothko expressed his beliefs about art:

> We favor the simple expression of the complex thought. We are for the large shape because it has the impact of the unequivocal. . . . We assert that . . . only that subject matter is valid which is tragic and timeless. That is why we profess spiritual kinship with primitive and archaic art.[8]

Rothko's paintings became compositionally simple, and he increasingly focused on color as the primary conveyor of meaning. In works such as *No. 14* (FIG. **30-10**), Rothko created compelling visual experiences consisting of two or three large rectangles of pure color with hazy edges that seem to float on the canvas surface, hovering in front of a colored background. His compositions present shimmering veils of intensely luminous colors that appear to be suspended in front of the canvases. Although the color juxtapositions are visually captivating, Rothko intended them as more than decorative. He saw

30-10 MARK ROTHKO, *No. 14,* 1960. Oil on canvas, 9′ 6″ × 8′ 9″. San Francisco Museum of Modern Art, San Francisco (Helen Crocker Russell Fund Purchase).

Rothko's chromatic abstractionist paintings—consisting of hazy rectangles of pure color hovering in front of a colored background—are compositionally simple but compelling visual experiences.

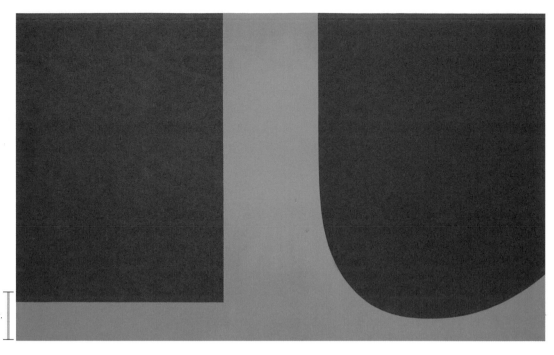

1 ft.

Post-Painterly Abstraction. Greenberg saw this art as contrasting with "painterly" art, characterized by loose, visible pigment application. Evidence of the artist's hand, so prominent in gestural abstraction, is conspicuously absent in Post-Painterly Abstraction. Greenberg championed this art form because it embodied his idea of purity in art.

color as a doorway to another reality, and insisted color could express "basic human emotions—tragedy, ecstasy, doom. . . . The people who weep before my pictures are having the same religious experience I had when I painted them. And if you, as you say, are moved only by their color relationships, then you miss the point."[9] Like the other Abstract Expressionists, Rothko produced highly evocative paintings reliant on formal elements rather than on specific representational content to elicit emotional responses in the viewer.

Post-Painterly Abstraction

Post-Painterly Abstraction, another postwar American art movement, developed out of Abstract Expressionism. Indeed, many of the artists associated with Post-Painterly Abstraction produced Abstract Expressionist work early in their careers. Yet Post-Painterly Abstraction, a term Clement Greenberg coined, manifests a radically different sensibility from Abstract Expressionism. Whereas Abstract Expressionism conveys a feeling of passion and visceral intensity, a cool, detached rationality emphasizing tighter pictorial control characterizes

ELLSWORTH KELLY Attempting to arrive at pure painting, the Post-Painterly Abstractionists distilled painting down to its essential elements, producing spare, elemental images. One of the primary practitioners of one variant of Post-Painterly Abstraction, *hard-edge painting,* was ELLSWORTH KELLY (b. 1923). Born in Newburgh on the Hudson River north of New York City, Kelly studied at the Pratt Institute in Brooklyn and later in Boston and Paris. *Red Blue Green* (FIG. **30-11**) is a characteristic example of his work. With its razor-sharp edges and clearly delineated shapes, the painting is completely abstract and extremely simple in composition. Further, the composition contains no suggestion of the illusion of depth. The color shapes appear resolutely two-dimensional.

FRANK STELLA Another artist associated with the hard-edge painters of the 1960s is Massachusetts-born FRANK STELLA (b. 1936). Stella studied history at Princeton University and moved to New York City in 1958, but did not favor the rough, expressive brushwork of the Abstract Expressionists. In works such as *Mas o Menos (More or Less;* FIG. **30-12**), Stella eliminated many of the variables associated with painting. His simplified images of thin, evenly spaced pinstripes on colored grounds have no central focus, no painterly or expressive elements, only limited surface modulation, and no tactile quality. His systematic painting illustrates Greenberg's insistence on purity in art. The artist's own famous comment on his work, "What you see is what you see," reinforces the notions that painters interested in producing advanced art must reduce their work to its essential elements and that the viewer must acknowledge a painting is simply pigment on a flat surface.

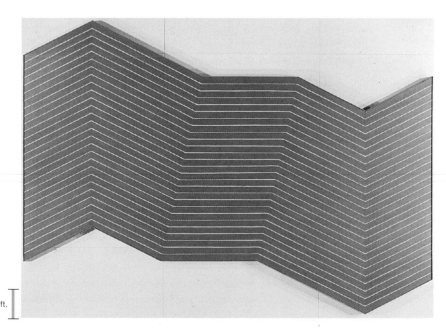

1 ft.

30-12 FRANK STELLA, *Mas o Menos,* 1964. Metallic powder in acrylic emulsion on canvas, 9′ 10″ × 13′ 8½″. Musée National d'Art Moderne, Centre Georges Pompidou, Paris (purchase 1983 with participation of Scaler Foundation).

Stella tried to achieve purity in painting using evenly spaced pinstripes on colored grounds. His canvases have no central focus, no painterly or expressive elements, and no tactile quality.

Helen Frankenthaler on Color-Field Painting

Helen Frankenthaler, the daughter of a New York State Supreme Court justice, began her study of art at the Dalton School in New York City under Rufino Tamayo (FIG. 29-74A). She has painted in New York for virtually her entire career. In 1965, the art critic Henry Geldzahler (1935–1994) interviewed Frankenthaler about her work as an abstract painter. In the following excerpt, Frankenthaler described the approach she took to placing color on canvas in *The Bay* (FIG. 30-13) and similar color-field paintings she produced in the early 1960s, and compared her method with the way earlier modernist artists used color in their paintings.

> I will sometimes start a picture feeling "What will happen if I work with three blues and another color, and maybe more or less of the other color than the combined blues?" And very often midway through the picture I have to change the basis of the experience....
>
> When you first saw a Cubist or Impressionist picture there was a whole way of instructing the eye or the subconscious. Dabs of color had to stand for real things; it was an abstraction of a guitar or a hillside. The opposite is going on now. If you have bands of blue, green, and pink, the mind doesn't think sky, grass, and flesh. These are colors and the question is what are they doing with themselves and with each other. Sentiment and nuance are being squeezed out.*

*Henry Geldzahler, "Interview with Helen Frankenthaler," *Artforum* 4, no. 2 (October 1965), 37–38.

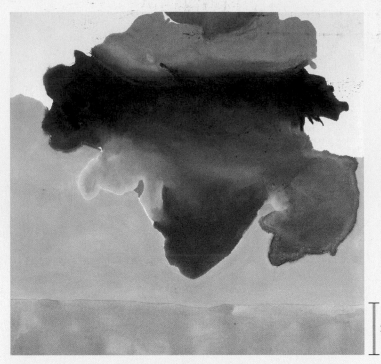

1 ft.

30-13 HELEN FRANKENTHALER, *The Bay*, 1963. Acrylic on canvas, 6′ 8⅞″ × 6′ 9⅞″. Detroit Institute of Arts, Detroit.

Frankenthaler and other color-field painters poured paint onto unprimed canvas, allowing the pigments to soak into the fabric. Their works underscore that a painting is simply pigment on a flat surface.

HELEN FRANKENTHALER *Color-field painting,* another variant of Post-Painterly Abstraction, also emphasized painting's basic properties. However, rather than produce sharp, unmodulated shapes as the hard-edge artists had done, the color-field painters poured diluted paint onto unprimed canvas and allowed the pigments to soak in. It is hard to conceive of another painting method resulting in such literal flatness. The images created, such as *The Bay* (FIG. 30-13) by HELEN FRANKENTHALER (b. 1928), appear spontaneous and almost accidental (see "Helen Frankenthaler on Color-Field Painting," above). These works differ from those by Rothko and Newman in that Frankenthaler subordinated the emotional component, so integral to hard-edge painting, in favor of resolving formal problems.

MORRIS LOUIS Baltimore native MORRIS LOUIS (1912–1962), who spent most of his career in Washington, D.C., also became a champion of color-field painting. Clement Greenberg, an admirer of Frankenthaler's paintings, took Louis to her studio, where she introduced him to the possibilities presented by the staining technique. Louis used this method of pouring diluted paint onto the surface of unprimed canvas in several series of paintings. *Saraband* (FIG. 30-14) is one of the works in Louis's *Veils* series. By holding up the canvas edges and pouring diluted acrylic resin, Louis created billowy, fluid, transparent shapes running down the length of the canvas. As did Frankenthaler, Louis reduced painting to the concrete fact of the paint-impregnated material.

CLYFFORD STILL Although not a member of the New York School, another American painter whose work art historians usually classify as Post-Painterly Abstraction was CLYFFORD STILL (1904–1980). Born in North Dakota, Still spent most of his career on the West Coast or in Maryland. He is best known for the large series of canvases he titled simply with their dates, underscoring his rejection of the very notion that the purpose of art is to represent places, people, or objects. Nonetheless, Still's paintings remind many viewers of vast landscapes seen from the air. But the artist's canvases make no reference to any forms in nature. His paintings, for example, *1948-C* (FIG. I-2), are pure exercises in the expressive use of color, shape, and texture.

Op Art

A major artistic movement of the 1960s was *Op Art* (short for *Optical Art*), in which painters sought to produce optical illusions of motion and depth using only geometric forms on two-dimensional surfaces. Among the primary sources of the movement was the work of Josef Albers, whose series of paintings called *Homage to the Square* (FIG. I-11) explored the optical effects of placing different

30-14 MORRIS LOUIS, *Saraband*, 1959. Acrylic resin on canvas, 8′ 5$\frac{1}{8}$″ × 12′ 5″. Solomon R. Guggenheim Foundation, New York.

Louis created his color-field paintings by holding up the canvas edges and pouring diluted acrylic resin to produce billowy, fluid, transparent shapes running down the length of the fabric.

colors next to each other. Ultimately, Op Art can be traced to 19th-century theories of color perception and the pointillism of Georges Seurat (see "Pointillism and 19th-Century Color Theory," Chapter 28, page 813, and FIG. 28-16).

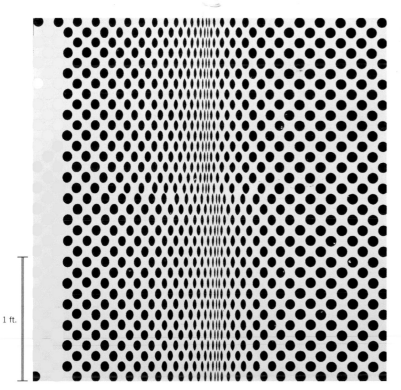

30-15 BRIDGET RILEY, *Fission*, 1963. Tempera on composition board, 2′ 11″ × 2′ 10″. Museum of Modern Art, New York (gift of Philip Johnson).

Op Art paintings create the illusion of motion and depth using only geometric forms. The effect can be disorienting. The pattern of black dots in Riley's *Fission* appears to cave in at the center.

BRIDGET RILEY The artist whose name is synonymous with Op Art is the British artist BRIDGET RILEY (b. 1931), who painted in a neo-pointillist manner in the 1950s before developing her signature black-and-white Op Art style. Her paintings, for example, *Fission* (FIG. **30-15**) of 1963, came to the public's attention after being featured in the December 1964 issue of *Life* magazine. The publicity unleashed a craze for Op Art designs in clothing. In 1965, the exhibition *The Responsive Eye* at the Museum of Modern Art, which also featured paintings by Ellsworth Kelly and Morris Louis, among others, bestowed an official stamp of approval on the movement.

In *Fission*, Riley filled the canvas with black dots of varied sizes and shapes, creating the illusion of a pulsating surface that caves in at the center (hence the painting's title). The effect on the viewer of Op Art paintings such as *Fission* is disorienting and sometimes disturbing, and some works can even induce motion sickness. Thoroughly modernist in the insistence a painting is a two-dimensional surface covered with pigment and not a representation of any person, object, or place, the Op Art movement nonetheless embraced the Renaissance notion that the painter can create the illusion of depth through perspective.

Abstraction in Sculpture

Painters were not the only artists interested in Clement Greenberg's formalist ideas. American sculptors also strove to arrive at purity in their medium. While painters worked to emphasize flatness, sculptors, understandably, chose to focus on three-dimensionality as the unique characteristic and inherent limitation of the sculptural idiom.

DAVID SMITH After experimenting with a variety of sculptural styles and materials, Indiana-born and Ohio-raised DAVID SMITH (1906–1965) produced metal sculptures that have affinities with the Abstract Expressionist movement in painting. In the

David Smith on Outdoor Sculpture

From ancient times, sculptors have frequently created statues for display in the open air, whether a portrait of a Roman emperor in a forum or Michelangelo's *David* (FIG. 22-13) in Florence's Piazza della Signoria. But rarely have sculptors taken into consideration the effects of sunlight in the conception of their works. American sculptor David Smith was an exception.

Smith learned to weld in an automobile plant in 1925 and later applied to his art the technical expertise in handling metals he gained from that experience. In addition, working in large scale at the factories helped him visualize the possibilities for monumental metal sculpture. His works, for example, *Cubi XII* (FIG. 30-16), created for display in the open air, lose much of their character in the sterile lighting of a museum.

> I like outdoor sculpture and the most practical thing for outdoor sculpture is stainless steel, and I make them and I polish them in such a way that on a dull day, they take on the dull blue, or the color of the sky in the late afternoon sun, the glow, golden like the rays, the colors of nature. And in a particular sense, I have used atmosphere in a reflective way on the surfaces. They are colored by the sky and the surroundings, the green or blue of water. Some are down by the water and some are by the mountains. They reflect the colors. They are designed for the outdoors.*

*Quoted in Cleve Gray, ed., *David Smith by David Smith* (New York: Holt, Rinehart, and Winston, 1968), 133.

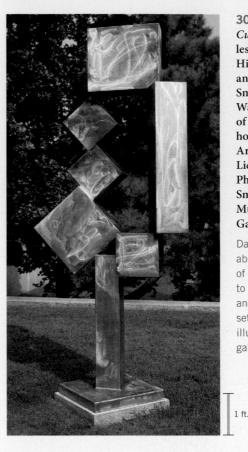

30-16 DAVID SMITH, *Cubi XII,* 1963. Stainless steel, 9′ 1⅝″ high. Hirshhorn Museum and Sculpture Garden, Smithsonian Institution, Washington, D.C. (gift of the Joseph H. Hirshhorn Foundation, 1972). Art © David Smith, Licensed by VAGA, NY. Photo by Lee Stalsworth, Smithsonian Hirshhorn Museum and Sculpture Garden.

David Smith designed his abstract metal sculptures of simple geometric forms to reflect the natural light and color of their outdoor settings, not the sterile illumination of a museum gallery.

1 ft.

1960s he produced a series of monumental works called *Cubi,* designed for display in the open air (see "David Smith on Outdoor Sculpture," above). *Cubi XII* (FIG. **30-16**), a characteristic example, consists of simple geometric forms—cubes and rectangular bars. Made of stainless-steel sections piled on top of one another, often at unstable angles, and then welded together, the *Cubi* sculptures make a striking visual statement. Smith added gestural elements reminiscent of Abstract Expressionism by burnishing the metal with steel wool, producing swirling random-looking patterns that draw attention to the two-dimensionality of the sculptural surface. This treatment, which captures the light hitting the artwork, activates the surface and imparts a texture to his pieces.

TONY SMITH A predominantly sculptural movement that emerged in the 1960s among artists seeking Greenbergian purity of form was *Minimalism.* One leading Minimalist was New Jersey native TONY SMITH (1912–1980), who created simple volumetric sculptures such as *Die* (FIG. **30-17**). Minimalist artworks generally lack identifiable subjects, colors, surface textures, and narrative elements, and are perhaps best described simply as three-dimensional objects. By rejecting illusionism and reducing sculpture to basic geometric forms, Smith and other Minimalists emphatically emphasized their art's "objecthood" and concrete tangibility. In so doing, they reduced experience to its most fundamental level, preventing viewers from drawing on assumptions or preconceptions when dealing with the art before them.

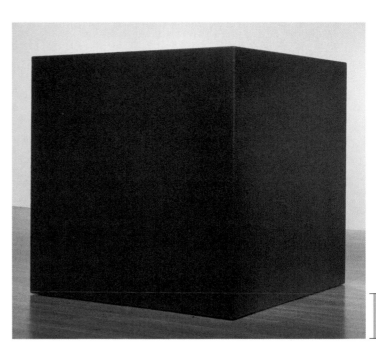

1 ft.

30-17 TONY SMITH, *Die,* 1962. Steel, 6′ × 6′ × 6′. Museum of Modern Art, New York (gift of Jane Smith in honor of Agnes Gund).

By rejecting illusionism and symbolism and reducing sculpture to basic geometric forms, Minimalist Tony Smith emphasized the "objecthood" and concrete tangibility of his sculptures.

Donald Judd on Sculpture and Industrial Materials

In a 1965 essay entitled "Specific Objects," the Minimalist sculptor Donald Judd described the advantages of sculpture over painting and the attractions of using industrial materials for his works (FIG. 30-18).

> Three dimensions are real space. That gets rid of the problem of illusionism . . . one of the salient and most objectionable relics of European art. The several limits of painting are no longer present. A work can be as powerful as it can be thought to be. Actual space is intrinsically more powerful and specific than paint on a flat surface. . . . The use of three dimensions makes it possible to see all sorts of materials and colors. Most of [my] work involves new materials, either recent inventions or things not used before in art. Little was done until lately with the wide range of industrial products. . . . Materials vary greatly and are simply materials—formica, aluminum, cold-rolled steel, plexiglas, red and common brass, and so forth. They are specific. If they are used directly, they are more specific. Also, they are usually aggressive. There is an objectivity to the obdurate identity of a material. . . . The form of a work of art and its materials are closely related. In earlier work the structure and the imagery were executed in some neutral and homogeneous material.*

*Donald Judd, *Complete Writings 1959–1975* (New York: New York University Press, 1975), 181–189.

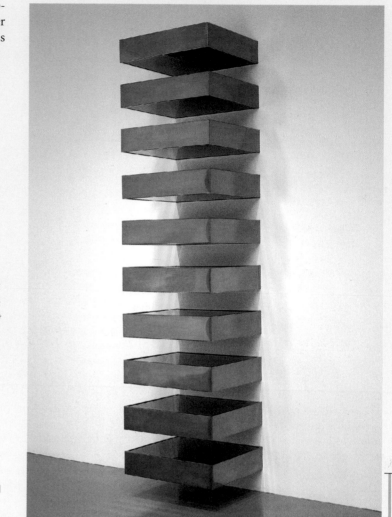

30-18 Donald Judd, *Untitled*, 1969. Brass and colored fluorescent Plexiglas on steel brackets, 10 units, 6⅛" × 2' × 2' 3" each, with 6" intervals. Hirshhorn Museum and Sculpture Garden, Smithsonian Institution, Washington, D.C. (gift of Joseph H. Hirshhorn, 1972). © Donald Judd Estate/Licensed by VAGA, New York.

Judd's Minimalist sculpture incorporates boxes fashioned from undisguised industrial materials. The artist used Plexiglas because its translucency gives the viewer access to the work's interior.

1 ft.

DONALD JUDD Another Minimalist sculptor, Donald Judd (1928–1994), embraced a spare, universal aesthetic corresponding to the core tenets of the movement. Born in Missouri, Judd studied philosophy and art history at Columbia University in New York City, where he produced most of his major works. Judd's determination to arrive at a visual vocabulary devoid of deception or ambiguity propelled him away from representation and toward precise and simple sculpture. For Judd, a work's power derived from its character as a whole and from the specificity of its materials (see "Donald Judd on Sculpture and Industrial Materials," above). *Untitled* (FIG. **30-18**) presents basic geometric boxes constructed of brass and red Plexiglas, undisguised by paint or other materials. The artist did not intend the work to be metaphorical or symbolic. It is a straightforward declaration of sculpture's objecthood. Judd used Plexiglas because its translucency enables the viewer access to the interior, thereby rendering the sculpture both open and enclosed. This aspect of the design reflects Judd's desire to banish ambiguity or falseness from his works.

Perhaps surprisingly, despite the ostensible connections between Minimalism and Greenbergian formalism, the critic did not embrace this direction in art:

> Minimal Art remains too much a feat of ideation [the mental formation of ideas], and not enough anything else. Its idea remains an idea, something deduced instead of felt and discovered. The geometrical and modular simplicity may announce and signify the artistically furthest-out, but the fact that the signals are understood for what they want to mean betrays them artistically. There is hardly any aesthetic surprise in Minimal Art. . . . Aesthetic surprise hangs on forever—it is there in Raphael as it is in Pollock—and ideas alone cannot achieve it.[10]

LOUISE NEVELSON Although Minimalism was a dominant sculptural trend in the 1960s, many sculptors pursued other styles. Russian-born Louise Nevelson (1899–1988) created sculpture combining a sense of the architectural fragment with the power of Dada and Surrealist found objects to express her personal

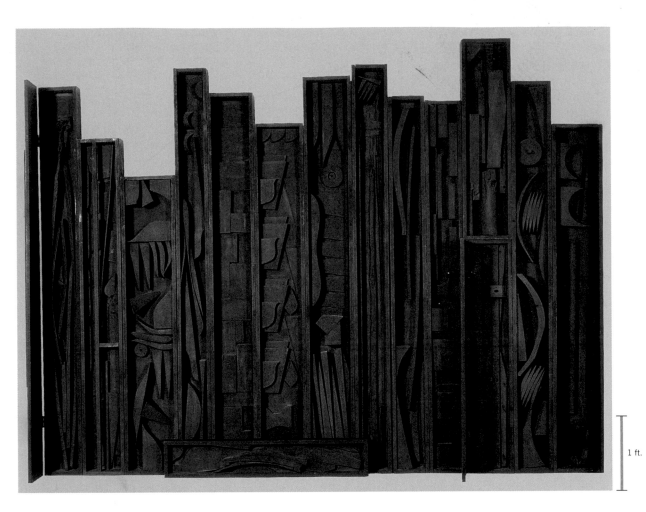

30-19 LOUISE NEVELSON, *Tropical Garden II*, 1957–1959. Wood painted black, 5' 11½" × 10' 11¾" × 1'. Musée National d'Art Moderne, Centre Georges Pompidou, Paris.

The monochromatic color scheme unifies the diverse sculpted forms and found objects in Nevelson's "walls" and creates a mysterious field of shapes and shadows suggesting magical environments.

1 ft.

sense of life's underlying significance. Multiplicity of meaning was important to Nevelson. She sought "the in-between place. . . . The dawns and the dusks"[11]—the transitional realm between one state of being and another.

Beginning in the late 1950s, Nevelson assembled sculptures of found wooden objects and forms, enclosing small sculptural compositions in boxes of varied sizes, and joined the boxes to one another to form "walls," which she then painted in a single hue—usually black, white, or gold. This monochromatic color scheme unifies the diverse parts of pieces such as *Tropical Garden II* (FIG. **30-19**) and creates a mysterious field of shapes and shadows. The structures suggest magical environments resembling the treasured secret hideaways dimly remembered from childhood. Yet the boxy frames and the precision of the manufactured found objects create a rough geometric structure the eye roams over freely, lingering on some details. The parts of a Nevelson sculpture and their interrelation recall the *Merz* constructions of Kurt Schwitters (FIG. 29-29). The effect is also rather like viewing the side of an apartment building from a moving elevated train or looking down on a city from the air.

LOUISE BOURGEOIS In contrast to the architectural nature of Nevelson's work, a sensuous organic quality recalling the evocative Biomorphic Surrealist forms of Joan Miró (FIG. 29-58) pervades the work of French-American artist LOUISE BOURGEOIS (1911–2010). *Cumul I* (FIG. **30-20**) is a collection of round-headed units huddled, with their heads protruding, within a collective cloak dotted with holes. The units differ in size, and their position within the group lends a distinctive personality to each. Although the shapes remain abstract, they refer strongly to human figures.

Bourgeois used a wide variety of materials in her works, including wood, plaster, latex, and plastics, in addition to alabaster, marble, and bronze. She exploited each material's qualities to suit the expressiveness of the piece.

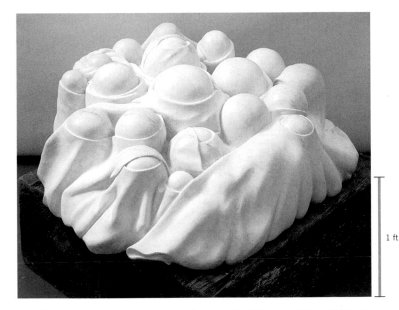

1 ft.

30-20 LOUISE BOURGEOIS, *Cumul I,* 1969. Marble, 1' 10⅜" × 4' 2" × 4'. Musée National d'Art Moderne, Centre Georges Pompidou, Paris. © Louise Bourgeois/Licensed by VAGA, New York. ◼◄

Bourgeois's sculptures are made up of sensuous organic forms that recall the Biomorphic Surrealist forms of Miró (FIG. 29-58). Although the shapes remain abstract, they refer strongly to human figures.

In *Cumul I,* the alternating high gloss and matte finish of the marble increases the sensuous distinction between the group of swelling forms and the soft folds swaddling them. As did Barbara Hepworth (FIG. 29-62), Bourgeois connected her sculpture with the body's multiple relationships to landscape: "[My pieces] are anthropomorphic and they are landscape also, since our body could be considered from a topographical point of view, as a land with mounds and valleys and caves and holes."[12] However, Bourgeois's sculptures are more personal and more openly sexual than Hepworth's. *Cumul I* represents perfectly the allusions Bourgeois sought: "There has always been sexual suggestiveness in my work. Sometimes I am totally concerned with female shapes—characters of breasts like clouds—but often I merge the activity—phallic breasts, male and female, active and passive."[13]

EVA HESSE A Minimalist in the early part of her career, EVA HESSE (1936–1970) later moved away from the severity characterizing much of Minimal art. She created sculptures that, although spare and simple, have a compelling presence. Using nontraditional sculptural materials such as fiberglass, cord, and latex, Hesse produced sculptures whose pure Minimalist forms appear to crumble, sag, and warp under the pressures of atmospheric force and gravity. Born Jewish in Hitler's Germany, the young Hesse hid with a Christian family when her parents and elder sister had to flee the Nazis.

She did not reunite with them until the early 1940s, just before her parents divorced. Those extraordinary circumstances helped give her a lasting sense that the central conditions of modern life are strangeness and absurdity. Struggling to express these qualities in her art, Hesse created informal sculptural arrangements with units often hung from the ceiling, propped against the walls, or spilled out along the floor. She said she wanted her pieces to be "non art, non connotative, non anthropomorphic, non geometric, non nothing, everything, but of another kind, vision, sort."[14]

Hang-Up (FIG. 30-21) fulfills these requirements. The piece resembles a carefully made empty frame sprouting a strange feeler extending into the room and doubling back to the frame. Hesse wrote that in this work, for the first time, her "idea of absurdity or extreme feeling came through. . . . [*Hang-Up*] has a kind of depth I don't always achieve and that is the kind of depth or soul or absurdity of life or meaning or feeling or intellect that I want to get."[15] The sculpture possesses a disquieting and touching presence, suggesting the fragility and grandeur of life amid the pressures of the modern age. Hesse was herself a touching and fragile presence in the art world. She died of a brain tumor at age 34.

ISAMU NOGUCHI Another sculptor often considered a Minimalist because of pure geometric works such as *Red Cube,* which he created in 1968 for the sidewalk in front of a New York City skyscraper, is Japanese American artist ISAMU NOGUCHI (1904–1988). His work defies easy classification, however, and in sculptures such as *Shodo Shima Stone Study* (FIG. 30-21A), Noguchi brilliantly wedded Western and Oriental themes and styles.

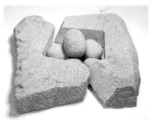

30-21A NOGUCHI, *Shodo Shima,* 1978.

Pop Art

Despite their differences, the Abstract Expressionists, Post-Painterly Abstractionists, Op Art painters, and Minimalist sculptors all adopted an artistic vocabulary of resolute abstraction. Other artists, however, observing that the insular and introspective attitude of the avant-garde had alienated the public, sought to harness the communicative power of art to reach a wide audience. Thus was born the Independent Group in London (FIG. 30-1) and the art movement that came to be known as Pop.

Although Pop Art originated in England, the movement found its greatest articulation and success in the United States, in large part because the more fully matured American consumer culture provided a fertile environment in which the movement flourished through the 1960s. Indeed, Independent Group members claimed their inspiration came from Hollywood, Detroit, and New York's Madison Avenue, paying homage to America's predominance in the realms of mass media, mass production, and advertising.

JASPER JOHNS One of the artists pivotal to the early development of American Pop Art was JASPER JOHNS (b. 1930), who grew up in South Carolina and moved to New York City in 1952. Johns sought to draw attention to common objects in the world—what he called things "seen but not looked at."[16] To this end, he did several series of paintings of numbers, alphabets, flags, and maps of the United States—all of which are items people view frequently but rarely scrutinize. He created his first

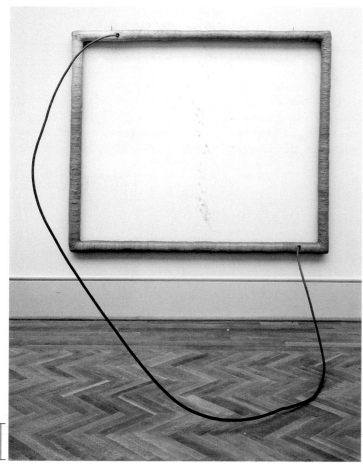

1 ft.

30-21 EVA HESSE, *Hang-Up,* 1965–1966. Acrylic on cloth over wood and steel, 6′ × 7′ × 6′ 6″. Art Institute of Chicago, Chicago (gift of Arthur Keating and Mr. and Mrs. Edward Morris by exchange).

Hesse created spare and simple sculptures with parts extending into the room. She wanted her works to express the strangeness and absurdity she considered the central conditions of modern life.

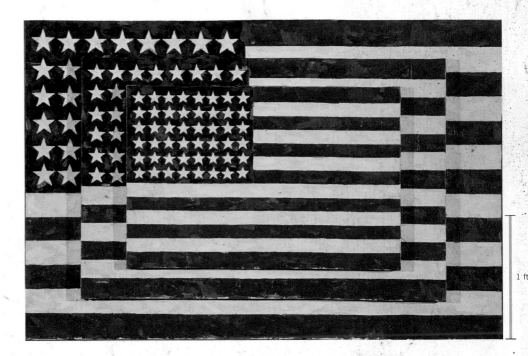

American Pop artist Jasper Johns wanted to draw attention to common objects people view frequently but rarely scrutinize. He made many paintings of targets, flags, numbers, and alphabets.

flag painting in 1954 at the height of the Cold War. Initially labeled a Neo-Dadaist because of the kinship of his works to Marcel Duchamp's readymades (FIG. 29-27), Johns also had strong ties to the Surrealists, especially René Magritte, whose painting of a pipe labeled "This is not a pipe" (FIG. 29-56) is conceptually a forerunner of Johns's flags—for example, *Three Flags* (FIG. **30-22**), which could easily carry the label "These are not flags." In fact, when asked why he chose the American flag as a subject, Johns replied he had a dream in which he saw himself painting a flag. The world of dreams was central to Surrealism (see Chapter 29).

In *Three Flags*, Johns painted a trio of overlapping American national banners of decreasing size, with the smallest closest to the viewer, reversing traditional perspective, which calls for diminution of size with distance. Johns drained meaning from the patriotic emblem by reducing it to a repetitive pattern—not the flag itself but three pictures of a flag in one. Nevertheless, the heritage of Abstract Expressionism is still apparent. Although Johns rejected the heroic, highly personalized application of pigment championed by the 1950s action painters, he painted his flags in *encaustic* (liquid wax and dissolved pigment; see "Encaustic Painting," Chapter 7, page 218) mixed with newsprint on three overlapping canvases. His flags thus retain a pronounced surface texture, emphasizing that the viewer is looking at a handmade painting, not a machine-made fabric. The painting, like the flags, is an object, not an illusion of other objects.

ROBERT RAUSCHENBERG

A close friend of Johns's, ROBERT RAUSCHENBERG (1925–2008) began using mass-media images in his work in the 1950s. Rauschenberg set out to create works that would be open and indeterminate, and he began by making *combines*, which intersperse painted passages with sculptural elements. Combines are, in a sense, Rauschenberg's personal variation on *assemblages*, artworks constructed from already existing objects. At times, these combines seem to be sculptures with painting incorporated into certain sections. Others seem to be paint-

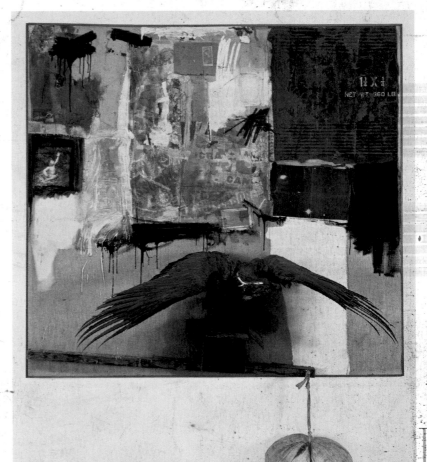

30-23 Robert Rauschenberg, *Canyon*, 1959. Oil, pencil, paper, fabric, metal, cardboard box, printed paper, printed reproductions, photograph, wood, paint tube, and mirror on canvas, with oil on bald eagle, string, and pillow, 6' 9¾" × 5' 10" × 2'. Sonnabend Collection, New York. © Robert Rauschenberg/ Licensed by VAGA, New York.

Rauschenberg's "combines" intersperse painted passages with sculptural elements. *Canyon* incorporates pigment on canvas with pieces of printed paper, photographs, a pillow, and a stuffed eagle.

Roy Lichtenstein on Pop Art

In November 1963, Roy Lichtenstein was one of eight painters interviewed for a profile on Pop Art in *Art News*. Gene R. Swenson posed the questions. Some of Lichtenstein's answers follow.

[Pop Art is] the use of commercial art as a subject matter in painting . . . [Pop artists portray] what I think to be the most brazen and threatening characteristics of our culture, things we hate, but which are also so powerful in their impingement on us. . . . I paint directly . . . [without] perspective or shading. It doesn't look like a painting *of* something, it looks like the thing itself. Instead of looking like a painting *of* a billboard . . . Pop art seems to be the actual thing. It is an intensification, a stylistic intensification of the excitement which the subject matter has for me; but the style is . . . cool. One of the things a cartoon does is to express violent emotion and passion in a completely mechanized and removed style. To express this thing in a painterly style would dilute it. . . . Everybody has called Pop Art "American" painting, but it's actually industrial painting. America was hit by industrialism and capitalism harder and sooner . . . I think the meaning of my work is that it's industrial, it's what all the world will soon become. Europe will be the same way, soon, so it won't be American; it will be universal.*

30-24 Roy Lichtenstein, *Hopeless*, 1963. Oil and synthetic polymer paint on canvas, 3′ 8″ × 3′ 8″. Kunstmuseum Basel, Basel. © Estate of Roy Lichtenstein.

Comic books appealed to Lichtenstein because they were a mainstay of popular culture, meant to be read and discarded. The Pop artist immortalized their images on large canvases.

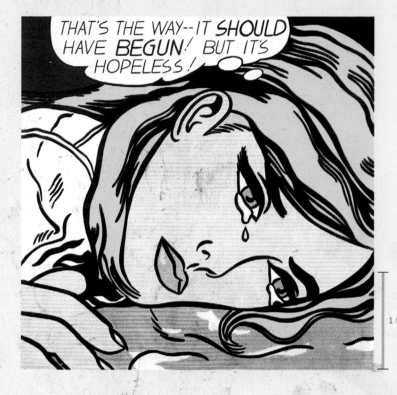

1 ft.

*G. R. Swenson, "What Is Pop Art? Interviews with Eight Painters," *Art News* 62, no. 7 (November 1963), 25, 64.

ings with three-dimensional objects attached to the surface. In the 1950s, assemblages usually contained an array of art reproductions, magazine and newspaper clippings, and passages painted in an Abstract Expressionist style. In the early 1960s, Rauschenberg adopted the commercial medium of *silk-screen printing*, first in black and white and then in color, and began filling entire canvases with appropriated news images and anonymous photographs of city scenes.

Canyon (FIG. **30-23**) is typical of his combines. Pieces of printed paper and photographs cover parts of the canvas. Much of the unevenly painted surface consists of pigment roughly applied in a manner reminiscent of de Kooning's work (FIG. 30-8). A stuffed bald eagle attached to the lower part of the combine spreads its wings as if lifting off in flight toward the viewer. Completing the combine, a pillow dangles from a string attached to a wood stick below the eagle. The artist presented the work's components in a jumbled fashion. He tilted or turned some of the images sideways, and each overlays part of another image. The compositional confusion may resemble that of a Dada collage, but the parts of Rauschenberg's combines maintain their individuality more than those, for example, in a Schwitters piece (FIG. 29-29). The eye scans a Rauschenberg canvas much as it might survey the environment on a walk through a city. The various recognizable images and objects seem unrelated and defy a consistent reading, although Rauschenberg chose all the elements of his combines with specific

meanings in mind. For example, Rauschenberg based *Canyon* on a Rembrandt painting of Jupiter in the form of an eagle carrying the boy Ganymede heavenward. The photo in the combine is a reference to the Greek boy, and the hanging bag is a visual pun on his buttocks.

ROY LICHTENSTEIN As the Pop Art movement matured, the images became more concrete and tightly controlled. ROY LICHTENSTEIN (1923–1997), who was born in Manhattan not far from Madison Avenue, the center of the American advertising industry, developed an interest in art in elementary school and as a teenager took weekend painting classes at the Parsons School of Design before enrolling at Ohio State University. He served in the army during World War II and was stationed in France, where he was able to visit the Musée du Louvre and Chartres Cathedral. In the late 1950s, however, he turned his attention to commercial art and especially to the comic book as a mainstay of American popular culture (see "Roy Lichtenstein on Pop Art," above).

In paintings such as *Hopeless* (FIG. **30-24**), Lichtenstein excerpted an image from a comic book, a form of entertainment meant to be read and discarded, and immortalized the image on a large canvas. Aside from that modification, Lichtenstein remained remarkably faithful to the original comic-strip image. His subjects were typically the melodramatic scenes that were hallmarks of

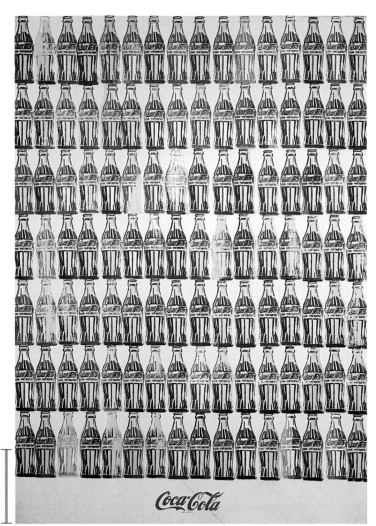

1 ft.

30-25 ANDY WARHOL, *Green Coca-Cola Bottles,* 1962. Oil on canvas, 6′ 10½″ × 4′ 9″. Whitney Museum of American Art, New York.

Warhol was the quintessential American Pop artist. Here, he selected an icon of mass-produced, consumer culture, and then multiplied it, reflecting Coke's omnipresence in American society.

romance comic books popular at the time and included "balloons" with the words the characters speak. Lichtenstein also used the visual vocabulary of the comic strip, with its dark black outlines and unmodulated color areas, and retained the familiar square dimensions. Moreover, his printing technique, *benday dots,* called attention to the mass-produced derivation of the image. Named after its inventor, the newspaper printer Benjamin Day (1810–1889), the benday-dot system involves the modulation of colors through the placement and size of colored dots. Lichtenstein thus transferred the visual shorthand language of the comic book to the realm of monumental painting.

ANDY WARHOL The quintessential American Pop artist was ANDY WARHOL (1928–1987). An early successful career as a commercial artist and illustrator grounded Warhol in the sensibility and

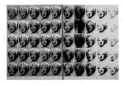

30-25A WARHOL, *Marilyn Diptych,* 1962. ◼◀

visual rhetoric of advertising and the mass media. This knowledge proved useful for his Pop artworks, which often depicted icons of mass-produced consumer culture, such as *Green Coca-Cola Bottles* (FIG. **30-25**), and Hollywood celebrities, such as Marilyn Monroe (1926–1962; FIG. **30-25A**). Warhol

favored reassuringly familiar objects and people. He explained his attraction to the ubiquitous curved Coke bottle:

> What's great about this country is that America started the tradition where the richest consumers buy essentially the same things as the poorest. You can be watching TV and see Coca-Cola, and you can know that the President drinks Coke, Liz Taylor drinks Coke, and just think, you can drink Coke, too. A Coke is a Coke and no amount of money can get you a better Coke.[17]

As did other Pop artists, Warhol used a visual vocabulary and a printing method that reinforced the image's connections to consumer culture. The silk-screen technique allowed Warhol to print the image endlessly (although he varied each bottle slightly). The repetition and redundancy of the Coke bottle reflect the saturation of this product in American society—in homes, at work, literally everywhere, including gas stations, as immortalized by GEORGE SEGAL (1924–2000) in 1963 (FIG. **30-25B**). So immersed was Warhol in a culture of

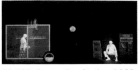

30-25B SEGAL, *Gas Station,* 1963.

mass production that he not only produced numerous canvases of the same image but also named his studio "the Factory."

CLAES OLDENBURG In the 1960s, CLAES OLDENBURG (b. 1929) also produced Pop artworks that incisively commented on American consumer culture, but his medium was sculpture. The son of a Swedish diplomat who moved to the United States in 1936, Oldenburg attended school in Chicago and graduated from Yale University in 1950. His early works consisted of plaster reliefs of food and clothing items. Oldenburg constructed these sculptures of plaster layered on chicken wire and muslin, painting them with cheap commercial house enamel. In later works, focused on the same subjects, he shifted to large-scale stuffed sculptures of sewn vinyl or canvas, many of which he exhibited in a show he titled *The Store*—an appropriate comment on the function of art as a commodity in a consumer society.

Oldenburg is best known, however, for his mammoth outdoor sculptures. In 1966, a group of graduate students at the Yale School of Architecture, calling themselves the Colossal Keepsake Corporation, raised funds for materials for a giant sculpture that Oldenburg agreed to create (in secret and without a fee) as a gift to his alma mater. The work, *Lipstick (Ascending) on Caterpillar Tracks* (FIG. **30-26**), was Oldenburg's first monumental public sculpture. He installed *Lipstick* on Ascension Day, May 15, 1969, on Beineke Plaza across from the office of the university's president, the site of many raucous protests against the Vietnam War. Oldenburg's characteristic humor emerges unmistakably in the combination of phallic and militaristic imagery, especially in the double irony of the "phallus" being a woman's cosmetic item, and the Caterpillar-type endless-loop metal tracks suggesting not a tractor-earthmover for construction work but a military tank designed for destruction in warfare. *Lipstick* was to be a speaker's platform for protesters, and originally the lipstick tip was a drooping red vinyl balloon the speaker had to inflate, underscoring the sexual innuendo. (Oldenburg once remarked that art collectors preferred nudes, so he produced nude cars, nude telephones, and nude electric plugs to please them.)

Vandalism and exposure to the elements (the original tractor was plywood) caused so much damage to *Lipstick* that it had to be removed and reconstructed in metal and fiberglass. Yale formally accepted the controversial and unsolicited repaired gift in 1974,

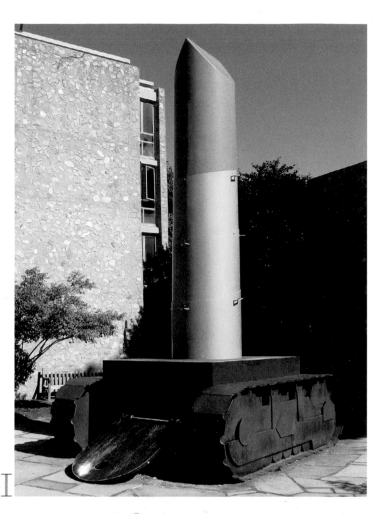

30-26 CLAES OLDENBURG, *Lipstick (Ascending) on Caterpillar Tracks,* 1969; reworked, 1974. Painted steel, aluminum, and fiberglass, 21′ high. Morse College, Yale University, New Haven (gift of Colossal Keepsake Corporation).

Designed as a speaker's platform for antiwar protesters, *Lipstick* humorously combines phallic and militaristic imagery. Originally the lipstick tip was soft red vinyl and had to be inflated.

when the architectural historian Vincent Scully (b. 1920), then master of Yale's Morse College, offered a permanent home for *Lipstick* in the college courtyard.

Also usually classified as a Pop Art sculptor was French-born NIKI DE SAINT-PHALLE (1930–2002), because her sculptures remind many viewers of dolls and folk art. Her most famous works are the series of polyester statues of women she called *Nanas* (FIG. **30-26A**), oversized, brightly colored sculptures that are feminist commentaries on popular stereotypes of female beauty.

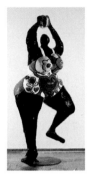

30-26A SAINT-PHALLE, *Black Venus,* 1965–1967.

Superrealism

Like the Pop artists, the artists associated with *Superrealism* sought a form of artistic communication more accessible to the public than the remote, unfamiliar visual language of the Abstract Expressionists, Post-Painterly Abstractionists, and Minimalists. The Superrealists expanded Pop's iconography in both painting and sculpture by making images in the late 1960s and 1970s involving scrupulous fidelity to optical fact. Because many Superrealists used photographs as sources for their imagery, art historians also refer to this postwar art movement as *Photorealism*.

AUDREY FLACK One of Superrealism's pioneers was lifelong New Yorker AUDREY FLACK (b. 1931), who studied the history of art at New York University's Institute of Fine Arts after graduating from Yale. Her paintings, such as *Marilyn* (FIG. **30-27**), were not simply technical exercises in recording objects in minute detail but were also conceptual inquiries into the nature of photography and the extent to which photography constructs an understanding of reality. Flack observed: "[Photography is] my whole life, I studied art history, it was always photographs, I never saw the paintings, they were in Europe. . . . Look at TV and at magazines and reproductions, they're all influenced by photo-vision."[18] The photograph's formal

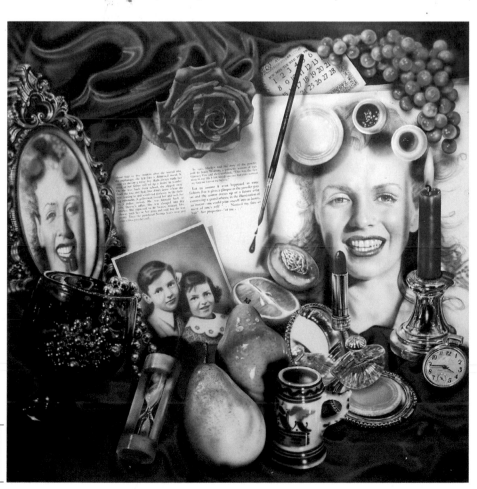

30-27 AUDREY FLACK, *Marilyn,* 1977. Oil over acrylic on canvas, 8′ × 8′. University of Arizona Museum, Tucson (museum purchase with funds provided by the Edward J. Gallagher Jr. Memorial Fund).

Flack's pioneering Photorealist still lifes record objects with great optical fidelity. *Marilyn* alludes to Dutch vanitas paintings (FIG. 25-1) and incorporates multiple references to the transience of life.

Painting, Sculpture, and Photography **917**

Chuck Close on Photorealist Portrait Painting

In a widely read 1970 interview in the journal *Artforum,* art critic Cindy Nemser asked Photorealist painter Chuck Close about the scale of his huge portraits (FIG. 30-28) and the relationship of his canvases to the photographs that lie behind them. He answered in part:

> The large scale allows me to deal with information that is overlooked in an eight-by-ten inch photograph . . . My large scale forces the viewer to focus on one area at a time. In that way he is made aware of the blurred areas that are seen with peripheral vision. Normally we never take those peripheral areas into account. When we focus on an area it is sharp. As we turn our attention to adjacent areas they sharpen up too. In my work, the blurred areas don't come into focus, but they are too large to be ignored. . . . In order to . . . make [my painted] information stack up with photographic information, I tried to purge my work of as much of the baggage of traditional portrait painting as I could. To avoid a painterly brush stroke and surface, I use some pretty devious means, such as razor blades, electric drills and airbrushes. I also work as thinly as possible and I don't use white paint as it tends to build up and become chalky and opaque. In fact, in a nine-by-seven foot picture, I only use a couple of tablespoons of black paint to cover the entire canvas.*

*Cindy Nemser, "Chuck Close: Interview with Cindy Nemser," *Artforum* 8, no. 5 (January 1970), 51–55.

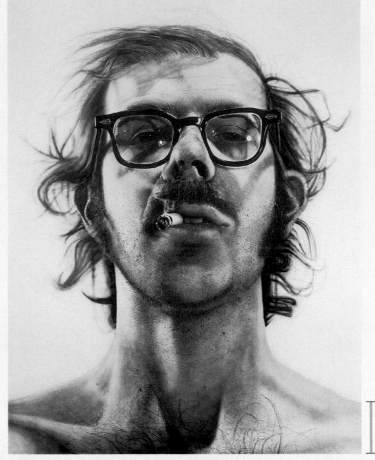

30-28 CHUCK CLOSE, *Big Self-Portrait,* 1967–1968. Acrylic on canvas, 8′ 11″ × 6′ 11″. Walker Art Center, Minneapolis (Art Center Acquisition Fund, 1969). ◼◀

Close's goal was to translate photographic information into painted information. In his portraits, he deliberately avoided creative compositions, flattering lighting effects, and revealing facial expressions.

1 ft.

---

qualities also intrigued her, and she used photographic techniques by first projecting an image in slide form onto the canvas. By next using an *airbrush* (a device originally designed as a photo-retouching tool that sprays paint with compressed air), Flack could duplicate the smooth gradations of tone and color found in photographs. Most of her paintings are still lifes that present the viewer with a collection of familiar objects painted with great optical fidelity. *Marilyn* is a still life incorporating photographs of the face of famed Hollywood actress Marilyn Monroe. It is a poignant commentary on Monroe's tragic life and differs markedly from Warhol's *Marilyn Diptych* (FIG. 30-25A), which celebrates celebrity and makes no allusion to the death of the glamorous star. Flack's still life includes multiple references to death and alludes to Dutch vanitas paintings (FIG. 25-1). In addition to the black-and-white photographs of a youthful, smiling Monroe, fresh fruit, an hourglass, a burning candle, a watch, and a calendar all refer to the passage of time and the transience of life on earth.

CHUCK CLOSE Also usually considered a Superrealist is CHUCK CLOSE (b. 1940), who grew up near Seattle and attended the University of Washington and Yale University. He is best known for his large-scale portraits, such as *Big Self-Portrait* (FIG. **30-28**). However, Close felt his connection to the Photorealists was tenuous, because for him realism, rather than an end in itself, was the

result of an intellectually rigorous, systematic approach to painting. He based his paintings of the late 1960s and early 1970s on photographs, and his main goal was to translate photographic information into painted information. Because he aimed simply to record visual information about his subject's appearance, Close deliberately avoided creative compositions, flattering lighting effects, and revealing facial expressions. Not interested in providing great insight into the personalities of those portrayed, Close painted anonymous and generic people, mostly friends. By reducing the variables in his paintings (even their canvas size is a constant 9 by 7 feet), he could focus on employing his methodical presentations of faces, thereby encouraging the viewer to deal with the formal aspects of his works. Indeed, because of the large scale of Close's paintings, careful scrutiny causes the images to dissolve into abstract patterns (see "Chuck Close on Photorealist Portrait Painting," above).

LUCIAN FREUD Born in Berlin, LUCIAN FREUD (1922–2011) moved to London with his family in 1933 when Adolph Hitler became German chancellor. The grandson of Sigmund Freud, the painter is best known for his unflattering close-up views of faces in which the sitter seems almost unaware of the painter's presence, and for his portrayals of female and male nudes in foreshortened and often contorted poses. Although Freud always used living

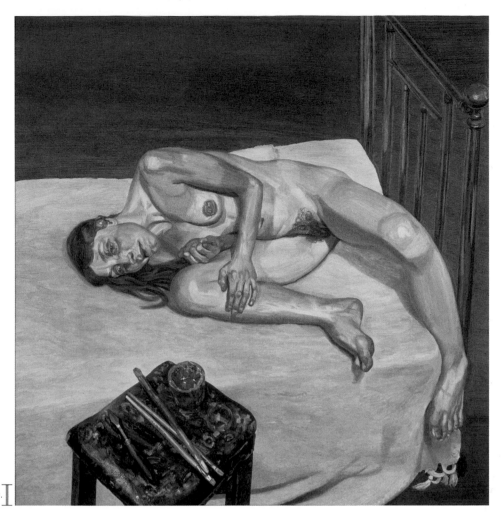

1 in.

30-29 LUCIAN FREUD, *Naked Portrait*, 1972–1973. Oil on canvas, 2′ × 2′. Tate Modern, London.

Freud's brutally realistic portrait of an unnamed woman lying on a bed in an awkward position gives the impression the viewer is an intruder in a private space, but the setting is the artist's studio.

DUANE HANSON Not surprisingly, many sculptors also were Superrealists, including Minnesota-born DUANE HANSON (1925–1996), who spent much of his career in southern Florida. Hanson perfected a casting technique that enabled him to create life-size figurative sculptures many viewers mistake at first for real people. Hanson began by making plaster molds from live models and then filled the molds with polyester resin. After the resin hardened, he removed the outer molds and cleaned, painted with an airbrush, and decorated the sculptures with wigs, clothes, and other accessories. These works, such as *Supermarket Shopper* (FIG. **30-30**), depict stereotypical average Americans, striking chords with the public specifically because of their familiarity. Hanson explained his choice of imagery:

> The subject matter that I like best deals with the familiar lower- and middle-class American types of today. To me, the resignation, emptiness and loneliness of their existence captures the true reality of life for these people. . . . I want to achieve a certain tough realism which speaks of the fascinating idiosyncrasies of our time.[21]

models whose poses he determined, his paintings convey the impression the artist and the viewer are intruders in a private realm.

In *Naked Portrait* (FIG. **30-29**), the viewer observes an unnamed woman lying in an uncomfortable, almost fetal, position at the foot of a bed. Freud depicted her from a sharp angle above and to the left. In the foreground is a small table with the painter's tools on it, revealing that this is not the woman's bedroom but the painter's studio and that the woman is the subject of intense scrutiny by the artist. Freud's models do not have perfect bodies. Some are overweight, and many are well beyond their prime. These are truly "naked portraits" of real people. They break sharply with the Western tradition from Greek antiquity to the Renaissance and into the modern era of depicting idealized Venuses, Eves, and courtesans in graceful and often erotic poses. Freud explained his interest in nudity: "I'm really interested in people as animals. Part of my liking to work from them naked is for that reason. Because I can see more."[19] Regarding the setting of his paintings, Freud observed: "I work from people that interest me, and that I care about and think about, in rooms that I live in and know."[20]

30-30 DUANE HANSON, *Supermarket Shopper,* 1970. Polyester resin and fiberglass polychromed in oil, with clothing, steel cart, and groceries, life-size. Nachfolgeinstitut, Neue Galerie, Sammlung Ludwig, Aachen. © Estate of Duane Hanson/Licensed by VAGA, New York.

Hanson used molds from live models to create his Superrealistic life-size painted plaster sculptures. His aim was to capture the emptiness and loneliness of average Americans in familiar settings.

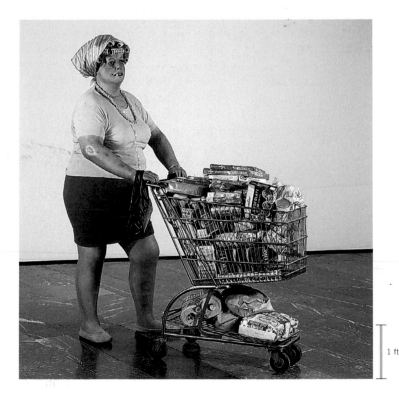

1 ft.

Painting, Sculpture, and Photography **919**

Photography

Although Superrealist artists admired the ability of photography to reproduce faithfully the appearance of people, objects, and places, photographers themselves used their medium to pursue varied ends. The photographs of Edward Weston (FIGS. 29-44 and 29-44A) and Dorothea Lange (FIG. 29-76) represent the two poles of American photography between the world wars—the art photograph (Weston), which transforms the real into the abstract, and the documentary photograph (Lange), which records people and events directly, without artifice. In the postwar period both approaches to photography continued to flourish.

DIANE ARBUS During the 1960s, the most famous photographer of people—with all their blemishes, both physical and psychological—was DIANE ARBUS (1923–1971). New York–born and –educated, Diane Nemerov married Allan Arbus when she was 18 and worked with her husband as a fashion photographer. After their divorce in 1959, Diane chose as her subjects the opposite of the beautiful people with perfect makeup and trendy clothes she had photographed constantly in the 1950s. Her photographs record ordinary people living ordinary lives, people with physical deformities, and people at the margins of society, for example, transvestites—in short, people who rarely were the chosen subjects of professional photographers.

One of Arbus's most memorable photographs (FIG. 30-31) is of a boy she encountered in New York City's Central Park in 1962 carrying a toy hand grenade. She asked him to stand still and pose

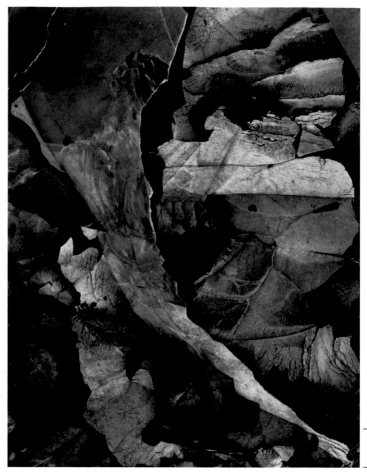

1 in.

30-32 MINOR WHITE, *Moencopi Strata, Capitol Reef, Utah*, 1962. Gelatin silver print, 1' ⅛" × 9¼". Museum of Modern Art, New York. © The Minor White Archive, Princeton University.

White's "straight photograph" of a natural rock formation is also an abstract composition of jagged shapes and contrasts of light and dark reminiscent of Abstract Expressionist action paintings.

for her, and as she moved around him searching for the perfect angle, he became impatient, his body tensed, and his face formed a menacing expression. She snapped the shutter and recorded his peculiar grimace and eerie clawlike left hand. The empty space all around the boy contributes to the sense he is a disturbed personality isolated from society, in contrast to the "normal" family at the top right of the photograph. Arbus's own life was not "picture perfect" either. She committed suicide in 1971.

MINOR WHITE Minneapolis native MINOR WHITE (1908–1976) moved to Portland, Oregon, in 1938 and became a photographer for the Works Progress Administration. He served in the United States Army in World War II and then settled in New York City in 1945, where he met Alfred Stieglitz, whose *Equivalent* photographs (FIG. 29-43A) he greatly admired. Deeply influenced by Zen Buddhism (see "Zen Buddhism," Chapter 34, page 1007), White sought to incorporate a mystical element in his own work. His 1962 photograph (FIG. 30-32) of a rock formation in Utah is a characteristic example. A "straight photograph" in the tradition of Stieglitz and Weston, it is also an abstract composition of jagged shapes and contrasts of light and dark reminiscent of Abstract Expressionist action paintings (FIG. 30-8C). Viewers of *Moencopi Strata, Capitol Reef, Utah* may recognize White's nominal subject as a detail of a landscape, but in his hands nature becomes the springboard for meditation. As one of the founders and the long-

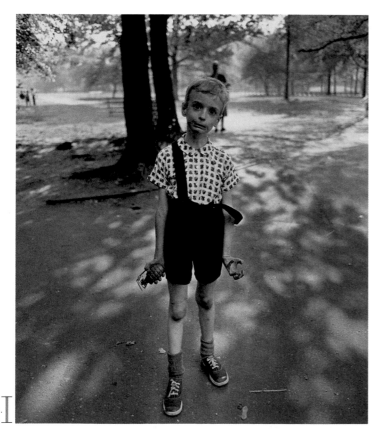

1 in.

30-31 DIANE ARBUS, *Child with Toy Hand Grenade, New York, New York*, 1962. Gelatin silver print, 7¼" × 8⅜". The Museum of Modern Art, New York.

Arbus specialized in photographs of people on the margins of society. Her photograph of a boy holding a toy hand grenade in New York's Central Park presents him as a menacing, isolated personality.

Judy Chicago on *The Dinner Party*

One of the acknowledged master-pieces of feminist art is Judy Chicago's *The Dinner Party* (FIG. 30-33), which required a team of nearly 400 to create and assemble. In 1979, Chicago published a book explaining the genesis and symbolism of the work.

[By 1974] I had discarded [my original] idea of painting a hundred abstract portraits on plates, each paying tribute to a different historic female figure.... In my research I realized over and over again that women's achievements had been left out of history... My new idea was to try to symbolize this.... [I thought] about putting the plates on a table with silver, glasses, napkins, and tablecloths, and over the next year and a half the concept of *The Dinner Party* slowly evolved. I began to think about the piece as a reinterpretation of the Last Supper from the point of view of women, who, throughout history, had prepared the meals and set the table. In my "Last Supper," however, the women would be the honored guests. Their representation in the form of plates set on the table would express the way women had been confined, and the piece would thus reflect both women's achievements and their oppression.... My goal with *The Dinner Party* was ... to forge a new kind of art expressing women's experience ... [It] seemed appropriate to relate our history through art, particularly through techniques traditionally associated with women—china-painting and needlework.*

*Judy Chicago, "The Dinner Party": *A Symbol of Our Heritage* (Garden City, N.Y.: Anchor Press, 1979), 11–12.

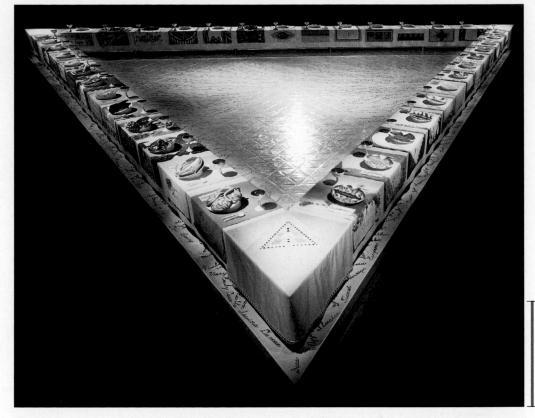

10 ft.

30-33 JUDY CHICAGO, *The Dinner Party,* 1979. Multimedia, including ceramics and stitchery, 48′ long on each side. The Brooklyn Museum, Brooklyn.

Chicago's *Dinner Party* honors 39 women from antiquity to 20th-century America. The triangular form and the materials—painted china and fabric—are traditionally associated with women.

---

time editor (1952–1975) of *Aperture,* the leading art photography magazine of the time, White had a profound influence on the development of the medium in the postwar period.

Feminist Art

With the renewed interest in representation the Pop artists and Superrealists introduced in the 1960s and 1970s, artists once again began to embrace the persuasive powers of art to communicate with a wide audience. In the 1970s, many artists began to investigate the social dynamics of power and privilege, especially in relation to gender, although racial, ethnic, and sexual orientation issues have also figured prominently in the art of recent decades (see Chapter 31). Women artists played a significant role in the feminist movement, which sought equal rights for women in contemporary society and focused attention on the subservient place of women in societies throughout history. Spearheading the feminist art movement of the 1970s were Judy Chicago (FIG. 30-33) and Miriam Schapiro (FIG. 30-34). Chicago and a group of students at California State University,

Fresno, founded the Feminist Art Program, and Chicago and Schapiro coordinated it at the California Institute of the Arts in Valencia. In 1972, as part of this program, teachers and students joined to create projects such as Womanhouse, an abandoned house in Los Angeles they completely converted into a suite of "environments," each based on a different aspect of women's lives and fantasies.

JUDY CHICAGO A major goal of Chicago native Judy Cohen, who took the name JUDY CHICAGO (b. 1939), was to educate the public about women's role in history and the fine arts and to establish a respect for women and their art. Chicago sought to forge a new kind of art expressing women's experiences and to find a way to make that art accessible to a large audience. Inspired early in her career by the work of Barbara Hepworth (FIG. 29-62), Georgia O'Keeffe (FIGS. I-5 and 29-42), and Louise Nevelson (FIG. 30-19), Chicago developed a personal painting style that consciously included abstract organic vaginal images. In the early 1970s, Chicago began planning an ambitious piece, *The Dinner Party* (FIG. **30-33**), using craft techniques (such as china painting and needlework)

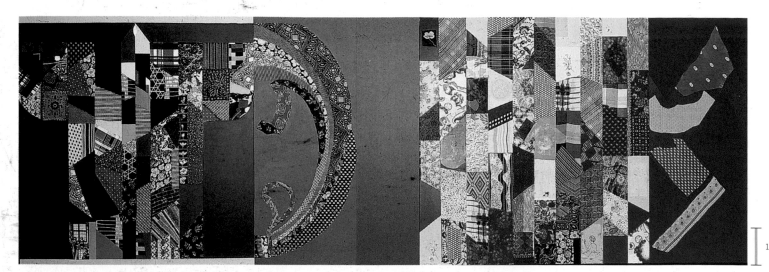

1 ft.

30-34 MIRIAM SCHAPIRO, *Anatomy of a Kimono* (detail of a 10-panel composition), 1976. Fabric and acrylic on canvas, entire work 6′ 8″ × 52′ 2½″. Collection of Bruno Bischofberger, Zurich.

Schapiro calls her huge sewn collages *femmages* to make the point that women had been doing collages of fabric long before Picasso (FIG. 29-16). This femmage incorporates patterns from Japanese kimonos.

traditionally practiced by women, to celebrate the achievements and contributions women had made throughout history (see "Judy Chicago on *The Dinner Party*," page 921). She originally conceived the work as a feminist *Last Supper* for 13 "honored guests," as in the biblical account of Christ's passion, but at Chicago's table the guests are women instead of men. The number of women in a witches' coven is also 13, and the artist intended her feminist *Dinner Party* additionally to refer to witchcraft and the worship of the Mother Goddess. But because Chicago had uncovered so many worthy women in the course of her research, she tripled the number of guests and placed table settings for 39 women around a triangular table 48 feet long on each side. The triangular form refers to the ancient symbol for both woman and the Goddess. The notion of a dinner party also alludes to women's traditional role as homemakers.

The Dinner Party rests on a triangular white tile floor inscribed with the names of 999 additional women of achievement to signify that the accomplishments of the 39 honored guests rest on a foundation other women laid. Among those with place settings at the table are American painter Georgia O'Keeffe, Egyptian pharaoh Hatshepsut (see "Hatshepsut," Chapter 3, page 69), British writer Virginia Woolf, Native American guide Sacagawea, and American suffragist Susan B. Anthony. Each woman's place has identical eating utensils and a goblet but features a unique oversized porcelain plate and a long place mat or table runner covered with imagery reflecting significant facts about that woman's life and culture. The plates range from simple concave shapes with china-painted imagery to dishes whose sculptured three-dimensional designs almost seem to struggle to free themselves. The designs on each plate incorporate both butterfly and vulval motifs—the butterfly as the ancient symbol of liberation and the vulva as the symbol of female sexuality. Each table runner combines traditional needlework techniques, including needlepoint, embroidery, crochet, beading, patchwork, and appliqué. *The Dinner Party* is more than the sum of its parts, however. Of monumental size, as so many great works of public art have been throughout the ages, Chicago's 1979 masterwork provides viewers with a powerful launching point for considering broad feminist concerns.

MIRIAM SCHAPIRO After enjoying a thriving career as a hard-edge painter in California in the late 1960s, Toronto-born MIRIAM SCHAPIRO (b. 1923) became fascinated with the hidden metaphors for womanhood she then saw in her abstract paintings. Intrigued by the materials she had used to create a doll's house for her part in Womanhouse, in the 1970s Schapiro began to make huge sewn collages, assembled from fabrics, quilts, buttons, sequins, lace trim, and rickrack collected at antique shows and fairs. She called these works *femmages* to make the point that women had been doing collages using these materials long before Pablo Picasso (FIG. 29-16) introduced them to the art world. *Anatomy of a Kimono* (FIG. 30-34) is one of a series of monumental femmages based on the patterns of Japanese kimonos, fans, and robes. This vast 10-panel composition (more than 52 feet long and almost 7 feet high) repeats the kimono shape in a sumptuous array of fabric fragments.

CINDY SHERMAN After studying painting in Buffalo, CINDY SHERMAN (b. 1954) switched to photography as her primary means of expression. She addresses in her work the way much of Western art presents female beauty for the enjoyment of the "male gaze," a primary focus of contemporary feminist theory, which explores gender as a socially constructed concept. Since 1977, Sherman has produced a series of more than 80 black-and-white photographs called *Untitled Film Stills*. She got the idea for the series after examining soft-core pornography magazines and noting the stereotypical ways they depicted women. She decided to produce her own series of photographs, designing, acting in, directing, and photographing the works. In so doing, she took control of her own image and constructed her own identity, a primary feminist concern.

In works from the series, such as *Untitled Film Still #35* (FIG. 30-35), Sherman appears, often in costume and wig, in a photograph that seems to be a film still. Most of the images in this series recall popular film genres but are sufficiently generic that the viewer cannot relate them to specific movies. Sherman often reveals the constructed nature of these images with the shutter release cable she holds in her hand to take the pictures. (The cord runs across

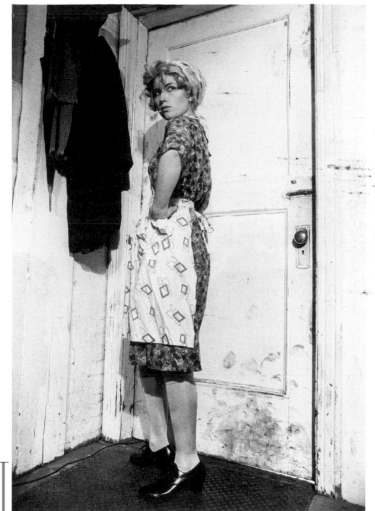

30-35 Cindy Sherman, *Untitled Film Still #35*, 1979. Gelatin silverprint, 10″ × 8″. Private collection. ◼◀

Sherman here assumed a role for one of 80 photographs resembling film stills in which she addressed the way women have been presented in Western art for the enjoyment of the "male gaze."

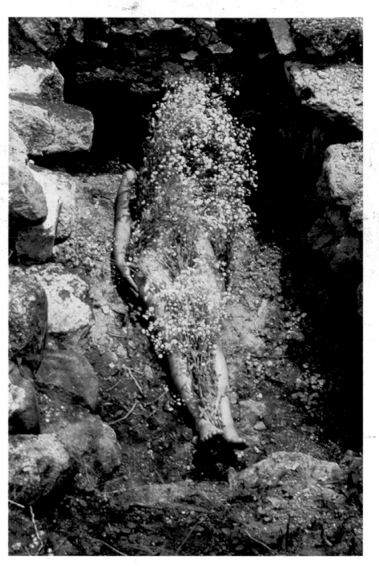

30-36 Ana Mendieta, *Flowers on Body,* 1973. Color photograph of earth/body work with flowers, executed at El Yagul, Mexico. Courtesy of the Estate of Ana Mendieta and Galerie Lelong, New York.

In this earth/body sculpture, Mendieta appears covered with flowers in a grave- or womblike cavity to address issues of birth and death, as well as the human connection to the earth.

the floor in *#35*.) Although the artist is still the object of the viewer's gaze in these images, the identity is one she alone chose to assume.

ANA MENDIETA Cuban-born artist Ana Mendieta (1948–1985) also used her body as a component in her artworks. Although gender issues concerned her, Mendieta's art also dealt with issues of spirituality and cultural heritage. The artist's best-known series, *Silueta* (Silhouettes), consists of approximately 200 earth/body works completed between 1973 and 1980. These works represented Mendieta's attempt to carry on, as she described, "a dialogue between the landscape and the female body (based on my own silhouette)."[22]

Flowers on Body (FIG. **30-36**) is a documentary photograph of the first of the earth/body sculptures in the *Silueta* series. In this work, Mendieta appears covered with flowers in an earthen, grave- or womblike cavity. Executed at El Yagul, a Mexican archaeological site, the work speaks to the issues of birth and death, the female experience of childbirth, and the human connection to the earth. Objects and locations from nature play an important role in Mendieta's art. She explained the centrality of this connection to nature:

I believe this has been a direct result of my having been torn from my homeland during my adolescence. I am overwhelmed by the feeling of having been cast from the womb (nature). My art is the way I re-establish the bonds that unite me to the universe. It is a return to the maternal source. Through my earth/body sculptures I become one with the earth.[23]

Beyond their sensual, moving presence, Mendieta's works also generate a palpable spiritual force. In longing for her homeland, she sought the cultural understanding and acceptance of the spiritual powers inherent in nature that modern Western societies often seem to reject in favor of scientific and technological developments. Mendieta's art is lyrical and passionate and operates at the intersection of cultural, spiritual, physical, and feminist concerns.

HANNAH WILKE Another artist who used her nude body as her medium was New Yorker Hannah Wilke (1940–1993), who studied art at Temple University. Enlarging images from her mixed media

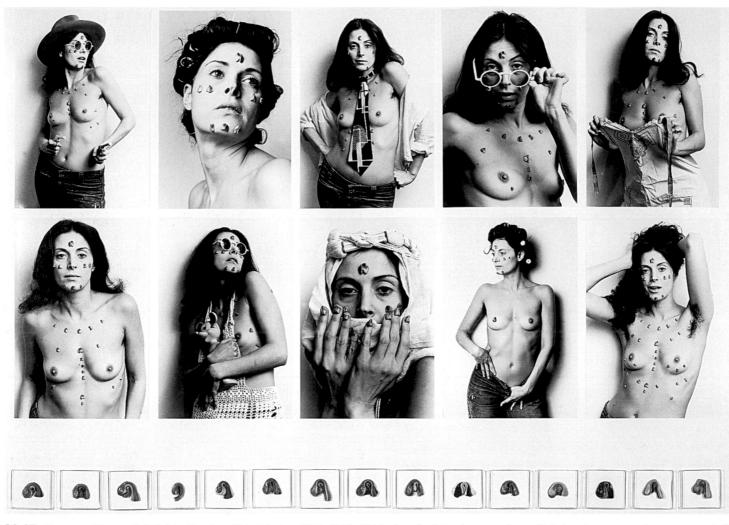

1 ft.

30-37 HANNAH WILKE, *S.O.S. Starification Object Series,* 1974–1982. 10 black and white photographs and 16 chewing gum sculptures mounted on ragboard, , 3′ 5″ × 4′ 10″ framed. © Marsie, Emanuelle, Damon, and Andrew Scharlatt/Licensed by VAGA, New York, NY. Courtesy Ronald Feldman Fine Arts, New York.

In this photographic series, Wilke posed topless decorated with chewing-gum sculptures of vulvas, which allude to female pleasure, but also to pain, because they resemble scars.

installation of 35 photographs, *S.O.S. Starification Object Series, An Adult Game of Mastication* (FIG. **30-37**), 1974–1975, Wilke, in *S.O.S. Starification Object Series,* 1974–1982, presented images of herself that trigger readings simultaneously metaphorical and real, stereotypical and unique, erotic and disconcerting, and that deal with both pleasure and pain. In these 10 black-and-white photographs, Wilke appears topless. In each, pieces of chewed gum shaped into small vulvas decorate her body. While these tiny vaginal sculptures allude to female pleasure, they also appear as scars, suggesting pain. Ultimately, Wilke hoped women would "take control of and have pride in the sensuality of their own bodies and create a sexuality in their own terms, without deferring to concepts degenerated by culture."[24]

MAGDALENA ABAKANOWICZ Not strictly feminist in subject, but created using materials traditionally associated with women, are the sculptures of Polish fiber artist MAGDALENA ABAKANOWICZ (b. 1930). A leader in the exploration of the expressive powers of weaving techniques in large-scale artworks, Abakanowicz gained fame with experimental freestanding figural works expressing the stoic, everyday toughness of the human spirit. For Abakanowicz, fiber materials are deeply symbolic:

I see fiber as the basic element constructing the organic world on our planet, as the greatest mystery of our environment. It is from fiber that all living organisms are built—the tissues of plants and ourselves. . . . Fabric is our covering and our attire. Made with our hands, it is a record of our souls.[25]

Abakanowicz's sculptures are to a great degree reflections of her early life experiences as a member of an aristocratic family disturbed by the dislocations of World War II and its aftermath. Initially attracted to weaving as a medium easily adaptable to the small studio space she had available, Abakanowicz gradually developed huge abstract hangings she called Abakans that suggest organic spaces as well as giant pieces of clothing. She returned to a smaller scale with works based on human forms—*Heads, Seated Figures,* and *Backs*—multiplying each type for exhibition in groups as symbols for the individual in society lost in the crowd yet retaining some distinctiveness.

This impression is especially powerful in *80 Backs* (FIG. **30-38**). Abakanowicz made each piece by pressing layers of natural organic fibers into a plaster mold. Every sculpture depicts the slumping shoulders, back, and arms of a figure of indeterminate sex and

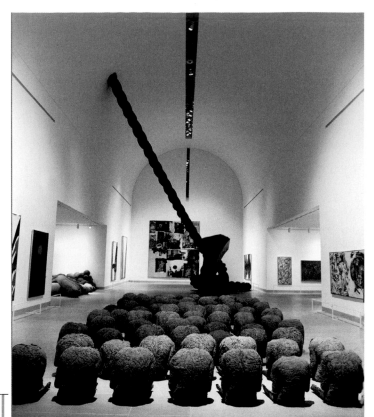

30-38 Magdalena Abakanowicz, *80 Backs,* 1976–1980. Burlap and resin, each figure 2′ 3″ high. Museum of Modern Art, Dallas.

Polish fiber artist Abakanowicz explored the stoic, everyday toughness of the human spirit in this group of nearly identical sculptures that serve as symbols of distinctive individuals lost in the crowd.

rests legless directly on the floor. The repeated pose of the figures in *80 Backs* suggests meditation, submission, and anticipation. Although made from a single mold, the figures achieve a touching sense of individuality because each assumed a slightly different posture as the material dried and because the artist imprinted a different pattern of fiber texture on each.

ARCHITECTURE AND SITE-SPECIFIC ART

Some of the most innovative architects of the first half of the 20th century, most notably Frank Lloyd Wright (FIGS. 29-45, 29-46, and 29-79), Ludwig Mies van der Rohe (FIG. 29-67), and Le Corbusier (FIG. 29-68), concluded their long and productive careers in the postwar period. At the same time, younger architects rose to international prominence, some working in the modernist idiom but others taking architectural design in new "postmodern" directions.

Modernism

In parallel with the progressive movement toward formal abstraction in painting and sculpture in the decades following World War II, modernist architects became increasingly concerned with a formalism stressing simplicity. They articulated this in buildings that retained intriguing organic sculptural qualities, as well as in buildings adhering to a more rigid geometry.

FRANK LLOYD WRIGHT The last great building Frank Lloyd Wright designed was the Solomon R. Guggenheim Museum (FIG. **30-39**) in New York City. Using reinforced concrete almost as a sculptor might use resilient clay, Wright, who often described his architecture as "organic," designed a structure inspired by the spiral of a snail's shell. Wright had introduced curves and circles into some of his plans in the 1930s, and as the architectural historian Peter Blake noted, "The spiral was the next logical step; it is the circle brought into the third and fourth dimensions."[26] Inside the building (FIG. 31-44), the shape of the shell expands toward the top, and a winding interior ramp spirals to connect the gallery bays. A skylight strip embedded in the museum's outer wall provides illumination to the ramp, which visitors can stroll up (or down, if they first take an elevator to the top of the building), viewing the artworks displayed along the gently sloping pathway. Thick walls and the solid organic shape give the building, outside and inside, the sense of turning in on itself, and the long interior viewing area opening onto a 90-foot central well of space creates a sheltered environment, secure from the bustling city outside.

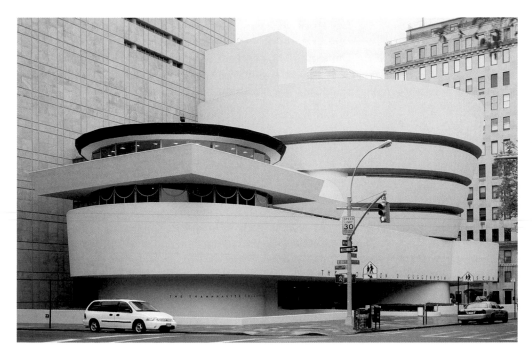

30-39 Frank Lloyd Wright, Solomon R. Guggenheim Museum (looking southeast), New York, 1943–1959. ◼◀

Using reinforced concrete almost as a sculptor might use resilient clay, Wright designed a snail shell–shaped museum with a winding, gently inclined interior ramp for the display of artworks.

LE CORBUSIER Compared with his pristine geometric design for Villa Savoye (FIG. 29-68), the organic forms of Le Corbusier's Notre-Dame-du-Haut (FIG. **30-40**) come as a startling surprise. Completed in 1955 at Ronchamp, France, the chapel attests to the boundless creativity of this great architect. A fusion of architecture and sculpture, the small chapel, which replaced a building destroyed in World War II, occupies a pilgrimage site in the Vosges Mountains. The monumental impression of Notre-Dame-du-Haut seen from afar is somewhat deceptive. Although one massive exterior wall (FIG. 30-40, *top*) contains a pulpit facing a spacious outdoor area for large-scale open-air services on holy days, the interior (FIG. 30-40, *bottom*) holds at most 200 people. The intimate scale, stark and heavy walls, and mysterious illumination (jewel tones cast from the deeply recessed stained-glass windows) give this space an aura reminiscent of a sacred cave or a medieval monastery.

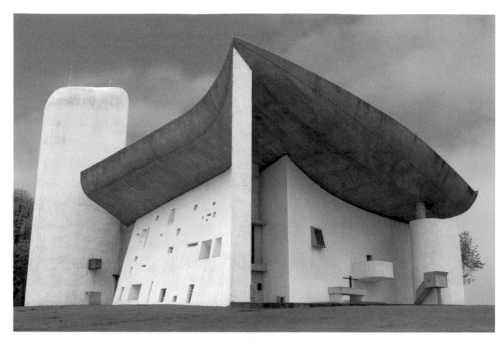

Notre-Dame-du-Haut's structure may look free-form to the untrained eye, but Le Corbusier based it, as did the designers of Romanesque and Gothic cathedrals, on an underlying mathematical system. The pilgrimage church has a frame of steel and metal mesh, which the builders sprayed with concrete and painted white, except for two interior private chapel niches with colored walls and the roof, which Le Corbusier wished to have darken naturally with the passage of time. The roof appears to float freely above the worshipers in their pews (FIG. 30-40, *bottom*), intensifying the quality of mystery in the interior space. In reality, a series of nearly invisible blocks holds up the roof. The mystery of the roof's means of support recalls the reaction to Hagia Sophia's miraculously floating dome (FIG. 9-8) a millennium and a half before in Byzantium. Le Corbusier's preliminary sketches for the building indicate he linked the design with the shape of praying hands, with the wings of a dove (representing both peace and the Holy Spirit), and with the prow of a ship (a reminder the term for

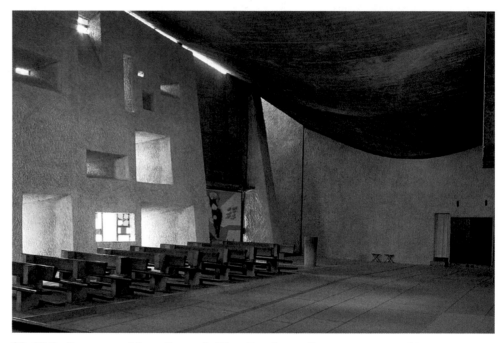

30-40 LE CORBUSIER, Notre-Dame-du-Haut, Ronchamp, France, 1950–1955. *Top:* exterior looking northwest; *bottom:* interior looking southwest. ◼◀

The organic forms of Le Corbusier's mountaintop chapel at Ronchamp present a fusion of architecture and sculpture. The heavy sprayed concrete walls enclose an intimate and mysteriously lit interior that has the aura of a sacred cave.

the central aisle in a traditional basilican church is *nave*—Latin for "ship"). Le Corbusier hoped that in the mystical interior he created and in the rolling hills around the church, men and women would reflect on the sacred and the natural. No one who has visited Notre-Dame-du-Haut, whether on a bright sunlit day or in a thundering storm, has come away unmoved.

EERO SAARINEN Dramatic, sweeping, curvilinear rooflines are also characteristic features of the buildings designed by Finnish-born architect EERO SAARINEN (1910–1961). One of his signature buildings of the late 1950s is the former Trans World Airlines terminal (now the Jet Blue Airways terminal, FIG. **30-41**) at John F.

Kennedy International Airport in New York. The terminal, which Saarinen based on the theme of motion, consists of two immense concrete shells split down the middle and slightly rotated, giving the building a fluid curved outline that fits its corner site. The shells immediately suggest expansive wings and flight. Saarinen also designed everything on the interior, including the furniture, ventilation ducts, and signboards, with this same curvilinear vocabulary in mind.

JOERN UTZON Saarinen was responsible for selecting the Danish architect JOERN UTZON (1918–2008) to build the Sydney Opera House (FIG. **30-42**) in Australia. Utzon's design is a bold

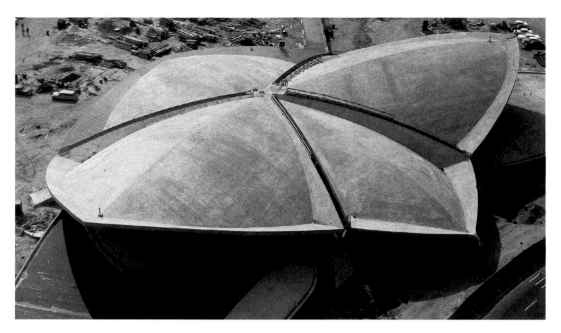

30-41 Eero Saarinen, Terminal 5 (Jet Blue Airways terminal, formerly the Trans World Airlines terminal; looking southeast), John F. Kennedy International Airport, New York, 1956–1962.

Saarinen based the design for this airline terminal on the theme of motion. The concrete-and-glass building's dramatic, sweeping, curvilinear rooflines suggest expansive wings and flight.

composition of organic forms on a colossal scale. Utzon worked briefly with Frank Lloyd Wright at Taliesin (Wright's Wisconsin residence), and the style of the Sydney Opera House resonates distantly with the graceful curvature of New York's Guggenheim Museum (FIG. 30-39). Clusters of immense concrete shells—the largest is 200 feet tall—rise from massive platforms and soar to delicate peaks. Recalling at first the *ogival* (pointed) shapes of Gothic vaults, the shells also suggest both the buoyancy of seabird wings and the billowing sails of the tall ships of the European settlers who emigrated to Australia in the 18th and 19th centuries. These architectural metaphors are appropriate to the harbor surrounding Bennelong Point, whose bedrock foundations support the building. Utzon's matching of the structure with its site and atmosphere adds to the organic nature of the design.

Though construction of the building began in 1959, completion of the opera house had to wait until 1972, primarily because Utzon's daring design required construction technology not yet developed. Today, the opera house is Sydney's defining symbol, a monument of civic pride that functions as the city's cultural center. In addition to the opera auditorium, the complex houses auxiliary halls and rooms for concerts, the performing arts, motion pictures, lectures, art exhibitions, and conventions.

MIES VAN DER ROHE Sculpturesque building design was not the only manifestation of postwar modernist architecture. From the mid-1950s through the 1970s, other architects created massive, sleek, and geometrically rigid buildings. They designed most of these structures following Bauhaus architect Mies van der Rohe's contention

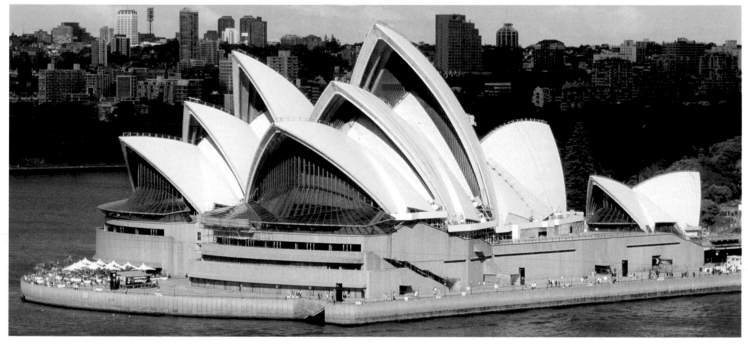

30-42 Joern Utzon, Sydney Opera House (looking southeast), Sydney, Australia, 1959–1972.

The soaring clusters of concrete shells of Utzon's opera house on an immense platform in Sydney's harbor suggest both the buoyancy of seabird wings and the billowing sails of tall ships.

that "less is more." Many of these more Minimalist designs are powerful, heroic presences in the urban landscape that effectively symbolize the giant corporations often inhabiting them.

The purest example of these corporate skyscrapers is the mid-1950s rectilinear glass-and-bronze Seagram Building (FIG. **30-43**) in Manhattan designed by Mies van der Rohe and American architect Philip Johnson (FIG. 30-46). By this time, the concrete-steel-and-glass towers pioneered by Louis Sullivan (FIGS. 28-40, 28-40A, and 28-41) and carried further by Mies van der Rohe himself (FIG. 29-67) had become a familiar sight in cities throughout the world. Appealing in its structural logic and clarity, the style, easily imitated, quickly became the norm for postwar commercial high-rise buildings. The architects of the Seagram Building deliberately designed it as a thin shaft, leaving the front quarter of its midtown site as an open pedestrian plaza. The tower appears to rise from the pavement on stilts. Glass walls even surround the recessed lobby. The building's recessed structural elements make it appear to have a glass skin, interrupted only by the thin strips of bronze anchoring the windows. The bronze metal and the amber glass windows give the tower a richness found in few of its neighbors. Mies van der Rohe and Johnson carefully planned every detail of the Seagram Building, inside and out, to create an elegant whole. They even designed the interior and exterior lighting to make the edifice an impressive sight both day and night.

SKIDMORE, OWINGS & MERRILL The architectural firm SKIDMORE, OWINGS & MERRILL (SOM), perhaps the purest proponent of Miesian-inspired structures, designed a number of these simple rectilinear glass-sheathed buildings, and SOM's success indicates the popularity of this building type. By 1970, the company comprised more than a thousand architects and had offices in New York, Chicago, San Francisco, Portland, and Washington, D.C. In 1974, the firm completed the Sears Tower (FIG. **30-44**), a mammoth corporate building in Chicago. Consisting of nine clustered shafts soaring vertically, this 110-floor building provides offices for more than 12,000 workers. Original plans called for 104 stories, but the architects acquiesced to Sears's insistence on making the building the tallest (measured to the structural top) in the world at the time. The tower's size, coupled with the black

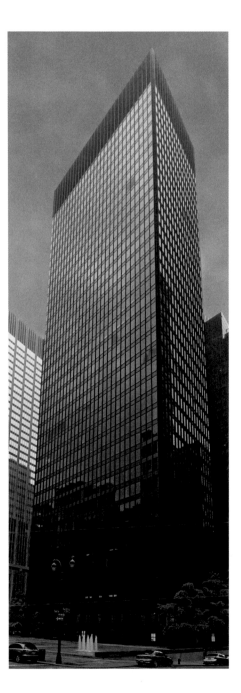

30-43 LUDWIG MIES VAN DER ROHE and PHILIP JOHNSON, Seagram Building (looking northeast), New York, 1956–1958. ◼◀

Massive, sleek, and geometrically rigid, this modernist skyscraper has a bronze and glass skin masking its concrete-and-steel frame. The giant corporate tower appears to rise from the pavement on stilts.

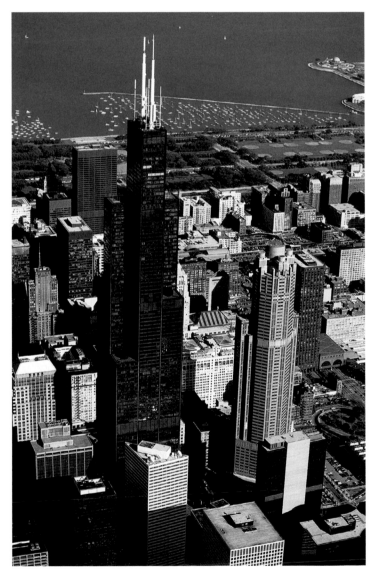

30-44 SKIDMORE, OWINGS & MERRILL, Willis Tower (formerly Sears Tower; looking east), Chicago, 1974. ◼◀

Consisting of nine black aluminum and smoked glass shafts soaring to 110 stories, the Willis (Sears) Tower dominates Chicago's skyline. It was the world's tallest building at the time of its construction.

aluminum sheathing it and the smoked glass, establish a dominant presence in a city of many corporate skyscrapers—exactly the image Sears executives wanted to project.

Postmodernism

The restrictiveness of modernist architecture and the impersonality and sterility of many modernist structures eventually led to a rejection of modernism's authority in architecture. Along with the apparent lack of responsiveness to the unique character of the cities and neighborhoods in which modernist architects built their structures, these reactions ushered in *postmodernism*, one of the most dramatic developments in later-20th-century architecture as well as in contemporary painting and sculpture (see Chapter 31). Postmodernism in architecture is not a unified style. It is a widespread cultural phenomenon far more encompassing and accepting than the more rigid confines of modernist practice. In contrast to the simplicity of modernist architecture, the terms most often invoked to describe postmodern architecture are pluralism, complexity, and eclecticism. Whereas the modernist program was reductive, the postmodern vocabulary of the 1970s and 1980s was expansive and inclusive.

Among the first to explore this new direction in architecture were Jane Jacobs (1916–2006) and Robert Venturi (FIG. 30-48). In their influential books *The Death and Life of Great American Cities* (Jacobs, 1961) and *Complexity and Contradiction in Architecture* (Venturi, 1966), Jacobs and Venturi argued that the uniformity and anonymity of modernist architecture (in particular, the corporate skyscrapers dominating many urban skylines) were unsuited to human social interaction and that diversity is the great advantage of urban life. Postmodern architects accepted, indeed embraced, the messy and chaotic nature of big-city life.

When designing these varied buildings, many postmodern architects consciously selected past architectural elements or references and juxtaposed them with contemporary elements or fashioned them of high-tech materials, thereby creating a dialogue between past and present. Postmodern architecture incorporates not only traditional architectural references but references to mass cul-ture and popular imagery as well. This was precisely the "complexity and contradiction" Venturi referred to in the title of his book.

CHARLES MOORE A clear example of the eclecticism and the dialogue between traditional and contemporary elements found in postmodern architecture is the Piazza d'Italia (FIG. **30-45**) by American architect CHARLES MOORE (1925–1993), who was educated at the University of Michigan and Princeton University and served as dean of the Yale School of Architecture from 1965 to 1970. Designed in the late 1970s in New Orleans, the Piazza d'Italia is an open plaza dedicated to the city's Italian-American community. Appropriately, Moore selected elements relating specifically to Italian history, all the way back to ancient Roman culture.

Backed up against a contemporary high-rise building and set off from urban traffic patterns, the Piazza d'Italia is accessible to pedestrians from three sides through gateways of varied design. The approaches lead to an open circular area partially formed by short segments of colonnades arranged in staggered concentric arcs, which direct the eye to the focal point of the composition—an *exedra*. This recessed area on a raised platform serves as a *rostrum* (speaker's platform) during the annual festivities of Saint Joseph's Day. Moore inlaid the piazza's pavement with a map of Italy centered on Sicily, from which the majority of the city's Italian families originated. From there, the map's Italian "boot" moves in the direction of the steps that ascend the rostrum and correspond to the Alps.

The piazza's most immediate historical reference is to the Roman forum (FIGS. 7-12 and 7-44). However, its circular form alludes to the ideal geometric figure of the Renaissance (FIGS. 22-3A and 22-21). The irregular placement of the concentrically arranged colonnade fragments inserts a note of instability into the design reminiscent of Mannerism (FIG. 22-55). Illusionistic devices, such as the continuation of the piazza's pavement design (apparently through a building and out into the street), are Baroque in character (FIG. 24-4). Moore incorporated all of the classical orders—most with whimsical modifications. Nevertheless, challenging the piazza's historical character are modern features, such as the stainless-steel columns and capitals, neon collars around the column necks, and neon lights framing various parts of the exedra.

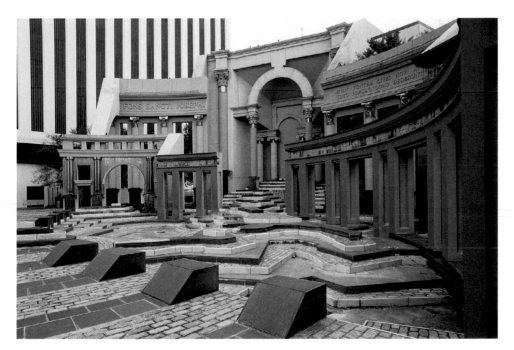

30-45 CHARLES MOORE, Piazza d'Italia (looking northeast), New Orleans, 1976–1980.

Moore's circular postmodern Italian plaza incorporates elements drawn from ancient Roman architecture with the instability of Mannerist designs and modern stainless-steel columns with neon collars.

Philip Johnson on Postmodern Architecture

Philip Johnson, who died in 2005 at age 98, had a distinguished career spanning almost the entire 20th century, during which he transformed himself from a modernist closely associated with Mies van der Rohe (FIG. 30-43) into one of the leading postmodernists, whose AT&T (now Sony) Building (FIG. 30-46) in New York City remains an early icon of postmodernism. In the following passages, Johnson commented on his early "Miesian" style and about the incorporation of various historical styles in postmodernist buildings.

> My eyes are set by the Miesian tradition . . . The continuity with my Miesian approach also shows through in my classicism. . . . [But in] 1952, about the same time that my whole generation did, I became very restless. . . . In the last decade there has been such a violent switch that it is almost embarrassing. But it isn't a switch, so much as a centrifugal splintering of architecture, to a degree that I don't think has been seen in the past few hundred years. Perfectly responsible architects build, even in one year, buildings that you cannot believe are done by the same person.*
>
> Structural honesty seems to me one of the bugaboos that we should free ourselves from very quickly. The Greeks with their marble columns imitating wood, and covering up the roofs inside! The Gothic designers with their wooden roofs above to protect their delicate vaulting. And Michelangelo, the greatest architect in history, with his Mannerist column! There is only one absolute today and this is change. There are no rules, surely no certainties in any of the arts. There is only the feeling of a wonderful freedom, of endless possibilities to investigate, of endless past years of historically great buildings to enjoy.†

*Quoted in Paul Heyer, *Architects on Architecture: New Directions in America* (New York: Van Nostrand Reinhold, 1993), 285–286.
†Ibid., 279.

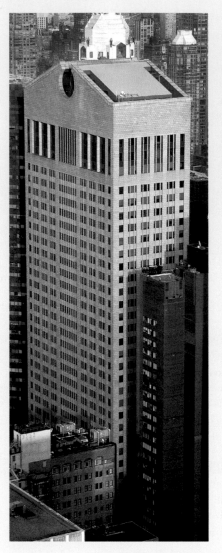

30-46 PHILIP JOHNSON and JOHN BURGEE (with SIMMONS ARCHITECTS), Sony Building (formerly AT&T Building; looking southwest), New York, 1978–1984.

In a startling shift of style, modernist Johnson (FIG. 30-43) designed this postmodern skyscraper with more granite than glass and with a variation on a classical pediment as the crowning motif.

In sum, Moore designed the Piazza d'Italia as a complex conglomeration of symbolic, historical, and geographic allusions—some overt and others obscure. Although the piazza's specific purpose was to honor the Italian community of New Orleans, its more general purpose was to revitalize an urban area by becoming a focal point and an architectural setting for the social activities of neighborhood residents. Unfortunately, the piazza suffered extensive damage during Hurricane Katrina in 2005.

PHILIP JOHNSON Even architects instrumental in the proliferation of the modernist idiom embraced postmodernism. Early in his career, PHILIP JOHNSON (1906–2005), for example, had been a leading proponent of modernism and worked with Mies van der Rohe on the design of the Seagram Building (FIG. 30-43). Johnson even served as director of the Department of Architecture at New York's Museum of Modern Art, the bastion of modernism, in 1930–1934 and 1946–1954. Yet he made one of the most startling shifts of style in 20th-century architecture, eventually moving away

from the severe geometric formalism exemplified by the Seagram Building to a classical transformation of it in his AT&T (American Telephone and Telegraph) Building (now the Sony Building, FIG. 30-46) in New York City. Architect JOHN BURGEE (b. 1933) codesigned it with assistance from the firm SIMMONS ARCHITECTS. This structure was influential in turning architectural taste and practice away from modernism and toward postmodernism—from organic "concrete sculpture" and the rigid "glass box" to elaborate shapes, motifs, and silhouettes freely adapted from historical styles (see "Philip Johnson on Postmodern Architecture," above).

The 660-foot-high slab of the former AT&T Building is mostly granite. Johnson reduced the window space to some 30 percent of the structure, in contrast to modernist glass-sheathed skyscrapers. His design of its exterior elevation is classically tripartite, having an arcaded base and arched portal; a tall, shaftlike body segmented by slender *mullions* (vertical elements dividing a window); and a crowning pediment broken by an *orbiculum* (a disklike opening). The arrangement refers to the base, column, and entablature system

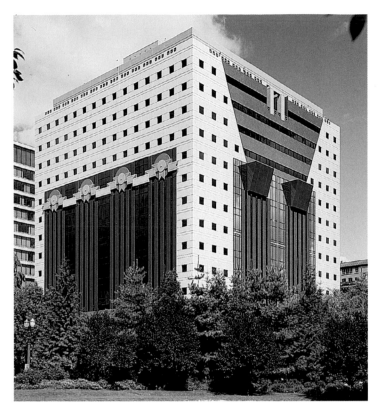

30-47 MICHAEL GRAVES, Portland Building (looking northwest), Portland, 1980.

In this early example of postmodern architecture, Graves reasserted the horizontality and solidity of the wall. He drew attention to the mural surfaces through polychromy and ornamental motifs.

wave of postmodernism than did his AT&T tower. The Portland Building (FIG. **30-47**) by Indianapolis-born architect MICHAEL GRAVES (b. 1934) reasserts the wall's horizontality against the verticality of the tall, window-filled shaft. Graves favored the square's solidity and stability, making it the main body of his composition (echoed in the windows), which rests upon a wider base and carries a set-back penthouse crown. Narrow vertical windows tying together seven stories open two paired facades. These support capital-like large hoods on one pair of opposite facades and a frieze of stylized Baroque roundels tied by bands on the other pair. A huge painted keystone motif joins five upper levels on one facade pair, and painted surfaces further define the building's base, body, and penthouse levels.

The modernist purist surely would not welcome the ornamental wall, color painting, or symbolic reference. These features, taken together, raised an even greater storm of criticism than greeted the Sydney Opera House or the AT&T Building. Various critics denounced Graves's Portland Building as "an enlarged jukebox," an "oversized Christmas package," a "marzipan monstrosity," a "histrionic masquerade," and a kind of "pop surrealism." Yet others approvingly noted its classical references as constituting a "symbolic temple" and praised the building as a courageous architectural adventure. Whatever history's verdict will be, the Portland Building, like the AT&T tower, is an early marker of postmodernist innovation that borrowed from the lively, if more-or-less garish, language of pop culture. The night-lit dazzle of entertainment sites such as Las Vegas, and the carnival colors, costumes, and fantasy of theme-park props, all lie behind the Portland Building design, which many critics regard as a vindication of architectural populism against the pretension of modernist elitism.

of classical architecture (FIG. 5-13). More specifically, the pediment, indented by the circular space, resembles the crown of a typical 18th-century Chippendale high chest of drawers. It rises among the monotonously flat-topped glass towers of the New York skyline as an ironic rebuke to the rigid uniformity of modernist architecture.

MICHAEL GRAVES Philip Johnson at first endorsed, then disapproved of, a building that rode considerably farther on the

ROBERT VENTURI As coauthor of *Learning from Las Vegas* (1972), Philadelphia native ROBERT VENTURI (b. 1925) codified these ideas about populism and postmodernism. An early example of Venturi's work is the house (FIG. **30-48**) he designed in 1962 for his mother. A fundamental axiom of modernism is that a building's form must arise directly and logically from its function and structure. Against this rule, Venturi asserted form should be separate from function and structure. Thus, the Vanna Venturi house has an

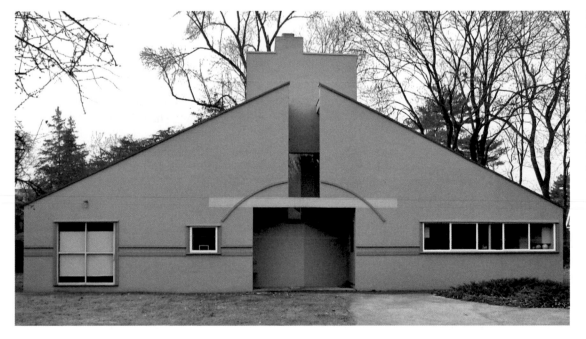

30-48 ROBERT VENTURI, Vanna Venturi House, Chestnut Hill, Pennsylvania, 1962.

Venturi asserted form should be separate from function and structure. In this house, the facade features an oversized roof recalling a classical temple, but split open at the middle and combined with an arch over the door.

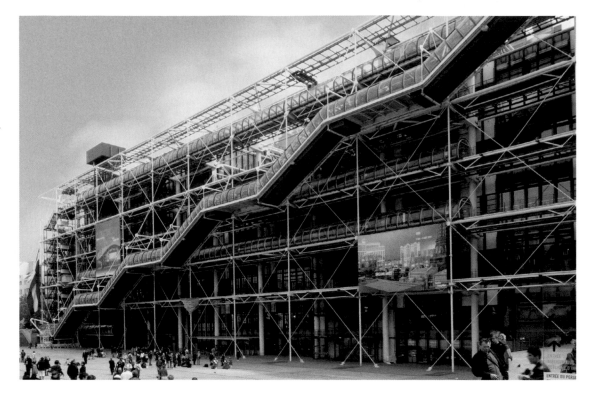

30-49 RICHARD ROGERS and RENZO PIANO, Centre Georges Pompidou (the "Beaubourg," looking northeast), Paris, France, 1977. ◼◀

The architects fully exposed the anatomy of this six-level building, as in the century-earlier Crystal Palace (FIG. 27-47), and color-coded the internal parts according to function, as in a factory.

oversized gable roof that recalls classical temple design more than domestic architecture. However, the gable has a missing central section, which reveals the house's "chimney" (a penthouse suite). Moreover, Venturi inserted an arch motif over the doorway's lintel, and the placement of the windows violates the symmetry of both classical and modernist design.

ROGERS AND PIANO During their short-lived partnership, British architect RICHARD ROGERS (b. 1933) and Italian architect RENZO PIANO (b. 1937) used motifs and techniques from ordinary industrial buildings in their design for the Georges Pompidou National Center of Art and Culture in Paris, known popularly as the "Beaubourg" (FIG. **30-49**). The architects fully exposed the anatomy of this six-level building, which is a kind of updated version of the Crystal Palace (FIG. 27-47), and made its "metabolism" visible. They color-coded pipes, ducts, tubes, and corridors according to function (red for the movement of people, green for water, blue for air-conditioning, and yellow for electricity), much as in a sophisticated factory.

Critics who deplore the Beaubourg's vernacular qualities disparagingly refer to the complex as a "cultural supermarket" and point out that its exposed entrails require excessive maintenance to protect them from the elements. Nevertheless, the building has been immensely popular with visitors since it opened. The flexible interior spaces and the colorful structural body provide a festive environment for the crowds flowing through the building and enjoying its art galleries, industrial design center, library, science and music centers, conference rooms, research and archival facilities, movie theaters, rest areas, and restaurant (which looks down and through the building), as well as dramatic panoramas of Paris from its terrace. The sloping plaza in front of the main entrance has become part of the local scene. Peddlers, street performers, Parisians, and tourists fill this square at almost all hours of the day and night. The kind of secular activity that once occurred in the open spaces in front of cathedral portals now takes place next to a center for culture and popular entertainment.

Environmental and Site-Specific Art

One of the most exciting developments in postwar art and architecture has been *Environmental Art,* sometimes called *earthworks.* Environmental Art stands at the intersection of architecture and sculpture. It emerged as a major form of artistic expression in the 1960s and includes a wide range of artworks, most of which are *site-specific* (created for a unique location) and in the open air. Many artists associated with the Environmental Art movement also used natural or organic materials, including the land itself. It is no coincidence this art form developed during a period of increased concern for the environment. The ecology movement of the 1960s and 1970s aimed to publicize and combat escalating pollution, depletion of natural resources, and the dangers of toxic waste. The problems of public aesthetics (for example, litter, urban sprawl, and compromised scenic areas) were also at issue. Widespread concern in the United States about the environment led to the passage of the National Environmental Policy Act in 1969 and the creation of the federal Environmental Protection Agency. Environmental artists used their art to call attention to the landscape and, in so doing, were part of this national dialogue.

As an innovative artistic genre challenging traditional assumptions about art making, Environmental Art clearly has an avant-garde, progressive dimension. But as Pop artists did in their time, Environmental artists insist on moving art out of the rarefied atmosphere of museums and galleries and into the public sphere. Most encourage spectator interaction with their works. Ironically, the remote locations of many earthworks have limited public access.

ROBERT SMITHSON One of the pioneering Environmental artists was New Jersey–born ROBERT SMITHSON (1938–1973), who used industrial construction equipment to manipulate vast quantities of earth and rock on isolated sites. Smithson's best-known project is *Spiral Jetty* (FIG. **30-50**), a mammoth 1,500-foot-long coil of black basalt, limestone rocks, and earth extending out into Great Salt Lake in Utah. As he was driving by the lake one

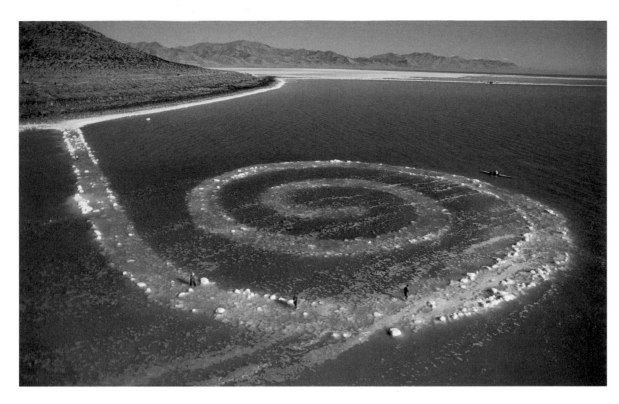

day, Smithson came across some abandoned mining equipment, left there by a company that had tried and failed to extract oil from the site. Smithson saw this as a testament to the enduring power of nature and the inability of humans to conquer it. He decided to create an artwork in the lake that ultimately became a monumental spiral curving out from the shoreline and running 1,500 linear feet into the water. Smithson insisted on designing his work in response to the location itself. He wanted to avoid the arrogance of an artist merely imposing an unrelated concept on the site. The spiral idea grew from Smithson's first impression of the location. Then, while researching Great Salt Lake, Smithson discovered that the molecular structure of the salt crystals coating the rocks at the water's edge is spiral in form.

> As I looked at the site, it reverberated out to the horizons only to suggest an immobile cyclone while flickering light made the entire landscape appear to quake. A dormant earthquake spread into the fluttering stillness, into a spinning sensation without movement. The site was a rotary that enclosed itself in an immense roundness. From that gyrating space emerged the possibility of the Spiral Jetty.[27]

Smithson not only recorded *Spiral Jetty* in photographs, but also filmed its construction in a movie describing the forms and life of the whole site. The photographs and film have become increasingly important, because fluctuations in Great Salt Lake's water level often place *Spiral Jetty* underwater. Smithson tragically died at age 35 in a plane crash while surveying a site for a new earthwork in Amarillo, Texas.

PERFORMANCE AND CONCEPTUAL ART AND NEW MEDIA

Environmental Art, although a singular artistic phenomenon, typifies postwar developments in the art world in redefining the nature of an "artwork" and expanding the range of works artists and the public at large consider "art." Some of the new types of artworks are the result of the invention of new media, such as computers and video cameras. But the new art forms also reflect avant-garde artists' continued questioning of the status quo.

Performance Art

An important new artistic genre that emerged in the decades following World War II was *Performance Art*. Performance artists replace traditional stationary artworks with movements, gestures, and sounds performed before an audience, whose members sometimes participate in the performance. The informal and spontaneous events Performance artists staged anticipated the rebellion and youthful exuberance of the 1960s and at first pushed art outside the confines of mainstream art institutions (museums and galleries). Performance Art also served as an antidote to the pretentiousness of most traditional art objects and challenged art's function as a commodity. In the later 1960s, however, museums commissioned performances with increasing frequency, thereby neutralizing much of the subversiveness characteristic of this new art form. Unfortunately, because the earliest Performance artists created their works before the widespread availability of inexpensive handheld video cameras, the only records of their performances are the documentary photographs taken during the events. Photographs are unsatisfying, if invaluable, records because they lack the element of time integral to Performance Art.

JOHN CAGE Many of the artists instrumental in the development of Performance Art were students or associates of the charismatic American teacher and composer John Cage (1912–1992). Cage encouraged his students at both the New School for Social Research in New York and Black Mountain College in North Carolina to link their art directly with life. He brought to music composition some of the ideas of Duchamp and of Eastern philosophy. Cage used methods such as chance to avoid the closed structures marking traditional music and, in his view, separating it from the unpredictable and multilayered qualities of daily existence. For

Carolee Schneemann on Painting, Performance Art, and Art History

Born in Pennsylvania, Carolee Schneemann (FIG. 30-51) studied painting at Bard College and the University of Illinois before settling in New York City in 1962, where she became one of the pioneering Performance artists of the 1960s. In notes she wrote in 1962–1963, Schneemann reflected on the nature of art production and contrasted her kinetic works with more traditional art forms.

> Environments, happenings—concretions—are an extension of my painting-constructions which often have moving (motorized) sections. . . . [But, the] steady exploration and repeated viewing which the eye is required to make with my painting-constructions is reversed in the performance situation where the spectator is overwhelmed with changing recognitions, carried emotionally by a flux of evocative actions and led or held by the specified time sequence which marks the duration of a performance. In this way the audience is actually *visually* more *passive* than when confronting a . . . "still" work . . . With paintings, constructions and sculptures the viewers are able to carry out repeated examinations of the work, to select and vary viewing positions (to walk with the eye), to touch surfaces and to freely indulge responses to areas of color and texture at their chosen speed.*

Readers of this book will also take special interest in Schneemann's 1975 essay entitled "Woman in the Year 2000," in which she envisioned what introductory art history courses would be like at the beginning of the 21st century:

> By the year 2000 [every] young woman will study Art Istory [sic] courses enriched by the inclusion, discovery, and re-evaluation of works by women artists: works (and lives) until recently buried away, willfully destroyed, [or] ignored.†

A comparison between this 14th edition of *Art through the Ages* and editions published in the 1960s and 1970s will immediately reveal the accuracy of Schneemann's prediction.

*Quoted in Bruce McPherson, ed., *More Than "Meat Joy": Complete Performance Works and Selected Writings* (New Paltz, N.Y.: Documentext, 1979), 10–11.
†Ibid., 198.

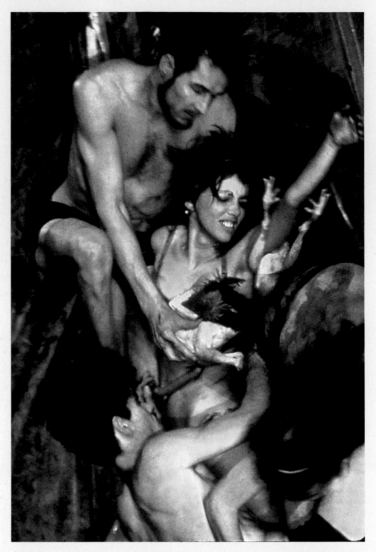

30-51 CAROLEE SCHNEEMANN, *Meat Joy* (performance at Judson Church, New York City), 1964.

In her performances, Schneemann transformed the nature of Performance Art by introducing a feminist dimension through the use of her body (often nude) to challenge traditional gender roles.

example, the score for one of Cage's piano compositions instructs the performer to appear, sit down at the piano, raise the keyboard cover to mark the beginning of the piece, remain motionless at the instrument for 4 minutes and 33 seconds, and then close the keyboard cover, rise, and bow to signal the end of the work. The "music" would be the unplanned sounds and noises (such as coughs and whispers) emanating from the audience during the "performance."

ALLAN KAPROW One of Cage's students in the 1950s was ALLAN KAPROW (1927–2006). Schooled in art history as well as music composition, Kaprow sought to explore the intersection of art and life. He believed, for example, that Jackson Pollock's actions when producing a painting (FIG. 30-7) were more important than the finished painting. This led Kaprow to develop a type of event known as a *Happening*. He described a Happening as

> an assemblage of events performed or perceived in more than one time and place. Its material environments may be constructed, taken over directly from what is available, or altered slightly: just as its activities may be invented or commonplace. A Happening, unlike a stage play, may occur at a supermarket, driving along a highway, under a pile of rags, and in a friend's kitchen, either at once or sequentially. If sequentially, time may extend to more than a year. The Happening is performed according to plan but without rehearsal, audience, or repetition. It is art but seems closer to life.[28]

Happenings were often participatory. One Happening consisted of a constructed setting with partitions on which viewers wrote phrases, while another involved spectators walking on a pile of tires. One of Kaprow's first Happenings, titled *18 Happenings in Six Parts,* took place in 1959 in the Reuben Gallery in New York City. For the event, he divided the gallery space into three sections with translucent plastic sheets. Over the course of the 90-minute piece, performers, including Kaprow's artist friends, bounced balls, read from placards, extended their arms like wings, and played records as slides and lights switched on and off in programmed sequences.

FLUXUS Other Cage students interested in the composer's search to find aesthetic potential in the nontraditional and commonplace formed the *Fluxus* group. Eventually expanding to include European and Japanese artists, this group's performances were more theatrical than Happenings. To distinguish their performances from Happenings, the artists associated with Fluxus coined the term *Events* to describe their work. Events focused on single actions, such as turning a light on and off or watching falling snow—what Fluxus artist La Monte Young (b. 1935) called "the theater of the single event."[29] Events usually took place on a stage separating the performers from the audience but without costumes or added decor. Events were not spontaneous. They followed a compositional "score," which, given the restricted nature of these performances, was short.

CAROLEE SCHNEEMANN Some artists, notably CAROLEE SCHNEEMANN (b. 1939) in the United States and members of the Concrete Art Association (FIG. 34-17) in Japan, produced artworks integrating painting and performance (see "Carolee Schneemann on Painting, Performance Art, and Art History," page 934). Schneemann's self-described "kinetic theater" radically transformed the nature of Performance Art by introducing a feminist dimension through the use of her body (often nude) to challenge "the psychic territorial power lines by which women were admitted to the Art Stud Club."[30] In her 1964 performance, *Meat Joy* (FIG. **30-51**), Schneemann reveled in the taste, smell, and feel of raw sausages, chickens, and fish.

JOSEPH BEUYS The leftist politics of the Fluxus group in the early 1960s strongly influenced German artist JOSEPH BEUYS (1921–1986). Drawing on Happenings and Fluxus, Beuys created actions aimed at illuminating the condition of modern humanity. He wanted to make a new kind of sculptural object that would include "Thinking Forms: how we mould our thoughts or Spoken Forms: how we shape our thoughts into words or Social Sculpture: how we mould and shape the world in which we live."[31]

Beuys's commitment to artworks stimulating thought about art and life derived in part from his experiences as a pilot during the war. After the enemy shot down his plane over the Crimea, nomadic Tatars nursed him back to health by swaddling his body in fat and felt to warm him. Fat and felt thus symbolized healing and regeneration to Beuys, and he incorporated these materials into many of his sculptures and actions, such as *How to Explain Pictures to a Dead Hare* (FIG. **30-52**). This one-person event consisted of stylized actions evoking a sense of mystery and sacred ritual. Beuys appeared in a room hung with his drawings, cradling a dead hare to which he spoke softly. Beuys coated his head with honey covered with gold leaf, creating a shimmering mask. In this manner, he took on the role of the shaman, an individual with special spiritual powers. As a shaman, Beuys believed he was acting to help revolutionize human thought so each human being could become a truly free and creative person.

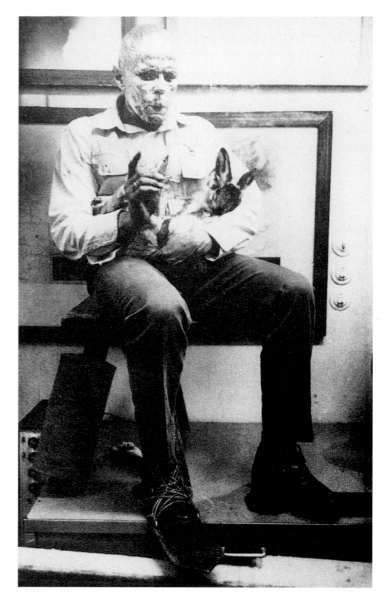

30-52 JOSEPH BEUYS, *How to Explain Pictures to a Dead Hare* (performance at Schmela Gallery, Düsseldorf), 1965. ■◀

In this one-person event, Beuys coated his head with honey and gold leaf. Assuming the role of a shaman, he used stylized actions to evoke a sense of mystery and sacred ritual.

JEAN TINGUELY The paradoxical notion of destruction as an act of creation surfaces in a number of kinetic artworks, most notably in the sculpture of JEAN TINGUELY (1925–1991). Trained as a painter in his native Switzerland, Tinguely gravitated to motion sculpture. In the 1950s, he made a series of *metamatics,* motor-driven devices that produced instant abstract paintings. He programmed these metamatics electronically to act with an anti-mechanical unpredictability when someone inserted a felt-tipped marking pen into a pincer and pressed a button to initiate the pen's motion across a small sheet of paper clipped to an "easel." Participants in his metamatic demonstrations could use different-colored markers in succession and could stop and start the device to achieve some degree of control over the final image. These operations created a series of small works resembling Abstract Expressionist paintings.

In 1960, Tinguely expanded the scale of his work with a kinetic piece designed to "perform" and then destroy itself in the sculpture garden of the Museum of Modern Art in New York City. He created

Tinguely produced motor-driven devices programmed to make instant abstract paintings. To explore the notion of destruction as an act of creation, he designed this one to perform and then destroy itself.

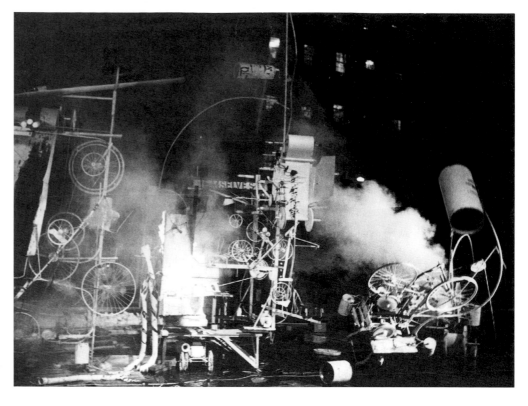

Homage to New York (FIG. 30-53) with the aid of engineer Billy Klüver (1927–2004), who helped him scrounge wheels and other moving objects from a dump near Manhattan. The completed structure, painted white for visibility against the dark night sky, included a player piano modified into a metamatic painting machine, a weather balloon that inflated during the performance, vials of colored smoke, and a host of gears, pulleys, wheels, and other found machine parts.

Homage to New York premiered (and instantly self-destructed) on March 17, 1960, with the state's governor, Nelson Rockefeller (1908–1979), an array of other distinguished guests, and three television crews in attendance. Once Tinguely turned on the machine, smoke poured from its interior and the piano caught fire. Various parts of the machine broke off and rambled away, while one of the metamatics tried but failed to produce an abstract painting. Finally, Tinguely summoned a firefighter to extinguish the blaze and ensure the demise of his artwork-machine with an ax. Like Tinguely's other kinetic sculptures, *Homage to New York* recalls the satiric Dadaist spirit and the droll import of Klee's *Twittering Machine* (FIG. 29-59). But Tinguely deliberately made the wacky behavior of *Homage to New York* more playful and more endearing. Having been given a freedom of eccentric behavior unprecedented in the mechanical world, Tinguely's creations often seemed to behave with the whimsical individuality of human actors.

Conceptual Art

The relentless challenges to artistic convention fundamental to the historical avant-garde reached a logical conclusion with *Conceptual Art* in the late 1960s. Conceptual artists maintained that the "artfulness" of art lay in the artist's idea, rather than in its final expression. These artists regarded the idea, or concept, as the defining component of the artwork. Indeed, some Conceptual artists eliminated the object altogether.

JOSEPH KOSUTH Born in Toledo, Ohio, and educated at the School of Visual Arts in New York City, JOSEPH KOSUTH (b. 1945) was a major proponent of Conceptual Art.

> Like everyone else I inherited the idea of art as a set of *formal* problems. So when I began to re-think my ideas of art, I had to re-think that thinking process . . . [T]he radical shift, was in changing the idea of art itself. . . . It meant you could have an art work which was that *idea* of an art work, and its formal components weren't important. I felt I had found a way to make art without formal

components being confused for an expressionist composition. The expression was in the idea, not the form—the forms were only a device in the service of the idea.[32]

Kosuth's work operates at the intersection of language and vision, dealing with the relationship between the abstract and the concrete. For example, in *One and Three Chairs* (FIG. 30-54),

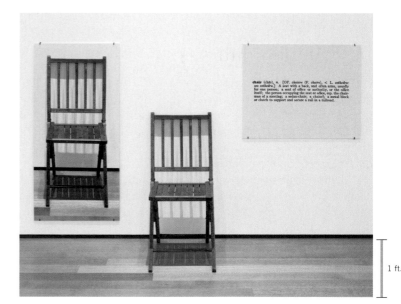

30-54 JOSEPH KOSUTH, *One and Three Chairs*, 1965. Wooden folding chair, photographic copy of a chair, and photographic enlargement of a dictionary definition of a chair; chair, 2′ 8⅜″ × 1′ 2⅞″ × 1′ 8⅞″; photograph, 3′ × 2′ ⅛″; text panel, 2′ × 2′ ⅛″. Museum of Modern Art, New York (Larry Aldrich Foundation Fund).

Conceptual artists regard the concept as an artwork's defining component. To portray "chairness," Kosuth juxtaposed a chair, a photograph of the chair, and a dictionary definition of *chair*.

Kosuth juxtaposed a real chair, a full-scale photograph of the same chair, and an enlarged reproduction of a dictionary definition of the word *chair*. By so doing, the Conceptual artist asked viewers to ponder the notion of what constitutes "chairness."

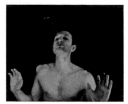

30-55A NAUMAN, *Self-Portrait as Fountain,* 1966–1967.

BRUCE NAUMAN In the mid-1960s in California, Indiana native BRUCE NAUMAN (b. 1941) made his artistic presence known when he abandoned painting and turned to object-making. Since then, his work, produced since 1979 in New Mexico, has been extremely varied. In addition to sculptural pieces constructed from different materials, including neon lights (FIG. **30-55**), rubber, fiberglass, and cardboard, he has also produced photographs (FIG. **30-55A**), films, videos, books, and large room installations, as well as Performance Art. Nauman's work of the 1960s intersected with that of the Conceptual artists, especially in terms of the philosophical exploration that was the foundation of much of his art, and in his interest in language and wordplay.

The True Artist Helps the World by Revealing Mystic Truths (FIG. 30-55) was the first of Nauman's many neon sculptures. He selected neon because he wanted to find a medium that would be identified with a nonartistic function. Determined to discover a way to connect objects with words, he drew on the method outlined in *Philosophical Investigations,* in which the Austrian philosopher Ludwig Wittgenstein (1889–1951) encouraged contradictory and nonsensical arguments. Nauman's neon sculpture spins out an

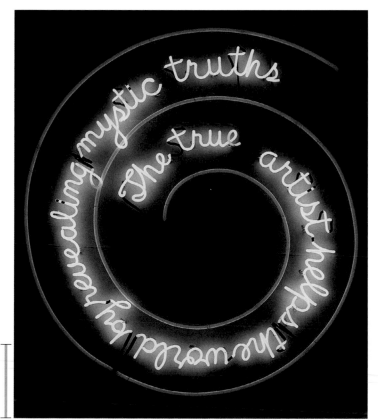

1 ft.

30-55 BRUCE NAUMAN, *The True Artist Helps the World by Revealing Mystic Truths,* 1967. **Neon with glass tubing suspension frame, 4′ 11″ high. Private collection.**

Nauman explores his interest in language and wordplay in his art. He described this Conceptual neon sculpture's emphatic assertion as "a totally silly idea," but an idea he believed.

emphatic assertion, which is also the work's title, but as Nauman explained, "[The statement] was kind of a test—like when you say something out loud to see if you believe it. . . . [I]t was on the one hand a totally silly idea and yet, on the other hand, I believed it."[33]

Other Conceptual artists pursued the notion that the idea is a work of art itself by creating works involving invisible materials, such as inert gases, radioactive isotopes, or radio waves. In each case, viewers must base their understanding of the artwork on what they know about the properties of these materials, rather than on any visible empirical data, and must depend on the artist's linguistic description of the work. Ultimately, the Conceptual artists challenged the very premises of artistic production, pushing art's boundaries to a point where no concrete definition of *art* is possible.

New Media

During the 1960s and 1970s, many avant-garde artists eagerly embraced technologies previously unavailable in their attempt to find new avenues of artistic expression. Among the most popular new media were video recording and computer graphics.

VIDEO Initially, only commercial television studios possessed video equipment, but in the 1960s, with the development of relatively inexpensive portable video recorders and of electronic devices allowing manipulation of recorded video material, artists began to explore in earnest the expressive possibilities of this new technology. In its basic form, video recording involves a special motion-picture camera that captures visible images and translates them into electronic data for display on a video monitor or television screen. Video pictures resemble photographs in the amount of detail they contain, but, like computer graphics, a video image consists of a series of points of light on a grid, giving the impression of soft focus. Viewers looking at television or video art are not aware of the monitor's surface. Instead, fulfilling the ideal of Renaissance artists, they concentrate on the image and look through the glass surface, as through a window, into the "space" beyond. Video images combine the optical realism of photography with the sense that the subjects move in real time in a deep space "inside" the monitor.

NAM JUNE PAIK When video introduced the possibility of manipulating subjects in real time, artists such as Korean-born NAM JUNE PAIK (1932–2006) were eager to work with the medium. Inspired by the ideas of John Cage and after studying music performance, art history, and Eastern philosophy in Korea and Japan, Paik worked with electronic music in Germany in the late 1950s. In 1965, after relocating to New York City, Paik acquired the first inexpensive video recorder sold in Manhattan (the Sony Porta-Pak) and immediately recorded everything he saw out the window of his taxi on the return trip to his studio downtown. Experience acquired as artist-in-residence at television stations WGBH in Boston and WNET in New York allowed him to experiment with the most advanced broadcast video technology.

A grant permitted Paik to collaborate with the gifted Japanese engineer-inventor Shuya Abe (b. 1932) in developing a video synthesizer. This instrument enables artists to manipulate and change the electronic video information in various ways, causing images or parts of images to stretch, shrink, change color, or break up. With the synthesizer, artists can also layer images, inset one image into another, or merge images from various cameras with those from video recorders to make a single visual kaleidoscopic "time-collage." This kind of compositional freedom permitted Paik to

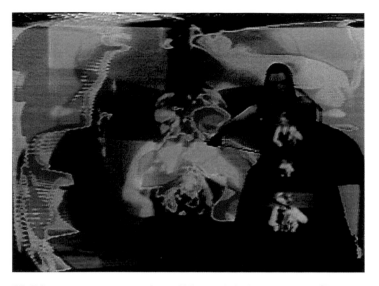

30-56 NAM JUNE PAIK, Video still from *Global Groove,* 1973. ¾″ video-tape, color, sound, 30 minutes. Collection of the artist. ◼◀

Korean-born video artist Paik's best-known work is a cascade of fragmented sequences of performances and commercials intended as a sample of the rich worldwide television menu of the future.

combine his interests in painting, music, Eastern philosophy, global politics for survival, humanized technology, and cybernetics. Paik called his video works "physical music" and said his musical background enabled him to understand time better than could video artists trained in painting or sculpture.

Paik's best-known video work, *Global Groove* (FIG. **30-56**), combines in quick succession fragmented sequences of female tap dancers, poet Allen Ginsberg (1926–1997) reading his work, a performance by Fluxus artist and cellist Charlotte Moorman (1933–1991) using a man's back as her instrument, Pepsi commercials from Japanese television, Korean drummers, and a shot of the Living Theatre group performing a controversial piece called *Paradise Now.* Commissioned originally for broadcast over the United Nations satellite, the cascade of imagery in *Global Groove* gives viewers a glimpse of the rich worldwide television menu Paik predicted would be available in the future—a prediction that has been fulfilled with the advent of affordable cable and satellite television service.

COMPUTER GRAPHICS Perhaps the most promising new medium for creating and manipulating illusionistic three-dimensional forms is computer graphics. This new medium uses light to make images and, like photography, can incorporate specially recorded camera images. Unlike video recording, computer graphic art enables artists to work with wholly invented forms, as painters can. Developed during the 1960s and 1970s, this technology opened up new possibilities for both abstract and figural art. It involves

electronic programs dividing the surface of the computer monitor's cathode-ray tube into a grid of tiny boxes called "picture elements," or *pixels.* Artists can electronically address pixels individually to create a design, much as knitting or weaving patterns have a grid matrix as a guide for making a design in fabric. Once created, parts of a computer graphic design can be changed quickly through an electronic program, enabling artists to revise or duplicate shapes in the design and to manipulate at will the color, texture, size, number, and position of any desired detail. Computer graphics pictures appear in luminous color on the cathode-ray tube. The effect suggests a view into a vast world existing inside the tube.

DAVID EM One of the pioneering artists working in this electronic painting mode, DAVID EM (b. 1952) uses what he terms *computer imaging* to fashion fantastic imaginary landscapes. These have an eerily believable existence within the "window" of the computer monitor. When he was artist-in-residence at the California Institute of Technology's Jet Propulsion Laboratory, Em created brilliantly colored scenes of alien worlds using the laboratory's advanced computer graphics equipment. He also had access to software programs developed to create computer graphics simulations of NASA's missions in outer space. Creating images with the computer afforded Em great flexibility in manipulating simple geometric shapes—shrinking or enlarging them, stretching or reversing them, repeating them, adding texture to their surfaces, and creating the illusion of light and shadow. In images such as *Nora* (FIG. **30-57**), Em created futuristic geometric versions of Surrealistic dreamscapes whose forms seem familiar and strange at the same time. The illusion of space in these works is immensely vivid and seductive. It almost seems possible to wander through the tubelike foreground "frame" and up the inclined foreground plane or to hop aboard the hovering globe at the lower left for a journey through the strange patterns and textures of this mysterious labyrinthine setting.

AFTER 1980 The decades following the conclusion of World War II were unparalleled in the history of art through the ages for innovation in form and content and for the development of new media. Those exciting trends have continued unabated since 1980—and with an increasingly international dimension that will be explored in Chapter 31.

30-57 DAVID EM, *Nora,* 1979. Computer-generated color photograph, 1′ 5″ × 1′ 11″. Private collection. ◼◀

Unlike video recording, computer graphic art enables the creation of wholly invented forms, as in painting. Em builds fantastic digital images of imaginary landscapes out of tiny boxes called pixels.

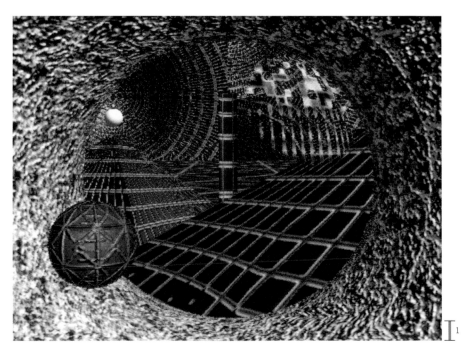

1 in.

MODERNISM AND POSTMODERNISM IN EUROPE AND AMERICA, 1945 TO 1980

PAINTING, SCULPTURE, AND PHOTOGRAPHY

I The art of the decades following World War II reflects cultural upheaval—the rejection of traditional values, the civil rights and feminist movements, and the new consumer society.

I The first major postwar avant-garde art movement was Abstract Expressionism, which championed an artwork's formal elements rather than its subject. Gestural abstractionists, such as Pollock and de Kooning, sought expressiveness through energetically applied pigment. Chromatic abstractionists, such as Rothko, struck emotional chords through large areas of pure color.

I Post-Painterly Abstraction promoted a cool rationality in contrast to Abstract Expressionism's passion. Both hard-edge painters, such as Kelly and Stella, and color-field painters, such as Frankenthaler and Louis, pursued purity in art by emphasizing the flatness of pigment on canvas.

I Pop artists, such as Johns, Lichtenstein, and Warhol, turned away from abstraction to the representation of subjects grounded in popular culture—flags, comic strips, Coca-Cola bottles—sometimes employing commercial printing techniques.

I Riley and other Op artists sought to produce optical illusions of motion and depth using only geometric forms on two-dimensional surfaces.

I Superrealists, such as Flack, Close, and Hanson—kindred spirits to Pop artists in many ways—created paintings and sculptures featuring scrupulous fidelity to optical fact.

I The leading sculptural movement of this period was Minimalism. Tony Smith and Judd created artworks consisting of simple and unadorned geometric shapes to underscore the "objecthood" of their sculptures.

I Arbus and White represent the two poles of photography in the postwar period—documentary photography and art photography.

I Many artists pursued social agendas in their work. Postwar feminist artists include Chicago, whose *Dinner Party* honors important women throughout history and features crafts traditionally associated with women; Sherman, who explored the "male gaze" in her photographs resembling film stills; and Mendieta and Wilke, whose bodies were their subjects.

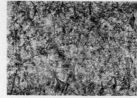

Pollock, *Lavender Mist*, 1950

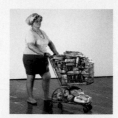

Hanson, *Supermarket Shopper*, 1970

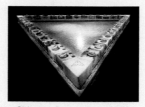

Chicago, *Dinner Party*, 1979

ARCHITECTURE AND SITE-SPECIFIC ART

I Some of the leading early-20th-century modernist architects remained active after 1945. Wright built the snail-shell Guggenheim Museum, Le Corbusier the sculpturesque Notre-Dame-du-Haut, and Mies van der Rohe the Minimalist Seagram skyscraper. Younger architects Saarinen and Utzon designed structures with dramatic curvilinear rooflines.

I In contrast to modernist architecture, postmodernist architecture is complex and eclectic and often incorporates references to historical styles. Among the best-known postmodern projects are Moore's Piazza d'Italia and Graves's Portland Building, both of which incorporate classical motifs.

I Site-specific art stands at the intersection of architecture and sculpture. Smithson's *Spiral Jetty* is a mammoth coil of natural materials in Utah's Great Salt Lake.

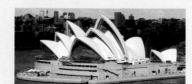

Utzon, Sydney Opera House, 1959–1972

PERFORMANCE AND CONCEPTUAL ART AND NEW MEDIA

I Among the most significant developments in the art world after World War II has been the expansion of the range of works considered "art."

I Performance artists, notably Schneemann and Beuys, replace traditional stationary artworks with movements and sounds performed before an audience. Performance Art often addresses the same social and political issues that contemporaneous painters and sculptors explore.

I Kosuth and other Conceptual artists believe the "artfulness" of art is in the artist's idea, not the work resulting from the idea.

I Paik and others have embraced video recording technology to produce artworks combining images and sounds.

I Em was a pioneer in exploring computer graphics as an art form. Unlike video recording, computer art enables artists to work with wholly invented forms, as painters can.

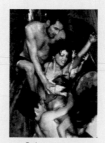

Schneemann, *Meat Joy*, 1964

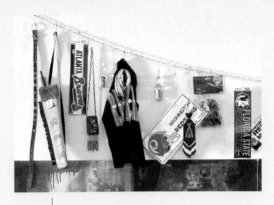

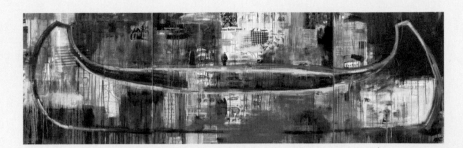

Smith's mixed-media canvases celebrate her Native American identity. Above the painting, as if hung from a clothesline, are cheap trinkets she proposes to trade for the return of confiscated land.

Overlapping the collage and the central motif of the canoe in Smith's anti-Columbus Quincentenary Celebration is dripping red paint, symbolic of the shedding of Native American blood.

The sports teams represented in *Trade* all have American Indian–derived names, reminding viewers of the vocal opposition to these names and to practices such as the Atlanta Braves' "tomahawk chop."

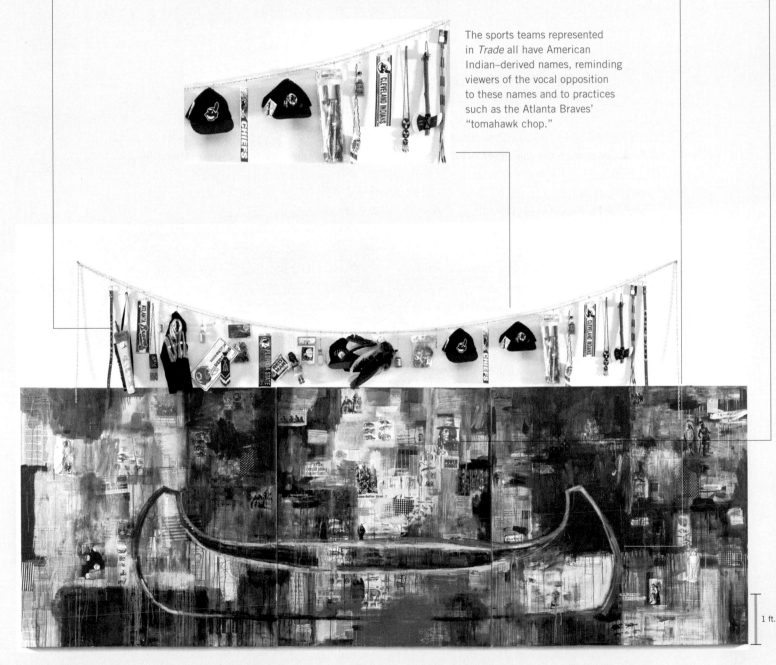

31-1 JAUNE QUICK-TO-SEE SMITH, *Trade (Gifts for Trading Land with White People)*, 1992. Oil and mixed media on canvas, 5′ × 14′ 2″. Chrysler Museum of Art, Norfolk.

1 ft.

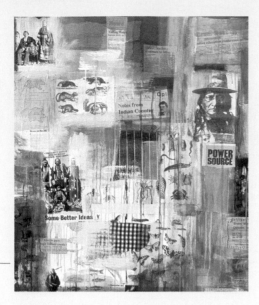

Newspaper clippings chronicle the conquest of Native America by Europeans and include references to the problems facing those living on reservations today—poverty, alcoholism, disease.

CONTEMPORARY ART WORLDWIDE

FRAMING THE ERA

ART AS SOCIOPOLITICAL MESSAGE

Although televisions, cell phones, and the Internet have brought people all over the world closer together than ever before in history, national, ethnic, religious, and racial conflicts are unfortunate and unavoidable facts of contemporary life. Some of the most eloquent voices raised in protest about the major political and social issues of the day have been those of painters and sculptors, who can harness the power of art to amplify the power of the written and spoken word.

JAUNE QUICK-TO-SEE SMITH (b. 1940) is a Native American artist descended from the Shoshone, Salish, and Cree peoples. Raised on the Flatrock Reservation in Montana, she is steeped in the traditional culture of her ancestors, but she trained as an artist in the European-American tradition at Framingham State College in Massachusetts and at the University of New Mexico. Smith's ethnic heritage has always informed her art, however, and her concern about the invisibility of Native American artists has led her to organize exhibitions of their art. Her self-identity has also been the central theme of her mature work as an artist.

In 1992, Smith created what many critics consider her masterpiece: *Trade* (FIG. **31-1**), subtitled *Gifts for Trading Land with White People*. A complex multimedia work of monumental size, *Trade* is Smith's response to what she called "the Quincentenary Non-Celebration," that is, White America's celebration of the 500th anniversary of Christopher Columbus's arrival in what Europeans called the New World. *Trade* combines collage elements and attached objects, reminiscent of a Rauschenberg combine (FIG. 30-23), with energetic brushwork recalling Willem de Kooning's Abstract Expressionist canvases (FIG. 30-8) and clippings from Native American newspapers. The clippings include images chronicling the conquest of Native America by Europeans and references to the problems facing those living on reservations today—poverty, alcoholism, disease. The dripping red paint overlaying the collage with the central motif of the canoe is symbolic of the shedding of Native American blood.

Above the painting, as if hung from a clothesline, is an array of objects. These include Native American artifacts, such as beaded belts and feather headdresses, plastic tomahawks and "Indian princess" dolls, and contemporary sports memorabilia from teams with American Indian–derived names—the Cleveland Indians, Atlanta Braves, and Washington Redskins. The inclusion of these objects reminds viewers of the vocal opposition to the use of these and similar names for high school and college as well as professional sports teams. All the cheap artifacts together also have a deeper significance. As the title indicates and Smith explained:

> Why won't you consider trading the land we handed over to you for these silly trinkets that so honor us? Sound like a bad deal? Well, that's the deal you gave us.[1]

SOCIAL AND POLITICAL ART

Jaune Quick-to-See Smith's *Trade* (FIG. 31-1) is the unique product of the artist's heritage as a Native American who has sought to bridge native and European artistic traditions, but her work parallels that of many other innovative artists of the decades since 1980 in addressing contemporary social and political issues. This focus on the content and meaning of art represents, as did the earlier work of the Pop artists and Superrealists (see Chapter 30), a rejection of modernist formalist doctrine and a desire on the part of artists once again to embrace the persuasive powers of art to communicate with a wide audience.

POSTMODERNISM The rejection of the principles underlying modernism is a central element in the diverse phenomenon in art, as in architecture, known as postmodernism (see page 929). No simple definition of *postmodernism* is possible, but it represents the erosion of the boundaries between high culture and popular culture—a separation Clement Greenberg and the modernists had staunchly defended.

For many recent artists, postmodernism involves examining the process by which meaning is generated and the negotiation or dialogue that transpires between viewers and artworks. This kind of examination of the nature of art parallels the literary field of study known as critical theory. Critical theorists view art and architecture, as well as literature and the other humanities, as a culture's intellectual products or "constructs." These constructs unconsciously suppress or conceal the real premises informing the culture, primarily the values of those politically in control. Thus, cultural products function in an ideological capacity, obscuring, for example, racist or sexist attitudes. When revealed by analysis, the facts behind these constructs, according to critical theorists, contribute to a more substantial understanding of artworks, buildings, books, and the overall culture.

Many critical theorists use an analytical strategy called *deconstruction*, after a method developed by French intellectuals in the 1960s and 1970s. In deconstruction theory, all cultural contexts are "texts." Critical theorists who employ this approach seek to uncover—to deconstruct—the facts of power, privilege, and prejudice underlying the practices and institutions of any given culture. In so doing, scholars can reveal the precariousness of structures and systems, such as language and cultural practices, along with the assumptions underlying them.

Critical theorists do not agree upon any single philosophy or analytical method, because in principle they oppose firm definitions.

They do share a healthy suspicion of all traditional truth claims and value standards, all hierarchical authority and institutions. For them, deconstruction means destabilizing established meanings, definitions, and interpretations while encouraging subjectivity and individual differences. Indeed, if there is any common denominator in the art of the decades since 1980, it is precisely the absence of any common denominator. Diversity of style and content and the celebration of individual personalities, backgrounds, and approaches to art are central to the notion of postmodernist art. The art of the 1980s and 1990s and of the opening decades of the 21st century is worldwide in scope, encompasses both abstraction and realism, and addresses a wide range of contemporary social and political issues.

Social Art: Gender and Sexuality

Many artists who have embraced the postmodern interest in investigating the dynamics of power and privilege have focused on issues of gender and sexuality in the contemporary world.

BARBARA KRUGER In the 1970s, some feminist artists, chief among them Cindy Sherman (FIG. 30-35), explored the "male gaze" and the culturally constructed notion of gender in their art. BARBARA KRUGER (b. 1945), who studied at Syracuse University and then at the Parsons School of Design in New York under Diane Arbus (FIG. 30-31), examines similar issues in her photographs. The strategies and techniques of contemporary mass media fascinate Kruger, who was a commercial graphic designer early in her career and the art director of *Mademoiselle* magazine in the late 1960s. In *Untitled* (*Your Gaze Hits the Side of My Face;* FIG. **31-2**), Kruger incorporated the layout techniques magazines and billboards use to sell consumer goods. Although she favored the reassuringly familiar format and look of advertising, Kruger's goal was to subvert the typical use of advertising imagery. She aimed to expose the deceptiveness of the media messages the viewer complacently absorbs. Kruger wanted to undermine the myths—particularly those about women—the media constantly reinforce. Her large (often four by six feet) word-and-photograph collages challenge the cultural attitudes embedded in commercial advertising. She has often used T-shirts, postcards, matchbooks, and billboards to present her work to a wide public audience.

In *Your Gaze*, Kruger overlaid a photograph of a classically beautiful sculpted head of a woman (compare FIG. 5-62A) with a vertical row of text composed of eight words. The words cannot be taken in with a single glance. Reading them is a staccato exercise, with an overlaid cumulative quality that delays understanding and

---

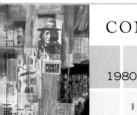

CONTEMPORARY ART WORLDWIDE

1980	1990	2000
▌ Social and political issues—gender and sexuality; ethnic, religious, and national identity; violence, homelessness, and AIDS—figure prominently in the art of Kruger, Wojnarowicz, Wodiczko, Ringgold, Weems, and many others	▌ Artworks addressing pressing political and social issues continue to be produced in great numbers by, among others, Quick-to-See Smith, Sikander, Bester, Hammons, and Neshat	▌ Modern, postmodern, and traditional art forms coexist today in the increasingly interconnected worldwide art scene as artists on all continents work with age-old materials and also experiment with the new media of digital photography, computer graphics, and video
▌ Stirling, Pei, and other postmodern architects incorporate historical references into designs for museums and other public buildings	▌ Realistic figure painting and sculpture (Kiki Smith, Saville) as well as abstraction (Schnabel, Kiefer, Donovan) remain vital components of the contemporary art scene	
▌ Site-specific artworks by Lin and Serra and exhibitions of the work of Mapplethorpe and Ofili become lightning rods for debate over public financing of art	▌ Deconstructivism (Behnisch, Gehry, Hadid) and green architecture (Piano) emerge as major architectural movements	

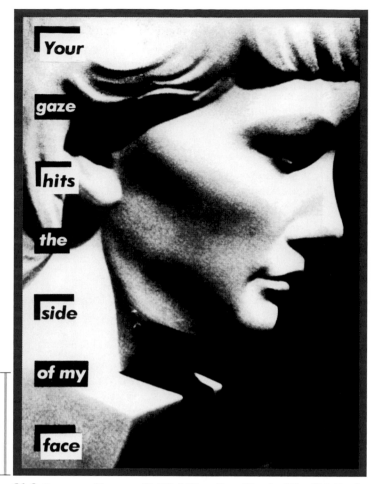

1 ft.

31-2 BARBARA KRUGER, *Untitled (Your Gaze Hits the Side of My Face)*, 1981. Photograph, red painted frame, 4′ 7″ × 3′ 5″. Courtesy Mary Boone Gallery, New York. ◼◖

Kruger has explored the "male gaze" in her art. Using the layout techniques of mass media, she constructed this word-and-photograph collage to challenge culturally constructed notions of gender.

intensifies the meaning (rather like reading a series of roadside billboards from a speeding car). Kruger's use of text in her work is significant. Many cultural theorists have asserted language is one of the most powerful vehicles for internalizing stereotypes and conditioned roles. Some feminist artists, most notably the GUERRILLA GIRLS (FIG. 31-2A), have created powerful artworks consisting only of words—presented in a style and format reminiscent of the same kinds of magazine ads Kruger incorporates in her photo-collages.

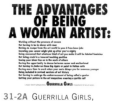

31-2A GUERRILLA GIRLS, *Advantages of Being a Woman Artist*, 1988.

DAVID WOJNAROWICZ For many artists, their homosexuality is as important—or even more important—an element of their personal identity as their gender, ethnicity, or race. Beginning in the early 1980s, unwelcome reinforcement for their self-identification came from confronting daily the devastating effects of AIDS (acquired immune deficiency syndrome) in the gay community. Some sculptors and painters responded by producing deeply moving works of art. DAVID WOJNAROWICZ (1955–1992) dropped out of high school in his hometown of Red Bank, New Jersey, and moved to New York City, where he lived on the streets before achieving success as an artist. A gay activist, he watched his lover and many of his friends die of AIDS. He reacted by creating disturbing yet eloquent works about the tragedy of this disease, which eventually claimed his own life. In *When I Put My Hands on Your Body* (FIG. 31-3), he overlaid a photograph of a pile of skeletal remains with evenly spaced typed commentary communicating his feelings about watching a loved one dying of AIDS. Wojnarowicz movingly describes the effects of AIDS on the human body and soul:

> When I put my hands on your body on your flesh I feel the history of that body. . . . I see the flesh unwrap from the layers of fat and disappear. . . . I see the organs gradually fade into transparency. . . . It makes me weep to feel the history of you of your flesh beneath my hands.

31-3 DAVID WOJNAROWICZ, *When I Put My Hands on Your Body*, 1990. Gelatin silver print and silk-screened text on museum board, 2′ 2″ × 3′ 2″. Private collection.

In this disturbing yet eloquent print, Wojnarowicz overlaid typed commentary on a photograph of skeletal remains. He movingly communicated his feelings about watching a loved one die of AIDS.

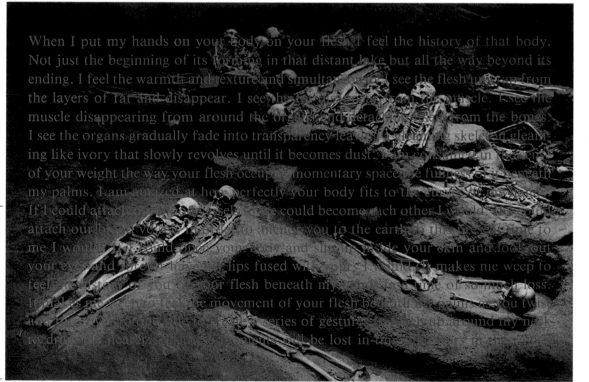

1 ft.

Public Funding of Controversial Art

Although art can be beautiful and uplifting, throughout history art has also challenged and offended. Since the early 1980s, a number of heated controversies about art have surfaced in the United States. There have been many calls to remove "offensive" works from public view (see "Richard Serra's *Tilted Arc*," page 967) and, in reaction, accusations of censorship. The central questions in all cases have been whether there are limits to what art can appropriately be exhibited, and whether governmental authorities have the right to monitor and pass judgment on creative endeavors. A related question is whether the acceptability of a work should be a criterion in determining the public funding of art.

Two exhibits in 1989 placed the National Endowment for the Arts (NEA), a U.S. government agency charged with distributing federal funds to support the arts, squarely in the middle of this debate. One of the exhibitions, devoted to recipients of the Awards for the Visual Arts (AVA), took place at the Southeastern Center for Contemporary Art in North Carolina. Among the award winners was Andres Serrano, whose *Piss Christ,* a photograph of a crucifix submerged in urine, sparked an uproar. Responding to this artwork, Reverend Donald Wildmon, an evangelical minister from Mississippi and head of the American Family Association, expressed outrage that this kind of work was in an exhibition funded by the NEA and the Equitable Life Assurance Society (a sponsor of the AVA). He demanded the work be removed and launched a letter-writing campaign that caused Equitable Life to cancel its sponsorship of the awards. To Wildmon and other staunch conservatives, this exhibition, along with *Robert Mapplethorpe: The Perfect Moment,* which included erotic and openly homosexual images of the artist (FIG. 31-4) and others, served as evidence of cultural depravity and immorality. These critics insisted that art of an offensive character should not be funded by government agencies such as the NEA. As a result of media furor over *The Perfect Moment,* the director of the Corcoran Museum of Art decided to cancel the scheduled exhibition of this traveling show. But Dennis Barrie, Director of the Contemporary Arts Center in Cincinnati, chose to mount the show. The government indicted Barrie on charges of obscenity, but a jury acquitted him six months later.

These controversies intensified public criticism of the NEA and its funding practices. The next year, the head of the NEA, John Frohnmayer, vetoed grants for four lesbian, gay, or feminist performance artists—Karen Finley, John Fleck, Holly Hughes, and Tim Miller—who became known as the "NEA Four." Infuriated by what they perceived as overt censorship, the artists filed suit, eventually settling the case and winning reinstatement of their grants. Congress responded by dramatically reducing the NEA's budget, and the agency no longer awards grants or fellowships to individual artists.

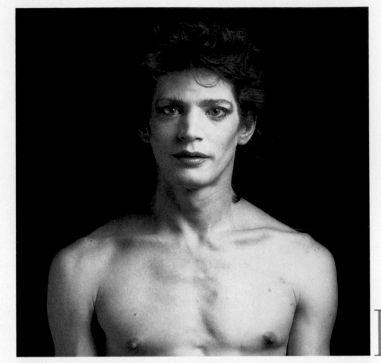

31-4 ROBERT MAPPLETHORPE, *Self-Portrait,* 1980. Gelatin silver print, $7\frac{3}{4}'' \times 7\frac{3}{4}''$. Robert Mapplethorpe Foundation, New York.

Mapplethorpe's *Perfect Moment* show led to a landmark court case on freedom of expression for artists. In this self-portrait, an androgynous Mapplethorpe confronts the viewer with a steady gaze.

Controversies have also erupted on the municipal level. In 1999, Rudolph Giuliani, then mayor of New York, joined a number of individuals and groups protesting the inclusion of several artworks in the exhibition *Sensation: Young British Artists from the Saatchi Collection* at the Brooklyn Museum. Chris Ofili's *The Holy Virgin Mary* (FIG. 31-10), a collage of Mary incorporating cutouts from pornographic magazines and shellacked clumps of elephant dung, became the flashpoint for public furor. Denouncing the show as "sick stuff," the mayor threatened to cut off all city subsidies to the museum.

Art that seeks to unsettle and challenge is critical to the cultural, political, and psychological life of a society. The regularity with which this kind of art raises controversy suggests it operates at the intersection of two competing principles: free speech and artistic expression on the one hand and a reluctance to impose images upon an audience that finds them repugnant or offensive on the other. What these controversies do demonstrate, beyond doubt, is the enduring power of art.

Wojnarowicz juxtaposed text with imagery, which, like works by Barbara Kruger (FIG. 31-2) and the Guerrilla Girls (FIG. 31-2A), paralleled the use of both words and images in advertising. The public's familiarity with this format ensured greater receptivity to the artist's message.

ROBERT MAPPLETHORPE One brilliant gay artist who became the central figure in a heated debate in the halls of the U.S. Congress as well as among the public at large was ROBERT MAPPLETHORPE (1946–1989). Born in Queens, New York, Mapplethorpe studied drawing, painting, and sculpture at the Pratt

Institute in Brooklyn, but after he purchased a Polaroid camera in 1970, he became increasingly interested in photography. Mapplethorpe's *The Perfect Moment* traveling exhibition, funded in part by the National Endowment for the Arts, featured his photographs of flowers and people, many nude, some depicting children, some homoerotic and sadomasochistic in nature. The show led to a landmark court case in Cincinnati on freedom of expression for artists and prompted new legislation establishing restrictions on government funding of the arts (see "Public Funding of Controversial Art," page 944).

Never at issue was Mapplethorpe's technical mastery of the photographic medium. His gelatin silver prints have glowing textures with rich tonal gradations of black, gray, and white. In many ways, Mapplethorpe was the heir of Edward Weston, whose innovative compositions of still lifes (FIG. 29-44) and nudes (FIG. 29-44A) helped establish photography as an art form on a par with painting and sculpture. What shocked the public was not nudity per se—a traditional subject with roots in antiquity, indeed at the very birth of art during the Old Stone Age (FIGS. 1-5, 1-6, and 1-6A)—but the openly gay character of many of Mapplethorpe's images. *The Perfect Moment* photographs included, in addition to some very graphic images of homosexual men, a series of self-portraits documenting Mapplethorpe's changing appearance almost up until he died from AIDS only months after the show opened in Philadelphia in December 1988. The self-portrait reproduced here (FIG. 31-4) presents Mapplethorpe as an androgynous young man with long hair and makeup, confronting the viewer with a steady gaze. Mapplethorpe's photographs, like the work of David Wojnarowicz (FIG. 31-3) and other gay and lesbian artists of the time, are inextricably bound with the social upheavals in American society and the struggle for equal rights for women, homosexuals, minorities, and the disabled during the second half of the 20th century.

SHAHZIA SIKANDER The struggle for recognition and equal rights has never been confined to the United States, least of all in the present era of instant global communication. In the Muslim world, women and homosexuals face especially difficult challenges, which SHAHZIA SIKANDER (b. 1969) brilliantly addresses in her work. Born in Lahore, Pakistan, and trained at the National College of Arts in the demanding South Asian/Persian art of miniature painting (see "Indian Miniature Painting," Chapter 32, page 979), she earned an MFA from the Rhode Island School of Design and now lives in New York City. So thoroughly immersed in the methods of miniature painting that she makes her own paper, pigments, and squirrel-hair brushes, Sikander nonetheless imbues this traditional art form with contemporary meaning. In *Perilous Order* (FIG. 31-5), she addresses homosexuality, intolerance, and hypocrisy by portraying a gay friend in the guise of the Mughal emperor Aurangzeb (r. 1658–1707), who was a strict enforcer of Islamic orthodoxy although reputed to be a homosexual. Sikander depicted him framed against a magnificent marbleized background ringed by voluptuous nude Hindu nymphs and behind the shadow of a veiled Hindu goddess. *Perilous Order* thus also incorporates a reference to the tensions between the Muslim and Hindu populations of Pakistan and India today.

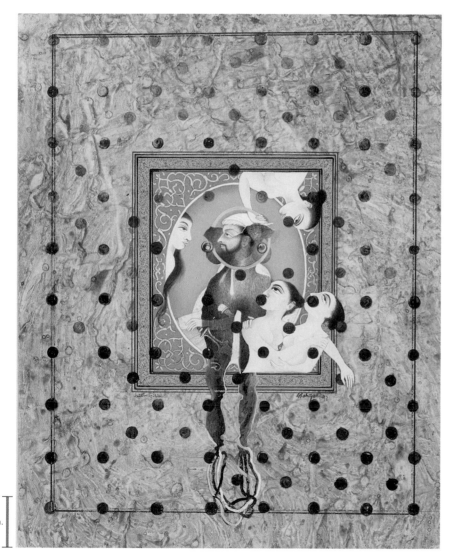

31-5 SHAHZIA SIKANDER, *Perilous Order,* 1994–1997. Vegetable color, dry pigment, watercolor, and tea on Wasli paper, $10\frac{1}{2}'' \times 8''$. Whitney Museum of American Art, New York (purchase, with funds from the Drawing Committee).

Imbuing miniature painting with a contemporary message about hypocrisy and intolerance, Sikander portrayed a gay friend as a homosexual Mughal emperor who enforced Muslim orthodoxy.

1 in.

Social Art: Race, Ethnicity, and National Identity

Gender and sexual-orientation issues are by no means the only societal concerns contemporary artists have addressed in their work. Race, ethnicity, and national identity are among the other pressing issues that have given rise to important artworks during the past few decades.

FAITH RINGGOLD One of the leading artists addressing issues associated with African American women is Harlem native FAITH RINGGOLD (b. 1930), who studied painting at the City College of New York and taught art education in the New York public schools for 18 years. In the 1960s, Ringgold produced numerous works that provided pointed and incisive commentary on the realities of racial prejudice. She increasingly incorporated references to gender as well and, in the 1970s, turned to fabric as the predominant material in her art. Using fabric enabled Ringgold to make more pointed reference to the domestic sphere, traditionally

31-6 FAITH RINGGOLD, *Who's Afraid of Aunt Jemima?* 1983. Acrylic on canvas with fabric borders, quilted, 7′ 6″ × 6′ 8″. Private collection.

In this quilt, a medium associated with women, Ringgold presented a tribute to her mother that also addresses African American culture and the struggles of women to overcome oppression.

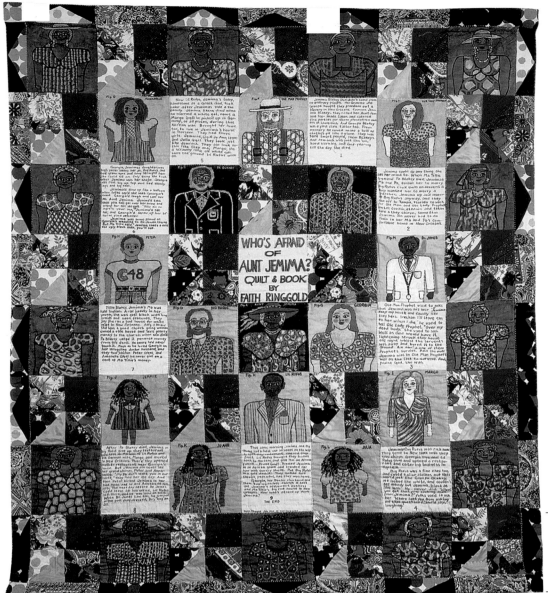

1 ft.

associated with women, and to collaborate with her mother, Willi Posey, a fashion designer. After her mother's death in 1981, Ringgold created *Who's Afraid of Aunt Jemima?* (FIG. **31-6**), a quilt composed of dyed, painted, and pieced fabric. A moving tribute to her mother, this "story quilt"—Ringgold's signature art form—merges the personal and the political. Com-

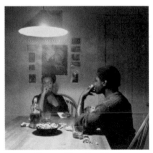

31-6A SIMPSON, *Stereo Styles*, 1988.

31-6B WEEMS, *Man Smoking/ Malcolm X*, 1990.

bining words with pictures, as did Barbara Kruger (FIG. 31-2) and David Wojnarowicz (FIG. 31-3), Ringgold incorporates a narrative in her quilt. *Aunt Jemima* tells the witty story of the family of the stereotypical black "mammy" in the mind of the public, but here Jemima is a successful African American businesswoman. Ringgold narrates the story using black dialect interspersed with embroidered portraits and traditional patterned squares. *Aunt Jemima*, while resonating with autobiographical references, also speaks to the larger issues of the history of African American culture

and the struggles of women to overcome oppression. Other contemporary feminist artists who have addressed similar racial and social issues are LORNA SIMPSON (b. 1960; FIG. **31-6A**) and CARRIE MAE WEEMS (b. 1953; FIG. **31-6B**).

MELVIN EDWARDS In his art, Californian MELVIN EDWARDS (b. 1937) explores a very different aspect of the black experience in America—the history of collective oppression of African Americans. One of Edwards's major sculptural series focused on the metaphor of lynching to provoke thought about the legacy of racism. His *Lynch Fragments* series, produced over more than three decades beginning in 1963, encompassed more than 150 welded-steel sculptures. Lynching as an artistic theme prompts an immediate and visceral response, conjuring chilling and gruesome images from the past. Edwards sought to extend this emotional resonance further in his art. He constructed the series' relatively small sculptures, such as *Tambo* (FIG. **31-7**), from found metal objects—for example, chains, hooks, hammers, spikes, knife blades, and handcuffs. Although Edwards often intertwined or welded together the individual metal components so as to diminish immediate identification of them, the sculptures still retain a haunting connection to the overall theme. These works refer to a historical act that evokes a

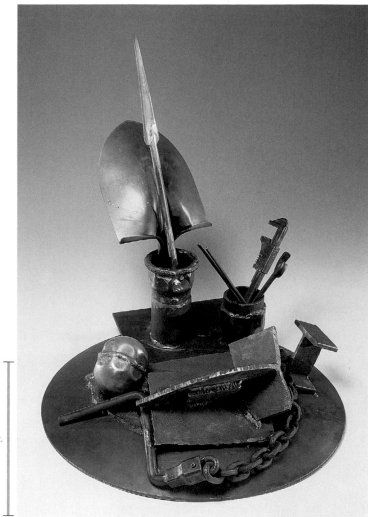

31-7 MELVIN EDWARDS, *Tambo*, 1993. Welded steel, 2′ 4⅛″ × 2′ 1¼″. Smithsonian American Art Museum, Washington, D.C.

Edwards's welded sculptures of chains, spikes, knife blades, and other found objects allude to the lynching of African Americans and the continuing struggle for civil rights and an end to racism.

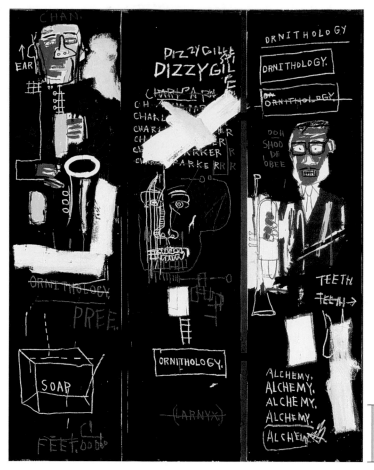

31-8 JEAN-MICHEL BASQUIAT, *Horn Players,* 1983. Acrylic and oil paintstick on three canvas panels, 8′ × 6′ 3″. Broad Foundation, Santa Monica.

In this tribute to two legendary African American musicians, Basquiat combined bold colors, fractured figures, and graffiti to capture the dynamic rhythms of jazz and the excitement of New York.

collective memory of oppression, but they also speak to the continuing struggle for civil rights and an end to racism. While growing up in Los Angeles, Edwards experienced racial conflict firsthand. Among the metal objects incorporated into his *Lynch Fragments* sculptures are items he found in the streets in the aftermath of the Watts riots in 1965. The inclusion of these found objects imbues his disquieting, haunting works with an even greater intensity.

JEAN-MICHEL BASQUIAT The work of JEAN-MICHEL BASQUIAT (1960–1988) focuses on still another facet of the minority cultural experience in America. Born in Brooklyn in a comfortable home—his father was an accountant from Haiti and his mother a black Puerto Rican—Basquiat rebelled against middle-class values, dropped out of school at 17, and took to the streets. He first burst onto the New York art scene as the anonymous author of witty graffiti in Lower Manhattan signed SAMO (a dual reference to the derogatory name *Sambo* for African Americans and to "same old shit"). Basquiat first drew attention as an artist in 1980 when he participated in a group show—the "Times Square Show"—in an abandoned 42nd Street building. Eight years later, after a meteoric rise to fame, he died of a heroin overdose at age 27.

Basquiat was self-taught, both as an artist and about the history of art, but he was not a "primitive." His sophisticated style owes a debt to diverse sources, including the late paintings of Pablo Picasso, Abstract Expressionism, and the "art brut" of Jean Dubuffet (FIG. 30-4). Many of Basquiat's paintings celebrate black heroes, for example, the legendary jazz musicians Charlie "Bird" Parker and Dizzy Gillespie, whom he memorialized in *Horn Players* (FIG. 31-8). The fractured figures, the bold colors against a black background, and the deliberately scrawled, crossed-out, and misspelled graffiti ("ornithology"—the study of birds—is a pun on Parker's nickname) create a dynamic composition suggesting the rhythms of jazz music and the excitement of the streets of New York, "the city that never sleeps."

KEHINDE WILEY Many African American artists have lamented the near-total absence of blacks in Western painting and sculpture, except as servants (compare FIG. 31-13), as well as in histories of Western art until quite recently. Los Angeles native KEHINDE WILEY (b. 1977) set out to correct that discriminatory imbalance. Wiley earned his MFA at Yale University and is currently artist-in-residence at the Studio Museum in Harlem, where he has achieved renown for his large-scale portraits of young urban African American men. Wiley's trademark paintings, however, are reworkings of historically important portraits in which he substitutes

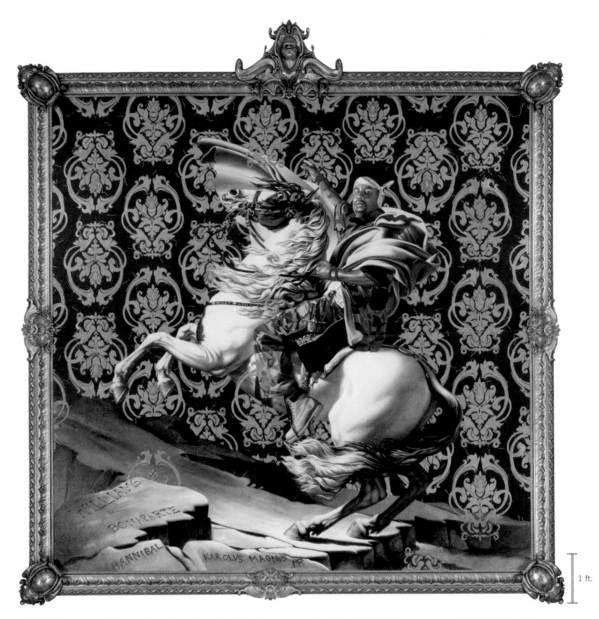

31-9 KEHINDE WILEY, *Napoleon Leading the Army over the Alps*, 2005. Oil on canvas, 9′ × 9′. Brooklyn Museum, Brooklyn (Collection of Suzi and Andrew B. Cohen).

Wiley's trademark paintings are reworkings of famous portraits (FIG. 27-1A) in which he substitutes young African American men in contemporary dress in order to situate them in "the field of power."

figures of young black men in contemporary dress in order to situate them in what he calls "the field of power." One example is *Napoleon Leading the Army over the Alps* (FIG. **31-9**), based on Jacques-Louis David's painting (FIG. 27-1A) of the same subject. To evoke the era of the original, Wiley presented his portrait of an African American Napoleon on horseback in a gilt wood frame. Although in many details an accurate reproduction of David's canvas, Wiley's version is not a slavish copy. His heroic narrative unfolds against a vibrantly colored ornate wallpaper-like background instead of a dramatic sky—a distinctly modernist reminder to the viewer that this is a painting and not a window onto an Alpine landscape.

CHRIS OFILI In the global artistic community of the contemporary world, the exploration of personal social, ethnic, and national identity is a universal theme. Three artists who, like Shahzia Sikander (FIG. 31-5), incorporate their

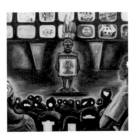

31-9A PIULA, *Ta Tele*, 1988.

national artistic heritages in their work are TRIGO PIULA (b. ca. 1950; FIG. **31-9A**), CHRIS OFILI (b. 1968; FIG. 31-10), and Cliff Whiting (FIG. 31-11).

One theme Ofili has treated is religion, interpreted through the eyes of a British-born Catholic of Nigerian descent. Ofili's *The Holy Virgin Mary* (FIG. **31-10**) depicts Mary in a manner that departs radically from conventional Renaissance representations. Ofili's work presents the Virgin in simplified form, and she appears to float in an indeterminate space. The artist employed brightly colored pigments, applied to the canvas in multiple layers of beadlike dots (inspired by images from ancient caves in Zimbabwe). Surrounding the Virgin are tiny images of genitalia and buttocks cut out from pornographic magazines, which, to the artist, parallel the putti often surrounding Mary in Renaissance paintings. Another reference to Ofili's African heritage surfaces in the clumps of elephant dung—one attached to the Virgin's breast, and two more on which the canvas rests, serving as supports. The dung enabled Ofili to incorporate Africa into his work in a literal way. Still, he wants the viewer to move beyond the cultural associations of the materials and see them in new ways.

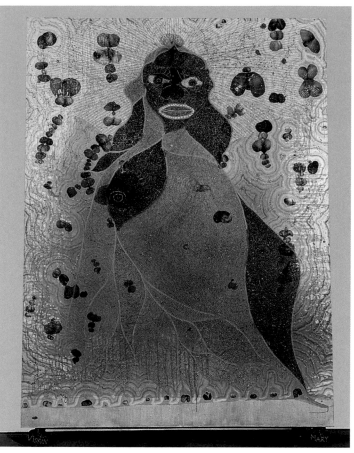

1 ft.

31-10 CHRIS OFILI, *The Holy Virgin Mary,* 1996. Paper collage, oil paint, glitter, polyester resin, map pins, elephant dung on linen, 7′ 11″ × 5′ 11$\frac{5}{16}$″. Saatchi Collection, London.

Ofili, a British-born Catholic of Nigerian descent, represented the Virgin Mary with African elephant dung on one breast and surrounded by genitalia and buttocks. The painting produced a public outcry.

Not surprisingly, *The Holy Virgin Mary* elicited strong reactions. Its inclusion in the *Sensation* exhibition at the Brooklyn Museum in 1999 with other intentionally "sensational" works by young British artists prompted indignant (but unsuccessful) demands for cancellation of the show and countercharges of censorship (see "Public Funding of Controversial Art," page 944).

CLIFF WHITING In New Zealand today, some artists draw on their Maori heritage for formal and iconographic inspiration. The historic Maori woodcarving craft (FIGS. 36-1 and 36-19A) brilliantly reemerges in what CLIFF WHITING (TE WHANAU-A-APANUI, b. 1936) calls a "carved mural" (FIG. **31-11**). Whiting's *Tawhiri-Matea* is a masterpiece in the venerable tradition of Oceanic wood sculpture, but it is a work designed for the very modern environment of an exhibition gallery. The artist suggested the wind turbulence with the restless curvature of the main motif and its myriad serrated edges. The 1984 mural depicts events in the Maori creation myth. The central figure, Tawhiri-Matea, god of the winds, wrestles to control the children of the four winds, seen as blue spiral forms. Ra, the sun, energizes the scene from the top left, complemented by Marama, the moon, in the opposite corner. The top right image refers to the primal separation of Ranginui, the Sky Father, and Papatuanuku, the Earth Mother. Spiral koru motifs symbolizing growth and energy flow through the composition. Blue waves and green fronds around Tawhiri suggest his brothers Tangaroa and Tane, gods of the sea and forest.

Whiting is securely at home with the native tradition of form and technique, as well as with the worldwide aesthetic of modern design. Out of the seamless fabric made by uniting both, he feels something new can develop that loses nothing of the power of the old. The artist champions not only the renewal of Maori cultural life and its continuity in art but also the education of the young in the values that made their culture great—values he asks them to perpetuate.

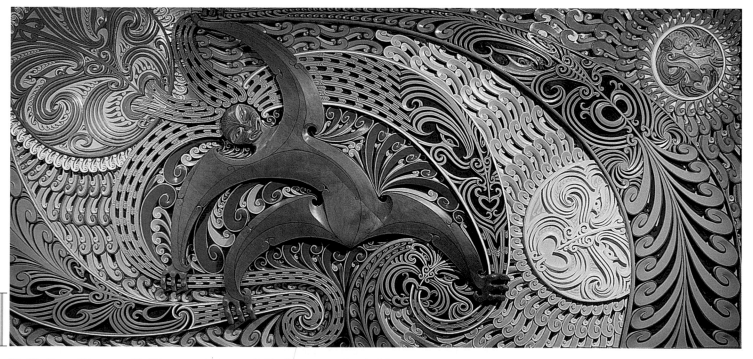

1 ft.

31-11 CLIFF WHITING (TE WHANAU-A-APANUI), *Tawhiri-Matea (God of the Winds),* 1984. Oil on wood and fiberboard, 6′ 4$\frac{3}{8}$″ × 11′ 10$\frac{3}{4}$″. Meteorological Service of New Zealand, Wellington.

In this carved wooden mural depicting the Maori creation myth, Cliff Whiting revived Oceanic formal and iconographic traditions and techniques. The abstract curvilinear design suggests wind turbulence.

Homage to Steve Biko is a tribute to a leader of the Black Liberation movement, which protested apartheid in South Africa. References to the injustice of Biko's death fill this complex painting.

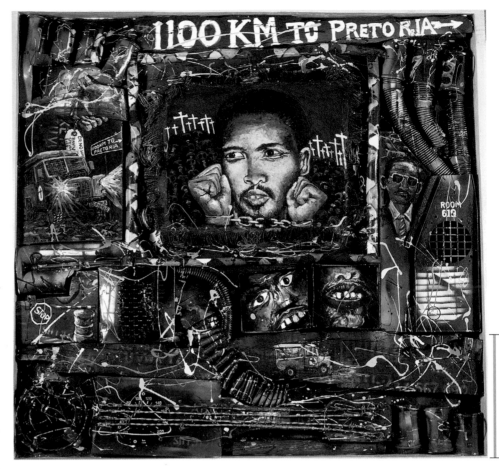

Political Art

Although almost all of the works discussed thus far are commentaries on contemporary society—seen through the lens of these artists' personal experiences—they do not incorporate references to specific events, nor do they address conditions affecting all people regardless of their gender, race, or national origin, for example, street violence, homelessness, and industrial pollution. Other artists, however, have confronted precisely those aspects of contemporary life in their work.

WILLIE BESTER Political oppression in South Africa figures prominently in the paintings of WILLIE BESTER (b. 1956), one of many South African artists who were vocal critics of apartheid (government-sponsored racial separation). Bester's 1992 *Homage to Steve Biko* (FIG. 31-12) is a tribute to the gentle and heroic leader of the South African Black Liberation Movement whom the authorities killed while in detention. The exoneration of the two white doctors in charge of him sparked protests around the world. Bester packed his picture with references to death and injustice. Biko's portrait, at the center, is near another of the police minister, James Kruger, who had Biko transported 1,100 miles to Pretoria in the yellow Land Rover ambulance seen left of center and again beneath Biko's portrait. Bester portrayed Biko with his chained fists raised in the classic worldwide protest gesture. This portrait memorializes both Biko and the many other antiapartheid activists, as indicated by the white graveyard crosses above a blue sea of skulls beside Biko's head. The crosses stand out against a red background, recalling the inferno of burned townships. The stop sign (lower left) seems to mean "stop Kruger," or perhaps "stop apartheid." The tagged foot, as if in a morgue, above the ambulance (to the left) also refers to Biko's death. The red crosses on this vehicle's door and on Kruger's reflective dark glasses repeat, with sad irony, the graveyard crosses.

Blood-red and ambulance-yellow are in fact unifying colors dripped or painted on many parts of the canvas. Writing and numbers, found fragments and signs, both stenciled and painted—favorite Cubist motifs (FIGS. 29-14 and 29-16)—also appear throughout the composition. Numbers refer to dehumanized life under apartheid. Found objects—wire, sticks, cardboard, sheet metal, cans, and other discards—from which the poor construct fragile, impermanent township dwellings, remind viewers of the degraded lives of most South African people of color. The oilcan guitar (bottom center), another recurrent Bester symbol, refers both to the social harmony and joy provided by music and to the control imposed by apartheid policies. The whole composition is rich in texture and dense in its collage combinations of objects, photographs, signs, symbols, and pigment. *Homage to Steve Biko* is a radical and powerful critique of an oppressive sociopolitical system, and it exemplifies the extent to which art can be invoked in the political process.

DAVID HAMMONS Racism of all kinds is a central theme of the work of DAVID HAMMONS (b. 1943). Born in Springfield, Illinois, Hammons, an African American, moved to Los Angeles in 1962, where he studied art at the Chouinard and Otis Art Institutes before settling in Harlem in 1974. In his *installations* (artworks creating an artistic environment in a room or gallery), Hammons combines sharp social commentary with beguiling sensory elements to push viewers to confront racism in American society. He created *Public Enemy* (FIG. 31-13) for an exhibition at the Museum of Modern Art in New York in 1991. Hammons enticed viewers to interact with the installation by scattering fragrant autumn leaves on the floor and positioning helium-filled balloons throughout the gallery. The leaves crunched underfoot, and the dangling strings of the balloons gently brushed spectators walking around the installation. Once drawn into the environment, viewers encountered the centerpiece of *Public Enemy*—large black-and-white photographs of a public monument in front of the American Museum of Natural History in New York City depicting President Theodore Roosevelt (1858–1919) triumphantly seated on a horse, flanked by an African American man and a Native American man, both men appearing in the role of servants. Around the edge of the installation, circling the photographs of the monument, were piles of sandbags with both real and toy guns propped on top, aimed at the statue. By selecting evocative found objects and presenting them in a dynamic manner, encouraging viewer interaction, Hammons attracted an audience and then revealed the racism embedded in received cultural heritage and prompted reexamination of American values and cultural emblems.

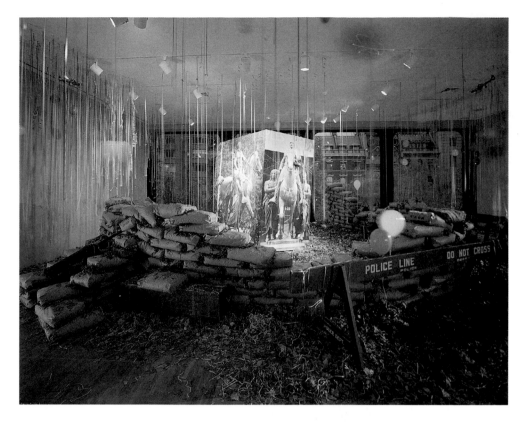

31-13 DAVID HAMMONS, *Public Enemy*, installation at Museum of Modern Art, New York, 1991. Photographs, balloons, sandbags, guns, and other mixed media. ◼◀

Hammons intended this multimedia installation, with Theodore Roosevelt flanked by an African American and a Native American as servants, to reveal the racism embedded in America's cultural heritage.

try to visualize the real products of the uses of power.[2]

Mercenaries IV (FIG. 31-14), a canvas rivaling the monumental history paintings of the 19th century in size, presents a mysterious tableau of five tough freelance military professionals willing to fight, for a price, for any political cause. The three clustering at the right side of the canvas react with tense physical gestures to something one of the two other mercenaries standing at the far left is saying. The dark uniforms and skin tones of the four black fighters flatten their figures and make them stand out against the searing dark red background. The slightly modulated background seems to push their forms forward up against the picture plane and becomes an echoing void in the space between the two groups. Golub painted the mercenaries so that the viewer's eye is level with the menacing figures' knees. He placed the men so close to the front plane of the work that the lower edge of the painting cuts off their feet, thereby trapping the viewer in the painting's compressed space. Golub emphasized both the scarred light tones of the white mercenary's skin and the weapons. Modeled with shadow and gleaming highlights, the guns contrast with the harshly scraped, flattened surfaces of the figures. The rawness of the canvas reinforces the rawness of the imagery. Golub often dissolved certain areas with solvent after applying pigment and scraped off applied paint with, among other tools, a meat cleaver. The feeling of peril confronts viewers mercilessly. They become one with all the victims caught in today's political battles.

LEON GOLUB During his long and successful career as a painter, LEON GOLUB (1922–2004) expressed a brutal vision of contemporary life. Born in Chicago and trained at the University of Chicago and the Art Institute of Chicago, he is best known for his two series of paintings titled *Assassins* and *Mercenaries*. In these large-scale works on unstretched canvases, anonymous characters inspired by newspaper and magazine photographs participate in atrocious street violence, terrorism, and torture. The paintings have a universal impact because they suggest not specific stories but a condition of being. As Golub observed:

> Through media we are under constant, invasive bombardment of images—from all over—and we often have to take evasive action to avoid discomforting recognitions.... The work [of art] should have an edge, veering between what is visually and cognitively acceptable and what might stretch these limits as we encounter or

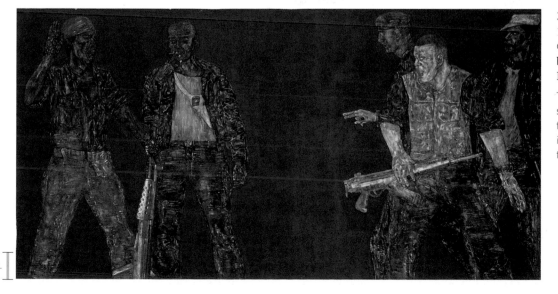

1 ft.

31-14 LEON GOLUB, *Mercenaries IV*, 1980. Acrylic on linen, 10′ × 19′ 2″. © Estate of Leon Golub/Licensed by VAGA, New York, NY. Courtesy Ronald Feldman Gallery.

The violence of contemporary life is the subject of Golub's huge paintings. Here, five mercenaries loom over the viewer, instilling a feeling of peril. The rough textures reinforce the raw imagery.

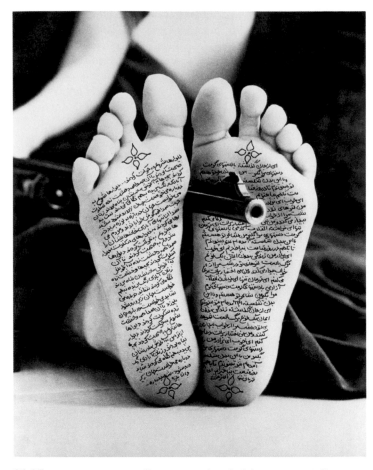

31-15 SHIRIN NESHAT, *Allegiance and Wakefulness,* 1994. Offset print. Israel Museum, Jerusalem.

Neshat's photographs address the repression of women in postrevolutionary Iran. She poses in traditional veiled garb but wields a rifle and displays militant Farsi poetry on her exposed body parts.

SHIRIN NESHAT Violence also plays a significant role in the art of SHIRIN NESHAT (b. 1957), who grew up in a Westernized Iranian home and attended a Catholic boarding school in Tehran before leaving her homeland to study art in California, where she earned undergraduate and graduate degrees from the University of California, Berkeley. Today, she lives in New York City and produces films, video, and photographs critical of the fundamentalist Islamic regime in Iran, especially in its treatment of women. Neshat often poses for her photographs wearing a veil—the symbol for her of the repression of Muslim women—and with her face and exposed parts of her body covered with Farsi (Persian) messages. A rifle often figures prominently in the photographs as an emblem of militant feminism, a notion foreign to the Muslim faith. In *Allegiance and Wakefulness* (FIG. **31-15**) from her *Women of Allah* series, the viewer sees only Neshat's feet covered with verses of militant Farsi poetry and the barrel of a rifle.

KRZYSZTOF WODICZKO Born in Poland, KRZYSZTOF WODICZKO (b. 1943) focuses on more universal concerns in his art. When working in Canada in 1980, he developed artworks involving outdoor slide images. He projected photographs on specific buildings to expose how civic buildings embody, legitimize, and perpetuate power. When Wodiczko moved to New York City in 1983, the pervasive homelessness troubled him, and he resolved to use his art to publicize this problem. In 1987, he produced *The Home-*

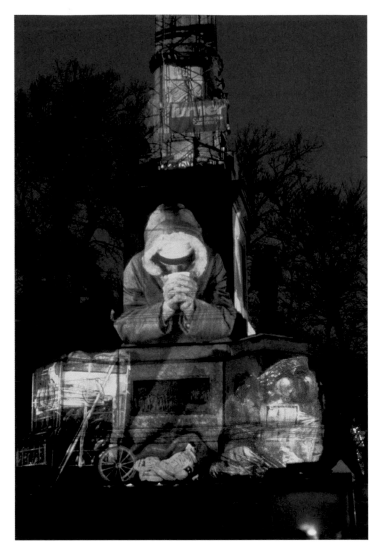

31-16 KRZYSZTOF WODICZKO, *The Homeless Projection,* 1986. Outdoor slide projection at the Civil War Soldiers and Sailors Monument, Boston. ◼◀

To publicize their plight, Wodiczko projected on the walls of a monument on Boston Common images of homeless people and their plastic bags filled with their few possessions.

less Projection (FIG. **31-16**) as part of a New Year's celebration in Boston. The artist projected images of homeless people on all four sides of the Civil War Soldiers and Sailors Monument on Boston Common. In these photos, the homeless appear flanked by plastic bags filled with their few possessions. At the top of the monument, Wodiczko projected a local condominium construction site, which helped viewers make a connection between urban development and homelessness.

HANS HAACKE Some contemporary artists have produced important works exposing the politics of the art world itself, specifically the role of museums and galleries in validating art, the discriminatory policies and politics of these cultural institutions, and the corrupting influence of corporate sponsorship of art exhibitions. German artist HANS HAACKE (b. 1936) has focused his attention on the politics of art museums and how acquisition and exhibition policies affect the public's understanding of art history. The specificity of his works, based on substantial research, makes them stinging indictments of the institutions whose practices he critiques.

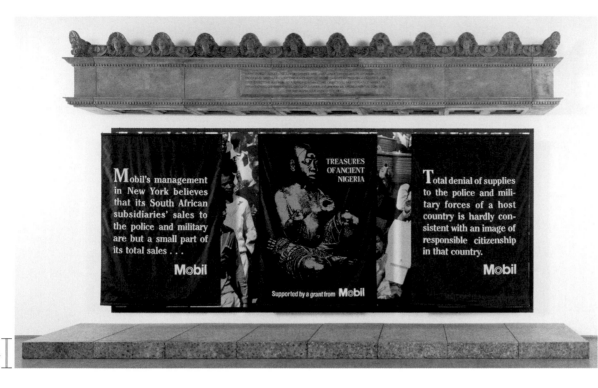

31-17 HANS HAACKE, *MetroMobiltan*, 1985. Fiberglass construction, three banners, and photomural, 11′ 8″ × 20′ × 5′. Musée National d'Art Moderne, Centre Georges Pompidou, Paris.

MetroMobiltan focuses attention on the connections between political and economic conditions in South Africa and the conflicted politics of corporate patronage of art exhibitions.

In *MetroMobiltan* (FIG. 31-17), Haacke illustrated the connection between the realm of art (more specifically, the Metropolitan Museum of Art in New York) and the world of political and economic interests. *MetroMobiltan* is a large sculptural work that includes a photomural of the funeral procession for black victims shot by the South African police at Cross Roads, near Cape Town, on March 16, 1985. This photomural serves as the backdrop for a banner for the 1980 Mobil Oil–sponsored Metropolitan Museum show *Treasures of Ancient Nigeria*. In 1980, Mobil was a principal investor in South Africa, and Haacke's work suggests one major factor in Mobil's sponsorship of this exhibition was that Nigeria is one of the richest oil-producing countries. In 1981, political activists pressured Mobil's board of directors to stop providing oil to the white South African military and police. Printed on the blue banners hanging on either side of *MetroMobiltan* is the official corporate response refusing to comply with this demand. Haacke set the entire tableau in a fiberglass replica of the Metropolitan Museum's entablature. By bringing together these disparate visual and textual elements referring to the museum, Mobil Oil, and Africa, the artist forced viewers to think about the connections among multinational corporations, political and economic conditions in South Africa, and the conflicted politics of corporate patronage of art exhibitions, thereby undermining the public's naive view that cultural institutions are exempt from political and economic concerns.

XU BING A different kind of political/cultural commentary has been the hallmark of XU BING (b. 1955), a Chongqing, China, native who was forced to work in the countryside with peasants during the Cultural Revolution of 1966 to 1976 under Mao Tse-tung (1893–1976). Xu later studied printmaking in Beijing at the Central Academy of Fine Arts. He moved to the United States in 1990 at the invitation of the University of Wisconsin, where two years earlier he had exhibited his most famous work, a large installation called *A Book from the Sky* (FIG. 31-18). First exhibited in China and Japan before being installed at Wisconsin's Chazen Museum of Art, the work presents an enormous number of woodblock-printed texts in characters evocative of Chinese writing but invented by the artist.

Producing them required both an intimate knowledge of genuine Chinese characters and extensive training in block carving. Xu's work, however, is no hymn to tradition. Critics have interpreted it both as a stinging critique of the meaninglessness of contemporary political language and as a commentary on the illegibility of the past. Like many works of art, past and present, Eastern and Western, Xu's postmodern masterpiece can be read on many levels.

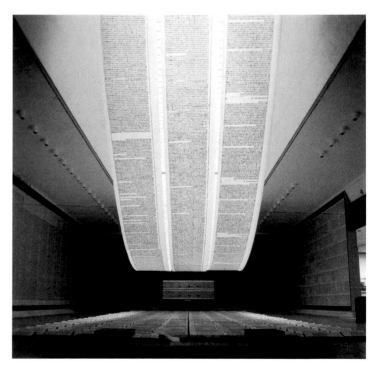

31-18 XU BING, *A Book from the Sky*, 1987. Installation at Chazen Museum of Art, University of Wisconsin, Madison, 1991. Moveable-type prints and books.

Xu trained as a printmaker in Beijing. *A Book from the Sky*, with its invented Chinese woodblock characters, may be a stinging critique of the meaninglessness of contemporary political language.

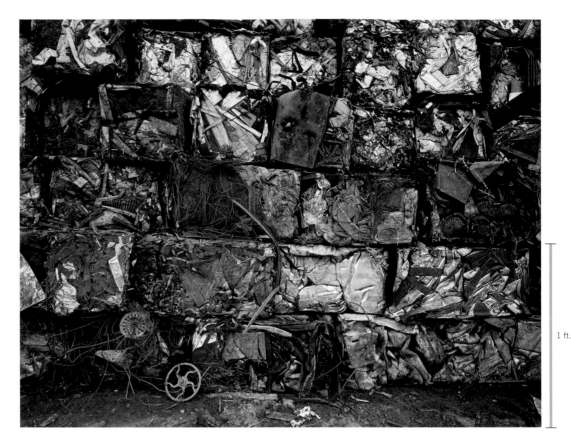

31-19 Edward Burtynsky, *Densified Scrap Metal #3a, Hamilton, Ontario,* 1997. Dye coupler print, 2′ 2¾″ × 2′ 10⅜″. National Gallery of Canada, Ottawa (gift of the artist, 1998).

Burtynsky's "manufactured landscapes" are commentaries on the destructive effects on the environment of industrial plants and mines, but his photographs transform ugliness into beauty.

1 ft.

EDWARD BURTYNSKY Concern with the destructive effects of industrial plants and mines on the environment has been the motivation for the photographs of "manufactured landscapes" by Canadian EDWARD BURTYNSKY (b. 1955). The son of a Ukrainian immigrant who worked in the General Motors plant in St. Catharines, Ontario, Burtynsky studied photography and graphic design at Ryerson University and Niagara College. He uses a large-format field camera to produce high-resolution negatives of industrial landscapes littered with tires, scrap metal, and industrial refuse. His choice of subjects is itself a negative commentary on modern manufacturing processes, but Burtynsky transforms ugliness into beauty in his color prints. His photograph (FIG. 31-19) of a Toronto recycling plant from his *Urban Mines* series converts bundles of compressed scrap metal into a striking abstract composition of multicolored rectangles. Burtynsky's work thus merges documentary and fine-art photography and bears comparison with the photographs of Margaret Bourke-White (FIG. 29-76) and Minor White (FIG. 30-32).

OTHER MOVEMENTS AND THEMES

Despite the high visibility of contemporary artists whose work deals with the pressing social and political issues of the world, some critically acclaimed living artists have produced innovative modernist art during the postmodern era. Abstraction remains a valid and compelling approach to painting and sculpture in the 21st century, as does more traditional figural art.

Abstract Painting and Sculpture

Already in the 1970s, Susan Rothenberg (FIG. 30-8D) had produced monumental "Neo-Expressionist" paintings inspired by German Expressionism and American Abstract Expressionism. Today, several important contemporary artists continue to explore this dynamic style.

JULIAN SCHNABEL New Yorker JULIAN SCHNABEL (b. 1951), who wrote and directed a 1996 film about fellow artist Jean-Michel Basquiat (FIG. 31-8), has experimented widely with media and materials in his forceful restatements of the premises of Abstract Expressionism. Schnabel's Neo-Expressionist works range from paint on velvet and tarpaulin to a mixture of pigment and fragmented china plates bonded to wood. He has a special interest in the physicality of objects, and by combining broken crockery and paint, as in The Walk Home (FIG. **31-20**), he has found an extension of what paint can do. Superficially, Schnabel's paintings recall the work of the gestural abstractionists, especially the spontaneous drips of Jackson Pollock (FIG. 30-6) and the energetic brushstrokes of Willem de Kooning (FIG. 30-8), but their Abstract Expressionist works lack the thick, mosaiclike texture of Schnabel's canvases. The amalgamation of media brings together painting, mosaic, and low-relief sculpture, and considerably amplifies the expressive impact of his paintings.

ANSELM KIEFER Neo-Expressionism was by no means a solely American movement. German artist ANSELM KIEFER (b. 1945), who studied art in Düsseldorf with Joseph Beuys (FIG. 30-52) in the early 1970s, and has lived and worked in Barjac, France, since 1992, has produced some of the most lyrical and engaging works of recent decades. Like Schnabel's canvases, Kiefer's paintings, such as *Nigredo* (FIG. **31-21**), are monumental in scale, recall Abstract Expressionist works, and draw the viewer to their textured surfaces, made more complex by the addition of materials such as straw and lead. It is not merely the impressive physicality of Kiefer's paintings that accounts for the impact of his work, however. His images function on a mythological or metaphorical level as well as on a historically specific one. Kiefer's works of the 1970s and 1980s often involve a reexamination of German history, particularly the painful Nazi era of 1933–1945, and evoke the feeling of despair.

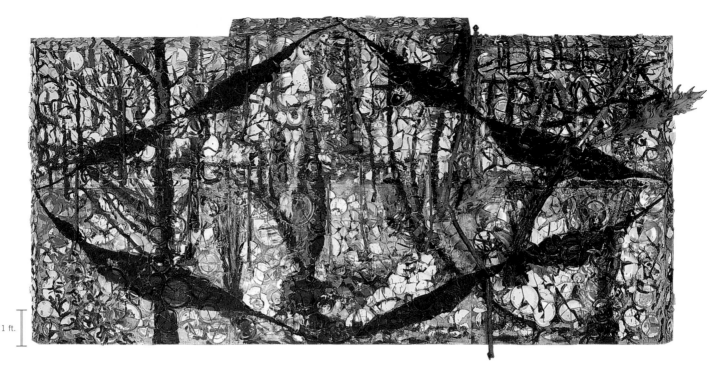

1 ft.

31-20 JULIAN SCHNABEL, *The Walk Home,* 1984–1985. Oil, plates, copper, bronze, fiberglass, and Bondo on wood, 9′ 3″ × 19′ 4″. Broad Art Foundation and the Pace Gallery, New York. ◼◀

Schnabel's paintings recall the work of the gestural abstractionists, but he employs an amalgamation of media, bringing together painting, mosaic, and low-relief sculpture.

Kiefer believes Germany's participation in World War II and the Holocaust left permanent scars on the souls of the German people and on the souls of all humanity.

Nigredo (blackening) pulls the viewer into an expansive landscape depicted using Renaissance perspective principles. This landscape, however, is far from pastoral or carefully cultivated. Rather, it appears bleak and charred. Although it does not make specific reference to the Holocaust, this incinerated landscape indirectly alludes to the horrors of that historical event. More generally, the blackness of the landscape may refer to the notion of alchemical change or transformation, a concept of great interest to Kiefer. Black is one of the four symbolic colors of the alchemist—a color referencing both death and the molten, chaotic state of substances broken down by fire. Because the alchemist focuses on the transformation of substances, the emphasis on blackness is not absolute, but can also be perceived as part of a process of renewal and redemption. Kiefer thus imbued his work with a deep symbolic meaning that, when combined with the intriguing visual quality of his parched, congealed surfaces, results in paintings of enduring power.

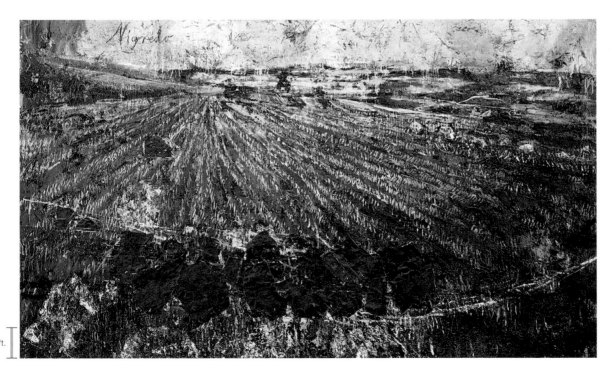

1 ft.

31-21 ANSELM KIEFER, *Nigredo,* 1984. Oil paint on photosensitized fabric, acrylic emulsion, straw, shellac, relief paint on paper pulled from painted wood, 11′ × 18′. Philadelphia Museum of Art, Philadelphia (gift of Friends of the Philadelphia Museum of Art).

Kiefer's paintings have thickly encrusted surfaces incorporating materials such as straw. Here, the German artist used perspective to pull the viewer into an incinerated landscape alluding to the Holocaust.

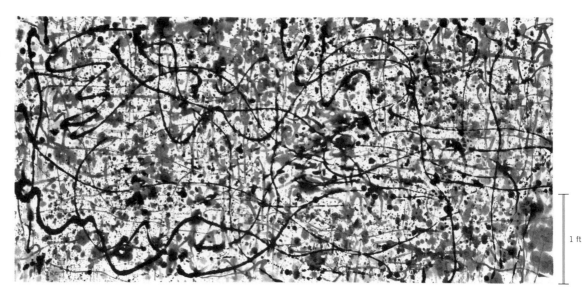

31-22 WU GUANZHONG, *Wild Vines with Flowers Like Pearls*, 1997. Ink on paper, 2′ 11½″ × 5′ 11″. Singapore Art Museum, Singapore (donation from Wu Guanzhong).

In a brilliant fusion of traditional Chinese subject matter and technique with modern Western Abstract Expressionism, Wu depicted the wild vines of the Yangtze River valley.

1 ft.

WU GUANZHONG Abstraction is a still-vital pictorial mode in Asia, where the most innovative artists working in the Neo-Expressionist mode have merged Western and Eastern traditions in their work. WU GUANZHONG (1919–2010) attended the National Art College in Hangzhou, graduating in 1942, and then studied painting in Paris at the École Nationale Supérieure des Beaux-Arts from 1946 to 1950, when he returned to China to take up teaching positions at several prestigious art academies. His early work, reflecting his exposure to the Western tradition, was primarily oil painting on canvas, but in the 1970s he began to embrace the traditional Chinese medium of ink and color on paper, later often restricting his palette only to ink. His mature work, for example, *Wild Vines with Flowers Like Pearls* (FIG. **31-22**), painted in 1997, combines the favored medium and subject matter of the centuries-old *literati* tradition—the 17th-century paintings of Shitao (FIG. 33-15) were important forerunners—with an abstract style strongly influenced by Pollock. American Abstract Expressionist painting was politically impossible to pursue during the Cultural Revolution, when Wu, like Xu Bing (FIG. 31-18), was sentenced to labor on a rural farm because of his refusal to conform to official doctrine.

The inspiration for *Wild Vines*, as for so many of Wu's paintings, was the mountainous landscape and forests of the Yangtze River. The free composition and bold thick brushstrokes brilliantly balance abstract, sweeping, crisscrossing lines with the suggestive shapes of vines and flowers. His work, like that of SONG SU-NAM (b. 1938; FIG. **31-22A**) in Korea and EMILY KAME KNGWARREYE (1910–1996; FIG. **31-22B**) in Australia, represents a highly successful fusion of traditional local and modern Western style and subject matter.

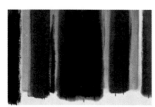

31-22A SONG, *Summer Trees*, 1983.

31-22B KNGWARREYE, *Untitled*, 1992.

KIMIO TSUCHIYA In contemporary Japan, as in China, no single artistic style, medium, or subject dominates, but much of the art produced during the past few decades springs from ideas or beliefs integral to the national culture over many centuries. For example, the Shinto belief in the generative forces in nature and in humankind's position as part of the totality of nature (see "Shinto," Chapter 17, page 479) holds great appeal for contemporary artists such as KIMIO TSUCHIYA (b. 1955), who studied sculpture in London and Tokyo. Tsuchiya is best known for his large-scale sculptures (FIG. **31-23**) constructed of branches or driftwood. Despite their abstract nature, his works assert the life forces found in natural materials, thereby engaging viewers in a consideration of their

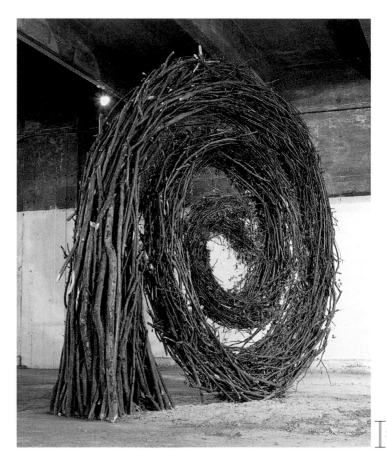

1 ft.

31-23 KIMIO TSUCHIYA, *Symptom*, 1987. Branches, 13′ 1½″ × 14′ 9⅛″ × 3′ 11¼″. Installation at the exhibition *Jeune Sculpture '87,* Paris 1987.

Tsuchiya's sculptures consist of branches or driftwood, and despite their abstract nature, they assert the life forces found in natural materials. His approach to sculpture reflects ancient Shinto beliefs.

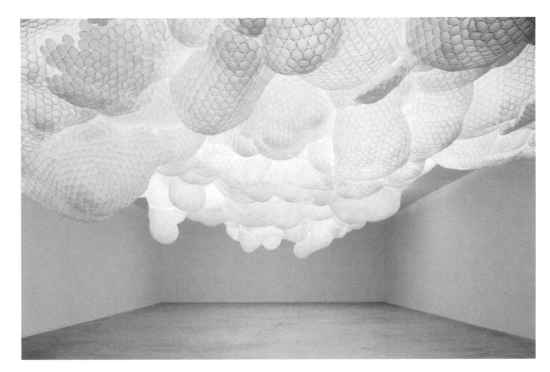

31-24 TARA DONOVAN, *Untitled,* 2003. Styrofoam cups and hot glue, variable dimensions. Installation at the Ace Gallery, Los Angeles, 2005.

Donovan's sculptures consist of everyday components, such as straws, plastic cups, and wire. The abstract forms suggest rolling landscapes, clouds, fungus, and other natural forms.

own relationship to nature. Tsuchiya does not specifically invoke Shinto when speaking about his art, but it is clear he has internalized Shinto principles. He identifies as his goal "to bring out and present the life of nature emanating from this energy of trees. . . . It is as though the wood is part of myself, as though the wood has the same kind of life force."[3]

TARA DONOVAN Brooklynite TARA DONOVAN (b. 1969) studied at the School of Visual Arts in New York City, the Corcoran College of Art and Design in Washington, D.C., and Virginia Commonwealth University in Richmond. She was the first recipient (in 2005) of the Alexander Calder Foundation's Calder Prize for sculpture. Donovan has won an international reputation for her installations (FIG. 31-24) of large sculptural works composed of thousands of small everyday objects, such as toothpicks, straws, pins, paper plates, plastic cups, and electrical wire. Her abstract sculptures often suggest rolling landscapes, clouds, fungus, and other natural forms, although she seeks in her work not to mimic those forms but to capture nature's dynamic growth. Some of Donovan's installations are unstable and can change shape during the course of an exhibition.

Figural Painting and Sculpture

Recent decades have brought a revival of interest in figural art, both in painting and sculpture, a trend best exemplified in the earlier postwar period by Lucian Freud (FIG. 30-29), who remains an active and influential painter.

JENNY SAVILLE Fellow Briton JENNY SAVILLE (b. 1970) is the leading figure painter in the Freud mold of the younger generation of European and American artists. Born in Cambridge, England, and trained at the Glasgow School of Art in Scotland, Saville lives and paints in an old palace in Palermo, Italy. Her best-known works are over-life-size self-portraits in which she exaggerates the girth of her body and delights in depicting heavy folds of flesh with visible veins in minute detail and from a sharply foreshortened angle, which further distorts the body's proportions. Her nude self-portraits deserve comparison not only with those of Freud but also

of Egon Schiele (FIG. 29-10), despite the vivid contrast between Schiele's emaciated body and Saville's obesity.

Saville's paintings are a commentary on the contemporary obsession with the lithe bodies of fashion models. In *Branded* (FIG. 31-25), she underscores the dichotomy between the popular notion of a beautiful body and the imperfect bodies of most people by "branding" her body with words inscribed in her flesh—*delicate, decorative, petite.* Art critic Michelle Meagher has described Saville's paintings as embodying a "feminist aesthetics of disgust."[4]

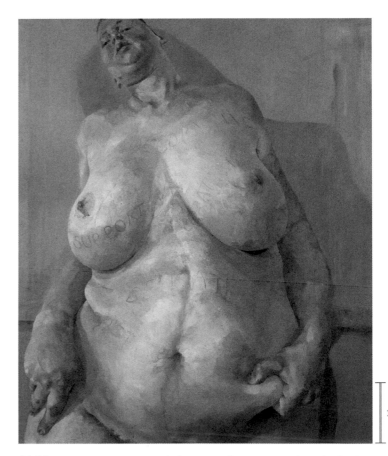

1 ft.

31-25 JENNY SAVILLE, *Branded,* 1992. Oil on canvas, 7′ × 6′. Charles Saatchi Collection, London.

Saville's unflattering foreshortened self-portrait "branded" with words such as *delicate* and *petite* underscores the dichotomy between the perfect bodies of fashion models and those of most people.

KIKI SMITH A distinctly unflattering approach to the representation of the human body is also the hallmark of New York–based KIKI SMITH (b. 1954), the daughter of Minimalist sculptor Tony Smith (FIG. 30-17). In her work, Smith has explored the question of who controls the human body, an interest that grew out of her training as an emergency medical service technician. Smith, however, also wants to reveal the socially constructed nature of the body, and she encourages the viewer to consider how external forces shape people's perceptions of their bodies. In works such as *Untitled* (FIG. 31-26), the artist dramatically departed from conventional representations of the body, both in art and in the media. She suspended two life-size wax figures, one male and one female, both nude, from metal stands. Smith marked each of the sculptures with long white drips—body fluids running from the woman's breasts and down the man's leg. She commented:

> Most of the functions of the body are hidden . . . from society. . . . [W]e separate our bodies from our lives. But, when people are

dying, they are losing control of their bodies. That loss of function can seem humiliating and frightening. But, on the other hand, you can look at it as a kind of liberation of the body. It seems like a nice metaphor—a way to think about the social—that people lose control despite the many agendas of different ideologies in society, which are trying to control the body(ies) . . . medicine, religion, law, etc. Just thinking about control—who has control of the body? . . . Does the mind have control of the body? Does the social?[5]

JEFF KOONS The sculptures of JEFF KOONS (b. 1955) form a striking counterpoint to the figural art of Kiki Smith. Trained at the Maryland Institute College of Art in Baltimore, Koons worked early in his career as a commodities broker. He first became prominent in the art world for a series of works in the early 1980s involving the exhibition of everyday commercial products such as vacuum cleaners. Clearly following in the footsteps of Marcel Duchamp (FIG. 29-27), Koons made no attempt to manipulate or

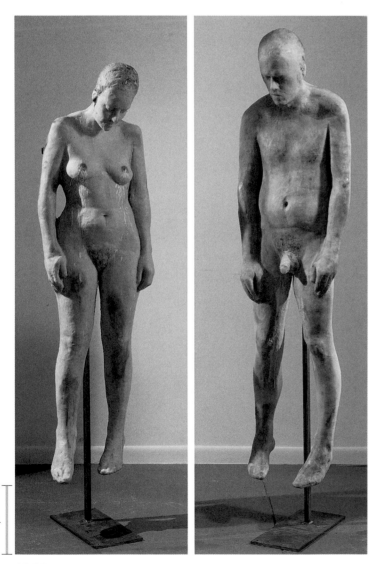

1 ft.

31-26 KIKI SMITH, *Untitled,* 1990. Beeswax and microcrystalline wax figures on metal stands, female figure installed height 6′ 1½″ and male figure installed height 6′ 5″. Whitney Museum of American Art, New York (purchased with funds from the Painting and Sculpture Committee).

Asking "Who controls the body?" Kiki Smith sculpted two life-size wax figures of a nude man and woman with body fluids running from the woman's breasts and down the man's leg.

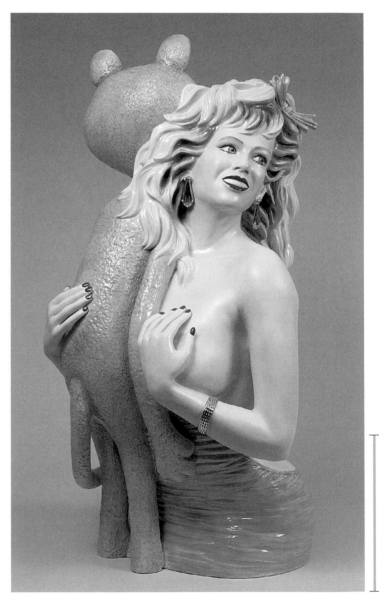

1 ft.

31-27 JEFF KOONS, *Pink Panther,* 1988. Porcelain, 3′ 5″ high. Museum of Contemporary Art, Chicago (Gerald S. Elliot Collection). ◼◂

Koons creates sculptures highlighting everything he considers wrong with contemporary American consumer culture. In this work, he intertwined a centerfold nude and a cartoon character.

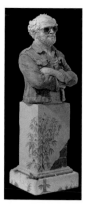

alter the machine-made objects. More recently, he, like Californian ROBERT ARNESON (1930–1992; FIG. 31-27A), turned to ceramic sculpture. In *Pink Panther* (FIG. 31-27), Koons, who divides his time between his hometown of York, Pennsylvania, and New York City, intertwined a magazine centerfold nude with a famous cartoon character. He reinforced the trite and kitschy nature of this imagery by titling the exhibition of which this work was a part *The Banality Show.* Some art critics have argued Koons and his work instruct viewers because both artist and artwork serve as the most visible symbols of everything wrong with contemporary American society. Regardless of whether this is true, Koons's prominence in the art world indicates he has developed an acute understanding of the dynamics of consumer culture.

MARISOL ESCOBAR

Known simply by her first name, MARISOL ESCOBAR (b. 1930) grew up in a wealthy, widely traveled Venezuelan family. Born in Paris and educated there, in Los Angeles, and in New York City, Marisol first studied painting and drawing, but after discovering Pre-Columbian art in 1951, she pursued a career as a sculptor. Marisol also spent time in Italy, where she developed a deep admiration for Renaissance art.

In the 1960s, Marisol was one of the inner circle of New York Pop artists, and she appeared in two of Andy Warhol's films. Some of her works at that time portrayed prominent public figures, including the Hollywood actor John Wayne and the family of U.S. president John F. Kennedy. Her subjects were always people, however, not the commercial products of consumer culture that fascinated most leading Pop artists and still are prominent in the art of Jeff Koons and others.

Marisol retained her interest in figural sculpture long after Pop Art gave way to other movements. One of her most ambitious works (FIG. 31-28) is a multimedia three-dimensional version of Leonardo da Vinci's *Last Supper* (FIG. 22-4), including the walls and windows of the dining room in order to replicate the Renaissance master's application of linear perspective. By reproducing the fresco in three dimensions, she transformed it into an object. Marisol's figures are painted wood, with the exception of Christ, whose stone body is the physical and emotional anchor of the composition. In many of her sculptures, the female figures have Marisol's features, and in this tableau she added a seated armless portrait of herself looking at the *Last Supper.* Catholic and deeply religious—as a teenager she emulated martyr saints by inflicting physical harm on herself—Marisol may have wanted to show herself as a witness to Christ's last meal. But more likely her presence here is a tribute to the 16th-century painter. (She also made a sculptural replica of Leonardo's *Madonna and Child with Saint Anne* [FIG. 22-3].)

Marisol's *Self-Portrait Looking at the Last Supper* is a commentary on the artist not only as a creator but also as a viewer of the works of earlier artists, a link in an artistic chain extending back to antiquity. One pervasive element in the work

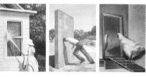

of contemporary artists is a self-consciousness of the postmodern painter or sculptor's position in the continuum of art history. No one better exemplifies that aspect of contemporary art than MARK TANSEY (b. 1949; FIG. 31-28A).

KANE KWEI AND PAA JOE

Painted wood sculpture remains a vital artistic medium in Africa, where it has a venerable heritage throughout the continent (see Chapters 19 and 37). Some contemporary African artists have pioneered new forms, however,

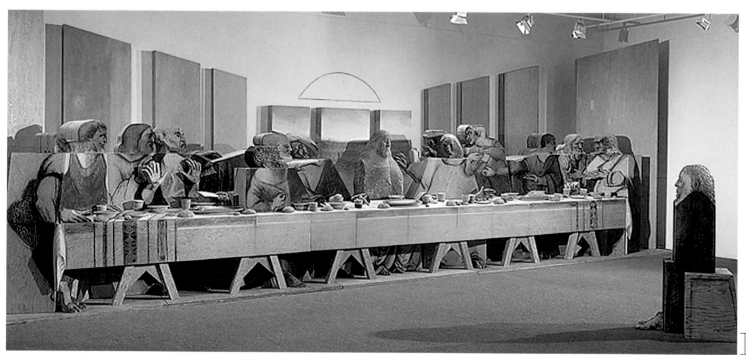

1 ft.

31-28 MARISOL ESCOBAR, *Self-Portrait Looking at the Last Supper,* 1982–1984. Painted wood, stone, plaster, and aluminum, 10′ 1½″ × 29′ 10″ × 5′ 1″. Metropolitan Museum of Art, New York (gift of Mr. and Mrs. Roberto C. Polo, 1986).

In a tribute to the Renaissance master, Marisol created a sculptural replica of Leonardo's *Last Supper* (FIG. 22-4), transforming the fresco into an object. She is the seated viewer as well as the artist.

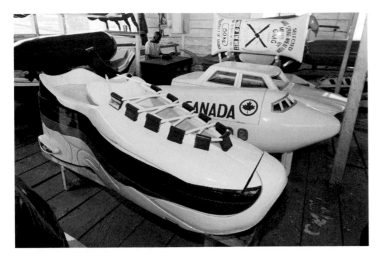

31-29 PAA JOE, running shoe, airplane, automobile and other coffins inside the artist's showroom in Teshi, Ghana, 2000. Painted wood.

The caskets of Paa Joe take many forms, including items of clothing, airplanes, and automobiles. The forms always relate to the deceased, but many collectors buy the caskets as art objects.

often under the influence of modern Western art movements. Kane Kwei (1922–1992) of the Ga people in urban coastal Ghana created a new kind of wooden casket that brought him both critical acclaim and commercial success. Beginning around 1970, Kwei, trained as a carpenter, created one-of-a-kind coffins crafted to reflect the deceased's life, occupation, or major accomplishments. On commission he made such diverse shapes as a cow, a whale, a bird, a Mercedes Benz, and various local food crops, such as onions and cocoa pods, all pieced together using nails and glue rather than carved. Kwei also created coffins in traditional African leaders' symbolic forms, such as an eagle, an elephant, a leopard, and a stool.

Kwei's sons and his cousin PAA JOE (b. 1944) have carried on his legacy. In a photograph (FIG. 31-29) shot around 2000 outside Joe's showroom in Teshi, several large caskets are on display, including a running shoe, an airplane, and an automobile. Many of the coffins Kwei and Joe produced never served as burial containers. Collectors and curators purchased them for display in private homes, art galleries, and museums. The coffins' forms, derived from popular culture, strike a familiar chord in the Western world because they recall Pop Art sculptures (FIG. 30-26), which accounts in large part for the international appeal of Kwei and Joe's work.

ARCHITECTURE AND SITE-SPECIFIC ART

The work of architects and Environmental artists today is as varied as that of contemporary painters and sculptors, but the common denominator in the diversity of contemporary architectural design and site-specific projects is the breaking down of national boundaries, with leading practitioners working in several countries and even on several continents, often simultaneously.

Architecture

In the late 20th and early 21st century, one of the by-products of the globalization of the world's economy has been that leading architects have received commissions to design buildings far from their home bases. In the rapidly developing emerging markets of Asia, the Middle East, Africa, Latin America, and elsewhere, virtually every architect with an international reputation can list a recent building in Beijing or another urban center on his or her résumé.

NORMAN FOSTER Award-winning architect NORMAN FOSTER (b. 1935) began his study of architectural design at the University of Manchester, England. After graduating, he won a fellowship to attend the master's degree program at the Yale School of Architecture, where he met Richard Rogers (FIG. 30-49). The two decided to open a joint architectural firm when they returned to London in 1962, but they established separate practices several years later. Their designs still have much in common, however,

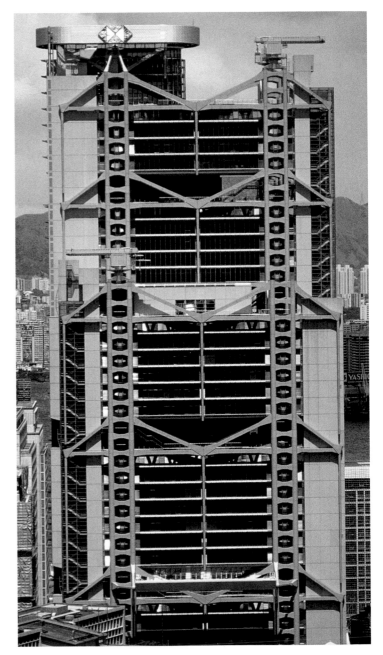

31-30 NORMAN FOSTER, Hong Kong and Shanghai Bank (looking southwest), Hong Kong, China, 1979–1986.

Foster's High-Tech tower has an exposed steel skeleton featuring floors with uninterrupted working spaces. At the base is a 10-story atrium illuminated by computerized mirrors that reflect sunlight.

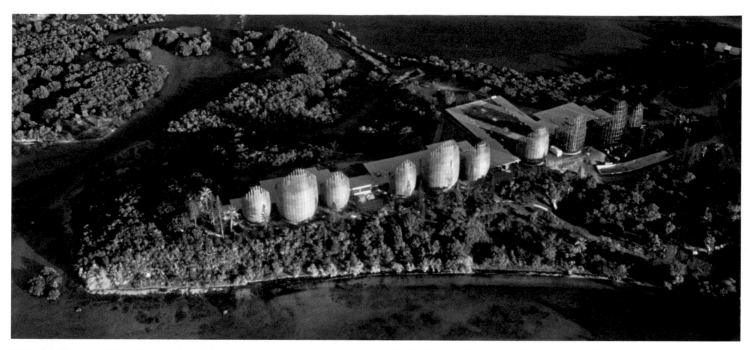

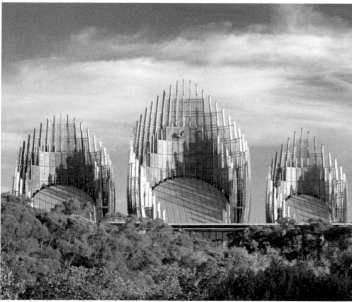

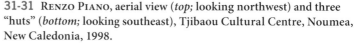

31-31 RENZO PIANO, aerial view (*top;* looking northwest) and three "huts" (*bottom;* looking southeast), Tjibaou Cultural Centre, Noumea, New Caledonia, 1998.

A pioneering example of "green architecture," Piano's complex of 10 bamboo units, based on traditional New Caledonian village huts, has adjustable skylights in the roofs for natural climate control.

each that he calls "villages," suspended from steel girders resembling bridges. Escalators connect the floors in each village—the floors are related by function—but the elevators stop at only one floor in each community of floors. At the base of the building is a plaza opening onto the neighboring streets. Visitors ascend on escalators from the plaza to a spectacular 10-story, 170-feet-tall atrium bordered by balconies with additional workspaces. What Foster calls "sun scoops"—computerized mirrors on the south side of the building—track the movement of the sun across the Hong Kong sky and reflect the sunlight into the atrium and piazza, flooding the dramatic spaces with light at all hours of the day. Not surprisingly, the roof of this High-Tech skyscraper serves as a landing pad for corporate helicopters.

GREEN ARCHITECTURE The harnessing of solar energy as a power source is one of the key features of what critics commonly refer to as *green architecture*—ecologically friendly buildings that use "clean energy" and sustain the natural environment. Green architecture is the most important trend in architectural design in the early 21st century. A pioneer in this field is Renzo Piano, the codesigner with Richard Rogers of the Pompidou Center (FIG. 30-49) in Paris. Piano won an international competition to design the Tjibaou Cultural Centre (FIG. **31-31**, *left*) in Noumea, New Caledonia. Named in honor of the assassinated political leader Jean-Marie Tjibaou (1936–1989), the center consists of 10 beehive-shaped bamboo "huts" nestled in pine trees on a narrow island peninsula in the Pacific Ocean. Rooted in the village architecture of the Kanak people of New Caledonia (see Chapter 36), each unit of Piano's postmodern complex has an adjustable skylight as a roof (FIG. 31-31, *right*) to provide natural—sustainable—climate control. The curved profile of the Tjibaou pavilions also helps the structures withstand the pressure of the hurricane-force winds common in the South Pacific.

because they share a similar outlook. Foster and Rogers are the leading proponents of what critics call *High-Tech* architecture, the roots of which can be traced to Joseph Paxton's mid-19th-century Crystal Palace (FIG. 27-47) in London. High-Tech architects design buildings incorporating the latest innovations in engineering and technology and exposing the structures' component parts. High-Tech architecture is distinct from other postmodern architectural movements in dispensing with all historical references.

Foster's design for the headquarters (FIG. **31-30**) of the Hong Kong and Shanghai Bank Corporation (HSBC), which cost $1 billion to build, exemplifies the High-Tech approach to architecture. The banking tower is as different from Philip Johnson's postmodern AT&T Building (FIG. 30-46) as it is from the modernist glass-and-steel Seagram Building (FIG. 30-43) and Sears Tower (FIG. 30-44). The 47-story Hong Kong skyscraper has an exposed steel skeleton with the elevators and other service elements located in giant piers at the short ends of the building, a design that provides uninterrupted communal working spaces on each cantilevered floor. Foster divided the tower into five horizontal units of six to nine floors

The roof, walls, and windows of the Deconstructivist Hysolar Institute seem to explode, avoiding any suggestion of stable masses and frustrating viewers' expectations of how a building should look.

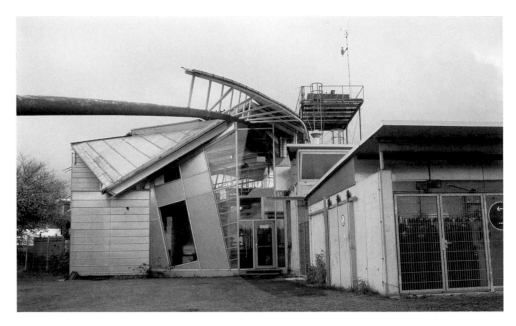

DECONSTRUCTIVISM

DECONSTRUCTIVISM In architecture, as in painting and sculpture, deconstruction as an analytical and design strategy emerged in the 1970s. The name given to this postmodern architectural movement is *Deconstructivism.* Deconstructivist architects attempt to disrupt the conventional categories of architecture and to rupture the viewer's expectations based on them. Destabilization plays a major role in Deconstructivist architecture. Disorder, dissonance, imbalance, asymmetry, irregularity, and unconformity replace their opposites—order, harmony, balance, symmetry, regularity, and clarity. The seemingly haphazardly presented volumes, masses, planes, borders, lighting, locations, directions, spatial relations, as well as the disguised structural facts of Deconstructivist design, challenge the viewer's assumptions about architectural form as it relates to function. According to Deconstructivist principles, the very absence of the stability of traditional categories of architecture in a structure announces a "deconstructed" building.

GÜNTER BEHNISCH Audacious in its dissolution of form is the Hysolar Institute (FIG. **31-32**) at the University of Stuttgart, Germany, by GÜNTER BEHNISCH (1922–2010). Behnisch, who gained international attention as the architect of the Olympic Park in Munich for the 1972 Olympic Games, designed the institute as part of a joint German–Saudi Arabian research project on the technology of solar energy. In the Hysolar Institute, Behnisch intended to deny the possibility of spatial enclosure altogether, and his apparently chaotic arrangement of the structural units defies easy analysis. The shapes of the roof, walls, and windows seem to explode, avoiding any suggestion of clear, stable masses. Behnisch aggressively played with the traditional concepts of architectural design. The disordered architectural elements of the Hysolar Institute seem precarious and visually threaten to collapse, frustrating the viewer's expectations of how a building should look.

FRANK GEHRY The architect most closely identified with Deconstructivist architecture is Canadian FRANK GEHRY (b. 1929). Trained in sculpture, and at different times a collaborator with Donald Judd (FIG. 30-18) and Claes Oldenburg (FIG. 30-26), Gehry works up his designs by constructing models and then cutting them up and arranging the parts until he has a satisfying composition. Among Gehry's most notable projects is the Guggenheim Museum (FIGS. **31-33** and **31-34**) in Bilbao, Spain, one

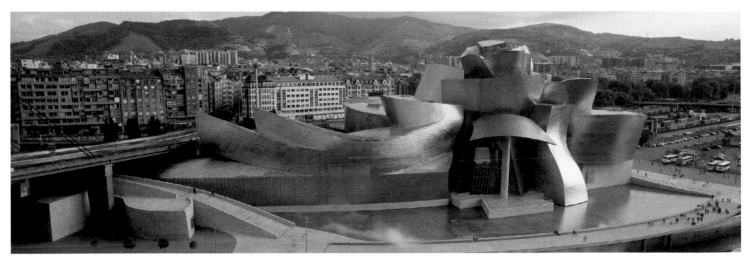

31-33 FRANK GEHRY, Guggenheim Bilbao Museo (looking south), Bilbao, Spain, 1997.

Gehry's limestone-and-titanium Bilbao museum is an immensely dramatic building. Its disorder and seeming randomness of design epitomize Deconstructivist architectural principles.

Frank Gehry on Architectural Design and Materials

Frank Gehry has been designing buildings since the 1950s, but only in the 1970s did he begin to break away from the rectilinearity of modernist architecture and develop the dramatic sculptural style seen in buildings such as the Guggenheim Museum (FIGS. 31-33 and 31-34) in Bilbao. In 1999, the Deconstructivist architect reflected on his career and his many projects in a book simply titled *Gehry Talks*.

> My early work was rectilinear because you take baby steps. I guess the work has become a kind of sculpture as architecture.... I'm a strict modernist in the sense of believing in purity, that you shouldn't decorate. And yet buildings need decoration, because they need scaling elements. They need to be human scale, in my opinion. They can't just be faceless things. That's how some modernism failed.*
>
> They teach materials and methods in architecture school, as a separate course. I'm a craftsman.... It seems to me that when you're doing architecture, you're building something out of something. There are social issues, there's context, and then there's how do you make the enclosure and what do you make it with? ... I explored metal: how it dealt with the light ... It does beautiful things with light.... Flat was a fetish, and everybody was doing that. I found out that I could use metal if I didn't worry about it being flat; I could do it cheaper. It was intuitive. I just went with it. I liked it. Then when I saw it on the building, I loved it.... Bilbao ... [is] titanium.... [I] prefer titanium because it's stronger; it's an element, a pure element, and it doesn't oxidize. It stays the same forever. They give a hundred-year guarantee!†

*Milton Friedman, ed., *Gehry Talks: Architecture + Process*, rev. ed. (New York: Universe, 2002), 47–48.
†Ibid., 44, 47.

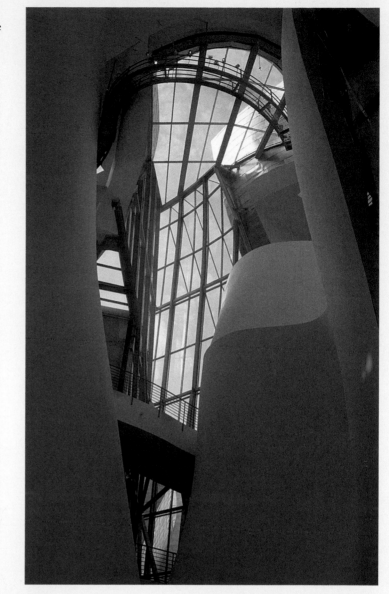

31-34 FRANK GEHRY, atrium of the Guggenheim Bilbao Museo, Bilbao, Spain, 1997.

The glass-walled atrium of the Guggenheim Bilbao Museum soars skyward 165 feet. The asymmetrical and imbalanced screens and vaults flow into one another, creating a sense of disequilibrium.

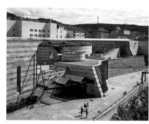

31-34A STIRLING, Neue Staatsgalerie, Stuttgart, 1977–1983.

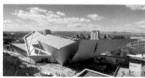

31-34B LIBESKIND, Denver Art Museum, 2006.

of several art museum projects of the past few decades as notable for their innovative postmodern architectural designs as for the important art collections they house. These include the Neue Staatsgalerie (FIG. **31-34A**) in Stuttgart, Germany, by British architect JAMES STIRLING (1926–1994); the Denver Art Museum (FIG. **31-34B**) by Polish-born DANIEL LIBESKIND (b. 1946); and the Grande Louvre Pyramide (FIG. 31-36) in Paris.

Gehry's Bilbao museum appears to be a collapsed or collapsing aggregate of units. Visitors approaching the building see a mass of irregular asymmetrical and imbalanced forms whose profiles change dramatically with every shift of the viewer's position. The limestone- and titanium-clad exterior lends a space-age character to the structure and highlights further the unique cluster effect of the many forms (see "Frank Gehry on Architectural Design and Materials," above). A group of organic forms Gehry refers to as a "metallic flower" tops the museum. In the center of the museum, an enormous glass-walled atrium (FIG. 31-34) soars 165 feet above the ground, serving as the focal point for the three levels of galleries radiating from it. The seemingly weightless screens, vaults, and volumes of the interior float and flow into one another, guided only by light and dark cues. The Guggenheim Museum in Bilbao is a profoundly compelling structure. Its disorder, its deceptive randomness of design, and the disequilibrium it prompts in viewers epitomize Deconstructivist principles.

have an emotional effect upon the viewer. A prime example of her work is the Vitra Fire Station (FIG. 31-35) in Weil-am-Rhein, Germany, completed in 1993. Composed of layers of reinforced concrete slabs and unframed window panes, the building features a boldly projecting (functionless) "wing" that suggests a burst of energy shooting out from the structure. It expresses the sudden mobilization of the firefighters within the time the alarm sounds and the time they jump into their trucks to race out to extinguish a blaze.

Zaha Hadid is the first woman to win the Pritzker Architecture Prize (in 2004), the architectural equivalent of the Nobel Prize in literature. The first recipient was Philip Johnson in 1979. Other previous winners include Norman Foster, Frank Gehry, Renzo Piano, James Stirling, Joern Utzon, Robert Venturi, and Ieoh Ming Pei.

IEOH MING PEI The latest chapter in the long architectural history of the Louvre—the former French royal residence (FIGS. 20-16, 23-14, and 25-25), now one of the world's greatest art museums—is a monumental glass-and-steel pyramid erected in the palace's main courtyard in 1988. Designed by the Chinese-American architect IEOH MING PEI (b. 1917), the Grand Louvre Pyramide (FIG. 31-36) is the dramatic postmodern entryway to the museum's priceless collections. Although initially controversial because conservative critics considered it a jarring, dissonant intrusion in a hallowed public space left untouched for centuries, Pei's pyramid, like Rogers and Piano's Pompidou Center (FIG. 30-49) a decade before, quickly captured the French public's imagination and admiration.

There are, in fact, four Louvre glass pyramids: the grand central pyramid plus the three small echoes of it bordering the large fountain-filled pool surrounding the glass entryway. Consistent with postmodern aesthetics, Pei turned to the past for inspiration, choosing the quintessential emblem of ancient Egypt (FIG. 3-7), an appropriate choice given the Louvre's rich collection of Egyptian art. But Pei transformed his ancient solid stone models (see "Building the Great Pyramids," Chapter 3, page 62) into a transparent "tent," simultaneously permitting an almost uninterrupted view of the wings of the royal palace courtyard and serving as a skylight for the new underground network of ticket booths, offices, shops, restaurants, and conference rooms he also designed.

Environmental and Site-Specific Art

When Robert Smithson created *Spiral Jetty* (FIG. 30-50) in Utah's Great Salt Lake in 1970, he was a trailblazer in the new genre of Environmental Art, or earthworks. In recent decades, earthworks

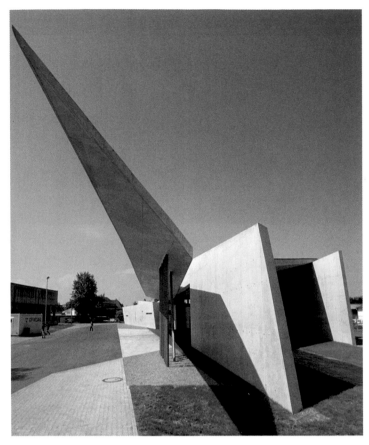

31-35 ZAHA HADID, Vitra Fire Station (looking east), Weil-am-Rhein, Germany, 1989–1993.

Inspired by Suprematism, Hadid employed dynamically arranged, unadorned planes for the Vitra Fire Station. The design suggests the burst of energy of firefighters racing out to extinguish a blaze.

ZAHA HADID One of the most innovative living architects is Iraqi Deconstructivist ZAHA HADID (b. 1950). Born in Baghdad, Hadid studied mathematics in Beirut, Lebanon, and architecture in London and has designed buildings in England, Germany, Austria, France, Italy, Spain, and the United States. Deeply influenced by the Suprematist theories and paintings of Kazimir Malevich (FIG. 29-30), who championed the use of pure colors and abstract geometric shapes to express "the supremacy of pure feeling in creative art," Hadid employs unadorned planes in dynamic arrangements that

31-36 IEOH MING PEI, Grand Louvre Pyramide (looking southwest), Musée du Louvre, Paris, France, 1988.

Egyptian stone architecture inspired Pei's postmodern entryway to the Louvre, but his glass-and-steel pyramid is a transparent tent serving as a skylight for the underground extension of the old museum.

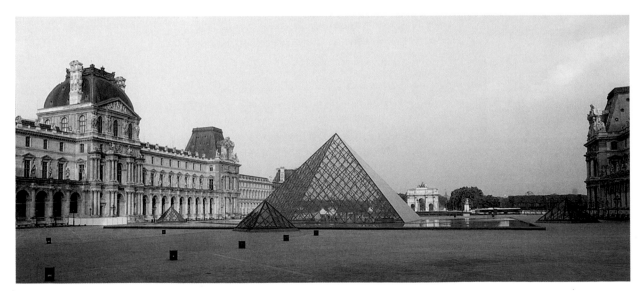

Maya Lin's Vietnam Veterans Memorial

Maya Lin's design for the Vietnam Veterans Memorial (FIG. 31-37) is, like Minimalist sculptures (FIGS. 30-17 and 30-18), an unadorned geometric form. Yet the monument, despite its serene simplicity, actively engages viewers in a psychological dialogue, rather than standing mute. This dialogue gives visitors the opportunity to explore their feelings about the Vietnam War and perhaps arrive at some sense of closure.

The history of the Vietnam Veterans Memorial provides dramatic testimony to this monument's power. In 1981, a jury of architects, sculptors, and landscape architects selected Lin's design from among 1,400 entries in a blind competition for a memorial to be placed in Constitution Gardens in Washington, D.C. Conceivably, the jury not only found her design compelling but also thought its simplicity would be the least likely to provoke controversy. But when the jury made its selection public, heated debate ensued. Even the wall's color came under attack. One veteran charged that black is "the universal color of shame, sorrow and degradation in all races, all societies worldwide."* But the sharpest protests concerned the form and siting of the monument. Because of the stark contrast between the massive white memorials (the Washington Monument and the Lincoln Memorial) bracketing Lin's sunken wall, some people interpreted her Minimalist design as minimizing the Vietnam War and, by extension, the efforts of those who fought in the conflict. Lin herself, however, described the wall as follows:

> The Vietnam Veterans Memorial is not an object inserted into the earth but a work formed from the act of cutting open the earth and polishing the earth's surface—dematerializing the stone to pare surface, creating an interface between the world of the light and the quieter world beyond the names.[†]

Due to the vocal opposition, a compromise was necessary to ensure the memorial's completion. The Commission of Fine Arts, the federal group overseeing the project, commissioned an additional memorial from artist Frederick Hart (1943–1999) in 1983. This larger-than-life-size realistic bronze sculpture of three soldiers,

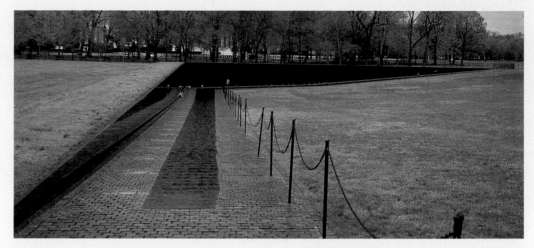

31-37 MAYA YING LIN, Vietnam Veterans Memorial (looking north), Washington, D.C., 1981–1983.

Like Minimalist sculpture, Lin's memorial to veterans of the Vietnam War is a simple geometric form. Its inscribed polished walls actively engage viewers in a psychological dialogue about the war.

armed and uniformed, now stands approximately 120 feet from Lin's wall. Several years later, a group of nurses, organized as the Vietnam Women's Memorial Project, received approval for a sculpture honoring women's service in the Vietnam War. The seven-foot-tall bronze statue by Glenna Goodacre (b. 1939) depicts three female figures, one cradling a wounded soldier in her arms. Unveiled in 1993, the work occupies a site about 300 feet south of the Lin memorial.

Whether celebrated or condemned, Lin's Vietnam Veterans Memorial generates dramatic responses. Commonly, visitors react very emotionally, even those who know none of the soldiers named on the monument. The polished granite surface prompts individual soul-searching—viewers see themselves reflected among the names. Many visitors leave mementos at the foot of the wall in memory of loved ones they lost in the Vietnam War or make rubbings from the incised names. It can be argued that much of this memorial's power derives from its Minimalist simplicity. Like Minimalist sculpture, it does not dictate response and therefore successfully encourages personal exploration.

*Elizabeth Hess, "A Tale of Two Memorials," *Art in America* 71, no. 4 (April 1983): 122.
[†]Excerpt from an unpublished 1995 lecture, quoted in Kristine Stiles and Peter Selz, *Theories and Documents of Contemporary Art: A Sourcebook of Artists' Writings* (Berkeley and Los Angeles: University of California Press, 1996), 525.

---

and other site-specific artworks that bridge the gap between architecture and sculpture have become an established mode of artistic expression. As is true of all other media in the postmodern era, these artworks take a dazzling variety of forms—and some of them have engendered heated controversies.

MAYA YING LIN Variously classified as either a work of Minimalist sculpture or architecture is the Vietnam Veterans Memorial (FIG. **31-37**) in Washington, D.C., designed in 1981 by MAYA YING LIN

(b. 1959) when she was a 21-year-old student at the Yale School of Architecture. The austere, simple memorial, a V-shaped wall constructed of polished black granite panels, begins at ground level at each end and gradually ascends to a height of 10 feet at the center of the V. Each wing is 246 feet long. Lin set the wall into the landscape, enhancing visitors' awareness of descent as they walk along the wall toward the center. The names of the Vietnam War's 57,939 American casualties (and those missing in action) incised on the memorial's walls, in the order of their deaths, contribute to the monument's dramatic effect.

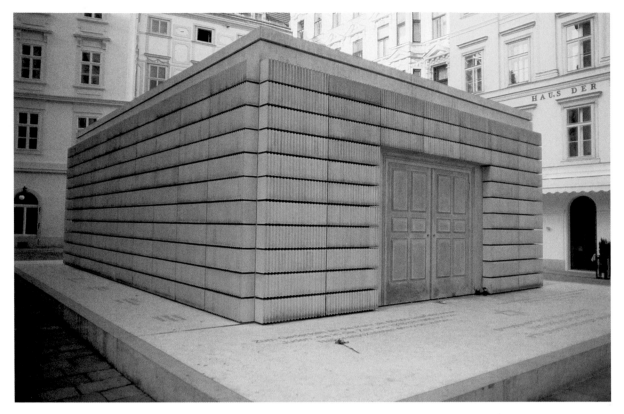

31-38 RACHEL WHITEREAD, Holocaust Memorial (looking northwest), Judenplatz, Vienna, Austria, 2000.

Whiteread's monument to the 65,000 Austrian Jews who perished in the Holocaust is a tomb-like concrete block with doors that cannot be opened and library books seen from behind.

When Lin designed this pristinely simple monument, she gave a great deal of thought to the purpose of war memorials. Her conclusion was a memorial

> should be honest about the reality of war and be for the people who gave their lives. . . . [I] didn't want a static object that people would just look at, but something they could relate to as on a journey, or passage, that would bring each to his own conclusions. . . . I wanted to work with the land and not dominate it. I had an impulse to cut open the earth . . . an initial violence that in time would heal. The grass would grow back, but the cut would remain.[6]

In light of the tragedy of the war, this unpretentious memorial's allusion to a wound and long-lasting scar contributes to its communicative ability (see "Maya Lin's Vietnam Veterans Memorial," page 965).

RACHEL WHITEREAD Another controversial memorial commissioned for a specific historical setting is the Viennese Holocaust Memorial by British sculptor RACHEL WHITEREAD (b. 1963). In 1996, the city of Vienna chose Whiteread as the winner of the competition to design a commemorative monument to the 65,000 Austrian Jews who perished at the hands of the Nazis during World War II (FIG. **31-38**). The decision to focus attention on a past most Austrians wished to forget unleashed a controversy that delayed construction of the monument until 2000. Also controversial was the Minimalist severity of Whiteread's massive block of concrete planted in a Baroque square at the heart of the Austrian capital—as was, at least initially, the understated form of Lin's Vietnam monument (FIG. 31-37) juxtaposed with the Washington and Lincoln Monuments in Washington, D.C.

Whiteread modulated the surface of the Holocaust memorial only slightly by depicting in low relief the shapes of two doors and hundreds of identical books on shelves, with the edges of the covers and the pages rather than the spines facing outward. The book motif was a reference both to Jews as the "People of the Book" and to the book burnings that accompanied Jewish persecutions throughout the centuries and under the Nazis. Around the base, Whiteread inscribed the names of Nazi concentration camps in German, Hebrew, and English. The setting for the memorial is Judenplatz (Jewish Square), the site of a synagogue destroyed in 1421. The brutality of the tomblike monument—it cannot be entered, and its shape suggests a prison block—was a visual as well as psychological shock in the beautiful Viennese square. Whiteread's purpose, however, was not to please but to create a memorial that met the jury's charge to "combine dignity with reserve and spark an aesthetic dialogue with the past in a place that is replete with history."

Whiteread had gained fame in 1992 for her monument commemorating the demolition of a working-class neighborhood in East London. *House* took the form of a concrete cast of the space inside the last standing Victorian house on the site. She had also made sculptures of "negative spaces," for example, the space beneath a chair or mattress or sink. In Vienna, she represented the space behind the shelves of a library. In drawing viewers' attention to the voids between and inside objects and buildings, Whiteread pursued in a different way the same goal as Pop Art innovator Jasper Johns (FIG. 30-22), who painted things "seen but not looked at."

RICHARD SERRA Also unleashing an emotional public debate, but for different reasons and with a decidedly different outcome, was *Tilted Arc* (FIG. **31-39**) by San Franciscan RICHARD SERRA (b. 1939), who worked in steel mills in California before studying art at Yale. He now lives in New York, where he received a commission in 1979 from the General Services Administration (GSA), the federal agency responsible for overseeing the selection and installation of artworks for government buildings, to install a 120-foot-long, 12-foot-high curved wall of Cor-Ten steel in the plaza in front of the Jacob K. Javits Federal Building in lower Manhattan. He completed the project in 1981. Serra wished *Tilted Arc* to "dislocate or alter the decorative function of the plaza and actively

Richard Serra's *Tilted Arc*

When Richard Serra installed *Tilted Arc* (FIG. 31-39) in the plaza in front of the Javits Federal Building in New York City in 1981, much of the public immediately responded with hostile criticism. Prompting the chorus of complaints was the uncompromising presence of a Minimalist sculpture bisecting the plaza. Many argued *Tilted Arc* was ugly, attracted graffiti, interfered with the view across the plaza, and prevented use of the plaza for performances or concerts. Due to the sustained barrage of protests and petitions demanding the removal of *Tilted Arc,* the General Services Administration, which had commissioned the sculpture, held a series of public hearings. Afterward, the agency decided to remove Serra's sculpture despite its prior approval of the artist's model. This, understandably, infuriated Serra, who had a legally binding contract acknowledging the site-specific nature of *Tilted Arc.* "To remove the work is to destroy the work," the artist stated.*

This episode raised intriguing issues about the nature of public art, including the public reception of experimental art, the artist's responsibilities and rights when executing public commissions, censorship in the arts, and the purpose of public art. If an artwork is on display in a public space outside the relatively private confines of a museum or gallery, do different guidelines apply? As one participant in the *Tilted Arc* saga asked, "Should an artist have the right to impose his values and taste on a public that now rejects his taste and values?"[†] One of the express functions of the historical avant-garde was to challenge convention by rejecting tradition and disrupting

the complacency of the viewer. Will placing experimental art in a public place always cause controversy? From Serra's statements, it is clear he intended the sculpture to challenge the public.

Another issue *Tilted Arc* presented involved the rights of the artist, who in this case accused the GSA of censorship. Serra filed a lawsuit against the federal government for infringement of his First Amendment rights and insisted "the artist's work must be uncensored, respected, and tolerated, although deemed abhorrent, or perceived as challenging, or experienced as threatening."[‡] Did removal of the work constitute censorship? A U.S. district court held it did not.

Ultimately, who should decide what artworks are appropriate for the public arena? One artist argued, "We cannot have public art by plebiscite [popular vote]."[§] But to avoid recurrences of the *Tilted Arc* controversy, the GSA changed its procedures and now solicits input from a wide range of civic and neighborhood groups before commissioning public artworks. Despite the removal of *Tilted Arc* (now languishing in storage), the sculpture maintains a powerful presence in all discussions of the aesthetics, politics, and dynamics of public art.

*Grace Glueck, "What Part Should the Public Play in Choosing Public Art?" *New York Times,* February 3, 1985, 27.
[†]Calvin Tomkins, "The Art World: Tilted Arc," *New Yorker,* May 20, 1985, 98.
[‡]Ibid., 98–99.
[§]Ibid., 98.

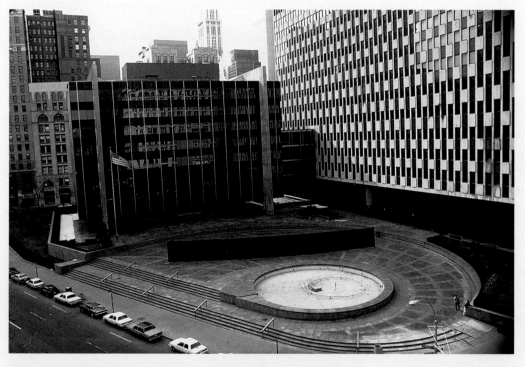

31-39 RICHARD SERRA, *Tilted Arc,* Jacob K. Javits Federal Plaza, New York City, 1981.

Serra intended his Minimalist *Tilted Arc* to alter the character of an existing public space. He succeeded but unleashed a storm of protest that caused the government to remove the work.

bring people into the sculpture's context."[7] In pursuit of that goal, Serra situated the sculpture so that it bisected and consequently significantly altered the space of the open plaza and interrupted the traffic flow across the square. By creating such a monumental presence in this large public space, Serra succeeded in forcing viewers to reconsider the plaza's physical space as a sculptural form—but only temporarily, because the public forced the sculpture to be removed (see "Richard Serra's *Tilted Arc,*" above).

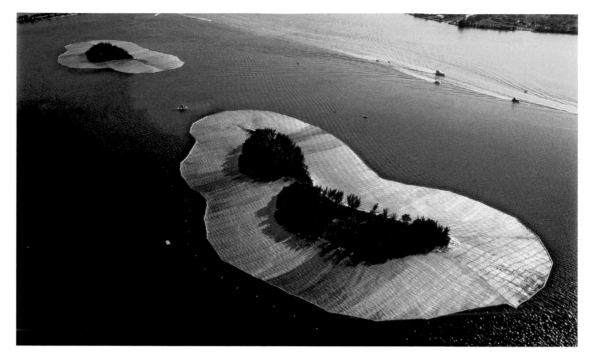

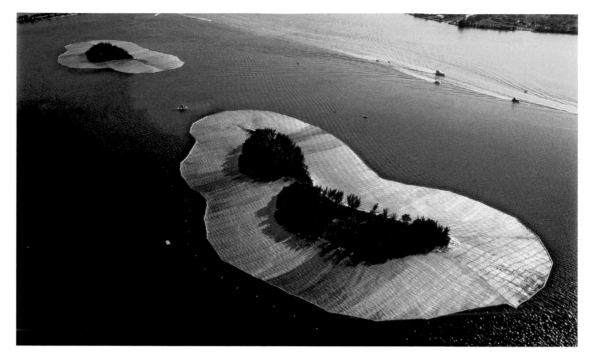

31-40 CHRISTO and JEANNE-CLAUDE, *Surrounded Islands, Biscayne Bay, Miami, Florida, 1980–1983.* ◼◀

Christo and Jeanne-Claude created this Environmental artwork by surrounding 11 small islands with 6.5 million square feet of pink fabric. Characteristically, the work existed for only two weeks.

CHRISTO AND JEANNE-CLAUDE The most famous Environmental artists of the past few decades are CHRISTO (b. 1935) and his deceased spouse JEANNE-CLAUDE (1935–2009). In their works they sought to intensify the viewer's awareness of the space and features of rural and urban sites. However, rather than physically alter the land itself, as Robert Smithson (FIG. 30-50) often did, Christo and Jeanne-Claude prompted this awareness by temporarily modifying the landscape with cloth. Christo studied art in his native Bulgaria and in Austria. After moving from Vienna to Paris, he began to encase objects in clumsy wrappings, thereby appropriating bits of the real world into the mysterious world of the unopened package whose contents can be dimly seen in silhouette under the wrap.

Starting in 1961, Christo and Jeanne-Claude began to collaborate on large-scale projects normally dealing with the environment itself. For example, in 1969 the couple wrapped more than a million square feet of Australian coastline and in 1972 hung a vast curtain across a valley at Rifle Gap, Colorado. Their projects require years of preparation and research, and scores of meetings with local authorities and interested groups of local citizens. These temporary artworks are usually on view for only a few weeks.

Surrounded Islands, Biscayne Bay, Miami, Florida, 1980–1983 (FIG. **31-40**), created in Biscayne Bay for two weeks in May 1983, typifies Christo and Jeanne-Claude's work. For this project, they surrounded 11 small artificial islands in the bay (previously created from a dredging project) with 6.5 million square feet of specially fabricated pink polypropylene floating fabric. This Environmental artwork required three years of preparation to obtain the required permits and to assemble the labor force and obtain the $3.2 million needed to complete the project. The artists raised the money by selling Christo's original preparatory drawings, collages, and models of works he created in the 1950s and 1960s. Huge crowds watched as crews removed accumulated trash from the 11 islands (to assure maximum contrast between their dark colors, the pink of the cloth, and the blue of the bay) and then unfurled the fabric "cocoons" to form magical floating "skirts" around each tiny bit of land. Despite the brevity of its existence, *Surrounded Islands* lives on in the host of photographs, films, and books documenting the project.

ANDY GOLDSWORTHY The most prominent heir today to the earthworks tradition of Robert Smithson is Environmental artist and photographer ANDY GOLDSWORTHY (b. 1956). Goldsworthy's medium is nature itself—stones, tree roots, leaves, flowers, ice. Because most of his works are ephemeral, the victims of tides, rainstorms, and the changing seasons, he records them in stunning color photographs that are artworks in their own right. Golds-

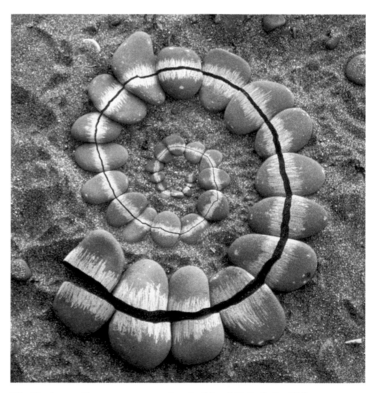

31-41 ANDY GOLDSWORTHY, *Cracked Rock Spiral,* St. Abbs, Scotland, 1985.

Goldsworthy's earthworks are "collaborations with nature." At St. Abbs, he split pebbles of different sizes in two, scratched white around the cracks using another stone, and then arranged them in a spiral.

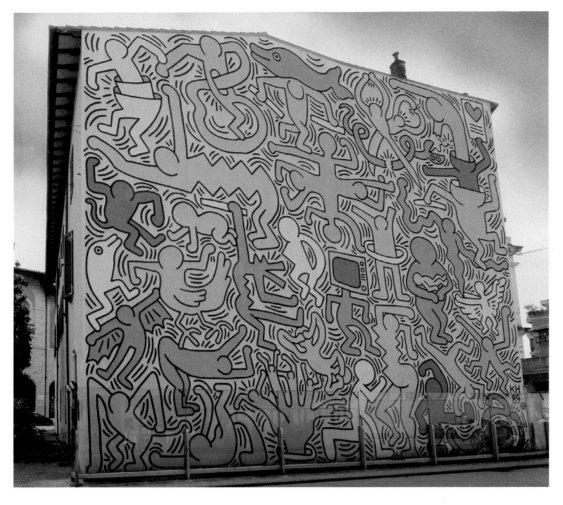

and displayed a genius for marketing himself and his work. In 1986, he parlayed his popularity into a successful business by opening The Pop Shop in the SoHo (South of Houston Street) gallery district of lower Manhattan, where he sold posters, T-shirts, hats, and buttons featuring his universally appealing schematic human and animal figures, especially his two most popular motifs—a crawling baby surrounded by rays and a barking dog.

Haring's last major work was a commission to paint a huge mural at the church of Saint Anthony in Pisa, Italy, a confirmation of his international reputation. *Tuttomondo* (*Everybody*) encapsulates Haring's style (FIG. **31-42**)—bright single-color cavorting figures with black outlines against a matte background. The motifs include a winged man, a figure with a television head, a mother cradling a baby, and a dancing dog. It is a hymn to the joy of life (compare FIG. 29-2A). Haring died of AIDS the next year. He was 31 years old.

worthy's international reputation has led to commissions in his native England, Scotland (where he now lives), France, Australia, the United States, and Japan, where his work has much in common with the sculptures of Kimio Tsuchiya (FIG. 31-23). Goldsworthy seeks not to transform the landscape in his art but, in his words, to "collaborate with nature."

One of Goldsworthy's most beautiful "collaborations" is also a tribute to Robert Smithson and *Spiral Jetty* (FIG. 30-50). *Cracked Rock Spiral* (FIG. **31-41**), which he created at St. Abbs, Scotland, on June 1, 1985, consists of pebbles Goldsworthy split in two, scratched white around the cracks using another stone, and then arranged in a spiral that grows wider as it coils from its center.

GRAFFITI AND MURAL PAINTING Although generally considered a modern phenomenon, the concept of site-specific art is as old as the history of art. Indeed, the earliest known paintings are those covering the walls and ceilings of Paleolithic caves in southern France and northern Spain (see Chapter 1). A contemporary twist on the venerable art of mural painting is the graffiti and graffiti-inspired art of, among others, Jean-Michel Basquiat (FIG. 31-8) and KEITH HARING (1958–1990). Haring grew up in Kutztown, Pennsylvania, attended the School of Visual Arts in New York, and, as did Basquiat, burst onto the New York art scene as a graffiti artist in the city's subway system. The authorities would constantly remove his chalk figures, which he drew on blank black posters awaiting advertisers, and arrested Haring whenever they spotted him at work. However, Haring quickly gained a wide and appreciative audience for his linear cartoon-inspired fantasies, and began to sell paintings to avid collectors. Haring, like Andy Warhol (FIGS. 30-25 and 30-25A), was thoroughly in tune with pop culture

NEW MEDIA

In addition to taking the ancient arts of painting and sculpture in new directions, contemporary artists have continued to explore the expressive possibilities of the various new media developed in the postwar period, especially digital photography, computer graphics, and video.

ANDREAS GURSKY German photographer ANDREAS GURSKY (b. 1955) grew up in Düsseldorf, where his father was a commercial photographer. Andreas studied photography at Düsseldorf's Kunstakademie (Academy of Art) and since the mid-1990s has used computer and digital technology to produce gigantic color prints in which he combines and manipulates photographs taken with a wide-angle lens, usually from a high vantage point. The size of his photographs, sometimes almost a dozen feet wide, intentionally rivals 19th-century history paintings. But as was true of Gustave Courbet (FIGS. 27-26 and 27-27) in his day, Gursky's subjects come from everyday life. He records the mundane world of the modern global economy—vast industrial plants, major department stores, hotel lobbies, and stock and commodity exchanges—and transforms the commonplace into striking, almost abstract, compositions. (Compare the photographs of Edward Burtynsky, FIG. 31-19.)

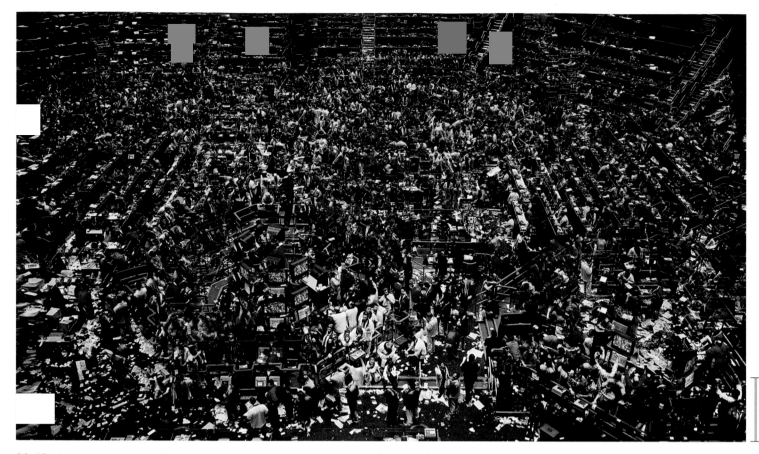

31-43 ANDREAS GURSKY, *Chicago Board of Trade II*, 1999. C-print, 6′ 9½″ × 11′ 5⅝″. Matthew Marks Gallery, New York.

Gursky manipulates digital photographs to produce vast tableaus depicting characteristic places of the modern global economy. The size of his prints rivals 19th-century history paintings.

Gursky's enormous 1999 print (FIG. **31-43**) documenting the frenzied activity on the main floor of the Chicago Board of Trade is a characteristic example of his work. He took a series of photographs from a gallery, creating a panoramic view of the traders in their brightly colored jackets. He then combined several digital images using commercial photo-editing software to produce a blurred tableau of bodies, desks, computer terminals, and strewn paper in which both mass and color are so evenly distributed as to negate the traditional Renaissance notion of perspective. In using the computer to modify the "objective truth" and spatial recession of "straight photography," Gursky blurs the distinction between painting and photography.

JENNY HOLZER Gallipolis, Ohio, native JENNY HOLZER (b. 1950) studied art at Ohio University and the Rhode Island School of Design. In 1990, she became the first woman to represent the United States at the prestigious Venice Biennale art exhibition. Holzer has won renown for several series of artworks using electronic signs, most involving light-emitting diode (LED) technology, and has created light-projection shows worldwide. In 1989, she assembled a major installation at the Solomon R. Guggenheim Museum in New York that included elements from her previous series and consisted of a large continuous LED display spiraling around the interior ramp (FIG. **31-44**) of Frank Lloyd Wright's landmark building (FIG. 30-39). Holzer believes in the communicative power of language, and her installation focused specifically on text. She invented sayings with an authoritative

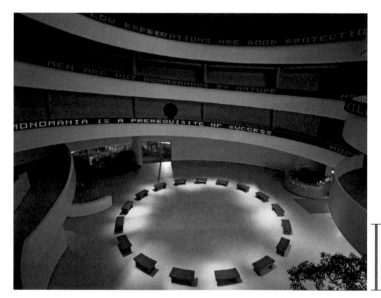

31-44 JENNY HOLZER, *Untitled* (selections from *Truisms, Inflammatory Essays, The Living Series, The Survival Series, Under a Rock, Laments,* and *Child Text*), 1989. Extended helical tricolor LED electronic display signboard, 16′ × 162′ × 6′. Installation at the Solomon R. Guggenheim Museum, New York, December 1989–February 1990 (partial gift of the artist, 1989).

Holzer's 1989 installation consisted of electronic signs created using LED technology. The continuous display of texts wound around the Guggenheim Museum's spiral interior ramp.

tone for her LED displays—for example, "Protect me from what I want," "Abuse of power comes as no surprise," and "Romantic love was invented to manipulate women." The statements, which people could read from a distance, were intentionally vague and, in some cases, contradictory.

ADRIAN PIPER Video artists, like other artists, pursue diverse goals. ADRIAN PIPER (b. 1948) has used video art to effect social change—in particular, to combat pervasive racism. Born in New York City, she studied art at the School of Visual Arts and philosophy at the City College of New York but now lives in Berlin, Germany. Her videos, such as the installation *Cornered* (FIG. **31-45**), are provocative and confrontational. *Cornered* included a video monitor placed behind an overturned table. Piper appeared on the video monitor, literally cornered behind the table, as she spoke to viewers. Her comments sprang from her experiences as a light-skinned African American woman and from her belief that although overt racism had diminished, subtle and equally damaging forms of bigotry were still rampant. "I'm black," she announces on the 16-minute videotape. "Now let's deal with this social fact and the fact of my stating it together. . . . If you feel that my letting people know that I'm not white is making an unnecessary fuss, you must feel that the right and proper course of action for me to take is to pass for white. Now this kind of thinking presupposes a belief that it's inherently better to be identified as white," she continues. The directness of Piper's art forces viewers to examine their own behaviors and values.

BILL VIOLA For much of his artistic career, BILL VIOLA (b. 1951) has also explored the capabilities of digitized imagery, producing many video installations and single-channel works. Often focusing on sensory perception, the pieces not only heighten viewer awareness of the senses but also suggest an exploration into the spiritual realm. Viola, who majored in art and music at Syracuse University, spent years after graduating seriously studying Buddhist, Chris-

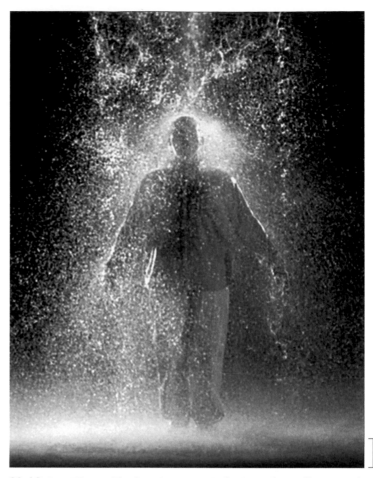

31-46 BILL VIOLA, *The Crossing*, 1996. Video/sound installation with two channels of color video projection onto screens 16′ high. ◼◀

Viola's video projects use extreme slow motion, contrasts in scale, shifts in focus, mirrored reflections, and staccato editing to create dramatic sensory experiences rooted in tangible reality.

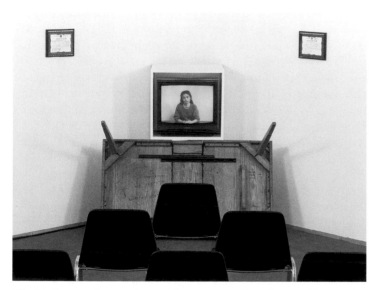

31-45 ADRIAN PIPER, *Cornered*, 1988. Mixed-media installation of variable size; video monitor, table, and birth certificates. Museum of Contemporary Art, Chicago. ◼◀

In this installation, Piper, a light-skinned African American, appeared on a video monitor, "cornered" behind an overturned table, and made provocative comments about racism and bigotry.

tian, Sufi, and Zen mysticism. Because he fervently believes in art's transformative power and in a spiritual view of human nature, Viola designs works encouraging spectator introspection. His video projects have involved using techniques such as extreme slow motion, contrasts in scale, shifts in focus, mirrored reflections, staccato editing, and multiple or layered screens to achieve dramatic effects.

The power of Viola's work is evident in *The Crossing* (FIG. **31-46**), an installation piece involving two color video channels projected on 16-foot-high screens. The artist either shows the two projections on the front and back of the same screen or on two separate screens in the same installation. In these two companion videos, shown simultaneously on the two screens, a man surrounded in darkness appears, moving closer until he fills the screen. On one screen, drops of water fall from above onto the man's head, while on the other screen, a small fire breaks out at the man's feet. Over the next few minutes, the water and fire increase in intensity until the man disappears in a torrent of water on one screen (FIG. **31-46**) and flames consume the man on the other screen. The deafening roar of a raging fire and a torrential downpour accompany these visual images. Eventually, everything subsides and fades into darkness. This installation's elemental nature and its presentation in a dark space immerse viewers in a pure sensory experience very much rooted in tangible reality.

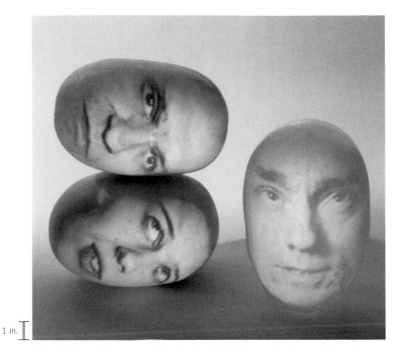

1 in.

31-47 TONY OURSLER, *Mansheshe*, 1997. Ceramic, glass, video player, videocassette, CPJ-200 video projector, sound, 11″ × 7″ × 8″ each. Courtesy of the artist and Metro Pictures, New York.

Video artist Oursler projects his digital images onto sculptural objects, insinuating them into the "real" world. Here, he projected talking heads onto egg-shaped forms suspended from poles.

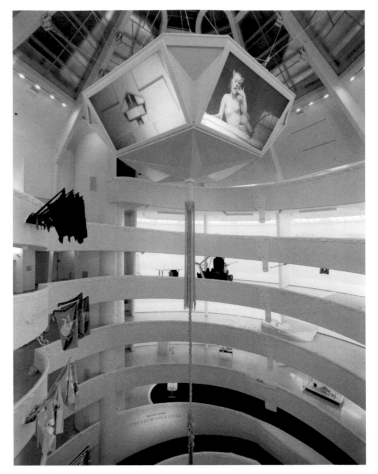

31-48 MATTHEW BARNEY, *Cremaster* cycle, installation at the Solomon R. Guggenheim Museum, New York, 2003.

Barney's vast multimedia installations of drawings, photographs, sculptures, and videos typify the relaxation at the opening of the 21st century of the traditional boundaries among artistic media.

TONY OURSLER Whereas Viola, Piper, and other artists present video and digital imagery to their audiences on familiar flat screens, thus reproducing the format in which we most often come into contact with electronic images, New Yorker TONY OURSLER (b. 1957), who studied art at the California Institute of the Arts, manipulates his images, projecting them onto sculptural objects. This has the effect of taking the images out of the digital world and insinuating them into the "real" world. Accompanied by sound tapes, Oursler's installations, such as *Mansheshe* (FIG. **31-47**), not only engage but often challenge the viewer. In this example, Oursler projected talking heads onto egg-shaped forms suspended from poles. Because the projected images of people look directly at the viewer, the statements they make about religious beliefs, sexual identity, and interpersonal relationships cannot be easily dismissed.

MATTHEW BARNEY A major trend in the art world today is the relaxation of the traditional boundaries between artistic media. In fact, many contemporary artists are creating vast and complex multimedia installations combining new and traditional media. One of these artists is MATTHEW BARNEY (b. 1967), who studied art at Yale University. The 2003 installation (FIG. **31-48**) of his epic *Cremaster* cycle (1994–2002) at the Solomon R. Guggenheim Museum in New York typifies the expansive scale of many contemporary works. A multimedia extravaganza involving drawings, photographs, sculptures, videos, films, and performances (presented in videos), the *Cremaster* cycle is a lengthy narrative set in a self-enclosed universe Barney created. The title of the work refers to the cremaster muscle, which controls testicular contractions in response to external stimuli. Barney uses the development of this muscle in the embryonic process of sexual differentiation as the conceptual springboard for the entire *Cremaster* project, in

which he explores the notion of creation in expansive and complicated ways. The cycle's narrative, revealed in the five 35-millimeter feature-length films and the artworks, makes reference to, among other things, a musical revue in Boise, Idaho (where San Francisco–born Barney grew up), the life cycle of bees, the execution of convicted murderer Gary Gilmore, the construction of the Chrysler Building (FIG. 29-47), Celtic mythology, Masonic rituals, a motorcycle race, and a lyric opera set in late-19th-century Budapest. In the installation, Barney tied the artworks together conceptually by a five-channel video piece projected on screens hanging in the Guggenheim's rotunda. Immersion in Barney's constructed world is disorienting and overwhelming and has a force that competes with the immense scale and often frenzied pace of contemporary life.

WHAT NEXT? No one knows what the next years and decades will bring, but given the expansive scope of postmodernism, it is certain no single approach to or style of art will dominate. New technologies will undoubtedly continue to redefine what constitutes a "work of art." The universally expanding presence of computers, digital technology, and the Internet may well erode what few conceptual and geographical boundaries remain, and make art and information about art available to virtually everyone, thereby creating a truly global artistic community. As this chapter has revealed, substantial progress has already been made in that direction.

CONTEMPORARY ART WORLDWIDE

SOCIAL AND POLITICAL ART

❚ Many contemporary artists use art to address pressing social and political issues and to define their personal identities.

❚ Gender and sexuality are central themes in the work of Barbara Kruger, the Guerrilla Girls, David Wojnarowicz, Robert Mapplethorpe, and Shahzia Sikander. Faith Ringgold, Lorna Simpson, Carrie Mae Weems, Melvin Edwards, Jean-Michel Basquiat, and Kehinde Wiley address issues of concern to African Americans. Jaune Quick-to-See Smith focuses on Native American heritage, Chris Ofili and Trigo Piula on their African roots, and Cliff Whiting on traditional Maori themes.

❚ Other artists have treated political and economic issues: Willie Bester, apartheid in South Africa; David Hammons, racial discrimination; Leon Golub, violence; Shirin Neshat, the challenges facing Muslim women; Krzystof Wodiczko, the plight of the homeless; and Edward Burtynsky, industrial pollution.

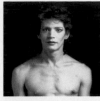

Mapplethorpe, *Self-Portrait*, 1980

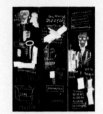

Basquiat, *Horn Players*, 1983

OTHER MOVEMENTS AND THEMES

❚ Contemporary art encompasses a phenomenal variety of styles ranging from abstraction to brutal realism, both in America and worldwide.

❚ Leading abstract painters and sculptors include Julian Schnabel and Tara Donovan in the United States, Anselm Kiefer in Germany, Emily Kame Kngwarreye in Australia, and Wu Guanzhong, Song Su-nam, and Kimio Tsuchiya in China, Korea, and Japan, respectively.

❚ Among today's best-known figural painters and sculptors are Kiki Smith, Jeff Koons, and Venezuelan Marisol in the United States, and expatriate Englishwoman Jenny Saville in Italy.

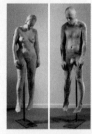

Smith, *Untitled*, 1990

ARCHITECTURE AND SITE-SPECIFIC ART

❚ Postmodern architecture is as diverse as contemporary painting and sculpture. Leading Hi-Tech architects include Norman Foster and Renzo Piano. Among the major champions of Deconstructivism are Günter Behnisch, Frank Gehry, Daniel Libeskind, and Zaha Hadid.

❚ The monuments designed by Maya Lin, Rachel Whiteread, and Richard Serra bridge the gap between architecture and sculpture, as do the Environmental artworks of Christo and Jean-Claude and of Andy Goldsworthy.

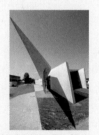

Hadid, Vitra Fire Station, 1989–1993

NEW MEDIA

❚ Many contemporary artists have harnessed new technologies in their artistic production: Andreas Gursky, digital photography; Jenny Holzer, LED displays; Adrian Piper, Bill Viola, and Tony Oursler, video; and Matthew Barney, complex multimedia installations.

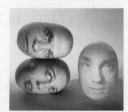

Oursler, *Mansheshe*, 1997

NOTES

Chapter 26

1. Translated by Robert Goldwater and Marco Treves, eds., *Artists on Art,* 3d ed. (New York: Pantheon Books, 1958), 157.

2. Quoted in Thomas A. Bailey, *The American Pageant: A History of the Republic,* 2d ed. (Boston: Heath, 1961), 280.

3. Translated by Elfriede Heyer and Roger C. Norton, in Charles Harrison, Paul Wood, and Jason Gaiger, eds., *Art in Theory 1648–1815: An Anthology of Changing Ideas* (Oxford: Blackwell, 2000), 451–453.

Chapter 27

1. Théophile Gautier, *Histoire de Romantisme* (Paris: Charpentier, 1874), 204.

2. Quoted in Helmut Borsch-Supan, *Caspar David Friedrich* (New York: Braziller, 1974), 7.

3. Translated by Jason Gaiger, in Charles Harrison, Paul Wood, and Jason Gaiger, eds., *Art in Theory 1815–1900: An Anthology of Changing Ideas* (Oxford: Blackwell, 1998), 54.

4. Quoted by Brian Lukacher, in Stephen F. Eisenman, ed., *Nineteenth Century Art: A Critical History* (New York: Thames & Hudson, 2007), 126.

5. Quoted in John W. McCoubrey, *American Art 1700–1960: Sources and Documents* (Upper Saddle River, N.J.: Prentice Hall, 1965), 98.

6. Quoted in Thomas A. Bailey, *The American Pageant: A History of the Republic,* 2d ed. (Boston: Heath, 1961), 280.

7. Quoted in Linda Nochlin, *Realism and Tradition in Art 1848–1900* (Upper Saddle River, N.J.: Prentice Hall, 1966), 42.

8. Quoted in George Heard Hamilton, *Manet and His Critics* (New Haven, Conn.: Yale University Press, 1954), 45.

9. Quoted in Eisenman, ed., *Nineteenth Century Art,* 336.

10. *New York Weekly Tribune,* September 30, 1865.

11. Quoted in Nikolai Cikovsky Jr. and Franklin Kelly, *Winslow Homer* (Washington, D.C.: National Gallery of Art, 1995), 26.

12. Quoted in Lloyd Goodrich, *Thomas Eakins, His Life and Work* (New York: Whitney Museum of American Art, 1933), 51–52.

13. Quoted in Nicholas Pevsner, *An Outline of European Architecture* (Baltimore: Penguin, 1960), 627.

14. Letter from Delaroche to François Arao, quoted in Helmut Gernsheim, *Creative Photography* (New York: Bonanza Books, 1962), 24.

15. Quoted in Naomi Rosenblum, *A World History of Photography,* 4th ed. (New York: Abbeville Press, 2007), 69.

16. Quoted in Kenneth MacGowan, *Behind the Screen* (New York: Delta, 1965), 49.

Chapter 28

1. Quoted in Linda Nochlin, *Realism* (Harmondsworth: Penguin, 1971), 28.

2. Clement Greenberg, "Modernist Painting," *Art and Literature,* no. 4 (Spring 1965): 193–194.

3. Quoted in Linda Nochlin, *Impressionism and Post-Impressionism 1874–1904: Sources and Documents* (Englewood Cliffs, N.J.: Prentice Hall, 1966), 35.

4. Translated by Carola Hicks, in Charles Harrison, Paul Wood, and Jason Gaiger, *Art in Theory 1815–1900* (Oxford: Blackwell, 1998), 595.

5. Quoted in John McCoubrey, *American Art 1700–1960: Sources and Documents* (Englewood Cliffs, N.J.: Prentice Hall, 1965), 184.

6. Quoted in Robert Goldwater and Marco Treves, eds., *Artists on Art, from the XIV to the XX Century* (New York: Pantheon, 1945), 322.

7. Ibid., 375.

8. Vincent van Gogh to Theo van Gogh, September 1888, in J. van Gogh–Bonger and V. W. van Gogh, eds., *The Complete Letters of Vincent van Gogh* (Greenwich, Conn.: New York Graphic Society, 1979), 3: 534.

9. Vincent van Gogh to Theo van Gogh, July 16, 1888, in W. H. Auden, ed., *Van Gogh: A Self-Portrait. Letters Revealing His Life as a Painter* (New York: Dutton, 1963), 299.

10. Quoted in Sam Hunter, John Jacobus, and Daniel Wheeler, *Modern Art,* 3d ed. (Upper Saddle River, N.J.: Prentice Hall, 2004), 28.

11. Cézanne to Émile Bernard, March 1904. Quoted in Goldwater and Treves, *Artists on Art,* 363.

12. Cézanne to Émile Bernard, April 15, 1904. Ibid., 363.

13. Translated by Akane Kawakami, in Harrison, Wood, and Gaiger, *Art in Theory,* 1066.

14. Quoted in George Heard Hamilton, *Painting and Sculpture in Europe 1880–1940,* 6th ed. (New Haven, Conn.: Yale University Press, 1993), 124.

15. Quoted in V. Frisch and J. T. Shipley, *Auguste Rodin* (New York: Stokes, 1939), 203.

16. Quoted in Eileen Boris, *Art and Labor: Ruskin, Morris, and the Craftsman Ideal in America* (Philadelphia: Temple University Press, 1986), 7.

Chapter 29

1. Quoted in John Elderfield, *The "Wild Beasts": Fauvism and Its Affinities* (New York: Museum of Modern Art, 1976), 29.

2. Translated by Charles Harrison and Paul Wood, eds., *Art in Theory 1900–2000: An Anthology of Changing Ideas* (Oxford: Blackwell, 2003), 65.

3. Quoted in Frederick S. Levine, *The Apocalyptic Vision: The Art of Franz Marc as German Expressionism* (New York: Harper & Row, 1979), 57.

4. Quoted in Sam Hunter, John Jacobus, and Daniel Wheeler, *Modern Art,* rev. 3d ed. (Upper Saddle River, N.J.: Prentice Hall, 2004), 121.

5. Quoted in George Heard Hamilton, *Painting and Sculpture in Europe 1880–1940,* 6th ed. (New Haven, Conn.: Yale University Press, 1993), 246.

6. Ibid., 238.

7. Quoted in Edward Fry, ed., *Cubism* (London: Thames & Hudson, 1966), 112–113.

8. Quoted in Françoise Gilot and Carlton Lake, *Life with Picasso* (New York: McGraw-Hill, 1964), 77.

9. Pablo Picasso, "Statement to Simone Téry," in Harrison and Wood, eds., *Art in Theory 1900–2000,* 649.

10. Quoted in Roland Penrose, *Picasso: His Life and Work,* rev. ed. (New York: Harper & Row, 1971), 311.

11. Filippo Tommaso Marinetti, *The Foundation and Manifesto of Futurism* (*Le Figaro,* February 20, 1909). Translated by Joshua C. Taylor, in Herschel B. Chipp, *Theories of Modern Art: A Source Book by Artists and Critics* (Berkeley and Los Angeles: University of California Press, 1968), 284.

12. Ibid., 286.

13. Quoted in Robert Short, *Dada and Surrealism* (London: Octopus Books, 1980), 18.

14. Quoted in Robert Motherwell, ed., *The Dada Painters and Poets: An Anthology*, 2d ed. (Cambridge, Mass.: Belknap Press of Harvard University, 1989).

15. Hans Richter, *Dada: Art and Anti-Art* (London: Thames & Hudson, 1961), 64–65.

16. Ibid., 57.

17. Quoted in Arturo Schwarz, *The Complete Works of Marcel Duchamp* (London: Thames & Hudson, 1965), 466.

18. Translated by Howard Dearstyne, in Robert L. Herbert, *Modern Artists on Art*, 2d ed. (Mineola, N.Y.: Dover, 2000), 117.

19. Ibid., 124.

20. Translated by Herbert Read and Leslie Martin, quoted in Chipp, *Theories of Modern Art*, 325–330.

21. Quoted in Sam Hunter, *American Art of the 20th Century* (New York: Abrams, 1972), 30.

22. Ibid., 37.

23. Charles C. Eldredge, "The Arrival of European Modernism," *Art in America* 61 (July–August 1973): 35.

24. Quoted in Gail Stavitsky, "Reordering Reality: Precisionist Directions in American Art 1915–1941," in *Precisionism in America 1915–1941: Reordering Reality* (New York: Abrams, 1994), 12.

25. Quoted in Karen Tsujimoto, *Images of America: Precisionist Painting and Modern Photography* (Seattle: University of Washington Press, 1982), 70.

26. Dorothy Norman, *Alfred Stieglitz: An American Seer* (Millerton, N.Y.: Aperture, 1973), 9–10.

27. Ibid., 161.

28. Quoted in Vincent Scully Jr., *Frank Lloyd Wright* (New York: Braziller, 1960), 18.

29. Quoted in Edgar Kauffmann, ed., *Frank Lloyd Wright: An American Architect* (New York: Horizon, 1955), 205, 208.

30. Quoted in Matthias Eberle, *World War I and the Weimar Artists: Dix, Grosz, Beckmann, Schlemmer* (New Haven, Conn.: Yale University Press, 1985), 54.

31. Ibid., 22.

32. Ibid., 42.

33. Quoted in William S. Rubin, *Dada, Surrealism, and Their Heritage* (New York: Museum of Modern Art, 1968), 64.

34. Quoted in Hamilton, *Painting and Sculpture in Europe 1880–1940*, 6th ed. (New Haven, Conn.: Yale University Press, 1993), 392.

35. Quoted in Richter, *Dada*, 155.

36. Ibid., 159.

37. Quoted in Rubin, *Dada, Surrealism*, 111.

38. Quoted in Hunter, Jacobus, and Wheeler, *Modern Art*, 179.

39. Quoted in William S. Rubin, *Miró in the Collection of the Museum of Modern Art* (New York: Museum of Modern Art, 1973), 32.

40. Translated by Norbert Guterman, quoted in Chipp, *Theories of Modern Art*, 182–186.

41. Translated by Nicholas Bullock, quoted in Harrison and Wood, *Art in Theory 1900–2000*, 281.

42. Quoted in Kenneth Frampton, *Modern Architecture: A Critical History*, 4th ed. (New York: Thames & Hudson, 2007), 147.

43. Quoted in Michel Seuphor, *Piet Mondrian: Life and Work* (New York: Abrams, 1956), 117.

44. Piet Mondrian, *Plastic Art and Pure Plastic Art* (1937), quoted in Hamilton, *Painting and Sculpture*, 319.

45. Mondrian, *Plastic Art*, quoted in Chipp, *Theories of Modern Art*, 349.

46. Ibid., 350.

47. Quoted in H. H. Arnason and Peter Kalb, *History of Modern Art*, 5th ed. (Upper Saddle River, N.J.: Prentice Hall, 2004), 154.

48. Quoted in Herbert, *Modern Artists on Art*, 173.

49. Ibid., 177.

50. Quoted in Hans L. Jaffé, comp., *De Stijl* (New York: Abrams, 1971), 185–188.

51. Piet Mondrian, *Dialogue on the New Plastic* (1919). Translated by Harry Holzman and Martin S. James, in Harrison and Wood, *Art in Theory 1900–2000*, 285.

52. Quoted in Wayne Craven, *American Art: History and Culture* (Madison, Wis.: Brown & Benchmark, 2003), 403.

53. Quoted in Vivian Endicott Barnett, "Banned German Art: Reception and Institutional Support of Modern German Art in the United States, 1933–45," in Stephanie Barron, *Exiles and Emigrés: The Flight of European Artists from Hitler* (Los Angeles: Los Angeles County Museum of Art, 1997), 283.

54. Quoted in Frances K. Pohl, *Ben Shahn: New Deal Artist in a Cold War Climate, 1947–1954* (Austin: University of Texas Press, 1989), 159.

55. Quoted in Henry Louis Gates Jr., "New Negroes, Migration, and Cultural Exchange," in Elizabeth Hutton Turner, ed., *Jacob Lawrence: The Migration Series* (Washington, D.C.: Phillips Collection, 1993), 20.

56. Wanda M. Corn, *Grant Wood: The Regionalist Vision* (New Haven, Conn.: Yale University Press, 1983), 131.

57. Quoted in Matthew Baigell, *A Concise History of American Painting and Sculpture* (New York: Harper & Row, 1984), 264.

58. Quoted in Milton Meltzer, *Dorothea Lange: A Photographer's Life* (New York: Farrar, Straus, Giroux, 1978), 133, 220.

59. Quoted in Philip Johnson, *Mies van der Rohe*, rev. ed. (New York: Museum of Modern Art, 1954), 200–201.

Chapter 30

1. Dawn Ades and Andrew Forge, *Francis Bacon* (London: Thames & Hudson, 1985), 8; and David Sylvester, *The Brutality of Fact: Interviews with Francis Bacon*, 3d ed. (London: Thames & Hudson, 1987), 182.

2. Clement Greenberg, "Toward a Newer *Laocoon*," *Partisan Review* 7, no. 4 (July–August 1940): 305.

3. Clement Greenberg, "Sculpture in Our Time," *Arts Magazine* 32, no. 9 (June 1956): 22.

4. Marcus Rothko and Adolph Gottlieb, quoted in Edward Alden Jewell, "The Realm of Art: A New Platform and Other Matters: 'Globalism' Pops into View," *New York Times*, June 13, 1943, 9.

5. Reprinted in Harold Rosenberg, *The Tradition of the New* (New York: Horizon, 1959), 25.

6. Quoted in Thomas Hess, *Barnett Newman* (New York: Walker and Company, 1969), 51.

7. Quoted in John P. O'Neill, ed., *Barnett Newman: Selected Writings and Interviews* (New York: Knopf, 1990), 108.

8. Rothko and Gottlieb, "The Realm of Art," 9.

9. Quoted in Selden Rodman, *Conversations with Artists* (New York: Devin-Adair, 1957), 93–94.

10. Clement Greenberg, "Recentness of Sculpture," in Gregory Battcock, ed., *Minimal Art: A Critical Anthology* (New York: Dutton, 1968), 183–184.

11. Louise Nevelson, quoted in John Gordon, *Louise Nevelson* (New York: Praeger, 1967), 12.

12. Quoted in Deborah Wye, *Louise Bourgeois* (New York: Museum of Modern Art, 1982), 22.

13. Ibid., 25.

14. Quoted in Lucy Lippard, *Eva Hesse* (New York: New York University Press, 1976), 165.

15. Ibid., 56.

16. Quoted in Richard Francis, *Jasper Johns* (New York: Abbeville, 1984), 21.

17. Andy Warhol, *The Philosophy of Andy Warhol* (New York: Harcourt Brace Jovanovich, 1975), 100.

18. Quoted in Christine Lindey, *Superrealist Painting and Sculpture* (London: Orbis, 1980), 50.

19. Quoted in Sebastian Smee, *Lucian Freud: Beholding the Animal* (Cologne: Taschen, 2009), 61.

20. Ibid., 7

21. Lindey, *Superrealist Painting*, 130.

22. Quoted in Susanna Torruella Leval, "Recapturing History: The (Un)official Story in Contemporary Latin American Art," *Art Journal* 51, no. 4 (Winter 1992): 74.

23. Ibid.

24. Hannah Wilke, "Visual Prejudice," in *Hannah Wilke: A Retrospective* (Columbia: University of Missouri Press, 1989), 141.

25. Quoted in Mary Jane Jacob, *Magdalena Abakanowicz* (New York: Abbeville, 1982), 94.

26. Peter Blake, *Frank Lloyd Wright* (Harmondsworth: Penguin, 1960), 115.

27. Quoted in Nancy Holt, ed., *The Writings of Robert Smithson* (New York: New York University Press, 1975), 111.

28. Quoted in H. H. Arnason and Peter Kalb, *History of Modern Art,* 5th ed. (Upper Saddle River, N.J.: Prentice Hall, 2004), 489.

29. Quoted in Barbara Haskell, *Blam! The Explosion of Pop, Minimalism, and Performance 1958–1964* (New York: Whitney Museum of American Art), 53.

30. Quoted in Bruce McPherson, ed., *More Than "Meat Joy": Complete Performance Works and Selected Writings* (New Paltz, N.Y.: Documentext, 1979), 52.

31. Quoted in Caroline Tisdall, *Joseph Beuys* (New York: Thames & Hudson, 1979), 6.

32. Quoted in "Joseph Kosuth: Art as Idea as Idea," in Jeanne Siegel, ed., *Artwords: Discourse on the 60s and 70s* (Ann Arbor, Mich.: UMI Research Press, 1985), 221, 225.

33. Quoted in Brenda Richardson, *Bruce Nauman: Neons* (Baltimore: Baltimore Museum of Art, 1982), 20.

Chapter 31

1. Quoted in Arlene Hirschfelder, *Artists and Craftspeople* (New York: Facts on File, 1994), 115.

2. Quoted in Richard Marshall and Robert Mapplethorpe, *50 New York Artists* (San Francisco: Chronicle Books, 1986), 448–449.

3. Quoted in Junichi Shiota, *Kimio Tsuchiya, Sculpture 1984–1988* (Tokyo: Morris Gallery, 1988), 3.

4. Michelle Meagher, "Jenny Saville and a Feminist Aesthetics of Disgust," *Hypatia* 18.4 (Fall/Winter 2003), 23–41.

5. Quoted in Donald Hall, *Corporal Politics* (Cambridge: MIT List Visual Arts Center, 1993), 46.

6. Quoted in "Vietnam Memorial: America Remembers," *National Geographic* 167, no. 5 (May 1985): 557.

7. Quoted in Calvin Tomkins, "The Art World: *Tilted Arc,*" *New Yorker,* May 20, 1985, 100.

GLOSSARY

Abstract Expressionism—The first major American avant-garde movement, Abstract Expressionism emerged in New York City in the 1940s. The artists produced *abstract* paintings that expressed their state of mind and that they hoped would strike emotional chords in viewers. The movement developed along two lines: *gestural abstraction* and *chromatic abstraction.* (902)

action painting—Also called *gestural abstraction.* The kind of *Abstract Expressionism* practiced by Jackson Pollock, in which the emphasis was on the creation process, the artist's gesture in making art. Pollock poured liquid paint in linear webs on his canvases, which he laid out on the floor, thereby physically surrounding himself in the painting during its creation. (905)

Analytic Cubism—The first phase of *Cubism,* developed jointly by Pablo Picasso and Georges Braque, in which the artists analyzed form from every possible vantage point to combine the various views into one pictorial whole. (847)

ancien régime—French, "old order." The term used to describe the political, social, and religious order in France before the Revolution at the end of the 18th century. (736)

Art Deco—Descended from *Art Nouveau,* this movement of the 1920s and 1930s sought to upgrade industrial design as a "fine art" and to work new materials into decorative patterns that could be either machined or handcrafted. Characterized by streamlined, elongated, and symmetrical design. (871)

Art Nouveau—French, "new art." A late-19th- and early-20th-century art movement whose proponents tried to synthesize all the arts in an effort to create art based on natural forms that could be mass produced by technologies of the industrial age. The movement had other names in other countries: Jugendstil in Austria and Germany, Modernismo in Spain, and Floreale in Italy. (828)

assemblage—An artwork constructed from already existing objects. (914)

automatism—In painting, the process of yielding oneself to instinctive motions of the hands

after establishing a set of conditions (such as size of paper or *medium*) within which a work is to be created. (875)

avant-garde—French, "advance guard" (in a platoon). Late-19th- and 20th-century artists who emphasized innovation and challenged established convention in their work. Also used as an adjective. (836)

bas-relief—See *relief.* (820)

batik—An Indonesian fabric-dyeing technique using melted wax to form patterns the dye cannot penetrate. (31-22B)

Bauhaus—A school of architecture in Germany in the 1920s under the aegis of Walter Gropius, who emphasized the unity of art, architecture, and design. (884)

Beaux-Arts—An architectural style of the late 19th and early 20th centuries in France. Based on ideas taught at the École des Beaux-Arts in Paris, the Beaux-Arts style incorporated *classical* principles, such as symmetry in design, and included extensive exterior ornamentation. (789)

benday dots—Named after the newspaper printer Benjamin Day, the benday dot system involves the modulation of *colors* through the placement and size of colored dots. (916)

Bharat Mata—Mother India; the female personification of India. (32-10A)

Biomorphic Surrealism— See *Surrealism.* (875)

calotype—From the Greek *kalos,* "beautiful." A photographic process in which a positive image is made by shining light through a negative image onto a sheet of sensitized paper. (791, 792)

camera lucida—Latin, "lighted room." A device in which a small lens projects the image of an object downward onto a sheet of paper. (791)

chromatic abstraction—A kind of *Abstract Expressionism* that focuses on the emotional resonance of color, as exemplified by the work of Barnett Newman and Mark Rothko. (903)

Classical—The art and culture of ancient Greece between 480 and 323 BCE. Lowercase *classical* refers more generally to Greco-Roman art and culture.

collage—A composition made by combining on a flat surface various materials, such as news-

paper, wallpaper, printed text and illustrations, photographs, and cloth. (835, 850)

color—The value, or tonality, of a color is the degree of its lightness or darkness. The intensity, or saturation, of a color is its purity, its brightness or dullness. See also *primary colors, secondary colors,* and *complementary colors.* (813)

color-field painting—A variant of *Post-Painterly Abstraction* in which artists sought to reduce painting to its physical essence by pouring diluted paint onto unprimed canvas and letting these pigments soak into the fabric, as exemplified by the work of Helen Frankenthaler and Morris Louis. (908)

combines—The name American artist Robert Rauschenberg gave to his *assemblages* of painted passages and sculptural elements. (914)

complementary colors—Those pairs of *colors,* such as red and green, that together embrace the entire spectrum. The complement of one of the three *primary colors* is a mixture of the other two. (813)

Conceptual Art—An American *avant-garde* art movement of the 1960s whose premise was that the "artfulness" of art lay in the artist's idea rather than its final expression. (936)

Constructivism—An early-20th-century Russian art movement formulated by Naum Gabo, who built up his sculptures piece by piece in space instead of carving or *modeling* them. In this way the sculptor worked with "volume of mass" and "volume of space" as different materials. (860)

Cubism—An early-20th-century art movement that rejected *naturalistic* depictions, preferring compositions of shapes and forms abstracted from the conventionally perceived world. See also *Analytic Cubism* and *Synthetic Cubism.* (847)

Dada—An early-20th-century art movement prompted by a revulsion against the horror of World War I. Dada embraced political anarchy, the irrational, and the intuitive. A disdain for convention, often enlivened by humor or whimsy, is characteristic of the art the Dadaists produced. (835, 856)

daguerreotype—A photograph made by an early method on a plate of chemically treated metal; developed by Louis J. M. Daguerre. (791, 792, 983)

De Stijl—Dutch, "the style." An early-20th-century art movement (and magazine), founded by Piet Mondrian and Theo van Doesburg, whose members promoted utopian ideals and developed a simplified geometric style. (880)

deconstruction—An analytical strategy developed in the late 20th century according to which all cultural "constructs" (art, architecture, literature) are "texts." People can read these texts in a variety of ways, but they cannot arrive at fixed or uniform meanings. Any interpretation can be valid, and readings differ from time to time, place to place, and person to person. For those employing this approach, deconstruction means destabilizing established meanings and interpretations while encouraging subjectivity and individual differences. (942)

Deconstructivism—An architectural *style* using *deconstruction* as an analytical strategy. Deconstructivist architects attempt to disorient the observer by disrupting the conventional categories of architecture. The haphazard presentation of volumes, masses, planes, lighting, and so forth challenges the viewer's assumptions about form as it relates to function. (962)

Der Blaue Reiter—German, "the blue rider." An early-20th-century *German Expressionist* art movement founded by Vassily Kandinsky and Franz Marc. The artists selected the whimsical name because of their mutual interest in the color blue and horses. (841)

Die Brücke—German, "the bridge." An early-20th-century *German Expressionist* art movement under the leadership of Ernst Ludwig Kirchner. The group thought of itself as the bridge between the old age and the new. (839)

divisionism—See *pointillism*. (812)

earthworks—See *Environmental Art*. (932)

eaves—The lower part of a roof that overhangs the wall. (457)

empiricism—The search for knowledge based on observation and direct experience. (775)

encaustic—A painting technique in which pigment is mixed with melted wax and applied to the surface while the mixture is hot. (914)

Enlightenment—The Western philosophy based on empirical evidence that dominated the 18th century. The Enlightenment was a new way of thinking critically about the world and about humankind, independently of religion, myth, or tradition. (727)

en plein air—See *plein air*. (798, 799, 801, 805, 806, 28-2A, 28-7A)

Environmental Art—An American art form that emerged in the 1960s. Often using the land itself as their material, Environmental artists construct monuments of great scale and minimal form. Permanent or impermanent, these works transform some section of the environment, calling attention both to the land itself and to the hand of the artist. Sometimes referred to as earthworks. (932)

Events—See *Fluxus*. (935)

exedra—Recessed area, usually semicircular. (929)

exemplum virtutis—Latin, "example or model of virtue." (746)

Expressionism (adj. **Expressionist**)—Twentieth-century art that is the result of the artist's unique inner or personal vision and that often has an emotional dimension. Expressionism contrasts with art focused on visually describing the empirical world. (839)

fasces—A bundle of rods with an ax attached, representing an emblem of authority in ancient Rome. (752)

Fauves—French, "wild beasts." See *Fauvism*. (836)

Fauvism—An early-20th-century art movement led by Henri Matisse. For the Fauves, *color* became the formal element most responsible for pictorial coherence and the primary conveyor of meaning. (836)

Favrile—A type of leaded stained glass patented by Louis Comfort Tiffany in the late 19th century. (28-36B)

femmages—The name American artist Miriam Schapiro gave to her sewn *collages,* assembled from fabrics, quilts, buttons, sequins, lace trim, and rickrack collected at antique shows and fairs. (922)

femme fatale—French, "fatal woman." A destructive temptress of men. (820)

femme savante—French, "learned woman." The term used to describe the cultured hostesses of *Rococo* salons. (729)

fête galante—French, "amorous festival." A type of *Rococo* painting depicting the outdoor amusements of French upper-class society. (732, 733)

fin-de-siècle—French, "end of the century." A period in Western cultural history from the end of the 19th century until just before World War I, when decadence and indulgence masked anxiety about an uncertain future. (823)

Floreale—See *Art Nouveau*. (828)

Fluxus—A group of American, European, and Japanese artists of the 1960s who created *Performance Art*. Their performances, or Events, often focused on single actions, such as turning a light on and off or watching falling snow, and were more theatrical than *Happenings*. (935)

formalism—Strict adherence to, or dependence on, stylized shapes and methods of composition. An emphasis on an artwork's visual elements rather than its subject. (902)

Futurism—An early-20th-century Italian art movement that championed war as a cleansing agent and that celebrated the speed and dynamism of modern technology. (853)

genius—Latin, "spirit." In art, the personified spirit of a person or place. (22-52A)

German Expressionism—An early-20th-century regional Expressionist movement. (839)

gestural abstraction—Also known as *action painting*. A kind of *abstract* painting in which the gesture, or act of painting, is seen as the subject of art. Its most renowned proponent was Jackson Pollock. See also *Abstract Expressionism*. (903)

Gothic Revival—See *Neo-Gothic*. (788)

gouache—A painting *medium* consisting of watercolor mixed with gum. (843)

Grand Manner portraiture—A type of 18th-century portrait painting designed to communicate a person's grace and class through certain standardized conventions, such as the large scale of the figure relative to the canvas, the controlled pose, the landscape setting, and the low horizon line. (742)

green architecture—Ecologically friendly architectural design using clean energy to sustain the natural environment. (961)

Happenings—A term coined by American artist Allan Kaprow in the 1960s to describe loosely structured performances, whose creators were trying to suggest the aesthetic and dynamic qualities of everyday life; as actions, rather than objects, Happenings incorporate the fourth dimension (time). (934)

hard-edge painting—A variant of *Post-Painterly Abstraction* that rigidly excluded all reference to gesture and incorporated smooth knife-edge geometric forms to express the notion that painting should be reduced to its visual components. (907)

High-Tech—A contemporary architectural *style* calling for buildings that incorporate the latest innovations in engineering and technology and expose the structures' component parts. (961)

hookah—A Moroccan water pipe. (27-17A)

hôtel—French, "town house." (728)

hue—The name of a *color*. See also *primary colors, secondary colors,* and *complementary colors.* (813)

illusionism (adj. **illusionistic**)—The representation of the three-dimensional world on a two-dimensional surface in a manner that creates the illusion that the person, object, or place represented is three-dimensional. See also *postmodernism*.

impasto—A layer of thickly applied pigment. (902)

Impressionism—A late-19th-century art movement that sought to capture a fleeting moment, thereby conveying the elusiveness and impermanence of images and conditions. (799)

incubus—A demon believed in medieval times to prey, often sexually, on sleeping women. (762)

installation—An artwork that creates an artistic environment in a room or gallery. (950, 30-25B)

International style—A style of 14th- and 15th-century painting begun by Simone Martini, who adapted the French *Gothic* manner to Sienese art fused with influences from northern Europe. This style appealed to the aristocracy because of its brilliant *color,* lavish costumes, intricate ornamentation, and themes involving splendid processions of knights and ladies. Also, a style of 20th-century architecture associated with Le Corbusier, whose elegance of design came to influence the look of modern office buildings and skyscrapers. (886)

Jugendstil—See *Art Nouveau.* (828)

lancet—In *Gothic* architecture, a tall narrow window ending in a pointed arch. (890, 27-43A)

literati—In China, talented amateur painters and scholars from the landed gentry. (956, 31-22A)

lithograph—See *lithography.* (778)

lithography—A printmaking technique in which the artist uses an oil-based crayon to draw directly on a stone plate and then wipes water onto the stone. When ink is rolled onto the plate, it adheres only to the drawing. The print produced by this method is a lithograph. (778)

local color—An object's true *color* in white light. (801)

medium (pl. **media**)—The material (for example, marble, bronze, clay, *fresco*) in which an artist works; also, in painting, the vehicle (usually liquid) that carries the pigment. See also *automatism, gouache.*

memento mori—Latin, "reminder of death." In painting, a reminder of human mortality, usually represented by a skull. (26-7A, 30-25B)

metamatics—The name Swiss artist Jean Tinguely gave to the motor-driven devices he constructed to produce instant abstract paintings. (935)

Minimalism—A predominantly sculptural American trend of the 1960s characterized by works featuring a severe reduction of form, often to single, homogeneous units. (910)

mobile—A kind of sculpture, invented by Alexander Calder, combining nonobjective organic forms and motion in balanced structures hanging from rods, wires, and colored, organically shaped plates. (895)

modernism—A movement in Western art that developed in the second half of the 19th century and sought to capture the images and sensibilities of the age. Modernist art goes beyond simply dealing with the present and involves the artist's critical examination of the premises of art itself. (801, 998)

Modernismo—See *Art Nouveau.* (828)

mosaic—Patterns or pictures made by embedding small pieces of stone or glass in cement on surfaces such as walls and floors; also, the technique of making such works. (28-24A)

Nabis—Hebrew, "prophet." A group of *Symbolist* painters influenced by Paul Gauguin. (819)

Naturalistic Surrealism—See *Surrealism.* (875)

Neoclassicism—A style of art and architecture that emerged in the late 18th century as part of a general revival of interest in *classical* cultures. Neoclassical artists adopted themes and styles from ancient Greece and Rome. (745)

Neo-Expressionism—An art movement that emerged in the 1970s and that reflects artists' interest in the expressive capability of art, seen earlier in *German Expressionism* and *Abstract Expressionism.* (905, 30-8D)

Neo-Gothic—The revival of the *Gothic style* in architecture, especially in the 19th century. (788)

Neoplasticism—The Dutch artist Piet Mondrian's theory of "pure plastic art," an ideal balance between the universal and the individual using an abstract formal vocabulary. (881)

Neue Sachlichkeit—German, "new objectivity." An art movement that grew directly out of the World War I experiences of a group of German artists who sought to show the horrors of the war and its effects. (872)

odalisque—A woman in a Turkish harem. (761)

ogive (adj. **ogival**)—The diagonal rib of a Gothic vault; a pointed, or Gothic, arch. (927)

Op Art—An artistic movement of the 1960s in which painters sought to produce optical illusions of motion and depth using only geometric forms on two-dimensional surfaces. (908)

optical mixture—The visual effect of juxtaposed *complementary colors.* (813)

orbiculum—A disklike opening. (930)

Orphism—A form of *Cubism* developed by the French painter Robert Delaunay in which color plays an important role. (848)

orrery—A mechanical model of the solar system demonstrating how the planets revolve around the sun. (727)

palette—A thin board with a thumb hole at one end on which an artist lays and mixes *colors;* any surface so used. Also, the colors or kinds of colors characteristically used by an artist. See also *palette knife.*

palette knife—A flat tool used to scrape paint off the *palette.* Artists sometimes also use the palette knife in place of a brush to apply paint directly to the canvas. (777)

papier collé—French, "stuck paper." See *collage.* (850)

pastel—A powdery paste of pigment and gum used for making crayons; also, the pastel crayons themselves. (809)

philosophe—French, "thinker, philosopher." The term applied to French intellectuals of the *Enlightenment.* (736)

photomontage—A composition made by pasting together pictures or parts of pictures, especially photographs. See also *collage.* (835)

Photorealism—See *Superrealism.* (917)

Picturesque garden—An "unordered" garden designed in accord with the *Enlightenment* taste for the natural. (750)

pier—A vertical, freestanding masonry support. (12, 72, 184)

pinnacle—In Gothic churches, a sharply pointed ornament capping the piers or flying buttresses; also used on church facades. (27-43A)

Pittura Metafisica—Italian, "metaphysical painting." An early-20th-century Italian art movement led by Giorgio de Chirico, whose work conveys an eerie mood and visionary quality. (875)

pixels—Shortened form of "picture elements." The tiny boxes that make up digital images displayed on a computer monitor. (938)

plein air—An approach to painting very popular among the *Impressionists,* in which an artist sketches outdoors to achieve a quick impression of light, air, and color. The artist then takes the sketches to the studio for reworking into more finished works of art. (798, 799, 801, 805, 806, 28-2A, 28-7A)

pointillism—A system of painting devised by the 19th-century French painter Georges Seurat. The artist separates *color* into its component parts and then applies the component colors to the canvas in tiny dots (points). The image becomes comprehensible only from a distance, when the viewer's eyes optically blend the pigment dots. Sometimes referred to as *divisionism.* (812)

Pop Art—A term coined by British art critic Lawrence Alloway to refer to art, first appearing in the 1950s, that incorporated elements from consumer culture, the mass media, and popular culture, such as images from motion pictures and advertising. (899)

positivism—A Western philosophical model that promoted science as the mind's highest achievement. (775)

Post-Impressionism—The term used to describe the stylistically heterogeneous work of the group of late-19th-century painters in France, including van Gogh, Gauguin, Seurat, and Cézanne, who more systematically examined the properties and expressive qualities of line, pattern, form, and color than the *Impressionists* did. (811)

postmodernism—A reaction against *modernist formalism,* seen as elitist. Far more encompassing and accepting than the more rigid confines of modernist practice, postmodernism offers something for everyone by accommodating a wide range of styles, subjects, and formats, from traditional easel painting to *installation* and from *abstraction* to *illusionistic* scenes. Postmodern art often includes irony or reveals a self-conscious awareness on the part of the artist of art-making processes or the workings of the art world. (929)

Post-Painterly Abstraction—An American art movement that emerged in the 1960s and was characterized by a cool, detached rationality emphasizing tighter pictorial control. See also *color-field painting* and *hard-edge painting.* (907)

Poussiniste—A member of the French Royal Academy of Painting and Sculpture during the early 18th century who followed Nicolas Poussin in insisting that form was the most important element of painting. See also *Rubéniste.* (733)

Precisionism—An American art movement of the 1920s and 1930s. The Precisionists concentrated on portraying man-made environments in a clear and concise manner to express the beauty of perfect and precise machine forms. (867)

primary colors—Red, yellow, and blue—the *colors* from which all other colors may be derived. (813)

primitivism—The incorporation in early-20th-century Western art of stylistic elements from the artifacts of Africa, Oceania, and the native peoples of the Americas. (845, 846)

Productivism—An art movement that emerged in the Soviet Union after the Russian Revolution; its members believed that artists must direct art toward creating products for the new society. (860)

Purism—An early-20th-century art movement that embraced the "machine aesthetic" and sought purity of form in the clean functional lines of industrial machinery. (853)

Rayograph—A photograph produced without a camera by placing objects on photographic paper and then exposing the paper to light; named for the American artist Man Ray. (864)

relief—In sculpture, figures projecting from a background of which they are part. The degree of relief is designated *high, low (bas),* or *sunken.* In the last, the artist cuts the design into the surface so that the highest projecting parts of the image are no higher than the surface itself. See also *Rococo.*

Rococo—A style, primarily of interior design, that appeared in France around 1700. Rococo interiors featured lavish decoration, including small sculptures, ornamental mirrors, easel paintings, *tapestries, reliefs,* wall paintings, and elegant furniture. The term *Rococo* derived from the French word *rocaille* (pebble) and referred to the small stones and shells used to decorate grotto interiors. See also *femme savante, fête galante.*

Realism—A movement that emerged in mid-19th-century France. Realist artists represented the subject matter of everyday life in a relatively *naturalistic* mode.

Regionalism—A 20th-century American art movement that portrayed American rural life in a clearly readable, *Realist* style. Major Regionalists include Grant Wood and Thomas Hart Benton. (889)

Romanticism—A Western cultural phenomenon, beginning around 1750 and ending about 1850, that gave precedence to feeling and imagination over reason and thought. More narrowly, the art movement that flourished from about 1800 to 1840. (762)

rostrum—Speaker's platform. (929)

Rubéniste—A member of the French Royal Academy of Painting and Sculpture during the early 18th century who followed Peter Paul Rubens in insisting that *color* was the most important element of painting. See also *Poussiniste.* (733)

Saint-Simonianism—An early-19th-century utopian movement that emphasized the education and enfranchisement of women. (779)

saturation—See *color.* (813)

satyr—A Greek mythological follower of Dionysos having a man's upper body, a goat's hindquarters and horns, and a horse's ears and tail. (27-33A)

secondary colors—Orange, green, and purple, obtained by mixing pairs of *primary colors* (red, yellow, blue). (813)

silk-screen printing—An industrial printing technique that creates a sharp-edged image by pressing ink through a design on silk or a similar tightly woven porous fabric stretched tight on a frame. (915)

Simultanéisme—Robert Delaunay's version of *Cubism* in which he created spatial effects and kaleidoscopic movement solely through color contrasts; also known as *Orphism.* (848)

simultaneous contrasts—The phenomenon of juxtaposed *colors* affecting the eye's reception of each, as when a painter places dark green next to light green, making the former appear even darker and the latter even lighter. See also *successive contrasts.* (813)

site-specific art—Art created for a specific location. See also *Environmental Art.* (932)

successive contrasts—The phenomenon of colored afterimages. When a person looks intently at a *color* (green, for example) and then shifts to a white area, the fatigued eye momentarily perceives the *complementary color* (red). See also *simultaneous contrasts.* (813)

Superrealism—A school of painting and sculpture of the 1960s and 1970s that emphasized producing artworks based on scrupulous fidelity to optical fact. The Superrealist painters were also called Photorealists because many used photographs as sources for their imagery. (917)

Suprematism—A type of art formulated by Kazimir Malevich to convey his belief that the supreme reality in the world is pure feeling, which attaches to no object and thus calls for new, nonobjective forms in art—shapes not related to objects in the visible world. (859)

Surrealism—A successor to *Dada,* Surrealism incorporated the improvisational nature of its predecessor into its exploration of the ways to express in art the world of dreams and the unconscious. Biomorphic Surrealists, such as Joan Miró, produced largely *abstract* compositions. *Naturalistic* Surrealists, notably Salvador Dalí, presented recognizable scenes transformed into a dream or nightmare image. (875)

Symbolism—A late-19th-century movement based on the idea that the artist was not an imitator of nature but a creator who transformed the facts of nature into a symbol of the inner experience of that fact. (819)

Synthetic Cubism—A later phase of *Cubism,* in which paintings and drawings were constructed from objects and shapes cut from paper or other materials to represent parts of a subject, in order to engage the viewer with pictorial issues, such as figuration, realism, and abstraction. (848)

tapestry—A weaving technique in which the *weft* threads are packed densely over the *warp* threads so that the designs are woven directly into the fabric. (730)

ukiyo-e—Japanese, "pictures of the floating world." During the Edo period, woodcut prints depicting brothels, popular entertainment, and beautiful women. (28-16B)

Usonian—Frank Lloyd Wright's term for the inexpensive houses he designed for ordinary people. *Usonian* derives from "United States of North America." (896)

value—See *color.* (813)

vanitas—Latin, "vanity." A term describing paintings (particularly 17th-century Dutch still lifes) that include references to death. (26-7A)

veduta (pl. **vedute**)—Italian, "scenic view." (744)

wainscoting—Paneling on the lower part of interior walls. (827)

warp—The vertical threads of a loom or cloth. See also *tapestry.*

weft—The horizontal threads of a loom or cloth. See also *tapestry.*

wet-plate photography—An early photographic process in which the photographic plate is exposed, developed, and fixed while wet. (792)

zoopraxiscope—A device invented by Eadweard Muybridge in the 19th century to project sequences of still photographic images; a predecessor of the modern motion-picture projector. (796)

BIBLIOGRAPHY

This list of books is very selective but comprehensive enough to satisfy the reading interests of the beginning art history student and general reader. Significantly expanded from the previous edition, the 14th edition bibliography can also serve as the basis for undergraduate research papers. The resources listed range from works that are valuable primarily for their reproductions to those that are scholarly surveys of schools and periods or monographs on individual artists. The emphasis is on recent in-print books and on books likely to be found in college and municipal libraries. No entries for periodical articles appear, but the bibliography begins with a list of some of the major journals that publish art historical scholarship in English.

Selected Periodicals

African Arts
American Art
American Indian Art
American Journal of Archaeology
Antiquity
Archaeology
Archives of American Art
Archives of Asian Art
Ars Orientalis
Art Bulletin
Art History
Art in America
Art Journal
Artforum International
Artnews
Burlington Magazine
Gesta
History of Photography
Journal of Roman Archaeology
Journal of the Society of Architectural Historians
Journal of the Warburg and Courtauld Institutes
Latin American Antiquity
October
Oxford Art Journal
Women's Art Journal

General Studies

Baxandall, Michael. *Patterns of Intention: On the Historical Explanation of Pictures.* New Haven, Conn.: Yale University Press, 1985.

Bindman, David, ed. *The Thames & Hudson Encyclopedia of British Art.* London: Thames & Hudson, 1988.

Boström, Antonia. *The Encyclopedia of Sculpture.* 3 vols. London: Routledge, 2003.

Broude, Norma, and Mary D. Garrard, eds. *The Expanding Discourse: Feminism and Art History.* New York: Harper Collins, 1992.

Bryson, Norman. *Vision and Painting: The Logic of the Gaze.* New Haven, Conn.: Yale University Press, 1983.

Bryson, Norman, Michael Ann Holly, and Keith Moxey. *Visual Theory: Painting and Interpretation.* New York: Cambridge University Press, 1991.

Burden, Ernest. *Illustrated Dictionary of Architecture.* 2d ed. New York: McGraw-Hill, 2002.

Büttner, Nils. *Landscape Painting: A History.* New York: Abbeville, 2006.

Carrier, David. *A World Art History and Its Objects.* University Park: Pennsylvania State University Press, 2009.

Chadwick, Whitney. *Women, Art, and Society.* 4th ed. New York: Thames & Hudson, 2007.

Cheetham, Mark A., Michael Ann Holly, and Keith Moxey, eds. *The Subjects of Art History: Historical Objects in Contemporary Perspective.* New York: Cambridge University Press, 1998.

Chilvers, Ian, and Harold Osborne, eds. *The Oxford Dictionary of Art.* 3d ed. New York: Oxford University Press, 2004.

Corbin, George A. *Native Arts of North America, Africa, and the South Pacific: An Introduction.* New York: Harper Collins, 1988.

Crouch, Dora P., and June G. Johnson. *Traditions in Architecture: Africa, America, Asia, and Oceania.* New York: Oxford University Press, 2000.

Curl, James Stevens. *Oxford Dictionary of Architecture and Landscape Architecture.* 2d ed. New York: Oxford University Press, 2006.

Duby, Georges, ed. *Sculpture: From Antiquity to the Present.* 2 vols. Cologne: Taschen, 1999.

Encyclopedia of World Art. 17 vols. New York: McGraw-Hill, 1959–1987.

Fielding, Mantle. *Dictionary of American Painters, Sculptors, and Engravers.* 2d ed. Poughkeepsie, N.Y.: Apollo, 1986.

Fine, Sylvia Honig. *Women and Art: A History of Women Painters and Sculptors from the Renaissance to the 20th Century.* Rev. ed. Montclair, N.J.: Alanheld & Schram, 1978.

Fleming, John, Hugh Honour, and Nikolaus Pevsner. *The Penguin Dictionary of Architecture and Landscape Architecture.* 5th ed. New York: Penguin, 2000.

Frazier, Nancy. *The Penguin Concise Dictionary of Art History.* New York: Penguin, 2000.

Freedberg, David. *The Power of Images: Studies in the History and Theory of Response.* Chicago: University of Chicago Press, 1989.

Gaze, Delia, ed. *Dictionary of Women Artists.* 2 vols. London: Routledge, 1997.

Hall, James. Hall, James. *Dictionary of Subjects and Symbols in Art.* 2d ed. Boulder, Colo.: Westview, 2008.

Harris, Anne Sutherland, and Linda Nochlin. *Women Artists: 1550–1950.* Los Angeles: Los Angeles County Museum of Art; New York: Knopf, 1977.

Hauser, Arnold. *The Sociology of Art.* Chicago: University of Chicago Press, 1982.

Hults, Linda C. *The Print in the Western World: An Introductory History.* Madison: University of Wisconsin Press, 1996.

Kemp, Martin. *The Science of Art: Optical Themes in Western Art from Brunelleschi to Seurat.* New Haven, Conn.: Yale University Press, 1990.

Kostof, Spiro, and Gregory Castillo. *A History of Architecture: Settings and Rituals.* 2d ed. Oxford: Oxford University Press, 1995.

Kultermann, Udo. *The History of Art History.* New York: Abaris, 1993.

Lucie-Smith, Edward. *The Thames & Hudson Dictionary of Art Terms.* 2d ed. New York: Thames & Hudson, 2004.

Moffett, Marian, Michael Fazio, and Lawrence Wadehouse. *A World History of Architecture.* Boston: McGraw-Hill, 2004.

Morgan, Anne Lee. *Oxford Dictionary of American Art and Artists.* New York: Oxford University Press, 2008.

Murray, Peter, and Linda Murray. *A Dictionary of Art and Artists.* 7th ed. New York: Penguin, 1998.

Nelson, Robert S., and Richard Shiff, eds. *Critical Terms for Art History.* Chicago: University of Chicago Press, 1996.

Pazanelli, Roberta, ed. *The Color of Life: Polychromy in Sculpture from Antiquity to the Present.* Los Angeles: J. Paul Getty Museum, 2008.

Penny, Nicholas. *The Materials of Sculpture.* New Haven, Conn.: Yale University Press, 1993.

Pevsner, Nikolaus. *A History of Building Types.* London: Thames & Hudson, 1987. Reprint of 1979 ed.

———. *An Outline of European Architecture.* 8th ed. Baltimore: Penguin, 1974.

Pierce, James Smith. *From Abacus to Zeus: A Handbook of Art History.* 7th ed. Upper Saddle River, N.J.: Pearson Prentice Hall, 1998.

Placzek, Adolf K., ed. *Macmillan Encyclopedia of Architects.* 4 vols. New York: Macmillan, 1982.

Podro, Michael. *The Critical Historians of Art.* New Haven, Conn.: Yale University Press, 1982.

Pollock, Griselda. *Vision and Difference: Femininity, Feminism, and Histories of Art.* London: Routledge, 1988.

Pregill, Philip, and Nancy Volkman. *Landscapes in History Design and Planning in the Eastern and Western Traditions.* 2d ed. Hoboken, N.J.: Wiley, 1999.

Preziosi, Donald, ed. *The Art of Art History: A Critical Anthology.* New York: Oxford University Press, 1998.

Read, Herbert. *The Thames & Hudson Dictionary of Art and Artists*. Rev. ed. New York: Thames & Hudson, 1994.

Reid, Jane D. *The Oxford Guide to Classical Mythology in the Arts 1300–1990s*. 2 vols. New York: Oxford University Press, 1993.

Rogers, Elizabeth Barlow. *Landscape Design: A Cultural and Architectural History*. New York: Abrams, 2001.

Roth, Leland M. *Understanding Architecture: Its Elements, History, and Meaning*. 2d ed. Boulder, Colo.: Westview, 2006.

Schama, Simon. *The Power of Art*. New York: Ecco, 2006.

Slatkin, Wendy. *Women Artists in History: From Antiquity to the 20th Century*. 4th ed. Upper Saddle River, N.J.: Prentice Hall, 2000.

Steer, John, and Antony White. *Atlas of Western Art History: Artists, Sites, and Monuments from Ancient Greece to the Modern Age*. New York: Facts on File, 1994.

Stratton, Arthur. *The Orders of Architecture: Greek, Roman, and Renaissance*. London: Studio, 1986.

Summers, David. *Real Spaces: World Art History and the Rise of Western Modernism*. London: Phaidon, 2003.

Sutton, Ian. *Western Architecture: From Ancient Greece to the Present*. New York: Thames & Hudson, 1999.

Trachtenberg, Marvin, and Isabelle Hyman. *Architecture, from Prehistory to Post-Modernism*. 2d ed. Upper Saddle River, N.J.: Prentice Hall, 2003.

Turner, Jane, ed. *The Dictionary of Art*. 34 vols. New ed. New York: Oxford University Press, 2003.

Watkin, David. *A History of Western Architecture*. 4th ed. London: Laurence King, 2010.

West, Shearer. *Portraiture*. New York: Oxford University Press, 2004.

Wittkower, Rudolf. *Sculpture Processes and Principles*. New York: Harper & Row, 1977.

Wren, Linnea H., and Janine M. Carter, eds. *Perspectives on Western Art: Source Documents and Readings from the Ancient Near East through the Middle Ages*. New York: Harper & Row, 1987.

Zijlmans, Kitty, and Wilfried van Damme, eds. *World Art Studies: Exploring Concepts and Approaches*. Amsterdam: Valiz, 2008.

Chapter 26: Rococo to Neoclassicism: The 18th Century in Europe and America

Beddington, Charles. *Venice: Canaletto and His Rivals*. London: National Gallery, 2010.

Bermingham, Ann. *Landscape and Ideology: The English Rustic Tradition, 1740–1850*. Berkeley: University of California Press, 1986.

Boime, Albert. *Art in the Age of Revolution, 1750–1800*. Chicago: University of Chicago Press, 1987.

Bowron, Edgar Peters, and Joseph J. Rishel, eds. *Art in Rome in the Eighteenth Century*. Philadelphia: Philadelphia Museum of Art, 2000

Braham, Allan. *The Architecture of the French Enlightenment*. Berkeley: University of California Press, 1980.

Brion, Marcel. *Art of the Romantic Era: Romanticism, Classicism, Realism*. New York: Praeger, 1966.

Conisbee, Philip. *Painting in Eighteenth-Century France*. Ithaca, N.Y.: Phaidon/Cornell University Press, 1981.

Craske, Matthew. *Art in Europe, 1700–1830: A History of the Visual Arts in an Era of Unprecedented Urban Economic Growth*. New York: Oxford University Press, 1997.

Crow, Thomas E. *Painters and Public Life in Eighteenth-Century Paris*. New Haven, Conn.: Yale University Press, 1985.

Gaunt, W. *The Great Century of British Painting: Hogarth to Turner*. New York: Phaidon, 1971.

Goodman, Elise, ed. *Art and Culture in the Eighteenth Century: New Dimensions and Multiple Perspectives*. Newark: University of Delaware Press, 2001.

Harrison, Charles, Paul Wood, and Jason Gaiger, eds. *Art in Theory, 1648–1815: An Anthology of Changing Ideas*. Oxford: Blackwell, 2000.

Hedley, Jo. *François Boucher: Seductive Visions*. London: Wallace Collection, 2004.

Herrmann, Luke. *British Landscape Painting of the Eighteenth Century*. New York: Oxford University Press, 1974.

Honour, Hugh. *Neo-Classicism*. Harmondsworth: Penguin, 1968.

Irwin, David. *Neoclassicism*. London: Phaidon, 1997.

Jarrassé, Dominique. *18th-Century French Painting*. Paris: Terrail, 1999.

Kalnein, Wend Graf, and Michael Levey. *Art and Architecture of the Eighteenth Century in France*. New York: Viking/Pelican, 1973.

Lee, Simon. *David*. London: Phaidon, 1999.

Levey, Michael. *Rococo to Revolution: Major Trends in Eighteenth-Century Painting*. London: Thames & Hudson, 1966.

Rosenblum, Robert. *Transformations in Late Eighteenth-Century Art*. Princeton, N.J.: Princeton University Press, 1970.

Roston, Murray. *Changing Perspectives in Literature and the Visual Arts, 1650–1820*. Princeton, N.J.: Princeton University Press, 1990.

Rykwert, Joseph. *The First Moderns: Architects of the Eighteenth Century*. Cambridge, Mass.: MIT Press, 1983.

Stillman, Damie. *English Neo-Classical Architecture*. 2 vols. London: Zwemmer, 1988.

Waterhouse, Ellis Kirkham. *Painting in Britain: 1530–1790*. 4th ed. New Haven, Conn.: Yale University Press, 1979.

Wilton, Andrew. *The Swagger Portrait: Grand Manner Portraiture in Britain from Van Dyck to Augustus John, 1630–1930*. London: Tate Gallery, 1992.

19th and 20th Centuries, General

Arnason, H. H., and Peter Kalb. *History of Modern Art: Painting, Sculpture, Architecture, Photography*. 6th ed. Upper Saddle River, N.J.: Prentice Hall, 2009.

Ashton, Dore. *Twentieth-Century Artists on Art*. New York: Pantheon Books, 1985.

Barnitz, Jacueline. *Twentieth-Century Art of Latin America*. Austin: University of Texas Press, 2001.

Brettell, Richard R. *Modern Art, 1851–1929: Capitalism and Representation*. New York: Oxford University Press, 1999.

Brown, Milton, Sam Hunter, and John Jacobus. *American Art: Painting, Sculpture, Architecture, Decorative Arts, Photography*. New York: Abrams, 1979.

Burnham, Jack. *Beyond Modern Sculpture: The Effects of Science and Technology on the Sculpture of This Century*. New York: Braziller, 1968.

Butler, Cornelia, and Alexandra Schwartz, eds. *Modern Women: Women Artists at the Museum of Modern Art*. New York: Museum of Modern Art, 2010.

Chipp, Herschel B. *Theories of Modern Art*. Berkeley: University of California Press, 1968.

Chu, Petra ten-Doesschate. *Nineteenth-Century European Art*. 2d ed. Upper Saddle River, N.J.: Prentice Hall, 2006.

Coke, Van Deren. *The Painter and the Photograph from Delacroix to Warhol*. Rev. ed. Albuquerque: University of New Mexico Press, 1972.

Colquhoun, Alan. *Modern Architecture*. New York: Oxford University Press, 2002.

Craven, Wayne. *American Art: History and Culture*. Rev. ed. New York: McGraw-Hill, 2002.

Dennis, Rafael Cardoso, and Colin Trodd, eds. *Art and the Academy in the Nineteenth Century*. New Brunswick, N.J.: Rutgers University Press, 2000.

Doordan, Dennis P. *Twentieth-Century Architecture*. New York: Abrams, 2002.

Doss, Erika. *Twentieth-Century American Art*. New York: Oxford University Press, 2002.

Driskell, David C. *Two Centuries of Black American Art*. Los Angeles: Los Angeles County Museum of Art; New York: Knopf, 1976.

Eisenmann, Stephen F., ed. *Nineteenth-Century Art: A Critical History*. 4th ed. New York: Thames & Hudson, 2011.

Elsen, Albert. *Origins of Modern Sculpture*. New York: Braziller, 1974.

Facos, Michelle. *An Introduction to Nineteenth-Century Art*. New York: Routledge, 2011.

Foster, Hal, Rosalind Krauss, Yve-Alain Bois, and Benjamin H. D. Buchloh. *Art since 1900: Modernism, Antimodernism, Postmodernism*. New York: Thames & Hudson, 2004.

Frampton, Kenneth. *Modern Architecture: A Critical History*. 4th ed. New York: Thames & Hudson, 2007.

Frascina, Francis, and Charles Harrison, eds. *Modern Art and Modernism: A Critical Anthology*. New York: Harper & Row, 1982.

Giedion, Siegfried. *Space, Time, and Architecture: The Growth of a New Tradition*. 4th ed. Cambridge, Mass.: Harvard University Press, 1965.

Goldwater, Robert, and Marco Treves, eds. *Artists on Art*. 3d ed. New York: Pantheon, 1958.

Greenough, Sarah, Joel Snyder, David Travis, and Colin Westerbeck. *On the Art of Fixing a Shadow: One Hundred and Fifty Years of Photography*. Washington, D.C.: National Gallery of Art; Chicago: Art Institute of Chicago, 1989.

Hamilton, George H. *Painting and Sculpture in Europe, 1880–1940*. 6th ed. New Haven, Conn.: Yale University Press, 1993.

Harrison, Charles, and Paul Wood. *Art in Theory, 1900–2000: An Anthology of Changing Ideas*. Oxford: Blackwell, 2003.

Herbert, Robert L., ed. *Modern Artists on Art*. Upper Saddle River, N.J.: Prentice Hall, 1971.

Hertz, Richard, and Norman M. Klein, eds. *Twentieth-Century Art Theory: Urbanism, Politics, and Mass Culture*. Englewood Cliffs, N.J.: Prentice Hall, 1990.

Heyer, Paul. *Architects on Architecture: New Directions in America*. New York: Van Nostrand Reinhold, 1993.

Hills, Patricia. *Modern Art in the USA: Issues and Controversies of the 20th Century*. Upper Saddle River, N.J.: Prentice Hall, 2000.

Hitchcock, Henry-Russell. *Architecture: Nineteenth and Twentieth Centuries*. 4th ed. New Haven, Conn.: Yale University Press, 1977.

Hunter, Sam, John Jacobus, and Daniel Wheeler. *Modern Art: Painting, Sculpture, Architecture, Photography*. Rev. 3d ed. Upper Saddle River, N.J.: Prentice Hall, 2004.

Janson, Horst W. *19th-Century Sculpture*. New York: Abrams, 1985.

Jencks, Charles. *Modern Movements in Architecture*. Garden City, N.Y.: Anchor; Doubleday, 1973.

Kaufmann, Edgar, Jr., ed. *The Rise of an American Architecture*. New York: Metropolitan Museum of Art; Praeger, 1970.

Krauss, Rosalind E. *The Originality of the Avant-Garde and Other Modernist Myths*. Cambridge, Mass.: MIT Press, 1985.

———. *Passages in Modern Sculpture*. Cambridge, Mass.: MIT Press, 1981.

Lewis, Samella S. *African American Art and Artists.* Rev. ed. Berkeley: University of California Press, 1994.

Licht, Fred. *Sculpture, Nineteenth and Twentieth Centuries.* Greenwich, Conn.: New York Graphic Society, 1967.

Marien, Mary Warner. *Photography: A Cultural History.* 3d ed. Upper Saddle River, N.J.: Prentice Hall, 2011.

Mason, Jerry, ed. *International Center of Photography Encyclopedia of Photography.* New York: Crown, 1984.

McCoubrey, John W. *American Art, 1700–1960: Sources and Documents.* Englewood Cliffs, N.J.: Prentice Hall, 1965.

Newhall, Beaumont. *The History of Photography.* New York: Museum of Modern Art, 1982.

Osborne, Harold. *The Oxford Companion to Twentieth-Century Art.* New York: Oxford University Press, 1981.

Pohl, Frances K. *Framing America: A Social History of American Art.* 2d ed. New York: Thames & Hudson, 2008.

Rose, Barbara. *American Art since 1900.* Rev. ed. New York: Praeger, 1975.

Rosenblum, Naomi. *A World History of Photography.* 4th ed. New York: Abbeville, 2007.

Rosenblum, Robert. *Modern Painting and the Northern Romantic Tradition: Friedrich to Rothko.* New York: Harper & Row, 1975.

Rosenblum, Robert, and Horst W. Janson. *19th-Century Art.* Rev. ed. Upper Saddle River, N.J.: Prentice Hall, 2005.

Ross, Stephen David, ed. *Art and Its Significance: An Anthology of Aesthetic Theory.* Albany: State University of New York Press, 1987.

Russell, John. *The Meanings of Modern Art.* New York: Museum of Modern Art; Thames & Hudson, 1981.

Scully, Vincent. *Modern Architecture.* Rev. ed. New York: Braziller, 1974.

Spalding, Francis. *British Art since 1900.* London: Thames & Hudson, 1986.

Spencer, Harold. *American Art: Readings from the Colonial Era to the Present.* New York: Scribner, 1980.

Steinberg, Leo. *Other Criteria: Confrontations with 20th-Century Art.* New York: Oxford University Press, 1972.

Szarkowski, John. *Photography until Now.* New York: Museum of Modern Art, 1989.

Upton, Dell. *Architecture in the United States.* Oxford: Oxford University Press, 1998.

Weaver, Mike. *The Art of Photography: 1839–1989.* New Haven, Conn.: Yale University Press, 1989.

Whiffen, Marcus, and Frederick Koeper. *American Architecture, 1607–1976.* Cambridge, Mass.: MIT Press, 1983.

Wilmerding, John. *American Art.* Harmondsworth: Penguin, 1976.

Wilson, Simon. *Holbein to Hockney: A History of British Art.* London: Tate Gallery & Bodley Head, 1979.

Chapter 27: Romanticism, Realism, Photography: Europe and America, 1800 to 1870

Amic, Sylvain, et al. *Gustave Courbet.* Ostfildern: Hatje Cantz, 2008.

Bartoli, Damien, and Frederick C. Ross. *William Bouguereau.* 2 vols. New York: Antique Collectors' Club, 2010.

Bellenger, Sylvain. *Girodet, 1767–1824.* Paris: Gallimard, 2005.

Bergdoll, Barry. *European Architecture 1750–1890.* New York: Oxford University Press, 2000.

Boime, Albert. *The Academy and French Painting in the 19th Century.* London: Phaidon, 1971.

———. *Art in the Age of Bonapartism, 1800–1815.* Chicago: University of Chicago Press, 1990.

Bordes, Philippe. *Jacques-Louis David: Empire to Exile.* New Haven, Conn.: Yale University Press, 2007.

Brown, David Blayney. *Romanticism.* New York: Phaidon, 2001.

Bryson, Norman. *Tradition and Desire: From David to Delacroix.* New York: Cambridge University Press, 1984.

Burns, Sarah, and John Davis. *American Art to 1900: A Documentary History.* Berkeley and Los Angeles: University of California Press, 2009.

Clark, T. J. *The Absolute Bourgeois: Artists and Politics in France, 1848–1851.* London: Thames & Hudson, 1973.

———. *Image of the People: Gustave Courbet and the 1848 Revolution.* London: Thames & Hudson, 1973.

———. *The Painting of Modern Life: Paris in the Art of Manet and His Followers.* Princeton, N.J.: Princeton University Press, 1984.

Clay, Jean. *Romanticism.* New York: Phaidon, 1981.

Eitner, Lorenz. *Neoclassicism and Romanticism, 1750–1850: An Anthology of Sources and Documents.* New York: Harper & Row, 1989.

Fried, Michael. *Courbet's Realism.* Chicago: University of Chicago Press, 1982.

———. *Manet's Modernism, or, The Face of Painting in the 1860s.* Chicago: University of Chicago Press, 1996.

Hilton, Timothy. *The Pre-Raphaelites.* New York: Oxford University Press, 1970.

Hofmann, Werner. *Caspar David Friedrich.* New York: Thames & Hudson, 2001.

———. *Goya.* New York: Thames & Hudson, 2003.

Holt, Elizabeth Gilmore, ed. *From the Classicists to the Impressionists: A Documentary History of Art and Architecture in the Nineteenth Century.* Garden City, N.J.: Anchor Books; Doubleday, 1966.

Honour, Hugh. *Romanticism.* New York: Harper & Row, 1979.

Koerner, Joseph Leo. *Caspar David Friedrich and the Subject of Landscape.* 2d ed. London: Reaktion, 2009.

Krell, Alain. *Manet and the Painters of Contemporary Life.* London: Thames & Hudson, 1996.

Kroeber, Karl. *British Romantic Art.* Berkeley: University of California Press, 1986.

Le Men, Ségolène. *Courbet.* New York: Abbeville, 2008.

Lewis, Michael J. *The Gothic Revival.* New York: Thames & Hudson, 2002.

Licht, Fred. *Goya.* New York: Abbeville, 2001.

Mainardi, Patricia. *Art and Politics of the Second Empire: The Universal Expositions of 1855 and 1867.* New Haven, Conn.: Yale University Press, 1987.

———. *The End of the Salon: Art and the State in the Early Third Republic.* Cambridge: Cambridge University Press, 1993.

Middleton, Robin. *Architecture of the Nineteenth Century.* London: Phaidon, 2003.

Middleton, Robin, and David Watkin. *Neoclassical and 19th-Century Architecture.* 2 vols. New York: Electa/Rizzoli, 1987.

Needham, Gerald. *19th-Century Realist Art.* New York: Harper & Row, 1988.

Nochlin, Linda. *Realism and Tradition in Art, 1848–1900: Sources and Documents.* Upper Saddle River, N.J.: Prentice Hall, 1966.

Novak, Barbara. *American Painting of the Nineteenth Century: Realism and the American Experience.* New York: Harper & Row, 1979.

Novak, Barbara. *Nature and Culture: American Landscape and Painting, 1825–1875.* 3d ed. New York: Oxford University Press, 2007.

Nature and Culture: American Landscape and Painting, 1825–1875. 3d ed. New York: Oxford University Press, 2007.

Novotny, Fritz. *Painting and Sculpture in Europe, 1780–1880.* 3d ed. New Haven, Conn.: Yale University Press, 1988.

Porterfield, Todd. *The Allure of Empire: Art in the Service of French Imperialism 1798–1836.* Princeton, N.J.: Princeton University Press, 1998.

Rosen, Charles, and Henri Zerner. *Romanticism and Realism: The Mythology of Nineteenth-Century Art.* New York: Viking, 1984.

Rubin, James Henry. *Courbet.* London: Phaidon, 1997.

———. *Manet: Initial M, Hand and Eye.* Paris: Flammarion, 2010.

Shelton, Andrew Carrington. *Ingres.* London: Phaidon, 2008.

Sloane, Joseph C. *French Painting between the Past and the Present: Artists, Critics, and Traditions from 1848 to 1870.* Princeton, N.J.: Princeton University Press, 1973.

Symmons, Sarah. *Goya.* London: Phaidon, 1998.

Taylor, Joshua, ed. *Nineteenth-Century Theories of Art.* Berkeley: University of California Press, 1987.

Tillier, Betrand, et al. *Gustave Courbet.* New York: Metropolitan Museum of Art, 2008.

Toman, Rolf, ed. *Neoclassicism and Romanticism: Architecture, Sculpture, Painting, Drawings, 1750–1848.* Cologne: Könemann, 2006.

Vaughn, William. *German Romantic Painting.* New Haven, Conn.: Yale University Press, 1980.

Wolf, Bryan Jay. *Romantic Revision: Culture and Consciousness in Nineteenth-Century American Painting and Literature.* Chicago: University of Chicago Press, 1986.

Wood, Christopher. *The Pre-Raphaelites.* New York: Viking, 1981.

Chapter 28: Impressionism, Post-Impressionism, Symbolism: Europe and America, 1870 to 1900

Baal-Teshuva, Jacob. *Louis Comfort Tiffany.* Cologne: Taschen, 2008.

Bergdoll, Barry. *European Architecture 1750–1890.* New York: Oxford University Press, 2000.

Bryson, Norman. *Tradition and Desire: From David to Delacroix.* New York: Cambridge University Press, 1984.

Calloway, Stephen. *Aubrey Beardsley.* New York: Harry N. Abrams, 1998.

Clark, T. J. *The Painting of Modern Life: Paris in the Art of Manet and His Followers.* Princeton, N.J.: Princeton University Press, 1984.

Cogeval, Guy, ed. *Claude Monet, 1840–1926.* Paris: Réunion des Musées Nationaux, 2010.

Distel, Anne. *Renoir.* New York: Abbeville, 2010.

Eitner, Lorenz. *Neoclassicism and Romanticism, 1750–1850: An Anthology of Sources and Documents.* New York: Harper & Row, 1989.

Facos, Michelle. *Symbolism in Context.* Berkeley: University of California Press, 2009.

Hauptmann, Jodi. *Beyond the Visible: The Art of Odilon Redon.* New York: Museum of Modern Art, 2005.

Loyrette, Henri, Sebastien Allard, and Laurence Des Cars. *Nineteenth Century French Art: From Romanticism to Impressionism, Post-Impressionism, and Art Nouveau.* Paris: Flammarion, 2007.

Masson, Raphaël, and Véronique Mattiussi. *Rodin.* Paris: Flammarion, 2004.

McShine, Kynaston, ed. *Edvard Munch: The Modern Life of the Soul.* New York: Museum of Modern Art, 2006.

Middleton, Robin. *Architecture of the Nineteenth Century.* London: Phaidon, 2003.

Middleton, Robin, and David Watkin. *Neoclassical and 19th-Century Architecture.* 2 vols. New York: Electa/Rizzoli, 1987.

Pfeiffer, Ingrid, et al. *Women Impressionists.* Ostfildern: Hatje Cantz, 2008.

Swinbourne, Anna. *James Ensor.* New York: Museum of Modern Art, 2009.

Thomson, Belinda, ed. *Gauguin: Maker of Myth.* London: Tate, 2010.

Zerbst, Rainer. *Gaudí: The Complete Buildings.* Cologne: Taschen, 2005.

Chapter 29: Modernism in Europe and America, 1900 to 1945

Antliff, Mark. *Cultural Politics and the Parisian Avant-Garde.* Princeton, N.J.: Princeton University Press, 1993.

Antliff, Mark, and Patricia Leighten. *Cubism and Culture.* New York: Thames & Hudson, 2001.

Arnaldo, Javier, and Max Hollein. *Kirchner.* Ostfildern: Hatje Cantz, 2010.

Baigell, Matthew. *The American Scene: American Painting of the 1930s.* New York: Praeger, 1974.

Barr, Alfred H., Jr. *Cubism and Abstract Art: Painting, Sculpture, Constructions, Photography, Architecture, Industrial Arts, Theatre, Films, Posters, Typography.* Cambridge, Mass.: Belknap, 1986.

Barron, Stephanie. *Exiles and Emigrés: The Flight of European Artists from Hitler.* Los Angeles: Los Angeles County Museum of Art, 1997.

———, ed. *Degenerate Art: The Fate of the Avant-Garde in Nazi Germany.* Los Angeles: Los Angeles County Museum of Art, 1991.

Bayer, Herbert, Walter Gropius, and Ise Gropius. *Bauhaus, 1919–1928.* New York: Museum of Modern Art, 1975.

Bearden, Romare, and Harry Henderson. *A History of African-American Artists from 1792 to the Present.* New York: Pantheon, 1993.

Bergdoll, Barry. *Bauhaus 1919–1933.* New York: Museum of Modern Art, 2009.

Bouvet, Vincent, and Gérard Durozoi. *Paris between the Wars 1919–1939: Art, Life & Culture.* New York: Vendome, 2010.

Breton, André. *Surrealism and Painting.* New York: Harper & Row, 1972.

Brown, Milton. *Story of the Armory Show: The 1913 Exhibition That Changed American Art.* 2d ed. New York: Abbeville, 1988.

Campbell, Mary Schmidt, David C. Driskell, David Lewis Levering, and Deborah Willis Ryan. *Harlem Renaissance: Art of Black America.* New York: Studio Museum in Harlem; Abrams, 1987.

Cowling, Elizabeth, ed. *Picasso: Challenging the Past.* London: National Gallery, 2011.

Cox, Neil. *Cubism.* London: Phaidon, 2000.

Curtis, Penelope. *Sculpture 1900–1945.* New York: Oxford University Press, 1999.

Curtis, William J. R. *Modern Architecture since 1900.* Upper Saddle River, N.J.: Prentice Hall, 1996.

Davidson, Abraham A. *Early American Modernist Painting, 1910–1935.* New York: Harper & Row, 1981.

Dietrich, Dorothea, ed. *Dada: Zurich, Berlin, Hannover, Cologne, New York, Paris.* Washington, D.C.: National Gallery, 2008.

Du Pont, Diana C. *Tamayo: A Modern Icon Reinterpreted.* Santa Barbara, Calif.: Santa Barbara Museum of Art, 2007.

Eberle, Matthias. *World War I and the Weimar Artists: Dix, Grosz, Beckmann, Schlemmer.* New Haven, Conn.: Yale University Press, 1985.

Edwards, Steve, and Paul Wood, eds. *Art of the Avant-Gardes.* New Haven, Conn.: Yale University Press, 2004.

Elderfield, John. *The "Wild Beasts": Fauvism and Its Affinities.* New York: Museum of Modern Art, 1976.

Fer, Briony, David Batchelor, and Paul Wood. *Realism, Rationalism, Surrealism: Art between the Wars.* New Haven, Conn.: Yale University Press, 1993.

Friedman, Mildred, ed. *De Stijl, 1917–1931: Visions of Utopia.* Minneapolis: Walker Art Center; New York: Abbeville, 1982.

Gale, Matthew. *Dada and Surrealism.* London: Phaidon, 1997.

Goldberg, Rose Lee. *Performance: Live Art 1909 to the Present.* New York: Abrams, 1979.

Golding, John. *Cubism: A History and an Analysis, 1907–1914.* Cambridge, Mass.: Belknap, 1988.

Gordon, Donald E. *Expressionism: Art and Idea.* New Haven, Conn.: Yale University Press, 1987.

Harrison, Charles, Francis Frascina, and Gil Perry. *Primitivism, Cubism, Abstraction: The Early Twentieth Century.* New Haven, Conn.: Yale University Press, 1993.

Herbert, James D. *Fauve Painting: The Making of Cultural Politics.* New Haven, Conn.: Yale University Press, 1992.

Herrera, Hayden, ed. *Frida Kahlo.* Minneapolis: Walker Art Center, 2007.

Hills, Patricia. *Painting Harlem Modern: The Art of Jacob Lawrence.* Berkeley and Los Angeles: University of California Press, 2009.

Hitchcock, Henry-Russell, and Philip Johnson. *The International Style.* New York: Norton, 1995.

Hurlburt, Laurance P. *The Mexican Muralists in the United States.* Albuquerque: University of New Mexico Press, 1989.

Jaffé, Hans L. C. *De Stijl, 1917–1931: The Dutch Contribution to Modern Art.* Cambridge, Mass.: Belknap, 1986.

Krauss, Rosalind. *The Originality of the Avant-Garde and Other Modernist Myths.* Cambridge, Mass.: MIT Press, 1986.

Kuspit, Donald. *The Cult of the Avant-Garde Artist.* Cambridge: Cambridge University Press, 1993.

Lloyd, Jill. *German Expressionism: Primitivism and Modernity.* New Haven, Conn.: Yale University Press, 1991.

Lodder, Christina. *Russian Constructivism.* New Haven, Conn.: Yale University Press, 1983.

Lozano, Luis Martin, and Juan Coronel Rivera. *Diego Rivera: The Complete Murals.* Cologne: Taschen, 2008.

Martin, Marianne W. *Futurist Art and Theory.* Oxford: Clarendon, 1968.

Motherwell, Robert, ed. *The Dada Painters and Poets: An Anthology.* 2d ed. Boston: Hall, 1981.

Mundy, Jennifer. *Duchamp, Man Ray, Picabia.* London: Tate, 2008.

Orvell, Miles. *American Photography.* New York: Oxford University Press, 2003.

Peters, Olaf. *Otto Dix.* New York: Prestel, 2010.

Rhodes, Colin. *Primitivism and Modern Art.* New York: Thames & Hudson, 1994.

Richter, Hans. *Dada: Art and Anti-Art.* London: Thames & Hudson, 1961.

Rochfort, Desmond. *Mexican Muralists: Orozco, Rivera, Siqueiros.* San Francisco: Chronicle, 1998.

Rosenblum, Robert. *Cubism and Twentieth-Century Art.* Rev. ed. New York: Abrams, 1984.

Rubin, William S. *Dada and Surrealist Art.* New York: Abrams, 1968.

———, ed. *Pablo Picasso: A Retrospective.* New York: Museum of Modern Art; Boston: New York Graphic Society, 1980.

———. *"Primitivism" in 20th-Century Art: Affinity of the Tribal and the Modern.* 2 vols. New York: Museum of Modern Art, 1984.

Selz, Peter. *German Expressionist Painting.* Berkeley: University of California Press, 1974. Reprint of 1957 edition.

Silver, Kenneth E. *Esprit de Corps: The Art of the Parisian Avant-Garde and the First World War, 1914–1925.* Princeton, N.J.: Princeton University Press, 1989.

Smith, Terry. *Making the Modern: Industry, Art, and Design in America.* Chicago: University of Chicago Press, 1993.

Stott, William. *Documentary Expression and Thirties America.* New York: Oxford University Press, 1973.

Taylor, Joshua C. *Futurism.* New York: Museum of Modern Art, 1961.

Taylor, Michael R., ed. *Arshile Gorky: A Retrospective.* New Haven, Conn.: Yale University Press, 2009.

Terraroli, Valerio, ed. *Art of the Twentieth Century, 1900–1919: The Avant-Garde Movements.* Milan: Skira, 2006.

———. *Art of the Twentieth Century, 1920–1945: The Artistic Culture between the Wars.* Milan: Skira, 2006.

Tisdall, Caroline, and Angelo Bozzolla. *Futurism.* New York: Oxford University Press, 1978.

Trachtenberg, Alan. *Reading American Photographs: Images as History—Mathew Brady to Walker Evans.* New York: Hill and Wang, 1989.

Troyen, Carol, ed. *Edward Hopper.* Boston: Museum of Fine Arts, 2007.

Tsujimoto, Karen. *Images of America: Precisionist Painting and Modern Photography.* Seattle: University of Washington Press, 1982.

Tucker, William. *Early Modern Sculpture.* New York: Oxford University Press, 1974.

Vogt, Paul. *Expressionism: German Painting, 1905–1920.* New York: Abrams, 1980.

Weiss, Jeffrey S. *The Popular Culture of Modern Art: Picasso, Duchamp, and Avant-Gardism.* New Haven, Conn.: Yale University Press, 1994.

Whitford, Frank. *Bauhaus.* New York: Thames & Hudson, 1984.

Chapter 30: Modernism and Postmodernism in Europe and America, 1945 to 1980

Alloway, Lawrence. *American Pop Art.* New York: Whitney Museum of American Art; Macmillan, 1974.

———. *Topics in American Art since 1945.* New York: Norton, 1975.

Altshuler, Bruce. *Isamu Noguchi.* New York: Abbeville, 1994.

Anfam, David. *Abstract Expressionism.* New York: Thames & Hudson, 1990.

Archer, Michael. *Art since 1960.* New ed. New York: Thames & Hudson, 2002.

Ashton, Dore. *American Art since 1945.* New York: Oxford University Press, 1983.

———. *The New York School: A Cultural Reckoning.* Harmondsworth: Penguin, 1979.

Ballantyne, Andrew, ed. *Architectures: Modernism and After.* Malden, Mass: Blackwell, 2004.

Battcock, Gregory, ed. *Idea Art: A Critical Anthology.* New York: Dutton, 1973.

———. *Minimal Art: A Critical Anthology.* New York: Studio Vista, 1969.

———. *The New Art: A Critical Anthology.* New York: Dutton, 1973.

———. *New Artists Video: A Critical Anthology.* New York: Dutton, 1978.

Battcock, Gregory, and Robert Nickas, eds. *The Art of Performance: A Critical Anthology.* New York: Dutton, 1984.

Beardsley, John, and Jane Livingston. *Hispanic Art in the United States: Thirty Contemporary Painters and Sculptors.* Houston: Museum of Fine Arts; New York: Abbeville, 1987.

Beardsley, Richard. *Earthworks and Beyond: Contemporary Art in the Landscape*. New York: Abbeville, 1984.

Broude, Norma, and Mary D. Garrard. *The Power of Feminist Art: The American Movement of the 1970s, History and Impact*. New York: Abrams, 1994.

Bürger, Peter. *Theory of the Avant-Garde*. Minneapolis: University of Minnesota Press, 1984.

Butler, Cornelia H., ed. *WACK! Art and the Feminist Revolution*. Cambridge, Mass.: MIT Press, 2007.

Causey, Andrew. *Sculpture since 1945*. New York: Oxford University Press, 1998.

Caws, Mary Ann. *Robert Motherwell*. New York: Columbia University Press, 1996.

Cockcroft, Eva, John Weber, and James Cockcroft. *Toward a People's Art*. New York: Dutton, 1977.

Cohn, Marjorie, and Eliza Rathbone. *Mark Rothko*. Ostfildern: Hatje Cantz, 2001.

Crow, Thomas. *The Rise of the Sixties: American and European Art in the Era of Dissent*. New Haven, Conn.: Yale University Press, 2005.

Finch, Christopher. *Chuck Close: Work*. New York: Prestel, 2010.

Frascina, Francis, ed. *Pollock and After: The Critical Debate*. New York: Harper & Row, 1985.

Gale, Matthew, ed. *Francis Bacon*. New York: Rizzoli, 2009.

Gaugh, Harry F. *Franz Kline*. New York: Abbeville, 1994.

Geldzahler, Henry. *New York Painting and Sculpture, 1940–1970*. New York: Dutton, 1969.

Godfrey, Tony. *Conceptual Art*. London: Phaidon, 1998.

Goldberg, Rose Lee. *Performance Art: From Futurism to the Present*. Rev. ed. New York: Abrams, 1988.

Goldhagen, Sarah Williams, and Réjean Legault. *Anxious Modernisms: Experimentation in Postwar Architectural Culture*. Cambridge, Mass.: MIT Press, 2002.

Goodman, Cynthia. *Digital Visions: Computers and Art*. New York: Abrams, 1987.

Goodyear, Frank H., Jr. *Contemporary American Realism since 1960*. Boston: New York Graphic Society, 1981.

Gouma-Peterson, Thalia. *Miriam Schapiro: Shaping the Fragments of Art and Life*. New York: Abrams, 2000.

Green, Jonathan. *American Photography: A Critical History 1945 to the Present*. New York: Abrams, 1984.

Greenberg, Clement. *Clement Greenberg: The Collected Essays and Criticism*. Edited by J. O'Brien. 4 vols. Chicago: University of Chicago Press, 1986–1993.

Grundberg, Andy. *Photography and Art: Interactions since 1945*. New York: Abbeville, 1987.

Guilbaut, Serge. *How New York Stole the Idea of Modern Art*. Chicago: University of Chicago Press, 1983.

Hays, K. Michael, and Carol Burns, eds. *Thinking the Present: Recent American Architecture*. New York: Princeton Architectural, 1990.

Henri, Adrian. *Total Art: Environments, Happenings, and Performance*. New York: Oxford University Press, 1974.

Hobbs, Robert. *Lee Krasner*. New York: Abbeville, 1993.

Hoffman, Katherine. *Explorations: The Visual Arts since 1945*. New York: Harper Collins, 1991.

Hopkins, David. *After Modern Art, 1945–2000*. New York: Oxford University Press, 2000.

Hughes, Robert. *The Shock of the New*. New York: Knopf, 1981.

Hunter, Sam. *An American Renaissance: Painting and Sculpture since 1940*. New York: Abbeville, 1986.

Jacobs, Jane. *The Death and Life of Great American Cities*. New York: Random House, 1961.

Jacobus, John. *Twentieth-Century Architecture: The Middle Years, 1940–1964*. New York: Praeger, 1966.

Jencks, Charles. *The Language of Post-Modern Architecture*. 6th ed. New York: Rizzoli, 1991.

———. *What Is Post-Modernism?* 3d ed. London: Academy Editions, 1989.

Johnson, Ellen H., ed. *American Artists on Art from 1940 to 1980*. Boulder, Colo.: Westview, 1982.

Joselit, David. *American Art since 1945*. New York: Thames & Hudson, 2003.

Kaprow, Allan. *Assemblage, Environments, and Happenings*. New York: Abrams, 1966.

Kirby, Michael. *Happenings*. New York: Dutton, 1966.

Kotz, Mary Lynn. *Rauschenberg: Art and Life*. New York: Abrams, 2004.

Kramer, Hilton. *The Age of the Avant-Garde: An Art Chronicle of 1956–1972*. New York: Farrar, Straus & Giroux, 1973.

Leja, Michael. *Reframing Abstract Expressionism: Subjectivity and Painting in the 1940s*. New Haven, Conn.: Yale University Press, 1993.

Lippard, Lucy R. *Mixed Blessings: New Art in a Multicultural America*. New York: Pantheon, 1990.

———. *Pop Art*. New York: Praeger, 1966.

———, ed. *From the Center: Feminist Essays on Women's Art*. New York: Dutton, 1976.

———. *Six Years: The Dematerialization of the Art Object from 1966 to 1972*. New York: Praeger, 1973.

Livingston, Jane, ed. *The Paintings of Joan Mitchell*. New York: Whitney Museum of American Art, 2002.

Lovejoy, Margot. *Postmodern Currents: Art and Artists in the Age of the Electronic Media*. Ann Arbor, Mich.: UMI Research Press, 1989.

Lucie-Smith, Edward. *Art Now*. Edison, N.J.: Wellfleet, 1989.

———. *Movements in Art since 1945*. New ed. New York: Thames & Hudson, 2001.

Mamiya, Christin J. *Pop Art and Consumer Culture: American Super Market*. Austin: University of Texas Press, 1992.

Marder, Tod A. *The Critical Edge: Controversy in Recent American Architecture*. New Brunswick, N.J.: Rutgers University Press, 1980.

———. *An International Survey of Recent Painting and Sculpture*. New York: Museum of Modern Art, 1984.

Mercurio, Gianni. *Lichtenstein: Meditations on Art*. Milan: Skira, 2010.

Meyer, Ursula. *Conceptual Art*. New York: Dutton, 1972.

Mitchell, William J. *The Reconfigured Eye: Visual Truth in the Post-Photographic Era*. Cambridge, Mass.: MIT Press, 1992.

Morris, Francis, ed. *Louise Bourgeois*. New York: Rizzoli, 2008.

Polcari, Stephen. *Abstract Expressionism and the Modern Experience*. Cambridge: Cambridge University Press, 1991.

Popper, Frank. *Origins and Development of Kinetic Art*. Translated by Stephen Bann. Greenwich, Conn.: New York Graphic Society, 1968.

Price, Jonathan. *Video Visions: A Medium Discovers Itself*. New York: New American Library, 1977.

Reichardt, Jasia, ed. *Cybernetics, Art, and Ideas*. Greenwich, Conn.: New York Graphics Society, 1971.

Robbins, Corinne. *The Pluralist Era: American Art, 1968–1981*. New York: Harper & Row, 1984.

Rorimer, Anne. *New Art in the 60s and 70s: Redefining Reality*. New York: Thames & Hudson, 2001.

Rosen, Randy, and Catherine C. Brawer, eds. *Making Their Mark: Women Artists Move into the Mainstream, 1970–1985*. New York: Abbeville, 1989.

Rosenberg, Harold. *The Tradition of the New*. New York: Horizon, 1959.

Rush, Michael. *New Media in Art*. 2d ed. New York: Thames & Hudson, 2005.

Russell, John, and Suzi Gablik. *Pop Art Redefined*. New York: Praeger, 1969.

Sandford, Mariellen R., ed. *Happenings and Other Acts*. New York: Routledge, 1995.

Sandler, Irving. *Art of the Postmodern Era*. New York: Harper Collins, 1996.

———. *The Triumph of American Painting: A History of Abstract Expressionism*. New York: Praeger, 1970.

Sayre, Henry M. *The Object of Performance: The American Avant-Garde since 1970*. Chicago: University of Chicago Press, 1989.

Schneider, Ira, and Beryl Korot. *Video Art: An Anthology*. New York: Harcourt Brace Jovanovich, 1976.

Shapiro, David, and Cecile Shapiro. *Abstract Expressionism: A Critical Record*. New York: Cambridge University Press, 1990.

Shiff, Richard. *Barnett Newman: A Catalogue Raisonné*. New Haven, Conn.: Yale University Press, 2004.

Sims, Lowery Stokes. *Wifredo Lam and the International Avant-Garde, 1923–1982*. Austin, Tex.: University of Texas Press, 2002.

Smagula, Howard. *Currents: Contemporary Directions in the Visual Arts*. 2d ed. Upper Saddle River, N.J.: Prentice Hall, 1989.

Smee, Sebastian. *Lucian Freud: Beholding the Animal*. Cologne: Taschen, 2009.

Sonfist, Alan, ed. *Art in the Landscape: A Critical Anthology of Environmental Art*. New York: Dutton, 1983.

Sontag, Susan. *On Photography*. New York: Farrar, Straus & Giroux, 1973.

Stiles, Kristine, and Peter Selz. *Theories and Documents of Contemporary Art: A Sourcebook of Artists' Writings*. Berkeley and Los Angeles: University of California Press, 1996.

Taylor, Brendon. *Contemporary Art: Art since 1970*. Upper Saddle River, N.J.: Prentice Hall, 2005.

Terraroli, Valerio, ed. *Art of the Twentieth Century, 1946–1968: The Birth of Contemporary Art*. Milan: Skira, 2007.

Tuchman, Maurice. *American Sculpture of the Sixties*. Los Angeles: Los Angeles County Museum of Art, 1967.

Varnedoe, Kirk. *Pictures of Nothing: Abstract Art since Pollock*. Princeton: Princeton University Press, 2006.

Venturi, Robert. *Complexity and Contradiction in Architecture*. New York: Museum of Modern Art, 1966.

Venturi, Robert, Denise Scott-Brown, and Steven Isenhour. *Learning from Las Vegas*. Cambridge, Mass.: MIT Press, 1972.

Waldman, Diane. *Collage, Assemblage, and the Found Object*. New York: Abrams, 1992.

Wallis, Brian, ed. *Art after Modernism: Rethinking Representation*. New York: New Museum of Contemporary Art in association with David R. Godine, 1984.

Wheeler, Daniel. *Art since Mid-Century: 1945 to the Present*. Upper Saddle River, N.J.: Prentice Hall, 1991.

Wood, Paul. *Modernism in Dispute: Art since the Forties*. New Haven, Conn.: Yale University Press, 1993.

Chapter 31: Contemporary Art Worldwide

Buchhart, Dieter, et al., *Jean-Michel Basquiat*. Ostfildern: Hatje Cantz, 2010.

Butler, Cornelia H., and Lisa Gabrielle Mark. *WACK!: Art and the Feminist Revolution*. Cambridge, Mass.: MIT Press, 2007.

Celent, Germano. *Anselm Kiefer*. Milan: Skira, 2007.

Chilvers, Ian, and John Glaves-Smith. *Oxford Dictionary of Modern and Contemporary Art*. 2d ed. New York: Oxford University Press, 2009.

Cook, Peter. *New Spirit in Architecture*. New York: Rizzoli, 1990.

Cummings, P. *Dictionary of Contemporary American Artists*. 6th ed. New York: St. Martin's, 1994.

Deepwell, K., ed. *New Feminist Art*. Manchester: Manchester University Press, 1994.

Enwezor, Okwui, and Chika Okeke-Agulu. *Contemporary African Art since 1980*. Bologna: Damiani, 2009.

Ferguson, Russell, ed. *Discourses: Conversations in Postmodern Art and Culture*. Cambridge, Mass.: MIT Press, 1990.

Fineberg, Jonathan. *Art since 1940: Strategies of Being*. 2d ed. Upper Saddle River, N.J.: Prentice Hall, 2000.

Galassi, Peter. *Andreas Gursky*. New York: Museum of Modern Art, 2001.

Ghirardo, Diane. *Architecture after Modernism*. New York: Thames & Hudson, 1996.

Goldsworthy, Andy. *Andy Goldsworthy: A Collaboration with Nature*. New York: Abrams, 1990.

Heartney, Eleanor, Helaine Posner, Nancy Princenthal, and Sue Scott. *After the Revolution: Women Who Transformed Contemporary Art*. New York: Prestel, 2007.

Hertz, Richard, ed. *Theories of Contemporary Art*. 2d ed. Upper Saddle River, N.J.: Prentice Hall, 1993.

Hopkins, David. *After Modern Art, 1945–2000*. New York: Oxford University Press, 2000.

Jencks, Charles. *The New Paradigm in Architecture: The Language of Post-Modernism*. New Haven, Conn.: Yale University Press, 2002.

Jodidio, Philip. *100 Contemporary Architects*. Cologne: Taschen, 2008.

Kasfir, Sidney Littlefield. *Contemporary African Art*. New York: Thames & Hudson, 1999.

Kolossa, Alexandra. *Keith Haring 1958–1990: A Life for Art*. Cologne: Taschen, 2009.

Kotz, Mary Lunn. *Rauschenberg: Art and Life*. New York: Abrams, 2004.

Lippard, Lucy R. *Mixed Blessings: New Art in a Multicultural America*. New York: Pantheon, 1990.

Mullins, Charlotte. *Painting People: Figure Painting Today*. New York: Thames & Hudson, 2008.

Nesbitt, Judith, ed. *Chris Ofili*. London: Tate, 2010.

Norris, Christopher, and Andrew Benjamin. *What Is Deconstruction?* New York: St. Martin's, 1988.

Paul, Christiane. *Digital Art*. 2d ed. New York: Thames & Hudson, 2008.

Pauli, Lori, ed. *Manufactured Landscapes: The Photographs of Edward Burtynsky*. New Haven, Conn.: Yale University Press, 2003.

Perry, Gill, and Paul Wood. *Themes in Contemporary Art*. New Haven, Conn.: Yale University Press, 2004.

Raskin, David. *Donald Judd*. New Haven, Conn.: Yale University Press, 2010.

Risatti, Howard, ed. *Postmodern Perspectives: Issues in Contemporary Art*. Upper Saddle River, N.J.: Prentice Hall, 1990.

Sandler, Irving. *Art of the Postmodern Era*. New York: Harper Collins, 1996.

Smith, Terry. *What Is Contemporary Art?* Chicago: University of Chicago Press, 2009.

Sollins, Susan, ed. *Art: 21 (Art in the Twenty-first Century)*. 5 vols. New York: Abrams, 2001–2009.

Stiles, Kristine, and Peter Selz. *Theories and Documents of Contemporary Art: A Sourcebook of Artists' Writings*. Berkeley and Los Angeles: University of California Press, 1996.

Taylor, Brendon. *Contemporary Art: Art since 1970*. Upper Saddle River, N.J.: Prentice Hall, 2005.

Terraroli, Valerio, ed. *Art of the Twentieth Century, 1969–1999: Neo-avant-gardes, Postmodern and Global Art*. Milan: Skira, 2009.

Wands, Bruce. *Art of the Digital Age*. New York: Thames & Hudson, 2007.

Warren, Lynne. *Jeff Koons*. New Haven, Conn.: Yale University Press, 2008.

Wines, James. *Green Architecture*. Cologne: Taschen, 2008.

CREDITS

Chapter 26—**Opener:** © Bridgeman-Giraudon/Art Resource, NY; **26-01A:** © Jason Hawkes/Terra/Corbis; **Map 26-1:** © Cengage Learning; **timeline:** © Bridgeman-Giraudon/Art Resource, NY; **26-2:** akg-images/Bildarchiv Monheim; **26-3:** © Erich Lessing/Art Resource, NY; **26-3A:** Hervé Champollion/akg-images; **26-4:** © Erich Lessing/Art Resource, NY; **26-5A:** akg-images/Bildarchiv Monheim; **26-5B:** © Erich Lessing/Art Resource, NY; **26-6:** The Art Archive/Musée du Louvre Paris/Gianni Dagli Orti; **26-7:** © Scala/Art Resource, NY; **26-7A:** © Bildarchiv Preussischer Kulturbesitz/Art Resource, NY; **26-8:** By kind permission of the Trustees of the Wallace Collection, London.; **26-9:** © Wallace Collection, London, UK/The Bridgeman Art Library; **26-10:** © Scala/Ministero per i Beni e le Attività culturali/Art Resource, NY; **26-11:** Image copyright © The Metropolitan Museum of Art/Art Resource, NY; **26-11A:** © National Gallery, London/Art Resource, NY; **26-12:** The Art Archive/John Meek/Picture Desk; **26-13:** © Réunion des Musées Nationaux/Art Resource, NY; **26-14:** The Art Archive/Musée du Louvre Paris/Gianni Dagli Orti; **26-15:** Summerfield Press, Ltd; **26-15A:** © Erich Lessing/Art Resource, NY; **26-16:** Image copyright © The Metropolitan Museum of Art/Art Resource, NY; **26-17:** National Gallery, London; **26-18:** The National Gallery of Art; **26-19:** © National Gallery, London, UK/The Bridgeman Art Library; **26-20:** National Gallery of Canada; **26-21:** Photograph © 2011 Museum of Fine Arts, Boston, 30.781; **26-22:** © Scala/Art Resource, NY; **26-23:** © Peter Aprahamian/CORBIS; **26-23A:** Electa/akg-images; **26-24:** Photo: Katherine Wetzel © Virginia Museum of Fine Arts; **26-25:** © Réunion des Musées Nationaux/Art Resource, NY; **26-26:** © Scala/Art Resource, NY; **26-27:** © Jonathan Poore/Cengage Learning; **26-27A:** akg-images/Bildarchiv Monheim; **26-28:** © Eric Crichton/Encyclopedia/Corbis; **26-28A:** akg/Bildarchiv Monheim; **26-29:** © ART on FILE/Corbis Art/Corbis; **26-30:** Thomas Jefferson Foundation; **26-31:** © Michael Freeman/Value Art/Corbis; **26-32:** Photo © The Library of Virginia; **26-33:** © Smithsonian American Art Museum, Washington, DC/Art Resource, NY; **UNF 26-01:** akg-images/Bildarchiv Monheim; **UNF 26-2:** © Bridgeman-Giraudon/Art Resource, NY; **UNF 26-3:** © Scala/Art Resource, NY; **UNF 26-4:** Photo: Katherine Wetzel © Virginia Museum of Fine Arts; **UNF 26-5:** © Jonathan Poore/Cengage Learning; **UNF 26-5:** © Jonathan Poore/Cengage Learning.

Chapter 27—**Opener:** © Réunion des Musées Nationaux/Art Resource, NY; **timeline:** © Réunion des Musées Nationaux/Art Resource, NY; **27-01A:** © Erich Lessing/Art Resource, NY; **27-2:** © Réunion des Musées Nationaux/Art Resource, NY; **27-2A:** © Erich Lessing/Art Resource, NY; **27-3:** © Jonathan Poore/Cengage Learning; **27-4:** © Scala/Ministero per i Beni e le Attività culturali/Art Resource, NY; **27-4A:** © Réunion des Musées Nationaux/Art Resource, NY; **27-5:** © Réunion des Musées Nationaux/Art Resource, NY; **27-5A:** © Réunion des Musées Nationaux/Art Resource, NY; **27-6:** © Réunion des Musées Nationaux/Art Resource, NY; **27-7:** © Réunion des Musées Nationaux/Art Resource, NY; **27-8:** © The Bridgeman Art Library International; **27-9:** © The Pierpont Morgan Library/Art Resource, NY; **27-10:** Image copyright © The Metropolitan Museum of Art/Art Resource, NY; **27-10A:** © Erich Lessing/Art Resource, NY; **27-11:** The Art Archive/Museo del Prado Madrid/Gianni Dagli Orti/Picture Desk; **27-12:** © Erich Lessing/Art Resource, NY; **27-13:** © Erich Lessing/Art Resource, NY; **27-13A:** © Réunion des Musées Nationaux/Art Resource, NY; **27-14:** © Giraudon/Art Resource, NY; **27-15:** © Réunion des Musées Nationaux/Art Resource, NY; **27-15A:** © Erich Lessing/Art Resource, NY; **27-16:** © Réunion des Musées Nationaux/Art Resource, NY; **27-17A:** © Erich Lessing/Art Resource, NY; **27-17:** The Art Archive/Musée d'Orsay Paris/Gianni Dagli Orti/Picture Desk; **27-18:** © Jonathan Poore/Cengage Learning; **27-19:** © Bildarchiv Preussischer Kulturbesitz/Art Resource, NY; **27-20:** © Bildarchiv Preussischer Kulturbesitz/Art Resource, NY; **27-21:** © National Gallery, London/Art Resource, NY; **27-22:** Photograph © 2011 Museum of Fine Arts, Boston, 99.22; **27-23:** Image copyright © The Metropolitan Museum of Art/Art Resource, NY; **27-24:** © Smithsonian American Art Museum, Washington, DC/Art Resource, NY; **27-25:** Photo copyright © The Cleveland Museum of Art; **27-26:** © Staatliche Kunstsammlungen Dresden/The Bridgeman Art Library; **27-27:** © Erich Lessing/Art Resource, NY; **27-28:** © Réunion des Musées Nationaux/Art Resource, NY; **27-29:** © Erich Lessing/Art Resource, NY; **27-30:** Image copyright © The Metropolitan Museum of Art/Art Resource, NY; **27-31:** Image copyright © The Metropolitan Museum of Art/Art Resource, NY; **27-32:** © Erich Lessing/Art Resource, NY; **27-33:** © Scala/Art Resource, NY; **27-33A:** © The Bridgeman Art Library International; **27-34:** © Bildarchiv Preussischer Kulturbesitz/Art Resource, NY; **27-35:** Image copyright © The Metropolitan Museum of Art/Art Resource, NY; **27-36:** Photo copyright © Philadelphia Museum of Art, 207-1; **27-37:** Photograph © 2011 Museum of Fine Arts, Boston, 19.124; **27-38:** © Art Resource, NY; **27-39:** Howard University Gallery of Art, Washington, D.C; **27-40:** © Tate, London/Art Resource, NY; **27-41:** © Tate, London/Art Resource, NY; **27-42:** akg-images/Bildarchiv Monheim; **27-43:** © Travel Pix/Robert Harding; **27-43A:** © Leo Sorel; **27-44:** © Roger Antrobus/CORBIS; **27-45:** © Jonathan Poore/Cengage Learning; **27-46:** © Collection Artedia/Leemage; **27-47:** Private Collection/The Stapleton Collection/The Bridgeman Art Library International; **27-46A:** © Bettmann/Corbis; **27-48:** © Louis Daguerre/Time & Life Pictures/Getty Images; **27-49:** Massachusetts General Hospital Archives and Special Collections, Boston; **27-50:** © Nadar/Bettmann/Corbis; **27-51:** Private Collection/The Stapleton Collection/The Bridgeman Art Library International; **27-52:** Courtesy George Eastman House; **27-53:** © New York Public Library/Art Resource, NY; **27-54:** Courtesy George Eastman House; **UNF 27-01:** © Jonathan Poore/Cengage Learning; **UNF 27-2:** © Réunion des Musées Nationaux/Art Resource, NY; **UNF 27-3:** © Staatliche Kunstsammlungen Dresden/The Bridgeman Art Library; **UNF 27-4:** © Travel Pix/Robert Harding; **UNF 27-5:** © Louis Daguerre/Time & Life Pictures/Getty Images.

Chapter 28—**Opener:** © Bildarchiv Preussischer Kulturbesitz/Art Resource, NY; **timeline:** © Bildarchiv Preussischer Kulturbesitz/Art Resource, NY; **28-2A:** Photograph: The Art Institute of Chicago.; **28-2:** © Erich Lessing/Art Resource, NY; **28-3:** Image copyright © The Metropolitan Museum of Art/Art Resource, NY; **28-4:** © Erich Lessing/Art Resource, NY; **28-5:** Photography © The Art Institute of Chicago, 1964.336; **28-6:** Photo © Los Angeles County Museum of Art; **28-7:** Photo © The Norton Simon Art Foundation; **28-7A:** © National Gallery, London, UK/The Bridgeman Art Library, **28-8:** © Réunion des Musées Nationaux/Art Resource, NY; **28-9:** © Samuel Courtauld Trust, The Courtauld Gallery, London, UK/The Bridgeman Art Library; **28-10:** © Culture and Sport Glasgow (Museums); **28-11:** © Réunion des Musées Nationaux/Art Resource, NY; **28-12:** © Réunion des Musées Nationaux/Art Resource, NY; **28-13:** Photography © The Art Institute of Chicago, 1910.2; **28-14:** © The Bridgeman Art Library International; **28-15:** Photography © The Art Institute of Chicago, 1928.610; **28-15A:** © The Bridgeman Art Library; **28-16:** Photography © The Art Institute of Chicago, 1926.224; **28-16A:** © The Bridgeman Art Library International; **28-16B:** © Hermann Buresch. Van Gogh Museum, Amsterdam/Bildarchiv Preussischer Kulturbesitz/Art Resource, NY; **28-17:** © Yale University Art Gallery/Art Resource, NY; **28-18:** Digital Image © The Museum of Modern Art/Licensed by © Scala/Art Resource, NY; **28-19:** © Art Resource, NY; **28-20:** Photograph © 2011 Museum of Fine Arts, Boston, 36.270; **28-21:** Photograph © Philadelphia Museum of Art, E1936-1-1; **28-22:** Photography © The Art Institute of Chicago, 1926.252; **28-22A:** © The Philadelphia Museum of Art/Art Resource, NY; **28-23:** Photography © The Art Institute of Chicago, 1922.445; **28-24:** akg-images; **28-24A:** © Réunion des Musées Nationaux/Art Resource, NY; **28-25:** © The Kröller-Müller Foundation, Otterlo; **28-26:** Digital Image © The Museum of Modern Art/Licensed by © Scala/Art Resource, NY; **28-26A:** © Scala/Art Resource, NY; **28-27:** © DACS/Lauros/Giraudon/The Bridgeman Art Library International; **28-27A:** © Victoria & Albert Museum, London/Art Resource, NY; **28-28:** © 2011 The Munch Museum/The Munch-Ellingsen Group/Artists Rights Society (ARS), NY. Photo: © Erich Lessing/Art Resource, NY; **28-29:** © Erich Lessing/Art Resource, NY; **28-30:** Image copyright © The Metropolitan Museum of Art/Art Resource, NY; **28-31:** Image copyright © The Metropolitan Museum of Art/Art Resource, NY; **28-31A:** © Giraudon/The Bridgeman Art Library; **28-32:** © Réunion des Musées Nationaux/Art Resource, NY; **28-32A:** © Vanni/Art Resource, NY; **28-33:** ©Peter Willi/The Bridgeman Art Library; **28-33A:** © Smithsonian American Art Museum, Washington, DC/Art Resource, NY; **28-34:** © Massimo Listri/CORBIS; **28-35:** © Culture and Sport Glasgow (Museums); **28-36:** © 2011 SOFAM/architect: V. Horta, photo Bastin & Evrard sprl; **28-36A:** © 2011 SOFAM

Architect V. Horta, Photo Bastin and Evrard sprl.; **28-36B:** Image copyright © The Metropolitan Museum of Art/Art Resource, NY; **28-37:** © Gala/Superstock/Photolibrary; **28-38:** © Jonathan Poore/Cengage Learning; **28-39:** Chicago Architectural Photographing Company; **28-40:** ©Thomas A. Heinz/Corbis; **28-40A:** © ART on FILE/CORBIS; **28-41:** © Hedrich Blessing Collection/Chicago History Museum/Getty Images; **UNF 28-01:** © Réunion des Musées Nationaux/Art Resource, NY; **UNF 28-2:** Digital Image © The Museum of Modern Art/Licensed by © Scala/Art Resource, NY; **UNF 28-3:** Digital Image © The Museum of Modern Art/Licensed by © Scala/Art Resource, NY; **UNF 28-4:** © Peter Willi/The Bridgeman Art Library; **UNF 28-5:** © Jonathan Poore/Cengage Learning.

Chapter 29—Opener: © 2011 Artists Rights Society (ARS), NY/VG Bild-Kunst, Bonn. Photo © Bildarchiv Preussischer Kulturbesitz/Art Resource, NY, NG 57/61; **29-2:** © 2011 Succession H. Matisse, Paris/Artists Rights Society (ARS), NY. Photo © San Francisco Museum of Modern Art.; **29-2A:** © 2011 Succession H. Matisse/ Artists Rights Society (ARS), New York. Photograph: © The Bridgeman Art Library; **Map 29-01:** © Cengage Learning; **29-3:** © 2011 Succession H. Matisse, Paris/Artists Rights Society (ARS); **29-4:** © 2011 Artists Rights Society (ARS), NY/ADAGP, Paris. © Erich Lessing/Art Resource, NY; **29-4A:** © 2011 Artists Rights Society (ARS), NY/ ADAGP, Paris. Photo: National Gallery of Art, Washington, John Hay Whitney Collection 1982.76.4; **29-5:** © The Museum of Modern Art/Licensed by © Scala/Art Resource, NY; **29-6:** Used by permission of Stiftung Seebull Ada & Emil Nolde, Neukirchen, Germany. Photo © Hamburger Kunsthalle, BPK, Berlin.© The Bridgeman Art Library International; **29-6A:** Used by permission of Stiftung Seebull Ada & Emil Nolde, Neukirchen, Germany. Photo © Jamison Miller, The Nelson-Atkins Museum of Art.; **29-7:** © 2011 Artists Rights Society (ARS), New York/ADAGP, Paris. Photo: © Solomon R. Guggenheim Museum; **29-8:** Oeffentliche Kunstsammlung Basel, photo Martin Bühler; **29-9A:** akg-images; **29-9:** © 2011 Artist's Rights Society (ARS), New York/VG Bild-Kunst, Bonn. Photo: © Erich Lessing/Art Resource, NY.; **29-10:** © Art Resource, NY; **29-10A:** © Burstein Collection/Corbis Art/Corbis; **29-11:** © 2011 Estate of Pablo Picasso. Licensed by Artist's Rights Society (ARS), NY. Photo © The Metropolitan Museum of Art/Art Resource, NY; **29-11A:** © 2011 Estate of Pablo Picasso/Artists Rights Society (ARS), New York. Photograph: © National Gallery of Art, Washington, D.C.; **29-12:** © 2011 Estate of Pablo Picasso. Licensed by Artist's Rights Society (ARS), NY. Digital Image © The Museum of Modern Art/Licensed by © Scala/Art Resource, NY; **29-13:** © 2011 Licensed by Artist's Rights Society (ARS), NY. Photo: © Réunion des Musées Nationaux/Art Resource, NY; **29-14:** © 2011 Artists Rights Society (ARS), NY/ ADAGP, Paris. Photo: © Bridgeman-Giraudon/Art Resource, NY; **29-15:** © Kunstmuseum Basel, Basel (Emanuel Hoffman Foundation).; **29-15A:** © The Art Institute of Chicago; **29-16:** © 2011 Estate of Pablo Picasso. Licensed by Artist's Rights Society (ARS), NY. Photo: © Réunion des Musées Nationaux/Art Resource, NY; **29-17:** © 2011 Artists Rights Society (ARS), NY/ADAGP, Paris. Photo: © The Bridgeman Art Library International; **29-18:** © 2011 Estate of Pablo Picasso/Artists Rights Society (ARS), NY. Photo: © Erich Lessing/Art Resource, NY; **29-19:** © 2011 Estate of Pablo Picasso/Artists Rights Society (ARS), NY. Photo: © The Museum of Modern Art/Licensed by © Scala/ Art Resource, NY; **29-19A:** © 2011 Estate of Pablo Picasso/Artists Rights Society (ARS), NY. Digital Image © The Museum of Modern Art/Licensed by © Scala/Art Resource, NY; **29-20:** © 2011 Estate of Aleksandr Archipenko/Artists Rights Society (ARS), NY. Photo: The Museum of Modern Art/Licensed by © Scala/Art Resource, NY; **29-21:** © 2011 Artists Rights Society (ARS), NY/ADAGP, Paris. Photo © The Museum of Modern Art/Licensed by © Scala/Art Resource, NY; **29-21A:** © The Estate of Jacques Lipchitz, courtesy Marlborough Gallery, New York. Photo: Jamison Miller, The Nelson-Atkins Museum of Art; **29-22:** © 2011 Artists Rights Society (ARS), New York/ADAGP, Paris. Photo: © The Philadelphia Museum of Art/Art Resource, NY; **29-22A:** © 2011 Artists Rights Society (ARS), New York/ADAGP, Paris. Photo: © The Museum of Modern Art/Licensed by © Scala/Art Resource, NY; **29-23:** © 2011 Artist's Rights Society (ARS), NY. © DACS/The Bridgeman Art Library; **29-24:** Digital Image © The Museum of Modern Art/Licensed by © Scala/Art Resource, NY; **29-25:** © 2011 Artist's Rights Society (ARS), New York/ADAGP, Paris. Photo: © Richard S. Zeisler Collection, New York/The Bridgeman Art Library; **29-26:** © 2011 Artists Rights Society (ARS), NY Photo Credit : Digital Image © The Museum of Modern Art/Licensed by © Scala/Art Resource, NY; **29-27:** © 2011 Artists Rights Society (ARS), New York/ADAGP, Paris/ Succession Marcel Duchamp. Photo: © Philadelphia Museum of Art, 1998-74-1; **29-27A:** ©2011 Artists Rights Society/ADAGP, Paris/Succession Marcel Duchamp. Photo: © Philadelphia Museum of Art. 1950-134-934; **29-28:** © 2011 Artists Rights Society (ARS), New York/ADAGP, Paris/Succession Marcel Duchamp. Photo: © Philadelphia Museum of Art, 1952-98-1; **29-29:** © 2011 Artists Rights Society, (ARS), NY/ VG Bild-Kunst, Bonn. Photo © Yale University Art Gallery/Art Resource, NY; **29-30:** Digital Image © The Museum of Modern Art/Licensed by © Scala/Art Resource, NY; **29-30A:** © The Bridgeman Art Library; **29-31:** © Naum Gabo. Photograph by David Heald © The Solomon R. Guggenheim Foundation, NY, 55.1429; **29-32:** Photo © akg-images, © Estate of Vladimir Tatlin; **29-33:** Artifice Images; **29-34:** © 2011 Artists Rights Society (ARS), NY. Photo: © The Philadelphia Museum of Art/Art Resource, NY; **29-35:** Photo © Philadelphia Museum of Art, 1950-134-59, © 208 Artists Rights Society (ARS), New York/ADAGP, Paris/Succession Marcel Duchamp; **29-36:** © The Estate of Arthur G. Dove, c/o Terry Dintenfass, Inc. Photograph: The Art Institute of Chicago.; **29-37:** © 2011 Man Ray Trust/Artists Rights Society (ARS), NY/ ADAGP, Paris. Digital Image © The Museum of Modern Art/Licensed by © Scala/Art Resource, NY; **29-38:** Image copyright © The Metropolitan Museum of Art/Art Resource, NY, 49.70.42; **29-39:** Art © Estate of Stuart Davis/Licensed by VAGA, NY. Digital Image © The Museum of Modern Art/Licensed by © Scala/Art Resource, NY; **29-40:** Fisk University Galleries, University of Tennessee, Nashville; **29-40A:** © SCHOMBURG CENTER/Art Resource, NY; **29-41:** © 203 Whitney Museum of American Art; **29-42:** © 2011 Georgia O'Keeffe Museum/Artists Rights Society (ARS), NYSheldon Memorial Art Gallery, Lincoln, Nebraska; **29-43:** Digital Image (c) The Museum of Modern Art/Licensed by © Scala/Art Resource, NY; **29-43A:** © 2011 Georgia O'Keeffe Museum/Artist Rights Society (ARS), New York. Reproduction, The Art Institute of Chicago.; **29-44:** Photograph by Edward Weston. Collection Center for Creative Photography ©1981 Arizona Board of Regents; **29-44A:** Photograph by Edward Weston. Collection Center for Creative Photography ©1981 Arizona Board of Regents; **29-45:** © 2011 Frank Lloyd Wright Foundation, Scottsdale, AZ/Artists Rights Society (ARS), NY. Photo © Dennis Light/Light Photographic; **29-46:** © 2011 Frank Lloyd Wright Foundation, Scottsdale, AZ/Artists Rights Society (ARS), NY; **29-47:** © Jonathan Poore/Cengage Learning; **29-48:** Art © Estate of George Grosz. Licensed by VAGA, NY. Photo © The Hecksher Museum of Art, Huntington, NY; **29-48A:** Art © Estate of George Grosz/Licensed by VAGA, New York, NY Digital Image © The Museum of Modern Art/Licensed by © Scala/Art Resource, NY, 243.1947; **29-49:** © 2011 Artists Rights Society (ARS), NY/VG Bild-Kunst, Bonn. Photo © Walter Klein; **29-50:** © 2011 Artists Rights Society (ARS), NY/VG Bild-Kunst, Bonn. Photo © Erich Lessing, Art Resource, NY.; **29-51:** akg-images/ullstein bild; **29-52:** © 2011 Estate of Giorgio de Chirico, Licensed by Artist's RIghts Society (ARS), NY. Photo: © The Museum of Modern Art/Licensed by © Scala/Art Resource, NY; **29-53:** © 2011 Artists Rights Society (ARS), NY/ADAGP, Paris. Digital Image © The Museum of Modern Art/ Licensed by © Scala/Art Resource, NY, 0256.37; **29-55:** © 2011 Salvador Dali, Gala-Salvador Dali Foundation/Artists Rights Society (ARS), NY. Digital Image © The Museum of Modern Art/Licensed by © Scala/Art Resource, NY, 162.1934.; **29-56:** © 2011 C. Herscovici, Brussels/Artists Rights Society (ARS), NY. Photo © Los Angles County Museum of Art, 78.7.; **29-56A:** © 2011 C. Herscovici, London/Artists Rights Society (ARS), New York. Photo: © The Museum of Modern Art/Licensed by © Scala/ Art Resource, NY; **29-57:** © 2011 Artist's Right's Society (ARS), NY/ProLitteris, Zürich. Digital Image © The Museum of Modern Art/Licensed by © Scala/Art Resource, NY; **29-58:** © 2011 Successió Miró/Artists Rights Society (ARS), NY/ADAGP, Paris. Digital Image © The Museum of Modern Art/Licensed by © Scala/Art Resource, NY, 229.1937.; **29-59:** © 2011 Artists Rights Society (ARS), NY/VG-Bild Kunst, Bonn. Digital Image © The Museum of Modern Art/Licensed by © Scala/Art Resource, NY, 564.1939.; **29-59A:** © 2011 Artists Rights Society (ARS), New York; Photo: Digital Image ©The Museum of Modern Art/Licensed by © Scala/Art Resource, NY; **29-60:** © 2011 Mondrian/Holtzman Trust c/o HCR International, VA, USA; **29-61:** © 2011 Artists Rights Society (ARS), NY/ADAGP, Paris. © Philadelphia Museum of Art/Corbis, 1950-134-14, 15.; **29-61A:** © 2011 Artists Rights Society (ARS), New York/ADAGP, Paris. Photograph: © The Philadelphia Museum of Art/Art Resource, NY; **29-62:** © Bowness, Hepworth Estate. Photo © Tate , London/Art Resource, NY; **29-63:** Photograph © 1985 The Detroit Institute of Arts, © The Henry Moore Foundation; **29-64:** Art © Estate of Vera Mukhina/RAO, Moscow/VAGA, NY Photo © Gregor Schmid/Corbis; **29-65:** Bildarchiv Monheim GmbH/Alamy; **29-66:** © 2011 Artists Rights Society (ARS), NY/ VG Bild-Kunst, Bonn. Photo © Vanni/Art Resource, NY.; **29-66A:** Digital Image © The Museum of Modern Art/Licensed by © Scala/Art Resource, NY; **29-66B:** © 2011 Artists Rights Society (ARS), New York/PICTORIGHT, Amsterdam. Photograph: © Bauhaus-Archiv Museum für Gestaltung, Berlin.; **29-67:** © 2011 Artists Rights Society (ARS), NY/VG Bild-Kunst, Bonn. Digital Image © The Museum of Modern Art/ Licensed by © Scala/Art Resource, NY.; **29-68:** © Jonathan Poore/Cengage Learning; **29-69:** Photography © The Art Institute of Chicago, 1942.51, Estate of Edward Hopper © The Whitney Museum of American Art; **29-70:** " © 2011 The Jacob and Gwendolyn Lawrence Foundation, Seattle/Artists Rights Society (ARS), NY. Photo: The Phillips Collection, Washington, D.C."; **29-71:** Art © Figge Art Museum, successors to the Estate of Nan Wood Graham/Licensed by VAGA, New York, NY Photography © The Art Institute of Chicago,1930.934; **29-72:** Art © T.H. Benton and R.P. Benton Testamentary Trusts/UMB Bank Trustee/Licensed by VAGA, New York, NY Photo © Lloyd Grotjan/ Full Spectrum Photo, Jefferson City; **29-73:** © 2011 © Orozco Valladares Family/ SOMAAP, Mexico. Artists Rights Society (ARS). Photograph: Hood Museum of Art, Dartmouth College; **29-74:** © 2011 Banco de México Trust. Licensed by Artist's RIghts Society (ARS), NY. Dirk Bakker, photographer for the Detroit Institute of Arts/The Bridgeman Art Library; **29-74A:** © D.R. Rufino Tamayo/Herederos/Mexico/2011. Fundacion Olga y Rufino Tamayo A.C. Photo: © 209 Museum Associates/LACMA; **29-75:** © 2011 Banco de México Trust. Licensed by Artist's RIghts Society (ARS), NY. Photo © Schalkwijk/Art Resource, NY; **29-76:** Courtesy The Dorothea Lange Collection, The Oakland Museum of California; **29-77:** © Margaret Bourke-White/Time & Life Pictures/Getty Images; **29-78:** © 2011 Estate of Alexander Calder/Artists Rights Society (ARS), NY. Digital Image © The Museum of Modern Art/Licensed by © Scala/ Art Resource, NY, 590.1939 a-d.; **29-79:** © 2011 Frank Lloyd Wright Foundation, Scottsdale, AZ/Artists Rights Society (ARS), NY. Photo © Peter Cook/View Pictures/ Photolibrary. **UNF 29-01:** © 2011 Artists Rights Society (ARS), NY/ADAGP, Paris. Photo: © Bridgeman-Giraudon/Art Resource, NY; **UNF 29-2:** Photograph by Edward Weston. Collection Center for Creative Photography ©1981 Arizona Board of Regents; **UNF 29-3:** Photograph © 1985 The Detroit Institute of Arts, © The Henry Moore Foundation; **UNF 29-4:** © 2011 Artists Rights Society (ARS), NY/VG Bild-Kunst, Bonn. Photo © Vanni/Art Resource, NY; **UNF 29-5:** © 2011 Banco de México Trust. Licensed by Artist's RIghts Society (ARS), NY. Photo © Schalkwijk/Art Resource, NY.

Chapter 30—Opener: © 2011 Artists Rights Society (ARS), NY/DACS, London. Photo © The Bridgeman Art Library; **timeline:** © 2011 Artists Rights Society (ARS), NY/DACS, London. Photo © The Bridgeman Art Library; **30-2:** © 2011 Artists Rights Society (ARS), NY/ADAGP, Paris. Photo: © Des Moines Art Center; **30-3:** © 2011 The Estate of Francis Bacon/ARS, NY/DACS, London. Digital Image © The Museum of Modern Art/Licensed by © Scala/Art Resource, NY, 229.1948; **30-3A:** © 2011 The Estate of Francis Bacon. All rights reserved./ARS, New York/DACS, London. Photograph by Bob Hashimoto. Reproduction, The Art Institute of Chicago.; **30-4:** © 2011 Artists Rights Society (ARS), NY/ADAGP, Paris. Photo © Tate Gallery, London/Art Resource, NY; **30-5:** © 2011 The Arshile Gorky Foundation/The Artists Rights Society (ARS), New York. Photograph: © The Museum of Modern Art/Licensed by © Scala/Art Resource, NY; **30-6:** © 2011 The Pollock-Krasner Foundation/Artists Rights Society (ARS), NY. Photo © National Gallery of Art, 1976.37.1; **30-7:** Courtesy Center for Creative Photography, University of Arizona © 1991 Hans Namuth Estate; **30-7A:** © 2011 Pollock-Krasner Foundation/Artists Rights Society (ARS), New York. Photograph: © The Whitney Museum of American Art; **30-8:** © 2011 The Willem de Kooning Foundation/Artists Rights Society (ARS), NY. Digital Image © The Museum of Modern Art/Licensed by © Scala/Art Resource, NY, 478.1953; **30-8A:** © 2011 The Franz Kline Estate/Artists Rights Society (ARS), New York. Photograph: Whitney Museum of American Art, New York.; **30-8B:** Art © Estate of Robert Motherwell/Licensed by VAGA, New York, NY Albright-Knox Art Gallery/Art Resource, NY; **30-8C:** © Estate of Joan Mitchell Photograph: © Butler Institute of American Art, Youngstown, OH, USA/ Gift of Marilynn Meeker, 1986 Courtesy of the Joan Mitchell Foundation, NYC/The Bridgeman Art Library International; **30-8D:** © 2011 Susan Rothenberg/Artists Rights Society (ARS), NY. Photo: Susan Rothenberg, Tattoo, 1979. Acrylic paint on canvas, 5′ 7″ x 8′ 7″. Collection Walker Art Center, Minneapolis. Purchased with the aid of funds from Mr. and Mrs. Edmond R. Ruben, Mr. and Mrs. Julius E. Davis, the Art Center Acquisition Fund, and the National Endowment for the Arts, 1979.; **30-9:** © 2011 Barnett Newman Foundation/Artists Rights Society (ARS), NY. Digital Image © The Museum of Modern Art/Licensed by © Scala/Art Resource, NY, 240.1969.; **30-10:** © 2011 Kate Rothko Prizel & Christopher Rothko. Licensed by Artists Rights Society (ARS), NY. Photo: © San Francisco Museum of Modern Art; **30-11:** © Ellsworth Kelly, photo Philipp Scholz Rittermann; **30-12:** © 2011 Frank Stella/Artists Rights Society (ARS), NY. Photo © CNAC/MNAM/Dist. © Réunion des Musées Nationaux/Art Resource, NY; **30-13:** © 2011 Helen Frankenthaler. Licensed by Artist's Rights Society (ARS), New York. © DACS/Founders Society Purchase, Dr & Mrs Hilbert H. DeLawter Fund/The Bridgeman Art Library; **30-14:** Solomon R. Guggenheim Museum, NY, 64.1685; **30-15:** The Museum of Modern Art/Licensed by © Scala/Art Resource, NY. © Bridget Riley 2011. All rights reserved. Courtesy Karsten Schubert, London; **30-16:** Art © David Smtih, Licensed by VAGA, NY. Photo: Smithsonian Hirschorn Museum and Sculpture garden; **30-17:** © 2011 Estate of Tony Smith/Artists Rights Society (ARS), NY. Digital Image © The Museum of Modern Art/Licensed by © Scala/Art Resource, NY, 333.1998; **30-18:** Art © Judd Foundation/Licensed by VAGA, NY Hirshhorn Museum and Sculpture Garden, Smithsonian Institution, photo Lee Stalsworth, 72.154; **30-19:** © 2011 Estate of Louise Nevelson/Artists Rights Society (ARS), NY. Photo © CNAC/MNAM/Dist. © Réunion des Musées Nationaux/Art Resource, NY; **30-20:** Art © Louise Bourgeois Trust/Licensed by VAGA, New York, NY Photo © CNAC/MNAM/Dist. Réunion des Musées Nationaaux/Art Resource, NY; **30-21:** Photography © The Art Institute of Chicago, © 208 The Estate of Eva Hesse/ Galerie Hauser & Wirth, Zürich; **30-21A:** © 2011 ISAMU NOGUCHI Licensed by Artist's Rights Society (ARS), New York. Collection Walker Art Center, Minneapolis (gift of the artist, 1978).; **30-22:** Art © Jasper Johns/Licensed by VAGA, New York, NY Photo:Whitney Museum of American Art, New York, USA/© DACS/The Bridgeman Art Library; **30-23:** Art © Estate of Robert Rauschenberg/Licensed by VAGA, New York, NY. Photo, Courtesy of the Sonnabend Collection; **30-24:** © Estate of Roy Lichtenstein; **30-25:** © 2011 Andy Warhol Foundation for the Visual Arts/ARS, NY. Photo © 204 The Whitney Museum of American Art; **30-25A:** © 2011 Andy Warhol Foundation for the Visual Arts/ARS, NY. Photo: © Tate Gallery, London/Art Resource, NY; **30-25B:** Art © Estate of George Segal/Licensed by VAGA, New York, NY Photo:National Gallery of Canada, Ottawa.; **30-26:** Art © Copyright 1969 Claes Oldenburg. Photo © 2009 Fred S. Kleiner; **30-26A:** © 2011 Niki Charitable Art Foundation. All rights reserved/ARS, NY/ ADAGP, Paris. Photograph: © Whitney Museum of American Art, New York.; **30-27:** Photo © University of Arizona Museum, Tucson, © Audrey Flack; **30-28:** Close, Chuck "Big Self Portrait" 1967-68, acrylic on canvas. Collection Walker Art Center Minneapolis. Art Center Acquisition Fund, 1969.; **30-29:** © Lucian Freud. Licensed by Goodman Derrick, LLP. Photo: © Tate, London/Art Resource, NY; **30-30:** Art © Estate of Duane Hanson/Licensed by VAGA, New York, NY Photo by Anne Gold; **30-31:** © The Estate of Diane Arbus. The Museum of Modern Art, New York, NY, U.S.A./Art Resource, Inc.; **30-32:** Reproduced with permission of the Minor White Archive, Princeton University Art Museum. © Trustees of Princeton University © The Museum of Modern Art/ Licensed by © Scala/Art Resource, NY; **30 33:** © 2011 Judy Chicago. Licensed by Artists Rights Society (ARS), NY. Photo: © The Brooklyn Museum; **30-34:** © Miriam Schapiro, courtesy Flomenhaft Gallery, NY; **30-35:** © Cindy Sherman, courtesy the artist and Metro Pictures; **30-36:** © The Estate of Ana Mendieta Collection Courtesy Galerie Lelong, New York; **30-37:** © Marsie, Emanuelle, Damon and Andrew Scharlatt/ Licensed by VAGA, New York, NY Courtesy Ronald Feldman Fine Arts, NY; **30-38:** © Magdalena Abakanowicz, courtesy Marlborough Gallery, NY; **30-39:** © Jonathan Poore/Cengage Learning; **30-40 (bottom):** © 2011 Licensed by Artist's Rights Society (ARS), New York. Photo: © Francis G. Mayer/CORBIS; **30-40 (top):** © 2011 Licensed by Artist's Rights Society (ARS), New York. Photo: © Jonathan Poore/Cengage Learning; **30-41:** Photo © Dmitri Kessel/Time & Life Pictures/Getty Images; **30-42:** © Jacob Halaska/Photolibrary; **30-43:** © Jonathan Poore/Cengage Learning; **30-44:** © Alan Schein Photography/Surf/Corbis; **30-45:** © Robert Holmes/Documentary Value/ Corbis; **30-46:** © Ambient Images Inc./Alamy; **30-47:** Photo Peter Aaron © Esto; **30-48:** Smallbones/Wikimedia Commons; **30-49:** © Jonathan Poore/Cengage Learning; **30-50:** © Estate of Robert Smithson. Licensed by VAGA, New York. Photo: © George Steinmetz/Corbis. **30-51:** © 2011 Carolee Schneemann/Artists Rights Society (ARS), NY. Photo © Al Geise, Courtesy PPOW Gallery; **30-52:** © 2011 Artists Rights Society (ARS), NY/VG Bild-Kunst, Bonn. Digital Image © The Museum of Modern Art/ Licensed by © Scala/Art Resource, NY. Photo: © Ute Klophaus; **30-53:** © 2011 Artists Rights Society (ARS), NY/ADAGP, Paris Photo Credit : Digital Image © The Museum of Modern Art/Licensed by © Scala/Art Resource, NY; **30-54:** © 2011 Joseph Kosuth/ Artists Rights Society (ARS), NY. Digital Image © The Museum of Modern Art/ Licensed by © Scala/Art Resource, NY, 383.1970 a-c; **30-55:** © Jean Baptiste Lacroix/ WireImage; **30-55A:** © Ted Thai/Time & Life Pictures/Getty Images; **30-56:** Courtesy Nam June Paik Studios, Inc.; **30-57:** David Em, Nora, 1979; **UNF 30-01:** © 2011 The Pollock-Krasner Foundation/Artists Rights Society (ARS), NY. Photo © National Gallery of Art, 1976.37.1; **UNF 30-2:** Art © Estate of Duane Hanson/Licensed by VAGA, New York, NY Photo by Anne Gold; **UNF 30-3:** © 2011 Judy Chicago. Licensed by Artists Rights Society (ARS), NY. Photo: © The Brooklyn Museum; **UNF 30-4:** © Jacob Halaska/Photolibrary; **UNF 30-5:** © 2011 Carolee Schneemann/Artists Rights Society (ARS), NY. Photo © Al Geise, Courtesy PPOW Gallery.

Chapter 31—Opener: Courtesy of Jaune Quick-to-See Smith (An Enrolled Salish, member of the Salish and Kootenai Nation Montana) Photo: © Chrysler Museum of Art, Norfolk, VA, Museum Purchase, 93.2; (timeline) Courtesy of Jaune Quick-to-See Smith (An enrolled Salish, member of the Salish and Kootemai Nation Montana) Photo © Chrysler Museum of Art, Norfolk, VA, Museum Purchase, 93.2; **31-2:** "COPYRIGHT: BARBARA KRUGER. COURTESY: MARY BOONE GALLERY, NEW YORK."; **31-3:** Courtesy of the Estate of David Wojnarowicz and P.P.O.W. Gallery, NY; **31-2A:** Copyright © 1988 Guerrilla Girls, courtesy www.guerrillagirls.com; **31-4:** Self-Portrait, 1980 © Copyright The Robert Mapplethorpe Foundation. Courtesy Art + Commerce; **31-5:** © Shahzia Sikander. Photograph: Sheldan C. Collins, courtesy Whitney Museum of American Art; **31-6:** © 1983 Faith Ringgold; **31-6A:** © Lorna Simpson; **31-6B:** Art: Courtesy of the artist and Jack Shainman Gallery, NY. Photo: Brooklyn Museum of Art, New York, USA/Caroline A.L. Pratt Fund/The Bridgeman Art Library International; **31-7:** © Smithsonian American Art Museum, Washington, DC/Art Resource, NY; **31-8:** © 2011 Estate of Jean-Michel Basquiat/ADAGP, Paris/Artists Rights Society (ARS), New York. Photography: Douglas M. Parker Studio, Los Angeles. Image courtesy of The Broad Art Foundation, Santa Monica; **31-9:** © Kehinde Wiley. Brooklyn Museum photograph, 2010; **31-10A:** Trigo Piula; **31-10:** © Chris Ofili, courtesy Chris Ofili-Afroco and Victoria Miro Gallery, photo by Stephen White; **31-11:** Meteorological Service of New Zealand Ltd. Collection, Wellington.; **31-12:** © Willie Bester; **31-13:** Photo Scott Frances © Esto, All rights reserved, © David Hammons; **31-14:** Art © Estate of Leon Golub/Licensed by VAGA, New York, NY Courtesy Ronald Feldman Gallery; **31-15:** © Shirin Neshat. Photo © The Bridgeman Art Library International; **31-16:** © Krzysztof Wodczizko Courtesy Galerie Lelong, New York; **31-17:** © 2011 Hans Haacke. Licensed by Artists Rights Society (ARS), NY/VG Bild-Kunst, Bonn. Photo: © CNAC/MNAM/Dist. © Réunion des Musées Nationaux/Art Resource, NY; **31-18:** Copyright © Xu Bing, courtesy Chazen Museum of Art (formerly Elvehjem Museum of Art), University of Wisconsin; **31-19:** © Edward Burtynsky, courtesy Nicholas Metivier, Toronto/Howard Greenberg & Bryce Wolkowitz, New York; **31-20:** Photo courtesy Broad Art Foundation and the Pace Gallery, NY, © Julian Schnabel; **31-21:** © Anselm Kiefer. Courtesy Gagosian Gallery. Photography by Robert McKeever. © Philadelphia Museum of Art, 1985-5 -1; **31-22:** Collection of National Heritage Board, Singpore Art Museum; **31-22A:** Heritage Images, © The British Museum; **31-22B:** © DACS/Mollie Gowing Acquisition Fund for Contemporary Aboriginal Art 1992/The Bridgeman Art Library; **31-23:** Association de la Jeune Sculpture 1987/2 photo © Serge Goldberg; **31-24:** © Tara Donovan. Ace Gallery, Los Angeles; **31-25:** Artwork © Jenny Saville; **31-26:** Photo © Whitney Museum of American Art, © Kiki Smith; **31-27:** Museum of Contemporary Art, Chicago © Jeff Koons; **31-27A:** Art © Estate of Robert Arneson/Licensed by VAGA, NY Photo: San Francisco Museum of Modern Art; **31-27A:** Art © Estate of Robert Arneson/Licensed by VAGA, New York, NY. Photo: San Francisco Museum of Modern Art; **31-28:** Art © Marisol Escobar/ Licensed by VAGA, New York, NY; **31-29:** © Johan Gerrits; **31-28A:** Mark Tansey, courtesy Gagosian Gallery, NY; **31-30:** © Martin Jones; Ecoscene/CORBIS; **31-31a:** © John Gollings/Arcaid/Corbis; **31-31b:** © John Gollings/Arcaid/Corbis; **31-32:** Photo Saskia Cultural Documentation; **31-33:** © Santiago Yaniz/Photolibrary; **31-34:** © Jacques Pavlovsky/Sygma/CORBIS; **31-34A:** Arcaid.co.uk; **31-35:** akg-images/ Hilbich; **31-36:** © Jonathan Poore/Cengage Learning; **31-36:** The Denver Art Museum; **31-37:** Kokyat Choong/The Image Works; **31-38:** Robert O'Dea/akg-images; **31-39:** © 2011 Richard Serra/Artists Rights Society (ARS), NY. Photo © Burt Roberts, courtesy of Harriet Senie; **31-40:** Wolfgang Volz ©1983 Christo; **31-41:** © Andy Goldsworthy Courtesy Galerie Lelong, New York; **31-42:** © Jonathan Poore/Cengage Learning; **31-43:** © 2011 ANDREAS GURSKY. Licensed by Artist's Rights Society (ARS) New York.; **31-44:** © 2011 Jenny Holzer/Artists Rights Society (ARS), NY. photograph by David Heald © The Solomon R. Guggenheim Foundation; **31-45:** Adrian Piper Research Archive; **31-46:** Bill Viola, photo: Kira Perov; **31-47:** Tony Oursler, courtesy of the artist and Metro Pictures, NY.; **31-48:** Photograph by David Heald © The Solomon R. Guggenheim Foundation, NY; **UNF 31-01:** Self-Portrait, 1980 © Copyright The Robert Mapplethorpe Foundation. Courtesy Art + Commerce; **UNF 31-2:** © 2011 Estate of Jean-Michel Basquiat/ADAGP, Paris/Artists Rights Society (ARS), New York. Photography: Douglas M. Parker Studio, Los Angeles. Image courtesy of The Broad Art Foundation, Santa Monica; **UNF 31-3:** Photo © Whitney Museum of American Art, © Kiki Smith; **UNF 31-4:** akg-images/Hilbich; **UNF 31-5:** Tony Oursler, courtesy of the artist and Metro Pictures, NY.

MUSEUM INDEX

Note: *Figure numbers in* blue *indicate bonus images.*

SUBJECT INDEX

Notes:
- *Page numbers in italics indicate illustrations.*
- *Page numbers in italics followed by* b *indicate bonus images in the text.*
- *Page numbers in italics followed by* map *indicate maps.*
- *Figure numbers in* blue *indicate bonus images.*

Russian Revolution (1917), 859, 860
Russolo, Luigi, 854
Rutherford, Ernest, 841

S

S.O.S.-Starification Object Series (Wilke), 923–924, *924*
Saarinen, Eero: Terminal 5, John F. Kennedy International Airport, New York, 926, *927*
Sacagawea (Native American guide), 922
Sacco and Vanzetti, 888
Sacred Grove (Puvis de Chavannes), 819–820, *819*
Sailboats on the Seine, Argenteuil (Monet), 799
Saint Mary of Egypt among Sinners (Nolde), 840, *840*
Saint Paul's Cathedral, London (Wren), 26-1A
Saint Peter's, Rome (Michelangelo Buonarroti)
  and 18th century European and American architecture, 748–749
  piazza (Bernini), 26-1A
Saint-Gaudens, Augustus: *Adams Memorial*, Rock Creek Cemetery, Washington, D.C., 827, *827b*, 28-33A
Saint-Lazare Train Station (Monet), 803–804, *803*
Saint-Phalle, Niki de: *Black Venus, Nanas* series, 917, *917b*, 30-26A
Saint-Simonianism, 779
Salome, 820
Salome (Wilde) (ill. by Beardsley), *822b*, 28-27A
Salon de la Princesse, Hôtel de Soubise, Paris (Boffrand, Natoire, and Lemoyne), 729–730, *729*
Salon des Indépendants (France), 802, 820–821, 29-2A
Salon des Refusés, Paris, 802
salons, 729, 733, 738, 760, 802, 820–821, 836, 28-7A, 29-2A
saltimbanques, 29-11A
San Diego, California (U.S.A.): *Jane Avril* (Toulouse-Lautrec), 28-15A
San Lorenzo, Florence (Brunelleschi), 31-32A
Sant'Agnese in Agone, Rome (Borromini), 26-3A
Sant'Antonio, Pisa, 969, *969*
Santería, 29-59A
Santi, Raffaello. *See* Raphael
Saraband (Louis), 908, *909*
sarcophagi: and Napoleonic era art, 759
Sardanapalus (Byron), 766, 767
Sargent, John Singer, 862
  The Daughters of Edward Darley Boit, 784, *784*
Sartre, Jean-Paul, 901
satire, 740–741, 778–779, 811, 835
saturation, 813
Saturn. *See* Kronos
Saturn Devouring One of His Children (Goya), 764, *765*
satyrs, 27-33A
Saville, Jenny: *Branded*, 957, *957*
Saying Grace (Chardin), 738–739, *738*
Scenes from the Massacre at Chios (Delacroix), 767, *767b*, 27-15A
Schapiro, Miriam, 921
  Anatomy of a Kimono, 922, *922*
Schiele, Egon, 842–843, 957
  Nude Self-Portrait, Grimacing, 843, *843*
Schinkel, Karl Friedrich: Altes Museum, Berlin, 787–788, *787*, 31-34A
Schnabel, Julian: *The Walk Home*, 954, *955*
Schneemann, Carolee
  Meat Joy, 934, *935*
  "Woman in the Year 2000," 934
School of Athens (Philosophy) (Raphael), Vatican Palace, Rome, 760
Schröder House, Utrecht (Rietveld), 884, *884*
Schubert, Franz, 767
Schwitters, Kurt, 864
  Merz 19, 858, *858*, 912
  and Nazi Germany, 877

science
  and 18th century European and American art, 726, 727, 743
  color theory, 813
  and the Enlightenment, 736–737
  and Marxism, 800
  and Modernism, 841, 847
  and photography, 796
  and pointillism, 812
  in Realist art, 783–784
  and Romanticism, 766, 767
The Scream (Munch), 822, *823*, 840, 30-3A
sculpture
  18th century European and American, 751–752
  American Modernist, 895–896
  Constructivist, 860
  contemporary, 946–947, 949, 956–957, 959–960, 966–967, 31-27A
  Cubist, 851–853, 29-20A
  European interwar Modernist, 874, 875, 879, 881–884, 29-61A
  Futurist, 854–855
  German Expressionist, 29-10A
  kinetic, 855
  late 19th century European and American, 824–827, 833, 28-31A, 28-32A, 28-33A
  late 20th century European and American, 901, 909–913, 916–917, 919, 30-21A, 30-26A
  Napoleonic era, 758–759, 27-4A
  Realist, 785–786
  relief. *See* relief sculpture
  Rococo, 735
  Romantic, 770
  techniques. *See* sculpture techniques
sculpture techniques: Neoclassical, 27-4A
Seagram Building, New York (Mies van der Rohe and Johnson), 928, *928*, 930, 961
Sears Tower (Willis Tower), Chicago (Skidmore, Owings, and Merrill), 928–929, *928*, 961
The Seasons (Krasner), *904b*, 30-7A
seated figure with drinking cup, Colima (sculpture), 29-74A
Seated Youth (Lehmbruck), 843, *843b*, 29-10A
secondary colors, 813
Segal, George: *The Gas Station*, 916, *916b*, 30-25B
Self-Portrait (Mapplethorpe), 944, 945
Self-Portrait (Vigée-Lebrun), 739–740, *739*, 26-15A
Self-Portrait as a Fountain (Nauman), *937b*, 30-55A
Self-Portrait Looking at the Last Supper (Marisol), 959, *959*
Self-Portrait with Amber Necklace (Modersohn-Becker), 842, *842b*, 29-9A
Self-Portrait with Two Pupils (Labille-Guiard), 740, *740*
self-portraits
  18th century European and American, 739–740
  Conceptual Art, 30-55A
  contemporary, 944, 945, 957, 31-27A
  Dadaist, 835
  German Expressionist, 843
  Photorealist, 918
  Post-Impressionist, 811
  in Romantic art, 27-10A
Senefelder, Alois, 778
Serra, Richard: *Tilted Arc*, New York, 944, 966–967, *967*
Serrano, Andres: *Piss Christ*, 944
Seurat, Georges, 802, 909
  A Sunday on La Grande Jatte, 802, 812, *812*, 813, 819–820, 822
Severini, Gino, 854
  Armored Train, 855, *855*
sexuality. *See* eroticism
Shahn, Ben: *The Passion of Sacco and Vanzetti*, 888
Shakespeare, William, 760, 786
Shchukin, Sergei, 844, 858
Sheeler, Charles, 868
Shelley, Mary Wollstonecraft, 767, 26-27A

Shelley, Percy Bysshe, 767
Sherman, Cindy, 942, 31-6A
  Untitled Film Stills series, 922–923, *923*
Shinto, 956, 957
Shodo Shima Stone Study (Noguchi), 913, *913b*, 30-21A
Shop Block, Bauhaus, Dessau (Gropius), 884, *885*
A Short History of Modernist Painting (Tansey), *959B*, 31-28A
Siddal, Elizabeth, 787–788
Signboard of Gersaint (Watteau), 733, *733b*, 26-7A
Sikander, Shahzia: *Perilous Order*, 945, *945*
silk-screen printing, 915
Silueta series (Mendieta), 923, *923*
Simmons Architects: Sony Building (AT&T building), New York, 930–931, *930*
Simpson, Lorna, 946
  Stereo Styles, *946b*, 31-6A
Simultanéisme, 848
simultaneous contrasts, 813
Sistine Chapel, Vatican, Rome: *Last Judgment* (Michelangelo Buonarroti), 754, 755, 826
site-specific art, 932–933, 964–969, 973
Sixth Avenue and Thirtieth Street, New York City (Sloan), 862, *862*
Skidmore, Owings, and Merrill (SOM): Willis Tower (Sears Tower), Chicago, 928–929, *928*, 961
skyscrapers, 830–832, 871–872, 886, 928–929, 28-40B
The Slave Ship (Slavers Throwing Overboard the Dead and Dying, Typhoon Coming On) (Turner), 772–773, *773*
slavery
  and Napoleonic era art, 27-5A
  Realism and, 785–786
  and Romanticism, 766
The Sleep of Reason Produces Monsters, Los Caprichos (Goya), 763–764, *763*
Sleeping Gypsy (Rousseau), 821, *821*
slide projections, 952
Sloan, John, 865
  Sixth Avenue and Thirtieth Street, New York City, 862, *862*
Smith, David, 909–910
  Cubi XII, 910, *910*
  on outdoor sculpture, 910
Smith, Jaune Quick-to-See: *Trade (Gifts for Trading Land with White People)*, 940, 941
Smith, Kiki: *Untitled*, 958, *958*
Smith, Tony: *Die*, 910, *910*
Smithson, Robert, 968
  Spiral Jetty, Great Salt Lake, Utah, 932–933, *933*, 964
Social Contract (Rousseau), 762
social Darwinism, 801
A Social History of the State of Missouri (Benton), 890, *891*
societal contexts of art
  18th century Europe and America, 728, 736–738, 739
  American Modernism, 862, 866, 887, 889, 894
  contemporary art, 941, 943, 945, 950, 965–966
  Cubism, 848, 849, 850–851, 29-15A
  Dada, 835, 856, 29-27A
  European interwar Modernism, 872, 876, 29-48A
  Futurism, 853–854, 855
  German Expressionism, 839, 842, 29-10A
  Impressionism, 804–805
  late 19th century European and American art, 799, 800–801, 806, 827
  late 20th century European and American art, 900–901
  Mexican interwar Modernism, 890–891, 893
  Modernism, 836
  Napoleonic era, 756–757
  Pop Art, 916
  primitivism, 846
  Productivism, 860
  Realism, 775, 777, 778, 782–783

Romanticism, 764, 771–772, 774, 775
Suprematism, 859–860
See also religion and mythology
Société des Artistes Indépendants (Society of Independent Artists) (France), 802
Socrates, 760
Solomon R. Guggenheim Museum, New York (Wright), 925, *925*, 927, 970
Song Su-Nam, 956
  Summer Trees, *956b*, 31-22A
Sony Building (AT&T Building), New York (Johnson and Burgee, with Simmons Architects), 930–931, *930*, 961
Soufflot, Jacques-Germain: Panthéon (Sainte-Geneviève), Paris, 748–749, *749*
South Asian art: contemporary, 945
Southworth, Albert Sands: *Early Operation under Ether, Massachusetts General Hospital*, 793, *793*
Soviet art, 859–861, 883–884
Spanish Civil War, 30-8B
Spanish Elegies series (Motherwell), *905b*, 30-8B
Spencer, Herbert, 801
Spiral Jetty, Great Salt Lake, Utah (Smithson), 932–933, *933*, 964
Split (Croatia): palace of Diocletian, 745
St. Abbs (Scotland): *Cracked Rock Spiral* (Goldsworthy), 968–969, *968*
St. Louis, Missouri (U.S.A.): Wainwright Building (Sullivan), 832, *832b*, 28-40A
Staffelstein (Germany): Vierzehnheiligen (Neumann), 731, *731*, 731
stained-glass windows
  Art Nouveau, 28-36B
  in late 20th century European and American architecture, 926
  in Neo-Gothic architecture, 27-43A
  and Post-Impressionist art, 817
Stanford, Jane, 865
Stanford, Leland, 796
Stanford Museum, Stanford, 865
Starry Night (van Gogh), 814–815, *815*
State Capitol, Jefferson City, 890, *891*
State Capitol, Richmond (Jefferson), 751
Statue of Liberty, New York (Bartholdi), 830
steel construction
  in early 19th century European and American architecture, 790, 791, 27-46A
  in European interwar Modernist architecture, 887
  in late 19th century European and American architecture, 830, 831, 832
The Steerage (Stieglitz), 869, *869*, 29-43A
Stein, Gertrude, 844, 858, 29-2A, 29-11A
Stein, Leo, 844, 858, 29-2A, 29-11A
Steiner, Lilly, 861
Steiner House, Vienna (Loos), 861, *861*
Stella, Frank: *Mas o Menos*, 907, *907*
Stereo Styles (Simpson), *946b*, 31-6A
Stieglitz, Alfred
  Equivalents series, 869, *869b*, 920, 29-43A
  and O'Keeffe, 868–869
  The Steerage, 869, *869*, 29-43A
  and the Steins, 844
Still, Clyfford: *1948-C*, 908
still life
  in American modernist art, 870
  in German Expressionist art, 29-6A
  in Post-Impressionist art, 818–819
Still Life in Studio (Daguerre), 792, 793
Still Life with Chair-Caning (Picasso), 848–849, *849*
Stirling, James: Neue Staatsgalerie, Stuttgart, 963, *963b*, 31-34A
Stölzl, Gunta, 885
  Gobelin tapestry, *885b*, 29-66B
The Stone Breakers (Courbet), 775, *775*, 776, 777
story quilts, 946
storytelling. *See* narrative art
Stourhead park (Flitcroft and Hoare), 750, *750*
Stra (Italy): Villa Pisani, 735, *735*
Strawberry Hill, Twickenham (Walpole and others), 749, *749b*, 26-27A
Street, Dresden (Kirchner), 840, *840*